*The Music
of the
Medieval Church Dramas*

The earliest surviving version of the 'Quem quaeritis . . .' trope; Paris, Bibliothèque Nationale, *MS lat. 1240*, fol. 30v (*c.* 933–6 A.D.). The neumes written above the text represent Aquitainian notation in its earliest form.

The Music
of the
Medieval
Church Dramas

WILLIAM L. SMOLDON

Edited by
CYNTHIA BOURGEAULT

London
OXFORD UNIVERSITY PRESS
New York   Melbourne
1980

Oxford University Press, Walton Street, Oxford OX2 6DP
OXFORD LONDON GLASGOW
NEW YORK TORONTO MELBOURNE WELLINGTON
KUALA LUMPUR SINGAPORE JAKARTA HONG KONG TOKYO
DELHI BOMBAY CALCUTTA MADRAS KARACHI
NAIROBI DAR ES SALAAM CAPE TOWN

British Library CIP Data

Smoldon, William Lawrence
 The music of the medieval church dramas.
 1. Music – History and criticism – Medieval,
 400–1500
 2. Music – History or criticism – 16th century
 3. Mysteries and miracle-plays, English –
 History and criticism.
 782.8'3   ML1702   80–40174
 ISBN 0–19–3163217

Set by Gloucester Typesetting Co Ltd
Printed by Ebenezer Baylis & Son, Ltd,
Worcester and London

Preface

In August, 1974, William L. Smoldon died, at the age of eighty-two, leaving to the University of London an extensive collection of manuscript photos and to Oxford University Press the complete but unrevised draft of *The Music of the Medieval Church Dramas*—both products of a lifetime of loving and painstaking scholarship.

Among the ranks of medievalists Smoldon holds a unique place. In a sense, he forged his own niche, plunging into that difficult 'no man's land' that separates literature from musicology and bridging the gap with imagination and common sense. It was one of his constant complaints that scholars approaching the drama from a purely 'textual' point of view neglect half the evidence. 'Few writers, it would seem, have realized that they are dealing not with dramas, but *music*-dramas, or, in other words, *operas*,' he commented ironically—and set out personally to rectify the mistake. His observations are all too true, although I have often suspected that the problem stems not so much from perversity (as he seemed wont to suppose) as from simple ignorance: in this era of academic overspecialization few burgeoning literary scholars have had the time or inclination to familiarize themselves with the discipline of music paleography; while budding musicologists, already overburdened with the chore of mastering the entire gamut of musical history from Guido of Arezzo to Penderecki, have had little spare time to explore the literary and historical aspects of medieval culture. It is to this problem that Smoldon addresses himself so energetically, and herein we find the uniquely valuable contribution of this book. If it were to accomplish nothing else, it would more than justify its existence by the mere fact of providing us with a bibliography which assembles most of the standard reference works in both musicology and literary history. Nor does Smoldon merely compile his sources; he also teaches us how to use them. For the literary historian his chapters on Gregorian chant and the techniques of music paleography are sure to be among the most valuable in the book, while for the musicologist his continuing attention to dramatic history and scholarship provides an excellent point of reference.

His scholarship itself is firmly orthodox. Smoldon makes no secret of his deep admiration for Karl Young; indeed, it would seem that in many ways *Medieval Music Drama* is envisaged as a kind of musicological companion piece to Young's monumental *Drama of the Medieval Church*. 'The adequate editing and exposition of the music associated with the dramatic texts might well require a separate treatise equal to the present one in extent,' writes Young in his Preface. In his own introductory remarks Smoldon takes up this challenge vigorously, and he never moves very far away from it (although he feels no hesitancy in correcting Young when the latter's 'textual' conclusions wander off into inaccuracy). As those readers who have been following the progress of literary/historical research on the liturgical drama will be quick to observe, this approach locks him immediately into controversy, particularly on the matter of the origins of the drama, where he strongly contests O. B. Hardison's 'dramatic ceremony' theory and comes down squarely on the traditional hypothesis that the drama arose out of the practice of troping, and specifically, out of the *Quem quaeritis* trope. On this point the reader will simply have to judge the evidence and come to his own conclusions. To my own mind it is quite clear that the origin of the drama is a still unfolding question and is going to be solved only by sensitive dialogue between literature, musicology—and also liturgy. To this end Smoldon contributes his evidence well and provides significant new credibility for Young's conclusions, while pointing the way toward the synthesis of the future. C. Clifford Flanigan summarizes the situation well in the course of a recent *Festschrift* dedicated to Smoldon:

It is perhaps not surprising that neither Young nor Hardison has been able to do much with the *Quem quaeritis* trope beyond chronicling its existence. Both labored under questionable methodological presuppositions about the trope form. For example, both believed a consideration of the music which accompanies liturgical texts to be of secondary importance. In a recent article Dr. William L. Smoldon has demonstrated how inadequate such an approach is, and in the process he has seriously called into question Hardison's thesis. It now seems certain that the melody which accompanied the *Quem quaeritis* dialogue, whether it was performed as a trope or as an independent ritual, was distinctly a trope melody. On the strength of Smoldon's musicological observations it must be concluded that 'the *Quem quaeritis* dialogue, whenever and wherever invented, took its first form as a *trope*; one that was *intended* to belong (as it clearly does) to the Introit of the Easter Mass.' Thus, despite the attractiveness of Hardison's arguments, a detailed understanding of the trope form of the *Quem quaeritis* is more essential than ever.[1]

Smoldon's comparative charts of the *Quem quaeritis* trope, his observations on the origin of the Fleury Playbook, his study of musical interlinkings in the *Zehnsilberspiel* drama: these and many other discoveries provide valuable insights into the development of the drama—insights which will need to be assimilated and explored further by future generations of scholars.

---

[1] C. Clifford Flanigan, 'The Liturgical Context of the *Quem quaeritis* Trope', *Comparative Drama*, Vol. 8, No. 1 (*Studies in Medieval Drama in Honor of William L. Smoldon on His 82nd Birthday*), Spring 1974, p. 46.

Preface

Before concluding, I would like to comment briefly on the particular style of Smoldon's approach. For him liturgical drama was above all a matter of high adventure and deep personal involvement: in a sense, a quest. His own words convey something of the nature of this quest, and also the particular flair and feeling that he brought to it. I quote from his original Foreword, unfortunately never completed:

About 1930, having just taken a music degree at London University, and seeking to know more about 'English language and literature', I began to attend King's College, London and came under the aegis of Dr. A. W. Reed. It was he who first encouraged me to undertake my research and gave me much guidance as to how to begin. It was after his lecture on the *Quem quaeritis* trope that I sought a personal word with him. He had just told us that the trope was not merely spoken, but 'chanted'. When I asked him if he could tell me what the music was like that was set to the text of the dialogue, he replied that he hadn't the faintest idea. Then he added, 'It might be a good move if *you* tried to find out'. I proceeded to try, but it took quite a time.

I found myself bound to follow the example set by the author of that outstanding work, *The Drama of the Medieval Church*, Professor Karl Young of Yale, who, as his pages show, returned time and again to a direct study of the original documents without trusting to someone else's version of a text, and acquiring, as he himself told me, quite a collection of photographs of relevant manuscript pages.

It was soon after I had started to do my own collecting of photographs in the early 1930s that I received a vital uplift, through the acquisition of Karl Young's two monumental volumes. I wrote to him; we met in London at his invitation, and then, through the rest of the 1930s and up to the year of his untimely death, we maintained a correspondence.

I was of course the gainer. Although my own collection of manuscript photos was growing rapidly, the Professor was at times able to inform me whether or no a remoter continental library manuscript contained its music. I can remember, on one joyful occasion, after I had badgered the librarian of Cividale Cathedral into instituting yet one more search for a long-lost *Visitatio Sepulchri*, and this proving successful, that I was able to send along prints to the Professor—a very small recompense for all the help and advice that I received from a very great scholar.

Meanwhile, my own collection of manuscript photographs was growing, and I was proceeding with my music transcriptions of the versions that I had acquired. On March 25, 1939, not long before we started our war with Hitler, I gave an address at the King's Weigh House Chapel, London, W.1 to the members of the Plainsong and Medieval Music Society on 'The Easter Play— an Early Medieval Music-Drama'. It was illustrated by dramatic activities (with costumes and simple 'properties'), carried out by members of the Society's choir, and by singers from Nashdom Abbey.

Soon afterwards, my photographs went into the safety of a vault, out of reach of bombings, until the end of World War II. Afterwards, it was some time before I resumed adding to my collection. When, to the best of my knowledge and ability, I had completed it, it was in the hope that I had photographs of all surviving Church dramas which showed their music. Of course,

I hadn't, as I'm so often finding, but here, I felt, was a solid foundation for my enquiry, my own property, and paid for out of my own pocket.

In these revealing glimpses we find Smoldon at his liveliest and most deeply personal. In a sense, his joy, freshness, and ingenuity, coupled with a certain naïveté, are qualities that belong far more to the amateur (in the real sense of the word, which implies love) than to the ranks of dry professionalism that so often pass for scholarship in this day and age. There is about Smoldon an originality and delight that makes everything he touches truly his. Even in the course of a work such as this there is still 'time out'—time out to wonder at the engineering of a Gothic cathedral or the beauty of a musical line.

It goes without saying that the editing of a posthumous manuscript is never an easy task—particularly in the case of a writer of such stature and individuality as William Smoldon. My 'editorial policy', therefore, has been to keep as low a profile as possible. I have confined my work primarily to the completion of footnotes and bibliographical details, the double-checking of transcriptions (some of which have undoubtedly still slipped by me), and where necessary, some streamlining and condensing. Many of the passages in the manuscript were sad and frustrating, written in an obvious losing battle against time. The conclusion, in Smoldon's first draft, reads '. . . to be completed'. And under that, in a shaky pencilled note: 'not really, unfortunately . . .' (I tapered it off as best I could).

Where Smoldon's conclusion might have gone is a matter of real conjecture. To the end, the manuscript gave evidence of its own life, with new information and possibilities evolving, seemingly, right before Smoldon's eyes. On the dust jacket of Plate II, for example, I found a tantalizing note, again scrawled hastily in pencil: 'my discussion of the *Quem quaeritis* trope will need to be revised in the light of Walter Lipphardt's recent discoveries as to dating . . .'—a job, unfortunately, which was not to be completed. But as the field of liturgical drama, its origins and development, comes increasingly alive, thanks in large part to Smoldon, we sense that the pioneer would have been right there, continuing to grow and explore.

While this opening of the field is exciting, it hardly makes life easy for an editor. As students of the liturgical drama know only too well, the past decade has seen a real explosion of scholarship, much of it of impressive quality and major significance. To keep a manuscript which is by now several years old up to date without violating its integrity has at times been a challenging task. I trust that the substance of what Smoldon has to say will carry its own weight and that readers will be forgiving of an occasional detail which is out of date. Nevertheless, it seems only fair to point out a few areas in which *The Music of the Medieval Church Dramas* is in need of revision or supplementation from more recent sources.

First, despite Smoldon's very great wish to be thorough, a number of new manuscripts have come to light since his death, and in some instances the new evidence they have to offer warrants a revision of certain conclusions which Smoldon draws. For bibliographical details, see the Supplementary Bibliography.

Second, a number of manuscripts have been recently recatalogued, so that their current library details are different from those recorded by Smoldon. Updated details are recorded in the Appendix, at the conclusion of the book; an effort has been made to be as thorough as possible in integrating these new numberings into the course of Smoldon's discussion.

Third, the provenance and dating of manuscripts are matters which in many cases are still far from settled. In these areas Smoldon tends to follow Karl Young rather uncritically, an approach which occasionally lands him in trouble since many of Young's ascriptions have recently come under sharp question and in some cases much-needed correction. I have felt that it far overstepped my authority as editor to replace Smoldon's ascriptions with those of other scholars, even in cases where such ascriptions have by now been generally accepted. Nevertheless, on these points readers are urged to check Smoldon's information against other sources. Similarly, his comments on the Limoges tropers need to be considered in the light of recent studies by Richard Crocker and Paul Evans. For details, see the Supplementary Bibliography. The Appendix represents more recent scholarly thinking on the provenance of the various 'Limoges tropers'.

Fourth, attention must be called to the publication in 1963–70 of René-Jean Hesbert's edition of the *Corpus Antiphonalium Officii* (*CAO*), an authoritative collection of the antiphons of the Church, which far supplants the *Paléographie Musicale* facsimile of *Hartker's Antiphonale* which Smoldon used as the basis of his investigation. Walther Lipphardt has graciously provided *CAO* numberings for most antiphons mentioned by Smoldon; these correlations are to be found in the index.

In conclusion, I need to express my gratitude to the several people who helped me in my editorial work: to the staff of O.U.P., who provided a steady stream of useful information and clarifications; to Thomas Connolly, of the music department at the University of Pennsylvania, who gave enormous assistance in corroborating Smoldon's commentary and bibliography on Gregorian chant; to O. B. Hardison, who offered valuable editorial advice and support; to James Gibson, who took time off from his own doctoral dissertation on the origins and development of the Christmas *Quem quaeritis* dialogue to double-check Smoldon's transcriptions and to offer additional bibliography. But most of all I would like to express my thanks to two scholars, Walther Lipphardt and Fletcher Collins, Jr., whose dedication both to scholarship and to their former colleague has been truly outstanding. Both men painstakingly read galley proofs, and both provided me with valuable supplementary materials—Lipphardt his detailed bibliography and

CAO numberings, Collins his extensive personal correspondence with Smoldon, which on many occasions clarified difficult points in the manuscript. In their actions we see an example of scholarly collegiality at its finest, and to them, above all, I owe an enormous debt of gratitude in bringing Smoldon's final words to the world.

CYNTHIA BOURGEAULT

February 1980
Swarthmore College

Acknowledgements

The publishers would like to express their deep gratitude to Cynthia Bourgeault for all her work on the preparation of this book.

Grateful thanks are also due to the authors and publishers of the books and articles quoted, and to the institutions which possess the manuscripts reproduced in the plates.

Contents

Contents

List of Plates

List of Plates

Introduction

M Y first task must surely be to offer some justification for the appearance of yet another book dealing with the dramatic works of the medieval Western Church.

It has been well over a hundred years now since scholarship first began to take an active interest in the recovery of the Church music-drama. The earliest efforts in this direction centered around the middle of the last century and involved such names as E. du Méril, F. Danjou, V. Luzarche, and above all, Edouard de Coussemaker. The last-named created a landmark in 1860 by publishing twenty-two transcriptions together with free-rhythm versions of their musical settings, under the title of *Drames liturgiques du moyen âge*. Coussemaker was a scholar and a pioneer to whom further attention will be given later.

More and more of these dramatic texts came into consideration in the late nineteenth and early twentieth centuries, involving such names as G. Milchsack, Carl Lange, M. Sepet, W. Creizenach, N. C. Brooks, and Sir E. K. Chambers, together with many more. Curiously enough, with the exception of a few people such as Oskar Schönemann and Ferdinando Liuzzi[1] (and of course Coussemaker) the transcribers made little or no mention of the musical settings to be found in the original manuscripts. As a result of these investigations there were more and more studies published by generations of 'literary' scholars, who edited and analyzed the texts and then theorized and argued concerning what could be learned from them. The medieval Church dramas (or 'liturgical dramas' as they are more frequently called) now possess a wealth of commentary from both sides of the Atlantic. A recent burst of scholarly activity, beginning in about the mid-1950s, has produced several important and influential commentaries, including Hardin Craig's *English Religious Drama* (1955), Richard Donovan's *The Liturgical Drama in Medieval Spain* (1958), and O. B. Hardison's *Christian Rite and Christian Drama in the Middle Ages* (1965).

In many respects the final word on the subject still belongs to Karl Young, whose monumental two-volume study, *The Drama of the*

---

[1] Oskar Schönemann, *Der Sündenfall and Marienklage* (Hanover, 1855); Ferdinando Liuzzi, *La Lauda e i primordi della melodia italiana*, 2 vols. (Rome, 1934), also his 'L'Espressione musicale nel Dramma liturgico', *Studi medievali*, 2 (1929), pp. 74–109.

1

Medieval Church (Oxford, 1933) has set both the direction and the style for forty years of scholarship. Although his work has lately fallen into a certain disfavour owing to his enthusiasm for finding 'evolutionary progress' in the drama even in defiance of chronology,[1] the overall effect is still one of great brilliance and a massive weight of documentation. There can be no doubt that every important observation concerning these dramatic works which can be gathered from textual, historical, and literary evidence alone has been summed up by Young with extraordinary thoroughness and insight. There is a thoroughness also in regard to the gathering of texts. Certainly a few more manuscripts have come to light since his time, as I shall occasionally show, but their appearance has in most cases made no significant impact upon the validity of his textual conclusions.[2] As Hardin Craig respectfully observes, 'His work is so complete and so intelligently presented that one might think it done for once and for all, and it is.'[3]

But is it? Certainly in this wealth of textual, historical, and literary information (both of Young and of his followers), it would seem that we have reached the end-point of one particular avenue of investigation. But is this the only avenue of investigation possible, and does it, in fact, bring us anywhere near to what this drama is all about? Here it would seem that a strange irony exists; for, having taken from my shelves one of the several leading volumes dealing with the subject and having proceeded to read orderly expositions of the texts of some of the dramas —these demonstrating in turn the rapid interchange of Latin dialogue, moving and poetic laments and meditations, passionate clashes of temperament between vividly drawn characters, and a host of other factors which impress us with the literary and dramatic skills of the creators—I find it all too easy to forget that even if the reader were to see all such scenes translated into verbal stage action, he would be receiving only a tiny portion of the dramatic impact that would have reached the medieval audience for such works, as they would have been performed in one of the medieval cathedrals or larger monasteries. There is one element not being taken into consideration: the music.

A point that appears constantly to be overlooked is the fact that the texts of these church dramas were always sung. They were, in fact, libretti, and the works themselves early examples of '*dramma per musica*'. Just as in the liturgical services, where text and chant, when brought together, existed as equal partners, so in these early dramatic works vocal musical effects played a direct and continuous part. Is it not naïve to assume that we may now simply ignore this part and still claim an accurate impression of the drama?

---

[1] The most extensive discussion of this matter is to be found in O. B. Hardison, *Christian Rite and Christian Drama in the Middle Ages* (Baltimore, 1965), pp. 1–34. For my own comments on the matter, see my pp. 33–5 and 129–34.

[2] A significant exception to this is the Wolfenbüttel music-drama. See my p. 306, pp. 389–94.

[3] Hardin Craig, *English Religious Drama* (Oxford, 1955), p. 2.

Karl Young was at least aware of this imbalance—an awareness much to his credit, though like others of a strongly literary orientation, he failed to recognize the significance of what he was missing. In a lengthy comment in his Preface he deals with the music, suggesting its possible functions with regard to dramatic analysis:[1]

> Another aspect of these plays which has been generally unexplored is their melodies. I do not feel called upon to apologize for having treated these pieces from an exclusively literary point of view, and were a defence required, one could cite eminent precedents. It is an obvious fact, however, that since the plays of the Church were actually sung, our knowledge of them cannot be complete until such of their music as exists has been published, elucidated and heard ... The adequate editing and exposition of the music associated with the dramatic texts might well require a separate treatise equal to the present one in extent. Such a study would undoubtedly aid in the interpretation of certain texts, would assist a demonstration of relationships, and would probably disclose unexpected traditionalisms or originalities throughout the body of the plays. Its chief contribution, however, would consist, I think, in opening to us the full charm of these dramatic pieces ... The sensitive auditor will then discover that certain dramatic utterances of no great distinction in their words are magically touching in their melodies.

There is much in this passage which is excellent—and which, as will be seen shortly, forms the basis for my own investigation. Yet I must decline to accept Young's statement that the *chief* contribution of the music is 'to open up to us the full charm of these dramatic pieces'. The charm is there in full measure, but to my mind, and as I propose continually to show, the *chief* contribution consists of the large amount of new evidence that a study of the music releases, that often enough corrects wrong ideas which in the absence of that evidence have been allowed to grow up.

In this regard Coussemaker proves to have had the far keener sense of proportion, realizing that the study of the Church music-drama without its music amounts to nothing less than a travesty. In the Preface to his *Drames liturgiques du moyen âge* he comments ironically on the practices of his fellow editors; his strictures, unfortunately, have remained largely unheeded throughout the decades:[2]

> Mais leurs publications, qui réproduisent des pièces dramatiques, sont incomplètes: elles offrent une lacune regrettable. Les éditeurs les ont dépouillées de la musique qui les accompagne, et qui en est une partie substantielle et intégrante ... Il est donc nécessaire, on ne saurait trop le répéter, qu'elle soit publiée avec le texte ... Que dirait-on d'un auteur qui, voulant nous initier aux opéras joués sous Louis XIV par exemple, se contenterait de réproduire les libretti de Quinault?

Philippe Quinault was, of course, the poet who dedicated all his life to

---

[1] Karl Young, *The Drama of the Medieval Church*, 2 vols. (Oxford, 1933), I, pp. xiii–xiv.
[2] E. de Coussemaker, *Drames liturgiques du moyen âge* (Rennes, 1860), pp. vi–vii, xii.

the famous composer, Jean Baptiste Lully. Coussemaker's irony remains very much to the point at the present day. The libretti of these *music-dramas* are still studied to the exclusion of the music. Few writers, it would seem, have realized that we are dealing not with drama, but with music-drama, or in other words, with *opera*. In their curious blindness to this fact, scholars have allowed themselves to disregard half the evidence that the original documents have to show, with, as I shall later demonstrate, quite a number of regrettable results, Karl Young being an offender among the rest.

Thus it is that the present book is based on a constant consideration of the vocal line, which in the original pages of these dramas must always be assumed to be present. I say 'assumed', since in a number of liturgical manuscripts in which these dramas have been found it will be discovered that the musical notation has not been written in. This, however, does not mean that in certain mysterious situations these plays were spoken and not sung; it means only that we are dealing with a manuscript which happens to be of an exceptional type, such as an *ordinarium*, in which the emphasis is concentrated mainly on ceremonial, in the form of rubric directions, rather than on performance. Even the texts themselves are at times found reduced to incipits, i.e. the opening words of a particular sentence. But the medieval performer knew well enough what it was that followed!

Let us pursue this point a bit further, for it brings neatly into focus what I have been saying about the usefulness of music as a tool for understanding the drama while at the same time issuing fair warning as to the miscalculations which can result when the music is ignored. Throughout the entire dramatic corpus this use of incipits is a common occurrence, and an entirely logical one. The scribes entrusted with the writing down of these plays could be quite confident that their colleagues and contemporaries would be able to supplement the abbreviations out of their own knowledge. Certainly they felt no obligations towards the needs of posterity. There can be no doubt, however, that in the use of these abbreviated forms they created an enormous puzzle for future generations of scholars working from textual resources alone. Karl Young himself once said that 'when only the *incipit* of the antiphon is given, it will hardly be possible to identify it exactly',[1] which shows how unaware even he was as to the resources of musical notation. I suspect that his comment may have arisen out of sheer exasperation: on this particular occasion he had fallen into error through expanding an incipit text by guesswork and guessing wrong!

In point of fact, through the collation and comparison of the settings of the various antiphons, responsories, and the like borrowed by the music-dramas from the liturgy, together with the numerous original items which had passed into common use between them, it is usually possible to identify an incipit by the few notes (or neumes) which accom-

---

[1] Young, I, p. 601.

pany the opening words. Only when no music is given, or when the material is entirely unfamiliar, does the technique fail.[1]

The more serious problem, however, lies not so much in deciphering the incipit as in understanding its fundamental nature and purpose. In the terms set forth in Young's Preface, this is a matter of 'the interpretation of certain texts', and it is here that scholarship working in ignorance of the music may so easily wander off into wild speculation.

Let me illustrate. We have already observed that in the extant corpus of Church music-drama a large number of manuscripts lack music. We have also observed the reason for this omission: that certain liturgical books such as missal, breviary, and *ordinarium*, because of their very purposes, are not supplied with the music that normally accompanies the service texts. It is when dramatic compositions (particularly those belonging to the Easter and Christmas seasons) crop up in these books that we meet them deprived of their music, even though there is no doubt at all that every one of these music dramas was *sung*. With regard to the *ordinarium*, Karl Young is careful to explain that it usually contains no complete part of the liturgical text itself, but merely the incipit.[2] Usually it sacrifices the music of the incipit, but not in every case. There are a number of occasions when music-dramas appear in *ordinaria* (and even in missals and breviaries) complete in text and setting.

Yet there are writers on the subject, concerned only with texts, who do not seem to realize the nature of an *ordinarium*. In 1923 a theory was advanced by a German, Joseph Klapper,[3] that the '*Quem quaeritis*' dialogue in its shortened form represented, not a temporary and convenient abbreviation in normal *ordinarium* style, but an actual separate type. The 'first stage' of the dialogue, it was argued, consisted of an exchange of extremely brief Biblical phrases ('*Quem quaeritis*'; '*Non est hic*'; etc.), from which the later form developed. Unfortunately this theory has now gained renewed prominence in the hands of O. B. Hardison, who shows little interest in the musical side.[4] I shall give this matter more attention later, since it will be necessary for me to defend Karl Young from attack. Meanwhile it must be noted that, as is so often the case with these speculative dramatic 'prototypes', the musical evidence proves too much for the theory.[5]

Let us return now to Karl Young and look in somewhat more detail at the functions and insights he assigns to the music in this process of

[1] As, for example, in the Barking Abbey *Visitatio* (*Oxford, Univ. Coll. MS 169, Ordin. Berkingense*, pp. 121–4), in which a number of the dialogue incipits employed are to be found neither in the liturgy nor anywhere else. For a discussion of the liturgical and dramatic activities of Barking Abbey see my p. 14. The manuscript itself is discussed on my p. 364.

[2] Young, I, p. 20.

[3] Joseph Klapper, 'Der Ursprung der lateinischen Osterfeiern', *Zeitschrift fur deutsche Philologie*, L (1923), pp. 46–58.

[4] Hardison, p. 197. For my own discussion of the matter, see my pp. 104–7.

[5] The same objection applies to Professor Hardison's theory, which has lately been widely disseminated, that the *Quem quaeritis* dialogue, whether in trope or dramatic use, originated in a previous 'Vigil Mass' liturgical ceremony. It is the musical evidence which wrecks the theory. I deal with the matter on pp. 69 ff.

recovering the Church music-dramas. In the past few pages I have perhaps been a bit severe with him, choosing to single out certain 'literary' prejudices which seem to me serious handicaps to a study of the drama. Now, however, I must hasten to re-affirm my great respect for the man and his work. As I have found over and again, Young's analysis remains uncannily clear, and his 'prophecies' with regard to the music find ample corroboration in the scores themselves. I have already dealt with his comments concerning the usefulness of music in 'the interpretation of certain texts'. I would like now to look at the several other functions he suggests.

The 'demonstration of relationships' prophecy is a particularly sound one. Numerous examples of such relationships will be made manifest in the course of this study, clarified through close similarities between the invented musical settings of similar texts. For the moment I would like to share just one such example of 'musical sleuthery': my discovery of the link (which only the music could have revealed) between the first 'Shepherd' scene in the *Herod* drama from the so-called 'Fleury Playbook' and the *Officium Pastorum* of Rouen Cathedral (*B.N. 904*). In both works the first item of the Angel ('*Nolite timere . . .*') is taken from St. Luke ii: 10–12. The music is plainly common to the two works, with but small and unimportant occasional note-differences. Moreover, this music, as far as I am aware, appears nowhere else and has no liturgical origins. Another unique sharing between the two music-dramas is the setting of St. Luke ii:15 ('*Transeamus usque Bethlehem . . .*'). Here again is an original musical composition; only a few notes difference between the two settings, and nothing at all to do, musically, with the same text in the ancient antiphon '*Pastores loquebantur*'.[1] Yet another strange piece of musical evidence in connection with these two works could be mentioned, this time involving the *Visitatio Sepulchri* alleged to belong to Fleury.[2] As is well known, the question put to the shepherds at the manger, '*Quem quaeritis in praesepe, pastores . . .*' was framed in imitation of the older Easter dialogue. What is not so well known is the fact that in practically all cases the musical setting of this text, while consistent with itself, is completely different from that of the Easter Introit trope. Yet in the Rouen 'Shepherds' and the Fleury 'Herod' the music of the '*Quem quaeritis in praesepe*' is precisely that of the '*Quem quaeritis in sepulchro*' setting, with, moreover, small rhythmic details which cause it to coincide with the phrase setting as given in the Fleury *Visitatio Sepulchri*. Afterwards, in each Christmas piece, the music moves to a melismatic passage characteristic of the Christmas trope.[3]

---

[1] This antiphon may be found on p. 54 of that extraordinary tenth-century document, *Hartker's Antiphonal* (*St. Gall, MSS 390–391*). The manuscripts, under the title *Antiphonale du B. Hartker*, appear in facsimile in *Paléographie musicale*, iie série, i, Solesmes, 1900.

[2] S. Corbin's speculation, in *Romania 74*, that the work may actually belong to St. Lomer of Blois has found widespread but by no means universal acceptance (*Ed.*).

[3] I cannot find that the circumstances of this linking of the *Herod* and *Officium Pastorum* '*quem quaeritis in praesepe . . .*' music can be matched anywhere else in the whole range of surviving manuscripts—except possibly in the case of an eleventh-century troper from a far-

There seems no doubt whatsoever that the *Officium Pastorum*, a unique work, belongs to Rouen Cathedral. I have long suspected that the extraordinary mixture of styles and merits known as the 'Fleury Playbook' represents nothing more than a compilation. I speculate now as to whether the *Herod* and *Visitatio* of the Playbook may not have had their origins in Rouen.[1]

Karl Young's next prediction concerns the possibility of the music disclosing 'unsuspected traditionalisms or originalities throughout the body of the plays'. Since a great deal of the material employed in the medieval music-dramas has been borrowed from the service books, it will be interesting, and perhaps at times useful, to find whether these redeployed texts transfer also the liturgical music. One discovers that this is sometimes the case and sometimes not. The antiphon '*Surrexit Dominus de sepulchro*', for example, appears in two settings, one retaining the ancient music and the other introducing an apparently original German composition. We shall look at this matter in more detail at a later point in our study.

An important 'traditional' take-over by the music-dramas was the sequence *Victimae paschali*. The various versions that employed it made great dramatic play with its question-and-reply opportunities, but preserved always the dignified music. Furthermore, its pervasiveness was such that we find the first powerful eight notes being 'quoted' in other compositions, as in the introductory choral item, '*Jesu, magne Rex aeterne*' from the Easter Sepulchre version found in *Rouen, Bibl. de la Ville MS 252*—eight notes and no more before the Rouen melody goes its own way. On the other hand, the text of another ancient sequence, '*Quem non praevalent propria*', appears in the already mentioned *Herod* music-drama in a balanced, apparently rhythmic setting which has plainly nothing to do with the original one and may represent a version unique to this drama. [2]

As for Karl Young's expectations of 'originalities' to be found in the musical settings, he would have been confronted with an embarrassment of riches. Many years ago I pointed out that in the *Adeodatus* ('Son of Getron') music-drama there was a foreshadowing of the leitmotif device, inasmuch as each of the principal participants had his individual stanza tune. Even more subtle for the period, and equally not to be perceived by readers of the text alone, is the fact that when the thoughts of the exiled Adeodatus turn towards home, he abandons his own melody in favour of his mother's. Another good example of originality of thought can be seen in the Angel's reply to the Marys' '*Jesum Nazarenum crucifixum . . .*' in the 'Playbook' *Visitatio Sepulchri*. Instead of its being the

---

distant centre, that of Novalesa in N. Italy (*Oxford, Bibl. Bodl. MS Douce 222*) fol. 19v. this manuscript shows the '*Quem quaeritis in sepulchro . . .*' dialogue; fol. 6v. the *Quem quaeritis in praesepe . . .*'. The unheighted neumes are exactly the same in each case and *could* indicate the same momentary and exceptional agreement between the two musics, as in the cases of the French manuscripts.

[1] I discuss this theory more fully in my Chapter X.

[2] This composition is quoted in full on p. 210.

usual '*Non est hic; surrexit . . .*' it takes the form of a rhymed and rhythmic fantasia on, and extension of, the sentence. The musician will note that the opening words '*Quid, Christicolae, . . .*' are fitted to the inevitable '*Quem quaeritis*' musical phrase, and when, later, '*Non est hic*' turns up, it is given the usual upward leap.

To my mind, the finest example of musical originality, a highlight of medieval craftsmanship, is to be found in the lament of Rachel over the bodies of the murdered children, in the music-drama of 'The Slaying of the Innocents'. Previously, the 'Mothers' had attempted to shield them against the swords of Herod's soldiery, their cry, '*Oremus tenerae natorum parcite vitae*', being set to a striking melodic phrase. Later, this succession of notes is taken up and used as a motif, being woven into Rachel's rhythmic music (and into that of her 'Consolers') as a constantly recurring cadence with infinitely pathetic effect. It is a device that seems to have stepped back out of a later century, and I shall refer to it again in due course.

Regarding Karl Young's final prediction as to 'certain dramatic utterances of no great distinction' proving to be 'magically touching in their melodies', there are too many instances of this for me to make distinction here, except to recall a single 'Alleluia' in one of the works which, by the beauty of the phrase and the pitch of the notes, seems to produce and effect out of proportion to its simplicity.[1]

From the foregoing discussion it should by now be clear that a thorough consideration of the music is essential to our understanding of the Church music-drama; without such a consideration we have no understanding at all. The music provides evidence and insight in a way that the texts alone simply cannot; at the same time it forces us to deal with the drama in all three dimensions and to come to know it as itself, not just as a literary abstraction of itself.

One final point has yet to be made, and this concerns the rather nebulous matter of 'artistic self-awareness'. I must confess a great impatience with a certain school of criticism which insists upon viewing the dramatic artistry of the Middle Ages as totally ingenuous, i.e. primitive in the same way that a child's painting is primitive. Such an opinion is clearly voiced by Hardin Craig in his *English Religious Drama of the Middle Ages*. Although his concern is mainly with the secular vernacular drama, he also includes in his criticisms the liturgical dramas, which he discusses at some length and on the reference base of Karl Young's volumes —again, wholly oblivious of the music. In his introduction (pp. 4–5) he writes:

Indeed, the religious drama had no dramatic technique or dramatic purpose, and no artistic self-consciousness. Its lifeblood was religion, and its success depended on its awakening and releasing a pent-up body of religious feeling . . . we have here the strange case of a drama that was not striving to

[1] The specific 'Alleluia' which Smoldon had in mind must remain unknown, for at his death this footnote remained incomplete. During the course of this study he will set forth several possible contenders (*Ed.*).

be dramatic but to be religious, a drama whose motive was worship and not amusement.

Whatever conclusions he may come to concerning the vernacular, spoken drama, it is a pity that he was not able to realize some of the thoroughly self-conscious and wholly artistic subtleties, such as we have reviewed above, that were practised by the devisers of the Church music-drama. It would perhaps have been a revelation to him to have witnessed any modern, sung performance of representative examples of these music-dramas, reasonably staged: say, the Beauvais *Peregrinus*, or the Cividale *Planctus Mariae*, the latter with its elaborate rubrics calling for various emotions, expressions, and gestures. He would have seen demonstrations of the fact that the Middle Ages could create an atmosphere which was both religious and, in the truest sense of the word, dramatic. In the best of the music-dramas there were conscious artists at work, highly equipped technically, and exercising their art with a grace and sophistication which is even to this day remarkable.

But this is a fact which is revealed not by the text alone, but only by the text and music together, taken as a single, unified art-form. Over the past century it is this art-form that has been curiously neglected by scholars—and this art-form that I now propose to examine.

CHAPTER ONE

THE LITURGICAL BACKGROUND
OF THE DRAMA

IF, in the celebrated phrase of Sir E. K. Chambers, the rebirth of drama in Western civilization began 'in the very bosom of the Church', it was there, also, that began the process of its modern-day recovery. In the course of the last hundred years, scholars concerned with the history of European drama became increasingly aware of certain manuscripts which showed themselves to be closely connected with the medieval Church liturgy, though not truly a part of it. These manuscripts clearly qualified for the term 'dramatic', since, unlike the ceremonials of worship with which they were surrounded, they seemed through their accompanying rubrics to call for impersonation, exchanges of dialogue, reflective solos, and some degree of costuming, dramatic movement, and gesture. Through the transcription and publication of these texts, the modern world came to share in the realization that on Easter morning in many of the important medieval centres of worship not only would a responsory be sung which told of the coming of the three Marys to the empty tomb, but shortly afterwards these same three characters would be seen and heard making their way to the 'Sepulchre', there to be confronted by an angelic questioner. Similarly, in places such as Rouen Cathedral, the Introit of the first Mass of Christmas day was preceded by the appearance and singing of a group of suitably attired 'shepherds'. These made their way to the 'Manger' and there gave homage to the Child in his mother's arms. Afterwards, still costumed, they took leading parts in the choral singing of the Mass—in liturgical terms, they 'ruled the choir'. Or again, during Epiphany in many places the 'Three Kings' followed a 'star' to 'Herod's court' and thence to the 'Manger' with their gifts. At other, lesser feasts of the Church other episodes of the Christian story received dramatic illustration. For more than five hundred years drama and liturgy were interwoven in a venture of unique artistic and religious proportions.

Let us begin our study of this interweaving with a general assessment of the dramatic material which has survived from medieval times. I say 'survived', since there is every reason to believe that it must represent only a fraction of what once existed. If the proportion between the subject-themes remains the same among the surviving examples as it stood originally, then it is clear that the overwhelmingly chief interest among these anonymous composer-playwrights resided in what was (and is) the greatest event of the Christian year, the celebration of Easter. Out of the total number of surviving dramatic works of every type, the vast majority turn out to be concerned with the visit of the Marys to the empty tomb on Easter morning and the declaration of the Angel (or Angels) of the Resurrection—the compositions to which were given the name *Visitatio Sepulchri*.

As might be expected, the next greatest interest concerned the other major Christian feast, that of the birth of Christ. Yet the surviving dramas dealing with the Manger and the three star-led Kings (in striking parallel to the Sepulchre and the three mourning Marys) amounts to only about a score, in contrast to the Sepulchre total, which may amount to hundreds.[1] Even smaller is the number of surviving brief 'Manger' dramas involving the Shepherds. The *Peregrinus* type, a dramatization of the 'Road to Emmaus' story' from St. Luke, Chapter xxiv, survives in seven examples and a few fragments. Large-scale 'comprehensives' for each season are represented by two Passion dramas from Benediktbeuern and one from Montecassino, and by the Christmas drama from Benediktbeuern. Representatives of the various other subjects, including the unique and impressive *Daniel*, the huge, unwieldy *Antichrist*, and the problematic *Sponsus* survive either in single manuscripts, or at the most in two or three versions.

The accumulated knowledge gained from the study of the rubrics of these dramatic works has resulted in a fairly consistent picture being recovered as to the general conditions of performance. First and most obvious is the fact that they were performed within church walls, almost all linked in varying degrees of closeness with official liturgical ceremonies. All texts were in Latin, but one finds incidental invasions of the vernacular throughout the movement's existence. Every word of the dramatic text was sung, a matter on which I have already laid much emphasis. At first the texts were in prose, but as the dramas expanded and the need for invention seemed to grow, Latin poetry was introduced, sometimes adaptations of previous prose material, sometimes new compositions.[2] The musical settings of these rhyming, rhythmic lines, though written in the same non-mensural plainsong notation as the settings of the prose sentences, are probably to be interpreted as being regularly rhythmic also, a matter which I shall go into more fully later. Rarely is more than monophonic musical notation (that of the singer's melody) to be found in any of the manuscripts.

The singer-actors were clerics of various grades, sometimes men-

---

[1] I am considering here only dramatic examples of the Sepulchre dialogue. Also, I discount the numerous instances of manuscripts which represent repeat copies. This matter will be discussed in more detail later.

[2] 'Free rhythm' chant music seems occasionally to have been composed for 'invented' (i.e. non-liturgical) speeches. As we shall see time and again, however, it was often found possible to use relevant service antiphons, responsories, and other liturgical material in their traditional settings.

tioned as being priests. Choristers are occasionally referred to as taking part. Some *Visitatio* manuscripts were associated with nunneries and with Augustinian canonries, and give evidence that the three Marys were sometimes acted and sung by women (in what amounted to 'mixed casts').[1] Details of costuming are mentioned in many of the versions. There are also calls for simple properties. These last two matters will be dealt with in more detail later. It would appear that, if needed, the whole of the church space up to the high altar itself would be used for the action, and that the players moved from place to place as the supposed locations were changed. A good deal more will be said in the matter of practical production after some of the longer and more striking versions have been discussed in detail.

The earliest forms of dramatic activity began in the mid-to-late tenth century and concerned the Easter Sepulchre, as has been noted. It is my firm contention that the dialogue was originally non-dramatic, having come into existence as no more than a trope (i.e. an unofficial, invented addition to a liturgical item) which had proved widely acceptable as a preface to the Introit of the Easter Mass. It was only when this dialogue (the so-called '*Quem quaeritis*') was transferred from the overwhelming proximity of the sacrificial rite of the Mass that it found opportunity to take on a truly dramatic form, set in the possible 'breathing-space' between the last responsory of Easter Matins, which told of the coming of the Marys, and the concluding hymn, '*Te Deum laudamus*'.[2] In recent years, however, this view has been vigorously challenged by Professor Hardison, and will need to be dealt with more thoroughly at a later point in our study.[3] Whatever else we may say, one point seems clear: that in the vast majority of instances, whatever the dramatic type and whatever the feast day, the end of Matins was the favoured place for it.[4]

Throughout the eleventh, twelfth, and thirteenth centuries the drama expanded, flourished, reached its peak, and then gradually tapered off. By the fourteenth century the movement was visibly in decline, with the exception of its earliest manifestation, the *Visitatio*, which continued widely in use in monasteries, cathedrals, and even in larger town churches. These later 'Sepulchre' versions continued to be of varying degrees of elaborateness, apparently in accordance with local needs and tastes, from examples that amounted to little more than the original brief threefold exchange of question, reply, and further question, to ambitious

---

[1] See, for example, my discussion on pp. 377–4 of the fourteenth-century *Visitatio* from a convent in Prague (*Prague, MS VI G 3b*). See also note, 1, p. 249.

[2] Young notes (I, p. 232) that this final responsory is to be found in four forms, of which the most common is the following: '*Dum transisset sabbatum, Maria Magdalena et Maria Jacobi et Salome emerunt aromata, ut venientes ungerent Jesum, alleluia, alleluia.* VERSUS: *Et valde mane una sabbatorum veniunt ad monumentum, orto iam sole.*'

[3] I consider this matter in more detail on pp. 69 ff.

[4] See Karl Young, I, pp. 231 ff., for a comprehensive exposition as to why Matins became the favoured position for the performance of such dramatic works. There were, however, a few striking exceptions to the practice. The *Peregrinus* music-drama from Beauvais (twelfth century) was performed during a halt made for that purpose in the very midst of Easter Monday Triple Vespers. After its conclusion, Vespers was resumed (see p. 194).

works of considerable length that made use of the vernacular as well as Latin. These plays continued to be performed, it would seem, until well into the sixteenth century, mostly in Germanic regions. The stern measures of the Council of Trent against extra-liturgical accretions to services spelled their final doom.

II

From the foregoing brief survey we can trace a relationship between the Church and the drama which was broad, stable, and long-lasting. If we are to approach our investigation in a truly three-dimensional fashion, however, it is clear that we need to know a good deal more about the actual mechanics of this relationship. In particular, we must come to an appreciation of both its uniqueness and its intimacy. Karl Young emphasizes these aspects on the very first page of his introduction:[1]

> The dramatic manifestations to be considered in these volumes were the independent creation and possession of the medieval Church in Western Europe. They are to be regarded not as a continuation of an ancient tradition, and not as a worldly importation from outside, but as a spontaneous new birth and growth from within the confines of Christian worship. From the date of its beginning, in the tenth century, throughout the Middle Ages and into modern times, this drama remained essentially free from the contamination of alien forms . . . No other dramatic tradition engendered it, or dictated its form or content.

If this is indeed the case—and few scholars have doubted it—then it seems inescapable that our quest for the medieval music-drama must begin with Christian ritual itself. Before we can understand the form and structure of 'liturgical drama', we must first understand the form and structure of liturgy. It is for this reason that Karl Young devotes considerable space in the first volume of his work to a generalized survey of 'the Roman system of daily collective worship' (I, p. 15)—an approach with which I heartily concur.

In his investigation of factors leading to this 'spontaneous new birth', Young does not hesitate to put even the Mass itself under consideration. In Chapters III to V he examines the dramatic elements inherent in the authorized liturgy of the Church and considers the extent to which these may have influenced the emergence of the drama.

On the whole, however, his conclusions turn out to be strongly negative. Basing his investigation upon a definition of drama which requires as its touchstone the presence of *sustained impersonation*, he asserts that Christian ritual consistently fails to make the leap into genuine drama. With regard to the Mass he writes:[2]

> The impossibility of there being impersonation in the liturgy of the Eucharist arises from the fact that since the early Christian centuries this rite has been

---

[1] Young, I, p. 1.   [2] Ibid., pp. 84–5.

regarded as a true sacrifice. The central act is designed not to represent or portray or merely commemorate the Crucifixion, but actually to repeat it. What takes place at the altar is not an aesthetic picture of a happening in the past, but a genuine renewal of it . . . The consecrated elements *are* Christ, and through the words and acts of the celebrant Christ accomplishes his own immolation, being Himself, in reality, both the victim and the priest. The celebrant remains merely the celebrant and does not undertake to play the part of his Lord . . . The Mass, then, is not a drama, nor did it ever directly give rise to the drama.

The same considerations hold true for the numerous dramatic ceremonies which, by early medieval times, had come to be a part of Christian tradition—particularly the extra-liturgical practices of Holy Week which involved the symbolic actions of the 'burying' of the Host, between Mass and Vespers on Good Friday, and its 'taking up' before Matins on Easter Monday—the so-called *Depositio* and *Elevatio*.[1] Though these ceremonies show striking resemblances to drama, particularly in their elaborate arrangements for stage-setting, they remain in essence liturgical ceremonies. Their texts are very much the standard liturgical forms for the season, and one finds no real attempts at either dialogue or impersonation. Young observes: 'As liturgical exercises they are uncommonly tender or vivid or splendid; but they lack the essential element of true drama.'[2] The same may be said, ultimately, of even the very colourful 'Harrowing of Hell' activities, which by late medieval times are often found in close connection with the *Elevatio*. Some of these, it must be admitted, do move very near to true drama. At the nunnery of Barking, for example, the autocratic Katherine of Sutton, abbess from 1363 to 1376, produced her very individual version of the *Elevatio* ceremony, in which the whole of her community of nuns were bundled into a small chapel to await the symbolic 'breaking down of the gates' (or '*Tollite portas*'), thereafter to be released, waving palm branches and impersonating the lost souls. The Bamberg *Elevatio* is even more dramatic in its organization. After the usual details of the Elevation, the liturgical procession, bearing Host and Cross, leaves the church, passes through the cemetery, and returns to conduct the '*Tollite portas*' exchange at three successive entrances. A voice from within, representing that of Satan, puts forth the question '*Quis est iste rex gloriae?*' From the chorus outside comes the reply, '*Dominus fortis et potens . . .*' At the third attempt and at the third portal the doors yield, the procession enters, and the ceremony is brought to a triumphant conclusion with the replacement of the Host and the singing of the sequence *Victimae paschali*. There is clear evidence that a lay congregation was present and that they were allowed to make their own contribution by singing lines of

---

[1] To these two ceremonies we may add a third, closely linked to the *Depositio* but far outdating it in antiquity: the Adoration of the Cross on Good Friday. In medieval practice this *Adoratio/Depositio* coupling resulted in the burial, not only of the Host, but of the Cross as well; a good many manuscripts, in fact, seem to call for the burial of the Cross alone. For a fuller discussion of the matter, see Young, I, pp. 117–22.

[2] Young, I, p. 148.

vernacular hymns such as *Christ ist erstanden*. To them, surely, the ceremony must have been a vivid reminder of the Death, the Harrowing, and the Resurrection. But promisingly dramatic as it is, it occurs far too late in the history of dramatic activities of the medieval Church to have had any bearing on their origin. At any rate, Young's conclusions are clear and firmly stated: 'The effectual beginnings of medieval religious drama are not to be found in the elaboration of elements present in the traditional forms of worship . . .'[1] Whatever these forms may have contributed indirectly, the liturgy itself remained 'always merely worship'.[2]

But although we must not look to the liturgy as the direct *source* of the drama, it is still undeniably the *context* in which the drama found its roots and strength. For our purposes here, the more important fact is that it is liturgy which provides the actual 'building blocks' for the drama, not only in terms of themes and plots, but in terms of specific textual and musical material. Clearly, if we are going to make effective use of this material in our discussion of the drama, it will be necessary to have some idea of where it comes from and how it functions in the overall pattern of Christian ritual. At this point, then, we need to turn our attention in somewhat more detail to the technical structure of Christian ritual. It will of course be noted that Karl Young has already treated this matter with great thoroughness in the first two chapters of his work. I have neither the time nor inclination to reproduce his efforts here: any serious student of the drama is urged to consult them at first hand. My ambition, rather, is to produce a general description of the liturgy of the Church of Rome as a background for some points of my own which have specific bearing on the music—the latter, as we have already seen, not being Karl Young's particular interest.

III

In considering Christian ritual, the first thing we need to bear in mind is that the basic daily worship of the Church falls into two parts: the Mass and the Canonical Office (or 'Hour services'). The Mass, which in Catholic tradition traces its institution to Christ himself, is the more ancient and sacred of the two observances. By the tenth century it was fairly well fixed in form—essentially as we know it in recent times—and established throughout most of Western Christendom.[3] The Office, lack-

---

[1] Ibid., p. 178.

[2] Ibid., p. 85. Young makes a valuable point (p. 100) when he corrects a widespread misunderstanding concerning the liturgical renderings of the four Gospel Passions during Holy Week. The chanting of the respective parts for Narrator, '*Christus*', and '*turbae*', as set down in modern Roman service books for three separate voices, might convince a listener that here, perhaps, were the roots of Church music-drama. It is Young's own researches which have made it clear that this manner of performing the passion dates from the fifteenth century, and that previously the whole item was sung straight through by a single deacon.

[3] Two significant exceptions were the permanently independent Ambrosian rite of Milan and the Mozarabic of Spain, then in its last throes. It will be noted, of course, that the

ing such basis in an 'explicit pattern enjoined by Christ' (Young, I, p. 44), shows a far less consistent history of development.

The various liturgical items comprising the Mass have been described in detail by Karl Young and need not be reproduced here. For our purposes, however, we need to be aware of two major dichotomies which function within the Mass as organizing principles: *Ordinary* versus *Proper*, and spoken versus sung. The Ordinary of the Mass includes those items which do not change their texts with the change of days and seasons. Of these, the musical items concerned are the Kyrie, Gloria, Credo, Sanctus (and Benedictus), and Agnus Dei. 'Proper' are those items whose texts change to conform with the season, or with the specific saint being commemorated. The musical items concerned here include the Introit, Gradual, Alleluia (or alternatively, the Tract), Offertory, and Communion. Willi Apel's table is useful in visualizing these matters, and I reproduce it here:[1]

THE MASS

CHANTS		SPOKEN OR RECITED	
PROPER	ORDINARY	PROPER	ORDINARY
1. Introit			
	2. Kyrie		
	3. Gloria		
		4. Collect	
		5. Epistle	
6. Gradual			
7. Alleluia (or Tract)			
		8. Gospel	
	9. Credo		
10. Offertory			
			11. Offertory Prayers
		12. Secret	
		13. Preface	
	14. Sanctus		
			15. Canon
			16. Pater Noster
	17. Agnus Dei		
18. Communion			
			19. Post-communion

Followed by the Dismissal ('*Ite, missa est*')

By the Middle Ages the time for the Mass seems to have been fixed in the morning, between the canonical hours of Terce and Sext. 'The' Mass

accepted 'Roman' form of the Mass is not that of Rome of the earlier centuries, but represents a fusion of Roman and Frankish elements. See Young, I, p. 17.

For a perceptive discussion of the Roman and Frankish (Gallican) elements in the Mass and the relationship between these elements and the origin of the drama, see Clifford Flanigan, 'The Roman Rite and the Origins of the Liturgical Drama', *University of Toronto Quarterly*, XL, No. 3 (Spring 1974), pp. 263–84 (*Ed.*).

[1] Willi Apel, *Gregorian Chant* (London, 1958), p. 26.

refers of course to the Mass of the day. 'Votive' Masses could be celebrated at any time for some special reason, and often upon request. It will later come to our notice in considering certain music-dramas that Christmas Day has three Masses, one after Matins, another after Prime, and a third after Terce.

The foregoing comment, of course, leads us into a consideration of that other major division of Christian worship: the Canonical Office. The Office, which is in fact a collective term, is comprised of eight separate devotional services, or *horae*, distributed throughout the course of the day: Matins, Lauds, Prime, Terce, Sext, None, Vespers, and Compline. As has already been mentioned, these services show an inconsistent history of development and tend to vary in their liturgical details from place to place, far more so than the Mass. Of the eight, the three most important are Matins, Lauds, and Vespers. It is these three also that are destined to have important connections with the history of the drama.

The Hour services based themselves more than anything else on the singing of the Psalms. As Gerbert, the historian of Christian music, proclaimed, quoting from St. Chrysostom: 'David is first, middle, and last.'[1] In all the services there were psalms with antiphons, together with hymns, lessons, various responsories, and introductory and concluding prayers. The lesser *horae* were brief in comparison with the major three, of which the longest was Matins. In this service one finds the main section to be the Nocturns, three almost identical divisions, each consisting of three psalms with their respective antiphons and three lessons with their respective responsories. There were thus in all nine psalms with antiphons and nine lessons with responsories—a lengthy business! A significant exception to this rule occurred, however, at Easter Matins, in which the number of Nocturns was reduced from three to one.[2]

The normal Lauds and Vespers are very similar to each other in organization. Lauds employs the Canticle of Zacharias, '*Benedictus Dominus Deus*' (Luke i:68–9); Vespers that of the Virgin, '*Magnificat anima mea Dominum*' (Luke i:46–55). It must be mentioned that the form of Vespers with which examples of the music-drama will be found associated was not the normal one, but a greatly expanded 'triple' version, which was enacted ceremoniously at various stations throughout the Church. More note will be made of this at a later point in our study.[3]

A not wholly resolvable question arises as to what times in the daily round the various medieval Hour services took place. The names of certain of them recall the classic Roman practice of successively numbering

[1] Quoted in Gustave Reese, *Music in the Middle Ages* (New York, 1940), p. 65.

[2] Normally there were nine psalms with antiphons in Matins, five in Vespers, four in Lauds, and three in the remainder. The psalms in their liturgical shapes do not always coincide with the Biblical ones, consisting sometimes of only a part of a normal text, sometimes of a combination of two or more. The liturgy visualized that each of the one hundred and fifty psalms would be sung once in the course of the Hour services for one week. This did not always work out exactly, since special festivals and other occasions for special psalms complicated matters.

[3] For a detailed description of this ceremony, see Young, I, pp. 456–8.

the hours of the day from 6 a.m. (*prima hora*) through midday (*sexta hora*) to 6 p.m. (*duodecima hora*), but in practice throughout Christendom there seems to have been neither a strict keeping to the 'hours' named nor a pattern of consistency generally. Karl Young (I, p. 74) speaks of the rule of St. Benedict in the Middle Ages as following 'in a general way' a *horarium* which runs thus: Matins, 2–2.30 a.m.; Lauds, 4.30– 5 a.m.; Prime, 6 a.m.; Terce, 9 a.m.; Sext, 12 noon; None, 4 p.m.; Vespers, 4.30 p.m.; Compline, 6 p.m. He continues: 'Although custom varied somewhat over Western Europe, some such distribution as this must have been followed in many monasteries and cathedrals. In modern times Matins and Lauds are usually sung continuously in early morning; and the other services of the day are combined in groups which differ from place to place.'

Young's exposition makes no mention of the mobility of Matins, which on special occasions could be found placed at midnight or before,[1] and the general differences in the Hour service timings from place to place which were certainly noticeable in medieval times. These matters, however, are taken up in considerably more detail by Professor Frank Harrison in his *Music in Medieval Britain*. Detailing the Sarum rite in Britain, he writes:[2]

The instructions to the ringers (of bells) show that the time of Matins varied with the seasons and feasts, beginning immediately after midnight on doubles in winter and summer until August, and otherwise at midnight in winter and at such a time as to end at dawn in summer. The exceptions were Christmas when Matins was finished before midnight, Easter Day and the following week when it began at first daylight, and certain festivals in midsummer, when it was allowed to be sung in the evening (*in sero*) after Vespers and Compline. When Matins was sung in the evening, Lauds, which normally followed it, was sung on the following morning. There was no significant variation in the times of the other offices. Prime was about nine, Terce about ten, Sext and None about eleven, Vespers and Compline about three.

In a footnote Professor Harrison adds that though the Hours services were not necessarily sung at the 'true' times of first hour, third hour, etc., they nevertheless respresented the times at which the events of Christ's Passion took place. In another footnote, on evidence from an *Ordinale* of St. Mary's, York, he further observes: 'In Benedictine communities the bell for Matins was rung at midnight all the year round and that for Prime at seven a.m.'

One is not surprised to find Willi Apel's contribution to the timings of the Hour services one of some caution.[3] For the time of Matins he commits himself to no more than 'before sunrise'; Lauds 'at sunrise'; Vespers 'at sunset'; Compline 'before retiring'. For the remaining four he confines himself to the Latin numberings (e.g. *ad primum horam*).

Anyway, since so much of our chief concern with the Hour services

[1] The term 'Nocturn' in itself suggests that Matins in the early centuries may have been celebrated in the middle of the night.
[2] Frank Harrison, *Music in Medieval Britain* (London, 1958), p. 55.   [3] Apel, p. 13.

will focus on the Easter ones, we will at least have the satisfaction of knowing that, as we imagine the last sounds of the third responsory of Matins dying away, to be succeeded by the sight of the 'Marys' themselves, they will be dimly and authentically revealed in the first light of day.

IV

Before leaving details of the liturgy we need to consider more closely, especially in matters connected with music, those items which played some part in the development of the music-dramas, beginning with the ubiquitous antiphon. In its original usage, which dates from the earliest centuries of Christian worship, the term *antiphona* referred to the practice of singing sentences such as psalm verses in alternation by two groups of voices. By about the sixth century, however, this meaning had been taken over by the term *alternatim*, and an antiphon had come to be accepted as a short text (often of Biblical origin) set to a chant and employed in the Office for use with a psalm, as an introduction and a rounding-off.[1] In the early centuries of Christian practice the antiphon was sung before and after the psalm and also between each verse, but this practice survived to later times only in special cases.[2] There are also certain occasions, such as processions and memorials, when antiphons are sung without attachment; these, however, are the exception rather than the rule.

As compared with other forms of the chant, antiphons are short and musically simple. The majority have settings consisting of single notes interspersed with two-note groups. Only occasionally do they develop melismatic passages. In quantity they far exceed any other type, numbering in the thousands. Their straightforward music and the quantity and variety of their texts caused them frequently to be borrowed, music and all, for use in the music-dramas. Here they served as ready-made passages of 'recitative'. The effect, especially when followed by a lyrical passage of Latin poetry, is that of an uncanny anticipation of the operatic technique of several centuries ahead.

Mention has already been made of the Nocturns of Matins, each with its three lessons. After each lesson came a musical postlude, the responsory. Longer and more melismatic in musical style than the antiphon, it was second to it in liturgical quantity. A responsory consisted of two parts. The opening respond was begun by one or a few voices and continued by the choir; then came a middle verse sung by the soloist (or soloists), after which the respond was repeated from mid point by the choir. This structural contrast was re-inforced by a musical one: the

---

[1] From an early date there was added at the end of the singing of the various types of psalmody, the Doxology (word of praise): '*Gloria Patri et Filio et Spiritui Sancto: Sicut erat in principio, et nunc, et semper, et in secula seculorum. Amen.*' Its presence is sometimes signalled in abbreviated form by the letters E u o u a e, the vowels of the two concluding words, '. . . *seculorum, Amen*'.

[2] For a listing of these cases, see Harrison, pp. 58–9.

B

respond chant-melody itself was a 'free' one, while the verse was normally sung to one of eight standard responsorial tones.[1]

A more elaborate form of the responsory is to be found in the Gradual of the Mass. Here the basic pattern is still visible, but with two significant differences; first, the respond itself is normally repeated in full after the verse (and not just from mid-point); second, the verse is sung to its own 'free' melody and not to a standard tone. Graduals tended to attain great ornateness and complexity and are among the most fully melismatic chants of the Gregorian repertory.

The Introit of the Mass, which in due course will be found to be deeply involved with the early stages of the Church music-drama, is another example of a form owing its origin to the complete psalm with antiphon. By the period with which we are concerned, however, the psalm has been reduced to a single verse, and the form has become: antiphon; psalm verse to a tone; antiphon repeat; '*Gloria Patri*' to the verse tone; antiphon repeat. The body of the Introit chants are in a consistently neumatic style, i.e. in any given Introit the great majority of syllables carry a group of notes numbering from two to five, very seldom more. In contrast to the elaborately melismatic Graduals, they are, as Apel describes them, 'moderately ornate'.[2] The various Introit melodies are also very individual and do not borrow phrases from each other, a practice sometimes found in the responsories and Graduals. A common Introit characteristic is the frequent use of *strophici* (repeated unisons on one syllable), usually *tristrophae*. We shall see this point illustrated when we consider our most relevant Introit, '*Resurrexi, et adhuc tecum sum*'. Again, there can be noted the frequent use in the antiphon section of single notes of the same pitch (as well as *strophici*), which gives to the melody a rather stationary character, not unlike a slightly ornamented recitative.[3]

The utterance '*Alleluia*' was taken over originally from the ancient Jewish services and occurs not only in the Mass, but as a general expression of praise and rejoicing. The various settings of the four syllables came to include a great deal of melismatic material, and in the repeat of the Alleluia the final 'a' was inevitably given a long vocal flourish (a choral one) termed a *jubilus*. The Alleluia at first stood by itself, but in its Mass form in the process of time it acquired a verse, usually from one of the psalms—this by simple addition, and not, as in the case of the psalmodic chants (such as Gradual and responsory) by the cutting down of a whole psalm. As for the form, it worked out to be the familiar ternary one, since the already-repeated Alleluia was repeated once more after the soloist's verse, *jubilus* and all. Nor was this the end of the repetition: in most cases the verses themselves concluded by incorporat-

---

[1] For a detailed discussion of responsorial psalmody and an enumeration of these eight tones, see the article on 'Psalmody' in *Grove's Dictionary of Music and Musicians*, 3rd edition (5 volumes and supplement), 1928.

[2] Apel, p. 305.

[3] For a fuller discussion of *Strophici*, and their notation, see Chapter III, pp. 40–1.

ing the *jubilus* music of the Alleluia, and at times even more of the first section music![1] Thus, the normal structure of the Mass Alleluia may be said to be: Alleluia; Alleluia with *jubilus*; Verse with *jubilus*; Alleluia with *jubilus*. It must be noted, however, that the various musical settings display many subtleties of structural detail, making a strict application of this rule frustrating if not impossible. It should be noted also that in the Mass of Easter the final Alleluia repeat is directed to be omitted. There follows immediately the sequence '*Victimae paschali*', with which the Easter music-dramas were destined to have much to do.

An occasional dramatic borrowing from the liturgy was that of the hymn, an item which (comparatively late) came to be established in the Office, and now and again in the Mass. The hymn, whose characteristic feature is an invented, poetic text, has a curious and stormy history. Although it is recorded that hymns were sung by the earliest Christians,[2] the Western Church (unlike the Byzantine) tended to frown upon the activity, taking a view which foreshadowed that of the Calvinists, that they were 'man-made', and having some early suspicions of a link between hymns and the Gnostic heresy.[3]

But then in Milan, towards the end of the fourth century, St. Ambrose actually encouraged the practice of hymn-singing and himself wrote a number of texts. Of the many hymns which have been ascribed to him, only four are now generally accepted as authentic: '*Aeterne rerum Conditor*'; '*Deus Creator omnium*'; '*Iam surgit hora tertia*'; and '*Veni Redemptor gentium*'.[4] All of these are written in a simple metrical pattern consisting of four-line stanzas with four iambic feet to each line—a metre which subsequently took on the name 'Ambrosian'. Trochaic patterns are of later date, one of the earliest examples being the still surviving hymn in the Good Friday Mass, '*Pange Lingua gloriosi*'. Much more elaborate metres, culled from classical sources, come into use during the eighth century Carolingian 'revival of learning', but their subtleties are less apparent since in the matter of accentuation the classical principle of quantity in Latin verse had given way to that of stress, the 'normal' accentuation that one finds marked in the Solesmes-edited service books. Although the hierarchy continued its coolness towards hymns through the mid-millennium, the support given to their use by St. Benedict (d.

---

[1] A magnificent example can be seen in the Mass, Common of Doctors (*Liber Usualis*, p. 1192). The verse, '*Justus germinabit*' soon takes up the music of the Alleluia *jubilus* for the setting of its words, and then, for the last two words ('*ante Dominum*') and its own *jubilus*, uses the whole of the Alleluia music.

[2] Perhaps the clearest reference to this practice dates from A.D. 269, when the Council of Antioch reproached Bishop Paul of Samosata for having forbidden the singing of hymns.

It must be noted that as late as *c.* 500 the word *hymnus* had not yet taken on its distinctive sense of a new composition in poetic form, and is used more frequently to designate the singing of a psalm. New compositions during this period are often referred to as *carmen*. See Apel, p. 421.

[3] For a time hymns were forbidden altogether—officially if not entirely effectively—by decree of the Council of Laodicea, which met between 360 and 381.

[4] The first of these survives to this day in the Roman rite.

547), their presence in the Offices of some sixth-century French monasteries, and finally the influence of the dominant Benedictine monastery of Cluny, caused the Benedictine Hymnal to be adopted by the Roman Church in the tenth century. Even so, the famous Hartker Antiphonal of the tenth century contains no hymns.[1]

When it comes to the matter of hymn melodies, one realizes that the firm organization to be found in the main portions of the liturgy is lacking in the hymn collections. The choice of a particular melody for a particular text is not constant even between the leading modern service books, the *Antiphonale Romanum*, the *Antiphonale Monasticum*, and the *Liber Usualis*. There are hymns with a double-figure number of alternative melodies. There are melodies that are employed for several texts.

As might be expected, the melodic styles of the free-rhythm hymn tunes are mostly basically simple, ranging from what amount to little more than reciting tones for some of the hymns of the lesser Offices, to melodies of some movement and charm, with incidental groups of two and three notes. Only for the more important feasts are there to be found examples of really melismatic moments, as in the *Alter Tonus* of '*Exsultet orbis gaudiis*'—a hymn in Second Vespers of the Common of the Apostles and Evangelists (*Liber Usualis*, p. 1116). Hymns were performed *alternatim*, the final doxology sung by all.

When the actual phrase-constructions of the hymn tunes are analysed, some interesting varieties of form are to be observed. Most hymn stanzas keep to four lines of fairly regular construction, easily enough fitted with four musical phrases. While often enough these phrases are all different, expressed musically as a b c d, what must be reckoned as an age-old desire to repeat an attractive phrase is sometimes irresistible, and as a result different patterns emerge. Such patterns are to be found in the secular music of the troubadours and trouvères of the eleventh and twelfth centuries, and must represent a widespread artistic inclination. Examples of such varied forms are also to be found in the shapely, regularly cadenced melodies occurring in the Church music-dramas, associated with invented, rhyming Latin poetry.

The most striking of these musical patterns must surely be the 'rounded bar-form'—a a b a; the microcosm of sonata-form, with its germ of a contrasting section and of a recapitulation. The hymn '*Splendor paterna gloria*' (Tuesday at Lauds, *Antiphonale Romanum*, p. 61) is a good example, the second 'a' with a slight variation, as is often the case. Even more striking is '*Tu Trinitatis Unitas*' (At Lauds, Feast of the Blessed Trinity, *Liber Usualis*, p. 907), where each version of the 'a' phrase repetition has its variation.[2]

Another pattern, using the important first repeat, a a b c, can be seen employed in the hymn '*Iste Confessor Domini*' (Second Vespers, Com-

---

[1] See footnote 1, p. 6.
[2] The a a b a form can be distinguished in the extensive stanza melody given to Gabriel in the famous and macaronic music-drama *Sponsus*.

mon of a Confessor Bishop, *Liber Usualis*, p. 1177, *second* tune).[1] The most common hymn-tune pattern employing a repetition is in fact a b c a, an example of which can be found in '*Nunc Sancte*' (First Sunday in Advent, at Terce, *Liber Usualis*, p. 318).

Other 'repetition' forms to be found among the official hymns include a b c b, a b b a, and even a b a b. All these patterns can be found used with music-drama poetry. A notable example, extended to six lines, has already been mentioned, '*Pange lingua gloriosi*' (Afternoon Liturgy, Good, Friday, *Liber Usualis*, p. 742). The pattern is a b c d c d, that used in the *Visitatio Sepulchri* for Mary Magdalene's stanza, '*Resurrexit hodie, Deus deorum*'.

One of the earliest of hymns is the immortal '*Te Deum laudamus*'. According to medieval legend, it is said to have been improvised jointly by Ambrose and Augustine while the former was baptizing the latter; but the more likely composer is now believed to be the Dacian Bishop Niceta of Remesiana (*c.* 335–414). By the sixth century the hymn was widely known, and at some period not long thereafter it found its way officially into the Roman liturgy. It normally concludes Matins, but apart from this use it has, through the generations, continually been employed on special ceremonial occasions to express a general emotion of thanksgiving. For the Church music-dramas its presence, indisputably in the right place, served as an ideal choral conclusion to whatever work was being performed.

Unlike the normal hymns in Latin poetry, the '*Te Deum*' is in prose, consisting of a succession of sentences in parallel construction. Three sections are apparent: (1) praise to God (the first thirteen verses); (2) praise to Christ (as far as the verse '*Aeterna fac*', which may possibly have marked the original end of the hymn); (3) a final section, from '*Aeterna fac*' to the end, which consists mainly of intercessory prayers and may well have been caught up from the versicle and response forms of the surrounding liturgy.

The music can be said to be mainly in psalm-tone style, with some brief and independent passages, and with occasional antiphon-like setting, as in the verses '*Aeterna fac*' and '*In Te Domine speravi*'. For all the wealth of polyphonic settings of the text which have come into existence, the plainchant version, by its dignity and power, continues to hold its own.

V

Before concluding this chapter, we need to attend to one final matter; namely, a consideration of the various types of service books in use by the Church, both in medieval times and in our own. This matter is important, for Church music-dramas occasionally turn up in unlikely places, and

---

[1] As in the case of the a a b a form, the repeat of 'a' suffers small variations at times. The same pattern is used in the music-drama tune sung by the King's Attendants in *Adeodatus*, one of the 'Fleury Playbook' works.

a failure to recognize the nature and function of the service book in which they appear may lead to unfortunate error. The texts of the Mass are found in the missal (*missale*).[1] The music (with the concomitant texts of course) is found in the gradual (*graduale*).[2] A number of lesser volumes existed in medieval times for meeting one or another particular purpose, such as a sacramentary (*sacramentarium*) containing the parts said by the celebrant; a Gospel book (*evangelarium*) containing the liturgical Gospels to be read; an epistle book (*epistolarium*) containing the epistles to be read; these last two sometimes found joined as a lectionary (*lectionarium*). Similarly in regard to music, an exclusive collection of texts and music of the Ordinary of the Mass (extracted from the gradual) was termed a *kyriale*.

Regarding the Canonical Office, the texts of the Hour services are found in the breviary (*breviarium*). The musical items (with texts of course) are found in the antiphonal (*antiphonale*). There is need also for a psalter (*psalterium*), giving words and music for the singing of the psalms. A *liber responsalis*, or *responsoriale*, contained the various other items sung by the choir, a *vesperale* contained the music for Vespers (also to be found in the *antiphonale*), while a hymnal (*hymnarium*) contained the hymns. Texts of homilies and Biblical passages, prayers and collects, and accounts of the lives of saints were to be found in separate books (*lectionarium, collectarium, martyrologium*). All the liturgical services needed an ordinary (*ordinarium*) for reference purposes. As we have already seen, this book was a directional one, the one most fully concerned with rubrics, at the expense of text and music.

Mention must be made of that comparatively modern service volume, the *Liber Usualis* ('Book for general use'), first published in 1896, with periodically revised editions later. As the name implies, it is a 'handy' volume, combining the main contents of missal, gradual, breviary, and antiphonal and giving a clear, single view of the structure of the liturgical day within manageable limits, at the cost of the sacrifice of a number of lesser-used chants. In the course of this present work references to it may prove convenient when examples from the official chant-music are called for.

---

[1] The missal nowadays contains all the rites of the Mass and certain other services closely connected with it. The book did not appear until about the tenth century, and during the Middle Ages there were missals of great variety. Pope Pius V issued a revised and definitive missal in 1570. Some re-editings have taken place since then.

[2] It will be noted that the same word occurs to describe one of the items of the Proper of the Mass, the term usually explained, in this case, as deriving from *gradus*, since the chant was sung from the steps leading to the pulpit.

CHAPTER TWO

THE MUSICAL BACKGROUND
OF THE DRAMA (1)

A brief history of the Gregorian Chant
The method of investigation in this book
The 'evolutionary hypothesis'

As soon as we commit ourselves to a study of the music-drama as music and not merely as drama, we are faced with a wide new range of responsibilities. Clearly, the prerequisites for our task include a knowledge not only of textual analysis and of liturgical tradition, but of musicology as well, and it is to this matter that we must now turn our attention.

Since the medieval music-dramas, closely attached to the liturgy as most of them were, used the same musical idiom and notations as did the service settings, it behoves us to begin our discussion with some attention to the subject of 'Gregorian Chant'. The name, of course, recalls the memory of Gregory the Great, Pope from 590 to 604. He played a great part in strengthening the authority of the See of Rome and in unifying the Church in the West, and he undertook various liturgical reforms; but modern research has become increasingly doubtful about what he ever produced or caused to be produced in the nature of a comprehensive chant repertory. Most assuredly he cannot be credited with the systematic and rigorous chant system which now bears his name. On the other hand, medieval tradition runs very strong here, particularly on the matters of his having founded (or reorganized) the *Schola Cantorum* and compiled the Roman Antiphonary; and in the absence of conclusive evidence to the contrary, it seems unwise to disregard tradition altogether. Perhaps the safest approach is to envisage a gradual process of evolution, in which Gregory played a significant, though as yet unknown, role.

As numerous records plainly show,[1] from the earliest Christian centuries singing (if at first little more than the simple rendering of psalms, antiphons, hymns, and responsories) has always been given its place in the liturgy of the day. Of this singing two things can be said: first, that it has been primarily vocal, the performance of service texts by either a solo voice or a group of voices,[2] and second, that it usually lacks any

---

[1] For an extensive listing of these records, see Apel, pp. 38–42.

[2] Instruments, however, are quite a different story! As early as Clement of Alexandria (*c.* 150–*c.*220), we find stern proscriptions against their use in churches—a battle which was to rage chronically for centuries thereafter. See Apel, p. 39, note 9.

impression of regular metre, since its texts are, for the most part, in prose. As to its development, the first general reorganization of the liturgy and the chant in the West as far as is known seems to be attributed to Damasus I, Pope from 366 to 384. It was modelled on the liturgical practices of the Church of Jerusalem.[1] Damasus is also supposed to have introduced antiphonal singing to Rome and to have added the Alleluia to the Mass service.[2] By the fifth century there had probably evolved some sort of rudimentary chant system organized to fill the whole ecclesiastical year.

The next several centuries are the story of its gradual growth and dispersion. It has already been pointed out (p. 15, note 3) that the early chant based in Rome was in fact only one of several branches that, with the firm adoption of Latin as the language of the liturgy, established themselves in the Western world. The history of the chant for the next few centuries was closely bound up in the struggle of the Roman rite for supremacy. The Ambrosian chant of Milan has maintained its differences to this day. The Spanish (Mozarabic) idiom soon faded. For our purposes, however, the most significant struggle was that which occurred between Rome and the powerful Gallican Church—and here the give and take lasted for a long period of time. As the liturgist J. A. Jungmann has written, describing the introduction of Roman usage into Franco-Germanic lands: 'The exotic seedling, when planted in a new soil and a new climate, was still pliant enough to be reshaped and modified by these influences.'[3] And reshaped it was: even though at first the rulers of the Frankish Empire, particularly Charlemagne, sought to placate Rome in matters ecclesiastical, it was nevertheless a Franco-Germanic hybrid developed in Franco-Germanic lands which finally returned to Rome to become what we now call 'Gregorian Chant'. As Jungmann further explains:[4]

About the middle of the tenth century the Roman liturgy began to return in force from Franco-Germanic lands to Italy and to Rome, but it was a liturgy which had meanwhile undergone radical changes and great development. This importation entailed supplanting the local form of the Roman liturgy by its Gallicized version even in the very centre of Christendom.

With regard to the final evolution of the chant, there can be no better

---

[1] This Jerusalem liturgy has been described in a fascinating and unique document known as the *Peregrinatio Etheriae* (formerly the *Peregrinatio Silviae*)—a first-hand account by the Spanish abbess Etheria, who in *c.* 385 undertook a pilgrimage to Jerusalem. Editions of this document are by W. Heraeus, *Peregrinatio Silviae vel potius Aetheriae ad loca sancta* (1921); and John H. Bernard, *The Pilgrimage of Saint Silvia* (1891). The liturgy which she describes is discussed in some detail in Apel, pp. 43–6.

[2] This second matter, however, is open to considerable question. The critical piece of evidence here is a letter of Gregory the Great; in recent years a number of scholars have argued convincingly that its meaning should be corrected to the exact opposite of what it seems to say. If this is the case, then we must conclude that Damasus did not introduce the Alleluia, but in fact abolished it! See Apel, pp. 376–7.

[3] J. A. Jungmann, *The Mass of the Roman Rite*, translated by Francis A. Brunner, 2 volumes (New York, 1951), Vol. 1, p. 76.

[4] Ibid., p. 95.

summary of the situation as far as we have pursued it than Willi Apel's:[1]

> The conclusion is almost inescapable that this chant, as found in the manuscripts of St. Gall, Einsiedeln, Metz, Chartres, etc., received its final form in France, in the period about 800, a form that differed considerably from its Roman model . . . We may then assume that what we call Gregorian Chant is the result of a development that took place in the Franco-German empire under Pepin, Charlemagne, and his successors. This does not mean to say that all the many thousands of melodies of the present-day repertory were composed during this time . . . It means that they represent the final stage, and the only one known to us, of an evolution, the beginnings of which may go back to the earliest Christian period and even to the chant of the Synagogue. What changes took place during the numerous formative stages we cannot say. Some chants may have changed relatively little, others so much that their original form was obscured or completely lost. On grounds of probability and plausibility we may assume that the simpler chants were less affected by the vicissitudes of a purely oral tradition than those of a highly ornate character . . . It is probably safe to think of certain very rudimentary types, such as the psalm tones . . . as being a heritage from early Christian, and ultimately pre-Christian days; of simple antiphons as dating possibly from the time of Gregory; and of an Introit, a Gradual, a Tract as being, in its present-day form, a product of the eighth or ninth century.

There now comes a crucial question. How was the *music* of all these various services (mentions of which often come down to us without any surviving service manuscripts) put on record?

In the time of Gregory the Great and for perhaps 150–200 years thereafter, the answer seems to be that it wasn't. In this obscure and difficult period of Christian history it would appear that all previous efforts towards a practical system of musical notation (as, for example, the Greeks of classical times had devised) had passed into oblivion, and it was that mainstay of a largely illiterate age, the strongly developed individual memory, that was relied on. It may be that in this early Church music there was a certain fluidity, a reliance upon formulae and a measure of improvisation rather than fixed melody, as is the case with Synagogue chant and other Eastern music. It is not only that no evidence, no hint of notation has come down from these early centuries; there is also the quite specific statement by Isidore of Seville (c. 570–636), a Spanish archbishop and a voluminous writer, well in the centre of affairs ecclesiastical, that 'Unless sounds are remembered by man, they perish, for they cannot be written down'.[2] He lived about a generation *later* than Pope Gregory I.

It seems quite incredible that Gregory (or his *Schola Cantorum*) could have evolved a system of music anywhere approaching the dimensions and the intricacy of what we have come to know as the Gregorian Chant, without the aid of some system of recording it. But what this

---

[1] Apel, pp. 82–3.
[2] Quoted in Oliver Strunk, *Source Readings in Music History* (New York, 1950), Vol. I, p. 93.

system may have been—if indeed, it ever was—remains lost in history. We have seen that Gregory is said to have compiled an *antiphonarium*, but if it were anything like the ones surviving from the next few centuries, it consisted of texts alone, with no sign of music.[1]

The date for the earliest appearance of a practical (even if imperfect) notation must remain in doubt. The first manuscripts to contain the (unheighted) neumes of the first 'Gregorian' notation come from the various religious centres belonging to the Frankish Empire, the earliest surviving being a St. Gall manuscript, *Cod. 359*, which dates from about the year 900.[2] Apel has pointed out that its neume notation is already an intricate one, which suggests that the manuscript had its predecessors, but to trace these predecessors is difficult indeed. There are a few eighth-century fragments that show brief but clear examples of neume notation;[3] and evidence of a system of notation is clearly implied in the following quotation from the Council of Clovesho (Glasgow) in 747: '(The Festivals of our Lord) . . . in the Office of Baptism, the celebration of Masses, *in the method of chanting*, shall be celebrated in one and the same way, namely, in accordance with the *sample* that we received *in writing* from the Roman Church.'[4] But what evidence there is points that we can go no further back than the eighth century for the rise and shaping of the early neume notation.[5]

Let us consider what the notation was like in its earliest surviving forms. The word *neuma*,[6] of Greek origin, seems to have implied merely a 'sign', a 'shape', and the most plausible theory seems to be that the various shapes of the neumes were expanded from basic grammatical accent-signs used by the Greek and Latin world of speech-study. Employed thus, a moving upward of the voice was indicated by a (right oblique) acute accent, a moving downward of the voice by a (left oblique) grave accent, and a combination of the two movements by a joining of the two accents into a circumflex form, whether normal or

---

[1] The two earliest chant books that have survived are (*a*) the Gradual of Monza (late eighth century) and (*b*) the Gradual and Antiphonary of Compiègne (*c*. 870). Neither manuscript contains any music.

[2] This manuscript is of a type known as a *cantatorium*; i.e. it contains only the *solo* chants of the Mass, the choral ones being designated by *incipits*.

[3] See Dom Gregory Suñol, *Introduction à la Paléographie Musicale Grégorienne* (Paris, 1935), p. 33. The author reproduces a photograph of a page of *Codex Bruxelles 10127–10144*, fol. 90.

[4] Ibid., p. 34. The translation is by Gustave Reese, p. 133 (italics are Reese's).

[5] Nevertheless, there remains a powerful temptation (and at least a certain amount of circumstantial evidence) for the inference of an earlier date. Reese writes (p. 133): 'Indeed, the history of Gregorian Chant would seem to support the assumption that neumes existed as early as the 6th century. For it is difficult to conceive how the complex task of codifying plainsong melodies could have been undertaken during the time of Gregory the Great without the aid of some system of notation. And it is extremely unlikely that the emissaries of the Schola Cantorum could have transmitted the musical repertory of the Church as faithfully and disseminated it as widely as they apparently did entirely by word of mouth.'

[6] Suñol (p. 2) says: '. . . le mot *Neume* est l'équivalent de *Figure*.'.

'anti-'.[1] Another simple sign borrowed from the grammarians was the apostrophe ('), employed to indicate unison with the previous note. The whole subject of Gregorian notation will be gone into far more fully and graphically in the next chapter. For the present we will speak in more general terms.

The up and down motions suggested by the accent-signs probably also pictured the gestures of the choirmaster as he indicated to his singers the risings and fallings of the melody, reminding them of a progress which indeed they should already have learned by heart. The information furnished by the neumes was, like that gained from the manual signs, only vaguely indicative of the pitch of the notes.[2] The main purpose of this early notation was to make clear beyond all doubt to the person reading the neume-forms the number of notes to be allotted to each syllable of the liturgical text (whether one, two, three, or more, up to a long vocal flourish).

In due course the practice began of placing the neumes at various distances 'above' the texts in order to indicate (roughly, at least) the relative pitches of the sounds, termed 'diastematic' or 'heighted' notation. Incidentally, it is a remarkable fact that even in the tenth century, while notation remained so uncertain, the various leading ecclesiastical centres in France, the Germanic countries, Italy, England, and Spain, had developed their own characteristic neume shapes,[3] internationally recognizable, but indicating with some certainty the sources of a manuscript's origin.[4] The move towards exactitude of pitch now gathered way. The single, scratched line with 'heighted' neumes developed, especially in Italy and France, into two distinctively coloured lines with clef signs indicating c' and f respectively. All such experiments finally crystallized into the system of Guido d'Arezzo (d. 1056), an inspired choirmaster who made a number of valuable musical innovations. To him is owed the final establishment of the stave of four lines, representing intervals of a third, and of regular clef letters, identifying c' and f mainly, but occasionally employing other letter values.

By the twelfth century there had evolved in France and Italy a system of notation using quadrate (square) neume-forms placed on four-line staves with clefs, the difference between b flat and b natural being distinguished. The larger size and rectangular shape of the note-heads were due to the abandonment of the reed pen in favour of the broader and more pliant quill type. The details differed very little from those employed in modern times by the Church of Rome in its service books. Even so, the Abbey of St. Gall persisted with the use of its characteristic

---

[1] These rhetorical signs are supposed to be of Byzantine origin, but were found all over Europe early in the Christian era. The earliest surviving copy of the works of Virgil, now in Florence, is marked in this way, the signs being plainly of later date than the text.

[2] This notation is termed 'oratorical' or 'cheironomic' (Gk. *cheir* = hand, and *nomos* = 'rule'); or said to be '*in campo aperto*', i.e. 'in the open field', referring to the lack of guidance.

[3] See the neume chart on p. 38.

[4] There were some exceptions, due perhaps to the 'visitor' scribes.

'campo aperto', level-pitched neumes up to the fourteenth century;[1] and the Aquitainian notation of the Limoges monasteries lagged behind in the matter of indicating unambiguous pitches to its notes, even though the breaking up of its neumes into separate 'points' served in some ways to clarify intentions.

With the establishment of absolute accuracy in regard to pitches, however, another factor which had existed in the earliest of the surviving manuscripts tended to fade and be forgotten. This was a system of indicating rhythm, i.e. different duration-values to the note-units, by various means. These means had included adding meaningful letters above the neumes, attaching to them a short stroke to indicate a lengthening, called an *episema*, and even modifying the normal shape of a neume, in order to imply a rhythmic significance. The early and important codex, *St. Gall. 359*, is full of such indications. Among the other early manuscripts with rhythmic features can be included *St. Gall 390–1* (*Hartker's Antiphonale*), *Einsiedeln 121*, *Laon 239*, and *Chartres 47*.

But by the twelfth century only the faintest signs remained of the system, which was probably not appreciated even at that time, since it would seem that the practice of 'rhythmic' performance of the chant died out soon after A.D. 1000. The famous Aribo Scholasticus, in his *De Musica* of about 1070, writes: 'In earlier times not only the inventors of melodies but also the singers themselves used great circumspection that everything should be invented and sung in proportion ("*proportionaliter et invenirent et canerent*"). This consideration perished some time ago and is now entirely buried.'[2] The loss of this system, and the various attempts in recent times to recover it, have had important consequences for the current state of chant scholarship, as we shall see shortly.

From A.D. 1000 onwards not only was there a fading of the 'rhythmic' tradition, but also something of an overall musical decline concerned with performances of the chant in general. The evidence is widespread. Many of the great scholars of the time, notably Aribo, Guido d'Arezzo, Berno of Reichenau, and John Cotto, bitterly denounced the falling standards of understanding and performance on the part of the singers, who were condemned, apparently with reason, as asses and fools. There seems little doubt that the development of polyphony, which gave to many items of the liturgy the new charm of part-singing, tended to bring about a lessening respect for the ancient music. The Renaissance was even harsher to the chant, referring to it sometimes as a relic of barbarism. In Italy in the early seventeenth century there occurred an almost incredible happening, an editorial cutting-down and mutilation of the melodies by church musicians of the Palestrinan school. The

[1] Credit must be given to the early attempts by scribes of the St. Gall school to settle pitch identities among the *campo aperto* neumes by the use of accompanying letters, such as 'e' (= *equaliter*) indicating the same pitch, or 's' (= *sursum*), a higher note.

[2] Quoted in Apel, p. 132. In speaking of 'rhythm' in this particular context, it is to be understood that we are dealing with various interpretations of prose rhythm, not the more regular forms to be met with in the 'rhythmic modes' (see Chapter XI), in the settings of Latin metrical poetry, and in medieval dance music.

result was even more deplorable: the issuing, in 1614, of the official 'Medicean' edition of the chant, in which the free and clear melodic lines were obscured in a heavy, slow-moving, organ-accompanied style. But all this was too bad to last, and dissatisfaction came to a head in the nineteenth century. In 1850 a Jesuit priest, L. Lambillote, took a step towards an actual approach to the original sources, the codex he took in hand being none other than *St. Gall 359*. There followed the great concerted effort of the Order of the Congregation of France, better known to us as the Benedictines of Solesmes, who, under the direction of a series of scholarly abbots, sought to recover the authentic chant of the golden age of plainsong by making a study of all the codices through the centuries that could be recovered. Thus members of the fraternity visited every library in Europe that possessed such manuscripts of service books, seeking to take photographs of their pages. The enormous number of reproductions thus gathered served as a basis for a comparative study. The melody of each liturgical item was traced back through the centuries, each on its separate comparative chart, to its earliest existence; its variants, where they arose, were considered; and finally its most likely authenticity was decided upon. In the 1880s began the publication of the results of their labours of decades—service books which the Solesmes choir put into practical use, as they developed a more authentic style of performance than the heavy handed Medicean tradition. In 1889 there began the publication of that famous series *Paléographie Musicale*, consisting of photographic facsimiles of various early and important codices (including *St. Gall 359*, and the *Hartker Antiphonale*) together with discussions of the various technical problems involved. The general appreciation of their achievements suffered delay for a number of years owing to the official recognition by the hierarchy in mid-century of the 'Ratisbon' edition of the Chant, which was little more than a rehash of the 'Medicean' travesty. But after the election in 1903 of Pius X, a Pope with a good understanding of music, a new edition (the 'Vatican') was soon launched, with the monks of Solesmes as the editors.

There can be no doubt as to the supreme beauty of the Solesmes version of the sung liturgy. Grounded in many years of painstaking scholarship, it has the merit of being authentically linked, melodically, with the tenth century; and in the manner of its delivery, it creates an atmosphere of consummate religious and artistic beauty.

It must be noted that the Solesmes method of performance is a 'free-rhythm' one, and this fact embroils it in a certain amount of controversy. As we have already seen, the secrets of the 'rhythmic' method of singing plainchant were fast fading by around the end of the first millennium and were considered by Aribo to be 'entirely buried'. This may be so, but there are men who wish to dig them up again! At various times in the present century the 'free-rhythm' of the established Solesmes system has been objected to by a number of scholars who might be bracketed together under the title of 'Mensuralists'. Unfortunately, as individuals they seem much divided as to what the various measured values should

31

be, and how managed. The whole question is a highly specialized one. Those wishing to pursue it further should consult Reese, pp. 140–8, where the pros and cons concerned with the Solesmes school, the Mensuralists, and their predecessors the Accentualists, are set forth with that scholar's usual clarity. For my own part, I can merely observe that it seems to me highly doubtful that details of a rhythmic system will ever be recovered with any certainty, judging, at least, from the wide disagreements that exist among those who seek it. It may well be that such interpretations, like the regional style of the neumes, differed from place to place. In the absence of definitive evidence, there seems little more to be said except to reiterate the beauty of the Solesmes melodic readings and to note that they have the authoritative support of the Church of Rome.

II

Having concluded our survey of the chant, let us now return to the subject of the Church music-dramas. As I have already indicated in Chapter One, the particular task which I set before myself was to recover their music, written down in the same notation as were the Gregorian chant melodies. It should now be clear that my problems, even though on a far smaller scale, were similar to some of those which had been overcome by the Benedictines of Solesmes; it therefore behoved me to follow their methods as far as I was able. To begin with, the separate dramas had each to be transcribed, along with their musical notations. This done, the second step was to isolate and compare the various textual and musical items which turned up in the transcriptions. Whenever an item was found in more than one work (and this was so in an overwhelming number of cases), it had to be transferred, with its music, to its own chart so that comparison could be made between the settings.[1] In many cases where unheighted neume versions were concerned, this process involved tracking a tune through several centuries, from 'campo aperto' notation to the fortunate goal of a 'line' version.

My first extensive investigation concerned the Easter dialogue '*Quem quaeritis in sepulchro* . . .' This, in its trope form the origin of the *Visitatio Sepulchri*, survived in hundreds of examples and called for the aid of large comparative charts before any certainty could be reached as to the note-pitches of the earliest examples. One significant piece of data that the charts quickly revealed was the essential uniformity and uniqueness of the Easter dialogue setting in whatever country it turned up. There were small differences of detail between the versions, but the melody remained manifestly the same; the 'differences', in fact, were frequently useful in terms of classification and evaluation.

As to the great wealth of other items to be found in the dramas (some of them liturgical, others representing new inventions), the need to make

---

[1] For an example of such a comparative chart, see my Chart Two.

comparisons between the settings involved well over a hundred lesser charts, some with only a few examples, others with a score or more. Besides the actual identification of a melody and its restoration to readability, my aim was to gain new facts concerning these dramatic works from the actual musical evidence. Such matters will be dealt with when we consider the music-dramas separately. By now, however, it should be clear that before any such investigation can be undertaken and its results discussed and interpreted, an understanding of the specific techniques of Gregorian notation is wholly necessary. It will be this matter to which we turn our attention in the following chapter.

One final point must be made with regard to the techniques of investigation and classification. In recent years there has been much criticism of the 'evolutionary' point of view so strongly maintained by Chambers and Young. Even Hardin Craig, in many ways a disciple of Young, is compelled to say:[1]

Young ... has presented us with a brilliantly executed arrangement of all the known texts of Easter dramatic offices, ... every possible form seems realised, but one must remember in the evolutionary study in this great body of texts and versions, and of other groupings of medieval religious plays similarly presented, that there is no unified sequential development except in the body of data regarded as a whole. Although every stage of theoretical completeness is to be found, this completeness was not achieved by gradual development, in which each more advanced stage grew out of an immediately preceding, less advanced stage. Some of the simplest forms seem to be of very late provenance, and some highly developed forms are certainly very early ...[2]

There is something to be said for Craig's objections. Certainly Young's methods of proceeding from the simple to the complex—of demonstrating a progress stage by stage from an Easter Introit trope to that of a 'third stage' Easter Sepulchre drama—are plausible enough only until it is realized that chronology has been neglected in the process. It is my purpose in this study to present my investigations of the Church music-dramas within the framework of the particular century to which each version belongs.[3] By this method an opportunity will be given for discerning from a historical point of view the progressions and fadings that occurred, as well as the incidences of any sequential developments.

---

[1] Craig, p. 8.

[2] Craig's reference to 'stages' reminds me that I have made no formal mention of Karl Young's nomenclature regarding his organization of the *Visitatio Sepulchri* manuscripts. Such a triple division had first been employed by that earlier scholar, Carl Lange. The 'first stage' was that which had already been given form in the trope versions—The Marys, the angelic interrogation, the reply; followed by varying supplementary sentences, and rounded-off by the dismissal. To these actions there was added the appearance of Peter and John, this comprising the 'Second Stage'. The 'Third Stage' involved the appearance of the Risen Christ to Mary Magdalen. Thereafter to be encountered were efforts to expand the drama further by the additions of other relevant episodes.

[3] It is to be remembered, of course, that the date of the writing down of a manuscript music-drama represents a *terminus ad quem*. It could be, and sometimes proves to be, a copy of an earlier version. Note will be taken of any such instances.

In the Appendix are set out, century by century, the library details of the most important of the Church music-drama manuscripts, each type in its own particular column. With some knowledge of the individual contents of the various versions a good deal can be learned from even a cursory survey of the columns thus organized. It is apparent that even though the Easter activities were the first to be launched, the Christmas music-dramas were close in their wake. The first known surviving Christmas Introit trope dialogue (from St. Martial de Limoges: *Paris, B.N. MS lat. 1118*) is of the late tenth century (not the eleventh, as several leading authorities mistakenly aver), while the Magi-Herod works begin to appear in the eleventh century in an extraordinarily advanced stage of expansion, dramatically and musically—a matter that needs more explanation than it has yet obtained.

Apparent also is the fact that France after the thirteenth century was losing interest in longer Easter dramas (even though the 'Dublin Play', *Oxford Bodl., MS Rawlinson lit. d. iv* and *St. Quentin 86*, seems to have appeared in the fourteenth). Germany was experimenting with a differently framed '*Quem quaeritis*' dialogue (complete with new music), and producing its *Zehnsilberspiel* type of bulky 'stanza' dramas. The first sign of this pattern is to be seen in the fragmentary *Vich 105* and expanded in the more orderly *Einsiedeln 300* and a number of lengthy dramas employing somewhat melismatic stanza tunes, the type lasting well into the sixteenth century. Some kind of chronological development can perhaps be traced in this particular type.

Another fact stands out—the numerical poverty of all types other than the music-dramas of the Easter and Christmas seasons. One can also realize that, had the 'Fleury Playbook' not survived with its music (feeble as some of its lesser items are), our resources for any practical rendering of 'other types' would have been slender indeed.

Hardin Craig remarks with regard to the Easter dramas that some of the simplest forms seem to be of very late provenance. What we have in fact in these 'late-simple' examples are very largely copyings-out, texts and music, of centuries-old versions that were still to hand. Thus, when we take a brief *Visitatio* from Munich (*Staatsbibl. MS lat. 2988*) of the fifteenth century, and one from Hildesheim (*Dombibl. MS lat. 597*) of the sixteenth, both written with heavy German 'nail' notation, we find traditional texts and a music that has come straight down from *St. Gall 484*. Other examples will be found where an ecclesiastical centre keeps firmly to its own traditional product. The text and the 'nail' notation of the *Visitatio* of the fifteenth century *Bamberg 27* is an exact reproduction of the *Visitatio* of the late twelfth century *Bamberg 22*, with its 'campo aperto' neumes.

I cannot agree that the 'highly developed form' of the Easter music-drama took place at a date that was particularly 'early'. The expansion to include the scene of Christ appearing to Mary Magdalen is found earliest in four versions—all of the late twelfth or early thirteenth centuries: the sketchy example from the *Vich 105* troper (Spain); the *Visi-*

tatio from the 'Playbook' (France); the earlier of the two 'Dutch Easter Plays'; and *Einsiedeln 300* (Switzerland). The scene, a prose one, was handled in very much the same way in each case (Vich's being fragmentary)—the texts partly from the Gospels, partly adapted from antiphons; the music partly invented (each version showing individuality), partly liturgical. Here then, around the turn of the twelfth to thirteenth centuries, we meet for the first time the scene in use, and that over a wide area. It is a far cry back to the third quarter of the tenth century, where we may presume that the Easter Sepulchre activities had already begun. Also, there is a wide gap between the simplicity of a Winchester dramatic performance and all the textual and musical subtleties of the 'Playbook's' *Visitatio Sepulchri*. Certainly the longer Easter forms were small in number as compared with the brief, so-called 'first-stage' versions that proliferated during the eleventh and twelfth centuries, but there must surely have been other, and non-surviving, attempts at a 'Christ-Magdalen' scene, that would fill part at least of the hiatus of the centuries. The recovery of a few more such examples might help to demonstrate even more that signs of 'sequential development' are not lacking.

CHAPTER THREE

THE MUSICAL BACKGROUND
OF THE DRAMA (2)

The Gregorian system of musical notation,
medieval and modern

WE have already realized that any attempt to understand the notation to which the libretti of the Church music-dramas were linked involves a grasp of the system of plain-chant neume notation, since both the liturgy and these invented compositions made use of the same style of 'free rhythm' melody, set down in the same specialized way.[1] The earlier stages of this notation will need a certain amount of detailed exposition.

The neume system, as was mentioned on p. 28, was almost certainly founded on the three basic signs distinguished as 'acute', 'grave', and 'circumflex', and, incidentally, gave pictorial representation of a hand directing the 'upward' and 'downward' movements of voices. A note of high pitch, or one reached by an 'upward' movement (indicated by the acute accent) came to be written as the *virga*, a note of low pitch, or one reached by a downward movement, soon ceased to be indicated in writing by an equivalent to the grave accent, and became a mere dab of reed pen, the *punctum*. The grouping of two notes to a syllable became, respectively, the representation of either an upward progression, the *podatus* (or *pes*), or a downward one, the *clivis* (or *flexus*),[2] pictorially obvious (see table on p. 38).

As can be gathered from any modern Roman service book, neume-groups up to four notes, involving movements in various directions, are in common use. The notation plan which we have seen beginning was extended logically enough. It will be realized that three-unit neumes gave four different combinations,[3] and four-unit neumes, eight. For

---

[1] However, as the centuries passed, the admission into Church music-drama libretti of more and more rhyming Latin poetry of regular scansion made it obvious that settings of such lyrical compositions, though written in plainchant notation, were more than likely to have been interpreted (like the similarly notated melodies of the troubadours and trouvères) through some kind of use of the 'rhythmic modes', or at least, in something other than 'free rhythm'. This problem will be considered in Chapter XI.

[2] *Virga* = 'rod': *punctum* = 'point'. As the number of units making up a neume increased, so the medieval technical names grew more complicated. These labels are noted in the lists below, but there seems no reason for taking much heed of those past the three-unit stage.

[3] Actually, five, if the distinction between the rising three notes of *scandicus* and *salicus* is preserved. The former takes the accent on the first note, the latter on the second. See the chart on p. 38 (with comments on p. 37), and also p. 42.

clarity's sake no further extensions were normally classified, and long melismas on single syllables were suitably broken up.

It will be recalled that in free-rhythm chant the single note is the beat-unit, having the same value, in duration, as the single syllable to which it is united. Thus *virga* and *punctum* (each a single note), clarified as to pitch on a four-line stave, will have no distinctive purposes. In modern Roman service books the square *punctum* replaces the *virga* everywhere as a separate note. In editions where the chant is written in modern notation, the single note, the chant-unit, is represented by a quaver, or eighth-note. The table on p. 38 sets out (A) the basic neume forms, and (B) compound neume forms arising from various combinations of these

Some comments on this chart may be necessary. In modern use the *virga* is not employed singly, but only as part of a compound neume The *podatus* has its second note vertically above the lower one, but the latter is of course sung first. The *scandicus/salicus* differences seem to have been a matter of where performance stresses were placed, and whether on occasion the first two units of the *salicus* should be given the same pitch.[1] The diamond-shaped notes of the *climacus* have no special significance. They were the result of the sideways turn of the scribe's quill pen, as he shaped them. The 'bar' of the *porrectus* is again a scribe's convention. The first note coincides with the top of the bar, the second with its lowest limit. Consistency of pattern in neume shapes will not be found either in manuscripts or in modern printings, as I have indicated in the case of the *torculus resupinus*. The *climacus* form developed quite a shower of descending notes on occasions (the *conjunctura* of later measured notation). A music-drama free-rhythm example can be drawn upon, the wail of despair uttered by the Jew in *The Image of St. Nicholas*, which is achieved by a diatonic downward sweep from c to D.[2]

Certain modifications will be found in the basic neumes, which are aimed at smoothing the passage from one syllable to another, and in general facilitating correct pronunciation of the Latin, these changes found of course both in the manuscripts and in the modern reproductions. Both the normal term 'liquescent neume' and the alternative, *semivocalis*, imply that there was some special kind of vocal delivery involved, with the last note sung in a fluid or lightly-voiced manner, rather like the grace note of today. The rules governing their employment may be summarized as follows:[3]

1. At the meeting of two successive consonants: *palma, tempus, magnus, super coelos, ad te,* etc.
2. In the case of two vowels coming together to form a diphthong: *autem, euge,* etc.

---

[1] However, see p. 42.   [2] See p. 260.

[3] Liquescents are discussed to some length in *Paléographie Musicale*, II, pp. 37 ff., and in Apel, pp. 104 ff. Briefer notice is to be found in Reese, pp. 131–2. These are merely three among many accounts—which, incidentally, do not always agree in detail. It must be noted, moreover, that while the examples listed above represent the usual cases in which liquescents are to be found, even such rules have exceptions, depending upon the requirements of the melody.

Table of Neumes

	Name of Neume	Number of Neume Units to One Syllable	Primitive Neume Shape	Standard Neume Shape	Equivalent in Modern Notation
A	Virga	One			
	Punctum	One			
	Podatus (or Pes)	Two			
	Clivis (or Flexa)	Two			
	Scandicus	Three			
	Salicus	Three		or	or
	Climacus	Three			
	Torculus (or Pes flexus)	Three			
	Porrectus (or flexa resupina)	Three			
B	Scandicus flexus	Four			
	Porrectus flexus	Four			
	Climacus resupinus	Four			
	Torculus resupinus	Four			
	Pes subbipunctis	Four			
	Virga subtripunctis	Four			
	Virga praetripunctis	Four			
	Porrectus resupinus	Four	?		

NOTE:
Among both the primitive and standard neume shapes of Section **B** there occur alternative ways of writing a particular compound neume. I have given only one example.

Re. last entry (*Porrectus resupinus*), this is an addition to the standard classification by Willi Apel (p. 102). He points out that this grouping — high, low, high, high, — occurs in the liturgy (even though rarely) without having gained official recognition. The name given here is his suggestion.

There are inconsistencies of practice to be found, both medieval and modern. The usual liquescent neume forms as now written are given below. I have not included the 'campo aperto' manuscript forms, since these are frequently misleading to any but the expert. One finds, moving from region to region, too many different shapes implying the same thing, and contrariwise, single shapes seeming to have different meanings.[1]

The Liquescent Neumes – Modern Forms

Name	Modern Chant Notation	Modern Normal Notation
Liquescent *podatus (epiphonus)*		
Liquescent *clivis (cephalicus)*	[As in many MSS.] [1]	
Liquescent *scandicus*		
Liquescent *climacus (ancus)*	(specially small)	 
Liquescent *torculus*		
Liquescent *porrectus*		

I am adding, for convenience' sake, another exceptional form, the *quilisma*, a single jagged shape that served as some kind of link between two units, the second higher than the first:  as in

A few comments on the above forms follow:

An example of a liquescent *clivis (cephalicus)* has prominence in Church music-drama, since it is frequently to be found at the very beginning of the '*Quem quaeritis*' Easter dialogue. The *m* of *Quem* is not easy to link in vocal smoothness with the *q* of *quaeritis*. Thus, in the great majority of cases the manuscripts use a liquescent, usually in the form shown above. But in some instances there is a plain *clivis* for *Quem*, or very occasionally a simple *punctum*.

In the case of the liquescent *climacus*, two methods of notation are met with, according to whether the last note is thought of as having the liquescence, or the last two. In the latter case, the lozenge-shaped notes are smaller than usual.

Regarding the *quilisma*, the usual explanation is that it is another

[1] I have bracketed in the *cephalicus* line the St. Gall neume version of it, since, as I have said above, this liquescent, in various shapes, so often sets the first syllable of '*Quem quaeritis in sepulchro* . . .'. For a detailed chart of the cephalicus and its regional variants, see Suñol, p. 104.

example of a lightly-sung linking note, and that the preceding note should be emphasized and slightly lengthened. Incidentally, the gap to be filled is normally a minor third, sometimes a major third, occasionally a fourth. However, it has been pointed out that it is strange that so distinctive a shape should have been given to a mere passing-note, and there has been the suggestion that it might indeed indicate a more elaborate vocal ornament, such as a turn.[1] Anyway, at present no firm evidence has been advanced to support this view, even though it must be admitted that the 'passing note' explanation seems inadequate.

It remains to consider certain specialized neume forms (see facing page). There again remains some disagreement as to their renderings.

Some comments follow regarding this list:

The *Apostropha*, a 'comma'-like sign, was, like the acute and grave accents and their combinations, borrowed from grammatical practices, where it had been put to uses similar to our like-derived apostrophe.

This hook shape will be found in the manuscripts employed in various ways in association with other neumes, even as indicating an *oriscus*. Nothing is now known of the idea that it once indicated some kind of vocal nuance for the neume to which it was joined.[2] Its most obvious use is to represent the repercussive neumes, the *bistropha* and *tristropha*, which call for the immediate and emphatic repetition of a pitch. Their notes are nowadays normally written as *puncta*, but in certain editions the old distinction is restored by the use of special shapes; thus for a *tristropha*. There is no doubt as to the rapid repercussions given to the separate units of the *strophici* in medieval performances, but modern chant experts seem to be unwilling to recommend any present-day attempts by choirs to emulate their medieval brethren in this respect. The *Liber Usualis* (p. xxiii) is particularly cautious, and advises the joining of the notes in one sound (and in its 'modern notation' edition tying together the notes of each group). There is also to be a slight crescendo or decrescendo, according to the position of the group in regard to the words of the text, and with stresses only at the beginning of each group. Suñol (pp. 488–9), quoting Dom Mocquereau of Solesmes, admits to the 'coups de voix' being 'artifice vocal difficile à notre époque', and himself goes on to say, 'demandant pratiquement un léger *crescendo* suivi d'un *vibrato*, puis un *decrescendo*, doux et en *legato*, de chacun des sons'. He is also of the opinion that in medieval times the repeated notes were often sung with an 'oscillation' of a semitone. There can be quoted the occurrence of a *tristropha* with the word *simul* written above it, as if the scribe were giving due warning that, on this occasion at least, the notes must be sung on a level.

The two following items represent, of course, mere variations of the two *strophici*.

---

[1] On this point see Apel, p. 114.
[2] On this matter, and on the interpretation of the rather puzzling *oriscus*, see Apel, pp. 111–12.

40

The Repercussive and Other Special Neumes

Repercussive Neumes (Strophici)

Name	As in St. Gall MSS	Modern Chant Notation	Modern Normal Notation
Apostropha			(quaver)
Bistropha (Distropha)			
Tristropha			
Bistropha praepunctis			
Tristropha praepunctis			
Bivirga			
Pressus	[Some Alternatives] / [With the joining of two neumes]	[1 & 2] [3]	[1 & 2] [3]
Oriscus	[Included in] me – i	mè – i	mé – i
Trigon	[Included in] [i-ni] mi – cus	-mi – cus	-mi – cus
Franculus (virga strata)		or	or
Pes stratus			
Clivis strata (or Clivis strophicus)			
Pes quassus			
The Episcma Sign			The episema was used to indicate a prolongation, especially in early St. Gall manuscripts and the important Einsiedeln MS 121. The horizontal dashes in place of *puncti* are examples of the *punctum planum* (or *virga jacens*), this again indicating a prolongation.

[1] In the liturgy (and in the music-dramas) one finds repetitions of the *strophicus* groups—of groups of two or groups of three, or groups of two followed by three, up to six or seven notes. Re the 'modern notation' versions and their slurs, see opposite.

[2] Example from the Gradual, *Tribulationes* (see *Liber Usualis*, p. 546).

[3] Example from the Gradual, *Inveni* (see *Liber Usualis*, p. 1130).

I am indebted to W. Apel for directing me to these examples.

41

A *Bi-virga* is sometimes met with, both in the manuscripts and in printed service-books. It represents merely a high-pitched version of the bi-stropha, and involves no practical difference.

Regarding *Pressus*, I quote the *Liber Usualis* statement (pp. xxiv–xxv):

... two notes placed side by side on the same degree, the second of which is the first of a group. This may occur in two ways:
   a) By a *punctum* being placed before the first note of a group.
   b) By the juxtaposition of two neumes, the last note of the first being on the same degree as the first note of the second.

The two notes are sung in one sustained tone, the accent falling on the first of them.

The *Trigon* (Lat. *trigonum* = triangle) is another somewhat mysterious neume, one of infrequent occurrence in the manuscripts. The three dots that outline the shape suggest the melodic pattern of the *torculus*. Thus, it has been suggested that it was a staccato version of the normally *legato* neume, or again, that it was perhaps the note values that were made shorter than those of the *torculus*; guesswork, it would seem! The readings of the diastematic manuscripts nearly always show that the highest note of the *trigon* is either c', f, or b flat, each involving a semitone degree with the note below. Moreover, the later, 'fixed' notation given to the *trigon* represents it as a *bistropha flexa*, i.e. with the first two units set in unison (thus resembling a *pressus*). This causes Apel to suggest (p. 116) that the first interval may have been a microtonal one, perhaps a quarter-note. We may recall the suggestion as to 'tonal oscillation' in the case of the *tristropha*. Plainchant is a wholly melodic art, and, like other similar monophonic systems such as the music of India and that of ancient Greece, it may have developed a greater sensitivity to refinements of pitch than the normal musical ear of today would be likely to appreciate.

The *franculus* consists of a *virga* with a hook (*apostropha*) attached. The diastematic manuscripts write it occasionally as a single note, but more usually as a *podatus*, the hook assumed to be an upper ornamental note. In the same way, the *pes stratus* could take the form of a *scandicus*.

A final word about the *salicus*, differing from the *scandicus* in having an *apostropha* for its second unit. The official view is that this indicates only that the emphasis normal to the first unit has been transferred to the second. This explanation has been challenged by some scholars, who hold that some refinements of pitch in regard to the second note were involved. However, when it comes to modern performance this has but academic interest. The normal appearance of both *scandicus* and *salicus* is that of three-unit neumes, but occasionally in the service chants they rocket upward to six or more notes.

The *pes quassus* is an example of the deliberate alteration of the normal shape of a neume in order to indicate the prolongation of a sound. It could be equivalent to a *podatus* preceded by *pressus*. Other neumes among the early types of notation were similarly modified for rhythmic reasons.

Forms of the *episema* were found not only in St. Gall notation, but also in those of Metz, Chartres, Nonantola, Benevento, and Aquitaine.

Attached to early manuscripts of St. Gall neumes are to be found the first examples of the so-called 'Romanian letters',[1] these referring not only to matters of rhythm, but also helping to determine the pitch of some of the notes of the 'campo aperto' music; also sometimes directing the expression to be used momentarily, or even for a whole passage. Only a few of the more common letters can be given here. Of the 'rhythmic' ones there may be mentioned t (*trahere* or *tenere*—to drag or to hold); x (*expectare*—to retard); c (*celeriter*—quickly). There were 'qualifying' letters, such as v (*valde*—very, extremely); b (*bene*—well); and m (*mediocriter*—moderately). Some useful 'melodic' letters were: a (*altius*) and l (*levare*), both warning that there was to be a raising of pitch. In contrast there was d (*deprimatur*—should be depressed). A very useful one was e (*equaliter*—in unison, i.e. the following note was on the same level). The notations of Chartres and Metz also show such letters, but to a lesser degree. None of the early music-drama manuscripts in neumes show any sign of the letters, but, especially in St. Gall pages, there are plenty of examples of the *episema* and of modified shapes of the neumes.

It has already been remarked (p. 29) that early in the history of the neumes their individual shapes tended to show small differences, owing to the various regions evolving styles of their own to express the same melodies. It is apparent also that the earlier the example, the nearer it is to some common origin. A 'geographical' organization of the various neume notations gives us the following:[2]

1. Primitive Notation of N. Italy.
2. Notation of Nonantola.
3. Notation of Novalesa.
4. Notation of Milan.
5. Notation of the Centre of Italy.
6. Notation of Benevento.
7. English (Anglo-Saxon) Notation.
8. Notation of St. Gall.
9. German Notation (derived from St. Gall, later taking a 'Gothic' form).
10. Notation of Metz.
11a. Notation of the North of France.
11b. Norman Notation (derived from No. 11a).
12. Notation of Chartres.
13. Aquitainian Notation.
14. Visigothic Notation.
15. Catalonian Notation.

[1] From Romanus, the legendary chant specialist from Rome who was supposed to have brought the chant from Rome to St. Gall, in Charlemagne's day. The story was set down by Ekkehard, chronicler of St. Gall, some two hundred years after, and is likely to be apocryphal. The meanings of a large number of the letters were elucidated by the famous monk, Notker Balbulus (d. 912), in a letter to a friend which is still preserved. See Apel, p. 117.

[2] These various forms of notation are discussed individually in great detail in Suñol, with tables of neume formation and local characteristics.

Although often enough the native region of a manuscript can be settled from its neume type, this evidence cannot always be relied on. The Aquitainian notation moved far into Spain; there was the matter of the travelling, professional scribe; resettlements such as those of the Normans in Italy brought the notation of the newcomers.

To illustrate the differences to be found in these various styles of 'campo aperto' neumes a chart has been given (Plate I) which sets out first the Communion of the Mass for the third day after the first Sunday in Lent, together with its music.[1] This latter is in modern square notation, as it appears in the Vatican Edition, with its editorial *episemas* and duration dots. Below are representations of how the same music was written in service books from the various regions mentioned. Some curious differences of shape will be observed, especially regarding the *clivis*, which appears sometimes looking like a figure seven. Occasionally, small discrepancies appear, e.g. a *virga* for a two-unit neume, or vice versa, but the consistency is marvellous. The first seven of the examples in the chart show rhythmic notations; that is, by various means they have sought to indicate variations in the uniform rendering of the melodic line. Examples of the Romanian letters will be plainly observed, especially in the first example (No. 8), from *Einsiedeln 121*.

Within the space of a short Communion quite a variety of neume forms have been included. All that one may regret is that only one liquescent appears—at the first *torculus*. The single neume used by Metz (No. 10) which looks like a small *franculus* is in fact Metz's particular brand of *virga*. At times it uses two of them, one below the other, in place of an ordinary *clivis*, as a rhythmic device, to indicate the lengthening of the sound of each note. When these are seen, there will also be evident in most cases an *episema* attached to the corresponding St. Gall *clivis*, affecting both units. Metz shares with several other regions its preference for the 'seven' sign to represent the ordinary *clivis*.

The unique nature of the Aquitainian notation will be noted (No. 13) —the breaking-up of so many of its neumes into their elements as separate points. This was not so promising a move as might be expected, for the Aquitainian style, even when it becomes diastematic, neglected to use horizontal lines for a long time, or left them ambiguous as to their clef values.

No further comments on the chart will be made here, but other points concerning neume notation will certainly arise when the early Easter trope dialogues and music-dramas are considered.

II

Before the subject of notation is left, another form of it, that of sol-fa,

---

[1] Reproduced from *Paléographie Musicale Grégorienne*, by kind permission of the Benedictines of Solesmes. This same chart appears as 'Planche C', among the final appendices of Suñol's volume (*Ed.*).

I A comparative chart showing the various styles of neume notation.

45

must be mentioned, since some occasional use will be made of it in this study. The idea of giving short, distinctive names to the degrees of an octave scale is as ancient as the ancient Greeks, who distinguished between the four notes of their tetrachord in this way. We may recall Guido d'Arezzo's solmization methods, by which the names *ut, re, mi, fa, sol, la* were applied to the hexachord diatonic scale, resulting in an immense improvement in his choristers' sight-reading.[1] Other medieval uses were made of solmization, as can be seen, for example, by consulting Volume II of *The New Oxford History of Music* (London, 1954), f.p. 221, where there can be seen a reproduction of a page from a twelfth century manuscript from Monte Cassino. The melody of a rhythmic song, '*O Roma nobilis* . . .' is written in abbreviated solmization, l s f m r v (ut), each note in its diastematic position on a stave of six lines, each line given not only its sol-fa, but its scalic letter. Later centuries with a developed 'leading-note' sense added a seventh syllable, *si*, modified in some countries to *te* or *ti*. Also, *ut* was widely considered to be somewhat unvocal, and *do* was substituted. Thus, a modern version of the sol-fa diatonic major scale (in any key) could be assumed to be:

do re mi fa sol la si (te or ti) do'

—shortened for convenience (after the manner of the Monte Cassino example) to:

d   r   m   f   s   l   t   d'

This system will be employed for short music examples, assurance being gained from the fact that the learned Fathers of Solesmes make a working use of the same convenience.

The employment of an 'upper octave' mark (against the last *do*) will be noted. 'Lower octave' marks will also be used (thus, l,). Neume groups, i.e. more than one note to a syllable, will be indicated by an underlining of the notes concerned. Thus, if a free-rhythm setting of the words '*Quem quaeritis in sepulchro*', rendered as in the Limoges trope example on p. 74, were given a sol-fa transcription, this would be:

rd l,dt, drd r - d m mfs fr -

The extension of a sound is indicated by a dash, but I have not thought it worth while to give special indications for liquescents or *quilismae*.

It should be added that music examples capable of being rendered rhythmically will be shown in modern staff notation.

III

In modern Roman service books there will be noted before most liturgical items a single numeral, lying between one and eight. This figure indicates to which of the eight tonalities, known as the Church modes,

---

[1] The story of the derivation of the names from the *Ut queant laxis* hymn is recorded in Reese, pp. 149–50. The bottom note of Guido's medieval range (as on the bottom line of our bass clef) was G, written as the Greek letter *Gamma*. As the first note of a hexachord it was called *Gamma Ut*, or 'Gamut'. Eventually the term was applied to the whole scalic range, and used in this sense even after the modes had faded.

the composition is held to belong. This 'modal' system represents an attempt to codify and classify the whole of the melodies of the Chant. Evidence as to the formation of such an 'explanatory' system first appeared in the tenth century, being inspired, probably, by the much earlier and very similar scalic organization, the *octoechos* (eight tones) of the Byzantine Church. In view of the long pre-existence of the bulk of the Gregorian melodies to any such Western theories, it is not surprising to find that quite a number of those melodies that have come down to us cannot be made to fit comfortably into the modal strait-jacket.

The Gregorian melodic system is a diatonic one, and ('equal temperament' apart) can be demonstrated on the white notes of the pianoforte.[1] Four scales, of the *ambitus* (range) of an octave, were based respectively on the notes d, e, f, and g, and, as is clearly apparent, each preserved a distinctive succession of tones and semitones. The notes named were the respective 'finals' of the modes, on one or another of which a melody closed in accordance with its mode. Medieval writers sometimes used the term *maneria* when taking this 'four-categories' point of view.

However, the generally accepted organization was that reached by dividing each *maneria* into two parts, obtaining for each *finalis* two different ambits in relation to it. The authentic mode-scale began with the final and extended to its upper octave; the plagal mode-scale began a fourth below the final and extended to a fifth above it. The latter ambit allowed for melodies that ranged well below the final.

We have spoken of the ambit of a mode-scale as being that of an octave. It is written thus as a matter of convenience for illustration purposes. In practical use, however, a note below the octave range is frequently to be found. Also, as will be seen in any service book, the upward octave range is exceeded again and again. But even though it may seem that the eight-mode system leaves a great deal unaccounted for, we will give below a summary of the organization in diagram form.

Protus Maneria	⎧Mode I				D	E	F	G	*a*	b	c	d
	⎩ „ II	A	B	C	D	E	*F*	G	a			
Deuterus „	⎰ „ III				E	F	G	a	b	*c*	d	e
	⎱ „ IV	B	C	D	E	F	G	*a*	b			
Tritus „	⎰ „ V				F	G	a	b	*c*	d	e	f
	⎱ „ VI	C	D	E	F	G	a	b	c			
Tetrardus „	⎰ „ VII				G	a	b	c	*d*	e	f	g
	⎱ „ VIII	D	E	F	G	a	b	*c*	d			

The terms Dorian, Phrygian, Lydian, and Mixolydian are commonly applied to the four *maneriae*; names borrowed from Greek music by medieval writers and muddled in the process. The prefix, 'Hypo-' is sometimes used to distinguish the plagal ambit.

It will be noted that one tone in each of the above modal scales has been distinguished by being in italics. This is done to signalize the Tenor

---

[1] We have already met with evidence, none too firm, which suggests occasional use of chromaticisms and even microtones. See p. 42.

(sometimes called the Dominant) of the mode. Its importance is usually stated to be due to the fact that it was used as the 'reciting-note' of the mode. It is to be identified as the fifth above the final in authentic modes, and the third above in the plagal modes. Exceptions will be noted in the third and eighth modes, where c replaces b in each case, and in the plagal fourth mode, where G is raised to a in order to match the move in the corresponding authentic mode. The rejection of b as the Tenor has had more than one explanation; e.g. because of its less stable position than the other degrees, being liable to be replaced by b flat; or because of its 'tritone' relationship with F.

However, as Apel has pointed out (p. 136), with numerous quoted liturgical examples, 'the dominant can hardly be said to be a characteristic of the mode, because the great majority of the melodies of a given mode fail to show any clear evidence of the dominant . . . Actually, the dominant is a characteristic property, not of a mode in general, but of a few special melodies associated with that mode, such as the psalm tones and other recitation tones.'

While the close of a modal piece was strictly bound, there was a certain amount of freedom as to what note the piece could start on. Practically speaking, however, it would seem that particular initial figures became associated with particular modes. It is to be remembered also that in the course of a Gregorian composition of any length, inner sections would show characteristics and close in cadences belonging to modes other than the prevailing ones. In other words, *modulation* in the strict sense of the word would take place.

An important resource used by the Chant is the occasional substitution of a b flat for the normal natural. There are a few instances in the service books where it is employed as a clef sign, e.g. in the antiphons *'Alma Redemptoris Mater . . .'* and *'Regina caeli laetare . . .'* for Sunday at Compline (*Liber Usualis*, pp. 273 and 275). In music-drama examples there are numerous instances of the Easter Sepulchre dialogue being transposed upward a perfect fourth, and needing a b flat to bring about the exact reproduction. This the manuscript sometimes inserts, as in the case of the 'Dublin Play' (*Oxford, Bibl. Bodl. MS Rawlinson liturg., d. iv*), but often enough in medieval times it was assumed that the performer would know his rules of 'musica ficta', and the situation when a flat was necessary. As for its strictly melodic use, even in the case of the modern service books there are still places where scholars dispute between b natural and b flat readings.

With this point let us bring to a close our survey of musical matters concerning the Chant. It may be seen that the subject is a highly technical one, in which we have been able to do little more here than touch the surface. Those wishing to pursue the subject further may do so by consulting Apel and Suñol. Meanwhile, it may be stated that such musical matters as have been discussed above will prove to be quite relevant when we turn to the Church music-dramas themselves.

CHAPTER FOUR

TROPES AND SEQUENCES

IN the course of our discussion so far, even our very brief references to the Church music-dramas have revealed certain vital qualities inherent in them: imagination, adaptation, and invention. These qualities are not new to the drama, however; by the tenth century they had already been impressively demonstrated in the drama's parent body, that extra-liturgical activity which was responsible for the production of tropes (*tropae*).

The practice of troping, which represented a new flowering of artistic creation, began to reveal itself in the last decades of the eighth century and the beginning of the ninth, at a time when Charlemagne's empire was being firmly established in Western Europe and, 'paradoxically enough, when the liturgical chant of the Church was attaining the unity and stability of melodic tradition which it was to preserve for many centuries. But while the basic liturgical texts were firmly maintained, yet a new spirit was abroad, expressed in many ways under the patronage of Charlemagne himself, who, with the support of a band of scholarly advisers led by Alcuin of York, brought about a veritable religious and cultural revival in the Frankish realms. In education, the Emperor hoped and planned for the emergence of a more enlightened body not only of clergy, but also of leading laymen, through the further expansion of the cathedral and monastic schools, the royal school setting an example in development. A revival of interest took place in the study of the Latin Bible and the writings of the Church Fathers, and even of the precariously surviving manuscripts of classical prose and poetry. There was much copying of older manuscripts of every sort, written in the new and beautiful Carolingian script, an activity for which the later Western world owes the era a profound debt of gratitude. A closer critical eye was employed on standards of latinity. The practical arts blossomed, notably in the production of sacred books, with richly illuminated pages and ivory bindings, carved and bejewelled. It was also the age that saw the art of unaccompanied, monophonic church-singing reach its greatest heights.

'Troping', that is, the practice of making *additions* to those portions of the liturgy that appeared suitable for such treatment, was part of this desire to render both the liturgy itself and ceremonial in general as religiously impressive as possible. Thus it was that new compositions were joined to the beginnings and/or conclusions of liturgical items, or were interpolated between their parts. These additional texts explained further, commented on, or reinforced the sentiments expressed in the liturgical passages concerned. Some additions were purely musical, new and elaborate vocal flourishes on a vowel sound, such as passages of greater ambition than the melismas already met with at the rounding-off of the Mass Alleluia.

With regard to this new practice, we may readily identify both its good and bad points. For the good, we may cite its imagination and creativity, both musically and liturgically. Willi Apel views the movement as:[1]

... a final and not at all unsuccessful attempt to rejuvenate [the chant] and to prolong its creative life for another four or five centuries. It is a testimony to the force of the Gregorian tradition that this activity took the form, not of independent creation, but rather of amplification. In fact, the various phenomena to be considered have one thing in common, they are accretions to chants of the old repertory, accretions that may be compared to fresh branches grafted upon old trees ... Viewed in this light, the development ... represents a wholly valid contribution to the repertory of the chant.

On the other hand, such accretions, when allowed to run out of control, have the inevitable effect of cluttering and obscuring the contours of the liturgy; and for this reason the Church hierarchy felt a certain amount of discomfort in their proliferation. For a time the practice was tolerated —though the tropes remained at best only optional additions to the liturgy and never a part of the official Roman chant. By the thirteenth century a certain falling-off in trope-writing was becoming apparent, together with a firm tightening of the reins of authority. Only certain types of tropes, such as those attached to the Kyrie, continued to flourish, together with what by then was proving to be a veritable art-form, the sequence. The Council of Trent, in about 1560, dealt the death blow to the movement, abolishing all tropes and nearly all sequences. But long before that time the tropes had made their impact felt, gaining for themselves a firm place in that delicate give-and-take between clarity of form and individual creativity which has always been characteristic of liturgical art.

II

As we have already seen, the place in the liturgy which seems to have been most widely accepted as inviting melismatic treatment was the final 'a' of the Mass Alleluia. This region seems to have been regarded as a sort of liturgical 'liberty zone' throughout the whole of the Middle Ages, for we find a more or less continuous stream of newly composed

[1] Apel, pp. 429–30.

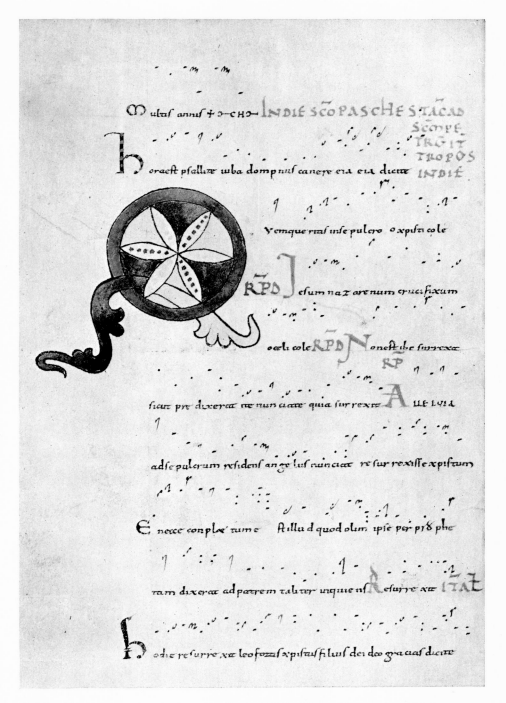

II The '*Quem quaeritis . . .*' trope; Paris, Bibliothèque Nationale, *MS lat.
1118*, fol. 40v (*c.* 988–96 A.D.), a troper from St. Martial de Limoges.
Compare the Limoges version in the frontispiece, more than fifty years
earlier. Note the scribal error '*Resurrexit*' for '*Resurrexi*'.

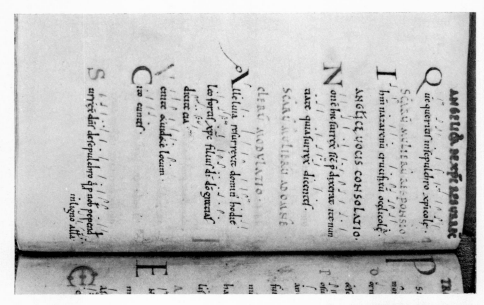

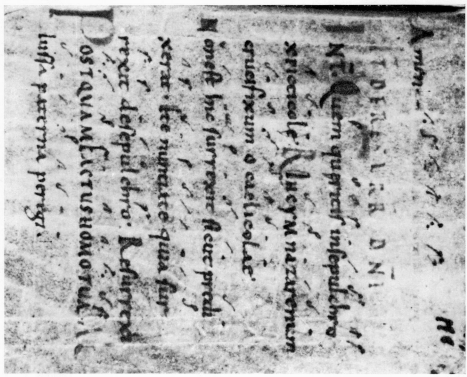

IIIa *Visitatio Sepulchri*; Cambridge, Corpus Christi College, *MS 473*, fol. 26v, an eleventh-century copy of the Winchester Troper (*c.* 980 A.D.). The music is shown in Anglo-Saxon neumes.

IIIb The simplest version of the '*Quem quaeritis . . .*' trope; St. Gall, Monastic Library, *MS 484*, p.111 (*c.* 950 A.D.). The music is given in characteristic 'St. Gall' unheighted neumes.

verses for existing Alleluias and even a number of new Alleluias. As early as the ninth century, however, certain of the Alleluia melismas were receiving a unique kind of expansion which was eventually to develop into a new art-form, the sequence. The sequence was a trope, but it was a special kind of trope, and one which was destined to play an important part in the musical history of the Middle Ages. Let us begin our study of tropes in general with a careful look at this new invention.

The characteristic feature of this type of Alleluia expansion was its length. The evidence of numerous manuscripts surviving from the period attests to the fact that there was everywhere in the Western Church a proliferation of very much extended melismas—or *longissimae melodiae*, as they were called. As with the original and more modest *jubili*, it would seem that a start was made with the original music of the Alleluia, the final 'a' sound of which was taken over—but then the composer took to his wings! Each melodic strophe was repeated—a result, it would seem, of each side of the choir singing in turn—and finally the rounding-off strophe was given a single performance, with everyone joining in. To this type of wordless composition there has nowadays been given the name of *sequela*, thus distinguishing it from the wholly developed, text-and-music *sequence*.[1] An example of a sequela, one of no great length, is here given, reproduced from *Anglo-French Sequelae* by Dom Anselm Hughes.[2] It is based on the Alleluia from the Mass *In Anniv. Dedic. Eccl.*, and is named *Digna culti*, for the usual reason of this being the first words of the original Alleluia Verse.[3, 4]

---

[1] The term 'sequela' is something of a modern choice. For the early stages of the text-with-music sequence, the name *prosa* was used in France, or even *sequentia cum prosa*. This in spite of the fact that the term *prosa* was sometimes applied to tropes of other items of the liturgy, e.g. responsories.

[2] *Anglo-French sequelae*, ed. from the papers of H. M. Bannister by Dom Anselm Hughes. Plainsong and Mediaeval Music Society (London, 1934), No. 14, p. 34.

[3] The Alleluia setting is the same as that used in the modern Roman liturgy for the Alleluia with the verse 'Adorabo . . .' (see *Liber Usualis*, p. 1251).

[4] For indicating the single rendering of a strophe, or for its repeat, I have made use of the sign 𝔵 (= *semel*) and 𝔡 (= *denuo*, *duplex*, or *dis*) as found in certain manuscript tropers.

When commenting upon the long-unrealized musical wealth of the sequelae, Hughes writes the following:[1]

... it cannot be too often or too strongly insisted that the primary value of these melodies is by no means antiquarian or liturgiological, for we have here nothing less than the first recorded School of Composition. Though it is all unison work, it is none the less Composition; and the curious may find many fine examples of artistic treatment in these simple and flowing melodies, an artistry which will develop in steady and surely marked progress until the superb architecture of the great classical polyphonists has reached its climax. Here is Composition in which, perhaps for the first time in the history of the Christian Church, the musician has had only musical laws to observe. In the sequela he is trammelled by no verbal texts—they are not added until later—he is free to express his soul, and to experiment with his rhythms and his parallelisms, his transpositions and modulations and variations. Again, it is the field which would presumably have attracted the men of the greatest musical ability, for there was scope here for initiative and discovery: and it was still the fashionable style of composition at the epoch when the stave came to be invented and standardised. This last fact has bearings of considerable importance: for the coming of the stave means that for the first time absolute music can not only be conceived for its own sake, but it can be recorded, preserved, transmitted, and embellished: and it is not too much to suggest, therefore, that the best and most progressive musicians in the Church of that age were giving their attention to Sequela and Sequence writing.

The development which followed is predictable. We meet in many surviving manuscripts examples of sequelae where isolated strophes of the melismatic music are found underlaid with passages of apparently invented prose, the neumes being broken up into single notes so that one syllable of the text could be fitted to each note,[2] and a second line of prose placed under the first in order to supply a text for the normal repeat of the music. Among the numerous sequelae brought together by Dom Anselm Hughes in the volume already mentioned can be seen five examples (on pp. 22, 23, 42, 65, and 73) where occasional strophes are thus treated. The facts concerned with these examples, as given in *Anglo-French Sequelae*, show that the practice of thus 'troping' the music was widespread in the Western Church. It needed nothing more than the whole of the succession of the sequela strophes to be treated in this fashion to for a unified literary text (with certain minor formal adjustments that we shall discover) for the sequence form to be born, and to pass into a veritable cult. During the medieval centuries thousands of sequences were written; new texts shaped to old melodies, and new

---

[1] Hughes, p. 12.
[2] The general rule of 'one syllable—one note' did not preclude the occasional use of two notes to a syllable, or, more rarely, three or four.

melodies and words written together. Peter Wagner suggests[1] that the very great attraction which the sequence form had for every class of listener was its essential simplicity (i.e. the syllabic nature of its melody and the straightforwardness of its form), and its possible resemblance in style to contemporary folk-song; this in contrast with the elaborateness of the liturgical music.

The production of sequences had at first two chief centres of inspiration, the monasteries of St. Martial de Limoges and St. Gall, representing French (or West Frank) and German (or East Frank) regions respectively; each with certain individual characteristics of style. The work of the English palaeographer H. M. Bannister (d. 1919) has shown conclusively that the original home of the sequence was Northern France rather than St. Gall. His evidence first appeared in the *Analecta Hymnica* series (where he was partnered by Fr. Clemens Blume), and is ably summarized by Dom Anselm Hughes in *Anglo-French Sequelae*, pp. 8–9.

As we have seen, one of the outstanding features of the sequence was its 'one note—one syllable' rule, which on occasion brought real power and dignity to the music. From time to time the appearance of two notes to the syllable was made obligatory by the need for a liquescent blending, but this was by far the exception rather than the rule. As to other characteristics of the sequence, we may note that the repeat of the musical strophe in order to set a second and corresponding text was almost everywhere observed, resulting in a series of paired lines of undeterminate number. Generally, the first and last lines were not repeated. Thus, if 'x' and 'y' represent the unpaired lines, the pattern of the normal, early-stage sequence could be written as follows:

x, aa, bb, cc, dd, ee, etc. . . . . y.

The sections (that is, the pairs of lines) kept to no pattern of length. There might be as few as eight syllables to a line, or as many as a score or more.[2] A general practice seems to have been that the first and last single strophes were sung by the whole choir, the paired lines antiphonally by alternate sides. The dimensions of some sequences were, quite early on, increased by repeating a whole group of internal pairs of musical strophes, such as: ee, ff, gg, ee, ff, gg, hh . . . etc.

A fairly regular distinction between French- and German-derived sequences is that the French ones (possibly because of being closer to the source of origin) usually called for the Alleluia to be sung first in its parent setting, while the German practice was to use the Alleluia music in the setting of the first line of the sequence. Early French sequences tended again to recall their Alleluia origins by causing their textual lines all to end on the assonance of the final 'a' (or sometimes 'am' or 'at'). This matter was generally disregarded in German examples. All texts

---

[1] Peter Wagner, *Introduction to the Gregorian Melodies*; translated by Agnes Orme and E. G. P. Wyatt (London, the Plainsong and Mediaeval Music Society, 1901), pp. 231 ff.

[2] A few surviving sequences show successions of strophe melodies without repeat, i.e. they appear as single lines, and not pairs. They may of course represent a primitive form, but on the other hand it may be that the melody was sung first as a vocalized melisma and then to the text (or vice versa).

53

were at this early stage non-metrical (hence 'prosa'). Only later came rhyme and regular rhythm.[1]

In past decades some writers held the view that the famous monk of St. Gall, Notker Balbulus, was the actual inventor of the sequence form —paired lines, single notes, and all; this, however, before the work of the investigators of which we have spoken and the recovery of a wealth of sequence examples such as has since taken place. Much of the strength of the Notker legend must be set down to a misunderstanding of the letter (probably a genuine one, and still preserved) which Notker sent to Liutward, Archbishop of Vercelli, a fellow countryman of Notker's, and and old acquaintance.[2] The letter came as an accompaniment to a volume of sequences which Notker had dedicated to his friend—a volume which was called, incidentally, the *Liber hymnorum*.

In the course of the letter Notker refers to the *longissimae melodiae*, recalling (no doubt like many another former chorister) that as a young man he had found them hard to memorize. Then he recounts how, in about 851, there came to the monastery a French monk, fleeing from the sack of Jumièges in northern France by the Norsemen. He brought with him his Antiphonal, and in it Notker found a mnemonic device—the insertion of words to fit the music of a melismatic passage. He was pleased with the idea, but not its execution, which he said was carried out clumsily. He endeavoured to improve on it by providing an Easter melody that was in use at St. Gall at the time with words of his own. This first effort, he tells us, was '*Laudes Deo concinat orbis*', still preserved.[3] On presenting the effort to Iso, his master, he received friendly encouragement, but was recommended to fit each syllable to a single note of the music. Three more sequences were the results of his renewed efforts.[4] They were performed, and he was advised to continue with the work, but it was not till *c.* 885 that the volume was completed and sent.[5]

No trace of it now remains, but we know that Notker continued sequence composition on those lines, and tradition has it that he wrote sequences for all the chief festivals celebrated at St. Gall. But what is implied by the word 'wrote', and what were the virtues that brought him fame? It happens that in the monastery of Einsiedeln (traditionally in

---

[1] Another variety of sequence was the Italian one, though on the whole it tended to make less impact. As a general description, Italian sequences seemed to share some of the German characteristics. One unusual Italian trick, however, was to recall the Alleluia melody by placing it between the first pair of repeat lines.

[2] The letter is printed in Gerbert *De Cantu*, I, pp. 412–13; Migne, *Patrologia Latina*, 131 pp. 1003–4; Dümmler, *St. Gallische Denkmale*, pp. 223–4. It should be mentioned that the genuineness of the letter has been questioned, and by no less an authority than Blume, in Vols. 53 and 54 of *Analecta Hymnica*. However, the weight of learned opinion seems against him. See J. M. Clark's statement of the case in *The Abbey of St. Gall* (Cambridge, 1926), pp. 179–80.

[3] In Einsiedeln MS 121, pp. 473–5.

[4] '*Christus hunc diem*'; '*Congaudent angelorum chori*'; '*Psallat ecclesia mater*'; all found in *Einsiedeln 121*.

[5] What the actual contents of the volume were remains a matter for debate. Schubiger's list of 78 sequences is now discredited. See Clark, p. 183, for a summary of the question.

close touch with St. Gall) there survives a *Codex 121*, an *Antiphonale-Missarum* of the tenth to eleventh century which contains versions of a number of Notker's sequences, including those already mentioned in the footnote. It happens also that in 1858, a monk of that monastery, Dom Anselm Schubiger, published a volume entitled *Die Sängerschule St. Gallens*, in which musical manuscripts from both St. Gall and Einsiedeln (from the eighth to the twelfth century) were dealt with, these including a number of Notker sequences. Fortunately for later generations the original neumes of the compositions were transcribed onto five-line staves. Such an author, with the centuries of tradition of his monastery behind him, would have been likely to be well equipped for such a task. However, some details of his transcriptions have come in for modern questionings.[1]

I have in front of me photographs of a number of Notker sequences from *Einsiedeln 121*, together with a copy of *Die Sängerschule St. Gallens*. Thus some interesting comparisons have become possible for me.

Let us consider first the sequence that Notker gives as his apprentice effort, '*Laudes Deo concinat*' (*Einsiedeln 121*, pp. 273–5; Schubiger, Exempla 14, pp. 16–17). The text is arranged in short and haphazard lines, some of them ending on a divided word, completed in the next. Beside each line (to the left on the left-hand page, to the right on the right-hand one) are numbers of multiple, unheighted neumes, representing no doubt the musical settings of each line, since the total number of syllables in a line corresponds with the total number of single units contained in the line of neumes. In Schubiger's stave transcription this is made plain; minims (half-notes) are written for each syllable. Whether Notker wrote out the music as single, separate notes we have no means of determining, but no such help was given the singers using the Einsiedeln manuscript version. They would have had to know the melody fairly well already if they were to pick it out from the frequently florid marginal neumes.[2]

A feature to note regarding this first sequence of Notker's concerns the first line, '*Laudes Deo concin—*'. In the margin are the letters A E U IA (Alleluia), with its original melismatic setting overhead. As we have learned to expect from this half of the Empire, the singing of the Alleluia would be disregarded, and the neumes used to set the '*Laudes Deo . . .*' line. But if we can believe Schubiger's transcription, the

---

[1] Apel adds the following cautionary note (p. 453): 'To the present day, musicologists must draw upon one of the earliest publications in the field of music history, that, is A. Schubiger's *Die Sängerschule St. Gallens* (1858), which contains the melodies for about fifty sequences. Two more recent publications, the *Variae preces* (Solesmes, 1901) and C. A. Moberg's *Ueber die schwedischen Sequenzen* (2 vols., 1927), contain a few additional examples from the early German repertory or, particularly in Moberg, better versions of those published by Schubiger.'

[2] Commencing on p. 578 of the Einsiedeln manuscript, the sequence '*Ecce solemnis diei*' has the usual florid marginal neumes, but above the syllables of the lines are the breakings-down into separate notes, represented by *virgae* and *puncta*, roughly diastematic and written apparently by a later hand.

music of these two words was set down as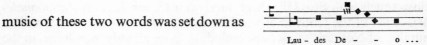

Lau - des De - - o ...

Obviously, Notker had not yet reached the stage of carrying out fully the one-note, one-syllable principle—which, as we have seen, was precisely his master's criticism!

Through the remainder of the sequence, however, the principle of the single-note setting prevails, except for the case of a pair of lines, one of them a syllable shorter than the other, making it necessary for a precautionary *podatus* to be put above the text at the critical place. Also, it is evident that the idea of using two lines of text to the same strophe of music is not regularly carried out. Finally, if it is to be supposed that the text was supplied for the (at least, partial) purpose of helping the singer to keep in mind the details of the originally wordless *jubilus* melody, it would on this particular showing have led to some breaking-up of the original rhythmic memories. I can afford to offer only a single example of what I mean. Above an early part of the text I have bracketed syllables, in order to show how the marginal neumes were spread as single notes.

[2 units] [5] [3]

Pér sum - mi pa - tris in - dul - gen - ti - am

Only in the last of the above groupings is there satisfactory agreement between the rhythms of text and neume group. A number of other places in the sequence could be faulted for the same reason. Clearly, Notker had a good deal to learn.

I turn now to one of the sequences which, according to the Liutward letter, Notker wrote after taking more to heart his teacher's counsel. It is '*Psallat ecclesia mater ...*' (*Einsiedeln 121*, pp. 508–9; Schubiger, Exempla 31, p. 31). Once again above the marginal A E U IA are placed the neumes of its original setting, waiting to be borrowed. But this time not only is the single-note pattern maintained, but the word accents and the neume rhythms are in excellent agreement. I give the first three lines of the manuscript version showing how the marginal neumes must have been spread.[1]

[3 units] [2] [4] [2]

Psal - lat ec - clé - si - a má - ter il - li - bá - ta et vir - go

[4] - [2] [5]

si - ne rú - ga ho - nó - rem hú - ius ec - clé - si - ae.

---

[1] The liquescent comes from the *Alleluia*, but it is handy for use with '*Psallat*'s' two middle consonants.

[2] Schubiger's transcription has a *podatus* for the third syllable of '*ecclesia*', the second note 'anticipating' that of the final 'a'; no doubt an accretion of the centuries. In others of the sequences there are small discrepancies between Einsiedeln and Schubiger. As I have said before, throughout sequence history two-unit neumes are to be met with, mingled sparingly with the single notes.

Throughout, this agreement of verbal and neume accent is maintained with great skill. We can perhaps forgive the fact that an extra syllable in one of the lines is without a note.[1] Otherwise, the pairing of the lines, each pair with its strophic melody is managed almost perfectly.

Notker's sequences seem soon to have found general fame, and travelled quickly to France and other countries of Christendom. But his reputation must rest on his being an improver of the form, and above all on being a master of original Latin prose-poetry.[2] We know that he adapted melodies for his sequences; it cannot be proved that he composed any of them.

As sequence writing progressed into the eleventh century a new type of text began to evolve, moving towards verse form without gaining absolute regularity. The original mnemonic purpose seems long to have faded, and the intention became that of creating a homogeneous textual and musical composition, the melody, possibly, as original as the text. The introductory sentence was often still retained, but the concluding single one tended to disappear. Rhyme was introduced, but tentatively. The most famous sequence of this period is the immortal '*Victimae paschali laudes*', one destined to survive the Council of Trent and hold its place in the liturgy of Rome. If tradition is to be believed, it was written by Wipo of Burgundy, court chaplain to the Emperor Conrad II, early in the eleventh century. The appearance of the melody, as set out in an eleventh-century manuscript (*Einsiedeln, Fragment I*) in single notes above the text and in the familiar unheighted neume style in the margin, may raise the question as to whether the musical setting was but an adaptation. Certainly there are several discrepancies between the two notations. The sequence is reproduced below in its eleventh-century version, text and music. There are a few differences in note-detail between it and the version found in the modern *Gradual* (or *Liber Usualis*). Also, one of the original sentences, '*Credendum est magis soli Mariae veraci*', is not to be found in the modern text.

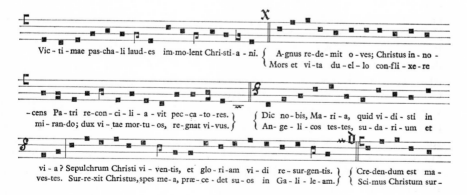

---

[1] That is, '*quae*' in the second of the second pair of lines. Schubiger had noticed it, and had supplied the necessary extra note.

[2] None of Notker's sequences contain any deliberate rhymings.

```
- gis  so - li  Ma - ri - æ  ve - ra - ci, quam Ju - de - o - rum tur - bæ  fal - la - ci. )
- re - xis - se  ex mor-tu - is  ve - re;  tu  no - bis  vic - tor Rex  mi - se - re - re. )
```

A number of *Visitatio Sepulchri* music-dramas made use of the sequence
as a concluding dramatic item, placed immediately before the *Te Deum*.
While its first part appears to be no more than a lyrical call to all
Christians to praise the Paschal Victim, the second contains (as did the
Quem quaeritis trope itself) the possibilities of a dramatic dialogue; in
this case between the three Marys (or a single one) returning from the
Tomb with news of the Resurrection, and the questioning disciples.
Some *Visitatio* versions employed the whole of the sequence. Others,
with better dramatic effect, began with the '*Dic nobis . . .*' question, as
coming from the disciples. The several reply phrases and sentences were
either divided among the three Marys or given to a single one, that is,
Mary Magdalen. Anyway, a considerable variety in the details of allocation can be found among the Sepulchre drama versions. Apart from the
omission, more often than not, of the lyrical first part, both the text and
the music of the sequence were very respectfully preserved, whenever
used.

We shall not be much concerned with the progress of the sequence
from the twelfth century onward, when its texts moved towards regularity of structure, rhythm, and rhyme scheme (approximating, that is,
to Latin poetry in hymn form), and reached a pitch of artistic perfection
in the work of the great poet-composer, Adam de St. Victor (d. 1192).
He wrote over fifty sequences in a smooth, regular, elegant style that was
universally admired, the verse patterns mostly variations on the '8 7
syllables' scheme, such as '8 8 7 : 8 8 7', or '8 8 8 7 : 8 8 8 7'. Normally,
the melody would occupy the first half of the stanza (three or four lines)
and be repeated for the second. A complete sequence would consist of
several such stanzas. There were other variations of technique that we
cannot touch on here.[1]

Adam de St. Victor's works were probably the main impulse which
brought about the remarkable passion for sequence writing that obtained
during the medieval centuries, to which we have already referred. Of all
this wealth of thousands of sequences, breathing religious devotion, the
Council of Trent allowed only five to survive in the Roman liturgy,
where they can still be encountered. These five are the venerable '*Victimae paschali*' already referred to, '*Lauda Sion*', '*Stabat Mater*', '*Veni
sancte Spiritus*', and the great and famous '*Dies irae*'. Even though our
survey of the music-dramas will not be concerned with them and a study
of them moves far beyond the scope of this work, it might well be useful
for the reader to take note of them at some time and to ponder the possible reasons for their representing a survival of the fittest.

---

[1] An exhaustive study of these particular sequences is E. Misset and P. Aubry, *Les Proses
d'Adam de Saint Victor* (Paris, 1900).

III

Let us turn now to a consideration of the main body of the tropes, examples of which for centuries attached themselves to nearly every type of liturgical chant, but which were set out mainly in their own special manuscripts, the Tropers.[1] The most considerable were designed for the Mass, the 'greater' tropes being those of the Ordinary (Kyrie, Gloria, Sanctus, and Agnus Dei); the 'lesser' those of the Introit, Alleluia, Offertory, and Communion.[2] Tropes were even to be found for a while applied to the Lessons and to the '*Ite missa est*' and '*Benedicamus*'. The Credo, however, seems almost never to have been touched;[3] and the Gradual, in spite of the melismatic opportunities that it presented, seems also to have escaped comparatively lightly.

In the case of the Hour Services the main attention was given to the responsories, especially when these were sung in processions.

There appear to have been three categories of tropes:

1. The purely musical trope, taking the form of a vocal flourish; a melisma in the style of an improvisation added to the normal item.
2. The purely textual type; the addition of a new text alone, fitted to the notes of an already existing melisma.
3. The musical-textual type. Here we have both new text and new music —complete originality.

The purely musical tropes appeared early and seem to have flourished best among the responsories of Matins, the form of which, as we have seen, is respond, verse, respond repeated. Even in the music of the long-purged modern service books, considerable melismas can be found on one or another of the concluding syllables of a respond (see responsory 2 at Corpus Christi Matins, *Liber Usualis*, p. 927). But in certain surviving manuscripts examples of responsories can be found where the melisma has been extended to fantastic lengths when the respond is repeated, this obviously representing a case of troping. Apel (pp. 441–2) quotes the example of '*Ecce jam coram te*' from the Feast of St. Stephen. In this responsory the word 'intercedere', which has a modest melisma of 12

---

[1] W. H. Frere, discussing tropes in general on p. vi of his edition of the Winchester Troper (London, 1894), mentions that 'the tropers practically represent the sum total of musical advance between the ninth and twelfth century . . .' but that the compositions, 'failing to gain admission into the privileged circle of the recognized service books, were thrown together so as to form an independent music-collection supplemental to the official books; and that is exactly what a troper is'.

[2] Besides the expansion of the conclusion of the Alleluia repeat, which developed into the Sequence, both the first Alleluia and its verse suffered a certain amount of troping.

The distinction between 'greater' and 'lesser' tropes belongs to Frere and has not generally been adopted by later scholars. For some recent critical viewpoints on the origin of the trope and the matter of terminology, see Paul Evans, 'Some Reflections on the Origin of the Trope', *Journal of the American Musicological Society*, 14 (1961), pp. 119–30; Ibid., *The Early Trope Repertory of St. Martial de Limoges* (Princeton, 1970); Richard Crocker, 'The Troping Hypothesis', *Musical Quarterly*, 52 (1966), pp. 183–203. (*Ed.*)

[3] 'Almost'; since H. Villetard (*L'Office de Pierre de Corbeil*, 1907) makes mention of a troped Credo in an Office of the thirteenth century.

note-units in the opening respond, is expanded hugely in the repeat to one of 76 units!

The textual method, as we have seen in the case of the sequence, permitted a considerable lengthening of the original item. Let us consider a very modest example, the brief versicle '*Benedicamus Domino*' with its equally brief response, '*Deo gratias*'. These, having originally been given somewhat melismatic settings, were joyfully seized upon by trope composers. Here is the Roman service book version of the versicle as at Lauds, on Solemn Feasts (see *Liber Usualis*, p. 124):

And here is a trope of it as found in *Aachen, Staatsbibl., Codex 7* of the fifteenth century (a late survival). It will clearly be seen how the flourishes on the first syllable of *Domino* have provided the musical setting for the inserted sentences, and how *Deo* and the inserted *dicamus* use the single notes of the *Benedicamus* music, while the original music of the second syllable of *Deo* is employed to provide a much longer flourish for the first syllable of *gratias*. A few small note-differences between the Aachen setting of the Verse and that of the modern Solesmes edition will be noted.

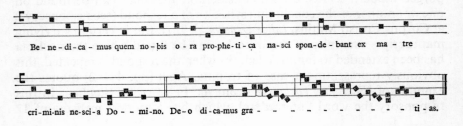

A much more extensive use of this principle is to be found in the numerous examples of troped (or 'farsed') Kyries. A Kyrie in full performance consists of nine acclamations: the initial '*Kyrie eleison*' ('Lord, have mercy') sung three times; '*Christe eleison*' sung three times; and a final '*Kyrie eleison*' sung three times.[1] To the medieval trope-composers this structure seemed ready-made for expansion. Syllabic melodies were shaped from the *Kyrie* and *Christe* melismas, and a troping was devised by inventing nine appropriate sentences and inserting them between the *Kyrie* or *Christe* starts and their concluding *eleisons*. A famous example

---

[1] Nowadays, '*Kyrie eleison*' is performed as seven syllables, the settings of the two middle 'e's being kept separate. In medieval times only five divisions were made (*Ky-ri-e-lei-son*), the single 'e' taking over the middle melismas.

is the '*Kyrie fons bonitatis*', so called because the first of the nine tropings started with those two words. The Kyrie itself (*Kyrie II*) with its music, can be seen on p. 19 of the *Liber Usualis*, and the first three sentences of the troping with their syllabic music on Apel, p. 431.

Another method employed in Kyrie tropes was to present the sentence first with its syllabic music, and then to complete the line with its normal '*Kyrie (Christe) eleison*'. The best-known example of this technique is undoubtedly the '*Kyrie Omnipotens (Cunctipotens) genitor*', based on *Kyrie IV* of the service books (*Liber Usualis*, p. 25). Schubiger has transcribed it into modern stave notation (*Sängerschule*, Exempla No. 42), and both *Kyrie* and troped *Kyrie* may be found in the *Historical Anthology of Music*, Vol. I, Item 15.[1] Both '*Kyrie fons bonitatis*' and '*Kyrie Omnipotens genitor*' have been attributed to the famous monk-musician Tuotilo of St. Gall (d. 913), but this rests on very doubtful evidence.[2]

The *Kyries* were the longest survivors among the tropes. W. H. Frere notes that in some cases, when the trope text itself disappeared, the music survived to make an even more elaborate setting for the words *Kyrie eleison*.[3]

When it comes to a consideration of the *Gloria, Sanctus*, and *Agnus Dei*, we find that these lack sufficiently florid melismas to pursue what we now might term the sequence or '*Kyrie*' technique. It is now a matter of the third category of trope, the musical-textual type. This method of troping begins in the process of intercalation, i.e. the insertion of invented sentences between sentences or phrases of the liturgical text. This being done, there is no help but to invent the music as well.

As an example of this kind of troping, I take a *Gloria, Sanctus*, and *Agnus Dei* from a *Graduale-Troparium* of the twelfth century from Nevers (*Paris, Bibl. Nat., Nouv. Acq., MS lat. 1235*), a very beautiful manuscript having its music on four-line staves with clefs. Photographs of the relevant pages are before me.[4]

Here are the texts of the first three sentences of the *Gloria*, along with the texts of the first three Nevers tropings:

'GLORIA IN EXCELSIS DEO. ET IN TERRA PAX HOMINIBUS BONAE VOLUNTATIS. Pax sempiterna Christus illuxit gloria tibi pater excelse.

'LAUDAMUS TE. Hymnum canentes hodie quem terris angeli fuderunt Christo nascente.

'BENEDICIMUS TE. Natus est nobis hodie salvator in trinitate semper colendus.' [etc.]

---

[1] The latter work, in setting out the troped version, has not included the *Kyrie* and *Christe* acclamations which were a part of it. A further example is discussed in Reese, p. 431: '*Kyrie Cunctipotens dominator*', based on *Kyrie XIV* (*Liber Usualis*, p. 54).

[2] For a more thorough discussion of this question, see Clark, p. 194.

[3] Frere, p. xiv.

[4] The respective folio details of the *Gloria, Sanctus*, and *Agnus Dei* are 185r.–186r.; 210r. and v.; 218v. We find the special term '*Laudes*' frequently applied to tropes of these three items.

A transcription of this *Gloria* trope appears on p. 192 of the Crocker article already mentioned above (footnote 1, p. 59) (*Ed.*).

It will be realized that by the time six more troping sentences have been inserted into an already fairly lengthy liturgical piece, the item has become one of formidable dimensions, and I can do no more than report on the settings of the trope sentences. These proceed in a moderately neumatic style with only a few instances of brief melismas. Also, I seek in vain for anything that could be described as a repetition of a musical phrase, or any borrowings from the liturgical music.

As for the troped *Sanctus* that follows, one finds seven intercalatory sentences, set almost exclusively to single notes. Once again there is not the slightest sign of any link between the trope settings and the liturgical music. The trope settings, however, show some relationship one with another. While the first seems independent, the second and third amount to the same tune, while the rest of the sentence settings (4 to 7) represent variations on what is another melody.

The *Agnus Dei* a shorter composition, has only three intercalatory trope sentences. These settings have little to do with each other except in one particular, the few notes of the Phrygian (E) cadence which they share with four of the liturgical sentences. The last of the latter ('*Dona nobis pacem*') closes in the Dorian (D) mode.

When, with the advent of the twelfth century, the gradual fading of the whole trope movement began, the *Gloria* tropes shared something of the longer life won by those of the *Kyrie*. Tropes of the *Sanctus* and *Agnus Dei* were fewer and disappeared far sooner.

The last body of Mass tropes that we need to consider are those of the Introit—and here we must spend some time, since the intimate relationship between these tropes and the origins of the music-drama will be made apparent as the subject of our next chapter.

The Introit itself, as we have already seen, is normally characterized by a moderately ornate (i.e. neumatic) style, with a predilection for the use of *strophici*. Introit tropes tend to conform to the neumatic style of their parent item, unlike the tropes of the *Gloria* and *Sanctus*, which are more syllabic. Once again we have, in the Introit, an item lacking in melismas; thus once again the troping must take the form of invention, both of texts and music. A striking feature of the composed music is that it not only imitates the style of the Introit to which it is attached, but usually keeps to the same range and tonality.[1] On occasions it will even be found to have borrowed a *motif* from the Introit melody.[2]

Two different methods seem to have been used for troping the Introit. The first was the usual intercalation, the interpolation of new texts and new music between successive Introit sentences. The other method was to frame an original, continuous, and relevant prose passage with origi-

---

[1] Peter Wagner calls attention to an opposite tendency, which is less common, this seen in a '*Puer natus . . .*' Introit trope from the *B.N. MS lat. 1235* from which I have already quoted. It is to be found on fol. 184, immediately before the '*Gloria*' which I mentioned. It seems deliberately to make a contrast between tonalities, G for the Introit, A for the intercalatory trope.

[2] Apel (p. 438) quotes a troping of that so-frequently troped Introit, '*Puer natus est . . .*' that illustrates this point.

nal, continuous, and relevant music (at least in style). The whole homogeneous composition acted as a preface to the Introit.

These introductory tropes of the Introit seem to stand in a class by themselves. Not being circumscribed as to meaning, as are the 'internal' tropes, nor framed to some degree in accordance with a previously existing musical scheme, as are the tropes founded on melismas, they represent a somewhat higher standard of inventive ability, in regard to both the text and the setting.

Such tropes are among the earliest of which we have knowledge, and one of the most famous of them is the '*Hodie cantandus est nobis puer*', ascribed with fair certainty to the already mentioned Tuotilo of St. Gall, and being a trope of (yet again) the '*Puer natus*' Introit. Its popularity in early medieval times seems to have been immense, and already in the tenth century it was known far and wide. It is to be found in the venerable Winchester Troper (*c*. 980)[1] as well as in many other manuscripts.

Its form should be noted; an introductory sentence, and then question and reply. The latter device was a familiar enough medieval procedure.[2] It may be useful to give the details of the interrogatory passage that follows the introduction. I have relied on the unheighted neumes of the Winchester Troper version (10v.–11r.), these interpreted by Schubiger's stave transcription of the music of the trope as given in *St. Gall, MS 378*.[3] In the example, I have placed above the notes the B flats suggested by Schubiger, and not of course indicated by the unheighted neumes of either *St. Gall. 378* or the Winchester Troper. Also, I have marked with asterisks the places where there are slight discrepancies between the notes of *St. Gall 378* (via Schubiger) and those of the Winchester Troper.

Quis est i - ste pu — er, quem tam ma - gnis præ - co - ni - is · di - gnum vo - ci - fe - ra - tis?

Di - ci - te no – bis ut con - lau ·- da - to — res es - se pos - si - mus.

[1] The text is printed in Frere, pp. 4–5.
 The Winchester Troper is preserved in two known manuscripts, which contain a good deal of overlapping material: Oxford, *Bibl. Bodl. MS 775* (tenth century), and *Corpus Christi College, Cambridge, MS 473* (eleventh century). Frere's edition (which deals only with the text) makes principal use of the latter which he judges to be 'more pure' and to contain 'a good deal of matter of great interest'. See Frere, p. xxviii (*Ed.*).
[2] Tropes from other parts of the liturgy may be found containing question and reply. Karl Young (I, p. 195) quotes an excellent twelfth-century example from *A.H. 47*, a trope of the *Kyrie*. There is, of course, the dialogued conclusion of '*Victimae paschali*'. But the prefacing Introit tropes (including '*Quem quaeritis in sepulchro* . . .') of the tenth century seem to be the earliest to be cast in this form.
[3] See Schubiger, Exempla No. 41, p. 39. He assumed, further, that the *internal* tropings of '*Puer natus est* . . .' belonging to *St. Gall MS 378*, were also the work of Tuotilo. This view is now discredited. It would seem that Tuotilo was concerned only with prefixing tropes.

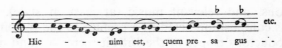

Hic - - - nim est, quem pre - sa - gus - - -

When we seek to identify the area in which tropes first developed we find that, as in the case of the sequence, scholarly opinion is once again inclined to favour Northern France. Clemens Blume, co-editor of *Analecta Hymnica*, in the volumes of which thousands of tropes have been gathered, takes this view. The vast majority of the collection derives from France and England, the Germanic regions seeming comparatively uninterested in their development. Again, however, we have to contend with strong traditional claims from St. Gall, with the name of Tuotilo put forward as the first deviser of tropes, and the early and widespread fame of '*Hodie cantandus* . . .' used to support the argument. However, that authoritative chronicler of the achievements of the Abbey of St. Gall, J. M. Clark, will allow no more to Tuotilo than the composition (prose-texts and music) of a few prefacing Introit and Offertory tropes of high quality. Clark suggests (p. 192) that we should look to Jumièges again. He speculates as to whether Tuotilo received his inspiration from the same source as did Notker, i.e. the antiphonary of the Norman monk, which, it is more than likely, contained Norman-French trope material. We know from the St. Gall chronicler Ekkehard IV that Tuotilo presented his first trope composition to the Emperor Charles III some years after Notker's first sequences appeared.

However sternly the disapproving Church may finally have treated these extra-liturgical compositions, they had some important secular results. Like the sequences, they seem to have been immensely popular with lay listeners, as the charming lines of French poetry so happily quoted by Karl Young (I, pp. 194–5) readily show.[1] The verse-forms which the tropes developed were imitated for secular use, and in the vernacular. The songs of the 'goliards' (the wandering scholars), at times devout, at times scurrilous, were undoubtedly directly influenced by them, as was medieval poetry in general. Modern writers have shown what a debt the troubadours and trouvères owed to the Church in regard to both verse forms and music.

Since the use of tropes and sequences was not a matter of direction but of toleration on the part of the hierarchy, the repertory varied a great deal from place to place, dependent on the preferences of each particular region and the material available. We shall notice, when deal-

[1]
       Chantons, chantons, clercs et clergesses,
       Les samedis les bèles messes
       De la Dame de paradis,
       Chantons, chantons les samedis
       Les déliteuses kyrièles,
       Les séquences plaisans et bèles
       A haute voiz et à haut tons.
       (Gautier de Coinci, *c.* 1220)
It will be noted that not only were the plain and straightforward melodies of the sequences appreciated, but also the vocal flourishes of the *Kyries.*

ing with the miscellaneous materials that made up the Church music-dramas, that there were tropes that were exclusively Franco-English, or Germanic, or Italian; also that established tropes had their own accretions. ('Trope d'un trope!'—to recall Léon Gautier's celebrated exclamation.)

It has already been said that the rise of the trope movement represented a new flowering of artistic creation. That authority on tropes and sequences, Jacques Handschin, has had much to say about the new spirit to be perceived in this music, stressing particularly the vividness and impressiveness of the melodies; and he makes what may seem to some a daring suggestion:[1]

... Agobard [an early ninth-century commentator], speaking of the danger that such music would swamp the liturgy, quotes passages from St. Jerome directed against 'theatrical art'. We must therefore conclude that the influx comes largely from the secular music of the period, which would otherwise have left no traces—or perhaps it would be more correct to say that the Church musicians worked on the same lines as their secular colleagues.

On the next page of the same volume he raises another important consideration:

Once the trope and sequence appeared with texts, the possibility of transferring a trope to a different Gregorian chant disappeared, and every trope was attached to a definite melody; only the sequence preserved a large measure of freedom in association with the Alleluia verse.

He again emphasizes this last statement in another monograph:

Every trope is in principle intended to combine with a given Gregorian song, as an introduction to it, or as an interpolation . . .[2]

This is a point to which we shall return later.

It can be fairly said that the music of the tropes and the fully developed sequences belonged to a new phase in the art of medieval monody. As we shall now be showing, to this phase there belongs also the music of the Latin dramas of the medieval Church.

---

[1] In *New Oxford History of Music* (London, 1954), Vol. II, p. 148.
[2] 'The Two Winchester Tropers', *The Journal of Theological Studies*, XXXVII (1936), p. 35.

CHAPTER FIVE

THE TENTH CENTURY (1)

The origin and function of the 'Quem quaeritis' trope

FOR many decades the view of most scholars has been that the *fons et origo* of the medieval Church's dramatic activities had been the Easter Introit trope of which we have already made so much mention. It is an opinion which I share, and I shall in due course be dealing with certain dissentient views that have of late come into prominence.

Our first task will be to try to settle the matter of the original home of this trope, one that has up to now remained a matter of uncertainty, principally because so little effort has been made in the past to examine the problem in terms of music. There are hundreds of examples of this Easter dialogue still in manuscript existence, and my investigations have shown me that in whatever part of Western Christendom the three familiar sentences turn up, the music to which they are set is manifestly derived from a single source. In other words, they represent variations on one basic melody, the small differences often proving to be distinctive characteristics of different centres.

It is clear that this setting (wherever it may have sprung from) 'caught on' with the same spontaneity as did other famous tunes which we know to be single acts of composition, such as the '*Hodie cantandus*' trope music of Tuotilo, several of the major sequences, the '*Alma Redemptoris Mater*'[1] of Hermannus Contractus, and that mysterious anthem with supposed magical powers, '*Media vita*'.[2] Also to be remembered are the swarms of lesser tropes that turned up all over the place, with texts that could have been anybody's pickings from the Bible and in some cases from the liturgy, but whose 'multiple' origins are contradicted by the fact that individual examples maintained a common musical setting over a wide area.

We find the two abbeys of St. Martial de Limoges and St. Gall once more prominent, as having the two earliest versions of the '*Quem quaeritis*' trope that have survived, contained in manuscripts mostly devoted to tropes. The St. Martial de Limoges version, now in the

---

[1] This composition is included among the 'Marian Anthems' of the Roman liturgy (a late addition). See *Liber Usualis*, p. 273, Sunday at Compline. The melody, with its constant B flat, is actually in the 'major mode'. Hermannus Contractus died in 1054.

[2] Wrongly attributed to Notker. Peter Wagner suggests a Gallican origin. See Reese, p. 129.

Bibliothèque Nationale (*Ms lat. 1240*, fol. 30v.) is found in one of the older portions of the volume, which consists of several different fascicles of different dates. Differing opinions among scholars seem to have hardened to the approximate dating of 933–6 for the writing down of the trope.[1] The St. Gall version, a good deal tidier than that of Limoges, was written down probably around 975.

Although the Limoges example is the older, its three sections (question, reply, and further statement) have already themselves been troped by the addition of further invented sentences, found both before and after the dialogue. 'Trope d'un trope' once again! The St. Gall version contains no more than the three sections, the final words, '*de sepulchro*', not being found in the Limoges version. The musical settings are manifestly very similar, but the small differences between them can be shown to be respectively characteristic of the centre and its dependents.

Let us consider each in turn, beginning with the older manuscript, from Limoges. *B.N. lat. MS 1240*, fol. 30v. is written in an early style of Aquitainian notation, set down in horribly careless fashion.[2] No reliance can be placed on the accuracy of the heighting of the neumes, which are plainly influenced by the amount of space that the lines of the text have left available. Reference is now invited to the frontispiece, which is a photograph of the manuscript page.

The introductory trope to the first '*Quem quaeritis*' sentence is, as far as I am aware, unique in this position. Karl Young thinks so too, since '*Psallite regi magno, devicto mortis imperio*' appears only once in his index, as attached to the *B.N. 1240* version. Its normal position is to act as one of the innumerable internal trope sentences inserted into the Easter Mass Introit, '*Resurrexi, et adhuc tecum sum . . .*', sometimes close to the conclusion of the '*Quem quaeritis*' trope, as in *B.N. MS lat. 887*, fol. 119r. (Limoges troper of the early eleventh century), sometimes more distance, as in a troper from Autun, *Paris, Bibl. de l'Arsenal MS 1169 anni 996–1024*, fols. 18v.–19r. But, be it noted, it is always

---

[1] See J. Chailley, *L'École Musicale de Saint Martial de Limoges jusqu'à la Fin du XIᵉ Siècle* (Paris, 1960), pp. 78–80. The book reveals very clearly the monastery's *avant-garde* position in the field of musical invention during this period, one concerned not only with melody but with the beginnings of polyphony.

[2] The Aquitainian style of notation certainly derived some of its features from that of Chartres (see Suñol, p. 269 and Plate 66). However, it developed a unique characteristic, that of dissolving the neumatic signs into single units, mostly 'points', indicating roughly individual pitches. In Apel, following p. 122, Plate V is a reproduction of a page from *B.N. MS lat. 776* (eleventh century). It shows an example of the Easter Introit, '*Resurrexi . . .*', also in Aquitainian notation, carefully heighted above a single incised line. If *B.N. 1240* represents the notation at a very low level of merit, *MS 776* is an example *par excellence*. Yet there is no identifying letter to the line, and it is only our foreknowledge of the music which settles that the line represents F. That known, the pitch of the 'points' can be read almost exactly. Limoges notation had been in no hurry to introduce even the single line, and this without a letter value. Only towards the end of the eleventh century did such a line take over a fixed identity in Aquitainian use, but this applicable only to a single piece. Such an identity could be altered from one item to the next, and this without an informative clef sign or any other kind of notice, such as was being found elsewhere. St. Gall was similarly conservative, writing '*campo aperto*' neumes (mainly on a level) in some cases into the fourteenth century, at a time when four-line staves with clefs were freely in use everywhere, including other parts of Germany.

after the word '*Resurrexi*', whether this is given in full or as a couple of letters of incipit. A better known example is the Winchester Troper, which shows it on its page 19v. I could quote one or two more occurrences of it that I have met, always as an internal trope of the Easter Introit and well separated from the '*Quem quaeritis*'. A situation worth mentioning is in connection with the companion Winchester document, the *Regularis concordia*. Here is given (without music) the earliest known dramatic version of the '*Quem quaeritis*', and with this there occurs what is surely a paraphrase of '*Psallite regi magno . . .*' in rubric form. We are told that '*Finita antiphona, prior congaudens pro triumpho regis nostri, quod devicta morte surrexit, incipiat hymnum Te Deum laudamus.*'[1]

The three '*Quem quaeritis*' sentences of *B.N. 1240* contain one uniquely different phrase, '*ipse dixit*' instead of the '*praedixerat*', which is almost universal in later '*Quem quaeritis*' manuscripts. To be sure, two French versions, *B.N. MS lat. 904* and *Oxford, Bodl. MS Rawlinson d. iv* conclude the sentence with '*sicut dixit*', while a few Italian and Spanish versions have '*locutus est*'. But *B.N. 1240's* two words are, as far as I know, found nowhere else in '*Quem quaeritis*' texts, although their music is the same as the '*praedixerat*' of the Limoges group of tropers belonging to around the turn of the century. *B.N. 1240's* rounding-off trope, which links the '*Quem quaeritis*' sentence to the '*Resurrexi*' Introit, is a widely used one, in both France and Italy. '*Alleluia, resurrexit Dominus hodie, resurrexit leo fortis, Christus filius Dei, Deo gratias, dicite eia!*' served as a trope for numerous versions of the '*Quem quaeritis*' dialogue, both in France and Italy, but the two countries used settings that distinguish them apart. Germanic regions seem not to have been interested.[2]

As will be seen from the photograph, the setting-down of the two-column page is disgraceful. At the left-hand top is a scatter of internal tropings of the Easter Introit which must have been added as an after-thought, since some of the details have spilt across to the right-hand top and threatened the continuation of the '*Alleluia, resurrexit Dominus hodie . . .*' trope in the right-hand column.[3] There follows on the right-hand side another internal troping of the Introit, with the incipit versions of the Introit sentences reduced to '*Po*' (*Posuisti*) and '*Mirab*' (*Mirabilis*), without their music. Karl Young, in his printing of the text of the *B.N. 1240* page (I. pr 210), disregarded the added Introit troping at the left-hand top. After the end of the sentence, '*Alleluia, resurrexit Dominus hodie . . .*', while quite rightly inserting the missing Introit

---

[1] See Young, I, p. 250.

[2] I must record an exception. The somewhat enigmatic version from Mainz; (Vienna, *Nat. Libr. MS lat. 1888*, fol. 103r., of the tenth century) includes this trope, but the neume notation of the page is that of St. Gall, and there is a version of '*Surrexit Dominus de sepulchro, qui pro nobis . . .*' the music of which is not liturgical, but an independent German setting.

[3] The absence of the '*Resurrexi*' incipit will be noted. But '*Posuisti*' and '*Mirabilis*' are there and the neumes of the alleluias indicate the standard liturgical setting. Light comes when one turns back to the previous page (30r.) where '*Resurrexi, et ad(h)uc tecum . . .*' can be seen at the foot of the right-hand column. This column is plainly a palimpsest, and its scraping left the vellum perilously thin. Possibly it was written after the '*Quem quaeritis*' trope, some of the details of which can be seen in reverse, through the page.

incipit, '*Resurrexi, et adhuc tecum sum . . .*', and adding the following details of the first internal troping of the Introit, he stopped his transcription of the manuscript text at this point. What happened afterwards was the appearance of the incipit, '*Re*' (i.e. *Resurrexi*) which marks the beginning of another and different internal troping of the Introit, followed in due course by the other incipits, this time written as '*Posu*' and '*Mira*', and passing on to the next page. It is a state of affairs, the offering of two or more alternative tropings of the Easter Introit, which is so often found in '*Quem quaeritis*' trope versions after the first '*Resurrexi*' (often marked with the rubric '*Al*', or '*Item Alius*' (*Alius*) or (*Aliter*), the texts not recorded by Karl Young. The confusion caused by the original slipshod setting-down of the *B.N. 1240* page has caused writers who rely on texts alone, particularly O. B. Hardison, to attempt to deny Karl Young's reading of the situation. Hardison is perturbed by several 'problems' of the manuscript page. He writes:[1]

> The earliest Limoges version [he then refers the reader to the page in Karl Young where the text is printed] also presents problems. It is titled *Trophi in Pasche*, and Young's emendation to *Trophi in die pasche* is purely editorial. The placement of the text in the Limoges manuscript is also curious. It does not end with *Resurrexi* but with *Deo gratias, dicite eia!* followed by the standard trope of the Easter Introit, *Dormivi Pater . . .* Only after the first line of this trope is there an abbreviation (*Po*) referring to the Easter Introit itself. We can assume that the first words of the Introit, *Resurrexi, et adhuc tecum sum*, preceded the trope, but there is no reference to them in the manuscript. The effect is that of two separate liturgical pieces, the *Quem quaeritis* and the Introit trope, run together. Evidently the *Quem quaeritis* was used at Limoges as part of the Easter Introit, but the manuscript does not justify the conclusion either that the Limoges version is original or that the original was part of the Introit. The evidence supports the idea of the conflation of two separate pieces equally well, if not better.

It seems to me that there are several points here that need commenting upon, although the matter of 'Young's emendation' is hardly worth bothering about. Several of the '*Quem quaeritis*' versions that we have already met with are similarly ambiguous in their headings, such as '*De Pascha Domini*' (*Paris, B. de l'Arsenal MS 1169*), '*In Pascha*' *Apt MS 18(4)* and '*In Pasca ad Missam*', (*B.N. MS 887*). But there is no doubt in their cases as to how they are functioning—as prefacing tropes to the Introit of the Easter Mass! If we look closely at the photograph of *B.N. 1240*, we find near the bottom of the right-hand column the incipit '*Re*' (*Resurrexi*), starting, as is so often the case in '*Quem quaeritis*' trope versions, a second internal troping of the Easter Introit, this confirmed by the last word of the page, the incipit '*Posuisti*'.

It is unnecessary for Hardison to say 'It does not end with "*Resurrexi*" but with "*Deo gratias, dicite eia!*"' ('it', I assume, being the '*Quem quaeritis*' trope). Of course it ends thus, since these are the last words of the rounding-off '*Alleluia, resurrexit Dominus hodie, resurrexit leo fortis,*

---

[1] Hardison, p. 190.

Christus filius Dei . . . dicite eia!' It is after '*Deo gratias, dicite eia!*' that the first '*Resurrexi*' incipit should have come, followed by what Hardison apparently calls the 'standard' trope sentence ('*Dormivi . . .*') of the Easter Mass Introit.[1] To confirm our suspicion on this point, we may consult the Winchester Troper, page 19v, which gives a much tidier replica of the *B.N. 1240* right-hand column, from '*Dormivi Pater . . .*' right down to the bottom. As we might expect, placed immediately preceding '*Dormivi*' is the incipit '*Resurrexi*', with its correct Introit neumes above it. The musical settings in each manuscript for the whole of this first internal troping coincide all down the page. Two lines up from the bottom the '*Re*' of *B.N. 1240* is confirmed by Winchester's '*Resurrexi*', with its liturgical neumes, as another internal troping of the Introit starts. There is also a bonus on the Winchester page, the trope, '*Psallite regi magno . . .*' given in full, its neumes, in the beautiful Anglo-Saxon notation, corroborating those of *B.N. 1240*. The fact is that by putting in the missing '*Resurrexi*' incipit before '*Dormivi*' in *B.N. 1240* we obtain a quite acceptable '*Quem quaeritis*' prefacing trope to the Easter Mass Introit. What is the basic shape of the '*Quem quaeritis*' trope? It amounts simply to the three sentences of the 'dialogue', either by themselves or with the addition of minor troping sentences before and/or after the '*Quem quaeritis*', at the conclusion of which there comes the '*Resurrexi, et adhuc tecum sum*' Introit itself, which will betray often enough that it has also to submit to further extensive internal tropings (this nothing at all to do with the prefacing '*Quem quaeritis*'), and involving several rewritings of the Introit incipits.

This is exactly the shape of *B.N. 1240*, except for the omission of that '*Resurrexi*' incipit, which is quite the sort of happening to be expected from this particular scribe. The fact of the omission, however, is amply proved by the 'replica' section of the Winchester Troper.

This matter of the numerous internal tropings of the Introit is an important one, and one to which Karl Young has devoted little attention. The practice seems to have been limited to the tenth and eleventh centuries, but within this time period it frequently attained great elaborateness. W. H. Frere comments (*The Winchester Troper*, p. xviii):

We must now return to the real introit-tropes and notice that they coincide with a stage in the method of singing the introit which disappeared later. The amount of psalmody sung at the introit had already been greatly curtailed by the ninth century, but it was still the custom, at times at any rate, to sing after the Gloria patri, a selected verse from the psalm called ℣ ad repetendum or ℣ prophetalis, and then to repeat the introit-antiphon for the last time. This ℣ disappeared later, but it survives in some few places in the English tropers . . . while the custom has left its mark on nearly every page by causing the tropes of the Introit to be divided into two classes, Ad introitum and Ad repetendum.

---

[1] I have objected to Hardison's reference to the '*Dormivi*' trope as being 'standard', since, although it turns up first as an internal Introit trope in the *B.N. 1240* and Winchester manuscripts, it can claim no real pre-eminence. The literature of the internal tropings of the Easter Introit is, as we shall see, enormous.

Karl Young did not, and of course could not set down the texts of the lengthy stream of '*Resurrexi*' tropes that followed his early '*Quem quaeritis*' trope examples. But the fact is that a great deal of useful information can be gathered from comparing the various choices of textual and musical material to be found among the versions. Moreover, we find even stronger confirmation, amounting, in fact, to an operating principle, that our '*Resurrexi*' emendation to *B.N. 1240* was correct.

My Plate IV, a reproduction of the late tenth-century *Apt MS 18(4)*, fols. 33v.–34r., provides a good illustration of this practice of multiple tropings. Here, in Provençal notation but belonging in its musical setting to the Limoges group, is a clear demonstration of the make-up of a '*Quem quaeritis*' prefacing trope of the Easter Mass Introit. Beginning with the rubric '*IN PASCHA*', we have first an introductory trope, '*Hora est, psallite . . .*', found in both French and Italian tropers with a uniform setting. The normal 'dialogue' follows; then comes the familiar '*Alleluia, resurrexit Dominus . . .*' right down to '*dicite eia*', to the usual French music. Immediately after comes '*Resurrexi, et adhuc tecum sum*', the full liturgical music being given in neumes. There follow the usual internal tropings of the sentences, (a different set from those of *B.N. 1240* and *Winchester*), with the inevitable '*Posuisti*' and '*Mirabilis*' incipits. But on this occasion the plate will show three different groups, with another '*Resurrexi*' at the bottom promising the start of yet another troping. Before the third occasion comes the rubric '*IT(EM) ALIOS*', marking the alternative. Another point to comment on is the addition by a later hand at the top of fol. 34r. of the sentence '*En ecce completum est illud quod olim ipse per prophetam dixerat, ad patrum taliter inquiens*' with its standard music.[1] It is used by some dozen French and Spanish versions of the '*Quem quaeritis*' trope. Karl Young, in his writing out of the text of *Apt 18(4)* (I, p. 212), incorporates both this sentence and the '*Alleluia, resurrexit*', but in my opinion they should be regarded as alternatives. In its original use of '*Alleluia, resurrexit . . .*' *Apt 18(4)* was following *B.N. 1240*'s practice, but by the time we reach the group of St. Martial tropers belonging to the turn of the century and beyond, we find that, while the 'dialogue' music has remained almost exactly the same, '*Alleluia, resurrexit Dominus . . .*' has been dropped as a rounding-off trope, and its place has been taken by '*En ecce completum . . .*', preceded by what now becomes its companion in the group mentioned above, the sentence, '*Alleluia, ad sepulcrum residens angelus nunciat resurrexisse Christum*'. *Apt 18(4)* is an example of this change beginning to take place. *Apt MS 17(5)* has almost exactly the same prefacing and 'dialogue' music as *Apt 18(4)*, but has abandoned '*Alleluia, resurrexit Dominus . . .*' in favour of the new pair.[2]

[1] A curious feature of the Provençal notation can be seen in the first '*Posuisti*' and also in the inserted '*En ecce completum . . .*' trope at '*ipse*' and '*inquiens*', where a neume like a figure 8 can be found by comparison with other manuscripts to represent some special form of *torculus* (pes flexus).

[2] The reader will no doubt have noticed that the photograph of *Apt 18(4)* (Plate VI) shows no vocative '*o*' before '*Christicolae*'. This matter is put right in *Apt 17(5)*, *Apt 18(4)*'s

A word of warning is necessary with regard to fol. 34r. of *Apt 18(4)*. The original scribe, whose Latinity wasn't his strong point, and influenced probably by having written not long before, '*Alleluia, resurrexit Dominus . . .*', could not make up his mind regarding '*Resurrexi*', and got it right only once. To give somebody his due, there is at one of the places an attempt to blot out the errant 't'. The touchstone of the matter is the presence in each instance of the right and proper Introit neumes, quite individual and unmistakable. '*Resurrexit*', for what should be '*Resurrexi*', is an error to be found in a number of manuscripts. Karl Young, even though lacking that touchstone, but guided by his good sense, has corrected the error on most occasions. O. B. Hardison, also unaware of any musical considerations, has attempted to question the corrections. The point being raised I shall have to discuss it further.

I had best begin by once again quoting Hardison, who this time is concerned with doubts in respect to another manuscript from Limoges. The page is *B.N. MS lat. 1118*, fol. 40v.; the portion of the manuscript containing it dates from 988–96 (the reader is invited to consult my Plate V). I quote some of Hardison's misgivings concerning it:

> Another anomaly of this text is its ending. The last word of the piece is *Resurrexit*, and it is followed not by the Easter Introit but by the rubric *item alius*. Young emends *Resurrexit* to *Resurrexi* on the assumption that the word is an erroneous transcription of the incipit of the Easter Introit. The emendation is doubtless justified in context because it is evident that the Limoges *Quem quaeritis* was, in fact, used at the beginning of the Mass. On the other hand, tenth- and eleventh-century versions of the *Quem quaeritis* regularly end with the antiphons *Resurrexit Dominus* and *Surrexit Dominus*, even when they are a part of Matins rather than Mass. It is therefore not at all clear that *Resurrexit* is a simple scribal error. It could equally be a transcription of an antiphon incipit from a version not associated with the Easter Mass. The relative frequency of the same error and the same emendation in later manuscripts strengthens this possibility. If the original version ended with *Resurrexit* or *Surrexit*, it is easy to see how it could become associated with the Easter Introit and why the apparent error in transcription tends to recur.[1]

There is no anomaly as to the ending of the '*Quem quaeritis*' trope, as set down in *B.N. MS lat. 1118*. After the three 'dialogue' sentences there come the two rounding-off tropes that I have already mentioned, '*Ad sepulcrum residens . . .*' and '*En ecce completum . . .*', set to the normal music that they carry on each of their appearances. I must now contradict a statement of Hardison's. He says that the last word of the piece is '*Resurrexit*', and it is followed not by the Easter Introit but by the rubric '*item alius*'. This is not so. The last word of the piece is the last word of the second rounding-off trope, '*inquiens*', while '*Resurrexi(t)*', badly in need of Karl Young's correction, is the first word, the incipit,

---

counterpart (almost) in Aquitainian notation, where the '*o*' is inserted, and a note transferred from the three-unit neume above the last syllable of '*Christicolae*', to act as a setting. For other instances of this feature, see p. 86.

[1] Hardison, pp. 189–90.

with its correct neumes, of the Easter Introit. The '*item alius*' that Hardison refers to seems to indicate that one could have either the Introit plain and straightforward or proceed to another of these frequent internal tropings of the Introit. Hardison, to judge from his footnote, took his text from pp. 211–12 of Karl Young's volume, and his evidence, drawn from the latter's text transcription that stops short at '*item alius*', derives from that text alone. If he had continued with the next page of the *manuscript* (the photograph of which is now before me), he would have found precisely those internal tropings of the Introit, with their familiar '*Posuisti*' and '*Mirabilis*' incipits. Familiar also is the first troping of the '*Resurrexi*'. It is the second half of the trope sentence, '*Alleluia, resurrexit Dominus dicite eia*', displaced from the closer association with '*Quem quaeritis*' that it was given in *B.N. 1240* and *Apt 18(4)*, but retaining its usual music.[1]

I must also question Hardison's statement that tenth- and eleventh-century versions of the '*Quem quaeritis*' regularly end with the antiphons '*Resurrexit Dominus*' and '*Surrexit Dominus*' even when they are a part of Matins rather than Mass. I suppose that by '*Resurrexit Dominus*' he means, '*Alleluia, resurrexit Dominus hodie, resurrexit leo fortis, Christus filius Dei, Deo gratias, dicite eia*', (which is a trope, not an antiphon); and by '*Surrexit Dominus*', the composition, '*Surrexit Dominus de sepulchro, qui pro nobis pependit in ligno*', which appears sometimes with the music of a now obsolete antiphon (surviving in Hartker) and sometimes to quite a different setting, as a German trope. Checking through my tenth- and eleventh-century photographic files, I find that the evidence of Christendom is that the '*Quem quaeritis*', whether in trope or dramatic form, ended in a variety of different fashions, rendering the term 'regularly' virtually meaningless. In France we have the '*Ad sepulcrum . . .*' and '*En ecce completum . . .*' pair; in Germanic lands, '*Surrexit enim sicut . . .*';[2] and quite a choice in Italy, including allowing the end of the '*Quem quaeritis*' exchange to pass straight to '*Resurrexi*', as in a number of German trope examples. However, the point is of little importance, and I must turn to a more decisive way of settling this '*Resurrexi(t)*' question.

Below, I reproduce in their simplest style the neumes which represent the immemorial music of the first word of the Easter Mass Introit as found in early service books, and which is faithfully preserved in the four-line plainchant notation of modern ones.

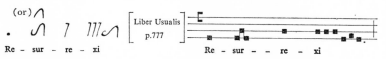

[1] The '*Resurrexit*' blunder occurs in several Limoges tropers, even though their concluding sentence before the Introit is '*En ecce . . . inquiens*', not '*Alleluia, resurrexit Dominus . . .*'. Occasionally, the error will be found corrected by smudging out the 't' (as in *B.N. MS lat. 887*, fol. 19r.); more commonly it is corrected by placing a *punctum* stab below the offending letter (as in *B.N. MS lat. 1120*, fol. 21r.).

[2] See p. 81.

I have given the alternative that is so often met with for the second neume, a *clivis* for a *torculus*. The fact of the first single neume (D) being of the same pitch as the first note of the *torculus* readily explains matters. The *tristropha* of the last syllable stands out like a beacon everywhere. Returning to Plate IV and the pages of *Apt 18(4)*, we can realise how clearly the first mistake of the scribe is revealed. He has written out the whole first sentence of the Introit, including the intrusive 't', but the music above betrays his error. Karl Young could guess. O. B. Hardison could doubt. The neumes *prove*. On every occasion when the Introit incipit reappears down the page, the scribe has obliging filled in the correct '*Resurrexi*' neumes, most of the time to his own betrayal. I wonder who tried to blot out the 't' of the second '*Resurrexi*'? He failed to finish his task of editing. It is amazing to realize the low state of scribal education that could permit such a slip at such an important point in the Gradual, the beginning of what must be the outstanding Mass of the liturgical year. Even the lowest level of cleric should surely have had text and music ringing in his head!

I shall now reproduce, in a readable modern form, what I think to be a reasonably correct interpretation of what was sung as the '*Quem quaeritis*' prefacing trope to the Introit of the Easter Mass at St. Martial de Limoges around A.D. 930 (*Paris, B.N. MS lat. 1240*, fol. 30v.). I will give it first (transposed up a perfect 4th with B flat in order to fit it comfortably on a G stave), and will proceed to justify it after.

I have not included Young's reading of the main rubric (*'TROPHI IN [DIE] PASCHE'*). However, in spite of objection by Hardison, it seems sound enough to me, for I believe that without doubt the *B.N. 1240* page represents a straightforward *'Quem quaeritis'* prefacing trope of the Easter Introit.[1] Although it is the earliest example extant, yet the accretions which have already attached themselves to its basic three sentences show that it cannot be the prototype. As for the claims made on behalf of *St. Gall 484*, I shall be dealing with those later. For the present, I will merely mention my belief that there was an original, three-sentence, prefacing trope of the *'Resurrexi'* Introit (not derived from any liturgical ceremony, or from St. Gall) and this, like other tropes of liturgical items, was a specially composed invention. In itself, it was intended for the *'Resurrexi'* Introit, and none other. This prototype lies further back in time from *B.N. 1240*, and owes its origin, almost certainly, to that highly active centre of trope production, St. Martial de Limoges. All this belongs to over a thousand years ago, and to a vellum-hungry world in which manuscript casualties were enormous, as a result not only of plain destruction, but from 'palimpsest' activities and uses as bindings for other manuscripts.

These causes must account for the strange fact that no further *'Quem quaeritis'* trope survives from Limoges until the late 980s or later. One reflects on what losses must have occurred over all those decades of trope composition at what was for a couple of centuries a most prolific centre. When, round the end of the tenth century, we meet with this new group of Limoges tropers and those from Apt, we find that while other ideas had grown up as to the troping of the trope (as well as to the internal troping of the Introit), the music of the three *'Quem quaeritis'* sentences had suffered remarkably little change. In fact it could be said that there was a 'house' version of the setting at Limoges and at places dependent on it, showing certain characteristics that made it recognizable anywhere.[2]

I have now to justify my reading of the *B.N. 1240* music, and I shall do so by consulting the neumes given to the three *'Quem quaeritis'* sentences as set out in the following versions, mostly belonging to St. Martial de Limoges and dating from the turn of the century and into the eleventh. These are (a) *B.N. MS 1118*, the earliest (988–96) [Plate II], (b) *B.N. MSS 1119, 1120, 1121*, together with *B.N. 1084, Apt 18(4)*

---

[1] I have also disregarded the left-hand top corner, a later addition of what I have already shown to be another attempt at an internal troping of the Introit. Included in the neumes of this item, and written above the first syllable of two of the alleluias, is a sign resembling a flat. Manifestly, it can't be. Comparison with other versions and the modern official music of the Introit gives a reading involving *strophici*, I have not met the sign elsewhere, and I don't think Suñol has taken note of it. It seems to me unlikely that it was meant as an *epiphonus*.

[2] This same 'house version' principle is visible in slightly varied but sufficiently distinctive configurations in a number of other places in France, the Germanic countries, Italy, and to a lesser degree, Spain (whenever the last-named can shake itself free from the Limoges influence), where the existence of 'groups' can be realized by certain special characteristics in their music.

[Plate IV], and *Apt 17(5)*, all these probably dating from round the end of the tenth to include the first half of the eleventh century: (c) *B.N. (Nouv. Acq) MS 1871* (eleventh century), probably from Aurillac: (d) *B.N. 779* (second half of the eleventh century), from Arles, near Avignon:[1] (e) *Huesca 4*, a Spanish manuscript (eleventh to twelfth century), but written in Aquitainian notation.[2] Every one of the manuscripts concerned except for *Apt 18(4)* makes some attempt at heighting the neumes, but with varying degrees of care. There is not the aid, even, of a single incised line, except for one doubtful instance. *B.N. 1119*, although vague at times in regard to heighting, supplies 'directs' at the end of each line of neumes to the beginning of the next. Possibly the most reliable of the versions is *B.N. (Nouv. Acq.) MS 1871*, with traces of an incised line and very clear directs. The page is a palimpsest, the trope written over other faintly discernible material. The scribe unfortunately never got down to writing the opening words; text and music start at '*o Christicolae.*'

The construction of a comparative chart[3] of the settings of all these versions brings a great deal of light to the neumes of *B.N. 1240*—and to the others as well. There seems no manner of doubt as to the authenticity of the music that I have set down for the first two sentences, that is, as far as '*caelicolae*', for the small disagreements between the versions are concerned only with *oriscus* signs for note lengthenings, and a disposition of almost all to add a final liquescent to the middle syllable of '*se-pul-chro*'. The juxtaposition of the two consonants, 'l' and 'c', makes this necessary, and there can be little doubt that, in practice, the effect would have been supplied by the singers of *B.N. 1240*. The one real difference between the music of the first '*Quem quaeritis*' sentence of *B.N. 1240* and the later Limoges-style versions is a simple rhythmic one at '*o caelicolae*': r̲m r̲d m f̲m- instead of *B.N. 1240*'s r̲m r̲d mf m r̲-. The music of the first half of the third sentence shows a similar consistency, except for a brief muddle in *MS 1120*, corrected by its twin, *MS 1121*; a division of preference as to whether the third syllable of '*praedixerat*' (or in the case of *B.N. 1240*, the first syllable of *dixit*) should have f̲r or f̲m̲r̲; and whether the final note should be 'm' or 'f'. The last part of the sentence, from '*Ite*' to '*surrexit*', shows the most disagreement, with doubts as to whether in some cases notes should be a tone higher than they appear to be, and some apparent independences on the part of *B.N. MS 1084*. I have had to puzzle a great deal over this last dialogue sentence ('*Ite*', etc.). The temptation is to follow the scribe of *B.N. (Nouv. Acq.) MS 1871*, who seemed very sure of himself, and wrote:

> r̲m m f̲m r̲m m m d m f̲s f-m̲ r-
> I - te, nun-ci - a - te qui-a sur- re- xit.

[1] *B.N. MS 779* is given by Karl Young (I, p. 569) as being of the thirteenth century; obviously an uncorrected slip in proofs.

[2] *B.N. MS 887* and *B.N. MS 1139*, both of the same period, I regard as 'odd men out', for reasons which I shall return to later. See pp. 111–12.

[3] See my Chart One.

Here, however, the heighting of the *B.N. 1240* neumes at this point (how I wish I could really rely on their pitch!) suggests rather those of *B.N. 1119, 1120* and *1121*. I therefore write:

$$\underline{r}f \quad f \quad \underline{fm} \quad \underline{r}f \quad f \quad f \quad m \, f \quad s \, \underline{f\text{-}r} \quad r \, \text{-},$$

I - te, nun-ci-a-te qui-a sur- re-xit.

for *B.N. 1240*'s last line. The penultimate neume differs from that of the other three versions, but I cannot go against what seem to be the firm intentions of *B.N. 1240*.[1]

Since I have more than once mentioned that the musical settings given to the three '*Quem quaeritis in sepulchro*' sentences as they exist throughout Christendom are readily recognizable as having sprung from one single source, let us try to discover, before we leave the music of *B.N. 1240*, what are the outstanding features of the melody which make its identity clear for all the editings of time and distance. I turn once more to the device of sol-fa, which even Solesmes finds useful at times for the quoting of short melodic phrases.

The melody is in the Dorian or *re* mode; more specifically, Mode II, starting and ending on D,[2] and with its melodic line ranging both above and below that pitch. At times during the centuries it will be found transposed to the fourth above with the use of B flat (or even with the flattening of the B no more than understood). It begins, almost always, with an opening dip, from r to l, ('*Quem quae-*'). Mostly, we find d (*do*) as an intermediate light note, a 'liquescent', as in our example, bridging the two awkward consonants, 'm' and 'q'. Sometimes the do liquescent is not written in; sometimes the leap from r to l, (liquescent) is taken with the first syllable. With '*quaeritis*' the tune returns to r, usually via two *torculus* forms (l,dt,,drd) but these sometimes simplify to dt,, dr. The next three notes again represent a characteristic, the upward triadic

---

[1] I imagine that a great deal of work remains to be done on tropes and tropers in general, with special attention regarding the information revealed by the music. The field is enormous and much territory is unexplored. I have found that, once again, too many investigators are concerned only with the texts, although of late years scholars like Handschin, Anglès, and Chailley have been altering that picture. Regarding the Aquitainian tropers, I have recently met with an analysis of their general contents (which I believe was based on texts alone) by David Hughes, 'Further Notes on the Grouping of the Aquitainian Tropers', *Journal of the American Musicological Society*, 19 (1966), pp. 3–12. Hughes' study divided the group into two families in the main, but with certain manuscripts that were considered to show considerable independence. In giving the identities I have omitted mention of those whose contents do not include the Easter '*Quem quaeritis*' trope. Family I included *B.N. 1119, 1120,* and *1121*; Family II included *B.N. 779* and *887*. *B.N. 1118* was reckoned as having an independent source, with 'preference' for Family I; *B.N. 1871* a similar independence but with preference for Family II. *B.N. 1240* was given as having some connection with *B.N. 887*. Certainly these divisions are not very discernible when the trope settings of the '*Quem quaeritis*' are considered. Except for *B.N. 887*, the versions we have met with are quite a happy musical family until the very last four-word sentence, when *B.N. 1240* appears to join up with *B.N. 1119, 1120,* and *1121*. Also, *B.N. 1118* shows no particular independence in its '*Quem quaeritis*' music until that last sentence, and even that may be due to faulty 'heighting'. Its only real difference is in starting off its internal Introit tropings with a couple of sentences that differ from those used by the rest of the later Aquitainian tropers, who all prefer '*Ecce Pater cunctus . . .*' and '*Victor ut ad caelos . . .*'.

[2] There are a very few instances of a start being made on E (A). These will be noted when met. But the general conformity is not affected by these small details.

stride, d m s, sometimes with the second or third note decorated, e.g.
d m mf̱s or d m̱s̱ s. The 'vocative' part, '*o Christicolae*', I shall pass over
for the time being. The setting of the reply, '*Jesum Nazarenum . . .*' is
clearly founded on the opening music, the essential do and re followed
once again by the upward-moving triad. The setting of '*Non est hic*' can
also be termed a 'characteristic' one. Almost all surviving examples,
whether French, German, Italian, or Spanish, and including the
Limoges group and the St. Gall versions, give the words the dramatic,
ringing uplift, ṟl l ḻṯd'. A few French versions, more modest as to pitch,
write d r ṟl. Small note-variants are to be found with each. I cannot of
course put on record every minor variation in melodic detail. What can
firmly be felt is that the framework, the solid structure, is there.

II

Within this solid structure, however, there occurs one important place of
variation—and one which I have been, I believe, the first to notice. It
concerns the two 'vocative' phrases, '*o Christicolae*' and '*o caelicolae*',
which we have up to this point bypassed in our discussion. The particular
notes of these settings are quite often the individual sign-manual, the
'thumb-print' of a particular group, and because of their distinctiveness
can be used as positive *musical* identification of groups and inter-
relationships. It is to this point that we must now turn our attention.

The St. Martial de Limoges rendering of '*Christicolae*' is, as we have
seen, r ḏṯ, ḏṟd r-, obviously derived from the opening music. The
'*caelicolae*' setting, however, is different: ṟd m̱f m r-.[1] When, however,
we come to consider the music of the other early '*Quem quaeritis*' trope,
that of *St. Gall 484*, we find quite another state of affairs. '*Christicolae*' is
set to a phrase that doesn't resemble the Limoges one; moreover, this
same phrase is used to set *caelicolae* as well. Thus, in the St. Gall version
we meet at the vocative words not only a verbal rhyme, but a musical one,
ṟd m̱s r r- in each case. Before continuing comparisons, let us see what a
modern reading of the St. Gall music looks like. The version given below
can be compared with Plate IIIb. (St. Gall, Stiftsbibl., *MS 484*, Trop.
Sangallense saec. X, p. 111.)

IT[EM] DE RESURR[ECTIONE] D[OMI]NI

Int[errogatio]·

Quem quae - ri - tis in se - pul - - chro, (o) Chri - sti - co - lae?

R[esponsio]

Je - sum· Na - za - re - num cru - ci - fi - xum, o cae - li - co - lae.

[1] The later Limoges tropers make the slight rhythmic alteration to ṟd m f̱m r–.

[2] The single note here is found in later versions sometimes as sol sometimes as la. I
believe that *MS 484* intends sol.

Non 'est hic, sur - re- xit si-cut præ-di- xe - rat. I - te, nun-ci - a - te qui-a sur - re - xit de se-pul-chro.

It has previously been mentioned that the earliest liturgical manuscripts with music made use of letters, signs, and special neume shapings, these affecting performance, especially in the matter of rhythm. By the time *B.N. 1240* and *St. Gall 484* were in being, most of these excrescences had vanished, an exception being the *episema*. I have recognized its presence (as I have the *oriscus*) by doubling the length of the note concerned. It could be contended that a more fluid view should be taken. Anyway, as far as the Church music-dramas are concerned, their notations were soon free even of the *episema*.

As regards the interpretations of the St. Gall neumes, there is the initial handicap that we have already discussed; namely that St. Gall persisted in writing down the music of so many of its liturgical mannscripts in *campo aperto* neumes without even the doubtful advantage of 'heighting', until well into the fourteenth century. It is fortunate, however, that there survive about a dozen or so derivative versions of the St. Gall '*Quem quaeritis*' dialogue on stave lines, from the eleventh to the sixteenth century. The earliest, *Einsiedeln, Stiftsbibl. MS 366* (*olim 179*), pp. 55–6, from a liturgical fragment of the eleventh to twelfth century, is quite remarkable (see Plate VI). The St. Gall neumes are accurately heighted round a single F line, and even at this early date the dialogue music has been transposed up a perfect fourth. Also, every B flat needed for the transposition is inserted.[1] Confirmation comes from the later versions, most of which are similarly transposed, with or without their B flats. Anyway, the result is that we are safely presented with a consistent 'St. Gall' version, with a number of 'thumb-prints' which make its identity unmistakable. The chief of these is the setting of the two vocative phrases, which present in all St. Gall versions the musical rhyme. In *St. Gall 484* it is:

> O   Chri - sti - co - lae
> O   cae - li - co - lae
> r̲m̲ r̲d̲   m̲s̲ r   r -

There are variants; the simplest, r̲m̲ r̲d̲ m̲s̲ m r-, or, r̲m̲ r̲d̲ m̲s̲ m̲r̲ r-, with at times a few other small note-elaborations, but always with the idea of a musical rhyme at the two vocative points. Another characteristic is to be seen by comparing the *B.N. 1240* setting of 'Chri-sti-co-lae' with the music of the same syllable in the St. Gall manuscript, where a feature of

---

[1] This manuscript is unique in having in a brief Easter Sepulchre music-drama, as an alternative to the usual dialogue exchange '*Quem quaeritis in sepulchro . . .*', the later German one '*Quem quaeritis, o tremulae mulieres . . .*'. It was as well that the flats were supplied, since it will be seen (if Plate VIII is consulted) that after the alteration of the pitch of the sixth line, the seventh and eighth lines have the value of A, a fact that mightn't have been apparent but for the presence of the flats. For a further discussion of this version, see p. 120.

the 'German chant-dialect' can be seen—'the frequent substitution of the interval of a third for that of a second',[1] also apparent elsewhere.

This trick of having, as well as the normal end-of-line verbal rhyme, an individual musical one, can be seen also in some French dialogue versions. The short musical motifs seem to link together several versions, calling attention at the same time to other common features. Such a musical rhyme links the early trope version, *Paris, Arsenal 1169* (A.D. 996–1024), to *B.N. 9449* (eleventh century) and *B.N. (Nouv. Acq.) 1235*. The Limoges setting of '*o caelicolae*' (rm rd m mfm r-) is used, but used twice, to make the rhyme. They have other links, e.g. the use of the (rarer) setting of '*Non est hic*', (d r rl). A different rhyme (rm mr d mfm r-) joins the twelfth to thirteenth century *Reims 265*, and the thirteenth-century *Paris, St. Geneviève 117*, and perhaps, if neume-shape similarities can be trusted, the eleventh-century *Cambrai 75*; also, a more startling suggestion, the eleventh-century pair from Silos (Spain), *Brit. Mus. Add. MSS 30848* and *30850*. All these use the d r rl setting of '*Non est hic*'. I have found at times that small musical clues such as these have certainly revealed a few of the 'unexpected relationships' prophesied by Karl Young.

No doubt it has not escaped notice (Plate IIIb having been consulted) that in the text of the Easter dialogue as written in *St. Gall 484*, '*Christicolae*' appears without its vocative '*o*', even though everywhere we meet with '*o caelicolae*'. This is paralleled in quite a number of other versions, including most of the Italian examples of the eleventh and twelfth centuries (but not, be it noted, in the cases of the Limoges tropers, including *B.N. 1240*, and the vast majority of the French versions). The fact has led to speculation in some quarters[2] that in the original dialogue '*Christicolae*' actually did stand alone, and that only later was the '*o*' added, in order to balance the two vocative phrases. One explanation offered has been that the composer of the text wished to expound the relationship of the angels towards humanity: the Marys are greeted without the '*o*', while the reverence of humanity towards the angels is expressed by the Marys' '*o caelicolae*'. I have met with writings that gravely classify the situations as being either 'mit o', or 'ohne o'. Needless to say, the subject of music had not been considered. In point of fact the '*o*' had been there in front of '*Christicolae*' from the beginning —in sound, if not always in script—and the explanation is in terms of paleography rather than piety. The situation is that the syllable before '*o Christicolae*' is the last syllable of '*sepulchro*'. Thus the effect in performance, unless meticulous care was taken, would be a running together of '*o*' sounds. The Middle Ages relied far more on retentive memories than the written sign; thus it seems plausible to suggest that, when it became necessary to put this particular passage into service-book

---

[1] See Reese, p. 122.

[2] Smoldon seems to have in mind here, though he does not actually cite it, Helmut de Boor's monumental study *Die Textgeschichte der lateinische Osterfeiern* (Tübingen, 1967). [*Ed.*]

record, in some instances only a single 'o' survived to receive its music. This explanation could indeed remain merely plausible without further proof, but musical notation is ready and waiting to supply this. When I turn to my charts of the dialogue, I find that where the vocative 'o' is omitted there is usually a small overplus of neume elements above the last syllable of 'sepul*chro*', as is evident in *St. Gall 484*. The situation is best seen expounded by the dialogue as it appears in two eleventh century St. Gall graduals from Minden, *Berlin, Staatsbibl. MS theo. lat. 4°. 11*, ff. 45v.–46r. and (ditto) *MS theo. lat. 4°. 15*, f. 120r. The versions are in fact twins, and their neumes indicate the same music as that of *St. Gall 484* (except for a following troping sentence, '*Surrexit enim sicut dixit Dominus . . .*')[1]. There is, however, this difference between the two: *4°. 11 omits* the vocative '*o*', and, above the '*o*' of '*sepulchro*', has a three-unit neume (*porrectus*) together with an *oriscus* to extend the last sound. *4°. 15* has the vocative '*o*'; it has two notes only (a *clivis*) for the '*o*' of '*sepulchro*', and has shifted across the third note with its extension (*virga* + *oriscus*) for use with the vocative '*o*'. By the same analogy I have inserted a vocative '*o*' before the '*Christicolae*' of *St. Gall 484*, and moved across two of the neume units. Anyone able to consult the eleventh-century St. Gall troper *MS 376* will find on p. 197 the '*Quem quaeritis*' dialogue text written out with the first vocative '*o*' omitted, but squeezed in over the top as an afterthought, with the necessary *podatus*. The music of the last syllable of '*sepulchro*' consists of two notes (a *clivis*). As in the case of *St. Gall 484* the musical rhyme of the two vocative phrases is r̠m r̠d m̠s r r-. I could show other such examples, including that pair of Apt manuscript versions already alluded to. The majority of the Italian Easter trope versions omit the vocative '*o*'; but most of them carry a three-unit neume (*porrectus*) for the '*o*' of 'sepul-chro', as do the Spanish (*Vich*) examples. Versions like *Verona 107*, *Ivrea 60*, and the *Vercelli* trio of tropers, all showing the vocative '*o*', just borrow the last of the three notes for the purpose, and thus indicate what was probably done in every case. Even if 'sepul*chro*' hadn't a note to spare (as in the case of the twelfth-century *Visitatio, Madrid MS 132*), I suspect that the '*o*' sound would have been given the necessary prolongation.

It will be noted that the only way of clinching a solution to this 'vocative "o" ' problem was through musical evidence.

III

In the course of my discussions concerning the two earliest existing manuscripts showing the '*Quem quaeritis*' sentences in trope form I have

---

[1] This sentence (see p. 73) crops up as a rounding-off to the *Quem quaeritis* dialogue in about a score of different versions, but in two different settings, (*a*) as a now obsolete antiphon, to be found in Hartker, p. 231, and (*b*) as a 'free' German composition. The latter setting is more popular among the surviving manuscripts. The text in full is: '*Surrexit enim sicut dixit Dominus, ecce præcedet vos in Galileam: ibi eum videbitis, alleluia*'.

more than once made mention of the theories of Professor O. B. Hardison, who in his book *Christian Rite and Christian Drama in the Middle Ages* has attacked the views of Karl Young as to the beginnings of the Easter Sepulchre drama. Karl Young, arguing only from the text, is content, as we have seen, to trace it to a trope form. O. B. Hardison, who operates within the same limits, thinks that the dramatic element was so strongly present within the services of the medieval Church as to make it probable that the three-stage question, reply, and further reply, which we find in both trope and dramatic forms, arose from already existing Church ceremonies of a dramatic nature. I quote his own words:[1]

An analysis of *Quem quaeritis* manuscripts in these terms consistently leads to the conclusion that the dialogue originated not as an Easter trope but as a ceremony associated with the vigil Mass.

The 'terms' on which he bases his analysis, however, include no reference to, nor quotation from the music of the Easter '*Quem quaeritis*' dialogue. Nor is it clear whether one is supposed to believe that all prefacing Introit tropes have been derived from previously existing liturgical ceremonies (how about that dialogued one of Tuotilo's mentioned on p. 68 ?), or that this origin is peculiar to '*Quem quaeritis in sepulchro . . .*'. It appears that he has not been able to discover surviving examples of the ceremony that he presupposes and can do no more than sketch a textual reconstruction (p. 215), which he confesses to be both 'theoretical' and 'extremely tentative'. He indicates further that 'concerning the date and place of origin of the ceremony there is no evidence at all. Here scholarship must yield to pure speculation' (p. 219). He believes that his 'vigil Mass' theory is supported by the existence of a text from Tours, written probably in the fifteenth century, and known only from the fact of its being reproduced by the eighteenth-century scholar, Martene, who printed it in his well-known publication.[2] Karl Young, who himself printed it (I, pp. 224–5), assumed it to be just another '*Quem quaeritis*' dialogue text, used in procession with some individual additional items, and most scholars, I imagine, would agree with him. The version appears to me to be of the normal *ordinarium* type, with incipits, and being an *ordinarium*, temporarily deprived of its music, which prevents me from investigating it further. However, when one consults the pages of Karl Young containing the Tours text, one finds on either side of it a number of other texts of processionals which in various ways and with various different items utilize the '*Quem quaeritis*' dialogue. Most of these other versions (from Ivrea, Monza, Heidenheim, St. Gall . . .) give texts and music in full, and in every case the music is 'standard' (I am checking from the photos of the originals). I have no doubt that were the incipit texts and the music of the Tours version restored (together with those of the other two *ordinarium* examples included in the

---

[1] Hardison, p. 219.
[2] E. Martene: *De Antiquis Ecclesiae Ritibus*, 4 vols., Venice, 1788.

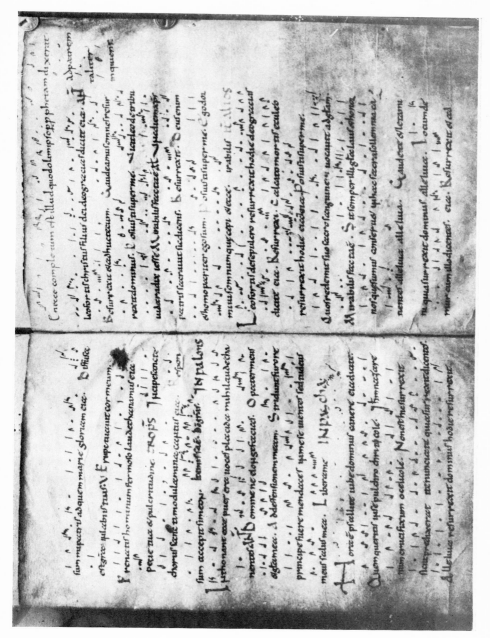

IV A version of the 'Quem quaeritis . . .' trope in the style of the later Limoges tropers; Apt, *MS 18(4)*, fol. 33v–34r (eleventh to twelfth century). The item (beginning five lines from the bottom of the first page) is written in Catalonian notation, with two of the sentences in Visigothic notation. '*Resurrexit*' appears several times for '*Resurrexi*'.

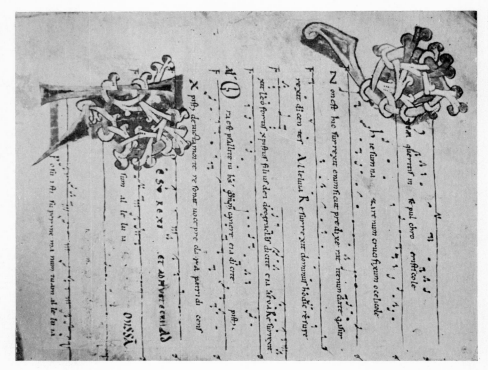

Va An Italian 'Quem quaeritis . . .' trope; Modena, Bibl. Capit., *MS O.1.7*, fol. 102v (eleventh to twelfth century). The neumes are almost exactly heighted round a line definitely marked as F. The '*Resurrexit*' mistake appears once.

Vb A badly damaged folio from Compostela Cathedral, Spain (mid-twelfth century), showing a brief *Visitatio* in Aquitainian notation, clearly deriving from Limoges.

chapter), everything would have been found to be 'normal'. I mention this because O. B. Hardison speaks of the Tours version as being given in the abbreviated form used in the *Regularis concordia*. His theory concerning abbreviated forms of the '*Quem quaeritis*' dialogue has been mentioned already, and I shall refer to it at greater length when I come to deal with the Winchester *Regularis*.[1]

Both Karl Young (I, p. 203) and O. B. Hardison (pp. 165, 171–2, 174) are at pains to marshal a number of liturgical items in the forms of Easter antiphons and responsories with their verses, pointing out very reasonably (Young on behalf of his trope text, Hardison for his liturgical ceremony) that here was the raw material to *suggest* the words of the three-item dialogue. All these sentences, together with their musical settings, are thoroughly well known to me. They are all to be found in Hartker's *Antiphonale*, together with their neume settings. I have rendered the music of all of them into modern notation (with, let me hasten to acknowledge, occasional help from the monks of Solesmes in cases of obsolete or more obscure antiphons). I can give here only a few examples from the list and thus have chosen the most familiar phrases. Here are the beginnings of three antiphons, the music rendered in space-saving sol-fa:

(a) *Karlsruhe, MS LX, fol. 93* (thirteenth century):

s   s   s̲l̲   s   s f l   d' t̲d̲'l̲s̲ l̲d̲' l̲d̲' s s
Je-sum, quem quae-ri-tis, non est hic, sed sur-re-xit . . .

(b) *Karlsruhe, MS LX, fol. 93r*:

s   s̲d̲' l l̲s̲ f s̲l̲ l   s   s   s   t   d' r̲'m̲' r'   r'   d̲'t̲ l̲s̲
No-li- te ex-pa-ve-sce-re; Je-sum Na-za-re - num quae-ri - tis
d' d̲'r̲'d̲' d' d̲'l̲   s   l̲d̲' d'
cru-ci - fi- xum; non est hic. . . .

(c) *Metz, MS 83, fol. 134* (thirteenth century):

s   s   s   s   s s̲f̲ s   l   d' d't̲s̲   t̲d̲' l̲s̲ l̲s̲ f   s̲f̲   s̲l̲ d' d' r' t
Je-sum, qui cru-ci-fi- xum est quae-ri-tis, al - le-lu-ia, non est hic, sur-re-xit
d' l   l̲s̲ f   s l   d' t
e - nim si-cut di-xit vo-bis . . .

All the music of all the items quoted by the two writers is straightforward Gregorian chant, the responsories (as is usual) a little more melismatic than the antiphons. But nowhere in that music is there a phrase of melody that suggests the patterned, balanced phrases of the '*Quem quaeritis*' music as we have seen it in the two earliest existing versions. The composition belongs to a new age, a different musical world from any ancient 'vigil Mass' liturgical ceremony (even if this particular ceremony ever existed, which seems to me very doubtful). I simply cannot imagine how phrases from such a Gregorian rite could turn into a trope

---

[1] See pp. 98–9.

composition, with its music, in the form that we find it in *B.N. MS 1240* and *St. Gall MS 484*. Tropes didn't happen like that; I cannot remember such a derivation ever having been proposed concerning any other famous trope. In Chapter IV of this book the history of tropes has already been traced at moderate length, and it seems clear that the spirit of the movement was that of new creation. Nor must we forget that other all-important point which Handschin has made, and which I raised at the end of the chapter (p. 65): '*Every trope is in principle intended to combine with a given Gregorian song . . .*' Here Willi Apel is even more specific; concerning Introit tropes he writes that 'the new music employs the same style (neumatic), the same range and tonality as the traditional chant, and occasionally even borrows a short motive from it'.[1] It is time now to examine the implication of these points.

What I propose to do is to make a comparison between the music of the '*Quem quaeritis*' trope and of the Easter Mass Introit, to which it was intended to act as a preface. I first give the Introit, with its setting in the same modern 'free' notation as that of the previous trope examples. Also, since these were for stave convenience transposed up a perfect 4th above the original, I have done the same in the case of the Introit. The version having been transcribed from the official plainchant with its Solesmes editing, I have treated the editorial dots at the cadences and elsewhere as representing doublings of note-lengths, a reading that is possibly too strict.

Certainly the Introit is *torculus*-haunted, and the first phrase of the trope music chimes well with this. If we seek for a common 'motive', then it is surely to be found between this '*Quem quaeritis . . .*' opening and the three '*Alleluias*' of the Introit that I have marked as A, B and A1. But in any case, I feel that the result of a practical performance is to confirm the feeling of a general melodic affinity in two items that blend in style, one having been intended and deliberately composed for attendance upon the other. Indeed, the whole nature and history of the trope

---

[1] Apel, p. 438. He points out, however, the matter of having the same tonality was not *strictly* kept to; sometimes a contrast was deliberately sought.

movement makes it wildly improbable that the '*Quem quaeritis*' dialogue with its individual setting could have been generated from a previous liturgical ceremony; particularly one that seems to have had no more than a 'theoretical' existence.

As for the place of origin of the trope, I have already ventured to say that, while obviously *B.N. MS 1240* cannot be the prototype, yet it is likely to have been at that famous centre of trope composition, St. Martial de Limoges, and at some earlier date, that the first framing of the sentences took place. Jacques Chailley has no doubts. He states in all confidence: 'Saint Martial de Limoges a sans doute inventé le trope "*Quem quaeritis*".'[1] I would prefer to be more cautious, and say merely that things seem to point that way, but that we lack the absolute proof. In my opinion the *St. Gall 484* setting represents a later, more sophisticated version, the presence of the musical rhyme and the somewhat more florid melodic line seeming to support that view. If the *original* pattern had included the device of the musical rhyme, it seems unlikely to me that Limoges and other early French centres would have abandoned it.

As a final matter, note must be taken of a few more surviving '*Quem quaeritis*' trope versions of some significance belonging to the late tenth or early eleventh centuries. *Paris, Bibl. de l'Arsenal MS 1169*, fol. 18v.–19r., coming from Autun and dating from 996 to 1024, has un-heighted French Primitive neumes, the dialogue followed by the usual French setting of '*Alleluia, resurrexit Dominus, hodie . . . dicite eia*' before reaching the '*Resurrexi . . .*', incipit. The neumes suggest (indeterminately, of course) the St. Martial music, but also include a musical rhyme at the vocatives, obtained by using the Limoges '*o caelicolae*' setting (r̲m̲ r̲d̲ m f̲m̲ r-) twice over. Here then, if the neumes are read correctly, is a very early French use of the musical rhyme.[2]

I am somewhat baffled by the late tenth-century trope version from *Vienna, Nat. Libr. MS lat. 1888*, fol. 197. It comes from Mainz, and is written in *campo aperto* St. Gall neumes (!), complete with *episemae* and occasional Romanian signs and letters. Yet the neumes show that while the general curves of the melody are being followed, the usual characteristics of St. Gall are not always being maintained: the *christicolae—caelicolae* musical rhyme. It is unique of its kind, and I am in fact unable to transcribe parts of the setting of the dialogue with any certainty. In spite of the fact that in the third sentence it uses the exceptional phrase '*sicut locutus est*', this does not seem to link it in any other way with the other '*locutus*' manuscript versions (*Arsenal 1169, Monza K.11*, and *Brit. Mus. (Silos) Add. MSS 318348/50*). Its following sentences, before

---

[1] Chailley, p. 373.
[2] The same musical rhyme is found in two actually dramatic versions from Nevers, *B.N. MS lat. 9449*, fol. 34r. (eleventh century) and *B.N. (Nouv. Acq.) MS lat. 1235*, fol. 205r. (twelfth century), as well as *B.N. MS lat. 12044*, fol. 100v. and r. (twelfth century) from Fossata. None of them in their settings seems to have strayed very far from St. Martial de Limoges. All make use of the item '*Alleluia, resurrexit Dominus, hodie . . . dicite eia*' to succeed the dialogue sentences.

reaching the *Resurrexi* incipit, are first, '*Alleluia, resurrexit Dominus, hodie . . .*' with its usual French music, to be succeeded by the distinctly German music of the independent setting of '*Surrexit Dominus de sepulchro, qui pro nobis pependit in ligno*'. Altogether a unique sort of hybrid, about which I shall endeavour to learn more.

There remain two more surviving '*Quem quaeritis*' compositions, belonging possibly to the turn of the century, that should receive notice. These are *B.N. MS lat. 9448*, fol. 33v. and *Bamberg, Staatsbibl. MS lit. 5* [Ed. V9] fol. 45r & v.). I reserve considerations of these until I have gone into the matter of the emergence of the dialogue as a miniature music-drama, having had its position moved from the Mass to the end of Easter Matins. Both the above versions seem to belong to this category.

But, as students of Church music-drama will be aware, even before the end of the tenth century indisputable evidence was in existence as to the dialogue having appeared in dramatic form in documents belonging to the diocese of Winchester, the date being *c.* 980. This metamorphosis will be the subject of our next chapter.

Karl Young, and others before and after him, have called attention to certain tropes of Introits of Masses on other feast days which are of the same dialogued pattern as the '*Quem quaeritis*' Easter Introit trope, and which therefore might represent imitations. I have my reservations regarding that famous composition '*Hodie cantandus*' There seems little reason to doubt the tradition that the composer was Tuotilo (d. 915). As we are already aware, he produced a number of tropes, but as far as is known, none of them Easter ones. Anyway, the music of the question and answer in '*Hodie cantandus*' (beginning, '*Quis est iste puer . . .*') bears no relation to that of the '*Quem quaeritis*' trope, and there is no attempt to maintain the pattern and balance which is so manifest in the Easter exchange.

The affinities between the texts of the Easter trope and the 'Shepherds' Christmas trope ('*Quem quaeritis in praesepe, pastores*? *Dicite!*') are quite apparent. But as I shall in due course point out, there is no link between the melodies.[1] The earliest surviving manuscript showing the 'Shepherds' trope of the Christmas Mass Introit is the St. Martial de Limoges *B.N. MS lat. 1118* of the late tenth century (fol. 8v.–9r.), wrongly attributed by E. K. Chambers and Karl Young to the eleventh century. I shall reserve consideration of it until later, when dealing with Christmas dramatic activities.

The texts of other dialogued Introit prefacing tropes, these of later date than the earliest '*Quem quaeritis*' examples, are often put on record to show obvious verbal imitations of the pioneer one. These include a trope for the Introit of the Mass of Ascension Day. A twelfth-century version from Nevers (*B.N. (Nouv. Acq.), MS lat. 1235*, fol. 215v.), while keeping its musical independence yet remembers to contrive two vocative phrases and give them a musical rhyme reminiscent of the '*o*

---

[1] There are a couple of occasions when the Christmas dialogue seems deliberately to be quoting a phrase from the Easter music. These will be noted in their place.

caelicolae' of the Limoges tropers. The two first lines with its music are perhaps worth reproducing. The 'speakers' may be assumed to be, respectively, angels and disciples:

<pre>
m̲r   f   m r r d   r̲m̲ m̲r f l̲s   l   s   f-m̲ r̲d   m f̲m̲ r -
Quem cre-di-tis su-per as-tra a-scen-dis-se, o Chri-sti-co-lae?
</pre>

<pre>
d̲r r   f r̲d r̲m̲ m̲r f   l̲s l   s   f-m̲ r̲d   m f̲m̲ r -
Je-sum qui sur-re-xit de se-pul-chro, o cae-li-co-lae.
</pre>

There is quite a pleasant balance in the setting. The 'borrowing' of the music for 'Jesum' will be noted, together with a musical rhyme; but thereafter the version goes its own way. There are other versions of the same trope with different musics, e.g. from St. Martial de Limoges and Vich; these are perhaps not so attractive as the Nevers (*B.N. MS 1235*) setting, and I do not propose to give space to them. I similarly pass over the imitative troping of the Mass of the Nativity of St. John the Baptist, found in the St. Martial tropers, '*Quem creditis natum in orbe, o Deicolae* . . .'. The exchange maintains a textual rhyme with '*o caelicolae*', but not a musical one, and the setting is altogether independent.

All the same, medieval Christendom seemed to find the music of the '*Quem quaeritis*' opening difficult to forget. I am reminded that Karl Young (I, p. 567) prints the text of an Easter sequence, from an unnamed eleventh-century manuscript, the first line of which is '*Quem quaeritis, mulieres, ad sepulcrum Domini?*' I have a photograph of a page from an eleventh century Italian manuscript (*Ivrea, Bibl. Cap. MS 60*, fol. 69v.) which shows almost the same text, but also gives the musical setting above, in unheighted neumes. These of course are strictly untranslatable without some other clue, but in the case of the first line (the line that in sequence form is not repeated) the neumes above the first eight syllables ('*Quem quaeritis, mulieres . . .*') are: *liquescent clivis; torculus; torculus; virga; clivis* with *oriscus; punctum,* which seem to suggest that the notes were those of a normal *Quem quaeritis* setting. But thereafter nothing else is recognizable, and the item continues in the normal plain style of a sequence setting, each musical sentence repeated. It rather looks as if somebody may have taken the pleasure of making a brief musical quotation, one that he felt would be recognized and appreciated.

Lastly, I give an example of a use of the *Quem quaeritis* composition in what can be described as a 'parody' form (in the best sense of the word). In a fourteenth-century manuscript from Vich Cathedral Library (*MS 118*, fol. 158v.–160) is a little music-drama which celebrates the feast of the Assumption of the Blessed Virgin by borrowing the trope pattern and its music.[1] Even the familiar introductory trope, '*Ubi est Christus, meus filius . . .*' is parodied as '*Ubi est Mater nostri Domini . . .*', and set to be established music. The second '*Quem quaeritis*' sentence has to be modified to '*Matrem Nazareni crucifixi . . .*', but the music is

---

[1] My attention was called to this manuscript by Dr. Richard B. Donovan, of the University of Toronto. I refer to his book, *The Liturgical Drama in Medieval Spain*, pp. 96–7.

that usual to Vich's Easter trope, including the musical rhyme m r̠d m fm r-. '*Non est hic*' is set to the normal rising passage, but thereafter text and music suffer some modification. A fourteenth-century manuscript such as this brings home the fact that the memory of the '*Quem quaeritis*' music lived long in medieval ears.

CHAPTER SIX

THE TENTH CENTURY (2)

True drama
The Marys at the sepulchre
The first Christmas tropes

So far, we have concerned ourselves with the versions of the '*Quem quaeritis*' dialogue which, by the evidence of the rubrics and the presence of the incipit '*Resurrexi*', have shown themselves to be nothing more than tropes of the Easter Mass, or at the most contained in processionals that have strayed but a short distance from that ceremony. However, the same style of dialogue, its identity confirmed by the musical setting, is found in versions (the earliest survivor dating from the second half of the tenth century) which show by their context that a complete change of position had occurred relative to the liturgy. Instead of the dialogue leading to the Introit of the Easter Mass we find it (directly or ultimately) rounded off by the Matins hymn '*Te Deum laudamus . . .*'. In other words, it has moved from being a prefixing trope of the Easter Introit, to a place at the end of Easter Matins. Here it is preceded by the third responsory. The wording is as follows:

Dum transisset sabbatum, Maria Magdalena, et Maria Jacobi, et Salome emerunt aromata, ut venientes ungerent Jesum, alleluia, alleluia. *Versus:* Et valde mane una sabbatorum veniunt ad monumentum, orto iam sole.[1]

Although, as we have seen, some of the trope versions and much liturgical ceremonial skated very near to dramatic action, it is only when the dialogue reaches this new position that there can be certainty as to real drama having arrived; that definite impersonation and true dramatic action had begun. The representation was now of an actual exchange between the Angel (or Angels) and the Marys at the empty Tomb, and a number of reasons for its permanent settlement at this point have been advanced.[2] The first and most obvious is the fact that the dialogue is a repetition in dramatic form of the scene pictured by the responsory.[3] It

---

[1] This of course comes from St. Mark xvi:1–2. There are three other versions of the responsory, variations of the same material, or employing a fourth verse: 'Et respicientes viderunt revolutum lapidem; erat quippe magnus valde'. These, however, are much more rare in their appearance. See Young, I, p. 232.

[2] With regard to this matter, see Young, ibid.

[3] In some manuscript versions of the *Visitatio Sepulchri*, given in full detail with its music but surrounded by mere textual incipits of the near-by liturgy, there appears the responsory '*Dum transisset . . .*', also written out in full with its music, in such fashion as to suggest that it was serving as a choral introduction to the drama.

would seem that no better place in the liturgy could have been found for it. This conclusion is reinforced by other considerations. It was, as we have seen, a medieval tradition that Matins should be completed before dawn, since Lauds was the office which indicated the beginning of the day. Thus the '*Te Deum*' of Matins came to be regarded as the transition from night to day. Thus also the Easter morning drama made a perfect approach to the conditions described in the Vulgate: '. . . *et valde mane sabbatorum . . . orto iam sole*'. Another reason for the conclusion that the position at the end of Easter Matins was the natural one for the drama, is found in the traditional use of incense there, and its connection with the 'sweet spices' carried by the Marys. It may well be that the thuribles mentioned in the rubrics of early examples were convenient 'properties', representing ointment boxes, but there was certainly a firm tradition for the censing of the altar at the singing of the '*Te Deum*', during that part of the year when the altar was most strongly associated with the idea of a 'sepulchrum'. There is much to be said for the idea that some detail of the drama, at least, derived from the censing ceremonial.

Having fixed itself at this point, it might seem to have taken on the appearance of the last part of a trilogy, the preceding stages being the *Depositio* and *Elevatio Crucis*, the continuity being emphasized by such common 'properties' as the 'sepulchrum' with its entrance stone, the grave clothes, and even, in some rare examples, the guard which was set round about. But such an association had its limitations, for as we have already seen, the two earlier ceremonies were constituted entirely of liturgical material, texts and music. Any truly dramatic features they developed (e.g. the 'Harrowing of Hell' theme) came late in the Middle Ages, in imitation of expanded examples of the liturgical music-drama. Many service books of the Middle Ages indicate a ritual which included a *Depositio* and *Elevatio* but no *Visitatio Sepulchri*.[1] The very different nature and origin of the last-named, it seems, were always felt. Authorized texts in their usual settings were the materials employed by the two earlier ceremonies, while the germ of the *Visitatio* was an original dramatic dialogue by a single author and composer, whatever further orthodox matter may have been added to it.

It has been a fashion lately to query a number of Karl Young's conclusions. Thus other explanations have been offered as to the settling of the *Visitatio Sepulchri* at the end of Matins. However, settle there it did, whatever the explanation.

A very complete idea of the aims, the resources and the techniques of the clerical actors of the period can be obtained from a document which represents the earliest surviving example of a dramatic *Visitatio Sepulchri*. The manuscript in which it is found is the *Regularis con-*

---

[1] I have already, in connection with these first truly dramatic activities at Easter Matins, used the term *Visitatio Sepulchri*, one widely accepted. It is no modern invention, but was a recognized medieval name for the Sepulchrum music-drama type. Several manuscripts (e.g. *St. Gall 360*, p. 31) use it as a rubric heading.

cordia.[1] This had been prepared by the Council of Winchester under the direction of their Bishop, Ethelwold, between the years 965 and 975, and laid down the ritual for the Benedictine order in England. The *Visitatio Sepulchri* is described in these terms:[2]

While the third lesson is being read, four of the brethren shall vest, one of whom, wearing an alb as though for some different purpose, shall enter and go stealthily to the place of the 'sepulchre'[3] and sit there quietly, holding a palm in his hand. Then, while the third respond is being sung, the other three brethren, vested in copes and holding thuribles in their hands, shall enter in their turn and go to the place of the 'sepulchre', step by step, as though searching for something. Now these things are done in imitation of the angel seated on the tomb and of the women coming with perfumes to anoint the body of Jesus. When, therefore, he that is seated shall see these three draw nigh, wandering about as it were and seeking something, he shall begin to sing softly and sweetly:

Whom seek ye [in the sepulchre, O followers of Christ]?

As soon as this has been sung right through, the three shall answer together:

Jesus of Nazareth [which was crucified, O celestial one.]

Then he that is seated shall say:

He is not here; he is risen, just as he foretold.
Go, announce that he is risen from the dead.

At this command the three shall turn to the choir saying:

Alleluia! The Lord is risen [today,
The strong lion, the Christ, the Son of God.
Give thanks to God, eia!]

When this has been sung he that is seated, as though calling them back, shall say the antiphon:

Come and see the place where the Lord was laid, Alleluia, alleluia!

---

[1] The *Regularis concordia* has survived in two separate manuscripts of the British Museum, (*a*) *MS Cotton Tiberius A.III, saec. xi*, fol. 21r.-v., and (*b*) *MS Cotton Faustina B.III, saec. xi*, fols. 188v.–189r.

[2] I give here a translation of this section, taken from the edition of the *Regularis Concordia*, by Dom Thomas Symons of Downside Abbey (London and New York, 1953), pp. 49–51. Dom Symons has printed the original Latin text, together with his translation of the whole work. Most of the sung texts are in incipit form. I have expanded them where needed.

[3] In Chapter I, p. 14, I made some reference to the symbolic *Depositio* and *Elevatio Crucis* ceremonies of Holy Week. Actually, the *Regularis concordia* contains the earliest extant texts of these ceremonies, the rubrics of which speak of the likeness of a sepulchre having been prepared in a vacant part of the altar, and screened with a movable veil. It was to this Winchester 'sepulchre', from which the cross had been removed, that the Winchester 'Marys' came. On this point, see Young, I, pp. 132–3.

And then, rising and lifting up the veil, he shall show them the place void of the Cross and with only the linen in which the Cross had been wrapped. Seeing this the three shall lay down their thuribles in that same 'sepulchre' and, taking the linen, shall hold it up before the clergy; and, as though showing that the Lord was risen and was no longer wrapped in it, they shall sing this antiphon:

> *The Lord is risen from the sepulchre,*
> [*Who for us hung upon the Cross.*]

They shall then lay the linen on the altar.

When the antiphon is finished, the prior,[1] rejoicing in the triumph of our King in that He had conquered death and was risen, shall give out the hymn:

> *We praise thee, O God . . .*

And thereupon all the bells shall peal.

Undoubtedly here is a truly dramatic piece, developed from the pattern of the trope exchange. In it, setting, costuming, and action are carefully detailed, even to the length of the 'Marys' ' approach being 'as though searching for something' (no doubt the producer gave some thought to this!). Also, there are some new features, one of them the recall of the 'Marys' after their first dismissal; this brought about by the borrowing of a liturgical antiphon, '*Venite et videte locum ubi positus erat Dominus*', (derived from St. Matthew, xxviii: 6). This gives the 'Marys' the opportunity of taking possession of the grave clothes that had been abandoned from the *Elevatio* ceremony, and displaying them to the clergy while singing the antiphon, '*Surrexit Dominus de sepulchro, qui pro nobis pependit in ligno*'. As they conclude and move away towards the choir, there comes a most effective finale, the singing by the whole community of the '*Te Deum*', after which the heavy 'tower' bells clang out independently.

The costumes, it will be noted, are clerical, and thus simply contrived, with the brother representing the angel appropriately clad in an alb (a full-length vestment of white) and holding a palm-branch. The three others wear copes—full length capes—which effectively set the scene of a 'journey' to the tomb (it is quite likely that these three are also hooded to conceal their masculine identity as much as possible). We also learn that each carries a censer filled with incense, 'in imitation . . . of the women coming with spices to anoint the body of Jesus'. The link between the drama and the ceremonial thurible has already been remarked on.

Not only is the text of this *Regularis* version incomplete, but no music is given. This need not surprise us, for the drama had been set out in the form of an *ordinarium*; that is to say, its immediate purpose was to concentrate on rubrics; in this case details of production. We have not

---

[1] i.e. the Abbot.

far to seek for what probably represents the full sung text and the musical setting. At the same centre, and within a few years of the *Regularis concordia*, there was written the famous and also still surviving Winchester Troper, about which I have already spoken (p. 63). This manuscript contains a *Visitatio*,[1] with very brief rubrics, but representing the same form as the *Regularis* version with the addition of yet another sentence ('*Cito euntes, dicite discipulis quia surrexit Dominus*'), one which seems to indicate that the need was soon felt for a definite second dismissal of the Marys. The close accord between the two drama versions is further emphasized by the fact of the single angel. The *Regularis* directions insist that one only of the brethren should ask the angelic question, while the 'Troper' version (most exceptionally) is careful to alter the normal rhyming 'caelicolae' to 'caelicola'. *Visitatio* playwrights in general knew well that the four evangelists themselves were not unanimous as to the number of angels that were at the Tomb.[1] Matthew and Mark speak of a single one, Luke and John of two. However, in spite of mentions in rubrics of one or the other arrangement, the general practice was to preserve the end-rhyme of the first two lines by writing '*caelicolae*' (or '*celicole*', with or without cedilla). Winchester was unique in its scruples.

Karl Young (I, p. 250) does not seem pleased that the *Regularis* should tamper with the order of St. Matthew's text, whereby 'the angel's words, "*Venite et videte*" are decisively separated from his declaration "*Non est hic*",' this leading to a recall of the Marys after their announcement of the Resurrection. Myself, I feel no objection to this varying of the pattern. There is indeed something humanly pleasing in discovering that even an angel can have second thoughts. The method employed, the use of familiar antiphon material, '*Venite et videte*', and in the case of the Winchester Troper, '*Cito euntes, dicite discipulis quia surrexit Dominus*', is a fitting one.[3] The *Visitatio* from the Troper has its rubrics cut to a minimum, but supplies the musical setting; beautiful Anglo-Saxon neumes, heighted at times, but not with any accuracy.

I will now attempt a free-rhythm transcription of them. I find this possible, since I am convinced that the music indicated by them is based on the 'house' version of the dialogue setting belonging to St. Martial de Limoges, particularly that of *B.N. MS lat. 1240*. None other of the numerous and widespread '*Quem quaeritis*' versions shows such remarkable musical similarity. To begin with, the 'vocative' phrases, which indicate (a) (*o Christicolae*) r̲m̲ r d̲t̲, d̲r̲d r- and (b) ('*o caelicolae*')

---

[1] *Oxford, Bibl. Bodl., MS 775*, fol. 17r.–v. Another copy of the *Visitatio* is to be found in *Cambridge, Corpus Christi College, Trop. Wintoniense MS 473*, fol. 26v. The whole manuscript represents an eleventh-century copy of the Troper (see Plate II). See footnote 1, p. 63.

[2] Karl Young (I, p. 217) discusses the matter at some length.

[3] Both antiphons, with their neumes, are to be found on p. 226 of Hartker's *Antiphonale*. The second of them ('Go quickly, and say to the disciples that the Lord is risen'), turns up in slightly modified textual forms (one source is the verse of an antiphon), and with settings that differ from the Hartker one, but most of the versions using the sentence stick to the Hartker music. I refrain from commenting further on the 'modified texts'. These are dealt with briefly by Karl Young (I, p. 254).

rm rd mf m r- cannot be matched anywhere else in Christendom; at least, that is what my charts seem to tell me. Again, while the later Limoges tropers, for example, *B.N. 1118, 1119, 1120, 1121, (Nouv. Acq.) 1871*, and the Limoges-influenced, Aquitainian-neumed *Apt 18(4)* and the (Spanish) *Huesca 4*, have for '*o caelicolae*' the setting rm rd m fm r-, differing in one small rhythmic detail from the earlier *B.N. 1240's* rm rd mf m r-, yet it is this *latter* setting which matches the music of '*caelicola*' as found in the Winchester Troper. This may seem a small point to labour, yet the fact remains that the exact details of these two vocative settings (so I believe) cannot be found in any other '*Quem quaeritis*' version. I must clear up one more point before coming to the transcription. It is customary to print the Winchester '*Christicolae*' as it stands in the manuscript, without the preceding '*o*'. I am inserting it, being convinced that of the four units above the syllable '-*chro*', two of them belong to what is the '*o*' sound prolonged into the vocative syllable.[1] One notes also that the third unit is an *oriscus*, a neume indicating a unison prolongation.

The *Visitatio Sepulchri* from The Winchester Troper

[*Oxford, Bibl. Bodl. MS 775, Trop. Wintoniense saec. x, (978-80)*
fol. 17r.-17v.   the earliest surviving European music-drama.]

Angelica de Christi Resurrectione :

Quem que – ri – tis in se – pul – chro, (O) Chri – sti – co – lae?

Sanctarum Mulierum responsio :

Ihe – sum Na – za – re – num cru – ci – fi – xum, O ce – li – co – la.

Angelice vocis consolatio :

Non est hic, sur – re – xit si – cut pre – di – xe – rat; i – te, nun – ti – a – te

qui – a sur – re – xit, di – cen – tes:

Sanctarum Mulierum ad omnem clerum modulatio :

Al – le – lu – ia, re – sur – re – xit Do – mi – nus ho – di – e; le – o for – – tis, Chri – stus

[1] See pp. 80–1.

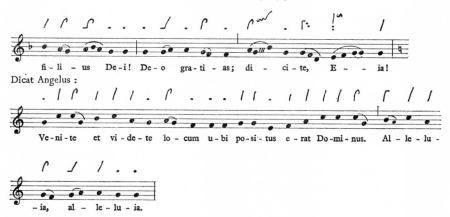

fi - li - us De - i! De - o gra - ti - as; di - ci - te, E — ia!

Dicat Angelus :

Ve - ni - te et vi - de - te lo - cum u - bi po - si - tus e - rat Do - mi - nus. Al - le - lu -

- ia, al - le - lu - ia.

Iterum dicat Angelus :

Ci - to e - un - tes, di - ci - te di - sci - pu - lis qui - a sur - re - xit Do - mi - nus.

Al - le - lu - ia, al - le - lu - ia.

Mulieres una voce canant iubilantes :

Sur - re - xit Do - mi - nus de se - pul - chro, qui pro no - bis pe - pen - dit in

li - gno. Al - le - lu - ia.

Some further comments on the transcription seem to be called for. Dealing as I am with 'campo aperto' neumes in all my comparisons with relevant manuscripts, there must be a certain amount of doubt and approximation regarding the pitches of some of the notes that set the dialogue. I mention once again my particular uncertainty when it comes to the latter half of the third sentence ('*Ite, nuntiate . . .*'). But I have no doubt as to the musical link with Limoges. I have, as in some previous examples, transposed the second mode dialogue music up a perfect fourth for the sake of fitting it comfortably into a five-line G-stave. I have restored the normal pitch at the liturgical item, '*Venite et videte*'. Such a move can be found between even service items. In any case, no sense of 'absolute pitch' existed in Gregorian music.

I mention some other features of the setting. The first *torculus* of the *Bodl. 775* '*quaeritis*' carries a *quilisma*, unlike the plain minor third of most versions of the music. As I have said previously, the vocal filling-in of such a gap as a third in suitable places seems to have occurred whether or not the *quilisma* itself was written. In point of fact, the eleventh-century copy of the Troper at Caius College, Cambridge, already mentioned (*MS 473*, fol. 26v.), has no *quilisma* at this point. The *C.C.C. 473* version is very nearly an exact copy of that of *Bodl. 775*, the differences being of no significance; e.g., one will attach an *oriscus* to a neume, while the other doesn't, and then at another place the reverse will occur. Reproducing the widely used French trope, '*Alleluia, resurrexit Dominus hodie*', both manuscripts choose to leave out the second '*resurrexit*' (found almost everywhere else) and proceed to the normal music for '*leo fortis*'. *C.C.C. 473*, however, has its own arrangement of the melismatic neumes of '*dicite eia!*'. Both texts conclude the '*Non est hic*' sentence with the extra word '*dicentes*'. Having traced the few other *Visitatio* versions which employ the word in this context (none of which has any other links with Winchester), I have concluded that the use has no significance. After all, it occurs often enough in the liturgy.[1] As regards the three concluding items, the liturgical antiphons '*Venite et videte . . .*', '*Cito euntes . . .*', and '*Surrexit Dominus de sepulchro . . .*', in every case both manuscripts use unmistakably the liturgical music. *C.C.C. 473* chooses to cut down to incipits the texts of the first two of them, and to omit the brief rubrics given to each of them by *Bodl. 775*. It should be mentioned that E. K. Chambers and others after him show concern (as Chambers puts it) 'as to whether the "*Quem quaeritis*" was intended in one or both of these manuscripts [i.e. *Bodl. 775* and *C.C.C. 473*] for use in Easter Matins'.[2] This nervousness was mainly due to the curious position of the *Visitatio* in *Bodl. 775*, placed in the Troper as if it belonged to Good Friday of all places! Karl Young (I, p. 587), commenting that the *C.C.C. 473* version occupies a sufficiently normal position, is of the opinion that 'Chambers probably takes this displacement [i.e. the Bodleian one] too seriously'. I, myself, also having some little experience of medieval scribes, certainly agree with Karl Young. At times there are some very queer displacements to be found, especially in tropers.

To me it seems apparent that, whatever the small differences in text (and in notes in the case of the two tropers) may be, we have in the combination of these three manuscripts, the Winchester *Visitatio Sepulchri*; as it were, the 'house' version. There comes to my mind an analogy to be found at another important centre, Rouen. Its very individual 'third stage' *Visitatio* can be found set out in a thirteenth-

---

[1] At the corresponding place in the *Regularis concordia* version the phrase is '*a mortuis*'. I have found this ending to the sentence nowhere else but in a printed service book of 1579 A.D. from Venice (*Brit. Mus. MS Legg. 51, Liber Sacerdotalis*, fol. 265r.–267r.). This late version of the '*Quem quaeritis*' dialogue has a setting which suggests a corrupted form of the usual music, certainly French in style.

[2] E. K. Chambers, *The Mediaeval Stage* (Oxford, 1903), Vol. II, p. 15.

century ordinarium, *Rouen, Bibl. de la Ville, MS 384*, with incipits for the texts, no music whatsoever, but ample 'production' rubrics. Of the same century, and representing exactly the same *Visitatio*, is a *graduale*, now lodged at the Bibliothèque Nationale, *MS lat. 904*; this latter with reduced rubrics, but with a clear and beautiful vocal score, the square notation on a four-line stave. Incidentally, another *ordinarium* version of the same *Visitatio* was written in the fifteenth century (*B.N. MS 1213*, p. 86), its incipits even more cut down.

As is well known, in the prologue of the *Regularis concordia* the unknown author tells us that the monastic customs of Fleury and Ghent have been borne in mind in preparing the Winchester document. It happens, however, that no evidence exists as to any dramatic activities at either of these Continental centres at that early date. On the other hand, there is no doubt that forms of the *Visitatio Sepulchri* were in existence on the Continent in the tenth century, and it would be rash to assume that the Winchester version represents anything but the earliest surviving one. I have already made it plain that I regard the dialogue music of the Winchester Troper (that of the question, reply, and further statement) as being linked uniquely with that of the Limoges troper, *B.N. MS lat. 1240*.[1] I will recall other links between the two entities that I have previously mentioned. *'Psallite regi magno, devicto mortis imperio'*, is a quite rare trope sentence, appearing (uniquely) as an introductory trope to the *'Quem quaeritis'* dialogue in *B.N. MS lat. 1240*. It is also to be found among the later Limoges tropers (e.g., in *B.N. MS 887*), but as an *internal* trope of the Easter Introit (*'Resurrexi'*); and as far as I am aware, nowhere else except at Winchester, where it can be found, once again as an internal trope of the Easter Introit, on p. 19v. of the Winchester Troper, (*Bibl. Bodl. MS 775*). Also, as we have seen, it is paraphrased in the last rubric of the *Regularis concordia* account.[2] All settings of the text, whether at Limoges or Winchester, show the same music.

I have also previously called attention to W. H. Frere's remarks in his edition of the Winchester Troper, as to the early, widespread, and extraordinarily numerous and varied internal tropings of the Easter Mass Introit.[3] A survey of French, German, and Italian tropers shows a wide variety of choice among the sentences that interrupt the liturgical *'Resurrexi'*, *'Posuisti'*, and *'Mirabilis'*, the Introit text often being repeated, with new and alternative sentences of troping. When I investigate the choices of *B.N. MS 1240* for the first presentation of the Introit, I find that they are: (*Resurrexi* . . .) *'Dormivi, pater exurgam diluculo, et somnus meus dulcis est mihi'*; (*Posuisti* . . .) *'Ita pater, sic placuit, ante te, ut moriendo mortis mors fuissem, morsus inferni et vita mundo'*; (*Mirabilis* . . .) *'Qui abscondisti haec sapientibus et revelasti parvulis. Alleluia, alleluia'*. The later Limoges tropers (dating from the turn of the century and the early eleventh) do not follow the pattern of *B.N. 1240*'s tropings, and present new inventions, even though several of the latter's sentences

[1] See p. 93.   [2] See p. 68.   [3] See p. 70.

turn up as later choices. But the outstanding fact is that *B.N. 1240*'s first Introit troping is almost exactly duplicated in the first Introit tropings of the two Winchester Troper manuscripts, the only differences being a doubtful neume or two and '*mundo vita*' instead of '*vita mundo*'. Repeat tropings of the Introit which follow show further correspondences, even though the order of the sentences is sometimes changed. Apart from these two Winchester Troper manuscripts, I have found no other *Quem quaeritis* version that links up in this particular way with *B.N. 1240*.

This series of items of evidence might seem to clinch the idea that the dramatic version of the Winchester '*Quem quaeritis*' as set forth in the *Regularis concordia*, together with the two manuscripts, *Bodl. 775* and *C.C.C. 473*, have unique links with the Limoges *B.N. 1240*.

However, O. B. Hardison disagrees. I have already (on p. 5) made mention of a theory first advanced in 1935 by J. Klapper, to the effect that the '*ordinarium*' form of a *Visitatio Sepulchri* represents a 'special type', to be accepted as its stands. Supporting Klapper's views, and dealing with the *Visitatio* as set out in the *Regularis concordia*, Hardison writes:[1]

... Its dialogue is in what will henceforth be called the 'abbreviated form'. Instead of the familiar *Quem quaeritis in sepulchro, o Christicolae*, the rubrics give only *Quem quaeritis*, and the Marys reply only *Ihesum Nazarenum*. Editors have assumed that the dialogue is given as a series of *incipits*, but the frequent recurrence of the abbreviated form in later manuscripts suggests that versions using it should be considered a distinct type. Since they have other features in common, they raise the possibility, first suggested by Klapper, that the dialogue was originally an extremely brief exchange of Biblical phrases supplemented by antiphons.

In support of his claim, Professor Hardison directs us, in a footnote, to eleven separate texts, printed in Karl Young's first volume.[2] The separate types of these are as follows—one from a missal, five from *ordinaria*, one from a '*directorium*', and four from unidentified sources, mostly reproduced by Martene. None of the manuscripts quoted writes out any music.

Looking at my photographs of the original manuscript pages that Hardison quotes from Karl Young, I note that they all tend to treat the antiphons that precede and follow the abbreviated '*Quem quaeritis*' dialogue in similar incipit fashion. On this showing, he should perhaps have written that the dialogue possibly 'was originally an extremely brief exchange of Biblical phrases supplemented by abbreviated antiphons'. Yet surely no choir ever sang, for example, '*Ardens est*'; '*Quis revolvet*'; '*Christus resurgens*'; '*Surrexit Dominus*'; and after each pair of words, promptly dried up! Surely Hardison, and others who have believed in this abbreviated form, should have realized the practical reasons for the use of incipits in the type of service book such as the

[1] Hardison, p. 197.
[2] The page numbers quoted by Hardison from Young are as follows: I: 214, 215, 221, 230, 240, 247, 262, 300, 302–3, 306, 591 [and *passim*].

ordinarium, in which, for the time being, the purpose is concentrated on rubrics and ceremonial rather than texts and chant.

Hardison, after quoting Young's page numbers, invites us by his phrase 'and *passim*' to seek further for examples. I turn to my photographs, recalling that some versions of the abbreviated type are not wholly strict as to the exclusion of music. I soon meet with such a one in a thirteenth-century ordinarium. *Zurich, Zentralbibl., MS Rheinau LIX, Ordin. Rhenoviense*, pp. 112–13. The abbreviated '*Quem quaeritis*' dialogue is surrounded by various liturgical sentences, also in incipit form. Karl Young refers to the text, but only to note its variants, in relation to a version from Prüm (*Munich, Staatsbibl., MS lat. 23037*) with which he is more concerned (I, pp. 596–7). The incipits for the '*Quem quaeritis*' dialogue are: '*Que(m) queritis*'; '*Ih(esu)m nazarenum*'; '*Non est hic*'; with the addition of '*Venite et videte locum*' (this last of course an antiphon incipit). All this is on the same lines as those of the versions quoted by Hardison, the difference being that most of the scattered liturgical incipits, and every syllable of the '*Quem quaeritis*' dialogue incipits, have their normal musical settings plainly indicated in neumes.

Must we think, then, that these snatches of '*Quem quaeritis*' dialogue music got invented to accompany an original abbreviated form, before the rest of the text and the rest of the music got thought of and written down? Or is the most obvious answer the right one? Here we have a normal type, an *ordinarium* (or a '*directorium*' or a missal, as the case may be) in which, another liturgical purpose taking the leading place for the time being, texts and music are suffering a temporary cutting-down to brief but nevertheless identifiable indications. I state confidently that the abbreviated form as a form, like the nebulous 'vigil Mass', is just another 'textual' myth; one that must be abandoned. Such a theory couldn't have grown up had the people who imagined it considered the value of musical evidence.

There seems little point in my continuing an examination of the quoted examples, which appear to me to be normal Easter trope or dramatic versions, given the treatment appropriate to a particular service book. However, I must linger over one of prime historical interest, being a *Visitatio Sepulchri* performed at the most fitting place on earth, at the Holy Sepulchre itself in the Anastasis (the building that enshrined it); this in the early twelfth-century Jerusalem that had not long before been captured by the first Crusaders. The text has survived in a Vatican manuscript; *Rome, Bibl., Vatic. MS Barberini lat. 659, Ordinarium ad usum Hierosolymitanum anni 1160*, fols. 75v.–76r. Printing the text, Karl Young speaks of it in the following terms:[1]

It is a French liturgical observance brought to Jerusalem by the Crusaders and adapted to the sanctity of the Holy Places. Some time between the date of their arrival (1099–1100) and the year 1160, however, the performance was discontinued, because of the throngs of pilgrims who came to see it. We must

[1] Young, I, p. 262.

be grateful for the vivifying phrase (in the rubrics)—*propter astancium peregrinorum multitudinem*, which enables us to visualize the jostling crowds of worshippers who had streamed into the none too ample church of the Anastasis and had turbulently surrounded the rock of the Holy Sepulchre in their desire to see a dramatization of a Christian mystery.

Karl Young has expanded the incipits, but even so, stretched to its full and with its melodies restored, the little music-drama would certainly have been on the brief side. However, the performance according to Hardison would have been briefer yet, amounting to just over a score of words, if we allow for the introductory four-word sentence to be sung three times, and exclude the added '*Te Deum laudamus*' incipit; (were only these three words sung?). The whole affair could have been over and done with before some of the turbulent pilgrims had got settled in. This certainly could explain their turbulence, but I prefer to believe that the manuscript, like the other 'examples', was in fact a normal *ordinarium* type, and that Karl Young's expansion, plus the restored music, is likely to represent what was actually performed in the Anastasis. The version is manifestly a French one and the music could be reconstructed with a fair amount of accuracy, to complete what is quite an interesting historical document. It is, in fact, something that I have already attempted and have had performed.

Continuing to speak of Winchester, Professor Hardison also says, 'It is impossible to think of the *Regularis Quem quaeritis* as the product of more or less haphazard embellishment and improvement on a St. Gall original composed about 910' (p. 194). I quite agree, especially as there is no evidence for the existence of a St. Gall original of that date. Moreover, if the Winchester documents had had anything to do with St. Gall, they would not have employed the item, '*Alleluia, resurrexit Dominus hodie leo fortis*', which is set in the Winchester Troper as a distinctly French composition.

II

Let us now turn our attention to the earliest Continental versions of the *Visitatio*. Karl Young (I, p. 582) briefly summarizes the evidence for the *Visitatio* form being in existence in Continental monasteries during the tenth century. However, actual surviving examples showing musical settings belong to the turn of the century or beyond. I consider a version from Reichenau (*Bamberg, Staatsbibl. MS lit. 5 [Ed.V,9]* fols. 45r & v.).[1] It reveals that monastery's close links with St. Gall, since its musical setting of the dialogue is a mere copy of *St. Gall 484*. The rounding-off of the brief drama is accomplished by the sentences beginning, '*Surrexit enim sicut dixit Dominus*'. This is almost exclusively a German use.[2] Originally it was an antiphon (see Hartker, p. 231), but in the present

---

[1] The text is given in Young, I, pp. 259–60.
[2] See pp. 73 and 81.

case and in the majority of instances of its use, it employs what seems to be an 'independent' setting of the text. The sentence used as an introduction is of more interest, and recalls that the *Visitatio* had inherited more than the 'sepulchre' and the grave clothes from the *Depositio* and *Elevatio* ceremonies; there was also the 'lapis', the property stone that was used to close the 'sepulchre' after the cross had been placed therein.

The liturgy had already made a borrowing of St. Mark xvi:3, in the shape of an antiphon (Hartker, p. 230). In this *Visitatio* version I find it employed for the first time, supposedly as a speech for the Marys as they approach the Tomb. The antiphon text is, '*Et dicebant ad invicem: Quis revolvet nobis lapidem ab hostio monumenti?*' Bamberg lit. 5 is one of the few versions that employ it as it stands. Most other *Visitatios* using it cut out the first four words, superfluous in the circumstances, and retain the second part with its antiphon music. Bamberg's rubrics are scanty; altogether, this early German *Visitatio*, its nature confirmed by the '*Te Deum laudamus*' conclusion, is not impressive.

One other version from the same turn-of-the-century period awaits our attention; the manuscript comes originally from Prüm in Germany, just over the present Belgian border. Its details are *Paris, B.N. MS lat. 9448*, fol. 33v. It is almost void of rubrics, its identity as a *Visitatio* made clear only by the heading '*DE SANCTO PASCHA*' and the concluding '*Te Deum*'. There are some blank places and uncertainties among its unheighted neumes. Nevertheless, it is not without interest, since it illustrates how, among the lesser *Visitatio* examples, occupying not too much time between Easter Matins and Lauds, and following a recognizable setting of the '*Quem quaeritis*' dialogue, these yet developed small variations of text and music, shared among several different versions. The Prüm example is almost duplicated by the eleventh- to twelfth-century *Visitatio* from Metz (*Bibl. Municipale, MS 452*, fol. 25r.),[1] its music written in characteristic Metz neumes. The Prüm setting, surprisingly, is in French primitive unheighted neumes, but there is a German ring about both versions, inasmuch as the concluding sentence of each, '*Surrexit Dominus de sepulchro, qui pro nobis . . .*', is given the widely used German setting instead of the Hartker music. Yet as far as I can judge from the pattern of the neumes, the '*Quem quaeritis*' exchange in both has the flavour of the Limoges music.

The two versions have in common an unusual detail, the insertion of the word '*quaerimus*' between '*Nazarenum*' and '*crucifixum*' in the second sentence (set to the notes s f̲m̲ r-). Also, surprisingly for German versions, the music of '*Non est hic*' is the rarer setting of the two; d r r̲l̲ (instead of r̲l̲ 1 l̲d̲'-), normally confined to French versions alone. The '*quaerimus*' matter leads us to another eleventh-century *Visitatio*, one from Arras (*Cambrai, Bibl. de la Ville, MS 75*, fol. 11v.),[2] which also makes use of that word and shows other similarities. However, it asserts its French origin by employing, instead of '*Surrexit Dominus de sepul-*

---

[1] The texts of both these can be found in Young, I, pp. 578–9.
[2] The text is given in Young, I, p. 245.

chro . . .', the truly French trope '*Alleluia, resurrexit Dominus hodie . . . dicite eia!*' Yet Arras finds room also for the sentence '*Karissimi verbis canite cuncti . . .*', a variation apparently of the otherwise exclusively Italian trope, '*Karissimi verba canite Christi*', for it certainly uses the Italian trope music.

Leaping ahead for the moment into the fourteenth century, one meets with two brief *Visitatios* from Châlons, *B.N. MS lat. 1269*, fols. 279r. and v., and *Paris B. de l'Arsenal MS 595*, fol. 164r. These could, with their '*quaerimus*' and other similarities, perhaps be added to the group. I could mention other such minor groupings, justified by small similarities in textual and musical details, especially in regard to 'rhymes' in the settings of the vocative phrases, '*o Christicolae*' and '*o caelicolae*'.[1] But at the moment I am not so much concerned with demonstrating these similarities in detail as with pointing out that the shapers of these dramatic works showed at times that there must have been enough regional inter-communication to allow for a great deal of knowledge of what other clerical bodies were doing, this with consequent borrowings and amendings of the compositions. On this point I shall have much more to say in the next chapter.

III

Regarding dramatic activities of the tenth century, we have concerned ourselves thus far only with those of the Easter Sepulchre. Late in the same century, however, there appeared the first signs of a similar interest concerned with the Nativity, which, as in the case of the *Visitatio*, first expressed itself as a non-dramatic trope, prefacing a Mass Introit. The materials for the writer were readily to hand, contained in St. Luke ii: 7–20. This gave an (exclusive) account of the Birth, with a manger as a cradle; also the episode of the shepherds in the fields, watching their flocks by night and terrified by the angelic vision, yet acting on the divine message and hastening to Bethlehem and the manger, thereafter to make known far and wide 'the saying which was told them concerning this child'. The pattern of the trope, a prefacing one to the third Mass of Christmas Day, was undoubtedly founded, textually, on the already widely known Easter '*Quem quaeritis in sepulchro . . .*'. St. Luke's words gave small suggestion as to authentic dialogue, even less than did the Easter morning narrations. Thus the structure and the very phrases of

---

[1] E.g. when the two *Visitatios*, *B.N. MS lat. 9449* of the eleventh century, and *B.N.* (*Nouv. Acq.*) *MS lat. 1235* of the twelfth century are investigated for the intrusion of the word '*Domini*' into the first line of each (in texts which are otherwise the same in a dozen other French versions), it would first be noted that in each of the two settings there is an unusual beginning ('*Quem quaeritis*' as d̲r r̲m̲r d̲r r–) that they have a common musical rhyme for the vocative phrases (r̲m r̲d m fm r–, which is the '*o caelicolae*' setting from Limoges), and that indeed from the evidence of the whole of the musical setting, that *MS 1235* is just a copy of the earlier version. This particular musical beginning is surprising, for it will presently become apparent that the phrase is employed also by *MS 1235* for the start of the Christmas Introit trope, where, among similar settings, it has a better right to be.

the Nativity trope frequently show obvious parallels to the Easter one.
Here is the text as given in the earliest surviving version, *B.N. MS lat.
1118*, fol. 8v.–9r. (988–96 AD.).[1] The manuscript belongs to St. Martial
de Limoges: once again the venerable Abbey can make a pioneer claim.

Quem quaeritis in præsepe, pastores? Dicite!
Whom do you seek within the manger? Say, o shepherds!

Salvatorem, Christum, Dominum, infantem pannis involutum,
The Redeemer, the Christ, the Lord, the infant wrapped in swaddling clothes,

secundum sermonem angelicum.
according to the words of the angel.

Adest hic parvulus cum Maria matre sua,   *de quo dudum vaticinando*
Behold, here with Mary his mother is the little child, whose coming the prophet

Isaias dixerat propheta:
Isaiah did of old foretell, saying:

'Ecce, virgo concipiet et pariet filium'; *et nunc euntes dicite quia*
'Behold, a virgin shall conceive and bear a son'; and now go forth, proclaim

natus est.'
that he is born.'

Alleluia, alleluia! Iam vere scimus Christum natum in terris, de quo
       Now surely we know that Christ is born into the world, of

(INTROIT)
canite, omnes cum propheta dicentes: *Puer natus est nobis...*
whom let all sing, proclaiming with the prophet: Unto us a child is born ...

It will be seen that the trope, whatever it owes to a parent composition,
is a very skilful piece of work. Even though it would merely have been
chanted antiphonally in choir, its latent drama must surely have been
felt. Its last sentence moves smoothly and logically into the *'Puer natus
est'* of the Introit.

On its way towards dramatization it had to face one difficulty that
the Easter trope had escaped. The latter could claim Gospel authority
for an angelic confrontation with the Marys, but who was it who
questioned the *'pastores'*? While the Christmas dialogue remained as a
trope, no text or rubric supplied the information, but later versions, in
the form of the *Officium Pastorum*, introduced the word *'obstetrices'*
(i.e. 'midwives'), derived from a tradition that seems to go back to the
second century, and certainly known in the West by the fourth through

[1] I have already noted that Karl Young, following E. K. Chambers, makes a curious error
(II, p. 5) when he speaks of 'the earliest extant texts of it, from the eleventh century'.
Modern scholarship is firm regarding the date 988 to 996 for that portion of *B.N. MS lat.
1118* which contains the Easter Sepulchre and 'Shepherd' tropes.

the Latin *Pseudo-evangelium Matthaei*. Speaking of this work, Karl Young says: 'Here the midwives are two in number, and from the sixth century onwards they are represented in art as serving Mary in her childbearing.'[1]

The total of surviving '*Quem quaeritis*' Christmas tropes amounts to a mere handful, and this also is true of its dramatization as the *Officium Pastorum*. The Church playwrights were more inclined to centre their attention on the Three Kings ('*Magi*') bearing their gifts to the Manger, allowing only occasional and subordinate appearances of the Shepherds on the scene.

But to return to the trope form: a remarkable fact concerning the '*Quem quaeritis*' Christmas dialogue is that its music, unlike its text, stands firmly independent, except perhaps for the suggestion of that upward 'triadic stride' to which I called attention in the case of the Easter music. Another striking fact is the extraordinary *consistency* of the setting. A chart, which I constructed, displays the music as found in the group of eleventh-century Limoges tropers (e.g. *B.N. MSS lat. 1119*; *1121*; *1084*; *887*; together with *Oxford, B. Bodl. MS Douce 222* from Novalese), manuscripts in which we have been interested before in connection with the Easter '*Quem quaeritis*'. These versions in roughly heighted neumes can be interpreted with almost total exactitude through the twelfth-century *B.N. MS lat.* (*Nouv. Acq.*) *1235*, with its precise notation on four lines. They show an even greater uniformity in small details than can be found in the Easter music of the same group. The differences that exist amount to little more than the pitch of an occasional single note—a *podatus* or *clivis* instead of a *punctum* or *virga*—and matters such as disagreements over the introduction of liquescents and *quilismas*. This French singlemindedness is perhaps no more than we might expect, but it is surprising to find that when we add to the chart some eleventh- and twelfth-century Italian examples, such as from Bobbio (*Turin, Bibl. Reg., F.IV 18*, fols. 9v.–10r.), from Ivrea (*Bibl. Capit. MS 60*, fol. 10v.) and from Mantua (*Verona, Bibl. Capit. MS 107*, fols. 5v.–6r.), the relative consistency is still maintained. This is true of a version from Spain (*Huesca Cathedral, MS 4*, fol. 123) of the eleventh to twelfth century.

We can thus approach the task of providing a line version of the earliest surviving '*Quem quaeritis*' Christmas trope setting with some confidence, being reasonably assured of a truly representative one.

It will be seen that the G mode setting, like the Easter one, keeps to a musical balance in the first question and reply section, but in its own fashion. The first four musical phrases could be described as being A B A B' (the last phrase ending on the fifth above), while the music of '*sermonem angelicum*' reappears at '(*I*)—*saias dixerat propheta*'. The whole setting has, as its 'motto' cadence, the mixolydian l t l s s -. Altogether, the music belongs to the 'new' style, which the trope movement made evident.

[1] Young, II, p. 5.

I set out below my reading of *B.N. MS lat. 1118*, fols. 8v.–9r.:

IN DIE N(ata)L(e) D(omi)NI STAC(io) AD S(an)C(tu)M PETRU(m)

(sic)
Incipiunt trop*us* antequa*m* dicat*ur* officium· [1]

Quem quae - ri - tis in prae - se - pe, pas - to - res, di - ci - te?

Respondent [3]

Sal - va - to - rem, Chri - stum Do - mi - num, in - fan - tem pan - nis in - vo - lu - tum,

se - cun - dum ser - mo - nem an - ge - li - cum.

Respondent

Ad - est hic par - vu - lus cum Ma - ri - a, ma - tre su - a, de qua du - dum

va - ti - ci - nan - do I - sa - i - as di - xe - rat pro-phe-ta: Ec-ce vir - go con-ci - pi - et

et pa - ri - et fi - li - um; et nunc e - un - tes di - ci - te qui - a na - tus est.

Respondent

Al - le - lu - ia, al - le - lu - ia! Iam ve - re sci - mus Chri-stus na - - tum in ter - ris, de quo

ca - ni - te o - mnes cum pro - phe - ta di - cen-tes, PU – ER NA – TUS EST NO - BIS.

(Introit of Third Mass)

We can thus conclude that before the close of the tenth century the Church had established within its fold the beginnings of an art that was

---

[1] '*Officium*', here = '*Introit*'.

[2] *B.N. (Nouv. Acq.) MS lat. 1235*, fol. 183v., of the twelfth century, writes this second neume as a *torculus* (G–A G).

[3] '*Respondent*', on each occasion restored from the manuscript letters, *R.P.D.*

peculiarly its own, the texts shaped from Bible and liturgy, the music based on and inspired by the traditional chant, which, while true Gregorian principles still continued to be maintained, relied solely on the resources of the unaccompanied human voice; solo, or in unison chorus.

IV

By A.D. 1000, the year which some Christian writers had feared would bring the end of the world and the Day of Judgement, the Dark Ages were safely past. It had been the era of the barbarian wanderers, and for the survival of the organized civilization of the West, it had almost been catastrophic. The Frankish empire of Charlemagne, which had stemmed the tide for a while, after the death of its founder in 814 soon dissolved into a shifting pattern of kingdoms and tribes. For the rest of the ninth century and into the tenth, the West reeled before the pitiless incursions from over land and sea of hordes of plunderers and destroyers; Vikings, Saracens, and Hungarians. Not until a couple of generations before the beginning of the eleventh century did the savagery slacken and cease, while a new Western 'empire' stood as the greatest secular power. A group of dukedoms, mostly to the east of the Rhine and including Saxony, Swabia, Franconia, and Bavaria (the nucleus of later 'Germany') gave recognition in 918 to Henry 'the Fowler' of Saxony as their overlord (albeit some of them very grudgingly). Accordingly, he became the first non-Frankish king of 'Germany', and spent the following decades fighting a number of his dukes as well as the Hungarians. It was his son, Otto the Great, who inflicted a final crushing blow on the Hungarians in 955, and ended the menace of the barbarian invasions once and for all.[1] Of his successful system of government (at least, for the time being) and his fencings with that other great power in the West, the Papacy, we shall have no more to say but that it led in 962 to another 'imperial' crowning at St. Peter's basilica in Rome, and a new 'Roman' empire in the West that had a longer life than its immediate predecessor. In 972 Byzantium gave grudging recognition to Otto's title. Even though the West was still haunted by the wish for no more than a revival of glories past and gone, a spirit of optimism and new endeavour began to prevail. Western Christendom had moved into what historians have since chosen to call the 'high Middle Ages', and, under the humanizing influence of a Church triumphant rather than that of local king or emperor, an expansion of the human spirit began.

---

[1] That is, until the deadly threat of the Mongols to eastern Germany in the mid-thirteenth century, followed by their inexplicable withdrawal.

CHAPTER SEVEN

THE ELEVENTH CENTURY (1)

Further development of the '*Quem quaeritis*' trope
and the *Visitatio Sepulchri*

BEFORE returning to our particular interest, the dramatic art-form that was growing up within the fold of an increasingly powerful Church, we will continue our survey of Western Christendom as it moved into the new century.

For a great part of the eleventh century the Church, or at least its prime authority, the Papacy, was far from triumphant. At its very headquarters a vicious Roman aristocracy and a turbulent Roman populace had much to do with the election of a series of popes of low calibre, a state of affairs of which Western Europe was largely unaware. But efforts towards reform continued, not only in favour of Papal election by the cardinal bishops, but against the general corruptions, particularly that of widespread simony among candidates for higher ecclesiastical posts. In these moves the religious-minded Henry III and the worthy Pope Leo IX played important parts. But in due course there came the inevitable clash of authorities. Whoever happened to be the reigning Emperor had too long had an interest in Church organization in general and Papal elections in particular not to react to any attempts to loosen his hold. The breach between Empire and Papacy (the 'Investiture Conflict'), began in 1058 with the activities of Pope Nicholas II; while the advent in 1073 (by means of a somewhat dubious election) of a Pope of such great intellect and determination as Gregory VII (Hildebrand) led to even greater frictions, culminating in the excommunication of the Emperor Henry IV and armed war. Neither protagonist gained a clear victory (the Pope died in exile), but before temporary chaos set in, Gregory had achieved much in asserting Papal authority, attacking corruption, and among other tightenings of control, renewing the insistence of the rule of celibacy among the priesthood. The Pope who eventually succeeded him, Urban II, had been prominent as a supporter of his. It was Urban who roused and directed that outburst of religious enthusiasm that led to the gathering of the forces of the First Crusade in 1095; it was to him that the warriors, mostly Frenchmen and Normans, rallied; and he it was who appointed the fighter-bishop Adhemar of le Puy, to lead the Crusade on the capacity of Papal legate. The Pope had neatly taken over from the Emperor the right to direct

Christian warriors against the heathen at a time when Germans and Lombards were busily engaged in slaying one another. Urban's growing reputation and influence led to the final retirement from Rome of an 'opposition' Pope, Guibert, the ally of the excommunicated Emperor, still reigning in Germany and parts of Italy.

But in spite of the intrigues, hatred, and strife among the hierarchy that were so apparent to the world, yet beneath it all, the heart of Christianity was beating very strongly. The next two centuries, the eleventh and the twelfth, witnessed the enormous expansion of a movement that in many ways rejuvenated the Church—monasticism. This institution, actually a pre-Christian one, was founded on the desire of certain religious-minded men and women to renounce the everyday world and to organize themselves into communities under some kind of common discipline, a 'rule' aimed at a strictly religious life, devoted to God in praise and prayer. Although the movement originated in the East, Celtic Christianity gave it an early welcome, while communities are to be traced in Italy and France from the mid-fourth century, introduced into the latter region, according to tradition, by St. Martin of Tours. For Latin Christianity the earliest great figure is that of St. Benedict (*c*. 480–*c*. 543), whose monastery at Montecassino, in spite of the periods of heathen devastation in Italy, came to be thought of as the monastic capital of the West, and St. Benedict's 'rule' as the firm basis of monasticism. Entering 'religion', the monk renounced the worldly life and joined a self-supporting community from whose precincts he was supposed never to stray. Although Benedict's wishes were that the life was to be austere without being unbearably harsh, there were three great vows of self-denial which the monk had to take (the 'Three Substantials'). These were: (1) *Obedience* to his superiors; (2) *Poverty* (he himself must own literally nothing); and (3) *Chastity*. Benedict included also the disciplines of frugality of diet and of working in the fields. But the most important of the duties of the monk was the '*opus Dei*', the 'work of God'; his long hours of chant and prayer in the monastic choir. The intercessions were not for the brethren themselves alone, but for all Christendom. On them the secular faithful relied for this supreme service.

All these were great ideals, and over long periods the exemplary lives of virtuous monks gained the respect of the outside world. But, human nature being what it is, the history of the institution was characterized by a persistent slow drift towards corruption, punctuated by vigorous outbursts of reform. Even so early a figure as the historian Bede (d. 735) spoke of monastic decay, as did Charlemagne himself, harrying his abbots unmercifully for the lapses of their underlings, and, when necessary, for their own. However, with the general revival of civilization during the centuries that we have spoken of, monasticism proceeded to expand in an unprecedented fashion. As R. H. C. Davis says:[1]

[1] R. H. C. Davis, *A History of Medieval Europe* (London, 1957), p. 260.

The Eleventh Century (1)

Religion in the Middle Ages was usually taken to be synonymous with monasticism. If a man was said to be 'converted to religion' the meaning was not that he had been baptised, but that he had become a monk; and the amazing thing is that in this sense one might almost talk of the 'conversion' of Europe in the eleventh and twelfth centuries. Hundreds and thousands of new monasteries were founded, and there was a whole series of monastic reforms . . .

The word 'reform' here takes on a dynamic cast. There was much voluntary overhauling and reshaping of 'rules', and reorganization in general. The greatest vigour was to be found at the establishment of Cluny in Burgundy. Founded in 910, it became the first 'reformed' community of leading importance. At the beginning of the twelfth century it possessed two hundred dependent monasteries, and gained the distinction of being the first to be 'exempted' by the Pope from control by the diocesan bishops. In the hundred years from 1120 there emerged a number of new monastic 'orders', each with its own distinctive 'rule'. They included the Carthusians (1084), Cistercians (1098), and Premonstratensians (1120). Of these the Cistercians became the most prominent. Under their great leader St. Bernard (1109–1153) they took the lead in bringing the communities back to the strict rule of St. Benedict, and for this they were richly rewarded, both in the spiritual vitality of their order and in the recognition afforded them by the world. As G. G. Coulton remarks,[1] commenting upon monasticism in general during the eleventh and twelfth centuries:

This period is the apogee of medieval monasticism. For two centuries wealth and worldly honour had flowed in upon the monks more freely than at any time since the earliest days; and, on the whole, they deserved it. True, the Benedictine rule of seclusion was very commonly neglected; but it was often neglected to admirable purpose . . .

It might even be claimed that the religious endeavours and aspirations of the age found their crystallization in the realization of a new art, that of the Gothic cathedral—its birthplace, central and northern France; its period, from the first half of the twelfth century onward. Suddenly there came to a Romanesque world such wonders as the Cluniac Abbey of St. Vezelay, and, shortly thereafter, the royal Abbey of St. Denis in Paris, reshaped under the direction of the great Abbot Suger (c. 1082–1152), for a time Regent of France. Suger's St. Denis may have originated many of the new developments that followed in architecture; in sculpture; and in the use of stained glass, which, filling the much enlarged window-spaces that the new techniques had made possible, brought a fresh and radiant light to the interiors. The pointed arch had been employed at times in Romanesque building, but Suger's consistent use of it, together with the ribbed vault that seemed to flow from it, as well as another new conception, the flying buttress, enabled roofs to be

[1] G. G. Coulton, 'Monasticism: Its Causes and Effects', in *Harmsworth Universal History*, p. 2280.

raised to unprecedented heights.[1] Between 1170 and 1270 more than 500 great French churches were built in Gothic style, and there is much to be said for Suger having introduced or perhaps even invented it. Also probably to his credit is the idea of the rose window and the symbolic 'Jesse Tree'.

One of the most wonderful of the French cathedrals is that of Chartres, first completed in 1164 in somewhat Romanesque style. Lord Clark says of it:[2]

> The main portal of Chartres is one of the most beautiful congregations of carved figures in the world. The longer you look at it, the more moving incidents, the more vivid details you discover ... We know from the old chronicles something about the men whose state of mind these faces reveal. In the year 1144, they say, when the towers seemed to be rising as if by magic, the faithful harnessed themselves to the carts which were bringing stone, and dragged them from the quarry to the cathedral. Men and women came from far away carrying heavy burdens of provisions for the workmen—wine, oil, corn. Amongst them were lords and ladies, pulling carts with the rest. There was perfect discipline, and a most profound silence. All hearts were united, and each man forgave his enemies ...

The Romanesque cathedral was destroyed by fire in 1194, but by heaven's mercy there survived the peerless west front. It was reconstructed on the new Gothic lines that Suger had pioneered at St. Denis, but even more ambitiously as to height and window spacing. The rebuilding of Chartres had behind it all the financial resources of one of the richest dioceses in France, but in this Age of Faith the chroniclers were moved once more to describe how people came from all over France to join in the work. Once more I borrow a passage from Lord Clark:[3]

> ... whole villages moved in order to help provide for the workmen; and of course there must have been many more of them this time, because the building was bigger and more elaborate, and required hundreds of masons, not to mention a small army of glass-makers who were to provide the hundred and seventy huge windows with stained glass. Perhaps it sounds sentimental, but I can't help feeling that this faith has given the interior of Chartres a unity and a spirit of devotion that exceeds even the other great churches of France, like Bourges and Le Mans.

As we all know, such human ideals were not to last, and centuries of religious strife lay ahead. I have lingered nostalgically, and, as Sir Kenneth has suggested, somewhat sentimentally, over those two extraordinary centuries, the eleventh and twelfth, but with, I trust, some excuse, for these were also the years during which, as I propose to show, the Latin music-dramas of the medieval Church in their various forms

[1] The St. Denis restoration soon led to other such activities, at Sens, Senlis, Noyon, and in 1163 Notre Dame in Paris. A rivalry seemed to develop as to whose vault could reach the greatest height. Chartres achieved 123 feet, but was surpassed by Amiens' 138 feet. Beauvais reached higher, but the roof collapsed; a second attempt met the same fate.

[2] *Civilisation* (London, 1969), pp. 55–6.

[3] Ibid., p. 59.

grew to their maturity, and then, before the thirteenth was past, began their decay.

II

As we have already seen, the '*Quem quaeritis*' dialogue probably began in a Benedictine monastery, and it was in Benedictine communities that, in the main, the music-dramas best flourished. Let us now pick up the threads of the Easter interest at the point where we had left them.

Although the tenth century had already witnessed, in several surviving examples, the development of the '*Quem quaeritis*' from a mere preliminary trope of the Easter Mass Introit into the dramatic *Visitatio Sepulchri* form situated at the end of Matins, yet everywhere in Christendom during the eleventh century there were monastic communities which were still satisfied to confine the dialogue of their tropers to a liturgical, non-dramatic use. The sum total of surviving manuscripts showing the '*Quem quaeritis*' exchange as a trope is a formidable one, and of these, the vast majority belong to the eleventh century.[1] Before we leave the trope stage altogether, then, it may be well to pause for a final accounting, and to consider some of those manuscripts listed in Appendices I and II which we have not yet discussed.

I give in Appendix Ic the details of the more important surviving tropers of the eleventh and eleventh to twelfth centuries. I have arranged them in three groups: (1) French (with Spanish);[2] (2) German; and (3) Italian.

With regard to the French tropers, Chart One (following p. 429) will show clearly how pervasive were the St. Martial de Limoges melodic characteristics, from *B.N. 1240* to the various other tropers found there and elsewhere well into the eleventh century, including versions from the cathedral of Apt, from Huesca in Spain, and of course (in Anglo-Saxon notation) from Winchester. Among the versions, the musical unanimity of the first three sentences of the dialogue (to '*praedixerat*') is remarkable. I have already spoken of the discrepancies of the last sentence ('*Ite, nunciate . . .*'), but apart from one or two exceptional examples, these really amount to variations on a single theme.

Among the significant variants within this group, however, are *B.N. 887* and *B.N. 1139*, manuscripts which I have already described (p. 76, n.2) as 'odd men out'. The early eleventh-century dialogue found in *B.N. 887*[3] has some musical differences which are indeed worthy of comment

---

[1] Thereafter, a mere handful can be traced, most of them Italian; the dialogue henceforward appearing, with few exceptions, in the Matins music-dramas.

[2] While the Spanish cathedrals and monasteries showed at times a certain independence in their treatment of the '*Quem quaeritis*' dialogue music, both in trope and dramatic use, especially at Vich, the influence of the Limoges musical characteristics (and notation) remained strong.

[3] It must always be remembered that these early tropers often consisted of fascicles of different dates and origins which happen to be bound together. The dates quoted concern only the relevant section in each case.

and which may help to confirm the doubts sometimes expressed as to whether St. Martial has a real claim to the manuscript's origin. Anyway, while the main shape of the music is not exceptional, it represents the Limoges group's only venture into a musical rhyme. '*O Christicolae*' and '*o caelicolae*' are each set by the musical phrase m̲r̲ d̲l̲, d̲t̲, d̲r̲d̲ r-. The unique sentence, '*Ite, nunciate in Galileam*' has already been commented upon by Karl Young (I, p. 569). His suggestion that the sentence represents a defective copying of an adaptation of a Vulgate verse, Matthew xxviii: 10, is a sound one, but I can go further than that. There are two other dialogue versions that show some close links with *B.N. 887*. One of these is *B.N. MS lat. 784*, which dates from the fourteenth to fifteenth century[1] and is probably a dramatic version. I shall have more to say of it later (p. 357); meanwhile, we may observe that it does give us the correct adapted sentence ('*Ite, nunciate discipulis eius quia praecedit vos in Galileam*') and probably the correct music.

The other version is *B.N. 1139*, a manuscript which has been described by the French musicologist Jacques Chailley as '. . . le plus célèbre et le plus riche des mss. de Saint-Martial.'[2] Certainly it contains much valuable material, to the extent of *c.* 230 pages. However, I fear that I can feel no enthusiasm for the '*Quem quaeritis*' dialogue version found on fol. 53r. It is headed '(*H*)*oc est de Mulieribus*', and this rubric has caused some writers to class it as a dramatic version. It may be, but there is no other evidence for it. There are no further rubrics; it is preceded by irrelevant *versus* matter, and immediately succeeded by the only known version of the 'mystère', *Sponsus*. Karl Young (I, p. 212) considers it to be an Easter Introit trope, and I see no reason for disagreeing with him. It is clear that on a number of musical details *B.N. 1139* and *B.N. 887* stand together, somewhat apart from the rest of the eleventh- to twelfth-century Limoges-style trope versions, as Section A of Chart One clearly shows. Regarding *B.N. 1139*, a textual omission is glaringly apparent, for the scribe passes from the '*Quem quaeritis*' question straight on to '*Non est hic . . .*' without writing in the reply; a gross piece of carelessness.[3] We have every opportunity to check up on the version, text and music, since the fourteenth- to fifteenth-century *B.N. 784* version from the same monastery is clearly a revival in more accurate form of the *B.N. 1139* version of centuries before. Both manuscripts employ an introductory trope to the dialogue, the sentence '*Ubi est Christus, meus Dominus et filius excelsus? Eamus videre sepulcrum*', which certainly has a dramatic ring about it and is found elsewhere in the trope version in *Vich MS 32*, and in the dramatic versions of *Vich MS 105* (formerly

---

[1] Karl Young (I, p. 271) dates this manuscript from the thirteenth to fourteenth century. My dating reflects Solesmes opinion.

[2] J. Chailley, p. 109. *B.N. 1139* is dealt with as a whole on pp. 109–15.

[3] I am inclined to wonder, since trope collections were not strictly 'official', whether they were given at times something less than the best quality of scribe available. As far as its eleventh- to twelfth-century section is concerned, *B.N. 1139* is set down in an atrociously careless fashion; this by one (or two) of the semi-literate scribes of the type that Dom Suñol castigates.

MS *111*) and the twelfth-century fragments from Compostela Cathedral (see Plate Vb). No clue is given anywhere as to the speakers, but the question certainly seems to belong to the Virgin rather than the three Marys. One of my comparative charts tells me that the settings given to this introductory trope represent, in each case, variations on a melody common to them all. It also enables me to settle that the scratched horizontal line of the *B.N. 1139* scribe is intended to represent the note D.[1] I shall have a great deal more to say later concerning this strange manuscript.

Both *B.N. 1139* and *B.N. 784* have as a rounding-off item to the dialogue the sentence: '*Vere surrexit Dominus de sepulchro cum gloria*', each set to the same music. I have not met this item elsewhere. It appears to be a free invention, and as far as I am aware, unique to these two manuscripts.

The second line of the dialogue of *B.N. 1139* being missing, we shall never know whether it brought off a musical rhyme, such as *B.N. 887* achieved and *B.N. 784* nearly did. *B.N. 1139* continues with its later and more sober companion as far as '*Non est hic, surrexit . . .*' and then its music goes wildly astray. I suspect a missing clef-change here, and similar troubles later. Anyway, a consultation of Appendix II, Chart One, will save further words. I have been harping on these errors in order to emphasise the unreliability of this particular scribe, and because it is the same person who in *B.N. 1139* passes on to make the uniquely surviving copy of the 'mystère', *Sponsus*. I shall have much to say about him in that connection.

A final member of this eleventh-century French group is the version from the Benedictine Abbey of Novalesa in Northern Italy (*Oxford, Bibl. Bodl. MS Douce 222*). Although the manuscript is written in the apparently Italian 'Novalese' unheighted neumes, Suñol mentions his belief that this particular style of notation derived from the north-west of France,[2] and I can contribute a modicum of confirmation by saying that the neumes of the dialogue seem to indicate a French setting, and that the '*Alleluia, resurrexit Dominus . . .*' incipit that links it to the Introit indicates exactly the musical phrase of *B.N. 1240*.

Let us continue with eleventh-century versions of the '*Quem quaeritis*' trope, by turning to St. Gall and its dependents. On these we need not dwell for long. Their individual identities can be seen in full detail in Appendix Ib, and a selection of some of their '*Quem quaeritis*' dialogue settings in Chart Two, written in unheighted St. Gall neumes. It will be observed how closely these settings maintain the original St. Gall-style music as found in *MS 484*. From the same chart, among examples of the dialogue showing 'fixed' notation and belonging to later centuries,

---

[1] This *B.N. 1139* version was transcribed by Edouard de Coussemaker in his *Histoire de l'Harmonie du moyen âge* (1852), under the title of 'Les Trois Maries'. Lacking the means for comparison that were later available, he assumed the horizontal line to represent F, and also added an unnecessary B flat to the reading.

[2] Suñol, p. 186.

can be seen the pattern clearly maintaining itself with no more than occasional variations.

A number of Italian '*Quem quaeritis*' versions have survived from the eleventh century, some of them quite interesting in the matter of musical notation. One of the earliest of these, belonging to the beginning of the century, is *Ivrea, Bibl. Capit., MS 60*, fol. 69v.

A curious fact concerning the *Ivrea 60* dialogue is that its music is closely linked to that of the eleventh- to twelfth-century *Vercelli 56* version.[1] It is evident that the two musical settings of the dialogue are almost wholly identical, and the identification is aided by the fact that we meet in the Vercelli notation an example of the fixing of exact musical pitch by means of a clef-labelled horizontal line, together with carefully heighted Central Italian neumes.

Another interesting feature to be observed is that the Ivrea version has a separated vocative '*o*' before '*Christicolae*', the last syllable of '*sepulchro*' having been given a single *virga*, the following '*o*' syllable, two notes. In the Vercelli version, the vocative '*o*' before '*Christicolae*' is absent, and the three notes concerned—the one for the final syllable of '*sepulchro*' and the two for the vocative—are brought together as a single neume, a *torculus*, which does duty for the '*chro*' of most of the eleventh century Italian versions. This, to me, appears as one more confirmation of the theory which I advanced on pages 80–1 in connection with the St. Gall version of the Easter dialogue.

In this eleventh-century Italian troper group there appears yet another clear example (in *Verona, Bibl. Capit. MS 107*, fol. 11r.) of a vocative '*o*' in the opening '*Quem quaeritis . . .*' question. The final syllable of '*sepulchro*' is given, not as a *torculus*, but as a *clivis*. A vocative '*o*' is then written, and the third and single sound, the *virga*, transferred to it.[2]

Continuing with the eleventh-century Italian tropers, we consider briefly *Turin, Bibl. Reale G.V. 20*, fol. 96r., from the monastery of Bobbio. As in other places in Northern Italy, use is made of St. Gall-style unheighted neumes. In this manuscript we find that one of the 'tropings of the trope' is a sentence which begins '*Resurrexit Dominus . . .*'[3] This sentence is found quite frequently amongst the Italian versions, but in a musical setting entirely different from the French. The Italian setting of *Turin G.V. 20* will be found, with minor variations, in such manuscripts as *Turin F. IV 18* (also from Bobbio), *Piacenza MS 65*, *Monza MS C. 13/76*, and a number of others. The French setting is less ornate.

The manuscript from the cathedral at Monza, *Bibl. Capit., 13/76*,

---

[1] Solesmes suspects that the relevant part of this manuscript actually comes from Ivrea. As to the notation in the Ivrea version, Suñol mentions (p. 229) that it was derived in the first place from that of Chartres. Here again we meet with evidence as to the widespread travelling of the professional scribe, who, apparently, on occasion launched into musical notations other than those with which he was most familiar.

[2] The scribe of *Verona 107*, in writing the first word of the Easter Mass Introit, appears to have obliterated an intrusive 't' and corrected '*Resurrexit*' to '*Resurrexi*'.

[3] The text of this version is given in Young, I, p. 207.

VI Two versions of the 'Quem quaeritis . . .' dialogue; Einsiedeln, MS 366, p. 55 (eleventh to twelfth century). A very exact rendering of the original Mode II music, transposed up a fourth, in carefully heighted St. Gall neumes around a line marked as F, followed by a later Germanic version, 'Quem quaeritis, o tremulae mulieres . . .'.

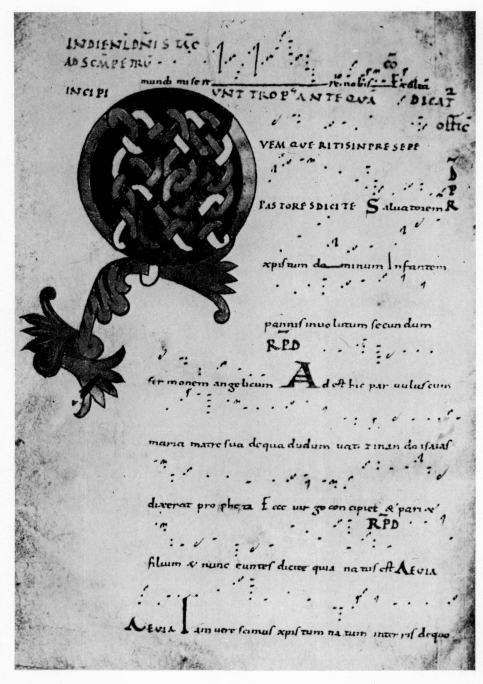

VII The earliest surviving example of the Christmas trope, '*Quem quaeritis in praesepe, pastores, dicite . . .?*'; Paris, Bibliothèque Nationale, *MS 1118*, fol. 8v (a troper from St. Martial de Limoges). While the text is clearly a parody of the Easter trope (which appears on fol. 40v of the same manuscript—see Plate II), the music is quite independent. See transcription on p. 105.

fol. 98v.–99r., is something of a transcriber's headache, the neumes very indistinct at times. The music seems, however, very much to follow a normal pattern, except that one notes that the first appearance of the Easter Mass Introit has already suffered that scribal correction, the obliteration of the added 't' to '*Resurrexi*' (the liturgical music is unmistakable), while at the subsequent appearance of the Introit incipit, there is no doubt as to the scribe's intentions, whether textual or musical; '*Resurrexi*', to the normal music, it is.

Now comes the first of several important manuscripts concerned with the famous centre of Vercelli.[1] *MS 161*, fol. 121r., of the Cathedral library, will immediately strike us in two respects. First, the neumes belonging to the opening two syllables of the familiar question ('*Quem quae-*') are most unusual. If one followed what seems to be a half-hearted attempt to 'heighten' the (Primitive Italian) neumes of the version, one might conclude that the setting of the words '*Quem quaeritis*' resolved itself into rm m-r dr r-, which appears to be the music of those words when they are used in relation to the Introit of the second Mass of Christmas, and later, in the 'Shepherds' Play'! The matter can be checked by reference to the 'Christmas tropes' of *B.N. MS 1118, 1119,* and *1235*. How seriously the coincidence must be taken appears to be a matter for debate.

A second point to be considered is the remarkable fact that in *Vercelli 161* we meet for the first time an example of the Easter '*Quem quaeritis*' trope which is shorter than the normally shortest form, that of St. Gall. Vercelli chooses to cut out half the Marys' reply, ('*o caelicolae*'). It is clear that this is no accident, but has been deliberately done, since there is plenty of room on the same line (after '*crucifixum*') for the phrase, while '*Non est hic*' is started on a new line.

Before leaving the tropes altogether, we need to concern ourselves briefly with one final matter: the growing number of textual elaborations —'tropes of tropes', which throughout the eleventh century seemed to be attaching themselves to the simple '*Quem quaeritis*' sentences. Karl Young has regarded these as the beginnings of a 'process of detachment', whereby the trope, in seeking greater dramatic freedom, found the means to put ever-increasing distance between itself and the Introit of the Mass. These more elaborate versions he classifies as 'tropes in transition' (I, p. 223).

To my mind, however, there seems little to be concerned about in this freer use of the '*Quem quaeritis*' dialogue. When such a 'trope in transition' is encountered, with its appendages, the texts and music of the latter turn out overwhelmingly to be familiar, whether liturgical item or subordinate trope. An investigation which I undertook showed something over a score of different sentence items preceding and/or following the '*Quem quaeritis*' exchanges. Of these, a little more than half-a-dozen of the compositions represented liturgical borrowings

---

[1] Students of medieval literature will be aware of the fame of the so-called 'Vercelli Book' (*Codex Vercellensis*), a manuscript (Old English in origin) still housed in the Cathedral Library at Vercelli, the writing down dating from the eleventh century.

E

(antiphons and the like). Some of the antiphons proved to be obsolete, no longer in the liturgy. In the case of a widely-used text, '*Surrexit enim sicut dixit Dominus* . . .' (mainly a German choice), one of the musical settings found is that of its liturgical antiphon, but another melody (met earliest in *Oxford, Bibl. Bodl. S.S. 27*) proved even more popular. I have previously made mention of the two different musical settings of '*Surrexit Dominus de sepulchro qui pro nobis pependit in ligno*'.

Generally speaking, the briefer tropes betrayed national preferences. '*Psallite, fratres, hora est* . . .' and '*Karissimi, verba canite* . . .' seemed mainly to belong to Italy, while '*Ad sepulcrum residens* . . .' and '*En ecce completum* . . .' appear French in origin, (in particular from Limoges) though straying over into Spain. Some of the brief 'internal' tropes that festooned the separate sentences of the Easter Introit occasionally spilt over the '*Resurrexi*' barrier, while more than once the popular French '*Alleluia, resurrexit Dominus hodie*' bisected itself on either side of the Introit sentence, its music scrupulously maintained.

Generally speaking, the musical settings of the invented sentences remained recognizable wherever met with, and were straightforward and tuneful. Here is a frequently mentioned twelfth-century example from a vich troper (*Vich, Museo, MS 32*, fol. 48v.):

Most of the 'invented' sentences that were used with the '*Quem quaeritis*' dialogue as 'tropes of the trope' did not reappear among the *Visitatio Sepulchri* type, but texts that did survive into longer *Visitatio* examples often found themselves amended and set to different music.

III

Let us return now to the true dramatic form, the *Visitatio Sepulchri*, and chart its progress in the eleventh century. As we have seen, by the end of the tenth century there had already been appearances in both French and German lands of brief dramatic actions at the end of Easter Matins. These continued, but not very ambitiously, into the next century. In a sense, there was no real need for expansion. What had been accomplished was perfectly congruent: a dramatic illustration of what had just been sung as the third responsory and was perhaps also present iconographically on a wall or window or on one of the illuminated pages of a service book in the monastic library.

Thus, the eleventh-century *Visitatio* from Nevers (*B.N. 9449*); that from Metz (*MS 452*) to which I have already referred on p. 101; and that from Arras (*Cambrai 75*), consisting like many a previous trope version of the '*Quem quaeritis*' exchange together with some rounding-off sentences, neither received nor seemed to need anything much in the way of additionally informative rubrics. *Nevers 9449* is reproduced in *Nevers (Nouv. Acq.) 1235*, a line version of a century later; a beautiful manuscript, but with *Interrogacio* and *Responsorio* as its sole rubrics.

An eleventh-century *Visitatio* version from the monastery of Silos in the Spanish province of Burgos, its music written in heighted Visigothic neumes, has survived in two breviaries, *Brit. Mus. add. MS 30848* and *add. MS 30850*. They are duplicates, but written by different hands. Instead of the vocative '*o*' of the first '*Quem quaeritis*' line, they prefer to write '*hoc*', a unique occurrence. A startling feature of the scanty rubrics is the first sentence: '*Interrogat Angelus et dicat ad Discipulos*'—a first-rate scribal blunder![1]

To me the most surprising feature of the version is revealed when it is compared with the twelfth- to thirteenth-century *Visitatio* from Reims (*Bibl. de la Ville, MS 265*, fol. 22r.). Reims has the normal '*praedixerat*' instead of the Silos '*locutus est*', and for the last two words of the dialogue, '*surrexit, dicentes*' instead of '*surrexit Dominus*'; also, the French music is on four lines with clefs, and in clear Metz notation. Yet the Spanish neumes of the '*Quem quaeritis*' dialogue seem to indicate an astonishingly close musical resemblance, including a musical rhyme on '*o caelicolae*' that looks like <u>rm</u> <u>mr</u> d <u>mfm</u> r-, together with some neume groups of three or four notes that coincide most convincingly. However, Reims concludes with the familiar '*Alleluia, resurrexit Dominus hodie*', while the neumes of Silos' single word '*Surrexit*' at the corresponding place show the sentence to be '*Surrexit Dominus de sepulchro, qui pro nobis . . .*', the music being not the liturgical, but the invented setting. With the free flow of communications such as existed between the great monasteries of Christendom from the eleventh century onward, it seems to me not impossible that this represents a real musical link.[2]

Nor is this the only link among the various manuscripts already mentioned. The musical setting of the words '*Non est hic*' was set down by both *B.N. 1240* and *St. Gall 484* as r l l(t)d', and taken up by the vast majority of settings elsewhere, as we shall see in due course. But it so happens that every one of the French versions mentioned so far in the present section of this chapter preferred to be less ambitious in pitch, and used in its place the phrase d r <u>rl</u>- (with an occasional small variant

---

[1] Also to be noted in *MS 30850* is that the *Visitatio* is out of place, and is referred to its correct position between third responsory and *Te Deum* by means of a cross.

[2] It will be recalled that Smoldon has already mentioned this '*o caelicolae*' link on pp. 76–8 in his discussion of the origin of the '*Quem quaeritis*' trope. In addition to *Reims 265* and the two Silos manuscripts, he includes within this (<u>rm</u> <u>mr</u> d <u>mfm</u> r-) group *Cambrai 75* and the thirteenth-century *Paris, Ste. Geneviève 117*.

A different musical rhyme (<u>rm</u> <u>rd</u> m <u>fm</u> r-), the Limoges setting of '*o caelicolae*', links *B.N. 9449* (and *1235*) to the early troper (*c. 996–1024*) *Arsenal 1169*, the first French version to contain a musical rhyme.

A distinction must be clearly drawn, however, between the musical rhyme found in this troper and the one found in *B.N. 887* (and *1139*?), which is <u>mr</u> <u>dl</u>, <u>dt</u>, <u>drd</u> r-. See p. 112 (*Ed.*).

such as d̲r̲ r l-). The earliest surviving instance of this choice is the trope version from Autun found in *Paris, Bibl. de l'Arsenal, MS 1169*, its remarkably early date being between 996 and 1024.[1] Its neumes are Primitive French, not Aquitainian. Signs like this and others previously mentioned make it plain that although Limoges may have had much—perhaps everything—to do with the launching of the '*Quem quaeritis*' trope text and the original pattern of its musical setting, the rest of France, as well as the other regions of Christendom, were very ready to practise their own variations on an original theme.

Turning to more easterly regions, we find that Italy remained concerned only with the '*Quem quaeritis*' dialogue as a trope. In seeking St. Gall-influenced *Visitatio* versions we meet again the previously mentioned pair from Minden, *Berlin 4⁰ 11* and *4⁰ 15* (see p. 81). Karl Young ranks them as being dramatic,[2] but there is no '*Te Deum*' to be seen, and the only justification for considering them to be acted examples is the heading, '*In die sancto Pasche primo mane ad visitandum Sepulchrum Domini*'. Otherwise the dialogue, together with its music, is almost exactly that of the basic *St. Gall 484*, except for the added sentence, '*Surrexit enim sicut dixit Dominus . . .*', previously met with in *St. Gall 376* and *Oxford S.S. 27*. Text and music are those of an official antiphon, to be found in Hartker, p. 232. Another doubtful case is to be met with in *B.N. 10510* (eleventh to twelfth centuries), a troper from Echternach near Trier. It has the simple dialogue (ending with '*dicentes*'), followed by '*Surrexit Dominus de sepulchro . . .*'. No *Te Deum*, no helpful rubrics; unheighted St. Gall neumes; St. Gall music; its '*Surrexit Dominus . . .*' setting the non-liturgical one.

More satisfactory are two Munich manuscripts from the eleventh to twelfth centuries. Both provide a concluding '*Te Deum*' to make their Matins position clear. The first, *MS 14083*, offers no really helpful rubrics, but provides a satisfactory introduction by means of the sentence (coming from the Marys), '*Quis revolvet nobis lapidem ab ostio monumenti?*'. This, as we have seen (p. 101), comes from a liturgical antiphon, which had a Gospel source, and was first employed by that early *Visitatio, Bamberg lit. 5*, with the hampering preliminary words, '*Et dicebant ad invicem*'. *Munich 14083* cuts out these words, but retains the rest of the antiphon with its music. In this modified form the introduction became widely used by *Visitatio* versions. Later, more elaborate musical settings were made; *Einsiedeln 300* (twelfth to thirteenth century) shows perhaps the earliest example of such treatment. *Munich 14083*, its neumes in St. Gall style, is remarkable for still writing *episema* signs when, in general, St. Gall had long abandoned them.

The other Munich manuscript, *14765*, gives a far better picture of dramatic action. The monastery remains anonymous[3] but there is some

---

[1] For previous references to this manuscript, see pp. 80 and 118.

[2] Young, I, p. 243.

[3] Walther Lipphardt reports that K. Hallinger has in fact identified this monastery as Siegburg, in the diocese of Cologne ('Die Provenienz der Consuetudo Sigiberti,' *Medievalia litteraria, festschrift für H. de Boorzum 80. Geburtstag*, Munich, 1971.) (*Ed.*).

detailed mention of the clergy involved, together with their liturgical garments and their actions. The term '*submissa voce*' is used for the first approach, which is given the usual music. The neumes, and the settings of the dialogue music, are those of St. Gall. One notes that the '*o caelicolae*' musical rhyme displays the small melodic variation that some St. Gall versions employ on the penultimate syllable, r̲m̲ r̲d m̲s̲ m̲r̲ r-. The dialogue completed, we meet the first evidence of a German use of that antiphon of invitation that had appeared so long before at Winchester, '*Venite et videte locum ubi positus*' (see p. 92). Also noteworthy is the rubric which directs the three Marys to enter the 'sepulchre' and take up the grave clothes, an action which gives point to the singing by all five of the antiphon, '*Surrexit Dominus de sepulchro . . .*' as these are displayed to the assembled company. Another significant sentence; the display is '*ad conventum vel ad populum*', a rare piece of rubric evidence of the fact that opportunity was sometimes given, despite the early hour, for folk other than clerics to witness the drama.

Another Germanic *Visitatio* of the same period comes, as does *Bamberg lit. 5*, from the famous abbey of Reichenau. This particular manuscript is to be found in *Zurich, Zentralbibl. MS 65*. Its position in Matins is clear, but there are no useful rubrics concerning performance, except that the final antiphon is, once again, 'announced to the people' ('populo'). This antiphon '*Surrexit Christus et inluxit populo suo, quem redemit sanguine suo, alleluia*', is now obsolete, but occurs in Hartker, as well as in a few German *Visitatio* examples later than *Zurich 65* (e.g. *B.N. 9486* and *Brit. Mus. 23922*). All these versions made use of the same liturgical music for the antiphon. In the St. Gall examples that we have considered in this section, the texts of the dialogues have wavered between '*Christicolae*' *solus* and '*o Christicolae*' for the first vocative phrase, but always my explanation given on pp. 80–1 holds good; a neume can be borrowed from the preceding '*o*' sound of '*sepulchro*', when needed.

In *MS 366* (eleventh- to twelfth-century) of the famous abbey of Einsiedeln a unique situation is met with. This manuscript, which we have already encountered briefly on p. 79, is something of a scrapbook with missing pages, and is in fact catalogued as *Fragmenta liturgica* for want of a better description. On pp. 55–6 there are to be found *two* brief *Visitatio* versions, interlocked as it were, before a final *Te Deum laudamus* is reached. The rubrics indicate only that they are to be sung by a single 'Angel' and the 'women'. After a first heading, '*In Resurrectione*',[1] there is the joyful sight, for a paleographer, of a normal St. Gall setting of the normal dialogue, the neumes carefully heighted round an F line, marked as such, and the pitch of every note identifiable.[2] I

---

[1] In the right hand margin, level with this heading, there has been written in a later hand the word, '*osterspiel*'.

[2] The pitch of the first two notes, the liquescent *clivis* (*cephalicus*) for '*Quem*', is revealed as being 'r̲d', and that of the next as being l,. In various neume versions the short *cephalicus* leaves the reading in doubt; might it not be 'r̲t,'? But later stave versions (e.g. *Utrecht 407*) clinch the matter. Here we have an example (there are others in the liturgy) of a liquescent note leaping a third. I have already mentioned that the long-tailed *cephalicus* for '*Quem*' normally indicates 'r̲l,'.

suggest now that Plate VI, which consists of a photograph of p. 55 of the manuscript, should be consulted, and the music compared with the transcription of the *St. Gall 484* dialogue and its photographed page, as given on pp. 78–9 and the frontispiece respectively. It will be seen that in *Einsiedeln 366* the neume that sets '*Quem*' is G plus liquescent F, this beginning the earliest surviving example of a transposition upward of a fourth from the original Mode II pitch. This transposition demands the use of B flat, and, sure enough, above the middle syllable of '*surrexit*', and subsequently whenever needed, the B flat is written in—the earliest instance that I know of its appearance in liturgical music-drama. Returning to the vocative musical rhyme, we see there yet another small variation of the melody on the penultimate syllable; 'm' instead of 'r', this variation being met with in some later St. Gall-type versions.

In this manuscript the apparently interlocking texts which we have already commented on lead to an impossible situation dramatically. After the initial three *Quem quaeritis* sentences we seem to come right back to where we started from, since the Marys are saying ('among themselves'): '*Quis revolvet nobis ab hostio lapidem quem tegere sanctum cernimus sepulchrum?*'[1] This sentence is clearly a reshaping of the 'approach' sentence that we first met with in that early *Bamberg lit. 5* version (see p. 101). Of more importance, this new text involves also new music, and that of *Einsiedeln 366* seems to represent the earliest surviving version, one that is found in a number of *Visitatios* which occur across the centuries to the sixteenth. These are all German or come from centres under German influence, with the exception of the notable and quite surprising inclusion of *St. Quentin 86* (fourteenth-century French). I have charted the examples using this sentence and find (even in the case of St. Quentin) that the settings represent variations on a single original tune. There is no traceable liturgical origin for either text or melody.

What is obviously happening in this manuscript is that another *Sepulchrum* dialogue is beginning. The angel makes his enquiry, the Marys reply, and are then told of the Resurrection and dismissed to inform the disciples. Although the general sense is the same, here is a new text set to altogether different music. This revised '*Quem quaeritis*' dialogue, its form obviously patterned on the original one, is to be found in a number of German versions,[2] including those that qualify for the term *Zehnsilberspiel*.[3] The rest of Christendom continued to favour the older dialogue, with its music. I set out below the new '*Quem quaeritis*' exchange as recorded by *Einsiedeln 366*, the earliest surviving version. I have transcribed it up a perfect fourth, as many of the manuscript versions that use it do.

---

[1] The complete text is given in Young, I, p. 598.

[2] This time, the *St. Quentin 86* version uses for the dialogue a unique poetic paraphrase, set to its own unique tune.

[3] See pp. 304 ff.

Angelus inquirit :
Quem que – ri – tis, o tre-mu- le mu-li- e - res, in hoc tu -mu-lo plo-ran - tes ?

Respond(ent) Mul(ieres) :
Jhe – sum Na-za- re-num cru-ci - fix – um que – ri - mus.

Angelus dicit :
Non est hic, sur - re - - xit; sed ci - to e - un-tes di-ci - te di‾- sci –

– pu - lis e – - ius et Pe -tro qui - a sur-re - - xit Jhe - sus.

If the reader has turned to Plate VI, he may have had doubts as to my interpretation of the three notes of '*Quem*', which appear ambiguous. However, I have at hand my 'through the centuries' chart of about 30 versions, two-thirds of which have settings of the dialogue written on staves. My study of them inclines me to read the Einsiedeln notes as '*frd*'. Actually, the two neumes of '*Quem quae-*' show quite a number of small variants. In the later centuries there were instances of simplification, e.g. *Wolfenbüttel Helmst 965* (fifteenth century) and *St. Gall 392* (sixteenth century) writing '*Quem quaeritis*' as m fm rm m-. In point of fact, this little motif (a common enough Gregorian one) seems to haunt the whole chart. We can fairly say that once again here is a musical setting that represents variations on a basic tune, invented for the occasion. I have previously referred to the pervasiveness of the older '*Quem quaeritis*' tune. An illustration of this is apparent in the new chart, where (uniquely) *Engelberg 314* (fourteenth century) writes for the first four syllables. 'rd l,dt, drd r-', and sets the word '*Ihesum*' to the equally traditional 'dr r-', as well as introducing into the text the words '*o caelicolae*', that had been abandoned by the new dialogue. Thereafter, it returns to the melodic style of the new setting.

Why was it that certain German centres found themselves desirous of replacing the older dialogue? Karl Young (I, p. 254) quotes the opinion that the text was revised to avoid the plural '*o caelicolae*' difficulty when a church desired to present a single angel, in accordance with the accounts of both Matthew and Mark. It has also been suggested that the use of '*tremulae mulieres*' and '*plorantes*' represented a desire to increase the emotional temperature.[1] If this were so, then I cannot but think that the new text-framers were not particularly fortunate in their tune, a Phrygian (E mode) one. It seems to me to represent rather a falling-away in melodic vigour and attractiveness as compared with the setting of the earlier dialogue. In any case, the latter held its own in Christendom to the end.

[1] Something over half a dozen versions of the text replace *plorantes* by *gementes*. These include *Nuremberg 22923* and *Oxford, Bibl. Bodl. 325*, both of the thirteenth century.

121

In the manuscript, after the second dialogue, there follow two more items before the 'Te Deum' is reached. The first consists of a borrowing of the processional antiphon *'Dicant nunc Judaei'*.[1] This anti-semitic composition, found in Hartker, p. 203, and in not more than a score of *Visitatios*, mostly German, is no longer in the Roman liturgy. Some of the musical settings, e.g. *Vienna 1890* (twelfth century), stray somewhat from the antiphon music, as far as can be judged from unheighted neumes.

The last item, *'Ad monumentum venimus plorantes, angelum Domini sedentem vidimus, ac dicentem quia surrexit Jhesus'* (again a first appearance), is one of several similar sentences which seem to have been composed specially for *Visitatio* use. It appears mostly in German versions, and there mostly in company with the revised dialogue, although we find exceptions to this, e.g. *Vienna 1890* and *Brit. Mus. MS Arundel 156* (fifteenth century), which manage to reconcile its use with the older dialogue. I have made a chart of more than thirty surviving *Visitatios* that use the item, and find that once again the list of settings is a matter of a single tune with but trifling variations between the versions. The list includes again the French *Visitatio* from St. Quentin.[2] The famous *Visitatio* from *Orléans, MS 201*, uses a unique rewriting of the text, set to its own music[3].

To consider the character of the *Einsiedeln 366 Visitatio* as a whole: it appears to be an attempt to give alternative versions, texts and music, for the performance of the dialogue part, and appears to show the earliest surviving writing-down of *'Quem quaeritis, o tremule mulieres ... ?'*. It seems reasonable to conclude that there had been established, either at the important monastery of Einsiedeln itself, or through some manuscript source that later perished, this new dialogue version. Opinion at Einsiedeln, it would seem, was that there was merit in both old and new, and that either might be used. It would seem that new invention had included a new 'approach' sentence for the Marys. The choice having been made and carried out, what was to come next? Did the older dialogue proceed to the *'Dicant nunc Judaei ...'* antiphon and then to the *'Te Deum'*, while the new invention took over the other new invention, *'Ad monumentum ...?'*. Each following item has its rubric; respectively, *'Mulieres redeuntes secum cantant'* and *'Venientes autem ad Discipulos dicunt'*. Perhaps both items were used together. Until (if ever)

---

[1] See Karl Young, I, p. 255 and p. 598 for the full text. Remarks on this liturgical piece are found on p. 587.

[2] St. Quentin's *Visitatio*, though quite markedly French, inasmuch as large portions of its text are in the vernacular, nevertheless belongs to a somewhat rigid type of Easter music-drama known to scholars as the *Zehnsilberspiel*, its surviving versions almost exclusively German. See pp. 304 ff.

[3] It may be of interest to mention the Italian manuscript *Udine F. 25*, which shows a twelfth-century *Visitatio* consisting of the revised dialogue together with an *'Ad monumentum venimus ...'*, written rather badly and incompletely, without rubrics, over an area of vellum which had been thoroughly scraped to obliterate something else. My guess is that this was the earlier dialogue, together with a different concluding item. See p. 157.

an earlier manuscript turns up displaying all this new material, *Einsiedeln 366* must be considered as rather an historical landmark.

One disappointment to be met with in considering these eleventh- and, it may be, early twelfth-century *Visitatios* is the shortage of 'stage direction' rubrics. There have occurred some useful 'headings', and final '*Te Deums*' to confirm their dramatic status, but only *Munich 14765* has given us some idea of a mise-en-scène and stage action; certainly nothing to equal the details provided by the long-past *Regularis concordia*.[1]

Let us summarize what we have learned as to the additional items attached to the versions, those that preceded and followed the dialogue exchange. The following—'*Surrexit Dominus de sepulchro, qui pro nobis . . .*' (with either setting); '*Alleluia, resurrexit Dominus hodie . . .*'; '*Eia, karissimi verba canite cuncti . . .*'; and '*Surrexit enim sicut dixit Dominus . . .*'—have been encountered before, in connection with Introit trope versions. The new additions include the use of '*Quis revolvet nobis lapidem ab ostio monumenti?*', by *Munich 14083*, the Gospel-derived antiphon having been stripped of its unnecessary '*Et dicebant ad invicem*'; the use by *Munich 14765* and *Einsiedeln 366* of a paraphrase of the same idea, a change to '*Quis revolvet nobis ab hostio lapidem quem tegere sanctum cernimus sepulcrum?*', with a new musical setting; the reappearance of the liturgical '*Venite et videte . . .*' as the Angel's recall of the Marys, in *Munich 14675* and *Zürich 65* (previously encountered only in the tenth-century versions); the advent of a new *Sepulchrum* dialogue ('*Quem quaeritis, o tremule mulieres . . .?*') in *Einsiedeln 366*, together with another apparent invention in its rounding-off sentence, '*Ad monumentum venimus . . .*'. All these new appearances were freely taken up by later *Visitatios*.

It seems hard to account for the absence from these versions, with the single exception of *Munich 14765*, of the 'recall' antiphon, '*Venite et videte . . .*', so useful in giving the excuse for the Marys to enter the Sepulchre to gather and afterwards display the grave clothes. A long time had passed since the advent of the *Regularis concordia* and the Winchester Troper, and I am reluctant to believe that until *Munich 14765* was written there was no other dramatic use of this antiphon, which led almost inevitably to the episode of the recovery and display of the grave clothes as proof of the Resurrection. I feel confirmed in my opinion that much manuscript concerned with the Easter Sepulchre music-dramas of the eleventh century either awaits discovery or (more likely) has irretrievably perished.

In a sense, however, what manuscript evidence we have seems to suggest that the real creative thrust of the eleventh-century dramatists lies not so much in the *Visitatio* forms as in the newly-emerging music—drama of the Christmas season. It is to this subject that we now turn our attention.

---

[1] See pp. 90 ff.

CHAPTER EIGHT

THE ELEVENTH CENTURY (2)

Further music dramas: Magi plays
(*Officium Stellae*), *Lamentatio Rachel, Sponsus,* and
Ordo Prophetarum

MENTION has already been made (pp. 102 ff.) of the first instances, towards the end of the tenth century, of the Christmas Introit trope '*Quem quaeritis in praesepe*', which suggested the scene of the Shepherds approaching the new-born Child in the Manger, as related by St. Luke. Throughout the eleventh century, however, the dramatic potential of this episode seems to have remained largely dormant. No full dramatic versions are to be found surviving.[1]

It was otherwise in the case of another Christmas season happening. One might argue, in fact, that the real creative interest of the eleventh century lay in the events of Epiphany (January 6): the visit of the Magi to the birthplace of Christ, as recounted in St. Matthew's Gospel.

Here was a dramatic and picturesque plot. No wonder the Shepherds remained for a time neglected! One recalls St. Matthew's vivid account of the 'wise men from the East' ('*Magi ab oriente*' in the Latin Bible) who had asked the question, 'Where is he who is born King of the Jews?', who had seen 'the star in the East' which 'went before them till it stood over where the young child was'. Matthew's second chapter continues with an account of the Magi's reception at Herod's court in Jerusalem; of their questioning by the King, who was already made uneasy by rumours and prophecies; of his crafty dispatching of them to seek for the young child and then bring him the news so that he might 'come and worship him also'; and finally, of his being baulked, since the wise men, having presented their gifts at the Manger, were warned by God in a dream and 'departed into their own country another way'.

In the manuscripts the dramas received, variously, such names as *Officium Stellae, Officium Regum Trium, Ordo Stellae,* or, remembering the other protagonist, *Versus ad Herodem faciendum* and *Ordo ad representandum Herodem.* In all, a dozen or so of these dramas survive, excluding examples which are difficult to separate from actual Mass liturgy, inasmuch as they appear as dramatized features closely associated with the Oblation ceremony.[2] Of what I would consider to be true

---

[1] A brief glimpse of the 'Shepherds in the fields' and the announcing Angel is given in the eleventh century *Officium Stellae* version from Freising (see pp. 130–1).

[2] Martene (III, p. 44) records from a Limoges *ordinarium* a brief scene of the Magi depositing their gifts at the high altar, as a preface to the Mass oblation ceremony. There they are

Officium Stellae music-dramas we have the following:

Eleventh century: from Nevers, Compiègne, and Freising.
Twelfth century: from Sicily, Montpellier (no music), the 'Fleury
                     Playbook', Strasburg, and Bilsen (Belgium).
Thirteenth century: from Laon (no music).
Thirteenth
   and
Fourteenth centuries: several manuscripts recording a drama from Rouen;
                     B.N. MS lat. 904, fols. 28v.–30r. is the only one to
                     have its music written down.

Besides these more or less complete manuscript versions there exist numerous fragments, together with mentions and hints of performances of such works. A curious case, to be mentioned in more detail in its place, is to be found in *Paris, B.N. MS (Nouv. Acq.) lat. 1235*, fols. 198r.–199v., of the twelfth century. Here is a jumble of familiar sentences, not intelligible as an actual Magi drama. It must represent some kind of scribal muddle, but is blest with a perfectly transcribable musical notation throughout, a gift to the musical paleographer if not to the textual one.

   Another useful, if incomplete, source of information is to be found in the previously mentioned 'Einsiedeln Fragments', (*MS 366*, p. 53). Schubiger, in his *Spicilegien*,[1] pp. 45–6, has transcribed relevant sentences with their musical settings. I have photographs of these pages. They contain the scene of the Kings at the Manger, with a hint of the Shepherds' scene, as well as that between Herod and his 'Armiger', who utters his warning concerning the Magi, '*Delusus es, Domine . . .*'. Schubiger's staff-notation versions of the Einsiedeln neumes of these few items agree very readily with the settings of the corresponding items found in the Freising version, similarly of the eleventh century and in close German association.

   But certainly we are in sore need of exact notation in connection with the Magi-Herod dramas. The eleventh-century examples all show unheighted neumes only (interspersed with some patches of illegibility). The twelfth century gives us the valuable *Madrid, MS 289*, one that had strayed from Norman-ruled Sicily. The notation is Norman, accurately heighted, and employing C and F clefs on faintly scratched horizontal lines. It can be given an accurate five-line stave transcription. The before-mentioned jumble of items that comprises *B.N. (nouv. acq.) MS lat. 1235* fol.s 198r.–199v. (coming from Nevers) is also musically valuable, its neumes accurately heighted between F and C clefs. The 'Fleury Playbook' (*Orléans, MS 201*, pp. 205–14) supplies a setting on a four-

---

greeted by an 'angel' with a verse from a Christmas hymn. The sentences are familiar, but no music has been preserved. It has not been definitely dated, but Wilhelm Meyer puts the version as being later than 1100. Some vague details have survived of a similar ceremony at Besançon, with realistic crowns and costumes. Again, dates are lacking. Young deals with these in II, pp. 34–42.

[1] A. Schubiger, *Musikalische Spicilegien* (Berlin, 1876).

line stave, a proportion of it individual, as we shall see. The Strasburg manuscript (*Brit. Mus. Add. MS 23922*, fols. 8v.–11r.) gives unheighted St. Gall neumes only, and the Montpellier example (*Bibl. de la Faculté de Médecine, MS H. 304*, fols. 41v.–42v.) most lamentably none at all. The same handicap concerns the thirteenth-century Laon version (*Laon, B. de la Ville, MS 263*, fols. 149r.–151r.), which Karl Young prints in his 'Slaughter of the Innocents' chapter, since this latter episode is found wholly attached to and continuing from the *Officium Stellae* part.

The most unequivocal of the musical settings of the *Officium Stellae* items are to be found in the thirteenth-century Rouen version (*B.N. MS lat. 904*, fols. 28v.–30r.), and it is for this reason that I have chosen to begin my discussion of the Magi drama here, for the time being disregarding chronology in favour of form. The play, which is one of the briefest, seems to have been intended for use in the Oblation ceremony of the Epiphany Mass,[1] and consequently limits itself to the pertinent subject matter from the Magi-Herod story. From the wealth of Rouen rubrics available, we learn that between Terce and the Mass following, three of the leading clergy, clad and crowned to represent the Three Kings, approach the main altar of Rouen Cathedral from separate directions. Each is followed by an attendant bearing the gift. At the altar they exchange the 'kiss of peace', comment on the Star, and follow it towards a 'corona' of lights hung over the altar of the Holy Cross, where, concealed by a curtain, are effigies of the Mother and Child. Two clerics (not here described as 'midwives') interrogate them, learn of their quest, and reveal the effigies, whereupon the Kings prostrate themselves in adoration and, in turn, present their gifts. Significantly, this latter action is followed by the movements of the clergy and members of the congregation bringing contributions of their own to the same altar. The 'oblation' link is a close one. The Kings then fall asleep. A boy-angel appears and sings his dream-warning, a paraphrase of St. Matthew ii: 12, telling them to avoid Herod's court and to return home another way. Awaking, the Kings rise and make their way to the choir, and, in the Mass that follows immediately after, 'rule' the ceremony in the sense of taking over the singing of a number of the principal items. With the advent of the oblation ceremony proper of the Mass, they 'leave the stage', as it were, by mingling with others, clerical and lay, who come forward to the altar bringing further gifts.

Rouen's staging of the little drama (see Young, II, pp. 43–4) consists of less than a score of brief items, of which a few are liturgical—processional responsories or antiphons carrying liturgical music. But there are ten other items which are more closely concerned with the dramatic action. These I have isolated, labelling them from (a) to (k) and

---

[1] As is the case with the Easter dramas, Matins seems to have been the normally favoured place for dramatic activity. Karl Young posits an evolutionary development for the *Officium Stellae* starting from these dramatic ceremonies associated with the Mass, but his hypothesis seems open to question from the standpoint of chronology. I discuss this matter in more detail on p. 129 and pp. 131–4.

setting them out below together with their *B.N. 904* free-rhythm music. The first three are the successive comments of the three Kings, after the first has pointed his staff at the 'blazing' Star. With (d) they express their united intention of seeking the 'King of kings' and offering their gifts. In my transcription I have omitted the liturgical items which follow, sung to cover the necessary movements, and pass immediately to the rhymed couplet (e) with which the three signal their arrival before the curtained second altar. Items (f), (g), and (h) are the materials for their encounter with the two attendants and the revelation of the Mother and Child. Item (j) represents the 'adoration' episode, and (k) the angelic warning. In the manuscript another liturgical responsory follows, linking the brief dramatic insertion with the beginning of the Epiphany Mass.

My reason for setting out these *B.N. MS lat. 904* items in this fashion is that their texts are to be found, in one order or another, in *every one* of the actual Epiphany music-dramas that are listed on p. 134,[1] and even among the jumbled collection of sentences found in *B.N., MS lat. 1235*. Mostly we find the same material repeated; at times we meet with variations, or extensions, or with rhyming paraphrases. Also with regard to the musical settings, those versions that manage to include them show that on most occasions the melodies as well as the texts have become traditional; often varied, but recognizable. In other words, in these ten items we have what can be called the 'core' of the Magi-Herod music-dramas,[2] most of which give evidence of having been produced in the traditional post-Matins position.

The 'Core' of the Magi-Herod Music-Dramas

— the music as given in *B.N. MS lat. 904, fol. 28v.-30r.*

Stel — la ful-go-re ni-mi-o ru-ti-lat, . Quæ re-gem re-gum na-tum 'de-'mon-strat.

Quem ven-tu-rum o-lim pro-phe-ti-'ae si-gna-ve-rant.

---

[1] The MS *Orléans 201* version chooses to leave out (b), the comment of the second Magus. However, *Orléans 201* is the most independent-minded of the Magi-Herod versions, as we shall see.

[2] For the purpose of comparing the musical settings or the items as met with in the various versions, we have only four manuscripts that have notations other than unheighted neumes. It must be admitted that when comparing versions, occurrences of *punctum* or *virga* in succession, or even *clivis* or *podatus*, do not offer safe identifications. However, the coincidental appearances of melismatic groups, such as at (a) '*Stella*', (e) '*nos*', and (k) '*de-la-to-res*', offer fair confirmations.

[1] The pitch of the notes here given is that of the four-line stave of the manuscript. In performance the pitch chosen would undoubtedly have been that most suitable in the circumstances.

2
'*Eamus ergo, et inquiramus . . .*' had apparently been adapted from an Epiphany antiphon. The music normally used by the dramas is not that of Hartker. In a few other Magi
versions (e.g. *B.N. MS lat. 16819*) some extra phrases are to be found.

³ These two rhyming lines concerning the Star were surely suggested by Matthew ii:9.
Most Magi versions are content with the two lines, but a few (including *B.N. MS lat. 904*)
add some further ones, sometimes including sentences from the ancient sequence '*Quem
non praevalent propria . . .*', and a responsory (to be found in Hartker, p. 34) beginning
'*Orietur stella ex Jacob . . .*'.

⁴ The usual reading is of course, '*I-te, viam . . .*', but the scribe seems here to have intended
the syllable '*ob-*' since he gives it a separate neume.

Having now identified the 'core' form of the *Officium Stellae*, we need to turn our attention to the question of when and where the drama first arose. As in the case of the Easter dramas, we have vivid Gospel vignettes, relevant liturgical antiphons and responsories, and Christian tradition ready at hand. But how did these inputs come together?

As we might by now expect, Karl Young's approach to this question is evolutionary. On II, p. 101, he summarizes the situation as follows:

... The original date of the dramatic ceremonies of Limoges and Besançon in which the impersonated Magi make offerings at the altar during Mass cannot be determined. Such ceremonies may, or may not, have antedated and inspired the more regular dramatic performances at the *praesepe* and at the throne of Herod. Whether or not a simple play such as that from Rouen had antecedents such as the performances at Limoges and Besançon, the general development from the Rouen type of play to that found at Fleury and Freising is not difficult to trace in broad outlines. To the play consisting essentially of the visit of the Magi to the *praesepe* was added a scene in which they appear before Herod. This is enlarged by a scene in which Herod confers with the scribes. To these two additional scenes—through a process that cannot be successfully unravelled in all its details—were added secondary actions in which the emissaries of Herod treat, more or less elaborately, with the Magi or the scribes, or with both. Finally the *Officium Stellae* included within its scope one or more scenes presenting the Shepherds.

As any student of Young's volumes will know, that scholar traces a development of the drama on the lines that he has detailed above (as did E. K. Chambers before him). Let us, for the moment, grant him his chronology as he moves from the comparative simplicity of the Rouen version (circa 17 sung items)[1] through those from, respectively, Nevers (*c*. 15), Compiègne (*c*. 34), Sicily (*c*. 36), Strasburg (*c*. 40), Montpellier (*c*. 53), Bilsen (*c*. 65),[2] Orléans (*c*. 60), and Freising (*c*. 68). There must also be included in the list the thirteenth century *Laon, Bibl. de la Ville, MS 263*, fols. 149r.–151r., which Karl Young places in his 'Slaughter of Innocents' chapter even though most of it (*c*. 37 items) consists of Herod's dealings with the Magi.

Within this evolutionary framework Young demonstrates the early stages and expansion of the scene in Herod's court in impeccably logical fashion. In the brief eleventh-century Nevers version (*Paris, Bibl. Mazarine MS 1708*, fol. 81v.), a well-informed and apparently well-mannered Herod suddenly appears in the course of the ten established 'core' items and asks, 'By what sign did you learn that the king you are seeking had been born?', and again, 'Tell me; do you believe that he reigns?' To which the Magi reply: 'In Eastern lands we learned that he was born; this the Star showed us'. These sentences are reproduced in

---

[1] I have ventured to add in parenthesis after each version, an approximation of the number of items involved. I have employed the word '*circa*', since it is not always easy to settle for what constitutes an item. No doubt my figures could meet with challenges.

[2] The Bilsen version (*Brussels, MS 299*), while employing over forty items to be found in other Magi dramas, contains also quite a number of brief but unique sentences.

every subsequent *Officium Stellae* version that we shall have to consider.[1] It would appear also that whosoever first designed these texts also composed the music, for even though most of the versions show only unheighted neumes, a comparative chart assisted by the fixed notes of *Madrid C.132* (*Sicily*), *Orléans 201*, and *B.N.* (*nouv. acq.*) *235*, indicates a basic unity. As usual *Orléans 201* shows the greatest degree of variation.

The second eleventh-century version (*B.N. MS lat. 16819*, fols. 49r.–49v.), from Compiègne, shows a great expansion of the Court scene with what are clearly new sentences and new music, as officials confront the Magi and conduct them to Herod, who, after questioning them, takes advice as to the significance of their news, and is told by his own learned men of the prophecy concerning Christ. Notable is the expansion of the '*Ecce stella . . .*' sentence (see p. 137, item 'e') by the incorporation of lines from a long-established sequence '*Quem non praevalent . . .*'.

Karl Young continues with his 'evolutionary' review by considering in succession the versions from Montpellier, Bilsen, Strasburg, and the particularly individual drama from *Orléans 201*. The Court scene becomes more and more crowded with people and incidents, and with new inventions of texts and music, while Herod approaches more and more towards the uncontrolled, raging tyrant of tradition. His frenzy, inflamed by his *Armiger*, is finally led to the pitch of handing over his sword to the latter, and ordering the massacre of the Innocents.

Karl Young declares (II, p. 92), '. . . the increasing violence of *Herodes iratus* . . . reaches its culmination in the Freising example'.[2] This version, coming at the end of Young's survey of 'the plays associated with the Nativity', is considered to be the climax of the expansion; the longest, and, it will be found, the most complete in all the recognized features of the Magi-Herod dramas, even if somewhat sparing of rubrics. It contains within itself all the dramatic situations and most of the dialogue sentences that happen to appear in any of the other versions. Let us now note the main details to be found in this most complete of the Magi-Herod music-dramas.

First, a choral introduction; six irregular lines beginning '*Ascendat rex et sedeat in solio . . .*', and rhyming a b b b a a. These may have served as a processional, probably to introduce Herod and the other actors who had to take their fixed places. The item is unique to Freising, as far as I am aware, and thus I can do nothing with the unheighted neumes.

Next, comes a brief scene disregarded by most of the Magi-Herod

---

[1] '*Regem quem quaeritis, natum esse quo signo didicistis?*'; '*Si illum regnare creditis, dicite nobis*'; and '*Illum natum esse didicimus in oriente stella monstrante*'.

[2] *Munich, Staatsbibl., MS lat. 6264a*, fol. 1r. This version is written on a single page of battered vellum (see Plate VIII), suffering numerous patches of obliteration to both texts and the unheighted St. Gall neumes that accompany them. Karl Young, and other text editors before him, have accomplished wonders in restoring indecipherable passages through comparisons with parallel sentences occurring elsewhere. In restoring the neumes I am not allowed the same kind of technique, but enough of the neumes can be distinguished to enable Freising to bear its part in the comparative charts that I found necessary to construct in the course of my study of the Magi-Herod music.

versions, 'the Shepherds in the fields'. An Angel greets the Shepherds, who express their intention of setting off to Bethlehem, and presumably do so. Each item owes its origin to a Hartker antiphon. Liturgical also is the '*Gloria*' sung by the chorus, representing the attendant angels.

The Magi then appear, hailing the Star with the first four of the standard items. Then comes a novelty, used later only by *Orléans 201*, an original sentence by the Magi appealing to the 'citizens of Jerusalem' for news of the 'new-born king'.

Then begins the interrogation of the three at Herod's Court, when the King puts the question as to the reasons for their journey ('*Quae sit causa . . . ?*'). He further demands, 'What race are you?'; 'Where is your home?'; 'Which do you bring to us, peace or war?'[1] The Magi reply in original verse ('We are Chaldaeans; bearers of peace we are . . .'), five lines which end by paraphrasing the second and third lines of their first appearance. These verses occur also in the Orléans version, but the musical settings are not the same, Freising's being the simpler. The Freising Court scene certainly continues as if it had laid contribution on all the other versions which we have mentioned, while including a number of unique sentences of its own, hexameters and otherwise.[2] One notes also a vivid cross-examination by Herod of each Magus, as he raps out such questions as '*Tu, ai unde es?*'.

Thereafter the material becomes increasingly that of the common store from the Magi-Herod dramas, with the free-rhythm settings indicating common musical traditions. Freising joins with the versions from Bilsen and Orléans in having the idea that the Epiphany antiphon, '*O Regem caeli . . .*' would be a suitable recessional for the Magi as they turn for home after the presentation of gifts and the angelic warning. Then come the counter-warnings of Herod's attendants and his violent reactions. One notes the unique Freising rubric, '*Rex prosiliens!*', as he utters the Sallustian line: '*Incendium meum ruina extinguam!*'[3] The Freising version concludes with, first, the frequently-encountered sentence of Herod's ordering the massacre, and then, uniquely, the alternative provision of a hymn verse. Finally, there is given a set of seven lines ('*Eia dicamus . . .*') to be sung by children (possibly the 'Innocents') in praise of the 'King', the purpose of which is not clear. The same lines, complete with unheighted neumes, are found as an introduction to the Bilsen version. Freising is here without any visible musical notation.

Thus far I have been following Karl Young's view of the *Officium Stellae* situation, which is that of a gradual progress through a crescendo

---

[1] These queries may in fact be founded on similar passages from Virgil's *Aeneid*, VII, 112–14; and IX, 376–7. See Young, II, pp. 66–7, in which these verbal parallels are discussed with regard to the Bilsen version.

[2] One unique and remarkable sentence, '*Adduc externos citius, vassalle, tyrannos!*' constitutes Herod's command for the recall of the Magi, after what seems to have been their temporary withdrawal. For Herod to 'call names' like this suggests a playwright with sardonic humour!

[3] See Young, II, p. 68, footnote.

of additional features, from the brief and simple Rouen and Nevers versions to the lengthiest and most closely-packed Freising example. But having reached the climax of what has been presented as a stage-by-stage evolutionary development, it will now be necessary for us to realize that all this has been no more than an academic exercise, bearing no relation to historical reality. The plain facts that are this eleventh-century Freising *Officium Stellae* happened to be in existence before, often long before, manuscripts that show much lesser developments came into being.

Certainly it could be speculated that these less expanded versions might represent copyings from others, belonging to pre-Freising times, that have since perished without trace, but such a theory will have to await a grain or two of evidence. At present, none exists.

What cannot be gainsaid is the existence of this large and battered single sheet,[1] recovered at the Cathedral of Freising, and representing a miracle of survival and an incredibly fortunate piece of evidence. In spite of the amount of damage and the many obliterations of its closely-packed texts and unheighted neumes, it demonstrates that the *Officium Stellae* music-drama had come to its fullest stature some time in the eleventh century.[2]

Hopeful seekings after evidence for less developed versions of the type in, say, the tenth century, may continue, and it may well be that some such earlier material will eventually emerge, but my own speculations are that the origin of the *Officium Stellae* music-dramas was a single act of composition by a single churchman, or perhaps a small group of them; the result, the Freising creation, or something very akin to it. I find an analogy in the production of the *Daniel* music-drama at Beauvais, proclaimed by its opening chorus as originating from the choir-school there. The fact that *Daniel* may very well have been based on the verse-drama of the same name, written by the goliard scholar Hilarius, merely calls our attention to the existence of another independent mind capable of taking a dramatic Biblical story and turning it into a music-drama out of hand. The not very numerous surviving *Officium Stellae* versions, whatever their stages of development, show us throughout very much the same material, both textual and musical, and are indeed too similar not to have been derived from a common source. To me it seems likely, given the early existence of such a full-scale version as Freising's, that from the eleventh century onward there was a good deal of this *Stella* material lying about as it were, and widely known in monastic circles. As in the case of the longer Easter music-dramas the various centres shaped their versions to the style and dimensions that best suited their own conditions, inserting their own little originalities (or big ones, as in

---

[1] See footnote on p. 130, and Plate VIII.

[2] I do not think it would be possible to interpret the neume music of the Freising version with the completeness that would be needed for an acting-version. The patches of illegibility in regard to the neumes are even worse than those concerned with the texts. It is also unfortunate that the four-line-staved *Orléans 201*, which uses on occasion important Freising texts (e.g. '*Chaldei sumus . . .*'), so often chooses to go its own independent way when it comes to the music.

the case of the *Orléans 201* version) as it pleased them. The result was differences in sizes and ambitions; thus, if the cards of these dramas are shuffled and dealt without any regard for the centuries, then apparent progress-patterns are bound to appear. But to my mind the close similarities of texts and music to be found in so many of the items throughout the series are due to their having come down from the basic conception of the *Officium Stellae* music-drama, of which the most authentic surviving representative is the eleventh-century Freising one. The attractive working from *Orléans 201* is the product of another clever mind, determined to be original when it could be, and giving its own twists, textual and musical, to the matter which it had inherited.[1] The Bilsen example has similar ambitions, but is not so successful artistically.

I cannot think that the full-scale *Officium Stellae* version owed its conception to any liturgical oblation ceremony. To my mind the reverse is likely—e.g. that the Rouen (*B.N. 904*) dramatic ceremony, with its handful of inherited items and tunes, represents a brief and convenient weaving together of materials that were already widely known to churchmen.

Let us also recall that the monastery of Freising shared with other great German centres such as those of Einsiedeln, Reichenau, Rheinau, Bamberg, Echternach, and a number of others, the reputation of being very actively allied with the greatest of them, that of St. Gall.[2] I have already (p. 125) called attention to the fact that the learned Einsiedeln community of the eleventh century seems to have been well aware of the existence of a major *Officium Stellae*. The evidence is contained in the monastery's *MS 366* fragments, which include texts and music of portions of both Shepherd's and Magi scenes at the Manger, and also a rounding-off that includes the *Armiger*'s warning to Herod, his suggestion as to the massacre, and Herod's final command for it, which includes the '*Incendium meum ruina . . .*' sentence. While a separate music-drama is clearly involved, the musical settings are all close to those of Freising.

Concerning St. Gall, there is an interesting piece of *Stella* evidence which does not seem generally to be known. It appears that St. Gall had a long memory for the eleventh-century *Stella*. There still remains in the monastery library a manuscript of the fourteenth century which is described as 'the oldest Christmas play in the German language'. It is in the vernacular, stage directions and all; it is spoken, not sung; but nevertheless it is undoubtedly based on the eleventh-century Freising *Officium Stellae*.[3]

I return to Karl Young. His views are, of course, that the *Officium Stellae* pursued an evolutionary development, from the simple to the complex, exemplified in the succession of versions which he has set out.

---

[1] I shall deal with the *Orléans* manuscript at greater length in its appropriate chapter, that concerned with the twelfth century.
[2] See Clark, p. 189.
[3] Ibid., pp. 223–4; also Chambers, II, pp. 49–50.

He has summarized his conclusions as follows:

From the plain fact that the simplest and oldest forms of the play are found only in France, one draws the obvious conclusion that it originated there. From the additional fact that French communities furnish most of the texts of the play in all its stages, one infers that it throve chiefly on French soil. As to the epoch during which the *Officium Stellae* arose there can be no substantial doubt. Both the records and the texts point to the eleventh century.[1]

I hold that such an evolution as Karl Young supposes cannot be reconciled with the admitted datings of the various versions which he handles, and particularly with the early date of the most fully developed example, from Freising, together with the total absence of any manuscripts that could effectively pre-date it. As for my own comments on Karl Young's summary, I certainly agree that, to judge by survivals, the *Officium Stellae* throve chiefly on French soil,[2] even though Germany had more to do with its early stages than Karl Young appears to recognize. But his statement that the oldest forms of the play are found only in France is one that I must question. It apparently rests on his belief that the simplest forms are necessarily the oldest, and this is far from having been proved. Thus, his conclusion that the drama arose in France is surely not an obvious one. I continue to maintain that our most likely guess with regard to origins is the one that I have already advanced in the case of *Daniel*: the supposition of a major invention by some first-class mind, or minds. But a more down-to-earth conclusion might be that we just don't know when and where this *Officium Stellae* first arose, and apart from the fortunate discovery of some further relevant early manuscript, the likelihood is that we never shall. I am still inclined to believe that Germany is not out of the running as its *fons et origo*.

II

Various of the *Officium Stellae* versions that we have encountered so far have concluded with sword-brandishings and foreshadowings of the massacre of the Innocents, as described in the latter half of St. Matthew's Gospel. In Compiègne, for example, we find a brief but vivid projection in this direction: the final appearance of an angel singing the Gospel verse and liturgical antiphon, 'Suffer little children' ('*Sinite parvulos*'). With such striking Biblical material at hand, it is not surprising that in ensuing centuries several music-dramatists made attempts to round off the story, and finally bring the Christ-child to safety at Nazareth.

For the most part, however, this development belongs to a period later than the eleventh century. As we might expect, the monastery of Freising is again early on the scene, and our same Munich, *MS 6264a* provides us, on fol. 27v., with the Freising version of the 'Slaying of the Innocents'. It is most likely, however, that this drama (and indeed, all

[1] Young, II, p. 101.
[2] Although England cannot show a manuscript version of an *Officium Stellae* music-drama, yet a number of accounts survive telling of such performances. See Young, II, p. 451.

the pages in this manuscript which follow the famous and dilapidated fol. 1r.) belongs to the turn of the century or beyond. Fol. 27v. shows St. Gall neumes and a text that is clearly and beautifully written, but in a different hand from that of the *Officium Stellae*. Dramatically, it represents quite a different approach from that of the latter. Such incidents as the angel's questioning of the shepherds; his warning to Joseph; even the agitated scenes at Herod's court, concluding with the not very convincing slaying of one Innocent at a time by 'Armiger', are told in rhyming verse throughout. I propose to take advantage of the fact that the Freising version *may* belong to the early twelfth century, to delay a detailed discussion of the 'Slaying of the Innocents' music-dramas in general until Chapter Ten, when the principal examples can be brought together in close comparison.

This leaves the eleventh century with one brief dramatic episode which might be included in that category, a short, lyrical, rhyming exchange between the lamenting 'Mother' and a consoling 'Angel'; a piece of pure invention by some unknown poet-musician and included in that 'problem' manuscript from St. Martial de Limoges, *B.N. MS lat. 1139* (fol. 32v.–33r.). It could be described as a trope of the responsory '*Sub altare Dei . . .*' which once belonged to Matins of Innocents' Day (December 28), and can still be seen with its St. Gall neumes on p. 65 of Hartker's *Antiphonal*, but is not now in the Roman liturgy. I give the text below, since phrases and sentences from it will later re-appear in both the Laon and *Orléans 201* 'Innocents' drama:[1]

Sub altare Dei audivi voces occisorum: Quare non defendis sanguinem nostrum? Et acceperunt divinum responsum: Adhuc sustinete modicum, donec impleatur numerus fratrum vestrorum. ℣(*ersus*) *Vidi sub altare Dei animas sanctorum, propter verbum Domini quod habebant, et clara voce dicebant. Quare non . . .*

The little episode succeeding it, introduced by the rubric *Lamentatio Rachel*, may not be of much dramatic importance, but it does give one of those sudden flashes of lyrical charm which show that there existed around 1100 a world of rhythmic melody, perhaps secular in origin, which through lack of notational resource has passed out of knowledge.

It is extremely unlikely that this little composition, which was written down probably at the end of the eleventh century, actually owed its origin to St. Martial de Limoges. However, the music is written in Aquitainian neumes, heighted apparently fairly reliably round a horizontal line the identity of which must simply be guessed at.

The first part, the words of the mourning Rachel, consists of nine 12-syllable lines, rhyming in pairs (aa, bb, etc.) and sometimes at the 6-syllable half-line. An extra rhyming line, involving the emotional highlight, '*Heu, mihi miserae . . . !*', precedes the third pair of lines.[2]

---

[1] In the case of the Orléans manuscript, this borrowing includes some reminiscences of the original responsory music.

[2] It involves also some slight scribal modifications of the melody which seem really to have been intentional.

The stanza of the Angel's reply is shaped entirely differently, and in ingenious fashion. Seven lines of 10-syllable verse are rhymed aa, bb/b, cc; but between the fourth and fifth lines is inserted a four-syllable interjection, '*Ergo gaude!*', repeated at the end, after another pair of rhyming lines.

The music is constructed on economical lines, but even so, is to my mind quite charming. Rachel's nine lines employ nine appearances of two musical sentences, the 'extra' line ('*Heu, mihi miserae . . .*') calling for some slight melodic adjustments. The Angel's seven lines mean seven appearances of a completely different melody, calmer and therefore less melismatic than Rachel's, except for the '*Ergo gaude*' flourish. Again, the changes of verbal accent that occur in the Latin lines bring about slight adjustments of the musical accents.

In attempting to transcribe into modern notation my own reading of the composition I am assuming that the horizontal line that was scratched on the manuscript is intended (for the time being) to represent G. I shall shortly go more fully into the vexed problem of such Aquitainian identifications, since we shall soon be meeting with other and longer compositions from *B.N. MS lat. 1139*. A further problem involved is the question of rhythm. There is no doubt in my mind that the melodies were performed rhythmically, their musical accents agreeing with the scansion of the Latin verse, and in this contention I am supported by the manner in which the musical scribe has differentiated his neume groupings. I read the line setting of Rachel's music as being in iambic rhythm, and render the first line thus, in 'three-four time':

The first half of the second line of verse scans slightly differently. In the manuscript the scribe has taken due note of this in his groupings of the Aquitainian neumes. The result is plainly:

(The second half-line setting is unchanged.)

The fifth line is given an extra note, due to the extra syllable occurring ('He-*u*'), and has also chosen in the fourth 'bar' to dwell a little more on the 'misery' being expressed,. I render it as:

In an attempt to be rhythmically tidy I have changed the quavers of the first bar to semiquavers. An eleventh-century performer, blissfully unaware of such matters as bar-lines and time-signatures, would probably not have bothered. Only in such things as dance-songs would the need for firm regularity be likely to be felt. The time for the strictness of the 'rhythmic modes', in the interests of early polyphony, was not yet.

The tune of the Angel, which followed, I have rendered thus (once again, iambic; or, if you choose to call it so, 'second rhythmic mode'):

I believe from the evidence of the previous stanza that the performers would be sensitive to the need for reconciling poetic and musical accents in the fashion that I have indicated. Finally, the melismatic 'burden' appears to me to transcribe thus, the second tune being in the 'Aeolian' mode:

III

The section of *B.N. MS lat. 1139* containing the *Lamentatio* which we have just discussed, the '*Quem quaeritis*' dialogue mentioned on p. 120, and the two other dramatic works, *Sponsus* and the *Procession of the Prophets*, with which we shall shortly be dealing, has at times been referred to as the 'liturgical drama' section of St. Martial de Limoges. I am inclined to question whether this term as applied to St. Martial de Limoges is strictly true. Certainly Professor Jacques Chailley, in his 'Le drame liturgique médiéval à Saint-Martial de Limoges',[2] mentions the centuries-old interest at the Abbey in miracle-plays, apparently in the open air, instancing performances in 1298 and 1302 (pp. 127–8). But he points out also (p. 129) that *B.N. 1139* is the sole witness for the existence of *liturgical* drama at St. Martial. It would be wise, therefore, for us to take a closer look at this particular manuscript and its history, as far as it can be traced. Seeing also that its musical notation is entirely that of Aquitaine, we would do well to recall some general characteristics of that style.

We have already noted that Aquitainian notation seems to have had early associations with that of Chartres, but, developing the independent feature of 'detached points', had from the tenth century onward spread

---

[1] Before leaving the 'Rachel' piece I feel bound to remark on the neatness and accuracy of the music copying of its manuscript pages (fols. 32v.–33r.), which is more than can be said of the other pages from *MS lat. 1139* with which we are concerned (from fols. 53r. to 58r.). These contain so many examples of carelessness and miscopying on the part of the music scribe that one could readily believe that a different person was involved. However, the hand appears to be the same. It must have been his good day.

[2] In *Revue d'Histoire du Théâtre*, 7 (1955), pp. 127–44.

far and wide from the Limoges region (its principal home), penetrating deeply into Spain, and even into Flanders and Italy.

The earliest surviving witness to the employment of the notation seems to be the famous troper, *B.N. MS lat. 1240* from St. Martial de Limoges, nowadays generally dated as A.D. 933–6. We have already noted some of its scribal crudities with regard to its '*Quem quaeritis*' dialogue, but I do not think that these crudities disqualify it as an attempt—however primitive—at diastematic notation, i.e., the accurate heighting of note symbols without a horizontal line. Here I must disagree with even that great authority Dom Suñol, who reserves this distinction for the later manuscript, *B.N. MS lat. 1118*, dated A.D. 987–96 To my way of thinking this classification is a bit too tidy. In connection with my '*Quem quaeritis*' charts I have found that in all the tenth- and early eleventh-century Limoges and other Aquitaine tropers there must be doubts at times as to the absolute accuracy of the heighting of the neumes, due either to plain carelessness or to the fact that if the line of text directly above got in the way of the music scribe, then so much the worse for the heighting. Even in the case of *B.N. 1118*, fol. 40v. (the page showing the '*Quem quaeritis*' dialogue),[1] the upward leap of a fifth followed by another of a minor third—the usual setting of '*Non est hic*'—has its accuracy temporarily baulked by the '*Nazarenum crucifixum*' text of the line above. On the other hand, in spite of frequent uncertainties of the heighting of the *B.N. 1240* neumes, the placings on fol. 30v. of the neumes of the trope '*Psallite regi magno*' could almost allow an accurate reading of the tune if only one knew the pitch of the first note, and if he'd been told that the 'g' of '*regi*' from the line above had pushed down the *cephalicus* of '*mortis*' a degree or so lower than it should be placed (see p. 79). Thus, while *B.N. 1118* may be the obvious choice for an early example of true diastematic notation, it would seem to me that *B.N. 1240*, has at least a certain claim.

As the eleventh century advanced, the 'dry-point' (i.e. scratched) line on the vellum, which had been used at first only as a guide for the writing of the texts, began to be employed as a basis for the 'heighting' of the neumes. However, there was a free-and-easy attitude among Aquitainian music scribes as to what the scratched line might signify in the matter of tonal values, and, as Jacques Chailley points out,[2] it could sometimes be found that in the repeat of precisely the same musical phrase (as in the case of a sequence setting) the notes might be reproduced at a different height in relation to the horizontal line. Only towards the end of the eleventh century can we expect the line to remain constant in value throughout the whole of a composition. And even so, there is no guarantee that if another pitch value is desired in the next item, any warning will be given of the change! Fortunately for palaeography the rest of Christendom went ahead with such matters as the progressive use of staves and clefs.

[1] See Plate V.
[2] See Note 2, previous page.

Let us now turn our attention once more to *B.N. 1139*, the writing down of which dates fortunately from a time when a dry-point line could be expected to remain constant throughout a composition. We have already seen on more than one occasion that (a) bound-up medieval manuscripts could consist of a number of separate fascicles of different periods and natures, which happened for some reason or another to find themselves in association; and (b) that the monastic library which happened to house a particular manuscript was not necessarily its place of origin.

Certainly *B.N. 1139* is a composite affair, a gathering together of fascicles of different dates. The first evidence of its existence at St. Martial is a scribbled note on the first folio to the effect that it was bound ('*relié*') in 1245. The 'dramas' are found in its earliest section (folios 32–118), which belongs to the late eleventh century (1096–9). Moreover, when we encounter the extraordinary *Sponsus* it is clear that the vernacular which occurs in this work belongs to a completely different region from Limoges, and that it certainly represents some very imperfect copying. Whether the unsatisfactory state of this particular music-drama is due to one or another of perhaps a succession of scribes (or to the lot), it is impossible to tell, but it adds point to the conclusions of Jacques Chailley, who says (if I translate him fairly) that it is with serious reservations that one ought to speak of the 'liturgical drama of St. Martial de Limoges'.

It appears then that all one can say is that these unique manuscripts, written between 1096 and 1099 by a scribe of the region for an unidentified Cluniac abbey—certainly not expressly for St. Martial—figured in the St. Martial library in the mid-thirteenth century. By this time the works were approximately a hundred and fifty years old, and there is no record that St. Martial ever took a practical interest in them.

IV

We will now give some closer consideration to the unique and highly original dramatic work which the manuscript itself names as '*Sponsus*' (i.e., 'The Bridegroom'). Its occurrence is from fol. 53r. to 55v., immediately following the imperfect '*Quem quaeritis*' dialogue with its prefacing and concluding tropes. The horizontal line supporting the music of the last words of the concluding trope ('. . . *cum gloria, alleluia.*') leads straight on to the music of the opening words of *Sponsus*. The libretto, altogether in rhyming verse, is based on the parable told by Jesus concerning the Wise and Foolish Virgins, as reported by St. Matthew, xxv: 1–13. I do not believe that the work should be described as 'liturgical'. The story may be a Gospel one, but the text owes nothing to the liturgy, and certainly the music does not. There is, moreover, no evidence at all that is was ever acted within Church walls. I prefer to use Professor L.-P. Thomas's term and call it a 'mystère' (see below, p. 140). Its use throughout of rhyming stanzas, set to rhythmic melody of 'troubadour' style, suggests a foreshadowing of the world of the open-air mystery-play which in due course expressed itself in spoken vernacular prose or verse, musical items being incidental only, and mainly in the hands of secular professionals.

A matter occasionally difficult to account for is that the stanzas of *Sponsus* are sometimes in Latin, sometimes in a vernacular dialect that (as we have already noted) is certainly not that of the Limoges region, and sometimes in a macaronic mixture of Latin with vernacular refrain. As I have previously mentioned, Jacques Chailley speaks of the 'drama' section of *B.N. 1139* as having been copied by a 'Cluniac scribe', and not necessarily for St. Martial. One certainty that has been realized for decades is that, as it stands in the single surviving version, the text is extremely corrupt. A number of fine scholars, among whom must be included Karl Young,[1] have given their attentions to clearing up a great many of the difficulties, errors, and even hiatuses that occur in the libretto. The latest and probably the most complete editing of the text is by the philologist Lucien-Paul Thomas.[2] The editing of the music to date has been, in my opinion, less satisfactory, and it will be my endeavour to make some practical suggestions concerning it.[3] The musical settings (as in the cases of 'Rachel's Lament' and the '*Quem quaeritis*' dialogue, written round a single dry-point horizontal line) call for the use of four stanza melodies only, but these, in spite of obvious evidences of scribal blunders, seem to me to work out as attractive rhythmic tunes, varied in style and mode, and belonging to the world of the troubadour. Professor L.-P. Thomas has transcribed them into modern notation without making an actual acting version of his edition. I fear that I must disagree with his musical readings on a number of counts.

The manuscript affords very little information as to mise-en-scène and production. As already said, there is no reason to believe that the work was performed within church walls. The first we hear of the manuscript concerns its binding at the St. Martial library in 1245. Before the century was out, mystery-plays were being produced in the St. Martial cemetery grounds. However, *Sponsus* might have been sited on the steps of the west front of a church, where there would be to hand a suitable door to act as the entrance to the 'nuptial feast-hall', and a higher level at which the Archangel Gabriel could appear. The few scattered rubrics in the manuscript refer only to the speakers (one such allocation clearly incorrect) and to a couple of stage directions. There is no hint as to costuming, but from the text it is clear that suitable lamps must be

[1] Young, II, pp. 361–9.

[2] Lucien-Paul Thomas, Le '*Sponsus*' (*Mystère des vierges sages et des vierges folles*) (Paris, 1951).

[3] I have in fact published an acting version of the music-drama—*Sponsus* (*The Bridegroom*), a '*Mystère*', *founded on the Parable of the Wise and Foolish Virgins*; the original version transcribed and edited, the music rendered into modern notation and rhythmed, the original Latin-French texts rendered into English, the whole shaped into an acting-version for four small choral groups and two soloists, with optional accompaniments for four solo instruments—portative organ, diatonic harp, shawm (oboe), and rebec (viola) (Oxford University Press, 1972).

provided for the Virgins, perhaps a booth for the Oil Merchants, and also possibly that familiar feature of the mystery plays, the 'gueule'—the Hell-Mouth (*'infernus'*) for the Demons.[1]

As for the participants, there is the question as to who sings the five introductory stanzas (*'Adest Sponsus qui est Christus . . .'*). Thomas suggests a chorus. I certainly agree, but must question his further suggestion that it should represent *Ecclesia*. The medieval view was, surely, that the Church was in fact the 'Bride' (who does not appear in the drama). However, Thomas argues the case for *Ecclesia* very strongly (pp. 44–46). With the evidence of the parable and the words of one of the merchants, we can be sure that there were five Wise and five Foolish Virgins who listened to the second section of stanzas, the Archangel Gabriel's warning. The introduction of Gabriel and the Merchants is of course the playwright's own idea, as is the appearance of the Demons, who enter music-drama for the first time. The entrance of *Christus*, held back until the last few moments, is overwhelmingly dramatic.

Thomas makes one point concerning the production that I must beg to question. He writes (p. 74): '. . . il est probable que la mise en scène ne se présentait pas a cette époque sous l'aspect matérialisé qui donnerait un corps précis a ces mouvements . . .', and goes on to suggest that the 'présentation plastique' of such properties as the door would not be undertaken, and that the '*Prudentes*' may well have remained to be present at the Hell-mouth dénouement, instead of disappearing into the feast-hall with the Bridegroom.

I must point out there is plentiful evidence in the rubrics of the eleventh- and twelfth-century Church music-dramas to show that material properties such as 'sepulchres' that could be entered, 'mangers', movable 'stars', armed attendants, the necessities for the supper at Emmaus (a table, bread, and wine) were all demanded by the particular rubrics. In a number of cases, entrances and exits are definitely indicated. The brief and early Easter Sepulchre dramatic representation acted out at Winchester, *c.* A.D. 1080, was, on the evidence of the manuscript, made as realistic as possible, with rubric directions as to costuming, movements, and tones of voice.

Briefly to summarize the action: the opening chorus, a dissertation on 'the Bridegroom who is Christ', may have allowed the two groups, *Fatuae* and *Prudentes*, to make their entry and to place themselves, probably in two distinct groups, ready for the appearance of Gabriel. The five stanzas are set to a single tune, which, editorially, I will call Melody I. Its hymn-derived pattern is, musically, a b a c.

The gist of the vernacular second section, Gabriel's four-stanza address to the Virgins, is the note of warning contained in the two-line refrain. As they await the Bridegroom's coming, they must 'scarcely sleep' (*'Gáire nói dormét!'*). Regarding this point Karl Young remarks

[1] Bernard Itier (d. 1225), a librarian of St. Martial de Limoges, records in his chronicle the purchase for the Abbey of an *infernus*. But this was in 1212, over a hundred years after the writing down of *Sponsus*. See Chailley, p. 374. Nothing is said in the chronicle as to the use to which the *infernus artificiose compositus* was put.

(II, p. 365), 'The most original aspect of the dramatic version is the centring of interest upon the foolish virgins, and the emphasis, not so much upon the failure of the '*Fatuae*' to provide themselves with oil, as upon their sleeping too long.' In the absence of any specific stage direction we must assume that the 'wise' group obey strictly the first '*vigilate*' exhortation, and stay awake and alert, while the 'foolish' ones fall asleep during the Archangel's address, and awake in due course unprepared. Gabriel's four stanzas are set by a flowing tune (editorially, Melody II), the first two lines and the final one using the same musical phrase.[1]

It is only from the sung text that we now assume the '*Prudentes*' to have placed themselves with lighted lamps ready for the Coming and the '*Fatuae*' to have awakened and realized their unpreparedness. The next section consists of three Latin stanzas with vernacular refrain, addressed by the '*Fatuae*' to their wiser sisters. Their plea is for the loan of oil for their neglected lamps, and they lament their error in the vernacular sentence: '*Doléntas, chaitívas, tróp i avém dormít!*' ('Unhappy, despairing, too long have we slept!'). Melody III, which sets these three stanzas, has the same musical sentence for the first three stanza-lines. Can the composer have intended this monotonous effect as an attempt to underline the foolishness of the group?[2]

The two-stanza reply of the '*Prudentes*' is firm and down-to-earth, both in text and music (Melody IV). They have no oil to spare; the '*Fatuae*' must seek to purchase some from the Merchants. After each manuscript stanza comes the incipit '*Dolentas . . .*', which suggests that they are to take up the '*Fatuae*'s refrain, modifying it to 'Unhappy, despairing, too long have *you* slept!' Unfortunately for certainty the few notes of music given here for '*Dolentas . . .*' are not those of the '*Fatuae*'s setting. Thomas has suggested that the line should be completed to '*Fatuae*'s music. This not wholly satisfactory solution seems the only thing to be done.

In the next section the '*Fatuae*', apparently debating among themselves, continue with two more stanzas of their previous pattern and setting. Then, apparently (there are no rubrics), they make a brief appeal in the vernacular to the '*Prudentes*', using, surprisingly enough, the first line of the '*Prudentes*' own melody for the purpose. The latter's reply, also in the vernacular and using the second and third lines of the music, reiterates their refusal and their advice to seek help from the Merchants.

It seems reasonable to suspect some kind of hiatus in the manuscript after this, since the next section consists of two stanzas in the vernacular sung by the Merchants, obviously replying to the '*Fatuae*', and using their tune for the purpose. Thomas has suggested that after their rejection by the '*Prudentes*', the '*Fatuae*' may have advanced towards the

---

[1] But see p. 146.

[2] I am reminded of the use of a continually repeated vocal phrase that so well illustrates the bafflement of Belshazzar's soothsayers when, in the Beauvais music-drama of *Daniel* (twelfth century), they are called on to interpret the message of the Hand.

Merchants, singing an additional line, in a final appeal for aid. Whatever the case, the Merchants profess themselves unable to assist, and give the barren advice that they should return to their 'five sisters' and try again.

The '*Fatuae*' appear to have lost hope. They move back with their unlighted lamps, lamenting among themselves in a Latin stanza, to their usual melody. Then arrives the moment for the entrance of the Bridegroom. (At last we have a directional rubric, even though slightly out of place.) We must assume that he opens the door of the 'feast hall' and allows the lamp-bearing '*Prudentes*' to pass through. The '*Fatuae*' rally themselves. In an incomplete stanza they plead to be allowed also to enter. But there is no mercy. 'Verily, I do not know you . . .' says the Bridegroom, and passes on to a threat of eternal doom. The Latin stanza is without music, but Melody I fits its rhythm quite smoothly. This must surely be the musical solution. His succeeding (and concluding) stanza of denunciation (also without music), involves a change of poetic rhythm, and this can be very well suited to the rhythm of Melody II, that of the other divine character.

The *dénouement* is swift. The Bridegroom presumably disappears into the feast hall, and the door is closed. A rubric states that the '*Fatuae*' are to be seized upon by demons and thrown into Hell.

A comparison with the concluding verses of the St. Matthew parable is inevitable. Christ's words, according to the Authorized Version, are as follows: 'Verily I say unto you, I know you not. Watch therefore, for ye know neither the day nor the hour wherein the Son of man cometh.'

Here is reproof, but no threat of everlasting fire. However, in the age of religious intolerance and swiftly aroused cruelty to which the drama belonged, the *Sponsus* conclusion was no doubt readily acceptable. Within another century the flourishing Provençal civilization of the south was to go down in blood and fire as the result of the Albigensian Crusade.

It has already been made clear that the text of *Sponsus*, as scribe-copied, contains many errors and omissions. When the musical notation as set down in the manuscript is closely scrutinized, a similar state of frequent carelessness becomes apparent. We have already realized that the work consists of distinctive sets of rhyming stanzas, each stanza of a set sharing the use of a patterned tune, the particular stanza tune being written out each time (except that where refrains are used they are given in brief incipit form). What the transcriber too often finds is that the notes of a setting are not reproduced in exactly similar detail; also, he may feel that the differences are not attempts at variation, but just plain errors. A minor example of what I mean can be met with at the very outset of the work. The first four neumes, setting the words '*Adest Sponsus*', appear in the sol-fa equivalents to amount to d̲r m r̲m, but after comparison with the frequent other occurrences of the phrase in the course of the five stanzas, it becomes clear that the correct reading must be d d̲r m d̲r.

This appears to be a suitable place for the setting down of my free-rhythm reading of Melody I:

In the manuscript the first note is written on the (anonymous) single horizontal line. I have assumed that on this occasion the line indicates F, and that also, for *musica ficta* reasons, the fourth above should take B flat. It is an opinion which I share with Coussemaker and with the Italian scholar, Ferdinando Liuzzi.[1] Thomas takes a different view and believes that the line represents G, thus giving a Mixolydian version of the tune instead of a major one. I shall in due course try to justify my own decision through musical evidence from the manuscript.

A more serious problem is met with in the next section, Gabriel's address to the Virgins. Following the text of the first stanza as printed by Karl Young, II, p. 362 (or that by L.-P. Thomas (p. 176); they disagree only in one place) we have:

> Oiét, vírgines, aisó que vós dirúm!
> Aiseét presén que vós comándarúm!
> Atendét ⌠un espós!   ⌡ Ihesú salváire a nóm
>   ⌊Sponsum!²⌋
> (Gáire nói dormét!)
> aisél espós que vós hor átendét.

The remaining three stanzas seem to follow just the same pattern. But each of them stops short at the single incipit '*Gaire*', it being generally accepted that this implies the re-employment of the last two lines of the first stanza as a refrain.

The shape of the music of the first stanza can be represented as a a¹ b a, a familiar hymn (or troubadour) pattern. The modification of the second line music amounts to a couple of notes. I agree with Thomas in his correction of one other note, to conform with its use in the later stanzas.

The top line on fol. 54r. of the manuscript happens to be '*Aisel espos que vos hor atendet*', i.e. the last line of the refrain of the first stanza. It also happens that it carries the same music as the first line of each stanza. It is at this point, I believe, that the music scribe went astray. He completed the music of '*Aisel espos . . .*' and passed on to '*Venit en terra . . .*', the first line of the second stanza, which has exactly the same setting. Then, seeing two versions of the music line 'a' in front of him, he

---

[1] Ferdinando Liuzzi, 'Le Vergini Savie e le Vergini Folli', *Studi Medievali*, Nuova Serie III (1930), pp. 82–109. Liuzzi's monograph is a study of *Sponsus*, not an acting-version.

[2] Thomas amends what appears to be '*un espos*' in the manuscript to '*Sponsum*'. I do not propose to concern myself with this particular matter. But see Thomas, p. 129.

attempted to set the second line of text, '*De la virgine . . .*' to a version of the third music line, 'b'; finally, when the third line of text came along ('*E flum Iorda . . .*') he could do no more than repeat line 'b' of the music, a trick not found anywhere else in the repeats of the stanza music. He then arrived at the incipit '*Gaire*' and was able to take a breath and start fair on the third stanza. At least, that is my attempted explanation of the manuscript's distortion of the second stanza tune.

Past editors have generally accepted the idea of Gabriel's four stanzas being uniform in pattern, each concluding with a two-line refrain ('*Gaire . . .*' and '*Aisel . . .*'). Ferdinando Liuzzi, however, presents a case for the '*Gaire . . .*' line being the only refrain, and for the second stanza to start with '*Aisel espos . . .*' and to have an extra 'b' line found in none of the others; in other words, to believe what is found in the manuscript. One of his objections to the generally accepted 'uniform stanza' view is that there is a capital A in the manuscript at '*Aisel*' which should indicate the beginning of a new stanza, and which, he says (referring to the most recent editing), Thomas has not taken seriously enough. In my opinion, it may well be that the capital A was written thus to signalize the beginning of the second line of the refrain, which was not written out again in the remaining stanzas, and which might need referring to if the incipit '*Gaire*' did not prove sufficiently a reminder. In any case, I am not as confident as Liuzzi that medieval scribes always got their capitals right; I believe (with Young and Thomas) in the uniform two-line refrain, and that the distorted music of the second stanza represents a scribal blunder.

Since we have now arrived at the beginning of the third stanza, and since I wish to present Melody II in a stave reading, I will do so with this particular text. The tune appears to be a flowing trochaic one in the Mixolydian mode.

[1] The scribe wrote F for the first syllable of '*gablet*', but probably meant G, which would correspond with other similar places.

In this third stanza we find the first two music sentences exactly alike, thus giving a stanza pattern of a a b a. In the case of the first stanza I had spoken of 'a' and 'a'', since the fifth and sixth syllables of the second line were set by F and E instead of by two G's as in the first line.

[2] '*Pendut*'; an editing by Thomas to replace '*batut*', the word found in the manuscript.

[3] Here, some further editing of the manuscript text by Thomas.

Having reached the fourth stanza the music scribe presents his final confusion. He sets the first line to the 'a¹' variation, while in the second, after showing a disposition to write the straightforward 'a' version, he gives us a muddle of notes at the words *'entrames aici'*. In my own acting version of *Sponsus* I came to the conclusion that it would be best to render Melody II in the uniform pattern of a a b a throughout the four stanzas, while at the same time giving due notice of the irregular occurrences of the 'a¹' variation.

When we pass on to the three Latin stanzas of the *'Fatuae'* set to Melody III, it is quite astonishing to find a sudden reform in the deportment of the music scribe. It *looks* like the same man, but whoever it was, the three versions of the tune are well and uniformly copied. The last line of the text, *'Dolentas, chaitivas . . .'*, being a refrain, is represented in the second and third stanzas by a brief incipit. This regularity of refrain rather tends to confirm my belief that this was the state of affairs in the 'Gabriel' section (Melody II).

I set out Melody III in the same fashion as before, applying it to the first stanza. The settings of the first three lines of the texts being uniform, I have used repeat signs with the music. In the manuscript everything was written out in full.

There follows Melody IV, the *'Prudentes'* stanza tune. serving the two Latin stanzas for the *'Prudentes'* which now occur, and also employed later. None of the versions of the melody agree exactly, note for note. The first stanza-text of the *'Prudentes'* is given below, together with a setting that represents, here and there, a compromise:[2]

[1] A very valuable section of L.-P. Thomas's volume is Chapter VIII, which is headed 'Les vers du "Sponsus" ' and consists of a detailed prosodic examination of the various types of verse-form, both Latin and French vernacular, employed by the poet. Thomas points out, as every editor of text with music soon discovers, that there are times when the normal textual stresses of a verse line clash with the musical accents of a particular melody. Some such situation can be seen above, complicated by the extra syllable of 'o-rá-re', for which the music scribe thoughtsully provides an extra note.

[2] On p. 151, in speaking of the *'Prudentes'* ' two stanzas, I mentioned the single-word incipit *'Dolentas'*, which suggested an adaptation of the *'Fatuae'*'s refrain, except for the fact that the music to *'Dolentas'* here is not that of the *'Fatuae'*. Thomas's idea is to complete the tune to the *'Fatuae'*'s music. This I have done, a smooth enough join, it seems; but whether this was the true solution we shall never know.

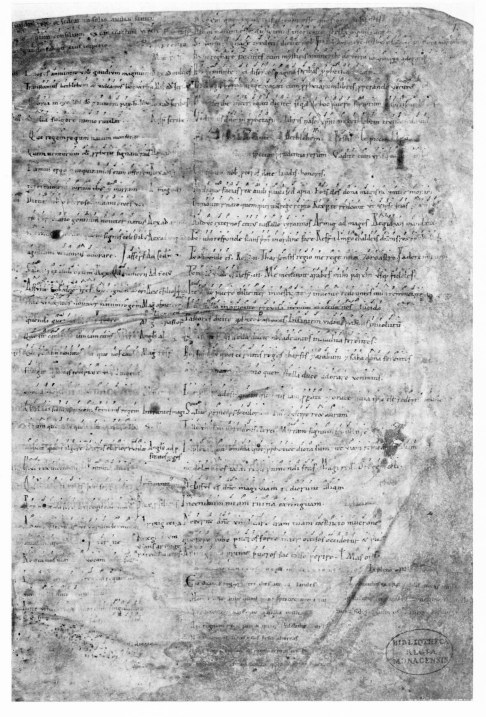

VIII One of the earliest surviving versions of the *Magi* drama; Munich, Staatsbibliothek, *MS Lat. 6264a*, fol. 1r (a single page from the Cathedral of Freising, eleventh century).

IX Elaborate vocal passages from the second of the Carmina Burana 'Passion' dramas; Munich, Bayerisches Staatsbibliothek, *Cod. 4660*, fol. 108r.

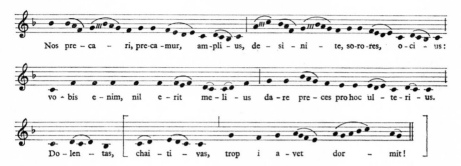

Nos pre – ca – ri, pre-ca -mur, am-pli – us, de – si – ni – te, so-ro-res, o – ci – us:

vo – bis e – nim, nil e – rit me – li – us da – re pre – ces pro hoc ul – te – ri – us.

Do – len – tas, chai – ti – vas, trop i a – vet dor – mit!

The four stanza melodies are the sum total of the musical material of *Sponsus*. I have already related how this material was employed as far as the remaining texts were concerned, and, where music was absent, how conveniently one or another of the tunes could be fitted to the bare texts, this seeming to suggest the reasons for the bareness.

The manuscript version breaks off with the appearance of the Demons, and there is no general and concluding Te Deum, such as would be found in the usual liturgical music-drama. It is a terrifying ending, and must have seemed very much so to the medieval audience, for whom the flames of hell were a constant threat and the Demons a lurking reality. Having taken part in an actual performance of the little drama I found that even a modern audience was left disturbed by the violent dénouement, part of the reason, possibly, being a certain sympathy for the unfortunate '*Fatuae*'. Our modern solution for this (the whole company having disappeared either through hall-door or Hell-mouth) was to call for their recessional through the audience; headed by *Christus*, followed by Gabriel, the opening choristers, the '*Prudentes*', the Merchants, the '*Fatuae*' (quite unscorched), and rounded off by a re;rguard of Demons, grinning masks, pitchforks, and all. This took place to the general singing of the Advent hymn, 'O come, Emmanuel . . .', lines from which are:

> O come, thou Lord of David's Key!
> The royal door fling wide and free . . .

and again:

> O come, thou Branch of Jesse! draw
> The quarry from the lion's claw;
> From the dread caverns of the grave,
> From nether hell, thy people save.
> Rejoice . . .

—which somehow gave the idea of a second Harrowing of Hell, and brought a more tranquil atmosphere to the conclusion.

I cannot agree with L.-P. Thomas's view that the melodies of the work are directly inspired by the music of the Church liturgy. Indirectly, yes; there is no doubt that the art of the troubadour-trouvères owed much to

F

the forms established over the centuries by the medieval Church—the litany, the hymn, the sequence, etc. I believe that the melodies of *Sponsus* represent, not the direct influence of Gregorian chant, but rather the troubadour-style invention inspired by that influence, the composer being undoubtedly a Church-trained musician. Gustave Reese has pointed out (*Music in the Middle Ages*, p. 197) that in *Sponsus* there are examples of the *lai* form, a characteristic troubadour framework. (He mentions also that the *lai* grew from the liturgical sequence.) I quote a few lines:

A particularly interesting form is displayed by the twelfth-century play *Sponsus* ('The Bridegroom'), based on the Parable of the Wise and Foolish Virgins (Matthew XXV, 1–13). Here the melodies accompanying the lines given to the virgins and oil merchants are paired and then repeated as a group, the melodies thus by themselves applying the principle of the sequence with doubled *cursus* . . . while the whole drama, with the music of the introduction recurring in the epilogue, presents the pattern of the reinforced *lai* . . .

Assuming, as I have done, that *Sponsus* is not 'liturgical', was probably not performed within church walls, and had taken on some of the attributes of the secular 'mystère', I did in my acting-version provide suggestions for preludes, accompaniments, and postludes to the texts, for solo secular instruments. In this present volume I am leaving the question of the employment (or otherwise) of instruments during the performances of medieval Church music-dramas to a later chapter.

Similarly, I have not attempted to 'rhythm' the four stanza-tunes (although I did so in my 'acting-version'). But again in a later chapter of this volume I have faced up to the general problem of giving rhythmic interpretations to neume notation when it is to be found connected with the regular scansions of rhymed Latin poetry.

One final matter. I have to defend my contention that the manuscript shows the music of *Sponsus* as starting on F, and that the incised line on which the first note is written had that identity throughout its previous existence on that particular folio of *MS 1139* (53r.). We have already dealt with the composition that precedes *Sponsus*, that very carelessly copied version of the '*Quem quaeritis*' dialogue (see p. 112). Its normal end is troped by an almost unique non-liturgical sentence, '*Vere surrexit Dominus de sepulcro cum gloria, alleluia*'. I can find elsewhere no discussion of the music of this last item, the '*alleluia*' of which immediately precedes the beginning of *Sponsus*. Also, I am fortunate in having a photograph of another manuscript from St. Martial, but this time of the fourteenth to fifteenth century, *B.N. MS lat. 784*, fol. 106v., which is a more careful version of the same '*Quem quaeritis*' dialogue, with the same prefacing and concluding tropes and with the same music. Thus I am perfectly sure that in *B.N. 1139* '*Vere surrexit . . .*' ends its '*alleluia*' on D, two degrees below the incised line, and halfway along its length. Another inch is occupied by the title, and then the *Sponsus* music begins, on the line, with a note that I have assumed to be F. However, according to Thomas, *Sponsus*, being a new composition, has the (Aquitainian) right to change, without a 'direct' or any other notice, the value of the line to G, and he argues at some length why the first tune should be Mixolydian. I can see no objection to beginning *Sponsus* (at an undisturbed pitch) with a 'major key' tune, and thus continuing with Mixolydian, Dorian, Dorian respectively. As a mere personal opinion, I think these sound rather better than does Thomas's choice. Liuzzi makes the same selection of modes as I do, and argues, with quotations from service music, why the first tune should be in the 'major key'.

I have devoted far more pages to *Sponsus* than I can afford to give to most examples of Church music-drama in a book of this scope. This is because I consider it (when its textual and musical misrepresentations have been, as far as can be judged, cleared away) to be one of the most artistic and imaginative dramatic productions of the medieval era. It is salutary to realize, when one reads Karl Young's consideration of the libretto (II, pp. 361–9) and Thomas's comprehensive philological study of the work and its background, that it has taken many decades of patient investigation by a number of scholars before the butterfly emerged from a particularly tangled-up cocoon.

V

Of less moment is the last 'dramatic' work to be included in *B.N. MS lat. 1139*. This is an example of the *Ordo Prophetarum*, 'one' (to borrow Karl Young's words) 'of a small body of pieces, presented on Christmas Day or a week later, containing utterances of the prophets concerning the coming of Christ'.[1] He goes on to tell us that the type of drama had been founded on a section of a famous Latin sermon against the Jews, the Pagans, and the Arians, written during the fifth or sixth century, and for long (but wrongly) attributed to St. Augustine. Much of the material of the sermon was widely used in medieval times as a *lectio*, read during Matins of Christmas, or some other day of the Christmas season.[2]

But with regard to dramatic actions one section only became relevant, that addressed specifically to the Jews; its object, 'to convict them of error through utterances of their own prophets and certain pagans. The preacher summons the selected witnesses singly by name and announces their successive testimonies.'[3] Almost inevitably any dramatization of such a theme would take the form of a pageant of relevant characters, suitably attired, each in turn summoned by the voice of authority, and each delivering, in verse, his testimony.

Only three dramatic, obviously 'acted', versions of the *Ordo Prophetarum* have survived, the *B.N. 1139* example much the earliest, and, unfortunately, the only one to have its music written down. Its deficiencies are in the matter of rubrics, which consist merely of the names

[1] Young, II, p. 125.
[2] Karl Young prints the text of the whole of the Latin sermon on his pp. 126–31.
[3] Young, II., p. 125.

of the prophetic witnesses and the incipit 'R' (of '*Responsum*'). There are no acting and costuming details, and nothing as to the when and where of the performance but an ambiguous mention of the item '*Benedicamus*' at its close. On the other hand, the thirteenth-century version from Laon (*B. de la Ville, MS 263*, fol. 147v.–149r.) and that from Rouen of the fourteenth century (*B. de la Ville, MS 384*, fol. 33r.–35r.)[1] supply later generations with abundant details regarding costumes, properties, and movements concerned with elaborately planned production, but although each was undoubtedly sung, neither manuscript has chosen to furnish the music. Each version has been thoroughly commented upon by Karl Young and many other writers whose work is concerned only with textual details, and very many people have been made aware of those striking episodes (dramas within a drama, one might say) of Nebuchadnezzar and the fiery furnace, and even more celebrated, the spurred and impatient Balaam mounted on his ass, with a boy in concealment ready to voice that animal's complaints.

My concern will be with the *B.N. 1139* version only, unique in retaining its musical setting. From the analogies afforded by the other versions, better equipped with directions, the general plan of its production can be realized. The opening three stanzas are introductory, sung possibly by a cantor or possibly the choir. Then whoever is the 'interrogator' puts a (usually two-line)[2] rhyming question to the 'witnesses' in turn. These comprise, in the following order, Isaiah, Jeremiah, Daniel, Moses, David, Habakkuk, Simeon, Zacharias, Elizabeth, John the Baptist, Virgil, Nebuchadnezzar, and the Sibyl. All reply to the interrogator with a rhyming stanza each, the stanzas being well varied both in regard to length and pattern. One type predominates, one that scans 4 4 7 4 4 7, and rhymes a a b c c b. As Karl Young (p. 143) very rightly says, 'The prophecies . . . in the Limoges text are, in general, free and pleasing versifications of the parallel utterances in the *lectio*.'

The pity is that the same clarity is not to be observed in the organization of the music. *Ordo Prophetarum* follows on immediately after *Sponsus*, and it appears to be the same scribe who contributes the Aquitainian notation around a faintly scratched line, which, I am continuing to suppose, still has the value of F.

The tune which sets the three introductory stanzas, and which I term 'A', is worth recording. I do so in the usual 'free' notation, although I have no doubt that it was interpreted rhythmically in performance. I give it as written to the first stanza, but checked and slightly amended by reference to the other ones, since there are small discrepancies among the three versions.

---

[1] Copies of this version survive in other Rouen manuscripts.
[2] The 'interrogator' occasionally puts a four-line question, but when dealing with John the Baptist he indulges in the extraordinary pattern of 4 4 2 4 4 2 8 8.

I have encountered the theory that the second half of 'Tune A' together with certain moments in 'Tune B' (set down below) present similarities of phrase that suggest a link with the first *Sponsus* melody (*'Adest Sponsus qui est Christus . . .'*) and thus some kind of affinity between the two works. I should like to believe this, but remain unconvinced. Arguments based on similarity of musical phrases always seem to me to be insecure. In the course of musical history there have evolved quite a variety of attractive melodic curves that have resulted in what might be described as 'stocks' of similar tunes. The *Sponsus* 'Melody I', which starts as: d dr m dr f m r d s f m dr m r d . . . (etc.), comes under one of these categories. Certainly the *'Dux de Juda non tolletur . . .'* setting (the 'Tune B' mentioned above) shows some resemblance, but so do the starts of the several versions of the *'Omnipotens pater . . .'* setting, the start of the antiphon music of *'Christus resurgens . . .'* (now obsolete), and that of the B.V.M. antiphon, *'Regina caeli laetare . . .'*. One could also recall the canon, *'Non nobis, Domine . . .'*, or even a theme from the second movement of Beethoven's 'Ninth'.

I turn now to *'Dux de Juda . . .'*. I have already suggested that it should be called 'Tune B'. It is sung by 'Israel', as the fifth item.

Previously, the 'interrogator' had sung his two lines to what appears as irregular snatches of some of its phrases. 'Tune B' is also used (with one or two small discrepancies), by 'Moyses', and the 'interrogator' returns to its motives at intervals from employing other tunes. The twists and differences of pitch in the similar patterns of notes that are so often encountered suggest errors rather than variations.

The phrase which I have labelled as the 'B cadence' makes periodic reappearances, not only with a recognizable version of the first part of the 'B' tune but as the cadence to other tunes.

The 'prophets' that immediately follow, 'Isias' and 'Jeremias', each have their own tunes, these quite melismatic and shapely. The music of

'Daniel's' brief contribution appears to be a skeleton version of the first two lines of 'B', while 'David', starting independently, rounds off with the 'B cadence'. 'Elizabeth' is even less original, employing 'tune B' with what may be termed 'variations'. 'Virgilius', still more brief and modest, uses the second half of 'B'. 'Johannes Baptista' has what appears to be an attractive 'major key' tune (a b a c). It is therefore somewhat bewildering to find 'Nabucodonosor's' music borrowing its opening phrase, going off on its own with an occasional reminiscent return to 'Johannes', and ending with the 'B cadence'.

I will pursue the analysis no further. There may be plenty else in the music of the Limoges composition that could be commented on and puzzled over, but with whatever animation its aid may have brought to the work, my opinion is that of Karl Young concerning the *Ordo Prophetarum* in general, that 'however carefully the personages may be differentiated through costume and other details of impersonation, an unrelieved succession of summonings and respondings cannot escape monotony.'[1]

As regards the music itself, there is a manifest state of disorder that nevertheless sometimes hints at intentions misplaced and schemes gone astray. Considering what we know of the history of this portion of *B.N. MS lat. 1139*, it may be that a true copy of the original has not come down to us.

A speculation that one sometimes meets with concerning *B.N. 1139* is that the proximity of *Sponsus* to the *Ordo Prophetarum* may imply that the former was acting as an introductory work to the latter. I find the theory difficult to credit. I cannot see why a drama on the subject of the Second Coming should serve as a preface to prophecies as to the First. Also, it is apparent that in the respective compositions there are two entirely different kinds of imagination at work. It is hard to think of their working together.

---

[1] Young, II, p. 170.

CHAPTER NINE

THE TWELFTH CENTURY (1)

The progress of the *Visitatio Sepulchri. Peregrinus*

IT has already been noted that after the millennium a period began when a new hope and a growing energy began to permeate Western Christendom. For all the struggles and bickerings between rival authorities, sacerdotal and secular, prospects for the common man were brightening. Great changes were occurring in agricultural methods, e.g., the growing use of the heavy plough, which made possible the opening up of the hitherto neglected clay soils. These changes, by the eleventh century, began to show beneficial results. From this time onward more and more of what had been regarded as 'waste' came under cultivation, and the starvation level among the peasantry began to fall. Population numbers were rising. Towns, the life of which had long been stagnant, also began to revive during the eleventh century, and by the beginning of the twelfth the employment of money had again become common. Its use gradually spread to the countryside, giving some aid to the liberalizing tendencies that were already beginning to be apparent.[1] The self-contained and self-supporting manorial system gave place to a realization of wider horizons and far-reaching trading prospects.

To the vigour of the bishops of the secular cathedrals and the enthusiastic support of the citizens of the expanding towns[2] must be given a great deal of the credit for the explosion of religious energy that throughout the twelfth and into the thirteenth century raised the mighty Gothic cathedrals of France and England. Some of these (Beauvais, for example) brought outstanding contributions to the art of the Latin music-dramas, which for long had been mainly the preserve of the monasteries.

---

[1] Charles T. Wood writes in *The Age of Chivalry* (London, 1970), p. 78: '... probably no more than ten per cent of the French farming population were serfs by the middle of the thirteenth century, whereas fully ninety per cent had lived under servile conditions three hundred years earlier.'

[2] Ibid., pp. 82 and 85: 'Although urban centres were initially small, they expanded rapidly until, by the end of the twelfth century, they dotted the landscape with a profusion far exceeding anything known at the height of the Roman Empire ... there was about the towns and cities of Europe an atmosphere of confident, devil-may-care exuberance.'

II

It will be seen from Appendix Ic that in the twelfth century the desire to produce further versions of the '*Quem quaeritis*' dialogue as a trope of the Easter Mass Introit was fast fading. To the best of my knowledge, only a handful of Italian versions and a single Spanish (Vich) example survive. They provide an interesting variety of notational styles in their settings.

Benevento MS 27, from south Italy, introduces the 'Beneventan' neumes, oddly thick and at times with stems unusually elongated, but carefully heighted, and in some examples with single horizontal lines, clef-labelled. The notation is famed, inasmuch as it was employed by the venerable Abbey of Montecassino.

Monza MS K.11 gives us an early example of a four-line stave with clefs and end-of-line 'directs', and thus absolute notational accuracy. The F and c lines are thickened and coloured, the neumes square (at times oblong).

Turin MS F.IV.18 uses the notation of Milan, a single heavy line indicating either F or c, but with plenty of other, faint lines to help to define all pitches past question. Also, unlike the Monza example, B flats are inserted where called for.

Vercelli MS 161 represents a notational retrogression; 'Primitive Italian' neumes, not reliably heighted; end-of-line directs, but no horizontal line. Like *Vercelli 146* and *162*, it omits the second vocative phrase ('*o caelicolae*'),[1] and has an exceptional setting of the first two '*Quem quaeritis*' syllables.

Vich MS 32 uses Catalonian notation with F and c lines together with faint assisting ones. As in the cases of the Benevento and Monza versions, the '*Quem quaeritis*' dialogue has been transposed up a fourth, but no B flats are indicated. However, it does look as if the intermediate note between 'a' and 'c' has been written a little nearer to the lowest note, suggesting 'mi, *fa*, sol'.

As for the dialogue settings, three of the five are fairly orthodox, the first phrase ('*Quem quaeritis*') varying between Benevento's rl̲ l̲,t̲,d̲t̲, d̲r̲ r- and Vich's plain r d̲t̲, d̲r̲ r-. The 'triadic stride' (decorated or otherwise) is generally observed, as well as the r̲l̲ l l̲td' of '*Non est hic*'. There are two curious exceptions to the usually orthodox start to the dialogue music. *Vercelli 161* writes for the first two words, r̲m̲ m-r̲ d̲r̲ r- (closely similar to the version of its eleventh century companions, *Vercelli 146* and *162*, who have r r̲m̲r̲ d̲r̲ r-). *Monza K. 11* starts even more surprisingly (I give something more than a phrase of it):

m	r̲d̲	r̲m̲	m	d	m	s̲l̲	s̲f̲		m	f̲m̲ r̲m̲	m-
Quem	quae-ri -	tis	in	se-pul-chro,					Chri-sti-co-lae?		

r̲m̲ m   d   m s̲l̲ s   . . . (etc.)
Je - sum Na-za-re-num . . . (etc.)

---

[1] See p. 114.

The musical differences, which could be described as variations interspersed with similarities, together with the quite deliberate action of three of the Vercelli versions in leaving out the vocative phrase, '*o caelicolae*', seem to point to some local independence that could bear further investigation.[1]

Regarding additional troping sentences occurring in the versions, the familiar '*Alleluia, resurrexit Dominus hodie, leo fortis . . .*' turns up; but musically, largely different from the usual French setting. On the other hand, another apparently Italian trope, '*Hodie exultent justi; resurrexit leo fortis, Deo gratias, dicite eia!*', found at Turin and Benevento, appears to have a music mostly derived from that first-mentioned French '*Alleluia, resurrexit Dominus hodie . . .*' trope.[2]

A newcomer, '*Pascha nostrum Christus est immolatus, agnus est . . .*', I have found associated with no other Easter '*Quem quaeritis*' but those of Turin. The music has nothing to do with the Easter Communion beginning with the same words.

Two tropes introducing the '*Quem quaeritis*' dialogue of *Vich 32*, '*Hora est psallite . . .*' and '*Ubi est Christus . . .*' have been encountered before.[3] Two 'following' tropes in the same version are also familiar, the Limoges-derived '*Ad sepulcrum residens . . .*' and '*En ecce completum . . .*'.[4] The musical settings remain consistent.

III

In this the twelfth century, with widespread religious fervour continuing to maintain itself, the production at ecclesiastical establishments of conveniently brief examples of the dramatic *Visitatio Sepulchri* continued in the simple form of the '*Quem quaeritis*' dialogue (with or without introductory material); then dismissal (with or without recall and second dismissal); and finally, choral rejoicings. Let us consider first a couple of French versions, notable more for their artistic appearance and notational interest than for their dramatic merits.

B.N. 1235 from Nevers, a beautiful Gradual, shows what swift progress had been made in France in notational exactitude of pitch. There are F and c clef-lines together with end-of-line 'directs'; also, since the '*Quem quaeritis*' dialogue is transposed up a fourth, the necessary B flats are provided. The version is indeed the twin of *B.N. 9449*, also from Nevers and belonging to the previous century, but notated only in unheighted neumes. Both of them make a most exceptional musical start to the first dialogue sentence, which I express as

---

[1] The fourth Vercelli trope version, *MS 56* (eleventh to twelfth century) has a normal musical beginning to the dialogue, and moreover, *includes* the second vocative phrase ('*o caelicolae*').

[2] '*Hodie exultent justi . . .*' seems to be an Italian trope as far as the *Quem quaeritis* dialogue is concerned. However, it appears as an internal trope of the Introit '*Resurrexi . . .*' in *St. Gall MS 484*, with what looks like very much the same music.

[3] See pp. 71, 112, 116.   [4] See p. 71.

dr rmr dr r-, reminiscent of the start of *Vercelli 146* and *162* (this latter fact I do not attempt to labour). Both the Nevers versions have a musical rhyme at the vocative phrases—rm rd m fm r-, borrowed apparently from the Limoges tropers' usual setting of '*o caelicolae*'. It is a privilege shared by *B.N. 12044*, *Brit. Mus. 37399* (thirteenth century), and the famous and more extensive 'Dublin Play' (*Oxford Bodl. Rawlinson liturg. d.iv*—fourteenth century). Like a few other French examples, *B.N. 1235* uses the less soaring setting of '*Non est hic*' (d r rl).[1]

B.N. 12044, from Fossata, is another beautiful but unambitious manuscript, its Norman-French notation utterly reliable on four stavelines with F and c clefs (on one occasion it actually marks an 'e' line). It also shows an early use of the 'hard B' (B *durum*) to cancel a B flat sign. This version, like the last, rounds off simply with the normal French trope, '*Alleluia, resurrexit Dominus hodie . . .*' to the usual setting, but, unlike *B.N. 1235*, the dialogue music, including '*Non est hic*', is normal.

Of much more dramatic interest and originality than the first two versions is the far-travelled *Madrid C. 132*. It is of Norman origin, as its carefully heighted neumes round a faintly scratched line plainly show. It represents a Sicilian use, brought there by Sicily's Norman conquerors. Yet it found its way to a Spanish abiding-place. Whoever the dramatist and composer was (or were), we have here, in brief, real composition instead of arrangement and adaptation. For example, here is the earliest appearance of an original 'lament' approach to the Tomb by the Marys, each in turn singing a short stanza, the first being[2]

He – u! mi-se-re cur con-ti-git vi-de-re mor-tem Sal-va-to-ris?
A – las!__ why this pit-iable hap-pen-ing to see the death of the Sa-vi-our?

The two other Marys follow, each with her individual tune. The probability is that the music was sung in rhythmic fashion. The actual lines are found in longer '*Visitatios*': in the 'Dublin Play' previously mentioned; in *Orléans 201* (in an appendix to the '*Visitatio*'); in *Tours 927* (thirteenth century); and finally, in the earlier version (twelfth to thirteenth century) of the so-called 'Dutch Easter Play' (*Hague, Royal Library, MS 71 J. 70*), the existence of which has not very long since come to the knowledge of scholars.[3] I have charted the three sets of double lines, together with the music as given by all the versions mentioned above, most of them later than *Madrid C. 132*. My chart

---

[1] As do *Paris, Ste Geneviève 117* (thirteenth century); *Paris, Arsenal 595* (fourteenth century); *B.N. 904* (twelfth century); *Rouen 252* (fourteenth century); *Reims 265* (twelfth to thirteenth century); *B.N. 269* (fourteenth century). I suspect a Rouen origin for the variation. For other links between these manuscripts, see p 80.

[2] I have transposed the original music up a fourth, adding B flat. See also p. 297.

[3] See p. 181.

shows a great deal of similarity between the settings, except that Madrid is a good deal more single-minded than the rest.

The next section again strikes an original note. The reaction of the three Marys at the sight of the stone ('*O Deus! Quis revolvet nobis . . .*') has nothing to do with the established music for this sentence. It is repeated by a single Mary, who once again brings a new touch of dramatic invention by crying out, '*Ecce lapis revolutus, et juvenis stola candida co-opertus!*'[1] The device, and a good deal of the music, seems to have been 'lifted' by the 'Dutch Easter Play', and by that prince of borrowers, the scribe of *Tours 927* (as we shall see in Chapter Thirteen). Madrid, again to original music, then neatly links on to the *Quem quaeritis* dialogue by the sentence, '*Nolite timere vos: dicite (quem quaeritis . . .*')', this device also used (and probably borrowed) by the Tours and 'Dutch' versions.

The Madrid dialogue music is normal, with a musical rhyme at the vocative words,[2] but after '*surrexit sicut predixerat*' the dramatist proceeds to reshape familiar material. The section is, in fact, a working of St. Matthew xxviii: 6–7, and St. Mark xvi: 6–7; and the '*Venite et videte . . .*' invitation is secured without any previous awkward dismissal. The whole of the section, from '*venite*' to '*sicut dixit vobis*', though containing familiar phrases, is, as far as I can discover, set to original music. Again, the dramatically fitting sentence '*Eamus, nuntiate mirum . . .*' seems unique, both words and setting. By contrast, the sentence which follows, '*Surrexit vere (enim) sicut . . .*' has already been met in a number of versions. The Madrid music follows one of the two regular melodies. The setting of '*Deo gratias, alleluia!*', sung by the choir in conclusion, is found among '*Visitatio*' versions elsewhere only in *Rouen MS 252*, as far as I am aware.

If I were seeing the *origin* of the far-journeying *Madrid MS C. 132*, I would incline towards the diocese of Rouen.

The German-derived 'first stage' *Visitatio* versions are on the whole as dull as they are brief. They are detailed in Appendix Ie, and it can be said that among them only *B.N. 9488, Stuttgart 4° 36*, and *Munich 23037* make any attempt to supply rubrics giving details of performances, these concerned mainly with the recovery and display of the *sudarium*. Only two versions have anything for their text settings but unheighted St. Gall neumes, these exceptions being *Utrecht 407*—Gothic ('horse-shoe nail') notation—; and *Udine F. 25*, the particular manuscript page of which has suffered rough handling, the area of vellum beginning at '*Quis revolvet nobis*' and continuing up to '*Te Deum laudamus*' having been thoroughly scraped and a rather blotty version of the new dialogue, '*Quem quaeritis, o tremulae mulieres . . .*' having been written in, probably substituting for the older dialogue. The manuscript comes from Tarvisio, north of Venice, and the notation, heighted round a single

[1] See St. Mark, xvi:3–5.

[2] *Madrid C. 132* writes in the second line of the dialogue: '*Jesum Nazarenum crucifixum querimus . . .*'. Uniquely, the scribe of *Tours 927*, does the same. A few other French versions include '*querimus*', but at a different place in the line.

157

horizontal line, appears to be that of Central Italy. Nevertheless, the influence is German. The rest of the German versions that we are considering chose to remain loyal to '*Quem quaeritis in sepulchro . . .*' (the music of course in the St. Gall style) in spite of the fact that two of them use the revised '*Quis revolvet nobis ab hostio . . .*', usually associated with the '*Quem quaeritis, o tremulae mulieres . . .*' dialogue.

The few introductory and rounding-off tropes or antiphons used by this group are all familiar. In the case of *Munich 14845* there is no sign of '*Te Deum laudamus*', but the version is certainly dramatic, and the unfamiliar sentences that follow '*Surrexit Dominus de sepulchro . . .*' are clearly irrelevant.

There must now be mentioned a Spanish *Visitatio* of the mid-twelfth century, belonging to the Cathedral Library of Santiago de Compostela. For centuries this torn and crumpled fragment had served the purpose of assisting in the binding of another manuscript. Yet somehow a brief *Visitatio Sepulchri* has survived, and can (with difficulty) still be read. Its music shows it to be linked with Limoges, particularly with *B.N. MS lat. 1139*, and also with the Vich versions.

A French gradual, *Reims 265*, belonging possibly to the first years of the new century, has a short *Visitatio* with some unusual features—an introductory threefold flourish, '*O Deus!*'; the first neume of the dialogue as dr (instead of rd); and the fairly rare appearance of the musical notation of Metz, written on a four-line stave. There is a musical rhyme (rm mr d mfm r-) at the vocative phrases; and (to return very much to normal) '*Alleluia, resurrexit Dominus hodie . . .*' at the end.

Another turn-of-the-century version, the German *Bamberg MS 22*, a short and simple St. Gall-style example with unheighted neumes, would scarcely merit our attention were it not for its striking introduction. Here, some talented medieval poet-musician has taken the familiar sentence, '*Ad monumentum venimus gementes . . .*', paraphrased it into five lines of verse, and not only set the words charmingly, but provided an echo effect as well. I have no doubt that the composition was sung rhythmically, and I feel that space must be found for such an excellent example of medieval artistry, which probably served as a choral accompaniment to the Marys' movements towards the Sepulchre. The 'echo' technique, whereby one side of the choir sang a phrase, the melody of which was vocalized to a vowel sound by the other, was a liturgical trick found more readily in later centuries. This present occurrence is the earliest that I have met. Incidentally, I should have been quite helpless in front of the unheighted St. Gall neumes of the paraphrase without my large-scale charts, which revealed to me a fifteenth-century Bamberg manuscript (*MS lit. 27*) that had faithfully preserved the melody and had written it on a four-line stave in heavy '*Hufnagel*' neumes.

In the manuscript the 'echo' music is indicated by the letter A, an extended horizontal line and a stream of close-packed neumes overhead. Karl Young, who printed the five lines of text (I, p. 585), wondered whether the neumes represented some kind of *jubilus*, or an '*Alleluia*' setting. A touch of medieval artistry can be seen in the composer's handling of the 'echo'. The first three lines proceed normally—sung text and vocalization. But since the fifth line is shorter than the rest the echo of the fourth is delayed, the two last lines of text-singing joined, and a 'combined' echo used to finish off. I give now a modern transcription of the item. The music is transposed upward a fourth, with B flat.

Bamberg, Staatsbibliothek, MS lit. 22, Grad. Bambergense, saec. xii–xiii, fol. 128r:

IV

In the twelfth century we first encounter *Visitatio* versions which take heed of the account given by St. John in the first ten verses of his twentieth chapter. This relates the discovery by Mary Magdalen of the empty Sepulchre; of her bewildered report to the chief disciple, Peter; and of the latter's hastening to the Tomb, accompanied (and indeed, outrun) by the 'other disciple', the youthful John himself. There, they find confirmation of Mary's words and take note of the abandoned grave

159

clothes. The final verse says simply that 'they went away to their own home'.

The music-dramas in due course made more of the episode than that, but at least there must have occurred something of a thrill among what onlookers there might happen to be at a performance, when two figures, issuing probably from the west end of the nave, hurtled through their surprised ranks on their way to the 'Sepulchre'. There seem to have been various attempts during the centuries to present the two disciples fittingly; Peter as old and bearded, in some cases as limping, and on one occasion, as holding a symbolic key (this in the so-called 'Dublin Play'); and John as young and smooth-cheeked. Some note will be taken of versions with informative rubrics, as we meet with them. It is curious to note that, with one exception only, the 'Dublin Play' (discussed on pp. 358–62), all of these so-called 'Second Stage' *Visitatio Sepulchri* versions surviving are German in origin.

The main action of the episode is described in the fourth verse of the Vulgate version in these terms: '*Currebant duo simul et ille alius discipulus praecucurrit citius Petro et venit prior ad monumentum, alleluia.*' As it happened, the verse had become a well-known antiphon,[1] and was borrowed by most second-stage *Visitatios* for use as most appropriate choral 'background music'[2] to the Race itself. Sometimes, directions for the Race were given without even *incipit* mention of the antiphon; sometimes the antiphon was called for without mention of the race of the disciples; but in each case it is probable that the naming of one presupposed awareness of the other. Karl Young (I, p. 354) mentions an extreme case, concerned with a breviary version (without music) of the fifteenth century from Herzogenburg, a performance in which Peter and John first chanted the verse, and then proceeded to suit the actions to the words.

Some versions, not content with a dumb-show for Peter and John, took over a sentence hitherto sung by the Marys, '*Cernitis, o socii . . .*', at the same time displaying the grave clothes, this in defiance of the Gospel account, but no doubt the playwright was determined to have a climax for his disciples at any cost. Let us now consider two twelfth-century *Visitatio* versions, which represent the earliest survivors of this 'Second Stage' type.

The text of the first, *Vienna 1890*, can be seen on p. 629 of Karl Young's first volume. The music, in St. Gall unheighted neumes, follows a normal sort of 'St. Gall' course in the dialogue, using the older ('*Quem quaeritis in sepulchro . . .*') exchange. Oddly enough, the introductory antiphon, '*Quis revolvet . . .*', sung by the Marys, still retains its prefacing, and here unnecessary, '*Et dicebant ad invicem . . .*'. An

---

[1] The antiphon, with its music, can be seen in *Antiphonale Romanum*, p. 380 (*Sabbato in Albis*).

[2] This choral description of something which is being simultaneously translated into action may seem incongruous to some people. But having listened to the episode on several cathedral occasions, I have found the combined effects of the vigorous action and the powerful antiphon to be very striking.

unusual feature is the use of a rare and now obsolete antiphon, '*Et recordatae sunt verborum eius . . .*' (the neumes given are those of Hartker, p. 232). The only notice as to the Race is the rubric *Duo Apostoli*, and the incipit, '*Currebant duo simul, et ille . . .*', with its neumes.[1] Afterwards, Apostles and Marys sing together (an unusual choral combination) the antiphon '*Dicant nunc Judaei . . .*', and the officiating priest, '*Surrexit enim sicut . . .*'. No mention is made of any display of the grave clothes.

The second twelfth-century version comes from the famous monastery of St. Lambrecht at Graz, *Graz, II. 798*. Here we meet with much fuller performance rubrics (see Karl Young, I, p. 363). As Young reports (p. 365) 'The angel sits upon a *lapis* placed outside the sepulchre, and raises a curtain to reveal the interior of the burial place. The grave-clothes are a fillet, or bandeau, in which the shaft and arms of the cross [i.e., the cross of the "Depositio" ceremony] were wrapped, and a sudary which was placed over the head of the cross. The persons chosen to act the parts of the apostles are of different ages; an old man to represent Peter, and a youth for the part of John. It is to be observed, however, that after the visit of the apostles to the tomb it is not they, but the Marys, who display the grave-clothes and elevate the cross. This re-entering of the women into the action at the close gives to the composition a certain effect of unity.'

Further features must be mentioned. The dialogue is cast in the newer mould—'*Quem quaeritis, o tremulae mulieres . . .?*'—with a preliminary '*Quis revolvet nobis ab ostio lapidem . . .?*'. Each item has its normal music. The tomb inspection is invited through the long-established '*Venite et videte . . .*', and the Marys retire to '*Ad monumentum venimus gementes . . .*'.

Then there occurs for the first time a feature that was to become well established in *Visitatio Sepulchri* versions, the dramatic use of the *Victimae paschali* sequence. Already, on pp. 57–8, I have set out this famous eleventh-century composition, and have mentioned that while the first part appears to be no more than a lyrical call to all Christians to praise the Paschal Victim, the second contains the possibilities of a dramatic dialogue between the three Marys (or a single one) returning from the tomb with news of the Resurrection, and the questioning disciples. I mentioned on that occasion that some *Visitatio* versions employed the whole of the sequence. Others, with better dramatic effect, began with the '*Dic nobis*' question, as coming from the disciples. With some few exceptions (our scribe from Tours among them), the versions that made use of the sequence texts were careful to preserve the music accurately.

Returning to the case of *Graz 798*, we find there that the first part of the sequence is disregarded, the episode beginning with the '*Dic nobis*'

---

[1] It becomes apparent that an ordinary brief 'first stage' *Visitatio* could be turned into a 'second stage' one, merely by adding a rubric and the '*Currebant duo simul . . .*' incipit; which was exactly what seems to have happened in some cases.

question—asked, however, not by the disciples but by the whole fraternity. The three reply-phrases are delivered, respectively and separately, by the three Marys; and then again the whole fraternity joins in to round off the sequence by singing the last lines. Later dramas using *Victimae paschali* found other ways of varying the procedure. Certainly the disciples were most often the questioners.

Graz 798 gives us yet another new feature, since, the sequence completed, it is revealed that there has been present a secular congregation. A rubric states that '*tunc incipiat ipsa plebs istum clamorem*', followed by a line in German ('Giengen dreie vrovven ce vronem grabe')[1] which bears no sign of music. As the 'clamour' dies away, the Race begins, as does '*Currebant duo simul . . .*', sung by a cantor. Then follows the display of the grave clothes already referred to, and the rendering of the phrase '*Surrexit Dominus de sepulchro*', in '*voce conclamantes*'. Unlike most of the uttered texts of the drama, this, like the German phrase, is given no neumes. It may be that it was shouted, as it were 'in excess of joy'.

We meet yet another item for the first time in Church music-drama. This is the famous vernacular hymn '*Crist*[2] *ist erstanden*'. The Graz version is the earliest known of its kind to make use of it. The rubric, placing its mention after the *Te Deum* of the liturgical choir, is somewhat ambiguous. It says merely '. . . *plebs conclamante "Crist ist erstanden"* ', and again there are no neumes. Was this another shouting, or was the phrase, or a stanza, or stanzas, to be sung to the established melody? The same *incipit* in the thirteenth-century *Nuremberg 22923* gives us recognizable neumes, while the fourteenth-century *Klosterneuberg 1213* includes a whole stanza. Karl Young discusses the composition on I, p. 636, and sets out the stanza most likely to have been used in connection with the Church music-dramas; this is indeed the one found in *Klosterneuberg 1213*.[3] I have myself gathered some photographs of manuscript pages that have recorded the music (these mostly of the fifteenth and sixteenth centuries) and have here transcribed what seems to be a representative version of the tune, based upon a Munich manuscript (*Codex 716*), and setting the stanza quoted by Karl Young. The stanzas can be found in somewhat varied forms,[4] as can remaining stanzas.

Christ ist er – stan – den von der mar-ter al – le, Des sul wir al – le
Christ is___ ri – sen from___ all___ suf – f'rings. For that we all___

---

[1] For further note of this sentence, see p. 163. Karl Young corrects a letter of the manuscript original.

[2] The rubric spellings vary between 'Crist' and 'Christ'.

[3] The Klosterneuberg manuscript is printed in Young, I, pp. 329–30. For my discussion of it, see p. 363.

[4] I have to admit that the *Codex 716*, the music of which I have used above, has as its second line, '*Judas ist derhangen*', instead of the more usual one that I give. I should add that, among the various versions, various spellings of '*Alleluia*' and '*Kyrieleyson*' will be met with.

fro sein; Christ wil un – ser   trost sein.__ } al – le – lu – ia!
re – joice; Christ will be our   com – fort.__ }

With regard to the vernacular line uttered earlier in the Graz version by the '*plebs*', '*Giengen dreie vrovven ce vronem grabe*', acknowledging the presence of the three Marys, this may have had something to do with a recognized stanza which began:

> Es giengen drei heylig Frawen
> sic wollen das grab beschawen . . .[1]

Before leaving *Victimae paschali*, we should note that, though the sequence seems to have been composed in the eleventh century, it was slow to enter the Church music-dramas. Only a few examples of its use are met with in the twelfth and thirteenth centuries, many more in the fourteenth to sixteenth. Yet, remembering the shattered state of such manuscripts as the Compostela fragment, we must allow for the likelihood of much material having been lost.

V

The Gospel authority for many of the details of the *Visitatio Sepulchri* has frequently been noted, including the last addition, the Race of Peter and John. With further material at hand from the Latin Gospels, it is not surprising to find other episodes being added, the first and most obvious being the appearance of Christ after his Resurrection. Dramas of this type have been classified by Karl Young as 'Third Stage'.

St. Matthew, St. Mark, and St. John in varying detail mention his meeting with one or more of the Marys. The factual differences account in part for the variety of treatment which the episode receives in the examples presently to be considered. St. Matthew's account is drawn on mainly because of verse 10 of Chapter xxviii; '*Nolite timere: ite, nuntiate fratribus meis ut eant in Galileam; ibi me videbunt.*' St. Mark (xvi: 9–10) relates in barest terms the meeting of Mary Magdalen with the Risen Christ and of her reporting the fact, while St. Luke makes no mention of the encounter at all. It is St. John who is the source of most of the material employed in the 'Third Stage' dramas, describing first Mary's meeting at the empty tomb with two angels and her speech with them; and then her turning away to encounter the supposed gardener. When treated dramatically, her question, the single gentle word from Jesus in reply, followed by her impassioned cry of recognition, make an effective and moving scene. Since so many sentences from St. John's account will be found unchanged in the Latin libretto texts, I have ventured to set down verses 11 to 18 in full:

---

[1] 'There went three holy women;
They wished to visit the sepulchre.'

Maria autem stabat ad monumentum foris, plorans: Dum ergo fleret, inclinavit se, et prospexit in monumentum:
Et vidit duos angelos in albis, sedentes, unum ad caput, et unum ad pedes, ubi positum fuerat corpus Jesu.
Dicunt ei illi: Mulier, quid ploras? Dicit eis: Quia tulerunt Dominum meum: et nescio ubi posuerunt eum.
Haec cum dixisset, conversa est retrorsum, et vidit Jesum: et non sciebat quia Jesus est.
Dicit ei Jesus: Mulier, quid ploras? Quem quaeris? Illa existimans quia hortulanus esset, dicit ei: Domine, si tu sustulisti eum, dicito mihi ubi posuisti eum, et ego eum tollam.
Dicit ei Jesus: Maria. Conversa illa dicit ei: Rabboni (quod dicitur, magister).
Dicit ei Jesus: Noli me tangere, nondum enim ascendi ad Patrem meum: vade autem ad fratres meos, et dic eis: Ascendo ad Patrem meum, et Patrem vestrum, Deum meum, et Deum vestrum.
Venit Maria Magdalene annuntians discipulis: Quia vidi Dominum et haec dixit mihi.

There are not many more than a couple of dozen surviving examples of the 'Third Stage' type of *Visitatio*, but most of them are accompanied by a musical setting. The majority of these versions are German, exploiting a great deal of common material, and that in a somewhat rigid fashion at times. The few French examples, notably one that has already been mentioned, a *Visitatio* from *Orléans 201*, show more individuality. An English manuscript, with some unusual moments, suffers from the fact that it is not furnished with its music.[1] The development of the Easter music-drama to this particular stage is thought to have taken place during the second half of the twelfth century. A fragmentary version from Vich,[2] in Spain, goes back to that period, while an argument for not seeking a much earlier date is derived from the existence of a work, hostile to the drama, written in about 1160 by a churchman, Gerhoh of Reichersberg. In his *Libri Tres de Investigatione Antichristi*, a special chapter, *De Spectaculis Theatricis in Ecclesia Dei Exhibitis*, is devoted to a detailed attack on Church drama, including Easter, Christmas, Biblical, and Saint plays. A representation of Christ himself would have been a crowning outrage, but such a happening is not mentioned. The fact of this omission has been used as an indication that either the scene had not yet been invented at that time, or, if it had, it could not have travelled far from its source, otherwise it would have come to the notice of the well-informed Gerhoh.[3]

---

[1] *Oxford, University College MS 169 (Ordinarium)*, pp. 121–4. This *Visitatio* was another product of the energies of Barking Abbey's forceful fourteenth-century Abbess, the Lady Catherine Sutton (see p. 14). The loss of the music of this fine composition is a loss indeed.
[2] *Vich, Museo, MS 105*, fols. 58v.–62r.
[3] This argument was advanced by E. K. Chambers (*Medieval Stage, II*, pp. 98–9), and supported by Karl Young, I, p. 369. Young cites the relevant passage from Gerhoh, (II, p. 524).

Whatever the truth of the matter, the fact is that some time (possibly late) in the twelfth century there was copied out in the so-called 'Fleury Playbook', in company with other Latin music-dramas (most of them of vastly less moment) a work of original genius, which, to my mind, deserves an honourable place in the history of the development of opera.[1] I do not at the moment propose to devote any general attention to the 'Fleury Playbook', once preserved at the monastery of St. Benoit de Fleury located at St. Benoit-sur-Loire (*Orléans, B. de la Ville, MS 201*) or its other contents in particular. This will be the subject of our Chapter Twelve. But I do wish to give some time to this particular Easter play.

The first rubric of the Orléans *Visitatio* (in translation) is as follows:

In representing the visit to the sepulchre let three of the brethren, prepared beforehand, and costumed in the likeness of the three Marys, advance slowly as if in mourning, singing in turn these stanzas:

Thus the scene is set. In some great twelfth-century church building Easter Matins were being concluded, and what lookers-on there happened to be in the nave had their attention fixed on the choir, who behind their screen were singing the last notes of the final responsory, '*Dum transisset sabbatum, Maria Magdalene, et Maria Jacobi, et Salome emerunt aromata, ut venientes ungerent Jesum*'. As they concluded, the word-picture took on living shape, and from the western end of the nave, possibly to the momentary bewilderment of the hearers, came the far-off, mournful cry of '*He-u!*', as the three Marys began their slow advance towards the distant 'Sepulchre'. The 'distance' can be vouched for, since no less than ten stanzas of vocal music are sung by the Marys, in turn— stanzas of lament and of purpose—before we learn from the rubrics that they have reached the entrance of the choir. Thus far, all has been invented material, words and music. Very similar texts for most of the stanzas can be found in other French *Visitatio* music-dramas, such as *Madrid 132*, the 'Dublin Play' from Oxford, *Tours 927*, even some scattered lines from German versions, such as *Nuremberg 22923*. But the *music* of the ten sections of the Orléans 'entrance' scene belongs just to itself, as far as I can discover—unique and beautiful.

It is obvious that we are dealing with not only a rhyming and rhythmic text, but with a rhythmic and novel setting as well. Music phrases are repeated and patterns maintained, such as that of the first line:

Pi - us   pas - tor   oc - ci - dit ...

while something quite out of the Gregorian world occurs at the refrains of the third and fourth stanzas (I quote the third):

[1] The text of *Orléans, MS 201, Visitatio Sepulchri* (pp. 220–5) is printed by Karl Young (I, pp. 393–7).

We have previously met with plenty of plainchant melismas, but never this most exotic chain of falling thirds![1]

In my own transcription of the work,[2] I rendered the music of the first six stanzas as in duple time, finding that, in my opinion, this suited best the scansions of the Latin verse. One could describe the setting as being in the transposed first (re) mode, the scribe himself having been responsible for the B flat at the beginning of each of the first six staves of the manuscript page. It is my belief that with the advent of the seventh stanza the original composer took heed of the change of mood apparent in the text. The Marys decide that they have mourned long enough; it is now time for positive action. The first says: *'Eamus ergo propere...'* ('Now let us therefore quickly go, with minds devout, to do the only thing possible...'), while the musician, having, even in the twelfth century, a resource that will enable him also to show his change of 'mood', that of 'modulation' in the medieval sense, cuts out the B flat as a clef sign and gives us

—that is, a temporary A mode.

I believe (although I cannot prove the idea) that at the same time another effect was obtained, in keeping with this new spirit of resolution —a change to triple time; a speeding-up. This is what I arranged for in my own rhythmic transcription; and with quite satisfactory results in regard both to Latin accents and to stage effects.

Having mended their paces and reached the entrance to the choir, the Marys become aware of the proximity of the 'Sepulchre', and recall a possible difficulty, one that had faced a couple of centuries of 'Marys' before them: *'Quis revolvet nobis lapidem ab ostio monumenti?'*. The Orléans playwright-composer (let us blend the two, for convenience and perhaps with likelihood) gracefully paraphrases the liturgical text in the form of a rhyming couplet, and sets it to a delightful and unique melody. I quote it here in rhythmic form and on a modern stave.[3]

---

[1] I have, unusually, written these two examples in plainchant notation; this for the edification of those readers accustomed to plainchant, who will realize how 'exotic' the *'Plebs'* passage looks in the circumstances.

[2] *Visitatio Sepulchri*, transcribed and translated by W. L. Smoldon (Oxford University Press, revised edition, 1967).

[3] We must credit *Orléans 201* with this composition, but must note that the 'Dublin Play' of the fourteenth century (see pp. 358–62), which shows a number of links with *Orléans 201*, knows of the same couplet, but has a tune of its own (also a very pleasant one) to fit to it. Incidentally, the key signatures of examples written in modern notation are merely those of convenience, as used in published editions.

The matter of the stone is forgotten as the Marys' attention is taken by the sight of the Angel 'seated outside at the head of the sepulchre'. His voice is 'quiet and grave' as he sings the familiar question' *'Quem quaeritis in sepulchro . . . ?'*. The music of *'O Christicolae'* is individual, and there is no attempt at a musical rhyme. The notes of the Marys' reply (*'Jesum Nazarenum . . .'*) could have come from one or another of the later Limoges tropers (e.g. *B.N. MS 1118*), but what follows displays the essential originality of the man who was shaping this music-drama. He proceeds to write a rhythmic and extended fantasy on the standard prose sentence *'Non est hic . . .'*. It is so altogether unique in medieval music-drama that I feel called on to quote it in full. The first phrase, *'Quid, Christicolae'* actually employs the previous *'Quem quaeritis'* setting, before breaking free; the mention of *'Non est hic'* is accompanied by the usual upward leap of a fifth; thereafter, text and music go their own original way.

Although there is no rubric to the effect, the Angel now apparently leaves the scene, since he is not there when Mary Magdalen inspects the tomb before uttering her solo lament. Meanwhile, the three women turn to the onlookers and sing what seems to be an antiphon, *'Ad monumen-*

tum Domini venimus . . .', one which apparently we have met before (see
p. 122) as being, not liturgical but specially composed for the *Visitatio*
type, and used by more than thirty versions to a standard tune. It turns
out, however, that the Orléans text is somewhat differently shaped and
the music altogether so—so often another instance of Orléans' great
individuality!

It would seem that the other two Marys now leave the scene, since
Mary Magdalen appears to be alone as she turns towards the tomb again
and utters her lament, a beautiful composition, unique to the Orléans
version. I give it in full, transcribed into modern notation:

A rubric now informs us that Mary has seen, at a distance, the two
disciples, Peter and John. She hastens to them and sings another finely
constructed, rhymed, and rhythmed composition, unique to *Orléans 201.*
Some of the same textual material from the Gospel is to be found in two
Easter pieces, a responsory and an antiphon, but there are no musical
links. The first line crops up in other *Visitatio* versions, but again
Orléans stands alone in its music. This time I give only the first two
sentences:

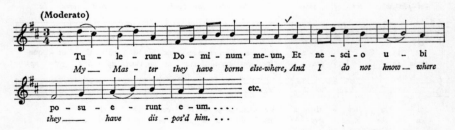

We can easily anticipate the next rubric, which begins (I translate):
'Hearing this, then let the disciples run swiftly to the Sepulchre . . .'.
What we might also anticipate, but will find lacking, is any mention of
the liturgical antiphon, '*Currebant duo simul . . .*', to accompany the Race;

but so usual is its incidence to the action, that I am firmly of the opinion that its employment here can be taken for granted.

In the Gospel account, as in the usual *Visitatio* Race, the disciples go to the Tomb, look within, and silently take their departure. This will not do for the writer of *Orléans 201*. He proceeds to invent a rhyming musical debate for the two after they emerge, on the meaning of what they have found; an item that no other *Visitatio* thought of imagining. I give no more than the first exchange, which is then continued for four more sentences:

Meanwhile, it would seem, the neglected Mary Magdalen has remained at a distance, a silent spectator, since a new rubric says: 'Then when they have gone away, Mary will come to the sepulchre, and will say . . .'.

What she says, in fact, is *'Heu, dolor! Heu! quam dira doloris angustia!'* She has received no comfort from the disciples' intervention; thus a repeat of her lament is dramatically fitting. The spoken words from St. John xx: 13–17 provide the libretto for the following scene, which is frequently called the 'Christ-Magdalen' scene.

At this point a short digression is in order. We may note that these same verses—St. John xx: 13–17—serve as a common 'libretto' for all 'third stage' *Visitatio* versions, but usually with very little agreement among the musical settings. Occasionally there are exceptions, however, and one of these seems particularly significant to me. Starting with the *'Mulier, quid ploras . . . ?'* of the Angels, there begins (to me) a notable partnership of Orléans with the thirteenth-century *Visitatio* from Rouen, *B.N. MS 904*. Time and again we shall find musical similarities between these two works, which have caused me to wonder whether the original home of the 'Orléans-Fleury' *Visitatio* might not have been the diocese of Rouen . . . I shall in due course mention other reasons for this suspicion. I continue with the Orléans version.

'Quia tulerunt Dominum meum . . .', Mary's reply, has no links with her previous rhymed and rhythmic address to Peter and John, nor indeed with any liturgical music such as that of the Easter Responsory using the same words (and following them with *'Mulier, quid ploras?'*). However, the *Orléans* item is duplicated in *Rouen B.N. MS 904*, the free-rhythm music coinciding almost note for note, though at different pitch-levels. Also, two other versions share the setting, with but a few notes difference. These are the twelfth- to thirteenth-century 'Dutch

Easter Play' and the thirteenth-century *Tours, MS 927*. Both are later than *Orléans 201*, as far as can be ascertained, and I suspect that both may have used material from other sources, especially Tours. I shall give adequate attention to each of them at the appropriate places.

Orléans' next item, the reassuring '*Noli flere, Maria . . .*', is an interpolation into the St. John account, and might be assumed to be the Easter Respond with that text, but once again Orléans is unique in its setting. However, a second interpolation, Mary's '*Ardens est cor meum . . .*', proves to be a borrowing; its music is that of the well-known antiphon, found in the *Antiphonale Romanum*, p. 391.

Both *Orléans* and *Rouen B.N. 904* use the same music for the '*Mulier, quid ploras?*' of the Angels—as well as re-using it when the 'Gardener' asks the same question, an economy practised by the versions from *Tours, St. Quentin* (fourteenth century), and the 'Dutch Easter Play', each with its own musical setting.

Orléans' next item, Mary's '*Domine, si tu sustulisti eum . . .*', though the text is from St. John, has its own non-liturgical setting. Those of *Rouen, St. Quentin*, and the 'Dutch Easter Play,' have a good deal in common, among themselves and also with *Orléans*.

Now comes the dramatic highlight of the scene. The *Orléans* writer continues his musical economy by using, for his setting of Christ's gentle '*Maria!*', the music of '*Mulier, quid ploras*'. Mary's glad cry of recognition ('*Rabboni*') is set to his own music, as is the succeeding '*Noli me tangere . . .*'.

After the withdrawal of Christ from Mary's touch, and his departure, Mary turns again to the onlookers. Once again *Orléans'* music seems to be original, even though the text, '*Congratulamini mihi omnes . . .*' is that of an Easter responsory, now obsolete (see Hartker, p. 233).

No clue is given in the manuscript as to when the other two Marys reappear. A good place seems to be towards the end of this, Mary Magdalen's joyful announcement. There follows the Angels' invitation to the Marys, '*Venite et videte . . .*'. Long before, the Winchester Troper had used this text, quoting an antiphon, a practice which, as we already know, was widely followed. But the music that the *Orléans* writer employs is a liturgical borrowing from the '*Angelus Domini . . .*' responsory of East Matins; (both *Rouen* and the 'Dublin Play' use the same setting). The appendage, '*Nolite timere vos*', is, as far as I am aware, *not* given liturgical music, but *Rouen* sets the same brief text very similarly.

'*Vultum tristem . . .*', sung by the Angels, is an original rhyming passage, set to rhythmic music, unique, and with music apparently of the *Orléans* writer's own composition. The same text is to be found in the somewhat later 'Dutch Easter Play' to a different and simpler tune.

Again the Angels hark back to earlier times to secure the Marys' dismissal, using the ancient liturgical antiphon, '*Cito euntes dicite discipulis . . .*'. Meanwhile the Marys seem to have gained possession of the grave-clothes. As they leave the Angels, they sing '*Surrexit Dominus de sepulchro . . .*', to the invented setting that we have met before, widely used among *Visitatio* versions, and then display the grave-clothes to the onlookers. As they do so they sing another '*Orléans* original', a unique paraphrase of the prose passage, '*Cernitis, o socii, ecce lintheamina . . .*', The *Orléans* composition is an attractive and balanced rhythmic tune in the Aeolian mode. I give a transcription of it, in full:

The Marys now dominate the scene. Having placed the cloths on the altar, they turn once more to the onlookers and sing another cleverly constructed and original effort by the *Orléans* writer, found nowhere else. It consists of two three-line rhyming stanzas, the rubrics directing that each set of three lines shall be divided between the three Marys. I give only the first stanza:

There follows now the moment of climax, the reappearance of the risen Christ. The original rubrics called for as splendid a robing as a medieval churchman could imagine. The effect on the assembled company is also imagined, and no doubt made plain in action, since his first words are '*Nolite timere vos!*'. He passes on to command them to announce his resurrection to all the disciples. The Gospel-derived liturgical phrases are familiar, but the free-rhythm setting seems to be the *Orléans* writer's own. Following this, '*omnes*' (whomever that comprises) take part in the singing of a modified text of the widely used trope, '*Alleluia, resurrexit hodie Dominus . . .*'; but as far as I know, *Orléans*' music to it is unique. Then comes the rounding-off which the fortunate position of the *Visitatio* type always affords. As the rubric now says: '*Et chorus dicat Te Deum laudamus.*'

The music-drama which we have just considered must surely rank as a work of art, judged by any standard. If the historical perspective is borne in mind, however, then we can hardly avoid a problem similar to that caused by the Freising 'Herod' example. When one seeks for signs of some kinds of evolutionary stages to account for the subtleties, the confident originalities that are to be found in this *Orléans* version; in its long progress, from the initial cry of despair and bewilderment, through item after item of original poetry and music to the choral triumph (*'omnes insimul'*) of '. . . *leo fortis, Christus, filius Dei!'*, then it will be realized that such evidence just isn't there. A streak of the same originality may perhaps be perceived in the much briefer (first stage) *Madrid 132* of the same century (and perhaps of the same Norman diocese). Also, there can be found other small signs of initiative (such as the 'echo' introduction of *Bamberg 22*) among the many straightforward *Visitatio* versions that we have so far considered, a fair proportion of which deserve no more than the description 'commonplace'. All these seem to indicate nothing very remarkable in the way of progress from the Winchester dramatic example of two centuries before, with its trope-adapted, straightforward *Quem quaeritis* exchanges followed by the exploitation of a few relevant antiphons.

Can we believe that in the intervening period of time all *Visitatio* versions that could have given suggestions to the framer of the much more ambitious *Orléans* structure have sunk without trace? Certainly much evidence exists to show that the destruction rate of vellum surfaces, especially those that were not wholly 'official', was a fairly high one. If this is the answer, then whatever attempts there were at expanding the *Visitatio* form in the twelfth century seem to have been particularly unlucky. That there were stirrings, attempts to expand from from the 'second stage', will be seen when we consider some few other surviving attempts to create 'third stage' *Visitatios* in the twelfth century, but doing so on more formal, less spontaneous and successful lines than the *Orléans* framework.

Before I leave *Orléans 201* I shall mention again that 'lament of the Marys' which I spoke of on p. 156 as appearing earliest in the 'first stage' *Madrid MS 132*. I also indicated that the items were found as an appendix to the actual *Orléans* drama, having been added, probably, so that they could serve as alternatives, or perhaps as additions, to those laments sung by the three Marys during their first advance. These items, together with one other not found in *Madrid 132* concern, henceforward, so many other *Visitatio* versions that I believe I am justified in transcribing them, together with the music that *Orléans* supplies:

Prima
He-u! mi-se-ræ cur con-ti-git vi-de-re mor-tem Sal-va-to-ris?
A-las! why this pi-ti-a-ble hap-pen-ing to see the death of the Sa-viour?

Secunda
He-u! Re-dem-pti-o Is-ra-el, ut quid mor-tem sus-ti-nu-it?
A-las! the Re-dee-mer of Is-ra:-el, why was it that he suf-fer'd death?

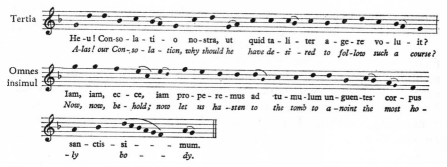

Tertia

He -u! Con-so-la-ti-o no-stra, ut quid ta-li-ter a-ge-re vo-lu-it?
A-las! our Con-so-la-tion, why should he have de-si-red to fol-low such a course?

Omnes insimul

Iam, iam, ec-ce, iam pro-pe-re-mus ad tu-mu-lum un-guen-tes cor-pus
Now, now, be-hold; now let us ha-sten to the tomb to a-noint the most ho-

san-ctis-si-mum.
-ly bo-dy.

There are enough similarities between the *Orléans* music and that of the same items in later *Visitatio* versions as to indicate that in spite of minor divergences, some sort of tradition was at the back of it all.

VII

But to return to the few 'third stage' *Visitatios* of the same period that I have proposed to survey—the first manuscript is a somewhat dis-ordered and quite impracticable one as far as Church music-drama is concerned, but is of considerable historical importance. It now belongs to the library of the Museum at Vich in Spain, a *Troparium-Prosarium* dating from the twelfth century.[1] Until comparatively recently it had been known as *MS 111*, but I am given to understand that its shelf number is now *MS 105*. I have previously mentioned it in connection with dialogued tropes that have imitated the Easter '*Quem quaeritis*' pattern. *Vich 105* contains examples of dramatic tropes of the Introit of the Mass for, respectively, the Feast of St. John the Baptist, and for Ascension Day. While the texts are clearly patterned on the Easter one, no links can be seen between musical settings. The manuscript also contains, on fol. 2r, another example of a '*Quem quaeritis*' Easter Introit trope, following *Vich MS 32*'s music almost exactly except that its own is not transposed.

The folios with which we are mainly concerned are 58v.–62r., the first page headed *VERSES PASCALES DE III M.*[2] The rhyming stanzas that follow are set to music that is, for the first two pages at least, clearly to be distinguished. There is a single, not very carefully drawn, horizontal line. An F clef is given throughout (for as long as the music lasts), and there are intermittent end-of-line directs and Aquitainian notation of reasonably accurate heighting. The latter shares with the text the occasional semi- or total obliterations that occur.

The music shows that the first four rhyming lines are a separate composition.[3] For the time being I propose to leave further considera-

[1] *Vich, Museo, MS 105 (olim 111) Trop.-Prosarium (Ripoll), saec. xii*, fols. 52v.–68r.

[2] '*Mariis*' or '*Mulieribus*' (Karl Young's comment). His valuable discussion of the text of the whole dramatic fragment and its implications will be found on I, pp. 678–82.

[3] Karl Young comments on these (I, pp. 678, 681–2) as having been given importance by K. Dürre. The latter considered them to have been the original literary kernel of the 'Mer-

tion of them and pass on to the second and larger item. This is a series of stanzas [115–33][1] beginning '*Omnipotens Pater altissime . . .*' which I have previously mentioned (p. 151) as having been known all over Europe from the twelfth to the sixteenth century. I have spoken also of the setting of these verses, which maintained its constant framework as an early example of a 'major mode' melody, beginning and ending on 'do' and having the pattern a a b c; 'b' reaching up to the fifth above, and 'c' comprising a refrain. I transcribe *Vich, MS 105*'s first stanza of the composition:

This stanza composition, sung apparently on the way to the sepulchre by the three Marys, continues for three more similar verses to the same music, the refrain indicated only by an incipit '*Heu*'. The gist of this could be summed up as a prayer and a decision to buy ointment ('*unguentum*'). The last stanza is indeed spoken to what proves to be a new figure in Easter music-drama, the *Mercator*—the 'Spice Merchant'. Might the 'Oil Merchants' of *Sponsus* have suggested such a figure? However, Gospel accounts and Easter antiphons have mentioned 'spices' and 'ointments' as having been carried by the Marys; also, there have been rubric mentions of the Marys having been handed their thuribles by an attendant, on the way to the sepulchre. It was a small step to dramatize these details. Anyway, it is *Mercator* who replies to the Marys ('*Mulieres, michi intendite, Hoc unguentum si cultis emere . . .*'), bargaining over his wares to the extent of nine lines, with 'e' rhymes throughout. The musical technique is subtle and artistic; the melody of the Marys' 'a' lines is taken and stripped to a blunter form:

---

chant Scene',—a theory to which Young attaches little credence. I discuss the matter more thoroughly on pp. 306–8.

[1] For the sake of convenience, I shall make use in the course of my discussion of Karl Young's line numberings.

Mu – li – e – res, mi – hi in – ten – di – te.
'La – dies, give ear to what I am say – ing.

The line 'b' setting is retained unchanged, but the refrain is cut out altogether. Thus, the nine lines are covered by three employments of the three line tune, while the Merchant states his terms. One of the Marys (Magdalen?) responds with a single stanza, lament and all, to the normal 'Mary' melody.

What has occurred thus far is what may be the first appearance of a set of stanzas which will soon be met with in certain other 'third stage' Easter Sepulchre music-dramas, these making use also, among themselves, of other groups of rhyming stanzas, which altogether cover, in their fashion, most of the situations found in the *Visitatio* action. Owing to the fact that most of these stanza groups are made up of lines of ten syllables, scholars have tended to follow Wilhelm Meyer in terming this type of music-drama *Zehnsilberspiel*. We shall have much more to say about it as our discussion proceeds.

With the '*Omnipotens Pater . . .*' stanzas completed (I, 33), we move on into what seems to be a major new division of the work, both in form and in content. From here onward (34–86) without any aiding rubrics, there succeed rhyming groups of lines of eight syllables. In a series of stanzas Mary Magdalen addresses her 'sisters', speaking (in unique passages both verbal and musical), of innocence suffering shame and crucifixion at the hands of enemies. She goes on to tell of their hope for the vision of the Resurrection, and then returns to the familiar theme of their having to seek the tomb and anoint the precious body. Altogether we have an episode intended apparently to occupy the time taken in moving from the merchant to the Sepulchre, where we shall meet with familiar material again. Whether the composition can be accredited to Vich or to some source now perished, we shall never know, but the techniques of its musical setting are worth putting on record. The condition of the worn vellum just here, and, altogether, the periodic partial and sometimes total obliterations of text throughout, makes the patient editing and suggestions by Karl Young (who first drew attention to the manuscript) of the utmost value. Any such 'restored' passages that I have used here, I have placed in brackets. The interpretation of the music is an equally difficult task. The whole of the 53 lines of this section is set to a tune (obviously rhythmic) of a pair of sentences, once repeated (X Y X X), together with a fifth (Z). The occurrence of sentence 'Z' is at times delayed through the 'X Y' sentences appearing for a third time. Actually, the scribe responsible for the dreadfully written manuscript, having a large amount of text set to a repeated melody, seizes his chance of effecting an economy of time and space. He supplies the musical material for a couple of times, and then gives nothing more than a close-packed text. The music is present from the last two notes of line 34 to halfway along line 44. Thereafter, it would appear, the singers had to fend for themselves all the way to line 86. One scribal concession was made. Above the beginning of lines 45, 54, 59, and 64 there is to be seen a letter-sign, ·a·. Karl Young (pp. 679–80) remarks on the first two occurrences in a couple of footnotes, and says that he cannot explain their significance. After what I have said above concerning the pattern of the setting, the reason should now be clear. While most of the time the singer could move ahead through the welter of text using sentences 'X' and 'Y' of the musical setting, when it was necessary to employ the rarer sentence, 'Z', the warning—the sign ·a·—was placed at the beginning of the line. The text is very difficult to read round about this point, and I cannot distinguish any more examples of ·a·. But since, from line 64 on, the lines proceed in even pairs, I am assuming that for the rest of the time they were set by the two musical sentences, 'X' and 'Y'.[1]

I now give a transcription with its music of the first five lines of the section. I have rendered the music in first-mode rhythm, and this material suffices to set the whole section (II, p. 34–86): I believe that all the notes B of the tune were intended to be flattened, and thus have given B flat as the clef-sign. The composition seems to me an attractive example of the lyrical, rhyming poetry set to rhythmic music that was beginning to be written everywhere in western Europe in the twelfth century:

Having arrived at line 86, the Marys seem also to have reached the Tomb area, since Mary Magdalen (presumably) asks the rhetorical question, '*Ubi est Christus . . .*'. This little composition, a French and Spanish trope, is found employed in that curious manuscript *B.N. MS 1139*, and also in a couple of other Vich Easter trope versions, one of them in the same (*105*) manuscript, the other in *Vich MS 32*. The trope music of the latter is almost exactly the same as that of the version we are discussing. This applies also to the respective layouts of the Sepulchre dialogue and its music. The trope which follows, leading to the closing '*Te Deum laudamus*', is '*Ad sepulcrum residens angelus nuntiat . . .*', used by a swarm of French and Spanish trope versions of the '*Quem quaeritis*' dialogue, to a common music.

What follows in the manuscript is curious, and is of historical importance. Although in fact not definitely linked with the completed Sepul-

---

[1] Here is another instance of a problem, found insoluble by textual reasoning, yet clarified by musical evidence.

chre drama, there is now sketched the earliest example we possess of the so-called 'Christ-Magdalen' scene, a playwright's dramatization of St. John's account in his Chapter xx of Christ's appearing to Mary in the guise of a gardener, and then revealing himself.

This Vich episode has to introduce itself in some way. It does so by heading the section 'Verses of the Pilgrims' and then supplying six rhyming lines of verse, beginning '*Rex*[1] *in acubitum* . . '. These are sung, apparently, by Mary Magdalen, and appear to place her in a 'garden', bearing her sweet-smelling 'nard', but finding that in spite of all her searchings for him, her 'King' had departed. The lines are set to a simple little rhythmic tune, beginning:

Rex in a - cu - bi - tum iam se con - tu - le - rat - - -

But with the advent of the Gardener and the Vulgate prose of St. John we have 'free rhythm' music. The settings in this Vich version of the Angel's and the Gardener's question, '*Mulier, quid ploras?*', together with Mary's reply to the Angel, seem not to be found elsewhere. Mary's second reply (to the Gardener), '*Tulerunt Dominum meum . . .*', is set to liturgical music.[2] But before Mary's recognition of Christ in the familiar '*Maria–Raboni*' exchange, the music ceases and is no more given. The drama of this moment is somewhat marred by the threefold repeat of both the words '*Maria*' and '*Raboni*', and the glimpse of an attempt to suggest the Gospel gloss ('*Magister*'). The next line is even more astonishing; Mary utters the cryptic sentence, '*Dic, impie Zabule, quid valet nunc fraus tua?*'. Gratefully, I learn from Dr. Richard Donovan[3] that this sentence was borrowed from the prose '*Fulgens praeclara rutilat . . .*', which, he says, was sung at Vespers during Easter week in many Catalan churches. The scene, still without any music, ends with a half-hearted use of some of the dialogued part of *Victimae Paschali*, disciples interrogating Mary, and an Angel intervening with the single sentence, '*Non est hic; surrexit sicut praedixerat . . .*'.

One might assume that this would represent the end of the episode— the 'Christ–Magdalen' scene rounded off in a fairly usual manner. However, on a new line there appear familiar sentences from St. Luke xxiv, the '*Peregrinus*' dialogue, beginning with the Stranger's question, '*Qui sunt hi . . .*' and concluding abruptly with the declaration of the 'two disciples'—'*De Jesu Nazareno, qui fuit vir propheta . . .*'.

This fragment of a *Peregrinus* drama, for that is what it must be, can have no real relevance with what has gone before. I should like to imagine that the initial *Visitatio Sepulchri* of the manuscript ended with the '*Te Deum laudamus*', a self-contained work, and that both the 'Christ-

---

[1] The first word, Rex, is given an elaborate initial 'R', as if a quite new item is to be signalized.

[2] See *Feria V infra Octavam Paschae: ad Vesperas*.

[3] Donovan, p. 86.

Magdalen' scene and the *Peregrinus* fragment represent separate 'jottings'. Perhaps the playwright had met these ideas in other manuscripts, and had thought to 'make a note of them'. I have already pointed out on p. 172 an example of some such practice at the conclusion of the *Visitatio* of Orléans, *201*, where, on p. 225 of the manuscript, there was a scribal decision to 'make a note of' an alternative set of verses for those used in the drama for the first appearance of the Marys.

However, in the case of the *Peregrinus* intrusion one must bear in mind the case of the 'Dutch Easter Play', soon to be encountered (p. 181), where a somewhat inept attempt is made to insert a similar truncated version of the 'road to Emmaus' episode into the Sepulchre story, cutting out the culminating Supper happenings. Perhaps the Vich playwright had met with this idea, or even an early version of an actual full-scale *Peregrinus*, and was recording the fact.

What has been gained from these extraordinary pages of *Vich 105* seems to be an earliest date for the afterwards widely known '*Omnipotens Pater altissime . . .*' stanza group, together with the first recorded advent of the 'Spice Merchant' bargaining with the Marys for the precious ointment, in verses that later also became standard ones. We are also given a hint that ideas concerning the 'Christ-Magdalen' scene and even the *Peregrinus* drama were beginning to be spread around.

VIII

At a somewhat later date, probably round the turn of the century, there was written at the famous German monastery of Einsiedeln, a *Visitatio* which goes much further in the development of the *Zehnsilberspiel* type mentioned on p. 175. A *Liber responsalis*, *MS 300*, of the twelfth to thirteenth centuries, sets out on its pp. 93–4 groups of rhyming stanzas that will find many near-duplicates in certain *Visitatios* of the succeeding centuries. Actually, the sum total of these different stanza-groups to be found among the *Zehnsilberspiel* type of *Visitatio* is six, plus a few 'floating' verses. Not all these groups were employed at once by individual versions. *Einsiedeln 300*, for example, contains only three and a bit, and none of these is '*Omnipotens Pater altissime . . .*'. These verse forms are free compositions, not merely metrical arrangements of Gospel or liturgical matter, and it will be found that the texts remain reasonably consistent throughout the various versions, although one or other of the usual verses, and even (as I have indicated) *sets* of verses, may be found omitted, according to the example considered. A similar reasonable consistency is to be found in the musical settings. I have constructed the usual comparative charts, and have found that, in spite of the notation of many of the melodies remaining in the form of unheighted neumes, the general unity is such that there is seldom any doubt as to the pitches of notes. A few difficulties, such as those concerned with *St. Quentin MS 86*, which wishes to bend the music to a vernacular translation of the Latin, will be dealt with when met. There are altogether six different stanza melodies, held in common. In the main these are faithful to their particular set of stanzas, although a certain amount of cross-borrowing will have to be mentioned. But more of that anon. I shall for the time being do no more than mention the purposes of each of the six groups of verses (most of them in lines of ten syllables) that form the body of the so-called *Zehnsilberspiel*, and quote the beginning of the first stanza of each group.[1]

A. The lament of the Marys as they set off to journey to the Sepulchre

    1. '*Heu! nobis internas mentes*

                Quanti pulsant gemitus . . .'

B. A prayer by the Marys and their decision to buy ointment (spices)

    1. '*Omnipotens Pater altissime,*

                Angelorum rector mitissime . . .'

C. The buying of the ointment—The Marys bargain with the Spice Merchant

    1. '*Aromata pretio quaerimus,*

                Corpus Jesu ungere volumus . . .'

D. The lament of Mary Magdalen, before the appearance of Jesus as the 'Gardener'

    1. '*Cum venissem ungere mortuum,*

                Monumentum inveni vacuum . . .'

E. Jesus' address to Mary Magdalen, in which he expounds the Resurrection

    1. '*Prima quidem suffragia*

                Stola tulit carnalia . . .'

F. Mary Magdalen's announcement to the Disciples, or to others, of her news

    1. '*Vere vidi Dominum vivere,*

                Nec dimisit me pedes tangere . . .'

When in the next century's discussions we meet with the bulk of the *Zehnsilberspiel* type versions, I will give the texts in full, and deal with the dramas in general, together with the *Zehnsilberspiel* music. I will, however, now take some note of the *Zehnsilberspiel*[2] version mentioned above (*Einsiedeln, MS 300, pp. 93–4*), a beautifully written manuscript, but with its music in unheighted St. Gall neumes, needing chart comparisons for their interpretation. (See Young, I, pp. 389–92.)

---

[1] These stanza groups, as delineated by Wilhelm Meyer, are set forth in Young, I, pp. 677–8. To these six Smoldon will later add a seventh, ZHN G, which figures prominently in his fuller discussion of the *Zehnsilberspiel* form. See pp. 304ff. and, particularly, the Chart on pp. 308ff. (*Ed.*).

[2] I shall henceforward abbreviate this word to ZHN, when using it for reference purposes.

The first item consists of ZHN A ('*Heu! nobis internas mentes . . .*'), all three stanzas, each sung by a separate Mary. The familiar text, '*Quis revolvet . . .?*', which follows, has a special musical setting, found elsewhere, as far as I know, only in the fifteenth-century *Visitatio* versions of St. Florian and Melk.

There now follows something quite unique; instead of the expected '*Quem quaeritis*' exchange, the Angel and the Marys are given incipits of sentences ('*Quem vos quem flentes . . .?*': '*Nos Jesum Christum . . .*') pointing to paraphrases that as far as I know, no scholar has yet solved. Certainly I cannot interpret their neumes.

The next item, '*Ad monumentum venimus . . .*', is a free composition that we have met before, earliest in *Einsiedeln 366*. Supplementing this is the ZHN G item, the additional stanza '*En angeli aspectum . . .*', here addressed to Peter. However, no reference is made at this point as to any 'Race' being in prospect, and there immediately follows ZHN D, all three stanzas of Mary Magdalen's Lament, beginning with '*Cum venissem ungere mortuum . . .*'. The ZHN B and C items, concerned with the ointment and its purchase from the Merchant, are conspicuous by their absence.

There follows a comment from the choir, an incipit ('*Una sabbati . . .*') of an obsolete antiphon. Mary Magdalen seems now to be left isolated at the Tomb. She is directed to sing the sequence *Victimae Paschali*, ceasing just before '*Dic nobis . . .?*', at which moment Christ, unrecognized as yet, puts the usual question, '*Mulier, quid ploras . . .?*'.[1] Seeing that Mary's last words have been, 'The Prince of life, who died, now lives and reigns!' ('*Dux vitae mortuus regnat vivus!*'), it is rather strange that she should be weeping! However, we have now the usual 'St. John' prose scene, except that Einsiedeln makes Christ's '*Maria!*' a threefold matter (as does *Vich 105*, and as do several other similar versions), thereby blunting somewhat the drama of the situation. Also Einsiedeln commits that too frequently met blunder of adding to Mary's '*Rabboni!*', St. John's gloss ('*quod dicitur, magister*').

ZHN E, Christ's address to Mary, beginning '*Prima quidem suffragia . . .*', then follows, with Mary's adoring comments ('*Sancte Deus!*', etc.) interspersing the stanzas. Next, a normal version of the antiphon '*Surrexit enim sicut . . .*' is sung by the chorus. They then proceed to question Mary Magdalen ('*Dic nobis, Maria . . .?*') in familiar terms, the second half of '*Victimae paschali*'. Then comes a somewhat unusual conclusion. Even though Mary Magdalen has gathered the most irrefutable evidence possible as to Christ's resurrection, and has proclaimed it in the sequence verses: 'I saw the tomb wherein the living one was laid: I saw his glory as he rose again', yet the incredulous Peter and John still insist on the Race to the Tomb, to the usual accompaniment of the choral antiphon, '*Currebant duo simul . . .*'. The final item is the singing of

---

[1] Normally, this question is first put by the Angel (or Angels), but on this occasion they appear to be cut out.

verses, given in incipit form, which as far as I know, have never been expanded. The '*Te Deum laudamus*' follows.

A fuller selection of the ZHN items A to G[1] will be found in later versions of the type, the variations in choice bringing about some variety between the works. But the repetitions of identically-shaped stanzas to repeated melodies certainly has the effect of slowing the dramatic pace—and interest—as compared with the constant changes in the techniques of presentation as carried through by the individual *Orléans 201*.

IX

One final Easter music-drama belonging to this period remains to be considered, the so-called 'Dutch Easter play'. Two manuscripts are concerned with it, and since its discovery is comparatively recent, the text will not be found in Karl Young. It is quite exceptional in its form and its pattern does not seem to have been imitated, even though some of its musical contents seem to have been reproduced in later *Visitatio* manuscripts. The version was discovered in the Royal Library of the Hague in the early 1950s. Actually, the finding consists of *two* manuscripts—two writings-down, centuries apart, of what is manifestly the same music-drama. One (*B*) in complete form, was found in a *Hymnarium* of the fifteenth century. The other (*A*) had been used for binding purposes concerned with an *Evangelarium*, and dates from either the late twelfth or early thirteenth century. It consisted originally, it would seem, of three folia, of which the first has perished. The Royal Library has registered the two manuscripts as (A) the 'Maastricht Easter play' (*MS 76, F.3.*) and (B) the 'Egmond Easter play' (*MS 71, J.20.*). The names refer to the probable places of their writings-down.

Both manuscripts have received scholarly notice in an article by the Dutch musicologist, Jos. Smits van Waesberghe, in *Musica Disciplina* (Vol. VIII, 1953, pp. 15–37). It was he who bracketed the two versions and called them 'a Dutch Easter play', since they represented essentially the same work. His article traces the evidence as to the origin of each manuscript and offers an assessment of the work based mainly on a study of the texts and a comparison of them with other *Visitatio* versions. I myself have written briefly of the discovery, on pp. 271–2 of *Grove's Dictionary of Music, Supplementary Volume* (Macmillan, 1961). I have obtained photographs of each manuscript, and the comments which follow are founded on a study of the music as much as of the texts.

The music of *MS 'A'* is written in German notation on four lines with F and c clefs. The discrepancies to be found between it and that of the fifteenth-century *MS 'B'* amount to not much more than occasional small pitch differences and different neume groupings, as between what are manifestly the same basic settings, this apart from the missing first

[1] See pp. 308ff.

page of 'A'.[1] *MS 'A'* may have received an editing, and *MS 'B'* may show the result, perhaps not at first hand.[2]

Though *MS 'B'* is even more outwardly German musically, written as it is in heavy *'Hufnagel'* notation, yet Smits van Waesberghe, arguing from the evidence of the texts, supposes a Norman-French origin for the work. In spite of the German notation, I hold that the evidence of the music supports that view. Except for a few passages that appear to be unique, the 'free' melodies have a French flavour, and there are links of sorts with *Vich 105* and *Madrid 132*; and, looking ahead, with the *Rouen B.N. 904*, *Tours 987*, and *St. Quentin 86*. There would appear to have been a great deal of common material 'loose' at the time. Once again the thought occurs as to untraced 'Third Stage' *Visitatio* versions of this period, unhappily perished.

To my mind the chief interest to be found in the 'Dutch Easter Play' is the novelty of its form. In this drama—uniquely, so far as I can discover—we find a radical departure from the 'normal' sequence of *Visitatio* events and an introduction of material (both textual and musical) which more properly belongs to the story of the *Peregrinus*, which we shall be examining shortly (see p. 185). I suspect a bit of individual creativity here: somebody, albeit at a lower level than that of the framer of the *Orléans 201 Visitatio*, was trying, like him, to get out of the rut. Our 'Dutch Easter Play' composer-playwright employs normally enough the ZHN B section[3] and his own choice of stanzas from ZHN C. Then comes the same four items as in the *Orléans 201* appendix (see p. 172), with music far too similar to be thought a separate inspiration. There are also several links with the earlier *Madrid 132*, as we shall see during the course of our discussion.

When we come to the *'Quem quaeritis'* dialogue we find musical differences between the two 'Dutch' manuscripts which, I believe, are of interest. I give below question and reply as in each version. My B flat stave sign is authorized by the free addition of B flat accidentals to the staves of both manuscripts:

---

[1] *MS 'A'* begins with the 28th line of the work, at *'Iam, iam, ecce . . .'*, but in view of the fact that the twelfth-century manuscript *Vich 105* shows almost the same succession of *'Omnipotens Pater . . .'* stanzas as the much later Dutch *MS 'B'*, it seems reasonable to assume that *MS 'A'* began, originally, in the same fashion.

[2] These differences, both textual and musical, can be ascertained by consulting Smits van Waesberghe's transcription in the article mentioned above.

[3] I have already mentioned above (note 1) that the 'Dutch Easter Play' (in its *MS 'B'* version anyway) follows what may be considered to be the usual pattern of setting for *'Omnipotens Pater . . .'*. Unlike *Vich 105* it begins the tune on G, but contrives to preserve its 'major mode' quality owing to the fact that the setting never touches the seventh of the scale.

The presence of the inserted '*quaerimus*' will be noted, probably picked up from *Madrid 132*. It is met with in a few other French Easter versions. There will also be seen samples of the small note-differences to be found between the two manuscripts, these not disturbing their essential identity. A matter of some interest, however, is the fact that the fifteenth-century *MS 'B'* has developed a 'musical rhyme' at its vocative phrases, certainly French in style, but as far as I know, not duplicated in detail elsewhere. That this pattern has evolved from the *MS 'A'* version seems to me to underline my supposition that 'vocative rhymes' in '*Quem quaeritis*' dialogue settings (as in *St. Gall MS 484*) developed later than the plainer statements of the Limoges school.

MS 'B' now contrives for a while to show considerable originality in its music. The second Angel's speech is shortened to '*Non est hic, sed surrexit*', with its music *not* following the almost inevitable upward leap, but making use of the melodic motif of '*caelicolae*', this continued through the newly composed setting of '*Venite et videte*' which follows. Incidentally, by making use of the liturgical text at this point, the Dutch work has avoided the recall and second dismissal which is so often found. *Madrid 132* uses the same trick, but the Dutch music, as far as I know, is quite original here, as are the settings of the (liturgical) '*Recordamini qualiter . . .*' and '*Sed cito euntes . . .*' texts.

After Mary's liturgical antiphon, '*Ardens est cor meum . . .*', the interchange between Mary and Christ begins, the 'Dutch' play, economical always, cutting out the Angel's question '*Mulier, quid ploras?*'. The Dutch music here is closely allied to the several French settings, all very similar. But it is strange to encounter here too the ineptitude (found, as we have seen, in the German *Zehnsilberspiel* but not in the French versions) of adding after '*Raboni*' the gloss of St. John—'*quod dicitur*

---

[1] The margin of the manuscript has here been trimmed, destroying the remaining notes of the line. The first neume of the bracketed part, however, can be guessed at as being a *torculus*.

[2] The *Musica Disciplina* transcription of the music of *MS 'B'* writes 'A,G' here; surely an uncorrected printer's error. The manuscript shows quite plainly 'G,F', as in the next line of the dialogue.

magister'. In the following '*Nolite me tangere . . .*' the musical links between the Dutch and the Orléans versions are apparent.

What next occurs sets the Dutch version apart from all others. Christ departs. As Mary at the tomb recovers the sudarium (and at the same time a small cross; no doubt a piece of symbolism) 'two disciples' enter, singing the first part of the sequence '*Victimae paschali*'. Most of us would expect these to turn out to be Peter and John, but the rubrics of *MS 'A'* (throughout more generous than those of *MS 'B'*) show that they are dressed as '*peregrini*' (i.e. wayfarers). Another surprise is that without any attempt to indicate a change of 'station' a rubric calls for the entry of Christ, clad in a shaggy cloak, barefooted, and with staff in hand; in other words, disguised as another wayfarer.

It will now be realized that we are being given an 'economical' glimpse of the *Peregrinus* drama,[1] *without* moving to the Emmaus road and then to the supper at the inn. Confirmation as to the identity of the '*peregrini*' now comes from a rubric mention of 'Cleophas' and 'the other disciple'. The complete episode, upon which the separate dramas were founded, is related in St. Luke xxiv:13–32. Many of the spoken Gospel sentences, especially those of the first encounter, were adapted into the liturgy as antiphons. The whole of the texts and music used by the 'Dutch' work for the 'Peregrinus' scene, can be found in the Hartker's Antiphonale.

Continuing with the 'Dutch' scene: after Christ's reproach, in terms of a part of the liturgical antiphon, '*O stulti et tardi . . .*', he vanishes from the sight of the two, who reproach themselves through another liturgical antiphon, '*Nonne cor nostrum . . .*'. Not being hampered by any thoughts of supper at the inn, and being in fact still on the spot where they questioned Mary Magdalen, they are able to follow the women to the sepulchre, and to be present at the final scene, which Smits van Waesberghe terms the *Apotheosis*. Here, the Angel at the head of the former resting-place sings the familiar antiphon, '*Cito euntes . . .*' while his companion at the foot follows with another, '*In Galilea Jesum videbitis . . .*'; these serve to cause the Marys to turn away. The latter's words to all the disciples, '*Eamus, nuntiate mirum . . .*' are found, to almost exactly the same music, in *Madrid 132*, and as far as I know, nowhere else. Once more the sudarium is displayed, this time to the '*populus*', while the familiar text, '*Surrexit Dominus de sepulchro, qui pro nobis . . .*', is sung. One notes that *MS 'A'* uses the non-liturgical setting found in a number of French and German *Visitatio* versions (beginning with *Vienna, MS 1888*), but that *MS 'B'* returns to the liturgical music. The cantor then begins the final '*Te Deum laudamus . . .*'.[2]

When we review the structure of this somewhat unusual work, it is apparent that the bulk of the scenes—the purchase of the spices, the lament of the Marys, the visit to the sepulchre, and the 'Christ-

---

[1] *Peregrinus*, as a separate music-drama, will be discussed in the next section of this chapter.

[2] The rubrics of the more informative *MS 'A'* are in a terrible jumble, from '*Nonne cor nostrum . . .*' to the end. Obviously the originals have been given additional phrases, added in haphazard fashion.

Magdalen' encounter—while containing some originalities, especially on the musical side, yet leave the 'Dutch Easter play' a normal *Visitatio*, one that has taken on the fashion of employing newly-circulating *Zehnsilberspiel* items,[1] but yet of no particular distinction. But the inserted '*peregrini*' section is quite another matter, and, in my opinion, not a successful innovation. The rubrics concerning it, moreover, seem to imply that the two disciples 'stayed put' after their '*Dic nobis*' exchanges with Mary Magdalen, and that the disguised *Salvator* enters to them there. After only a portion of the first questions and answers recorded by St. Luke are exchanged, he utters only a portion of the '*O stulti et tardi . . .*' antiphon reproach, and then proves his identity by just disappearing. The truly essential feature of the episode has been omitted altogether. This is the scene at the inn, where Christ, by re-enacting the details of the Last Supper, reveals himself in a much more subtle fashion. To use a colloquialism, I consider this truncated '*peregrini*' scene to be a flop, marring the accepted structures of both Church music-drama types.

The concluding *Apotheosis* gives us no other surprises. All the items have been met with before, and, except for the (probable) borrowing from *Madrid 132* of '*Eamus, nuntiate mirum . . .*', are of the antiphon type. Cleophas and his fellow-disciple are given no prominence in it. One would have expected them to be burning to proclaim their own irrefutable evidence of the Resurrection. It is a very tame conclusion as compared with some of the other major *Visitatios*, which make excellent play between solo and choral voices in shaping a dramatic use of the sequence *Victimae paschali*. But the Dutch drama had already exhausted that resource at an earlier stage. In sum, it would seem to me that the insertion of an incomplete and much 'edited' version of the '*peregrini*' episode produces a pattern that is unsatisfactory, both liturgically and artistically. Perhaps something of the failure if this experiment may be seen in the fact that, as far as has been discovered, there are no other Easter drama manuscripts which attempt to follow up this particular pattern.

X

It is time now to consider the Emmaus story as told in full and proper form in a number of music-dramas of the twelfth to fourteenth centuries, usually known by the generic name of *Peregrinus*.

As we have seen, St. Luke, Ch. xxiv, is the chief source of the story. Verses 13–32 tell of the meeting with the Stranger on the road to Emmaus by two disciples, one of them named in the rubric as Cleopas, the 'other disciple' supposed traditionally to have been Luke himself. The episode ends with their bewildered joy, after 'the breaking of bread'

---

[1] By 'newly-circulating' I am referring, of course, to *MS 'A'* and the twelfth to thirteenth century.

had caused them to realize the Stranger's identity and he had 'vanished out of their sight'. Verses 33–39 tell of the disciples' return to Jerusalem, to proclaim that 'the Lord had risen', but even as they spoke, Jesus stood in the midst of them, calming their fears as to his being a 'spirit' by showing them the wounds of his crucifixion.

St. John has nothing to say concerning the Emmaus episode, but we read (xx:19–23) that on Easter evening Jesus appeared to the body of the disciples in Jerusalem. Once again there is mention of the showing of the wounds, and the account goes on to mention (verses 24–29) the refusal of Thomas (absent on the occasion) to believe what he had been told. Eight days later, we are informed, Jesus again 'stood in the midst', and, confronting Thomas, invited him to make the material tests he had called for. Thomas's surrender was absolute—'My Lord and my God!'.

St. Mark's reference (xvi:12–14) makes a bare mention of Christ's confronting the two 'as they walked and went into the country', and then speaks of his afterwards appearing to the body of the disciples, upbraiding them for their 'unbelief and hardness of heart'.

This was the material available to the playwright-composers. Unlike most of the themes that received medieval church dramatization, a high proportion of the texts, especially those of the Emmaus episode, consisted of direct speech, which could, and indeed did, get taken over directly as drama dialogue. Moreover, many of the speech-sentences of the Gospel accounts had, long before, been turned into antiphons and given swift chant-settings, admirable for exchanges in 'recitative' style. Again, even some of the descriptions of actions given in the Gospel texts could be found in the form of antiphons; these were thus available for use by the liturgical choir, acting as a sort of Greek chorus, and commenting on what they saw taking place in action.

All this is not to say that in the best of the *Peregrinus* versions there would be any lack of features that were original both in regard to text and to music. However, the roll of surviving examples of the *Peregrinus* music-dramas is a woefully short one. Here are the library titles of the manuscripts in which they are to be found:

Twelfth Century: (1) Madrid, *Bibl. Nac. MS 289*; (2) Madrid, *Bibl. Nac. MS 132*; (3) Orléans, *B. de la Ville MS 201*; (4) Paris, *B.N. (Nouv. Acq.) MS lat. 1064.*
The 'Madrid' manuscripts are of course those adapted by the Normans in Italy to the Sicilian use but clearly derived from Northern France.
B.N. MS 1064, from Beauvais Cathedral, is surely the finest of the *Peregrinus* versions.

Thirteenth Century: (5) Rouen, *B. de la Ville MS 222*; (6) Munich, *Staatsbibl., MS lat. 4660a ('Carmina Burana').*

Fourteenth Century: (7) Paris, *B.N. MS lat. 16309* (a breviary used at Saintes).

Besides these complete examples there are some other 'evidences of existence'. As we have seen, at the very end of that confused attempt at a *Visitatio* found in the twelfth-century manuscript *Vich, MS 105,* there suddenly occurs the line, '*Qui sunt hi sermones quos confertis ad invicem ambulantes . . .*'. In other words, the first question of the Stranger on the road to Emmaus is, without warning, projected into the text. The counter-question which follows, '*Tu solus peregrinus es . . .?*' is preceded by a rubric which mentions the name of 'Cleophas', and the exchanges of St.Luke's sentences continue down to '*De Ihesum Nazareno . . . et omni populo*', and then cease, to be succeeded by the doxology and irrelevant verses. It would seem, then, that the Spanish cathedral of Vich had at least some glimmerings not only of the 'third stage' form of the Easter Sepulchre, but also the dramatic possibilities of the Emmaus story. A field of speculation is again opened; the idea of a music-drama on the 'Peregrinus' theme would seem to be quite widespread in the twelfth century. Evidence from two passages to be found in the medieval Lichfield Statutes[1] show that a *Peregrinus* (together with an *Officium Pastorum* and a *Visitatio Sepulchri*) had performances at Lichfield in the thirteenth or fourteenth centuries. No actual details are given. Probably associated with the same region are the well-known 'Shrewsbury Fragments', concerned with the same three types of drama, but consisting only of a single actor's part, with the necessary cues, and being largely made up of spoken verses in the vernacular.[2] There also must be mentioned a thirteenth-century *ordinarium* from Padua (*Bibl. Capit. MS S*, fol. 103r.–104r.),[3] which describes the action of a simple type of *Peregrinus*, with most of the familiar sentences given, but in incipit form and without their music. There are attempts at realistic costuming, and we learn that the 'altar of St. Daniel' was used as the 'supper table'. Still in the thirteenth century, an ordinarium of the collegiate church of St. Peter at Lille records a representation of a *Peregrinus*.[4] As for Spain—that the full-scale drama was not neglected at Vich can be seen from a *consueta* of the Cathedral, written in 1413, and declaring that if the clerics so desire, the *Peregrinus* may be presented at Vespers on Easter Monday.[5] Also in Spain, at least during the fourteenth to mid-sixteenth centuries, the Cathedral of Gerona, in Catalonia, records performances of not only *Visitatio Sepulchri*, but also *Peregrinus*.[6]

The Emmaus happenings having taken place late on Easter Sunday, that would seem to be the natural day, and Vespers the natural hour, for the drama to be given. However, only one of the surviving versions (*Madrid 132*) proposed to make room for it in what must have been a liturgically crowded period. Most versions settled for Vespers of Easter

---

[1] See Chambers, II, pp. 15, 23; Young, II, p. 522.

[2] The Library of the Shrewsbury School, *MS VI* (*Mus. iii, 42*), fols. 38r.–42v. See Young, II, Appendix B (pp. 514–22). I shall deal with the 'Fragments' in their place.

[3] Young (I, pp. 481–2) prints the Latin account as given in the ordinarium.

[4] Ibid., I, p. 694.

[5] See Donovan, p. 86.

[6] Ibid., p. 103. But as Donovan points out, the identification of the drama seems a little uncertain.

Monday, the most obvious reason being surely that the Gospel of that day was the passage from St. Luke which recounted the *Peregrinus* episode.

The *Peregrinus* drama is, of all the types, the one most closely inter-woven with the liturgy itself. Normally its performance occurred actually during the course of the elaborate 'triple Vespers' used throughout Christendom in medieval times on Easter Day and during the octave. Although details seem to have varied a great deal regionally, there was much processional movement and liturgical splendour. At Rouen, for example, at the beginning of the third part of the office, the procession set out upon its return to the choir, singing the psalm, '*In exitu Israel . . .*'. At the conclusion of this a halt was made in the nave, the figures of the two 'disciples', dressed for their parts, made their appearance, and the drama was carried through. At its conclusion the office was resumed and the clerical procession continued to the portals of the choir.

I shall in due course follow through chronologically the list of surviv-ing *Peregrinus* versions detailed on p. 186. But already a curious fact emerges, similar to that which became apparent when the surviving examples of the Magi-Herod dramas were considered (see pp. 129 ff.); namely, that when we explore the century which appears to be the earliest to produce the type (i.e. the twelfth) we find there the most advanced example, *B.N. MS lat. 1064*, from Beauvais, while a couple of centuries later a manuscript turns up showing the simplest, briefest form, *B.N. MS lat. 16309* from Saintes. It seems to me that a comparison might be drawn between this pair and the Magi-Herod pair, the full-length Freising drama of the eleventh century and the brief fourteenth-century 'Three Kings', *Rouen MS 384*. I cannot but conclude that Karl Young's attempt to reveal an evolution for the *Peregrinus* dramas by (once again) arranging versions in order of expansion while disregarding the chronology of their appearance must rest, as in the case of the Magi-Herod group, on an insecure foundation; even though it is open to say that the fourteenth-century Saintes breviary example may represent a copying from an earlier version.[1]

Our task now is to consider separately the *Peregrinus* dramas which show the earliest date of survival, that of the twelfth century. The briefest of them belongs to the Madrid Biblioteca Nacional (*MS 289*, fol. 117r.–118v.), and like its companion (*Madrid 132*) derives from Sicily, and, ultimately, Normandy. The music notation of the manu-script is plainly Norman, carefully heighted, with F and c clefs and the barely-to-be-distinguished assistance of faintly scratched stave-lines. Although the drama was set down for Easter Monday, nothing is said as to performance at Vespers, and directional rubrics are scanty. How-ever, we learn that the '*duo clerici*' wear copes, and that the 'inn table', with bread and wine, is 'at the altar'. However, a fitting introduction is

---

[1] The seven complete *Peregrinus* dramas which Karl Young presents in order of 'expan-sion' belong successively to the following centuries: (1) fourteenth; (2) twelfth; (3) thirteenth; (4) thirteenth; (5) twelfth; (6) twelfth; (7) twelfth.

provided; the two come into action to the choral sounds of the ancient hymn, '*Jesu, nostra redemptio . . .*',[1] an idea used by all the other versions except the Munich one. Before beginning the dialogue pattern of exchanged antiphon sentences, *Madrid 289* uses a phrase from Luke's verse 22 ('*Tertia dies est hodie quod haec facta sunt*'), set to a short tune that I cannot identify. *Orléans 201* has a very similar setting to the passage, but otherwise it seems unique to the two 'Madrid' manuscripts.

Regarding St. Luke's verses 17, 18 and 19, *Madrid 289* and all the other *Peregrinus* versions conform in using the antiphon setting of Hartker's *Antiphonale* with but few small differences of neume and pitch.[2] But verse 20 is not used by Hartker, and the two Madrid manuscripts seem to go their own way in providing a setting—as does *Orléans 201*, but with some expansions.

Borrowing the texts of the verses 25–6 of St. Luke (Christ's reproach to the disciples), *Madrid 289* shares with all the other surviving versions the borrowing also of the antiphon music. But in the case of the descriptive verses, 28 and part of 29, the only other versions to use them are *Madrid 132* and the one from Saintes.

With the '*Mane nobiscum . . .*' speech, all seven of the *Peregrinus* group take over the Hartker antiphon music. But immediately after comes the sentence, '*Mihi longum iter restat,*' which, text and music, is unique to the two 'Madrid' manuscripts, as far as I am aware.

Seemingly non-liturgical, also, as well as non-Gospel, is the passage:

Sol vergens ad occasum suadet ut nostrum velis hospitium; placent enim nobis sermones tui, quos refers de resurrexione magistri nostri.

One of my charts tells me that this text is found in five of the seven surviving versions, that the Munich example omits it, but that the (Beauvais) *B.N. MS 1064* paraphrases it into two attractive rhyming rhythmic stanzas, each scanning 8 7 8 7, and set to unique, original music. The free-rhythm, neumatic setting of the prose sentence, according to the five, represents a tune common to them all. This unanimity in all but small variations suggests that the prose composition may have been a recognized but now forgotten antiphon.

Continuing with *Madrid 289*, we find that its text for the entry of Christ to the inn, his sitting with the disciples and breaking the bread, is covered by a Hartker antiphon, this resource shared by *Madrid 132* and the Saintes and Beauvais dramas. However, the sentence, '*Et intravit cum illis, et factum est . . .*', a modification of the Gospel text, is the exclusive idea of the 'Madrid' dramas, and as far as I know, the music is as well.

Madrid 289 then presents its longest rubric, giving directions for the scene at the 'inn-table', at the altar. The breaking of the bread, the recognition, and the vanishing are all described.

[1] See *Antiphonale Romanum, Hymni antiqui*, p. 20.
[2] As it happens, I have given the settings (i.e. of the antiphon music of verses 17, 18, and 19) as found in the simplest of the *Peregrinus* versions, that of Saintes, in both *Grove's Dictionary of Music* (V, p. 328) and the *New Oxford History of Music* (II, p. 191).

The disciples' self-reproaches as expressed in Luke's verse 32 ('*Nonne cor nostrum . . . ?*') are given a Hartker antiphon setting, this found also in all the other versions except the Rouen one. Then comes what seems to be an invented passage, beginning, '*Heu! miseri! ubi erat sensus noster?*'. However, all the other versions except those of Rouen and Munich join Madrid's in making use of what seems to be a common setting, a somewhat melismatic one.

The brief Madrid rubric which follows calls for Christ's reappearance, but gives no hint of following St. Luke's account by transferring the scene to Jerusalem. His words, '*Pax vobis . . . Videte manus meas . . .*', derived from Luke's verses 36 and 40, are found as snatches of Hartker antiphons, and borrowed with a number of individual modifications and actual differences as to the settings of the sentences by all the versions except that of Rouen.[1] *Madrid 289* now concludes, swiftly and conventionally, with the disciples singing the 'non-liturgical' setting of '*Surrexit de sepulchro . . .*', and the choir rounding off with a '*Deo gratias, alleluia.*'

Certainly the *Madrid 289* version is undistinguished, but one imagines that it worked smoothly enough within the confines of Easter Vespers. I have here given it more attention than it really deserves, but with the intention of using it as a basis of reference when dealing with some of the longer ones. The first we turn to is its fellow 'Norman-Sicilian', *Madrid, MS C. 132*, fol. 105v.–108r., a beautiful manuscript that also houses the brief but very satisfactory *Visitatio Sepulchri*, with its novelty, a three-stanza 'entry' piece for the Marys (see p. 156). The music notation of the manuscript is plainly Norman, very clearly written on a scratched four-line stave, with 'directs' and F and alternative c clefs.

But the drama itself, which Karl Young terms 'the most comprehensive' among the surviving *Peregrinus* versions (II, p. 476), is a sad disappointment. Although its rubrics give us a few more facts as to the performance (we learn that it took place between the singing of the responsory '*Haec dies . . .*' and the procession to the font), and although alternative stanza introductions are provided, so that the work may be staged at Vespers either on Easter Day or on the Monday following, the actual 'Emmaus' affair, from '*Tertia dies est quod haec facta sunt*' to '*Pax vobis . . . Videte manus meas . . . sicut me videtis habere, alleluia!*', is nothing more than an exact reproduction, texts and music, of *Madrid MS 289.*[2]

The first introduction to *Madrid 132*, intended for Easter Day, consists of two four-line stanzas, scanning 8 8 8 8, the first beginning, '*Ego, sodes, dum recordor*', and the two founded (very broadly) on Luke's verses 14–16. The stanza tune, a 'major mode' one, is rather melismatic,

---

[1] These sentences also show up in *Tours 927*, though with blunders. For a fuller discussion of this 'problem' manuscript, see pp. 292ff.

[2] I must here record my appreciation of the accuracy of the scribal copying. Apart from *MS C. 132*'s indulging in a long melisma on the word '*sunt*' in the '*Tertia dies . . .*' item, there are only two or three trifling discrepancies between the music notations of the two manuscripts.

and to my mind, not at all distinguished. The alternative introduction, for Monday Vespers, is the usual one found, the hymn '*Jesu, nostra redemptio*'.

The large extension of the work which follows is made up, first, of familiar but surely unexpected material, the *Visitatio* scene at the sepulchre between the two interrogating Angels, Mary Magdalen, and in due course the interrogating Christ, in disguise and in person. The music, where it shows any resemblance to that of other versions, leans towards *Orléans 201*.

But the scene is all out of place chronologically; and furthermore, when the two disciples, apparently replacing Peter and John (as they do in the 'Dutch' *Visitatio*), proceed to question Mary in terms of the *Victimae paschali* exchanges, instead of proclaiming to all and sundry that they have just returned from their own contact with him in the flesh, the situation becomes somewhat absurd. It is the scheme of the 'Dutch Easter Play' in reverse, a *Sepulchre* scene inserted into a *Peregrinus* drama instead of the opposite—and to my mind, just as unsuccessful. No other surviving *Peregrinus* version chose to imitate the trick.

The final section of *Madrid 132* is based not on St. Luke, but on St. John xx:19–20 and 24–29. A rubric now introduces the 'doubting Thomas' incident.[1] Two appearances of Christ to the disciples at Jerusalem as reported by St. John, one eight days after the other, are here telescoped into one, with Thomas coming in to receive the '*Videmus Dominum*' report of the disciples, and to express his incredulity as in St. John xx:25. Jesus then appears, and after addressing all the disciples in terms of a Hartker antiphon ('*Data est mihi omnis potestas . . .*'— found with its liturgical music also in *Orléans 201*)—turns to Thomas. His text is a slightly modified verse 27; the music, as far as I am aware, invented for the situation.

According to a rubric, Thomas, convinced, now faces the '*populum*' and utters his testimony in words that paraphrase verses 27–28, but which, text and music, represent another Hartker antiphon. Yet another of the same, '*Quia vidisti me, Thoma, credidisti; . . .*', Jesus' final comment spoken in verse 29, closes the scene. The work concludes in the same fashion as in *MS 289*, with all the disciples singing the antiphon, '*Surrexit Dominus de sepulchro . . .*'.

A few touches of originality in the music can scarcely save the unwieldy *Madrid 132* from the censure expressed by Karl Young (I, p. 481) that 'As a dramatic composition this version of the *Peregrinus* can hardly be commended', an opinion with which I emphatically concur.

After the superb *Visitatio Sepulchri* found in the 'Fleury Playbook' of *Orléans 201*, the *Peregrinus* belonging to the collection appears to me

---

[1] Young (I, p. 481) notes that the number of the disciples are mentioned by the rubrics as being ten ('*decem*'), showing that heed had been taken of the absence of Thomas—and Judas.

not to have reached to the same standard.[1] However, I have a better opinion of it as a music-drama than Karl Young (I, p. 476) has of it as a 'literary composition'. He complains that it draws its speeches largely from the Vulgate and the choir-book; but since there is a high proportion of actual speech in the Gospel presentation of the Emmaus episode, especially at its beginning, what better texts could be found for the work? So many of the sentences having been re-employed as antiphons, their rapidly delivered musical settings served ideally for the 'parlante' dialogue. Actually, there are occasions when *Orléans 201* discards an antiphon setting and substitutes one of its own.

Karl Young also comments on the small proportion of original verse. As compared with the remarkable invention displayed by the deviser of the Beauvais version (which we shall consider next) this stricture may be true, but the two examples it provides are very fine ones, especially in their music. Also, I am not sure that I go along with Karl Young in his questioning of the success of the two choral passages, sentences taken from Isaiah lxiii:1. The choir here has somewhat of the function of a Greek chorus; it comments on the entry of Christ to the disciples, clad in a white tunic, a red cope, an embroidered head-dress, and bearing a cross of gold. Isaiah's, 'Who is this who cometh from Edom in dyed garments from Bozrah? this that is glorious in his apparel . . .' does not seem wholly out of place, especially as the texts were already employed as antiphons and would be known to the participating clergy. However, the music used, though straightforward and effective, is not that of the antiphons, and probably represents individual invention.

Let us now return to the opening rubrics, which mention that the performance took place (exceptionally) on the Tuesday after Easter. Throughout, details of costumes, properties, and actions are generous. The two disciples wear hats, arrange their vestments to resemble cloaks, and bear staves. Christ's first appearance approaches even more that of a traveller (*peregrinus*), with wallet and palm branch. Appropriately, it is the disciples (not the choir) who sing together the hymn, '*Jesu, nostra redemptio . . .*'. There is no need to detail the opening exchanges, which proceed according to pattern. However, it should be noted that the '*O stulti et tardi corde . . .*' sentence does not use the music of the liturgy.

I have mentioned in my examination of *Madrid 289* how the *Orléans* drama joins with other *Peregrinus* versions in using an antiphon setting for Luke's verse 29, but *Orléans* is unique in preceding it by eight rhyming lines, more or less foreshadowing Luke's words. *Orléans'* apparently original rhythmic music is attractive; sufficiently so for me to transcribe four of the lines with a rhythmic version of their setting, transposed up a perfect fourth:

---

[1] In the so-called 'Fleury Playbook' (the principal portion of *Orléans, MS 201*) there are four leading music-dramas: *Visitatio Sepulchri*; *Officium Stellae*; *Ordo Rachelis*; and *Peregrinus*. They are in a far higher class than the remainder.

The verses continue for four more lines, the music confirming that it is a 'major mode' melody.

There follows a good deal of originality on the *Orléans* writers' part that is not apparent in the texts alone, antiphon sentences but not the antiphon settings; even a communion text ('*Surrexit Dominus et apparuit Petro*'), but not its liturgical music. I have already noted the chorus's use of two passages from Isaiah commenting on Christ's first appearance to the apostolic group. Christ himself makes use of passages from St. Luke xxiv:38; Isaiah lxiii:3; and St. John xx:22–23, not met with elsewhere in *Peregrinus* versions, and set, apparently, to original music.

But the outstanding novelty in the *Orléans* drama is the processional music of the body of the disciples; the preliminary to the scene of 'doubting Thomas'. It is a first-class example of the sequence form, seven pairs of lines with the end-rhyme of 'a' throughout, and a single shorter line to conclude. It is not printed in Chevalier's collection,[1] and would appear to be unique to *Orléans 201*. A whisper of its existence elsewhere occurred long after, in the form of an *incipit* (that and no more, and without music), in a fifteenth-century *Visitatio* from a Coutances *ordinarium* (see Karl Young, I, p. 408).

I give the first two pairs of lines in rhythmic transcription. The tunes, of course, change with every pair. I should have been glad to have spared the space for the whole item:[2]

—together with the rounding-off sentence:

---

[1] U. Chevalier, *Repertorium Hymnologicum*, 6 vols., Louvain and Brussels, 1892–1920.

[2] The entire sequence may in fact be found, transcribed and interpolated into Smoldon's performing edition of the *Visitatio Sepulchri* (*Ed.*).

193

As we might expect, the rubrics direct that the item shall be sung *'alternando'*.

In the *Orléans* scene of Thomas's incredulity and conversion there is much that is textually familiar, and much that has been extracted from the Vulgate. As for the latter, St. John xx: 27–29, are called on. Also, when Christ appears with his thrice-spoken *'Pax vobis'*, he is chorally replied to by passages from Psalm cxviii. Christ is even given final sentences from St. Mark xvi:15–16. But it is difficult to find any resemblance between the music that Orléans supplies and the settings of any liturgical pieces that the texts might suggest. *'Haec est dies quam fecit Dominus . . .'* comes from Psalm cxvii[1] and is also a Gradual for Easter Mass; yet Orléans' music has nothing to do with that of the liturgy.

Sentences from St. John xx are employed by other versions as well as *Orléans 201*, to carry through the final Christ-Thomas scene, but *Orléans*, apart from some slight and possibly fortuitous resemblances to Beauvais and *Madrid* music, goes on its own individual way in its settings. Karl Young (I, p. 476, footnote) infers, quite rightly, that the work draws more from the Vulgate than the choir-book, but there is more in it than that. It draws a great deal on itself, and shows originality, especially in regard to its music.

The finest work of the whole *Peregrinus* type, whatever the century, is that from Beauvais Cathedral, contained in a 'miscellany' of the twelfth century,[2] The approbation that Karl Young (I, p. 466) gives to its structure and literary form must be supplemented by an appreciation of the good taste and originality shown by the music.

Apart from the information that the work was performed during Vespers on Easter Monday the rubrics are not informative. Very little is said as to properties, costuming, and general conditions of performance. However, after the conclusion, the mention of the responsory, *'Christus resurgens . . .'*, together with its verse and a following prayer, points to the resumption of Vespers, at the point when the clerical procession would move from the chancel to the font.

The work begins with the singing by the two disciples of four stanzas of the hymn, *'Jesu, nostra redemptio . . .'* (the usual *Peregrinus* start), this allowing for the approach of the 'Stranger'. Throughout the Emmaus episode, the disguised Christ is referred to as *Peregrinus*, while the name 'Cleophas' is used once only; otherwise the disciples are anonymous. The scene opens, as do all the *Peregrinus* versions, with the antiphon-set sentences of St. Luke, this time with a difference, since, after the swift rendering of verse 19, 'one of them' breaks into a rhyming paraphrase of verse 20 and part of 21. The impression it makes on me is that of *recitativo secco* followed by an *arietta*:

[1] Psalm cxvii in the Vulgate, but cxviii in the English Authorized Version.
[2] Paris, *B.N.* (*Nouv. Acq.*) *MS lat. 1064*, fols. 8r.–11v. I have transcribed an 'acting' version, published by Oxford University Press (1965).

—followed immediately by:

These four eight-syllable lines, set in the Mixolydian mode that rules the music for many succeeding items, are followed by another five, sung this time by the 'other disciple'. One has the impression of each interrupting the other in his anxiety to explain it all! I quote the 'other disciple's' first two lines:

The first disciple resumes with the paraphrased narrative concerned with St. Luke's verses 23 and 24, and in such meritorious fashion, verbal and musical, that I feel compelled to quote again, and at length:

¹ It will be realized that these expression marks are editorial.

Another excellent achievement of the Beauvais version is seen in the next item, that dealing with verses 25, 26, and 27 of St. Luke's account. Although the Stranger's first indignant outburst is a mere verse-paraphrase of the first two:

—yet in handling the last ('And beginning at Moses and all the prophets, he expounded unto them . . .'), *Beauvais* undertakes the task of an imagined actual exposition in detail, to the extent of a dozen original nine-syllable lines of poetry, rhyming in couplets. Below, I transcribe six of them, set to what seems to be the Beauvais writer's own original music:

One of the virtues of the Beauvais version is the flexibility and variety of the verbal rhythms of the Latin poetry, bringing a similar variety to the original musical settings. Christ's succeeding item, for example, expressing his wish to continue on his way, consists of a single rhyming couplet, ten syllables to a line, while the stanza lines with which the disciples attempt to restrain him can be represented as 7 7 7 3; all this set to music found nowhere else, as far as I am aware.

Before another lyrical passage of Beauvais invention, one of the disciples sings the antiphon version of St. Luke's verse 29. The long invented passage that follows (lines of fifteen syllables divided between the two disciples) is an extension of the same theme. There follows the scene within the 'Emmaus hostelry', for which, apparently, a table and bread were provided, while the chorus, exercising their function as commentators, describe what is happening in terms of St. Luke, expressed in liturgical antiphons belonging to Easter Week. Karl Young voices his displeasure in the fact that '*Mane nobiscum*' turns up twice in the early stages of the scene (I, p. 470). Apart from the fact that it is a phrase that might well be emphasised, however, it occurs for the second time in a different antiphon, and thus to a different setting.

A more serious objection by Karl Young is to the fact that the piece of antiphon description of Christ's actions in entering the inn, seating himself, and blessing and breaking the bread, are set down in a rubric as for *him* to sing, and in doing so, causing him to refer to himself in the 'third person' throughout. This complaint is manifestly absurd; since all other *Peregrinus* versions that use this particular antiphon (see *Antiphonale Romanum*, p. 400) for the same purpose, call for the *chorus* to perform it, it seems to me a reasonable assumption that the rubric has here gone astray, and that the chorus should sing the commentary, while the Stranger mimes the actions. Otherwise, the scene at the table is most effective. The Chorus says: 'He took bread and blessed it'— (rubric: 'he makes the sign of the cross'); Chorus: 'and brake'—(rubric: 'he breaks it'); Chorus: 'and divided it among them'.[1]

After the disappearance, and during the bewildered search by the disciples through the nave, there is a mingling of antiphon material with original texts and music. The '*Heu, miseri!*' text, of unknown derivation, employed by several *Peregrinus* versions, has a Beauvais music that is unique. As the disciples recover themselves and turn towards the chancel again, there comes a fitting comment from the chorus—Luke xxiv: 34 in the form of the liturgical Communion for Easter Monday, a splendidly vivid piece of plainchant, ending with the tremendous roll of a melismatic '*Alleluia!*'.

Contrary to the Gospel accounts, e.g., Luke xxiv: 34–39, the second appearance (and retirement) of Christ, 'in a different guise', is made at Emmaus instead of at Jerusalem. Also sited there, apparently, is the episode of 'doubting Thomas', the concluding episode of the drama. Still seemingly at Emmaus, Christ makes his final appearance, to convince the sceptical Thomas. One could reflect that the refusal of the Beauvais version to move the scene to Jerusalem obviated the need for the staging of all eleven disciples, as was done in some other *Peregrinus* music-dramas.

Christ's re-entry ('*Pax vobis . . .*') and the display of his wounds to the two disciples ('*Videte manus meas et pedes meos . . .*') has a Beauvais setting that disregards any liturgical sources, but shows fleeting similarities to the musics of Orléans and Madrid. The disciples' vigorous and rhythmic '*Vere, Thoma, vidimus Dominum!*' seems to represent a unique Beauvais setting—as also is Thomas's very firmly stated:

---

[1] I have seen the work performed several times, in English cathedrals and under the direction of Dr. E. Martin Browne, C.B.E. The atmosphere of the scene at the inn was that of a re-enactment of the Last Supper. Between each of the vital actions of the Stranger there came the stroke of a chime-bell. There may have been felt by some a foreshadowing of the ceremony of the Mass.

In my edition I introduced into this scene, as 'background music', the melody of the hymn '*Jesu, nostra redemptio . . .*', under the mistaken idea that the action would take longer than it did. It might be better omitted, as well as, if preferred, a great deal of the instrumental accompaniment throughout. See pp. 245ff.

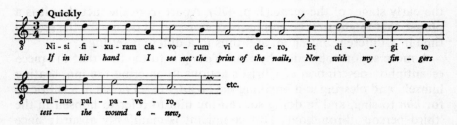

I call particular attention to the Beauvais writer's musical artistry that could convey something of Thomas's vigorous scepticism in his first tune, and contrast it in the setting of his phrases of utter abnegation after Christ had again appeared and offered to him in turn the material proofs. After an introductory rubric, 'Thomas, prostrating himself at his feet, says' [*Et Thomas procidens ad pedes eius dicat*], there comes his second solo, a Dorian one, full of his emotion:

With Christ's gentle reproach to Thomas the work ends quietly, once more to the Beauvais writer's own music:

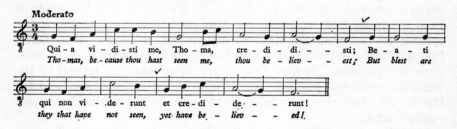

—And with the singing of the responsory '*Christus resurgens ...*' Vespers is resumed.

It was an independent and superior mind that put together this twelfth-century music-drama at Beauvais. Although for several centuries more the *Peregrinus* framework continued to be given dramatic and musical life, no other surviving version ever approached its quality.

CHAPTER TEN

THE TWELFTH CENTURY (2)

Music-dramas of the Christmas season
The earliest Old Testament plays

THE twelfth century saw the last of the surviving examples of the '*Quem quaeritis in praesepe . . .*' Introit trope of the Third Mass of Christmas. These two versions, Paris *B.N.* (*Nouv. Acq.*) *MS lat. 1235*, fol. 183v.– 184r., and Turin, *Bibl. Reg. F.IV 18*, fol. 9v.–10r., are both beautiful examples of the exactitude of pitch that could be achieved by neume notation. I record also the fact that the (quite normal) setting of the Christmas '*Quem quaeritis*' words in *B.N. 1235*, i.e., <u>dr</u> <u>rmr</u> <u>dr</u> r-, is used in the same manuscript to set the same two words to the Easter Sepulchre trope of the Introit for Easter Day, a most exceptional happening!

II

In Chapter VIII I have already discussed the nature of the *Officium Stellae* music-dramas in general before dealing with the versions of the eleventh century (the earliest), and in particular the one from the cathedral of Freising. My conclusion, as you will recall, is that the Freising version must constitute, not the climax of a steadily developing number of such music-dramas, but an entity which may well represent a single act of composition, from which later versions of the *Officium Stellae* may have derived much of their material, textual and musical.

In considering the twelfth-century versions, I mention first—but only in passing—the material found in *B.N.* (*Nouv. Acq.*) *MS 1235* (fol. 198r.–199v.), which, as we have already noted on p. 125, is in too much of a muddle to make dramatic sense. A more useful starting point is to be found in a manuscript which is by now an old friend to us—the Norman-Sicilian *Madrid 289*. On its folios 107v.–110r. it contains a practical version of moderate length, set to transcribable music. The drama begins with the appearance of the three Kings, following the Star, and closes with the singing of a rare Christmas hymn, '*Nuntium vobis fero de supernis*'.[1] Between, we meet with the ten-item 'core' (see pp. 127–8), texts and music normal, together with many added 'court' items, which seem to agree, most of the time, with the settings of parallel passages in the Freising and Compiègne versions of the eleventh century. *Madrid*

[1] For comments on this hymn, and the full text, see Young, II, p. 433 (*Ed.*).

follows *Compiègne* in extending 'core' Item E (*'Ecce stella . . .'*) to include some sentences that have clearly been gleaned from the ancient sequence, *'Quem non praevalent . . .'* (see p. 130). There are only two or three brief items in the work (including a hexameter) that cannot be matched in one or another of the *Officium Stellae* music-dramas. The 'Christmas hymn' mentioned above is a single Sapphic stanza, used also by the Beauvais *Daniel*. Both of them employ the music of the original hymn. *Madrid's* rubrics are not very informative, dramatically; we are told who is speaking to whom, and little more.

A Strasburg version belonging to the end of the century (*London, Brit. Mus., Add. MS 23922*, fol. 8v.–11v.) uses St. Gall unheighted neumes for its music, but the settings are mostly identifiable, with the exception of a few brief sentences (two of them apparently unique hexameters), and in particular an original rhyming passage assigned to Herod's *symmiste* (attendants), *'O principes sacerdotum . . .'*, for the neumes of which I have no clue.

Young (I, p. 67) calls attention to the appearance in the Strasburg version of a passage spoken by Herod, *'Quae sit causa vie . . .'*, which, as he proceeds to show, was perhaps composed under the influence of certain lines from Virgil's *Aeneid* (ix, 376–7). His mention of it as a 'first appearance' in the Strasburg manuscript is due to the fact that he was arranging his *Officium Stellae* dramas in the order of their apparent expansion, and not chronologically. We have already noted (p. 131) that it is the eleventh-century 'Freising' version that gives the earliest surviving example of the item, together with the Magi's reply, *'Rex est causa vie: reges sumus ex Arabitis . . .'*. Both the texts and the music of the passages from this particular area of the worn Freising vellum are very difficult to decipher, but what neumes remain readable seem to give evidence of a basic setting for the versions of Strasburg, Bilsen (*Brussels 299*), and *Orléans 201*, the last-named showing some elaborations, as we might expect. Karl Young also calls attention to Strasburg's use of the 'prophecy', *'Bethlehem, non es minima . . .'* (St. Matthew ii: 6–7). The musical settings of the six *Officium Stellae* versions of the verse available (in neumes or on staves, and meagre enough), show that when charted, a family likeness goes back once more, as far as neumes can indicate, to the Freising version.

One other feature of interest of which Karl Young makes mention in discussing the Strasburg work is Herod's emotional sentence, *'Incendium meum ruina extinguam'*, which, as Young says, has been borrowed from the writings of Sallust. But the Freising version had already laid claim to this item with a neume incipit close to Strasburg's.[1] The latter's setting of the first two words seems to be: r-dl, dr r r rf r-. We can even trace the borrowed sentence back to the eleventh-century *Einsiedeln MS 366*, where the first two words are definitely set to rd dr r r rf r-.

Karl Young seems inclined to dwell on the conscious 'literary' flavour of the Strasburg version. However, it appears to me that the work could

[1] See p. 131.

have taken over all its attributes from the eleventh-century Freising version, which had a similar taste for the construction of hexameters and for classical quotation.[1]

From the library of the Faculty of Medicine at Montpellier comes *MS H. 304*, fol. 41v.–42v. What could have proved to be a complete and thoroughly practical music-drama is disqualified by the fact that the folios are without their music. Also, owing to this absence we are deprived, probably, of a good deal of useful general evidence. Certainly out of the fifty and more items that the work contains only about half a dozen can be supposed to be unique to itself, but it would have been useful to have compared the settings of two important verse features, the sequence, '*Quem non praevalent propria . . .*' and Archelaus' fierce appeal to his father Herod in '*Salve, pater inclyte . . .*', with the music given to the same lines in *Orléans 201*, the latter being the only other *Officium Stellae* to employ them.

Karl Young (II, p. 68) mentions that the Montpellier version is in some way related to the traditions of Rouen. It is an opinion with which I concur, especially as I strongly suspect that the *Officium Stellae* from *Orléans 201* is likely to have originated in the diocese of Rouen.

Possibly the most unusual feature of the Montpellier version is the attempt to add verisimilitude to the court scene by allocating to two of the Magi what Karl Young describes (II, p. 73) as 'unintelligible gibberish' when addressing Herod; in other words, creating the impression of a use of exotic tongues. Seeing that almost immediately both of them revert to normal sung Latin, I should very much have liked to know if the 'gibberish' were indeed given music.

The rest of the court scene is on established lines, as is the Magi's brief encounter with the returning Shepherds. The adorations at the Manger and the giving of gifts are, however, marked by original slants and additions to the standard sentences.

Throughout the version the action is continually illuminated by the generously detailed rubrics, which contain such mentions as Herod's first reception of his visitors, when he gives each in turn a kiss and a seat beside him. The Star also comes in for much attention; apparently it was a 'travelling' one.

It is after the angelic warning to the Magi and their departure (during which they sing the now obsolete responsory, '*O magnum mysterium . . .*') that we have the appearance of Archelaus, son of Herod, and the stanzas of '*Salve, pater . . .*'. The concluding item, first found in the Freising version, is the cruel suggestion by Herod's attendant ('*Discerne, Domine . . .*') as to the necessity of the Massacre, and Herod is finally left brandishing a sword. It seems probable that Montpellier once possessed a sequel, dealing with the Innocents.

---

[1] I say 'Freising', but much similar eleventh-century material, perhaps actually set down as examples of *Officium Stellae*, may have existed at the time, now perished without trace. The condition of the single Freising folio is eloquent evidence as to the nearness of its escape from oblivion (see Plate XI).

I turn now to the *Officium Stellae* from the monastery of Bilsen (*Brussels, Bibl. des Bollandistes, MS 299*, fol. 179v.–180v.). Once again we have pages suffering from obliterations.[1] Although the version has its music, this takes the form of unheighted 'French primitive' neumes; the situation is not improved by the occasional use merely of incipits. Thus for some of the time it is impossible to interpret stretches of the settings with any certitude. The 'core' music is there, and that of other familiar items, but there is also an unusual proportion of sentences unique to Bilsen, especially leading up to and during the Herod scene.

What is immediately noticeable is the debt which Bilsen seems to owe to Freising. By way of a choral introduction there occurs a series of hexameters which have already turned up, almost exactly word for word, in the previous century in the Freising music-drama, but in this instance as a concluding choral item. In each case their exact relevance is not very clear. No comparison of the settings is possible. Bilsen gives unheighted neumes, Freising none at all, or at least, none visible.

Another Freising link follows in the choral singing of the antiphon, '*Super solium David, et super regnum eius sedebit in aeternum*', to mark the enthronement of Herod. There is something of dramatic irony in the use of this 'King David' antiphon, with its phrase, '*sedebit in aeternum*', in relation to the evil king soon to be dethroned. The same use is made of it, it will be found, in the *Ordo Rachelis* from *Orléans 201*.

Also, *Bilsen* shares with *Freising* (and *Orléans*) an inclusion of an opening scene of the angelic vision to the shepherds in the fields and the departure of the latter for Bethlehem. Then comes the entry of the Magi in familiar terms, both verbal and musical; but the development from this point up to their contact with Herod seems to be to the credit of the Bilsen playwright alone. The situation includes the unique moment of an eager messenger bursting in with the cry of '*Rex, rex, rex!*', anxious to give the news of the virgin birth.

After a good deal of court-scene material in common use, and including the 'Virgilian' feature, '*Quae sit causa vie . . . ?*', there comes what appears to be an original stroke, revealed in a rubric. After the Magi have declared their purpose to Herod and have displayed their gifts for the new-born king they are given some drastic treatment, namely, being committed to prison, where they remain until Herod has finished taking counsel with his scribes, and has called for their re-admittance.[2] His renewed cross-examination of the three again contains unfamiliar material, much of it in hexameter form—unfamiliar at least to all versions except eleventh-century *Freising*, which seems to be the source

[1] I believe that the particular folios are actually palimpsests, and that the semi-obliterations of the 'Stellae' material are complicated by the smears left by previous rubbings-out.

[2] The Bilsen version is the only one that, while Herod consults his own wise men, definitely orders the Magi out of earshot and then, afterwards, has them recalled. In *Freising* the Magi are also apparently absent—judging, at least, from Herod's command after the Scribes have given testimony, to 'lead them in' again ('*Adduc externos citius, vassalle, tyrannos*'). There is no clue as to their first exclusion, but one would hardly expect there to be in view of Freising's woeful shortage of rubrics. All other versions seem to call for the Magi to remain 'onstage' during the counsel of the Scribes.

of it, with some touches in Herod's questioning that seem to hark back to Virgil.

In the course of the interrogation the first Magus refers to himself as 'Zoroaster'. Karl Young comments (II, p. 83), that this appears to be a 'personal fancy' of the writer of this (Bilsen) play. This is not so; there is one other *Officium Stellae* version that ventures to give a personal name to one of the Magi. The version is from Freising and the name is 'Zoroaster'.

Bilsen next sends the Magi on their way with a half-dozen lines, found also in the versions from Compiègne and Madrid (i.e., Norman-Sicily). This item consists of an amalgam of the 'core' item E with some lines adrift from the sequence '*Quem non praevalent propria . . .*'. The music from the 'item E' part is derived, in the case of all three, from the stock setting; that from the sequence part a series of mostly single notes (as one might expect).

The Shepherds are met with on the way, in familiar verbal and musical terms, and as found in four other versions, including Freising. But in the presentation scene Bilsen has some unique material, three original but somewhat obscure hexameters. The version concludes with the usual warnings, by the Angel and by the *Armiger*, but by way of a change the Magi depart singing a Hartker antiphon '*O, Regem caeli . . .*', the chorus following with the ancient hymn, '*Hostis Herodes . . .*'.

Karl Young (II, p. 83) comments on 'the general absence from the rubrics of indications of costume or stage furnishings', and suggests that it might be 'that the text before us was not designed for use upon the stage'. This I cannot believe, since for the people who recorded it, the music of every word of the libretto-text was known, and was set down in neumes. The work is obviously a music-drama; that only a proportion of this notation can be interpreted after the lapse of centuries is just our misfortune, for like that from Montpellier, it is effectively shaped, with some original touches. However, its debts to the earlier music-drama from Freising are particularly apparent.

I deal now with one of the masterpieces of medieval music-drama, the *Officium Stellae* found in the so-called 'Fleury Playbook', contained in the manuscript now lodged in the municipal library at Orléans: *Bibl. de la Ville, MS 201*, pp. 205–14. I have already referred briefly to the 'Playbook' (see p. 165), saying that it was more likely to represent a collection than a repertoire. However, I shall further delay considerations of the 'Playbook' as a whole until the opportunity arises of meeting more of its items, and for the moment will deal only with its *Officium Stellae* representative.

This version has many advantages over the other surviving *Officium* examples. Both the text and the musical notation on a four-line stave are nearly always clearly rendered; and what incipits there are are capable of being safely expanded. The rubrics are generous in regard to dramatic action; gestures, movements, even emotions are plentifully described.

The drama begins with the scene of the angelic announcement to the

Shepherds in the fields. This type of opening to the drama of the Magi occurs elsewhere in *Officium Stellae* versions only in the Freising and Bilsen examples, and there in a briefer and more elementary fashion. The episode as treated by the Orléans manuscript amounts to an inclusion of an *Officium Pastorum* music-drama in itself, since it leads the Shepherds actually to the Manger, where they are confronted by the Midwives, and finally see the Child and adore him.

There can be found in this scene some interesting musical evidence. The opening rubrics give the official title as being *Ordo ad representandum Herodem,* and mention the appearance of the characters, among them Herod, and the Angel with his heavenly host. In the first item the Angel calms the manifest terror of the Shepherds with the words of St. Luke ii: 10, 'Fear not . . .'. His words to them continue to the end of verse 12. The chorus of angels which follows comprises verse 14. Then the Shepherds, 'rising up', utter the third item, their speech as in verse 15 ('Let us now go . . .'). These three settings of Vulgate text seem to represent free composition.

The question then arises—'Whose free composition?'. If we look ahead to a thirteenth-century *Officium Pastorum* undoubtedly belonging to the diocese of Rouen, (*Paris, B.N. MS lat. 904,* fol. 11v.–12v.), we find that the first item ('*Nolite timere . . .*') and the third ('*Transeamus usque . . .*'), as found in each work, are too much alike in their settings to be considered independent of each other. I give below the first sentence of the first item and the whole of the third item, from the respective manuscripts, together with renderings on G staves of their settings.

---

¹ The '*vos*' of *Orléans 201* is not to be found in the Vulgate verse.

The remainder of the first item in the respective manuscripts consists of the rest of the Angel's proclamation (verses 11 & 12), with the Orléans writer adding a bonus not found in St. Luke, a mention of the Child lying '*in medio duum animalium*', and thus providing places for the ox and the ass in the 'Christmas Crib' of future generations. The respective settings are strikingly similar, with differences of only a few notes: each scribe was plainly dealing with the same composition. Regarding the third Orléans item, the brief sentence comprising verse 14 (not a '*Gloria*' as such); here the two manuscripts each go their own way in setting the words. However, after the musical coincidence of '*Transeamus usque Bethleem . . .*' and the arrival of the Shepherds at the Manger, there comes yet another parallel. We have previously seen (see p. 104) that the Midwives' question, '*Quem quaeritis in praesepe . . . ?*' is uniformly set, all over Christendom, to a quite different music from

the Easter version: ♪ *Quem quae - ri - tis* ♪ represents the setting of the first two words. But not in the case of the *Officium Stellae* of *Orléans 201*; it proceeds to borrow from its manuscript companion, the Orléans

Visitatio of Easter, and writes: ♪ *Quem quae - ri - tis* ♪ The *Officium*

Pastorum of *B.N. 904* is similarly moved, and writes in its turn:

♪ *Quem quae - ri - tis* ♪ This to me is more than a coincidence. In all

the range of Church music-dramas I have met with no other instance of the Advent (Manger) question borrowing its *music* from the Easter (Sepulchre) one.[1] After those first two words, and after something like the 'triadic stride' of the Easter music, the two Christmas Season

[1] There is a curious reversal of this procedure in the case of the first stage *Visitatio* from Nevers (*B.N. MS 9449*, fol. 34r. and *B.N. MS lat.* (*Nouv. Acq.*) *1235*, fol. 205r.), which has the Christmas Season setting for the words '*Quem quaeritis*' in its Easter *Visitatio Sepulchri*.

205

music-dramas return to the usual Christmas Season settings,[1] but these two 'harkings-back' incline me towards the idea that, since there is no doubt that the *Officium Pastorum* of *B.N. 904* belongs to the diocese of Rouen, the *Officium Stellae* of *Orléans 201* may have had its origin in the same region, and only later have acquired the motley companionship of the 'Fleury Playbook'.

I continue with the progress of the Orléans music-drama. The reply of the Shepherds and the words of the Midwives as they reveal the Child are as in the normal Christmas trope form, text and music.[2] But *Orléans* proceeds further than any other 'Herod' drama in calling on the Shepherds to 'adore' the infant. This they do by borrowing one of the 'core' sentences, '*Salve, Rex (Princeps) saeculorum*', with its music. It is interesting to note that later in the work, the Magi, offering similar adoration, employ exactly the same music.

The Shepherds now address the onlookers, inviting them to join in the worship. The item is based on an obsolete Advent antiphon ('*Venite, adoremus eum . . .*'), surviving in Hartker (p. 74), and occurring elsewhere among the *Officium Stellae* only in the Norman-Sicilian version (*Madrid, MS 289*), where in fact it is sung by the Magi. There are similarities—and differences—in the two dramatic settings, but both look as if they might have owed something to the unheighted neumes of the now faded liturgical antiphon.

The Shepherds disappear from the scene, and attention is now given to the three Magi, who come forward from different directions, each 'as if from his own country'. As we might expect, the first words are those of the normal standard sentence, '*Stella fulgore . . .*', belonging to the 'core' that has already been detailed.[3] As we have seen, there is in all the versions an attractive musical start to the item. '*Stella*' is set, throughout, to the phrase r̠dl̠,d̠r r. This motif, it would seem, was borne in mind by a number of *Officium Stellae* versions, and recalled in later items and with varying consistency at such places as '*Regia (vos mandata vocant)*'; '*hoc venientes*' (in '*Rex est causa . . .*'); and '*nasci Christum*' (in '*Vidimus, Domine . . .*'). But it is *Orléans* that seems most committed to the phrase. Having in the first item written the music for '*Stel-la*' as r̠dl̠,d̠r r, the composer, quite uniquely, felt compelled to round off the item by setting '*ru-ti-lat*' as r̠dl̠,d̠r r. Leaving out the usual (b) item, he passes on to (c), '*Quem venturem . . .*', and sets '*si-gna-ve-rat*' as r̠d l̠, d̠r r-. Immediately afterwards, the kiss of peace is exchanged, a feature found elsewhere among the Magi only in the Montpellier version—and that without its music. *Orléans* has to set '*Pax quo-que ti-bi!*', and finds an easy solution in writing r d l̠, d̠r r-. In fact, the composer causes the whole short episode of the meeting of the Magi to echo with the phrase, as no other version does.

[1] In the case of *Orléans 201* the words '*in praesepe*' (together with their settings) are omitted. The next word, '*pastores*' takes on the usual Christmas Season music.

[2] Here, *Orléans* misses out the usual word '*hic*', after '*adest*'. A slip, since its four-note setting can be seen swallowed up by the long flourish of notes on the first syllable of '*parvulus*'. There is also a clef change that the scribe missed.　　　[3] See p. 127.

Their threefold cry at the sight of the Star ('*Ecce Stella, ecce stella, ecce stella!*') replaces the normal '*Ecce stella in oriente . . .*' for the time being.[1] The next two items—the enquiries made to the 'citizens of Jerusalem' by the Magi on their way to Herod, and Herod's question, '*Quae rerum novitas . . . ?*', when he catches sight of them—are each confined to Orléans and Freising only. Even so, Orléans has its own musical settings.

It is in the next item that Orléans really comes into its own. The few irregular lines of verse, beginning '*Caldei sumus . . .*' had already appeared in the Freising version, but set to what appear to be somewhat unenterprising neumes. Orléans' music, written on a stave, must surely have been sung rhythmically; a true lyric. I venture on a modern transcription.

On present evidence it would seem that this graceful tune owes its existence solely to the composer of the music of the *Officium Stellae* from *Orléans 201*.

The Orléans version of the scene at Herod's court, which follows, contains much that is familiar, though given distinction by some entirely unique items. For example, the phrases '*Leti inquisitores . . .*' and '*Reges sunt Arabum . . .*' appear only in *Orléans*; and it seems to be almost 'standard policy' of this composer-playwright to vary the usual melody of a widely accepted text, or to vary the text itself. Perhaps the most noticeable of the originalities, however, is the strong dramatic appearance of Herod's son Archelaus. As we have already seen, most versions, from Freising onward, make use of the St. Matthew 'prophecy' verse, '*Bethleem non minima . . .*', marking the moment when Herod most plainly betrays his apprehensions. But it is only *Orléans* that further heightens the drama of the hurling down of the book of prophecies by bringing in Archelaus, both to soothe his father's apprehen-

---

[1] This item in its standard setting, appears later in the drama, when the Magi, having taken their leave of Herod, proceed to the *praesepe*. See p. 209.

sions and to inflame him further to 'make war against this petty king!',[1] through the means of a vigorous rhythmic melody of most attractive quality. I offer a modern transcription:

[Herod replies :]

Herod continues for another stanza, to the same melody:

'*Rex est natus fortior,   Nobis et potentior*
('Yet we hear of stronger still, Who as a kingly babe is born)

'*Vereor ne solio   Nos extrahet regio.*'
('Truly there is fear that we   May from our royal throne be torn.')

Then, in the words of a rubric, 'let the son, speaking slightingly of Christ, offer himself as a defender' ['*Tunc filius despective loquens de Christo offerat se ad vindictam . . .*']. The same setting is used, but with an additional stroke of energy in the musical phrase of the first and fifth bars:

con – tra . . .

Archelaus' final stanza is one of firm resolve:

'*Contra illum regulum,   Contra natum parvulum,*
(' 'Gainst this king of little worth,   'Gainst the babe, new brought to birth,)

'*Iube, pater, filium,   Hoc inire praelium.*'
('Give word, father, to thy son,   That this strife be now begun.')

With restored confidence Herod now sends away the Magi to seek the Child, assuring them of his wish to join them in doing homage. As the Magi follow the Star, *Orléans* in a rubric affords us a delightful glimpse

---

[1] The composition occurs elsewhere only in the version from Montpellier, unfortunately without music, and set at the very end of the work—a less effective place.

of Herod and Archelaus brandishing their swords at it ('*Magis egredientibus, precedat stella eos, que nondum in conspectu Herodis apparuit. Quam ipsi sibi mutuo ostendentes, procedant. Qua visa, Herodes et filius minentur cum gladiis*').[1]

The Magi move away to one of the standard items, the couplet '*Ecce Stella in oriente praevisa . . .*'. Then occurs one of the less common happenings, the re-introduction of the Shepherds, returning from the Manger. Even rarer is the fact that they are singing the Christmas antiphon, '*O Regem caeli . . .*', a privilege usually allocated to the Magi. In the Shepherds' extended reply to the Magi's brief question there is a point of musical interest. The second moiety of the text becomes increasingly a quotation from the very first item of the work, the proclamation of the Angel. Increasingly, also, the Angel's music is taken over, until, with the last half-dozen words or so, everything has been borrowed.

The next item is another major instance of *Orléans*' musical originality. The Shepherds have departed; the Magi, in their turn, are on the way to the Manger, and the composer sets about providing them with a rhythmic, melodious processional. The text was already well known as a sequence,[2] and had been employed by the Montpellier *Officium Stellae* version, though without any music being given. *Compiègne*, *Madrid*, and *Bilsen* employed some of its sentences, tacking them on to the end of the widely used '*Ecce stella in oriente . . .*' couplet, and using for them the single-note sequence music. But *Orléans* makes a unique and unified composition of it, to what I have no doubt is an original setting. It is worth quoting in full.

---

[1] Late in 1963, I transcribed the Orléans *Officium Stellae* manuscript, rendering the music into modern barred notation, and giving, where necessary, rhythmic readings. This was done as part of my contribution towards the production of 'The Play of Herod', which in due course was performed at 'The Cloisters' by the New York Pro Musica, in the city of New York. The work, which included also my transcription of the Orléans 'Innocents' manuscript, was afterwards published by Oxford University Press, Inc. (New York, 1965). There were aspects of the production with which I was not in agreement, one of them concerned with the episode that has just been discussed.

In the actual performance (and in the published copy) Herod's confession to his son ('*Rex est natus fortior . . .*') is turned into a duet, the son sharing his father's apprehensions. Archelaus apparently so far recovers as to sing his defiant solo ('*Contra illum regulum . . .*'), but what happens next is a totally unauthorized climb-down, both Herod and Archelaus repeating together the stanza, '*Rex est natus fortior . . .*'. Thus the episode concludes in a mood not of defiance but fear, and all this, apparently, for the sake of ending up the scene with a duet.

Fortunately, I have an appendix in 'The Play of Herod', headed 'Literal Transcription'. This includes photographs of each of the manuscript pages concerned and my transcriptions of the texts and the music, the notation rendered as black semibreves and slurred to show the neume-groupings. From this appendix a clear distinction can be drawn between 'original' and 'editorial'. I shall have more to say of this New York Pro Musica production later (see p. 255).

[2] It still exists, with a setting in unheighted neumes, in *Brit. Mus. Add. MS 19768*, fols. 70–71. Karl Young prints the *Analecta Hymnica* version of the text on II, p. 446.

For the episode of the interrogation of the Magi by the Midwives and their revealing of the Child, *Orléans* keeps more or less to the standard settings, but the threefold '*Salve . . .*' homage to the Child is a feature unique to the *Orléans* and *Madrid* versions (and a small piece of further evidence as to what I think is their 'Norman' link). Of the two closely similar settings, *Madrid's* is slightly the more elaborate.

But the presentation of the gifts once more shows the Orléans writer shaping a tune to his own pattern, after beginning it in the 'normal' fashion. The item starts out (see J, p. 120):

210

—but then expands to:

Secundus:

Sus - ci - pe   myrr-ham, si -gnum se - pul - tu - rae.
Ac - cept   myrrh,.   em - blem of bu - ri - al.

This same melody, with different texts ('*Suscipe thus, tu vere Deus*') is repeated by the Third King.

After the giving of the gifts comes the 'dream' episode, the Angel's '*Impleta sunt . . .*' warning common to all the 'Magi' versions, and then three final items, found only in *Orléans*, the Christmas antiphon, '*O admirabile commercium . . .*' (still to be met in the Roman liturgy), and two other free-rhythm items which seem to represent new composition, the last with a vivid opening:

Gau - - de - te, fra - tres, ...   etc.

—and being followed with the last item of Matins, the '*Te Deum*'. All in all, a strikingly original and cohesive composition.

III

In Chapter VIII (pp. 124 ff.) I made reference to the 'Slaying of the Innocents' music-drama type, referring to a rhyming version contained in the same Freising manuscript-binding as the *Officium Stellae* of that library, but probably representing a later writing-down, by a different hand. Indeed, one might imagine that the composition was intended for the study rather than for a clerical performance staged within a church building, were it not the for fact that fairly melismatic musical settings in the form of unheighted St. Gall neumes accompany the rhyming couplets that make up the bulk of the libretto. One must also recall that the work is headed *Ordo Rachelis*, and that it concludes with the usual clue to a Matins performance, the '*Te Deum*' incipit.

Whoever undertook the shaping of the text created what appears to be largely an original poetic composition, with minor borrowings of familiar *Officium Stellae* sentences, and a major item from the liturgy. But in my opinion the dramatic value of the work cannot be rated very highly. It creaks at the joints; or perhaps it would be truer to say that there are no real joints, and that the work crashes disconcertingly from one scene to another.

Without any introductory rubric an Angel sings a five-line paraphrase of the Gospel message to the Shepherds. The Shepherds' reaction, a six-line rhyming stanza, is somewhat more sophisticated than the simple prose of St. Luke. They set off for Bethlehem singing what appears to be

H

a paraphrase of the liturgical antiphon '*O Regem coeli . . .*', its neumes bearing no relationships to the standard liturgical music. As for the settings of the two earlier stanzas, they reveal a practice which is followed almost throughout when providing music for the ubiquitous rhyming couplets—a succession of meandering melodies that seem to show no sign of repetition of phrase. This type of stanza tune seems to have been largely a German development. We shall make a closer acquaintance with the style when, in the next century, we encounter more examples of what I consider to be an unwieldy type, the *Zehnsilberspiel* brand of the *Visitatio Sepulchri*.

The only evidence we have as to the Shepherds having reached the *praesepe* is the face that a 'Chorus' (*not* the Midwives) sing the familiar sentence '*Pastores, dicite . . .*' to the usual music, and the shepherds reply with the equally familiar '*Infantem vidimus . . .*'. Then, it would appear, the whole scene disappears into thin air, for in the next line an Angel is addressing Joseph.

In point of fact, it is probable that the system of having different 'stations' was being employed, and that the onlookers were supposed to have turned their attention in a new direction. However, there is no denying that the *praesepe* scene has been broken off in a most unsatisfactory manner. The new situation is concerned with the Angel's warning to the Holy Family concerning Herod, and the need for the flight to Egypt. Joseph and Mary exchange distichs set in the same style as before, without repeats or patterns. Then by way of a change they depart on their way, to the singing by Joseph of a liturgical (and quite relevant) piece, the Matins responsory, '*Ægypte, noli flere . . .*'. The *incipit* neumes indicate the traditional setting.

The succeeding rubric informs us that we are at Herod's court, where a messenger exchanges rhyming couplets with the King, telling him of the escape of the Magi. Herod is actually more interested in the possibility of slaying the Christ-child, and promptly accepts the drastic suggestion of the messenger as to the despatching of *all* the young children of Bethlehem. The task is undertaken, apparently, by a single soldier, who deals with them one at a time, accompanying himself with the phrase: '*Disce mori, puer!*' (I can do nothing towards interpreting the neumes). The whole of this scene—the strong emotions of the King, his messenger, and his '*Armiger*' having to be expressed in somewhat stilted, end-stopped rhyming lines instead of swift prose—is surely less successful than similar moments in any of the major *Officium Stellae* versions. The few familiar phrases that turn up in this versified scene show no link with their usual settings. Even the '*Hostis Herodes impie . . .*' incipit of the ancient hymn with which the chorus rounds off the sketchy scene does not show in its unheighted neumes any likeness to the liturgical settings normally found with the verses.

Once again a scene seems to vanish, and we hear no more concerning Herod. A new rubric makes us aware of the following scene, Rachel weeping over the slaughtered children. The same technique is again

apparent, a succession of distichs, the unheighted neumes showing no
sign of repetition of phrase. I shall give below four of the lines of
Freising's particular version of 'Rachel's Lament' together with the
particular Freising neumes that accompany them. I imagine that very
little has been lost through our not possessing the key to the pitches of
this music. Its obvious formlessness contrasts strangely with the
regularity and rhythm of the verses.

The same four lines of poetry (and in fact quite a number of other
matching lines) will be met with in the Orléans version of the 'Slaying of
the Innocents', the composer's melodies in this work being given their
pitch values.

Here are the Freising lines mentioned above:

Ah!ˈ teneri partus, laceros quos cernimus artus!

Heu! dulces . nati, sola rabie jugulati!

The corresponding lines of the Orléans version, together with a
rhythmic reading of their setting, will be found on p. 217. I can say
nothing more in regard to the unheighted St. Gall neumes which set the
Freising lines except to mention again the lack of any indication of any
sort of musical repetition; and this, together with the presence of
a fair number of multiple neumes, makes it unlikely that we have here
the borrowing of a now forgotten sequence. When the same rhyming
lines are encountered in the 'Innocents' version belonging to the Orléans
manuscript there will be found a much more vivid musical treatment.

Another indispensable feature of the 'Slaying of the Innocents'
drama was the presence of a 'Comforter' (or 'Comforters'), offering to
the mourning mother whatever consolation is possible. Freising winds
up its version by a plain and straightforward piece of borrowing, that of
the whole of the famous (and in this case quite relevant) '*Quid tu,
virgo . . .*' a sequence attributed to Notker of St. Gall. The text clearly
takes the form of a dialogue between a bereaved mother and a com-
miserating chorus. The music of the Notker original is safely known,[1]
and the paired lines of neumes in the Freising manuscript, noted almost
wholly as *puncta* and *virgae*, are consistent with it.[2]

With the singing of this sequence the Freising drama comes to an
abrupt and unsatisfactory conclusion. There is little more to say

---

[1] The music is to be found in neume form in the eleventh-century Einsiedeln fragment,
MS 366, but is given a stave transcription by Schubiger in his *Spicilegien* (Berlin, 1876),
pp. 48–9. The notes are confirmed by the version given in St. Gall ,*MS 546*, pp. 282–3, with
only minor differences.

[2] Freising omits one pair of the usual lines.

concerning it, except that every single scene appears almost as if broken off. The Shepherds show no sign of offering their homage; we learn nothing of the Holy Family's return; the court scene is a mere sketch; and, particularly, no dramatic use is made of the Innocents, who are represented as mere supernumeraries, waiting to be slain. There were contemporaries with keener imaginations than those of the poet and composer of this Freising work, as we shall now see. Let us return to the *Orléans 201* manuscript.

It appears certain to me that the Orléans 'Slaying of the Innocents' was planned as a sequel to the *Officium Stellae* (which precedes it immediately in the manuscript), and that the same skilful hands wove it. Since the first work ends very definitely with a '*Te Deum laudamus*', one must suppose that the 'Innocents' drama is an entirely separate composition and intended for performance on a different day, but no internal evidence exists as to when this was.[1] What does appear is the same sense of order and quickness of imagination, whether in adaptation or invention, whether in the handling of prose, poetry or music.

When the wideness of the activities shown in the drama is considered, it seems plain that something more than the chancel and the space in front of the choir would be needed for performances.[2] We must again suppose the common enough techniques of the widely-separated 'stations'; Herod enthroned at his court (and the court would need plenty of space); the *praesepe* still remaining whence Joseph and Mary in due course will flee; the Angel standing on high, ready to give his warning to Joseph; the wide sweep needed for the procession of Innocents to make their choral excursions, and to be surrounded by Herod's swordsmen.

Not much is said regarding costuming in the rubrics of the work, but we do learn that the children taking the parts of the Innocents (no doubt of the choir) are to be clad in white stoles. They are the first to appear, making their way in procession round the church, and uttering their praises for the 'Lamb of God' in terms of an antiphon, '*O quam gloriosum . . .*', one that is still in the Roman liturgy. *Orléans* sets it to the liturgical music. Now comes a striking episode; the 'Lamb' having been mentioned, a rubric ensures that reality should succeed symbolism.[3] The directions are 'Then the Lamb, carrying a cross and coming unexpectedly, goes before them hither and thither, while those following sing'.[4] What they sing is a (now obsolete) antiphon of Lauds, '*Emitte*

---

[1] Performances on Innocents' Day seem the most obvious date, but see Young, II, pp. 116 and 455.

[2] In the performances at 'The Cloisters' in New York, to which I have previously referred, of the two *Orléans* dramas, 'Magi' and 'Innocents', the restricted space in the chancel of the reconstructed Spanish chapel caused great ingenuity to be shown in regard to production devices.

[3] The idea of the Innocents having with them a lamb, or some kind of representation of one, is met with also in the thirteenth century Laon *Officium Stellae* (see p. 129), a work which, unfortunately, is without its music. But the mention of the lamb is confined to no more than two words in a rubric concerned with the Innocents—'. . . *agnum portantes . . .*'.

[4] '*Tunc Agnus ex improviso veniens, portans crucem, antecedat eos huc et illuc, et illi sequentes cantent . . .*'.

Agnum, Domine . . .' ('Send forth, O Lord, the Lamb, the ruler of the whole earth . . .'). In medieval painting and carving the symbolic figure of the Lamb bearing a cross is familiar enough, but *Orléans* seems unique among medieval Church music-dramas in presenting a living, active representation—that is, if the rubrics is to be taken literally.[1]

While the Innocents are continuing their movements, Herod at his court assumes his throne, his armed attendant (*Armiger*) singing before him yet another relevant liturgical piece, the Lauds antiphon, '*Super solium David . . .*' ('He shall sit on David's throne . . .'). We have already noted its occurrence in the *Officium Stellae* versions from Freising and Bilsen. As I have remarked previously, it seems apparent that this inclusion was intended satirically, since the passage (found with the same music in Hartker, p. 24) was addressed to the occupant of the eternal throne, not to a king so soon to suffer corruption.

It is then that the Archangel, high above the *praesepe*, sings his warning to Joseph. The text is that from St. Matthew ii:13, but the mildly melismatic, free-rhythm music is, as far as I know, unique to the Orléans work. Joseph, Mary, and the Child take their departure for Egypt 'unseen by Herod'. Once again a liturgical piece is called on, and once again no better choice could have been made. Joseph sings the responsory '*Aegypte, noli flere . . .*'. We have already noted the item employed thus by the creator of the Freising 'Innocents' version.

It will be recalled that the last we have seen of Herod and his court in the Orléans *Officium Stellae* was the King and his son brandishing their swords at the Star that was guiding the departed Magi to their goal. With the sequel in mind the creators of the two dramas have held back from the first of them any employment of those sentences that will tell Herod of the failure of his schemes, until the Innocents are at hand on whom to vent his wrath.

It is following the departure of Joseph, then, that Herod's *Armiger* brings the news of the Magi's escape, with the familiar sentence, '*Delusus es, Domine . . .*', whereupon Herod, despairing, is according to a rubric prevented by his attendants from slaying himself, and then, more pacified, utters the equally familiar '*Incendium meum ruina . . .*'. Regarding the Orléans settings of each, I can see very little likeness between them and those of other versions, even those of Freising. The Orléans writer once again seems to be going his own way.

Meanwhile, it must have been apparent to any onlookers that a dramatic tension was being built up. The Innocents, following the Lamb, are continuing their devout processional, but by now Herod and his sinister *Armiger* have become aware of them. The children begin a new choral song, five pairs of rhymed lines set to a gently rhythmic Phrygian-mode tune. Both poem and music I believe to be unique to the Orléans drama. I quote its opening bars, transcribed up a fourth:

[1] In the New York performances previously spoken of, the device used was for a standard-bearer to precede the procession, holding a banner-representation of the cross-bearing Lamb.

In harsh succession comes the cruel suggestion from the *Armiger* that if all the Innocents are slain, then the Christ-child may perish among them. Herod's reply is to hand the *Armiger* his sword and order him to deal with the affair. The two sentences, '*Discerne, Domine . . .*' and '*Armiger eximie . . .*', go back to the Freising *Officium Stellae* and *Einsiedeln 366*, but in each case the Orléans music is similar only in places. The scene is now tense with dramatic irony. A rubric details that 'as the slayers approach, the Lamb secretly withdraws, and the Innocents acclaim him as he departs'.[2] Quite unconscious of their peril from the encircling swordsmen the Innocents break into a new song in praise of him, another lilting, rhythmic tune; another composition that, as far as I am aware, is unique to the Orléans work.[3] I quote it:

The doom of the Innocents is upon them, but another rubric is to be noted: 'The mothers of the victims then intercede with the slayers.' The appeal of the women, a six-bar phrase with a striking and significant cadence, will be found, musically, to have an important part to play in the rest of the drama. I quote it below. It was probably repeated several times, as the frantic mothers strove in vain to protect their children.

One must now visualize a pause in momentary silence. Herod, the *Armiger*, and the swordsmen have departed; the Innocents lie slaughtered; the mothers remain stunned and immobile in their grief. It is the Angel, far removed above the strife, who now speaks, bidding the

---

[1] A sense of chronology is not always to be found among medieval librettists.

[2] '*Interim occisoribus venientibus, subtrahatur agnus clam quem abeuntem salutant Innocentes*'. It does seem as if there must have been some kind of animate figure representing the 'Lamb' in the original medieval performances, about which, apart from the rubric evidence, we know nothing.

[3] That is, the rhythmic music; the text, with '*ecce*' instead of '*salve*', is to be found in St. John i:29. This same text is used as a responsory for Matins of Innocents' Day, but the liturgical music, as seen in Hartker, p. 49, is thoroughly melismatic plainchant.

victims awake and lift up their voices—a curious request! As far as I know this item ('*Vos qui in pulvere estis, expergiscimini et clamate!*') is unique to Orléans. What we must surely imagine as a dying voice replies with a very reasonable question; why were they not given divine protection? There comes the Angel's assurance ('*Adhuc sustinete modicum tempus . . .*') that in a little while they will once again join their brethren. The last two items have been borrowed (by the versions from both Orléans and Laon) from the responsory '*Sub altare Dei . . .*', which I have already referred to on p. 135. Orléans seems to have shaped its free-rhythm music on that of the responsory.

There now enters a principal figure, that of Rachel, accompanied by two *Consolatrices*. No doubt it is to be imagined that her own children were to be found among the victims. The rubrics concerning her say that she is 'led in' (*inducatur*). Apparently, the effects of her emotion were to be made obvious; moreover, as she stands there she 'sometimes falls' (*cadens aliquando*), with the Consolers having to 'support her as she falls' (*consolatrices excipientes eam cadentem*).

The rhyming stanzas of the next three items—Rachel's first solo, the Consolers' intervention, and Rachel's resumed lament—consist of lines that can almost all be found in either the Freising or the thirteenth-century Laon versions, often in different orders of arrangement. One might well think that the Orléans texts show the easiest flow, but whether the Orléans writer can be given the credit for them, or whether perhaps they come down from an earlier source, we have no means of knowing. It is worth noting that the scribe of the Orléans manuscript, while writing the lines of the stanzas in continuous prose fashion, went to the unusual trouble of indicating the fact that here was poetry, the line-endings being marked by stops and following capital letters; a trouble, incidentally, that he had already taken in the case of the Innocents' item, '*Agno sacrato . . .*'.

The music seems to fall readily into the first rhythmic mode. I regard Rachel's first item of such musical importance that I am quoting it in full.

217

nec ves - tra co - er - cu - it ae - tas! He - u! ma - tres mi - se - rae,
nor ten - der af - fec - tion could save you! He - u! pi - teous mo - thers,

quae co - gi - mur is - ta vi - de - re! He - u! quid nunc
hav - ing to real - ize what we have wit - ness'd! He - u! what shall

a - gi - mus! Cur non haec fa - cta su - bi - mus! He - u! qui - a
we do now! We can - not bear such hap - pen - ings! He - u! all these

me - mo - res no - stro - que le - va - re do - lo - res. Gau - di - a
me - mo - ries, a - las, can but serve to re - new our grief! No more can

non pos - sunt, nam dul - ci - a pi - gno - ra de - sunt!
there be glad - ness, since our sweet pledges of love have per - ish'd!

This beautiful Mixolydian composition I regard as an outstanding example of medieval melodic art. The composer has seized on the pathetic cadence of the '*Oremus tenere* . . .' item, the plea of the anguished mothers, and has produced a setting which is permeated by the haunting phrase, s l m f s s—; a 'working', as it were, of this *motif*. It will be noted that the last textual sentence ('*Gaudia non possunt* . . .') is set by, first, a variation of the motif, then a return to the curves of the opening bars, and, finally, a broadened version of the now familiar notes. I marvel at the beauty that has been maintained over a wide stretch of melody, without any aid from the device of modulation as we know it.

Apparently Rachel now sinks into the arms of her Consolers, as they take up the theme; this quite literally, since their first sentence is:

No - li, vir - go Ra - chel, no - li, dul - cis - si - ma ma - ter! . . .
Do not, O fair Ra - chel, do not, O sweet - est of mo - thers! . . .

—a variation of Rachel's opening sentence, followed by the inevitable cadence. The Consolers' stanza is a skilful weaving of new musical phrases with borrowed ones from Rachel's items, and it concludes:

Nam - que tu - i na - ti vi - vunt su - per as - tra be - a - ti.

218

Rachel now appears to rally herself. After a threefold cry of '*Heu!*' she again makes use of the main motif. There is something of a late eighteenth-century 'development' in the manner in which it has been packed more closely. She passes on to a melismatic cry of sorrow:

I shall quote no further from this twelve-line stanza of rhythmic couplets, but content myself by mentioning that the motif is employed twice more before its ending. Wisely, the composer makes no further use of it. The succeeding item, sung by the Consolers, employs a gentle, lilting theme, beginning thus:

The new melody continues in repeated, patterned phrases, and as for the text, it will be immediately apparent that here once more is the famous '*Quid tu, virgo . . .*' sequence, which we have seen borrowed *in toto* by the Freising 'Innocents'. But Orléans will have nothing to do with the plain sequence-melody which satisfied Freising, and has apparently created one of its own.

When the Orléans version reaches the point in the sequence text where Rachel is supposed to resume speaking, then the musical style changes. Rachel's indignation against the strokes of Fate is expressed by a rapid, free-rhythm recitative. I quote its beginning:

The Consolers' reply is also in plainchant, somewhat more melismatic. With their contribution the text of the sequence is completed. The line of the Orléans free-rhythm setting of these last two items bears no relation to the melodic line of the original sequence music. I can only conclude that the Orléans music was newly composed.

The succeeding '*Anxiatus est . . .*' item, Rachel's last solo, represents a borrowing of a liturgical antiphon from Lauds of Good Friday (Hartker, p. 220), the Orléans music derived from this setting.[1] We learn from rubrics that Rachel, in her passion of grief, throws herself forward on to the bodies, and is afterwards raised by the Consolers, and led away.

From above, the voice of the Angel is again heard, as he sings (I translate) 'Suffer little children to come unto me . . .', a happy borrowing of a liturgical antiphon (Lauds of Innocents Day) no longer extant,[2] and serving as the miraculous sentence which causes the Innocents to revive, to arise, and to 'enter the choir' ('*intrent chorum*'; clearly, they must previously have been strewn about the nave).

Regarding the chorus sung by the Innocents as they move 'off-stage' ('*O Christe, quantum patri . . .*'), Karl Young points out that the text comes from the sequence *Festa Christi*. He prints the poem in full (II, p. 454) as from *Analecta Hymnica*, liii, 50–1, but the melismatic music appears to be *Orléans*' own.

A rubric now informs us that Herod has died, and in his place Archelaus, his son, reigns as King. It is very probable that these happenings would have been represented in dumb show. We have examples in other Church dramas of such representations.

The voice of the Angel is now heard. Once more he summons Joseph (using the same musical phrase as before); and then informs him that the Holy Family may return to Judaea, since 'those enemies have perished who once did seek the life of the Child'. Like the earlier warning, this seems to be entirely an Orléans composition. Although the message ('*Revertere in terram Iudam . . .*') begins with an unfamiliar 'free rhythm' setting, as it progresses there are some note-groupings that are to be found in the music of the Angel's first warning, and finally, the two cadences coincide.

A rubric indicates that the Holy Family will be seen returning to Galilee; at which time Joseph sings a solo, represented only by an

---

[1] In the setting of this portion of the Notker text there are two notes (a *clivis*) which seem to be going spare. Also, by comparison with other versions of the text, *Orléans* appears to have left out two words—'*qui solus*' (three syllables) between '*meam*' and '*curaret*'. In the acting version I have inserted them and have compromised on their setting. The liquescent of '*angustos*' might perhaps be A B instead of B C'.

I will take the opportunity here of mentioning that in the 'Lament' scene the number of obvious scribal textual errors in the original manuscript seems higher than usual. Eminent textual scholars, from Du Meril to Karl Young, have corrected them and I have reproduced these amendments, not only in the Lament, but in earlier items of the work, and usually without comment.

[2] *Orléans* writes only an incipit ('*Sinite parvulos*'). I completed the item, with its music, from Hartker, p. 68, through the kind help of the Benedictines of Solesmes.

incipit ('*Gaude, Maria Virgo; cunctas hereses*'). As Young points out (II, p. 113, footnote 5), the text suggests an antiphon (no longer extant) for the Assumption. But the music is not the same, and none of the Gregorian scholars whom I consulted (even those of Solesmes) could identify its source. The concluding words are '*sola intemeristi in universo mundo*'. It would appear that any knowledgeable editor, if he wishes to see the music of the item completed, will have to undertake the task himself.

Here the drama ends, with the Matins '*Te Deum*' following, but the actual day of the *Ordo Rachelis* is never made clear. Karl Young (II, pp. 116 and 455) discusses the question, and favours the most likely possibility, the Feast of the Innocents (December 28th).

The New York Pro Musica performances, to which I have referred from time to time, of both these Orléans dramas, *Officium Stellae* and *Ordo Rachelis*, joined under the (modern) title of 'The Play of Herod', are, I believe, in some of their features, misleading to the ordinary observer in relation to the *mise-en-scène* and general features of a twelfth-century Church performance, but they certainly do illuminate the originalities, the great dramatic virtues, and the general actability of the works, which I consider to be the best of a leading half-dozen or so medieval Church music-dramas. They must be reckoned as representing artistic achievements that are ahead of their age; prophetic in their musical techniques.

IV

The twelfth century marked the beginning of dramatic activities concerned with Old Testament stories. These, however, seem never to have been numerous within the Church, and in any case, only four such manuscripts survive. These are detailed in Karl Young, II, pp. 258–306, and with the exception of one of them I can add no more to what that scholar has detailed so clearly concerning their texts. The first, an incomplete twelfth-century text from Vorau in Austria (rescued from the binding of a later book of sermons) tells the story of the deceit of Rebecca and Jacob which robbed Esau, eldest son of Isaac, of his father's blessing. The dramatization is carried on by a succession of rhyming couplets of eight syllables to the line. For something over 60 lines of the 160 surviving, the text is supplied with unheighted neumes showing changing stanza tunes, but I can do nothing towards resolving their pitches. I fear that it would not prove very rewarding even if I could. The rubrics, as Karl Young points out, are quite detailed and vivid at times, the 'properties' concerned with Esau's pursuit of venison being particularly lavish, and including a hunting-horn, termed, very classically, *bucina*. The lack of rhythmic variety in the incomplete verse libretto, which would probably have continued in eight-syllable lines to the bitter end, leaves the fragment of little practical value, except to demonstrate how strong was the dramatico-musical urge at the time, even when expressed clumsily. The acting-text of this Vorau work contains nothing that could have come direct from the liturgy. There is no concluding *Te Deum*, or any other evidence to confirm that the drama was ever performed within church walls.

CHAPTER ELEVEN

THE TWELFTH CENTURY (3)

The *Daniel* music-dramas
The rhythmic modes
The question of instrumental accompaniment

I come now to two closely connected dramatic works, both remarkable, one of them outstanding; both founded on the Old Testament story of the prophet Daniel as related in Chapters V and VI of that Book, but both also making use of the apocryphal story of the bringing of food to Daniel in the lions' den by the prophet Habakkuk, and of the former being defended there by an angel; both written in rhyming Latin poetry, the stanzas expertly varied in their rhythms; both providing solos expressing a variety of emotions; both staging impressive processional movements and powerful choruses; both, in fact, creating outstanding spectacles. Certain small similarities in dramatic detail, and certain lines of verse which appear in both, create some interesting problems as to authorship.

The first of these works, although of literary merit, is not to be given equal rank with the other. Moreover, a sad handicap as far as the purposes of this present book is concerned, it is without the vocal music which certainly must have accompanied the stanzas. It can, however, be given one almost unique distinction among Church music-dramas—we can with fair certainty give a name to its creator. There still exists a brief manuscript (*Paris, B.N. MS lat. 11331*) which represents what has survived of the writings of the goliard scholar, Hilarius. In the sixteen leaves which make up the manuscript there are found, besides short poems and verse-letters, three liturgical verse-dramas. One of these, our present concern, is headed '(*H*)*istoria de Daniel Representanda*'. The other two will receive later notice.[1]

Briefly to consider Hilarius. By his own testimony a pupil of the famous Abelard (1079–1142), he was for a time one of the fraternity of *goliards*—wandering scholars—young men in minor orders who, from the early eleventh to the early thirteenth century, travelled the roads of France, Germany, and England, their movements being, nominally,

---

[1] See pp. 265–7 and p. 281–2.

Though the drama is normally ascribed to Hilarius, it seems likely that he may have had collaborators. Scrawled in various places on the pages of his *Daniel* are his own name and those of, apparently, three companions—Jordanus, Simon, and Hugo. Young (II, pp. 288–9) discusses the various scholarly theories that attempt to account for the presence of these names, and seems finally to favour the idea that they signalized the collaboration of poet-friends in the composition of some of the stanzas—to my mind a reasonable explanation.

between the various European centres of learning. A proportion of their lyrical art, most of it racy and boldly satirical, has survived in such collections as the famous *Carmina Burana*.

To judge by the manuscript, which to my mind must surely be a later copy of a music-provided original, Hilarius visualized a performance of his work within church walls and in close association with the liturgy, since a final rubric directs that 'if it be given at Matins, Darius shall begin the '*Te Deum laudamus*'; if at Vespers, '*Magnificat anima mea Dominum*' ('*Quo finito, si factum fuerit ad Matutinas, Darius incipiat Te Deum laudamus; si vero ad Vesperas, Magnificat anima mea Dominum*'). I cannot think that, if and when Hilarius managed to get his work performed, he would still have been a goliard. The resources demanded for this considerable dramatic production—costumes; properties needed for the furnishing of a monarch's feast-hall; the onset of a 'stage' army; a representation of the fingers writing 'upon the plaister of the wall'; a pit for Daniel, complete with stage-lions; together with a dozen or more additional production needs—would surely call for the approval and support of a fairly important ecclesiastical authority, one likely to have little time for people belonging to that free-and-easy world of the wandering scholar.

II

In the circumstances of the Hilarius *Daniel* lacking its music, I shall go into no further separate details concerning it except when comparing or contrasting its features with the more developed *Daniel* that is to be found in a service manuscript which belonged originally to Beauvais Cathedral, but is now cared for by the British Museum (*MS Egerton 2615*). Its chief liturgical content is the Office of the Circumcision (1 January). There are also included two versions of the celebrated *Prose of the Ass*, associated with that Office. The first one, beginning on folio 1, has a single-line musical setting. The other, beginning on fol. 41, is in three parts.

Concerning the manuscript as a whole, the Catalogue of Additions to MSS at the British Museum (1882–7), p. 336, informs us:

Written in the thirteenth century, probably during the pontificate of Gregory IX (1227–41) and before the marriage of Louis IX to Marguerite of Provence in 1234.

The Department of Manuscripts arrived at this conclusion from the fact that on fol. 42r. & v. there are prayers for Gregorius Papa and Ludovicus Rex. There is no mention of a queen. The limiting dates seem therefore to be 1227–34.[1]

Since *Daniel* (fol. 95r.–108r.) occurs in juxtaposition with the Office of the Circumcision, it seems likely (although of course not certain) that

[1] Karl Young (II, p. 486) in a moment of error, described the Egerton manuscript as belonging to the twelfth century. He had already correctly ascribed it to the thirteenth.

the drama was performed on the same day, 1 January. Another, and somewhat slender, piece of evidence concerns Darius' reply to his evil counsellors, who are trying to trap Daniel into breaking a decree that they have suggested to the King. They finish each of their stanza choruses with the words '*O Rex!*'. Darius in his reply confirms the decree, but playwright and composer appear to hint at his foolishness by causing him to conclude his own stanza with

O hez!

—an astonishing happening when it is realized that this is the ass's bray, as it is found in the unison version of *The Prose of the Ass* in the same manuscript. The occurrence, besides being, an excellent example of artistic subtlety, appears to serve as another link with 1 January.

Although, as we have seen above, the manuscript *Egerton 2615* belongs to the thirteenth century, there is every reason to believe that the 'Daniel' version contained in it must be pre-dated, one of those reasons being the work that we have already considered, the *Daniel* of Hilarius. Although the two are independent, yet there are unmistakably a few common features which do not result from the common use of Biblical material. For example, the refrain of the vessel-bearing chorus in the Beauvais version—'*Gaudeamus; laudes sibi debitas referamus!*'—is found also in a Hilarius chorus (if only we could compare the two musics!). Again, the introductory Beauvais phrase, '*Ad honorem tui, Christe*', is paralleled by '*Ad honorem tui, Dari*', in a later part of the Hilarius work. Both dramas use the idea of a concluding prophecy by Daniel as to the coming of Christ, which of course owes nothing to the Old Testament chapters. Mention has already been made of the use by both versions of the apocryphal episodes at the lions' den, the visits of the sworded angel and of Habakkuk. The texts of these happenings are, however, independent, as are the respective versions of Daniel's prophecy. One last coincidence is the singing by an angel of the concluding item, the Christmas hymn, '*Nuntium vobis . . .*'.

Beauvais is alone in having such felicities as Daniel's Lament, and the recurrent and appropriately used sentence '*Rex, in aeternum vive*', to a constant setting. Hilarius uses the greeting once only. One feels also that there is some attempt by Beauvais at character drawing. For instance, Darius emerges as a just and merciful prince, torn between respect for '*lex Parthorum et Medorum*' and his desire to preserve Daniel. In contrast, Hilarius' Darius appears as an edition of '*Herod iratus*'. Altogether, it seems reasonable to conclude that one version has drawn from the other, but that Beauvais is much the better work of the two. The temptation is to assume that Beauvais improved on the Hilarius model. We are having, of course, to judge solely on literary considerations. Another possible theory, but without any evidence to support it, is that both worked from some earlier text.

Karl Young (II, p. 303) makes the suggestion that 'as a possible avenue of communication between Hilarius and Beauvais can be mentioned a certain Raoul, who taught at the Cathedral school of Beauvais in the twelfth century. Both he and Hilarius appear to have been pupils of Abelard.' Altogether, in view of the considerable evidence advanced, there seems little reason to quarrel with the conclusions of the German scholar Wilhelm Meyer, that both the Beauvais drama and that of Hilarius were written round about 1140, almost a century before the inclusion of the former in *Egerton 2615*.

We have seen that there may have been something of a goliardic background to the *Daniel* of Hilarius. The Beauvais *Daniel* may have been carried through, during its earlier existence, in rather the same atmosphere. By the twelfth century the medieval festivities of the Christmas season included a number of special celebrations, ruled in turn by four different ranks of the ecclesiastical community—the deacons on St. Stephen's Day (26 December); the priests on the Feast of St. John (27 December); the choristers on Innocents' Day (28 December), when the licensed rule of the 'Boy Bishop' was permitted; and finally the subdeacons, who presided, according to varying use, on the Feast of the Circumcision (1 January), or on Epiphany (6 January), or on the Octave of Epiphany (13 January). The activities of the subdeacons, most notorious in France, received a variety of names, none of them complimentary, e.g., *festa fallorum*, or *stultorum*, or *fatuorum*, which phrases can be summed up in the term 'Feast of Fools'.[1]

The first mention of these four *tripudia*, as they are significantly called (the term is derived from *tripudium*, the name of a Roman sacred dance, with which was also associated the idea of 'joy'), is by Joannes Belethus, Rector of Theology at Paris, some time between 1182 and 1190, when a movement towards the checking of excesses was already beginning. The reforms called for in 1199 by Eudes de Sully, Bishop of Paris, by Pierre de Corbeil a little later at Sens, by Pope Innocent III himself in 1207, and by a number of other ecclesiastical authorities, point to a state of affairs much in need of a curb. Of particular interest in this regard are some rather baffling references by seventeenth- and eighteenth-century historians to an unidentified twelfth-century document from Beauvais which describes such farcical rites as a 'pudding and sausage' censing, a drinking bout in the porch, and the bringing of an ass into church.[2] Similar scenes seem to have been enacted elsewhere. One of the results of the movement for reform was the issuing of a new Office of the Circumcision at Sens in the early thirteenth century, traditionally ascribed to Pierre de Corbeil. This banished the burlesque ceremonies. The thirteenth century Beauvais Office, contained in *MS Egerton 2615*, similarly shows no indiscretions (several leaves, however, are missing). It is a curious and significant fact that both of these 'expurgated' Offices retain the *Prose of the Ass*. In 1212 a national council under the Papal legate directed that both regular and secular clergy must abstain from

---

[1] For a detailed account of this festival, and its outrageous abuses, see E. K. Chambers, *The Mediaeval Stage*, I, pp. 274–335.

[2] Details of this document are recorded by Chambers, ibid., pp. 285–8.

the *festa fallorum*. In spite of all these strictures, however, ecclesiastical denunciations through the following centuries mark the continued lurking existence of the Feast of Fools.

The question arises as to what extent the *Daniel* production at Beauvais could have been affected by the possibility of its being in the hands of the Cathedral subdeacons, and further, what influence the Feast of Fools may have had on its atmosphere. We must of course always remember that there is no actual record in existence of the work ever having been performed at all![1] But the existence of the beautifully written score, and the assurance of the first sung item that '*Danielis ludus iste in Belvaco est inventus, et invenit hunc iuventus*' makes it difficult to imagine that medieval performances were neglected. That the 'young men' (of the song-school?) actually 'invented' the work, in the modern sense of the word, seems highly unlikely to me, whatever helping hand they may have been given. In my opinion, we have at Beauvais another example of a single first-class mind which took over the suggestions of a good but far from outstanding work (the Hilarius *Daniel*) and transformed it into a medieval masterpiece.[2] At any rate, whatever circumstantial associations we may have linking the play to the Feast of Fools, the fact remains that the work as it stands in the thirteenth-century manuscript is a wholly dignified and serious music-drama.

Let us now consider the manuscript in somewhat more detail. It will be recalled that the libretto is a dramatic poem, and owes nothing to the liturgy except for the Angel's concluding Christmas hymn, '*Nuntium vobis*'. As for its debts to the Hilarius *Daniel*, these have already been detailed above (p. 225). As matters stand, however, it must be granted that if indeed Beauvais made some small borrowings, these are smoothly absorbed into a finely constructed piece of dramatic writing. The poetic lines are organized very largely in rhyming couplets, but in the lengthier items, those consisting of several stanzas, there is to be found a great variety of formal patterns, as we shall presently discover.

One of the most significant features of this work is its rubrics, which, while lacking in specific details of costume and 'set', reveal a tight control over the direction of the actors: their movements, their manners of speech, and the emotions that they must express. One of the highlights of the play is given in this stage-direction:

[1] A printed announcement concerned with a performance of a modern transcription of the work stated that *Daniel* was a favourite with medieval audiences. I have sought in vain for any confirmation of this statement.

An inventory found in the treasury of Beauvais Cathedral, and dating from 1464, describes a black silk costume intended (so it is stated) for a 'man-at-arms' ('*homme ferré*'). G. Desjardins makes mention of it in his book, *Histoire de la Cathédrale de Beauvais* (Beauvais, 1865), pp. 119 and 169–70. His suggestion that it was a relic left from a performance of *Daniel* appears to me to be pure speculation.

[2] Karl Young suggests (II, pp. 303–4), that the man in question may, in fact, have been the already-mentioned 'Raoul' (p. 225), who taught at Beauvais and who had known Hilarius, sharing with him a pupilage to the great scholar Abelard. It is a fascinating suggestion, but of course, nearly impossible to prove. I can second Young's complaint as to the difficulty of finding facts concerning the cathedral school at Beauvais during the twelfth and thirteenth centuries.

Meanwhile there will appear in the King's sight a right hand, writing on the wall *Mane, Thechel, Phares*: seeing it, the King will be amazed and will cry out:

(*Interim apparebit dextra in conspectu Regis scribens in pariete: Mane, Thechel, Phares; quam videns Rex stupefactus clamabit:*)

Similarly, in the moment in which Darius unwittingly condemns Daniel to death, the rubric which precedes the pronouncement says:

The King, hearing this [i.e. the quotation of the law by the plotters], will say, willy-nilly (*'velit, nolit . . .'*)

Darius comes later to the pit of the lions, expecting to find that Daniel has perished. He speaks 'tearfully' (*'lacrimabiliter'*). Then, met with a cheerful *'Rex, in aeternum vive!'* from the prophet, he is directed to 'exclaim joyfully' (*'gaudens exclamabit'*) as he orders Daniel's release.

Excellently contrived as the libretto is, it is above all the nature and quality of the music which causes the Beauvais *Daniel* to be so outstanding. As in the case of the verses, we meet with much variety of style and structure. The settings are of course entirely monodic, and proceed on the principle of 'new speaker, new tune'. There are some deliberate exceptions to this rule, subtly contrived, as we shall show.[1] Of the fifty or so separate melodies that represent the total of the settings there is hardly one that is without points of formal interest. But, more striking still, there is a quality in some of them not easily paralleled in other Church music-dramas—a breath of the outside, secular world. Some of the rapid, lilting choruses may perhaps have been reminiscent of dance tunes, and certainly many of the solo settings could not be distinguished from examples taken from a trouvère's *chansonnier*. Half the item melodies belong to the Dorian (re) mode, although the frequent appearance of a manuscript B flat might cause some of them to be considered as Mixolydian (sol), notably Daniel's *Lament* (beginning at line 342 of Karl Young's printing of the text, II, p. 299), and his *Prophecy* (beginning at line 385 on p. 301). Nine seem to be in the 'wanton' Ionian, our 'major' key, notably the Queen's 'Conductus' (Young, II, p. 292, l. 75), her 'aria' (p. 293, l. 102), and also, strangely enough, the despair of Belshazzar (p. 295, l. 179). Pathos, and the gentler emotions generally, seem to be represented by the five examples of the Phrygian mode (mi), notably Daniel's prayer (p. 300, l. 352), his thanks (p. 300, l. 370), and the Angel's hymn-stanza (p. 301, l. 389). The dignified music of the two Kings is predominantly Dorian, although Darius mourns in the Phrygian mode (p. 300, l. 373). The choice of modes for Daniel's items is much wider. He uses them all, for he is made to express a variety of emotions.

The music of *Daniel* is written in staved Gregorian 'free-rhythm' notation; one that defines exactly the pitch of the notes, but offers no

---

[1] A plain and straightforward exception to the rule is the oft-repeated *'Rex in aeternum vive'*, already referred to, which is always set to the same melody, whoever the speaker.

clue as to any rhythmic interpretation of the music. This second condition regarding settings of Latin verse is what we ourselves have regularly encountered in Church music-dramas. However, the reader will have noted that this has not discouraged me from offering modern renderings of the melodies on five-line staves with time-signatures.

III

This may be a suitable moment for us to pause and consider what principles and methods have been employed by scholars of the present century in order to discover how medieval singers interpreted solo melodies written in 'free rhythm', when these were linked with texts which were in themselves regularly rhythmic. The pioneers of modern investigation were Pierre Aubry, Johann Beck, and, to some degree, Friedrich Ludwig, followed by such later names as Friedrich Gennrich, Higini Anglès, and Jacques Handschin. Results were obtained, certainly not by dealing with the lyrical examples of Latin poetry found with their settings in the Church music-dramas (very little notice, so far, has been taken of them), but by investigating the far greater amount of available vernacular material that has survived of the activities of the aristocratic troubadours and trouvères of France, which lasted from the eleventh century until the fading of the art during the second half of the thirteenth. The troubadours flourished among the cultivated upper-class society of Provence,[1] until this was shattered by the forces of the Albigensian Crusade (1208). The trouvères practised a similar lyrical art in the northern parts of France, from the latter half of the twelfth century.[2] For long, both movements represented an aristocratic 'closed shop', but there were some notable exceptions to this, and towards the end of the period we find 'citizen' trouvères, even academies of such, most notably at Arras.

Records of the troubadour-trouvère art are enshrined in the small, handy *chansonniers*, many of which have survived. These were used by performers, and were the means by which the knowledge of a composition could be spread widely. On a page of one of them a poem would be set out, with a single melody at the head doing duty for whatever stanza groupings were given below. As we have indicated, the music was written in staved, free-rhythm Gregorian notation, normally quadrate neumes and neume-groups. The modern experts, while differing among themselves in minor matters, are in general agreement with the assump-

---

[1] Provence was for long an anomaly as far as France was concerned. It was not definitely annexed to the kingdom until the fifteenth century.

[2] Troubadours and trouvères were divided by their two different vernaculars. The troubadour wrote in the '*langue d'oc*', the trouvère in the '*lange d'oil*' (the respective words for 'yes'). Regarding their names, Gustave Reese remarks (*Music in the Middle Ages*, p. 205): 'The simplest and most plausible derivation of the French verb *trouver* and noun *trouvère*, as of the Provençal *trobar* and *trobador*, connects their origin with that of the Latin *tropus* (trope).'

tion that the rhythm of the music was latent in the words and must be in accord with the poetic stresses. It is held that solutions were found at the time by making use of the 'rhythmic modes'.[1] The rhythmic mode scheme is found established (apparently first in France) in the second half of the twelfth century, being employed in connection with the earlier stages of contrapuntal part-writing. The problem of keeping several simultaneous parts together without a scheme of mensural notation (this not yet having been invented), was solved by making use of several patterns of rhythm, differing one from another in the various parts, but all conforming to an overall triple pattern. Medieval writers recognized six such modes (later amended to five)—various patterns of the 'long' and 'short' which could most simply be represented by ♩ ♪

I give these below, noting that the first three are the ones with which we shall be primarily concerned in the *chansonniers*.

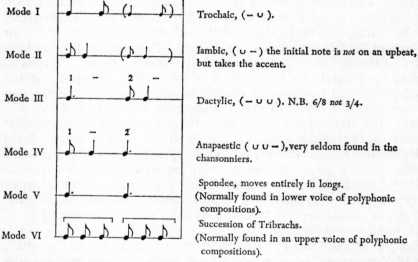

Mode I — Trochaic, (– ∪).

Mode II — Iambic, (∪ –) the initial note is *not* on an upbeat, but takes the accent.

Mode III — Dactylic, (– ∪ ∪). N.B. 6/8 *not* 3/4.

Mode IV — Anapaestic (∪ ∪ –), very seldom found in the chansonniers.

Mode V — Spondee, moves entirely in longs. (Normally found in lower voice of polyphonic compositions).

Mode VI — Succession of Tribrachs. (Normally found in an upper voice of polyphonic compositions).

The medieval version of the dactyl was something of a compromise, the idea being that when it came to polyphony, such a version, when combined with other, different rhythmic modes, would fit satisfactorily into the ternary pattern. Concerning the troubadour-trouvère music Anglès,[2] among others, claims that binary rhythm has had as long a history as ternary, and that, if occasion demanded it, the third rhythmic

---

[1] Not to be confused with the ecclesiastical, Gregorian modes; *Modus* in the Middle Ages was an overworked word. It had yet another, quite different implication connected with later, mensural notation.

The 'rhythmic modes' are sometimes described as being derived, with some adjustments, from the metres of classical prosody. One might be inclined to reflect that a sense of natural rhythm has been common to all mankind, throughout the ages.

[2] Higini Anglès, *La Música a Catalanya fins al segle XIII* (1935), p. 352, quoted in Reese, p. 210. Anglès also makes the claim (one that seems nowadays to be widely admitted) that if necessary the modes can be 'mixed', e.g. for that sake of a more satisfactory reading Mode II can replace Mode I, or vice versa.

mode could be rendered as ♩ ♪♪ . Another reading of the dactyl

is that it could be represented by the tribrach (♪ ♪ ♪) . Many of

the modern versions of *chansonnier* tunes move in straightforward triple
rhythm, most of the time one note to the syllable.

Support for the modal interpretation theory appears to be given by
the existence of the twelfth-century *Chansonnier Cange*,[1] in which there
are to be found songs in these rhythms, written in mensural notation.
But it is widely recognized by modern interpreters that the art of the
troubadour-trouvère was that of the solo performer, ready to rely a
great deal on his musical instinct. To tie down such a singer to the strict
notation of a 'barred stave and time-signature' age is to create a misleading strait-jacket. It may well be that a song, when sung on a second
occasion, even by the same singer, would be far from exactly reproduced.
Among musicologists we find a widespread unwillingness to insist upon
a rule-of-thumb. Sir Jack Westrup, commenting in the *New Oxford
History of Music* upon his own readings of numerous medieval troubadour and trouvère songs, remarks that 'the transcriptions in this chapter,
made in accordance with the rhythmic modes, are to be regarded merely
as the framework from which a skilled singer will re-create a living art'.[2]
Nevertheless, it seems clear that some sort of rhythmic organization
seems to have been understood by performers of the period. What could
it have been?

In approaching this problem, the two pioneers of modern rhythmic
mode interpretation, Pierre Aubry and Jean Beck,[3] have both laid
emphasis on one basic principle. We are asked to imagine that a
medieval performer, seeking to determine the rhythmic pattern of his
song, would read the first line of text to determine the placing of stresses,
finding that the most convenient method of doing so would be to check
backward from the *rhyming* syllable, which always took the accent. The
scansion completed, the most suitable rhythmic mode would become
apparent.

As an illustration of this principle, I take two phrases from a song by
the famous Provençal troubadour, Bernart de Ventadorn (*c.* 1130–95):

'É-ra·m cos-sel-hátz, sen-hór,   Vós, c'a-vétz sa-ber e sén:'

---

[1] Paris, *B.N. 846*; edited with facsimile by J. Beck in two volumes (Paris and Philadelphia,
1927).

[2] *The New Oxford History of Music*, Vol. II, 'Early Medieval Music up to 1300', edited
by Dom Anselm Hughes (London, 1967), p. 227.

[3] Pierre Aubry, *Trouvères et Troubadours* (Paris, 1909).
J. Beck, *La Musique des Troubadours* (Paris, 1910). Medieval French and Provençal both
possessed the syllable accentuations that modern French largely does without. We have
already met with such vernacular stress-patterns in *Sponsus* examples (see Chapter VIII, p.
140), offering exotic contrast to the Latin poetry of the work. However, Latin verse had long
become one of accent, not quantity, and responds satisfactorily to interpretations of its
settings by some of the rhythmic modes.

marking the poetic stresses and counting back in the case of each phrase from the rhyming stresses '*-hor*' and '*sen*' (shortly to rhyme with ('*s'a*) *-mór*' and ('*lon-ja*) *-men*'. The plainchant notation then resolves itself as a 'first mode' melody, thus:

E – ram cos – sel – hatz, sen – hor, Vos, c'a – vetz sa – ber e sen: ...
Main – te – nant con – seil – lez - moi, Seig-neurs de science et de sens:_ ...

I give another example, somewhat more varied in rhythm, from a song by the troubadour Jean Rudel (twelfth century), as transcribed by Jean Beck (p. 79):

Lan-quand li jorn son lonc. en mai, M'es bels douz. chans d'au-zels. de lonh,
Lors-que les jours sont longs en mai,— Me plaît le__ chant d'oi-seaux_ de__ loin, —

In dealing with the second rhythmic mode, Jean Beck takes a sentence from a song by the music-loving Thibaut of Champagne, later King of Navarre (1201–53) (p. 48):

Ro-bért ve-éz de Per-rón ...

He points out that, together with the rhyming accent, '-ron', the stresses are on '-bert' and '-ez', and that if the first rhythmic mode is attempted, the result will be:

Ro-bert ve – ez dé Per-ron

—which, as he says, produces a rather unpleasant sensation. However, he then writes the rhythm to which Thibaut's song is normally sung:

Ro - bert ve – ez de Per – ron (etc.)

—and states that now 'on ne sentira rien de choquant'.

Gustave Reese (p. 208), in his comment on Beck's example, puts the situation much more clearly. In condemning the 'first mode' attempt as unsatisfactory he explains that 'the two other accented syllables fall not only on off-beats but on shorter time-values than the preceding unaccented syllables'. But, as he points out, an entirely satisfactory solution is obtained by the use of the second mode, when the other text-accents are interpreted musically by means of length of time-values rather than stress.[1]

---

[1] The second rhythmic mode, even though it may seem at times a little strange to modern ears, seems to have been widely employed in the *chansonniers*. Also, the reader will have noted that a number of the Church music-drama examples encountered thus far in the present book have been rendered in this rhythm, including the warlike solo of Archelaus in the Orléans' *Herod* (p. 208).

With regard to the third rhythmic mode, Pierre Aubry remarks (*Trouvères et Troubadours*, pp. 200–1) that a stanza of a song composed in ten-syllable verse with a caesura after the fourth syllable, one of seven syllables with the same caesura, or one requiring a mingling with verse of four syllables, normally calls for the use of the third rhythmic mode. I give an extract from another Thibaut de Champagne song as an example of its use:[1]

De bone a — mour vient se – – ance   et bon – té,   Et   a – mors   vient de ces...

—and one from the troubadour Peirol (1190–1220), of seven-syllable verse:[2]

Quant A-mors   tro – – bet par – tit   Mon cor de ¨ son pes-sa – – men, ...

Regarding the problem of the choice of a rhythmic mode, Gustave Reese supplies a useful hint: 'If accents divide the syllables into groups of two, the mode will be the first or second; if into groups of threes, probably the third.'[3] However, chances seem to occur for the first two modes to suit even ten-syllable lines.

In such a brief discussion as this the details of many lesser problems must remain neglected—such as how to divide among two or more notes the time-value to which a single syllable is entitled, and how to deal with a line beginning on a weak beat (anacrusis). Mention should be made of a small matter connected with the rhyming (and therefore, accented) syllable. When the rhyme is 'masculine', i.e. involving a single note, all is straightforward. But when we have a 'feminine' cadence (as in 'bē - lĕ') there will be a weak syllable following the accented one, either as ♩ ♩ or ♩. ♩ ♪ depending on the circumstances.

be – le   be – le

I quote the first two lines of a charming song by the trouvère Moniot d'Arras (thirteenth century),[4] transcribed by F. Gennrich (p. 31), which may illuminate some matters. Incidentally, the song is in the 'major mode'.

---

[1] Transcribed from F. Gennrich, *Troubadours, Trouvères, Minne- und Meistergesang* (Köln, 1953), p. 33.

[2] Ibid., p. 18.

[3] Reese, p. 208.

[4] Moniot d'Arras, like the leading troubadour Bernart de Ventadorn, was not of the aristocratic class but represented the art very worthily as the leading figure of a burgher 'academy' in the flourishing city of Arras; this at a time when the movement was failing among the nobles.

I cannot refrain from adding the whole of a song by the trouvère Robert de Reims (again as transcribed by F. Gennrich, p. 32). Not only does it show a tribrach-style triple rhythm, but both poem and setting are fascinatingly constructed. The verse-lines of each of the three stanzas, counted in syllables, give the pattern 8 2 5 2 8 2 5 3 7 2 5 3 7. The song seems to exemplify that sense of rhythmic freedom inherent in the troubadour-trouvère's art, to which we have previously referred. One can imagine the performer, very conscious of his ingenious rhymes and echoed phrases, pausing, taking his 'own time' as he makes his points:

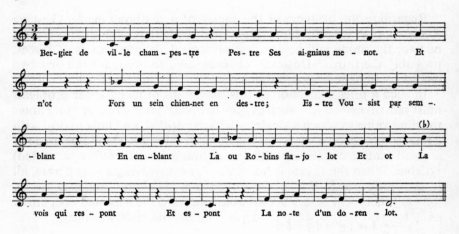

IV

We will now be turning back to our survey of the Beauvais *Daniel*, not only to evaluate its music, but to test how practical the rhythmic modes prove when applied to Latin accentuations. The introductory four lines, sung probably by a chorister, show a transposed Aeolian tune in the first rhythmic mode, with feminine cadences:

234

The prefacing rubric to the second item (Young, II, p. 290, ll. 5–34) terms it a *prosa*. We have previously met with the word 'prose' as being another name for the early sequence, but this particular item is not in sequence form. The label was probably given since the music shares a sequence-characteristic of 'one syllable—one note'. It is a brief and vigorous first rhythmic-mode melody which does duty for eight more stanza repetitions:

The text is a quaint example of medieval insensitivity to dramatic suspense. It is Belshazzar's nobles who sing it as he is coming to his throne, and what they are doing is proclaiming the 'plot' of the drama. They speak of the writing on the wall and its interpretation by Daniel, and follow it with the episode of the lions. However, they stop short at any mention of Darius. At this point the King ascends to his throne and the Satraps break off with:

—destined to be sung again and again (eight times, in fact) in the course of the work, and always to the same music. I have rhythmed the neumes, but they may well have been sung in free rhythm.

The next item consists of the King's command to his Satraps to bring to the feast the plundered Temple vessels. His four lines of music may be passed over; a straightforward Mixolydian tune in triple time. But the item that follows (Young, II, p. 291; ll. 40–59) is a notable one. Sung by the Satraps as they bear the vessels to the King and pay homage to him, it is a melody of great vitality. Again, in the rubric we find the term *prosa*; and, it would seem, for the same reason, for only seldom do the syllables get more than one note each. But there is no sequence-pattern in the musical phrases. If we use the usual letter analysis, we start off with 'a,b,a,b,' . . . but get to somewhere about 'k' before we finish, with occasional repetitions of phrase. It appears to me that the verbal accents permit of a musical duple time, affording a respite from the sometimes overworked triple. In this case we shall have for the first two lines:

The B flat is a delightful touch! Incidentally, the whole item-setting (there are eighteen more lines) turns out once again to be in the major mode.

The single line of the Satraps' presentation of the vessels takes the form of plainchant, with *bistrophae* and two long melismas; obviously to be sung in free rhythm.

Then comes the appalling moment of the appearance of the Hand, writing upon the wall. The terrified King calls for his soothsayers. The item (p. 292; ll. 61–4) has a Dorian setting, clearly in triple rhythm, and beginning on a weak beat. It seems to me that either Mode I or II would be appropriate. Possibly the iambic rhythm would suit Belshazzar's agitation better.

The soothsayers introduce themselves with '*Rex in aeternum vive!*'—the inevitable salutation. Meanwhile, the King has recovered his nerve, and, in giving his promise to reward richly whoever can interpret the message of the Hand, utters one of the most beautiful of the melodies; one, indeed, that could have come from the *chansonnier* of a master trouvère. I transcribe it in full (p. 292; ll. 67–72):

I have mentioned before the imagination shown in setting the bewildered verdict of the soothsayers (p. 292; ll. 73–4). The music of the two lines consists of the repeated two phrases:

Ne - sci-mus per-sol - ve re nec da - re con - si - li - um.
que sit su – per- scrip - ti - o nec ma-nus in - di - ci - um.

—which very well represented thoughts that were moving in circles!

This failure is succeeded by the *Conductus* of Belshazzar's Queen (p. 292; ll. 75–98), her escort singing four stanzas in her praise. This Beauvais manuscript (together with another celebrated one, the Spanish *Codex Calestinus*, of the same period) puts on record for the first time in history the term *Conductus*. Its first significance, applied to single-line metrical compositions, was of a song to accompany movements from place to place. This is the *Daniel* implication, but later it seems to have taken on a very wide meaning, to include many sorts of monodic compositions, religious or secular, grave or gay.[1]

The Queen's conductus is a remarkable piece of music. The neumes show that the composer was trying to put on record, within the limits of Gregorian notation, several rhythmic subtleties. I quote from the manuscript the first half of the (major mode) stanza melody:

Cum doc - to - rum et ma — go -rum o - mnis ad – sit con - ti - - o,

The fourth neume shows a *pressus*, as does the sixth, while the eleventh and fourteenth provide examples of *oriscus*. The ninth neume is a *cephalicus*—a liquescent *clivis*. I give a rhythmic reading, 'mixing' the modes towards the end:

Cum doc.- to -rum ¡et, ma go-rum o – mnis ad – ·sit con-ti – - o,

The second line is varied melodically, but with syncopation and *oriscus* still playing their part, and with the same 'major' cadence employed. It will be noted that I have ventured to 'mix' Modes I and II. The two *pressus* syncopations make a rather pleasant rhythmic effect. With regard to that rather mysterious neume the *oriscus*, I have treated it in one of the standard ways, as being in unison with the previous note. Some scholars would deal with the latter as if to be read a step below the

---

[1] The *polyphonic* conductus was quite another matter, a composition for up to four voices' with a Latin text the same in each part, and the voices tending to move in block chords. The Sens Cathedral version of *The Prose of the Ass* ('*Orientis partibus adventavit asinus . . .*') is a well-known example.

[2] I cannot think that certain of the items of *Daniel* were sung at the pitch shown in the manuscript. To take Daniel's own *tessitura*; he is called on in the course of the work to have a range from low A to top g, However, I have written the conductus at the given pitch.

oriscus. It has also been suggested that the *oriscus* might indicate some kind of rapid ornamentation. In the case of the St. Gall shape (ς), I have met with some liquescent intention. The hook-shape given in the Beauvais manuscript has been referred to on p. 40 of the present book. While Solesmes prints the neume as a plain square punctum, the *Antiphonale monasticum* still uses the special shape.

Whatever uncertainties there may be regarding the conductus tune, it is certainly a fine one. We may say the same about each of the Queen's two solos that follow, items that might be termed 'introduction and arietta'. Both '*Ut scribentis noscas . . .*' and '*Cum Judaeae captivis . . .*' (Young, II, p. 293; ll. 100–1 and 102–9) move smoothly enough in the first rhythmic mode. The Queen's advice to Belshazzar to summon Daniel having been given, the King proceeds to act on it. His orders, '*Vos Dániélem quaerité . . .*' are set to a simple Dorian first-mode tune.

I am henceforward dealing in detail only with points of special musical interest. However, in the long scene that involves the summoning and the escorting of Daniel by the Nobles (pp. 293–4; ll. 112–39), there are certainly some that call for comment. In places the items afford quite an insight into medieval techniques of variation writing.

The Nobles begin:

—and then continue their summons in French, possibly to give the impression that they are addressing the prophet in his native language. Two more stanzas follow, to the same melody (p. 293; ll. 112–17), and then Daniel ponders on it all:

—using phrases from the Nobles' tune to begin with, and afterwards snatches from it, concluding, not in the major mode, but its own transposed Dorian:

A most effective episode follows. The Nobles sing an item, labelled '*Conductus*', which is twice more repeated; a stirring triple-rhythm tune:

which concludes with a trumpet-like Mixolydian cadence:

Ces - tui man - da li Rois par nos!

Each stanza is devoted to praise for Daniel, but each time, between them, the prophet meekly inserts his own refrain comment ('*Pauper et exulans envois al Roi par vos*'). His variations of the tune, ending quietly in the major mode, make it almost a parody.

Pau - per et e - xu - - lans ...

Having reached the King and given him the usual salutation, Daniel is told by Belshazzar of the 'wealth beyond measure' that he will receive if he can interpret the writing. The King's address is musically simple— one note to each syllable, and the Dorian phrases represented by a, b, c, b, d, b.

Daniel's interpretation (pp. 294–5; ll. 147–76) is musically of the same Dorian simplicity, the one-syllable, one-note scheme interspersed only by an occasional *cephalicus* liquescent. It appears to me that the music of the four stanzas (four versions of a single tune) could be interpreted either in the first rhythmic mode, in continual lilt, or in straightforward, recitative-like, duple time. Myself, I prefer the latter.

After Daniel's unsparing interpretation of the prophecy, there occurs a magnificent piece of musical and dramatic imagination. With the fateful exegesis of '*mane*', '*thechel*', and '*phares*', Daniel ceases on the *third* line of his last stanza. The fourth:

Qui sic sol - vit la - ten - ti - a or - ne - tur ves - te re - gi - a.
Since he has read the hid - den words, let him be· vest - ed roy - al - ly.

still set to the prophet's music, comes unexpectedly and dramatically from the King, his noble answer to the pronouncement of his doom. He has apparently lost hope, for in another deep-toned, triple-rhythm passage he bids his Satraps bear away the vessels. Meanwhile the Queen prepares to leave her escort, again singing a *conductus*. To modern ears the style and subject matter of the music, in the circumstances, may appear rather incongruous. A charming tune, but surely dance-derived (Karl Young, p. 295, ll. 181–94).

Sol - vi ·- tur in li - bro Sa: - lo - mo - nis di - gna laus et con - gru - a ma - tro - nis.
In the book of So - lo -mon is gi - ven fit and wor-thy praise to vir - tuous wo - - men.

The Queen disappears to six more stanzas in her praise. It is now the turn of the Satraps to make their exit with the vessels. There is once again no sense of doom in their chorus, a thoroughly jolly Dorian one devoted to the praise of Daniel, and one with a fascinating refrain, (p. 295; ll. 195–215). There is a tremendous rhythmic vitality in the music, which must surely have had a secular source. Here is the first stanza:

—which, musically, can be represented as a, a, b, Refrain. The second stanza, in the same rhythm, has new material for three sentences, a return to 'b', and the refrain; thus; c, c, d, b, R. The third stanza has the same pattern as the first; and the fourth stanza's pattern is that of the second. It is all very highly organized and tidy, and the chorus fades into the distance to leave Belshazzar deserted and alone. A dramatic device, certainly, but possibly an economic one. Although the next rubrics state that 'Darius will immediately appear with his nobles' ('*statim apparebit Darius rex cum Principibus suis*') I wonder whether time was not spared for Belshazzar's Satraps to leap into different garments, take up helmet and arms, and reappear as the Persian Army.

The next item (p. 296, ll. 216–45) is another impressive chorus, the procession advancing, as it sings, towards the hapless Belshazzar. The theme is naturally the power and the glory of the Persian king. It is a 'straight-through' poem, seeming to move at first in two groups of three short lines, and then in succession of four-line groups for most of the rest of the way. The neumes seem to give the transcriber a choice between triple and duple rhythm. I prefer the latter. There has been a plethora of lilting first-mode tunes. The music of the opening group is given below:

The melodic pattern a, b, a¹ ('a¹' representing the slight variation) is repeated for the second group. The rest of the lines of the item are 'through-composed', with the occasional (and apparently inexplicable)

repetition of the 'a¹' line and a couple or so more. The concluding lines are well worth quoting; an excellent climax:

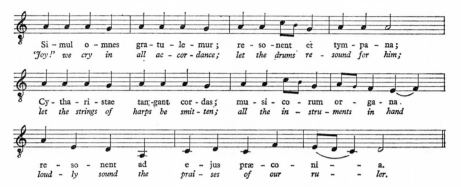

Si – mul o – mnes gra – tu – le – mur; re – so –nent et tym – pa – na;
'Joy!' we cry in all ac – cor – dance; let the drums re – sound for him;

Cy – tha – ri – stae tan;-gant cor – das; mu – si – co – rum or – ga – na.
let the strings of harps be smit – ten; all the in – stru – ments in hand

re – so – nent ad e – jus præ – co – ni – a.
loud – ly sound the prai – ses of our ru – ler.

Some time during the conclusion of the item Belshazzar is torn from his throne and slain. Darius replaces him, to the fifth repetition of '*Rex, in aeternum vive!*', and immediately two high officials offer secret advice to the new King that Daniel should be summoned for consultation. This the King apparently agrees to; and another long Daniel episode is launched. It begins with the 'advisers' passing on their orders to 'messengers'. The item (p. 297; ll. 247–56) is made up of a two-sentence Aeolian melody and four more repetitions of it; not very distinguished and appearing to go best in duple rhythm.

The next item (ll. 257–68), the orders to Daniel, continues with the repetitive style of a two-sentence tune spread over several stanzas, this time clearly a 'first mode' one. Daniel briefly replies. There comes now one of that type of leaping—almost dancing—triple-rhythm choruses that we have met before, again labelled '*conductus*' (pp. 297–8, ll. 270–84). This time the structure of the music is well worth considering. In point of fact its fifteen headlong lines have as their total musical material no more than two sentences:

A Fast

Con – gau – den – tes ce – le – bre – mus na – ta – lis so – lem-- ni – a ...
Let us joy to – geth – er ce – le – bra – ting the na – ti – vi – ty ...

and

B

In hoc na – ta – li – ti – o ...
On 'this Birth – day fes – ti – val ...

The form of the setting can be described as consisting of six lines, employed identically for each of two stanzas, the pattern being a, a, a',

---

[1] In the manuscript, the first musical note of the item is given as C. Whenever the phrase turns up later (which is rather often) the C is replaced by D.

a', a, a. The middle pair (a', a') represent the first pair transposed up a perfect fifth.

The '*Congaudentes . . .*' stanza is rounded off by the use of the musical sentence B, twice more repeated to set the three phrases, '*In hoc natalitio, Daniel, cum gaudio Te laudat haec contio*'—as a sort of summing-up refrain. This passage is missing from the end of the second stanza as given in the manuscript, but I believe that it was indeed added as a matter of course.

The extraordinary text of the item calls for mention. It is once more a paean of praise for Daniel, again mentioning the Apocryphal episodes of the prophet's rescue of Susannah, and of his bringing about the destruction of the false god, Bel, and of a dragon, similarly worshipped. But it also demonstrates how the Christian poet, in his enthusiasm for his faith, tended to discard any chronological sense that he ever possessed. The opening lines (this being the Christmas season) celebrate the Nativity, and the fact that 'the wisdom of our God has ransomed all mankind from death'. The last lines recall (before the event) the preservation of Daniel from the lions (he would have been glad to be told that); and finally, they offer praise 'to Him, the Word of God, the Virgin-born'!

There follow the exchanges between the King, and the conspirators planning to trap Daniel. The conspirators suggest that Darius should establish a decree, calling for the general worship of his own godhead; one that they know Daniel will surely disregard. The King, unsuspecting, agrees, and in due course the conspirators confront him with evidence of the prophet's transgression through his worship of his own deity; Darius, against his own desire, is compelled to condemn him to the lions.

There is nothing much of outstanding musical interest in the comparatively brief items of the episode—successions of triple-rhythm, 'first-mode' melodies. I have already commented on Darius' '*O hez*', the 'ass's bray' that marks his falling into the conspirator's trap. There is one other small musical trick to note. The King has told the conspirators (p. 298; ll. 307–11):

E - go man - do et re - man - do ne sit spre - tum hoc de - cre - tum...
I af - firm and re - af - firm that this de - cree must not be bro - ken ...

—followed by the bray.

When the conspirators return to denounce Daniel, they remind the king of his own decree by asking: 'Did you not, Darius, fix a law . . . ?' The four notes with which they start, used again and again in their following debate with the King, surely represent an additional jolt to his memory, in terms of music:

Num - quid, Da - ri ...

The King's final yielding (the rhythm probably a duple one) still harps on the same musical phrase (p. 299; ll. 340–1):

Daniel, condemned, betrays a momentary human weakness, and utters his celebrated lament.[1] Myself, I am doubtful as to any strict rhythming of the very effective music, as emotional a conception as any to be found in the period (p. 299; II. 342–9), and to be bracketed with Mary Magdalen's Lament in the *Visitatio* of *Orléans 201*, and that of Rachel from the *Ordo Rachelis* of the same manuscript.

No strict musical pattern is followed, but there are some workings of the descending phrase:

and the briefer descent of:

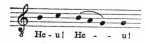

Darius offers a sympathetic but ineffective comment, and then, as he goes into the pit, Daniel sings a shapely '*Kyrie eleyson*', beginning (p. 300; l. 352):

—the second sentence a slightly varied version of the given one. In the meantime there have been angelic activities. The lions have been threatened by a celestial sword, while another angel, further removed, encounters the prophet Habakkuk, who is taking a dinner (*prandium*) to his harvesters. Two quite straightforward tunes mark their exchanges (p. 300; ll. 358–65), which end with the rather drastic action of the angel in seizing the reluctant prophet by the hair of his head, and conducting him thus, dinner and all, to Daniel. Habakkuk's stanza (p. 300; ll. 366–72) is set to another interesting melody, the opening phrase:

[1] Daniel's Lament will be found recorded (in 'free rhythm') in *The History of Music in Sound Vol. II: Early Medieval Music up to 1300* (London, Oxford University Press, 1953). Recorded by RCA Victor (His Master's Voice), LM–6015.

—being employed again in making its Dorian cadence. There is a hint of the same music in Daniel's following stanza of thanksgiving. The Angel leads back Habakkuk 'to his own place', but without further mention of '*capillo capitis sui*'. Also, we hear no more regarding the dinnerless harvesters.

There comes the scene of Daniel's deliverance by the King, who has come to the pit fearing the worst. I pass over these brief exchanges of Mixolydian or Dorian tunes, except to note that the plotters, condemned to the fate they intended for Daniel, show a proper repentance before being devoured, in terms of a chant on free, Gregorian lines (pp. 300–1; ll. 373–82).

Daniel, restored by the King to his honours, sings his final item, his prophecy of the coming of Christ, two stanzas set to a strictly organized a, b, a, b, melody, which, I think, goes best in the second rhythmic mode. It begins:

It remains for an Angel 'suddenly to appear', and sing, to its ancient and standard tune, the Christmas hymn '*Nuntium vobis* . . .' followed by the '*Te Deum*'.

This review of the Beauvais *Daniel* has been based only on the characteristics of the work as it stood in the original manuscript itself. This has revealed a masterly composition, subtly constructed not only in regard to the poetic text with its ever-changing patterns, but in the music settings given to the verse, which show themselves to possess a similar variety of technique.

In this our own day the work has become known for nearly two decades to a wide audience in many countries, through the modern re-staging of it by Noah Greenberg and the New York Pro Musica.[1] It is perhaps a desire to make the drama more attractive to unsophisticated ears that has led to editorial additions to the original features that are undoubtedly both unauthorized and anachronistic, and which must have given to the ordinary listener some strange ideas as to what music-dramas of the medieval Christian Church amounted to in the thirteenth century or thereabouts. I refer particularly to the swollen instrumental forces together with an exotic percussion, which have

---

[1] *The Play of Daniel*, edited for modern performance by Noah Greenberg; based on the transcription from *British Museum Egerton 2615* by The Rev. Rembert Weakland, o.s.b. (New York, 1959).

accompanied such performances. I will now take the opportunity of using my preoccupation with *Daniel* to debate a general problem (as I did in the case of the rhythmic modes). Let us consider now what evidence there is for the employment of musical instruments during the performances in medieval times of these Church works.

V

We have seen often enough how closely these music-dramas were linked with the actual services of the medieval Church. Thus it seems justified to enquire what the attitude of the Christian hierarchies of early and medieval times was, in relation to solo musical instruments. With regard to the former, the answer, derived from the writings of early Christian fathers such as Clement of Alexandria (d.*c.* 220), Eusebius (d.*c.* 340), and St. Jerome (d. 420), as well as from the strictures of Church councils, appears uniformly hostile, the reason being the long association of such instruments with 'heathen' festivals, and particularly with the degenerate late classical theatre. St. Jerome, advising a mother as to her daughter's education, says, 'Let her be deaf to the sound of the organ, and not know even the uses of the pipe, the lyre, and the cithara'.[1] Regarding the cithara, it will be recalled that the very similar harp was, in the medieval mind, closely associated with David, resulting in the numerous medieval pictures of the Old Testament king in the act of playing, but without any liturgical implications.[2]

The Greek Orthodox Church throughout its long history kept entirely to vocal resources in its services, excluding even the aid of the organ. Organs (of a portable type) were in fact secular instruments, used by the rival citizen factions assembled in the Byzantium amphitheatre.

As for the Western Church in the period under consideration, there are available nowadays the results of a great deal of research in the matter. To begin with our own country, Dr. Frank Harrison, in his *Music in Medieval Britain*,[3] writes: '. . . there is no evidence that any instruments but the organ were normally played in church.' This naming of the organ as the sole liturgical instrument receives confirmation from a thirteenth-century source. Joannes Aegidius (otherwise, 'Gilles') de Zamora was a learned Franciscan employed at the court of Alfonso X (1252–84), King of Castile and Leon—who was himself a learned man and a good musician. Gilles held a responsible post, being the tutor to the King's son and eventual successor, Sancho; and at the court, churchman though he was, he must have found himself steeped in the secular musical activities which went on around him. The King himself was responsible for the production of the still surviving two volumes of *Cantigas de Santa Maria*, a collection of no less than four hundred

[1] Quoted in Reese, *Music in the Middle Ages*, p. 63.
[2] For a more detailed description of the early Christian world and solo instruments, see Reese, pp. 61–7.   [3] Harrison, p. xiv.

songs in troubadour style, the poetry in Gallican-Portuguese vernacular, the forms mainly that of the *virelai*, and the single vocal lines written in mensural notation.[1] The theme of the whole collection, as the title shows, was the glorification of the Virgin Mary, and relation of the many miraculous incidents attributed to her. But the style of both verse and music was that of the troubadour. One of the many illustrations contained in the manuscripts depicts King Alfonso dictating to a scribe, while singers and instrumentalists stand by. Certainly we may safely imagine the songs being reinforced by the sounds of solo instruments. Many such are depicted on the pages of the *Cantigas*.

It is therefore impressive that Gilles de Zamora, well acquainted with both musical worlds, should, when he came to write his celebrated treatise, *Ars Musica*, speak of the use of the organ in relation to the liturgy of the Church in the following terms:

... et hoc solo musico instrumento utitur ecclesia in diversis cantibus, et in prosis, in sequentiis, et in hymnis, propter abusum histrionum, ejectis aliis communiter instrumentis ...[2]

That is to say, that the Church has employed this instrument (i.e. the organ) *alone* in various kinds of singing; in prose, sequence, and hymns, other instruments being generally rejected by reason of their association with the secular world of the jongleur.[3]

It is time now to mention a remarkable contribution to the general subject, an article by Dr. Edmund A. Bowles, entitled 'Were Musical Instruments used in the Liturgical Service during the Middle Ages?' which appeared in *The Galpin Society Journal* for May 1957.[4] Dr. Bowles advances a large amount of source-evidence, drawn from pronouncements of Church councils, medieval musical and critical writings, reports of church ceremonies, and extracts from registers of accounts. His conclusions, gathered from evidence from all over Christendom, agree with those of Dr. Frank Harrison, namely, that it was the intention of higher authority that the organ should be the sole

---

[1] For a fuller discussion of the *Cantigas*, and of the activities of Alfonso X, see Reese, pp. 244–8.

[2] *Ars Musica* was reproduced in print by the Benedictine scholar-abbot Martin Gerbert, in Vol. II (No. 13) of his great work *Scriptores ecclesiastici ...* (1794).

In 1797, moved possibly by Gilles de Zamora's opinion, Abbot Gerbert banished all instruments but the organ from his monastic church.

[3] It must of course be remembered that until the thirteenth century organs had been somewhat clumsy in construction and noisy in performance, and opinions were even expressed that such an instrument was unfit to accompany the human voice. It will be noted that hymns (e.g. '*Te Deum laudamus*') and sequences (e.g. '*Victimae paschali*') were compositions which were undertaken by the whole community in full tones, and also, ones which made use of the growing practice of *alternatim*, in which the verses were divided between unaccompanied singing and solo organ playing. (Manifestly, when the organ took over, the liturgical text was lost.)

[4] The *Galpin Society Journal*, No. X, pp. 40–56. *G.S.J.*, XI (1958) contained some criticisms of Dr. Bowles' article, to which he replied in *G.S.J.*, XII (1959), in my opinion getting the better of the exchanges. Also, in his final statement he adds some new and useful evidence in support of his thesis.

instrument to be played in church services. Dr. Bowles does not attempt to conceal records of the numerous infractions which brought about the oft-repeated injunctions of one Church Council after another concerning the exclusion of solo instruments from the services. He cites the Council of Milan, which in 1287, 'promoting various ecclesiastical reforms, decreed that only the organ was to be used inside the church; instruments like recorders and clarions being excluded'.[1] This seems to indicate that the use of recorders and clarions had been attempted by somebody or other. Dr. Bowles freely admits that 'the innumerable proscriptions in themselves point towards violations. However, this does not make the practice correct, nor does it lend the mantle of historical authenticity to present day performances replete with instruments, *within the sphere of the liturgy*.'[2]

One can speculate that, in hours of ease, clergy might well have listened to, and even handled, secular instruments. Chaucer's Monk would not have been the first of his kind. It has been cynically noted that when great Church councils assembled, there, drawn to the same place, the jongleurs swarmed. The naves of parish churches were put to some queer uses at times—or so a modern reader might think. But the fact that in such a parish church 'minstrels played' while a statue of the Virgin was being addressed does not mean that a jongleur would be permitted to enter the choir and perform at an actual service. Time and again it was emphasized by ecclesiastical authorities that his presence at medieval liturgical ceremonies was anathema.

There has been so much insistence so far on the isolation of the organ as the instrument of the liturgy, that it may be necessary to remind ourselves that in the period the sound of bells was frequently associated with it. In the form of the large 'tolling bell' (*campana, signum, clocca*—all three names were in use) we have seen them called for during the '*Te Deum*' singing that rounded off the *Visitatio* performance at tenth-century Winchester. Not an effect of musical instruments, one might claim, for the festival ringing of heavy tower bells could not possibly blend tonally with the vocal music. But early in the period another and smaller type was being used in churches. An increased mastery of bell-casting and tuning finally permitted examples of the *cymbalum* (*tintinnabulum, nola*[3]) to be hung on a bar in some kind of order of musical interval, and, struck with a wooden rod or a hammer, take the form of a musical instrument. *Cymbala* represent indeed a modification of the type of percussive metal plates which has been in ceremonial use since times immemorial. There is much mention of them in the Bible: (the Vulgate word is '*cymbalis*'). Nowadays, the modern version, 'cymbals', calls to mind the picture of a pair of large, slightly concave metal plates with a small hollow at the centre, intended to produce a sonorous clash

---

[1] Bowles, *Galpin Society Journal*, No. X, pp. 49–50.
[2] Bowles, *Galpin Society Journal*, No. XII, p. 89 (italics are Dr. Bowles').
[3] '*nola*': a diminutive (*campana—campanola—nola*). Nowadays the name normally used is 'chime-bells'.

of no particular pitch. This indeed seems to have been their ancient use, with mention also of much smaller plates fastened to short wooden bars and struck together. But the desire in medieval times to produce a chiming bell resulted in the development of a shape resembling half an egg-shell, modified later to something like a tulip form. Although in some of the surviving illustrations of *cymbala* only a few bells are depicted, from contemporary information it would seem that the most common demand was for C, D, E, F, G, a, b flat, b; b flat was sometimes omitted. At other times the octave was completed with the addition of c.

To what employment were the-chime-bells put? First of all, there was the obvious and valuable aid which they gave to the *teaching* of the chant. But there is also evidence of their ceremonial use.[1]

One final point concerning solo instruments and medieval church services requires elucidation. How must we view the large amount of pictorial representation, in the period, of the playing of single instruments, the types of performers ranging from multitudes of angels down to the grotesqueries of donkey-performers? Dr. Bowles in his above-mentioned study gives the question a great deal of attention (pp. 42–5). He is of the opinion that 'most of the paintings and illuminations were primarily religious and symbolic in inspiration' (p. 43). He comments also on 'the disconcerting number of instruments usually shown'. He remarks later, 'The final reason for generally discarding paintings and illuminations as evidence is that many of the details, arrangements, and indeed the traditions found in later medieval art, were based upon the usages of mystery plays, rather than upon the practices of the liturgy' (p. 44). Certainly there was enough inspiration for the iconographers who represented celestial and mundane groupings of instruments, in the very real practices of the open-air, vernacular, spoken drama, when the professional minstrels came into their own.[2]

I am as interested as Dr. Bowles in another query that he raises. He asks (*Galpin Society Journal*, XII, p. 90): 'Is there a single picture showing instruments being played during a service? No—at least I've never been able to find one so far'.[3] I also have undertaken such a quest, and have been equally unsuccessful.

In any case, what matters most is the massed evidence of the medieval church authorities in favour of the barring of 'secular' instruments from the services.

Only later do we find the gradual admission of solo instruments into church activities, beginning with the pomp of ecclesiastical processions. The larger participation of instruments reported in the fifteenth century was mainly due to the expansion of the princely chapels, which en-

---

[1] Professor J. Smits van Waesberghe's study, *Cymbala (Bells in the Middle Ages)* (Rome, 1951) is a valuable source of information on the history and use of chime bells.

[2] Dr. Bowles' failure to heed his own advice here leads him into trouble in another study, dealing with the use of instruments in the medieval music-drama. See my pp. 254–5.

[3] Dr. Bowles is referring of course only to the *medieval* centuries.

couraged private chaplains to co-operate with the numerous secular minstrels employed at courts. But, as musical history is well aware, the *a cappella* tradition did not perish.

VI

It is now my turn to undertake some investigations into the use of musical instruments—not in relation to the medieval Church liturgy, but during performances of the Latin music-dramas. It appears that only half a dozen or so of the Easter Sepulchre type (mostly German, and all later than the thirteenth century) put on record their use of the organ in choral items such as '*Te Deum*', '*Magnificat*', '*Gloria*', or the '*Victimae paschali*' dialogue used as a final item.[1] There is nowhere any mention of an organ being employed in any type of music-drama except towards the conclusion.[2] There are calls for the use of chime-bells, and/or for the *campana* type. Even these mentions (which include that of the *campana* bells of the earliest of *Visitatio* examples surviving, that from Winchester) do not amount to a score.

It is also to be recorded that in the rubrics of the longer *Visitatio Sepulchri* versions (the 'third stage' and the *Ludus Paschalis* of Karl Young's naming) there is not the whisper of an instrument; not a chime-bell, not an organ note. This absence applies also to the *Peregrinus* series, to the Christmas season dramas, to the *Orléans 201* 'Playbook' with its ten works of various types, and most of the rest. There are a few exceptions to mention.

Two fourteenth-century dramas from the Cathedral of Padua (*MS 56*) deal respectively with the Annunciation and the Purification of the Blessed Virgin Mary. In each case the participants assemble to the sound of a single *campana*. The Annunciation concludes with the singing of the '*Magnificat . . .*', the Purification with the '*Nunc dimittis . . .*'. In each of these final items the organ bears its part with the chorus in an *alternatim* performance.

Also in connection with the Blessed Virgin Mary there is a sixteenth-century 'Assumption' to be considered (*Bamberg, MS lit. 119*). All the sung items are liturgical and there is much dumb-show. The Virgin is represented by an effigy, which is finally drawn up through a hole in the roof. Joyous background music is supplied by organ and trumpets (or pipes). The late date of the manuscript (1532) and the fact of the action being ceremonial rather than dramatic robs it of significance as far as

---

[1] One of these German dramas, a fourteenth-century *ordinarium* from Essen (*sine sig.*) belonged to a collegiate church of canons and canonesses. Both parties took part in the 'second stage' *Visitatio*. The 'Angels' were men; the 'Marys', three women. My main reason for mentioning the work specially is due to the fact that the '*Te Deum*' is set down to be performed *alternatim*, the organ dealing with the first verse, the *conventus* the second, the *clerici* the third; '*et sic de aliis*'.

[2] By the term 'organ' I have thus far been intending to imply the 'fixed' type. We will shortly be meeting the unique mention in these Church dramas of the small 'portative' kind, which was apparently given processional use during the action.

our discussion is concerned. I refrain from detailed mention of similar mimed ceremonies, all belonging to the fifteenth century. They include a Pentecost from the same Bamberg manuscript, complete with descending dove and entirely liturgical in texts and settings. It has a similar background music, on occasion, of trumpets and pipes. The hymn '*Veni, Creator . . .*' is called on to be performed *alternatim* by organ and chorus, with the sound of trumpets interspersed.

Much more to the point is the remarkable work, also concerned with the Virgin, which was performed at Avignon late in the fourteenth century. Well might Karl Young refer to it as 'this astonishing *ordo*' (II, p. 242).

We owe our knowledge of it and its survival in manuscript form to one person, the famous French nobleman Philippe de Mézières (d. 1405). He was a gifted man—warrior, diplomat in the service of King Charles V, scholar, poet, well informed musically, and widely travelled in Europe and the Near East. Also, it would appear, singularly devout. Returning to France in the early 1370's he speaks, in a still surviving letter, of a 'Feast of the Presentation of the Blessed Virgin Mary at the Temple', which, based on apocryphal stories of the childhood of the Virgin, he found established by the Eastern Church, for November 21st. He, apparently, 'collected' it, and himself brought about an observance of it in Venice. Back home, he submitted his written version to the hierarchy at Avignon, in which city the Papacy was established, 'in exile'. The new dramatic 'office' gained the approval of Pope Gregory XI, and the result was a performance in an Avignon church in 1372.[1]

Pope Gregory returned to Rome in 1376 and soon died there. The election of his successor sparked off one of the greatest crises that the Roman Church has had to endure. There emerged two rivals for the office, one at Rome, one at Avignon, and the Great Schism had begun. It would appear that the new Avignon pontiff (Clement VII, elected in 1378) was as favourably disposed towards the new *ordo* as Gregory has been, to judge by the fact that at Avignon, on the 21st of November, 1385 and preceding the Mass of the day, Philippe's dramatic office was performed with no less than a bishop taking the part of 'The High Priest of the Temple at Jerusalem', and with the utmost elaboration of production—if, that is, we accept the monumental manuscript version as applying to this Avignon performance, as seems likely. This text (alas! the music of the sung items is lacking) is printed in full by Karl Young (II, pp. 227–42), and represents the most elaborate and detailed 'production details' by far to be found in Church music-drama. The costumes of the twenty-two characters, which, apart from New Testament personages, included the Archangels Gabriel, Raphael, and Michael, a group of nine Angels, and the living symbolisms of *Ecclesia* and *Synagoga*, are painstakingly described. The sworded Archangel

---

[1] The manuscript containing the letter and the text of the 'Presentation', as well as much other relevant matter, survives as *MS lat. 17330* of the Bibliothèque Nationale in Paris. It actually once belonged to Philippe.

Michael drags along a chained and reluctant Lucifer. The 'properties' include two high platforms, with steps up, and railings, all dimensions carefully detailed. In all, the rubrics, introductory or interspersed, amount to the extraordinary total of over five thousand words! This is by far the most ambitious set of rubrics concerned with Church music-dramas ever assembled.

However, for the time being I am concentrating on two minor participants, quietly introduced by the sentence '*Ceterum erunt duo iuvenes cum instrumentis pulsantes*' (Young, II, p. 228). These two young musicians are instructed to play during the numerous processional movements of the actors, but as one might expect, no music is given. They are also called on during the singing by the angels of a *cantilena* in the vernacular tongue in praise of the Virgin, but no further details of this are given, and there is no mention of the instruments being used during any of the sung items in Latin.

The question must arise, 'What instruments were being used?' I have not yet met with any answer to this. One clue is the employment of the verb *pulso*: at times the players themselves are termed '*pulsatores*' (e.g. '*et . . . duo pulsatores pulsantes instrumenta sua . . .*', Young, II, p. 232). The verb, meaning 'to strike', 'to beat', is found in the period applying to keyboard instruments, in contradistinction to stringed instruments, plucked or bowed, which use '*tango*', implying a 'touching' ('*Cytharistae tangant cordas . . .*'). Elsewhere among the directions the word '*dulcia*' (Young, II, p. 230) is applied to Philippe's instruments, so we have to assume that their tone was quiet and unobtrusive. The two musicians always played together; their instruments were apparently of the key-board variety; yet the performers moved freely with the processions, from place to place. I am assuming from all this that what were employed were a couple of hand-organs (portatives)[1] that could each be managed by a single player, whose left hand manipulated the small bellows, while his right played single notes on the somewhat limited keyboard.

This was the sum total of Philippe's instrumental demands, yet from his other writings it is clear that he was keenly interested in solo instruments. He seems to have supported the idea that trumpets should be sounded at the moment of the Elevation in the Mass. During this period France was swarming with open-air, secular mystery-play performances to the sound of jongleur music of many different instruments, and Philippe himself would certainly have known how to pile up colourful instrumental accompaniments if he had wanted to. Yet all he demanded was a couple of the gentlest of instruments, keeping to what we might term Gilles de Zamora's rule, that these should be organs. As for the possible suggestion that other instruments may have been used without their having been mentioned, I would offer the counter-suggestion that one should take a long, hard look at the full text of the *ordo* as transcribed in Karl Young's second volume—over fourteen pages of single-

---

[1] This was also the opinion of Anthony Baines of the Galpin Society, well known for his writings on ancient and medieval instruments.

space printing! Philippe's monumental directions include the tiniest of details concerning costumes, properties, movements, gestures, and manners of speech; everything right down to the provision of a cushion for Mary to kneel on. If Philippe had wanted any more instruments for his elaborate production, he would manifestly have said so very firmly in black and white. We must surely believe that his omissions were wholly intended.

There is no doubt in my mind that this austerity so plainly stated in the case of the immemorial liturgical vocal music applied also to the whole range of the unofficial music-drama that grew up within the Western Church, more or less attached to certain offices. Also, it appears likely to me that this tradition lingered on. I am thinking of certain compositions by the great seventeenth-century composer Heinrich Schütz. He had all the sixteenth-century intricacies of contrapuntal vocal resource at his command, together with a firm grasp of the new Italian ideas of the Venetian School concerning the use of orchestral colour. These techniques he used brilliantly in many a major work. Yet the three Passions (according to Sts. Matthew, Luke, and John), which he composed in his old age, are written in the starkest of styles. Apart from introductory and closing brief choruses, the German texts are a follow-through of the evangelical Passion accounts, set to solo chant-recitatives of Schütz's own devising, interspersed with mildly contrapuntal four-part choruses when any group of people is supposed to be speaking.

But not a single note is given any instrumental accompaniment in the original manuscript versions, not even the single continuo line so often met with. In past performances unauthorized organ support has been sometimes added, especially to the choruses, but of late opinion has hardened into believing that Schütz knew his own mind, and preferred voices alone—and throughout.

With all this evidence in mind I am returning to a further consideration of the Beauvais work, this time in its modern guise as *The Play of Daniel*, and in particular to my concern about the reinforcements given to the action during performances by the New York Pro Musica, by rebec (oboe),[1] recorders, bowed vielle (viola), bell carillon (chimes), handbells, psaltery (zither or autoharp without dampers), portative organ (soprano recorder or modern organ), minstrel's harp (guitar), straight trumpet (trumpet in C). In addition, the performances also made use of the following percussion instruments—small drum, large drum, small triangle, tambourine, finger cymbals, sleigh bells mounted on handle, wood block.

I can well remember my amazement when I encountered the explanation as to how *The Play of Daniel* happened to acquire such a list. It was revealed in an article by Dr. Edmund Bowles—whom we have met with already—in *The Musical Quarterly* for January 1959, entitled, 'The Role

---

[1] In brackets are given the alternative instruments suggested in the published edition of *The Play of Daniel*.

of Musical Instruments in Medieval Sacred Drama'. Dr. Bowles begins the article by saying (p. 67):

> The performances by the New York Pro Musica Antiqua of the Beauvais *Play of Daniel* furnishes us with an opportunity to review generally the role of musical instruments in medieval drama, especially northern European specimens of the 14th and 15th centuries. This writer was privileged to act as an adviser to the Pro Musica in the selection of instruments, which was based upon typological considerations. It is the thesis of this article that instruments used in sacred drama fell into a symbolic framework which served to underline the dramatic and iconographic features of the plays.

Remembering the calibre of Dr. Bowles' exploration of evidence when he tackled the question of instrumental accompaniment in relation to the medieval liturgy, I should have expected that, when the matter of *Daniel* arose, he would have investigated to some extent the nature of the Church music-dramas, attached as they were to the services of the Church, and actually written into service books. He would have found (and this probably would not have surprised him) that what little hard evidence there is shows them to conform with the liturgical 'Gilles de Zamora' rule. But it seems apparent to me that in his article he fails to realise the essential differences between the Church-bound Latin music-dramas and the open-air dramas, shaped for the ordinary citizen, and *spoken* in the vernacular of whatever country produced them. A further contrast is that the plentiful stage directions so often found in the open-air, vernacular dramas demand time and again a wealth of jongleur instruments (as well as organ), singly, or in various group selections. The examples from which Dr. Bowles draws his long lists of instruments all belong to the world of the mystery-play, and, as he indicates, they come mostly from those of the fourteenth and fifteenth centuries.

Much as Dr. Bowles is bound up with descriptions of the use of jongleur instruments in mystery plays of the fourteenth and fifteenth centuries, the main purpose of his essay is to show how these aided the permeation of the 'sacred drama' with the 'symbolism' of the medieval religious writers, when 'the belief prevailed that behind each concrete object or event lay a hidden meaning relating to the Scriptures . . .' (p. 67). I echo him again: '. . . instruments used in sacred drama fell into a symbolic framework'. Yet the first 'play' that he calls on for mention in his text is a twelfth-century music-drama from Beauvais.

What evidence is there that the original performance of *Daniel* would have included the presence of any instruments at all? In the rubrics there is mention that when the army of Darius invades Belshazzar's hall, the Persian King is to be preceded by 'harp-players' (*cytharistae*)—that and no more. The '*Te Deum*' even escapes any mention of bells and organ.

One fact that must certainly be noted, of course, is that in the powerful chorus of the army of Darius there occur the phrases: '. . . *cytharistae tangant cordas; musicorum organa resonent . . .*'.[1] These could be held to

[1] See p. 256.

prove that all the instruments named were present and were used. On the other hand they could also be said to be no more than poetic colouring, and that the writer who followed through the events related in Chapter V of the Old Testament *Book of Daniel* would be just as thoroughly acquainted with Chapter III, where an instrumental group is twice mentioned, and (according to the Authorized Version) is made up of: '. . . the sound of the cornet, flute, harp, sackbut, psaltery, dulcimer, and all kinds of music'.[1] Could the passage have given him ideas?

However, Dr. Bowles is not concerned in seeking for any proofs that the original *Daniel* was given instrumental aid. *The Play of Daniel* is merely *assumed* to be so equipped. After a number of pages of discussion concerning the symbolic use of instruments, the instances drawn from various examples of vernacular mystery plays dating from the fourteenth and fifteenth centuries, Dr. Bowles continues:

> The use of instrumental accompaniment reviewed above is too consistent and stereotyped when compared to its scenic contexts to suggest other than deliberate typological pattern. Consequently, for the New York Pro Musica performances of *The Play of Daniel* (from a new transcription of Egerton MS 2615, British Museum) *the selection of instruments was based upon symbolical considerations obtained by extrapolating backwards in time from the practices just discussed . . .*[2] Daniel himself is clearly the prophet image of Christ and the New Law, so the psaltery was selected to accompany his music. To make the allusion more complete, the psaltery player in the production was the constant companion of Daniel, following him throughout the play. The organ was employed to accompany the music of Daniel during dramatic occasions warranting a symbolic reference to the prophetic. The angel appearing before Habakkuk carried a harp, since this instrument was associated with heavenly figures in medieval drama, and foreshadowed the Crucifixion, as the writings of the scholastics clearly show. For the oriental Queen finger-cymbals were selected, underlining her essentially feminine role and at the same time retaining the basic Eastern feeling . . . During the processional of Darius the bagpipe was used, an instrument with pejorative connotations because of its association with the common people, beggars and scoundrels of all sorts . . .[3]

I will not attempt to question Dr. Bowles' theories when it comes to the techniques of the mystery plays, but there is little sign of this 'symbolic' preoccupation in the corpus of the Church music-dramas (and certainly not in association with instruments). The only recorded small efforts in that direction which I can recall are Peter's symbolic 'key', carried in the 'Dublin' *Visitatio*, Christ's brilliant costume and phylactery for his triumphant after-Resurrection appearance, when he also bears a cross, and some scattered mentions elsewhere of other cross-bearing occasions.

In regard to all those instrumental symbolisms in the case of the

---

[1] The last-mentioned phrase is rendered in the Vulgate as *'universi generis musicorum'*. Nowadays, the seventeenth-century versions of the names of some of the instruments would probably be given amendment.

[2] The italics are those of the present writer.

[3] Bowles, pp. 83–4 (footnote).

mystery plays, Dr. Bowles may indeed be right, but I decline to accept them for Church-music dramas in general and the Beauvais *Daniel* in particular. In fact, there is no justification at all for bringing the instrumentation of the 'spoken' mystery plays into a Church music-drama. The process by which it was achieved is described by Dr. Bowles himself as 'interpolating backward in time from the practices just discussed' (i.e. those of the mystery plays). Surely this is a very dangerous technique, and not that of sound scholarship? This practice justified, anachronisms of any sort have a free hand!

I once attempted to come to a compromise concerning the modern instrumental extravaganzas of *The Play of Herod*, also produced by the New York Pro Musica, by mentioning the possibilities of an influence from the 'Feast of Fools'. There is very little evidence for this, and I now think that I was wrong not to have stood firm on the results of research evidence. I reflect, moreover, that in the same famous Beauvais Cathedral in the same century there had been produced the finest of the *Peregrinus* music-dramas, and this, on the evidence of the rubrics, was performed in the very *midst* of the threefold Vespers of Easter Monday. At the conclusion of this 'Emmaus' interlude, the antiphon '*Christus resurgens . . .*' was sung as Vespers resumed. In the rubrics there is no whisper of instruments in the liturgical service. Are we to assume that they were imported for the *Peregrinus* and thereafter banished? I am more inclined to think that it never occurred to the Cathedral staff that any were needed.

With regard to *Daniel* I fear that the damage is done. The majority of people who have seen it in America and Europe in its 'Pro Musica' form will probably continue to imagine that this was its staging in the twelfth to thirteenth centuries, and may be disappointed if and when they meet with any other medieval Church music-dramas produced in more sombre, if in more authentic fashion. It can certainly be claimed that these 'Pro Musica' additions were good 'box-office'. But for the very sake of scholarship I must make this protest.[1]

---

[1] I have mentioned before that I happened to be concerned with the preparations of the New York Pro Musica for *The Play of Herod*, a Christmas music-drama from *Orléans 201*, inasmuch as I deciphered, transcribed, and rhythmed the musical settings and wrote one of the articles in the published edition. I managed to have my way in certain features, but there was much else that I objected to—unsuccessfully. However, I was glad to be able to be responsible for an Appendix, a 'literal transcription' of the manuscript, together with photos of the original pages. From it one could at least see plainly enough what was in the original version and what had been imposed on it.

The version to which Smoldon here refers is *The Play of Herod*, edited by Noah Greenberg and William Smoldon (New York, 1965). See note 1, p. 209 (*Ed.*).

CHAPTER TWELVE

THE TWELFTH CENTURY (4)

The Fleury Playbook
Dramas of St Nicholas
The *Conversio Pauli Apostoli* and *Resuscitatio Lazari*

I return now to the manuscript *Orléans, Bibliothèque de la Ville, MS 201*
for a closer consideration of that part of it which has come to be termed
(without justification, I believe), the 'Fleury Playbook'.[1] *MS 201* is of
small dimensions: 168 × 144 mms. A few extra and even smaller leaves
are inserted at an early place in the manuscript. The pages that comprise
the 'Playbook' part are numbered from 176 to 243. The previous section
is devoted to homilies concerning the Virgin, while the pages following
the 'Playbook' contain two sequences, (a) '*Launemari patris pii . . .*'
(devoted to St. Lomer), and (b) '*Ave mater Domini . . .*' (for the Virgin).
Both texts are to be found in the *Chevalier* and *Analecta Hymnica*
collections. The manuscript ends with p. 251.

The texts, considered throughout, represent at least four different
hands. That of the homilies appears to belong to the twelfth century,
while that of the insertion, previously mentioned, is different and seems
of a somewhat later date. The 'Playbook' section, with the additional
evidence of its musical notation, is almost certainly of the late twelfth
century, while the sequences may belong to over a century later.

The 'Playbook' itself has musical notation throughout—what appears
to be French-style neumes written on staves of four red lines, with C or
F clefs. Both the setting-down of the neumes and the ruling of the stave-
lines show lack of care at times. The normal number of staves to the
page is nine, but for some reason or other there was a scribal nervousness
regarding space towards the end of the 'Playbook', with staves per page
increasing to eleven, and once, even to thirteen. To me the notation
appears as a decadent style, contrasting to its disadvantage with the
neatly written French neumes of the '*Launemari patris pii . . .*' sequence
that follows. The quite competent hand responsible for the *texts* of the

---

[1] The manuscript was described and studied by Otto E. Albrecht in his book, *Four Latin
Plays of St. Nicholas* (Philadelphia, 1935). A more comprehensive handling of the manuscript
is that of Solange Corbin, 'Le Manuscrit 201 D'Orléans—Drames liturgiques dits de
Fleury', *Romania*, 36 (1953), pp. 1–43. The 'Playbook' is also considered to some length by
Charles W. Jones in his book, *The Saint Nicholas Liturgy and its Literary Relationships*
(University of California Press, Berkeley, 1963). Only Professor Corbin pays any heed to the
music of the 'Playbook'. She makes out a convincing case for connecting the early history of
the manuscript as a whole with the Abbey of St. Lomer at Blois, and not Fleury as was
previously thought.

dramas throughout is not found elsewhere in the Orléans manuscript.

A peculiarity of the 'Playbook' music-scribe is his version of the *virga* form. Nowhere else have I encountered this particular shape—a lozenge with the shaft both below and above it, thus: ◖|.[1] This single neume form is used in company with the normal blob or short stroke (◼) for the *punctum*. Obviously a single and somewhat unusual music-scribe tackled the whole ten compositions of the 'Playbook' section.

The first four to be met with (a very mixed bag, technically) are all concerned with the cult of St. Nicholas, the most popular saint of the Middle Ages, and the most widely reported in regard to saintly miracles. They comprise:

I	*Tres Filiae* (The Three Daughters)	pp. 176–82
II	*Tres Clerici* (The Three Clerks)	pp. 183–7
III	*Iconia Sancti Nicholai* (The Image of St. Nicholas)	pp. 188–96
IV	*Filius Getronis* (The Son of Getron)	pp. 196–205

The next four have already been met with and discussed. In my opinion they are the finest plays in the collection:

V	*Officium Stellae* (The Coming of the Magi)	pp. 205–14
VI	*Ordo Rachelis* (The Slaying of the Innocents)	pp. 214–20
VII	*Visitatio Sepulchri* (The Visit to the Sepulchre)	pp. 220–5
VIII	*Peregrinus* (The Stranger)	pp. 225–30

The final two represent attempts to dramatize two New Testament stories. They are:

IX	*Conversio Sancti Pauli* (The Conversion of St. Paul)	pp. 230–3
X	*Resuscitatio Lazari* (The Raising of Lazarus)	pp. 233–43

It has already been noted that the vast majority of surviving Church dramas are connected with the two major feasts of the liturgical year, those of Easter and Christmas. The more independent attempts at drama, such as those connected with Old and New Testament episodes, stories of the Virgin Mary and the saints, etc., make very poor numerical showing against the Easter and Christmas ones. In fact, probably by the accidents of fortune, the 'Playbook' collection (its own Easter and Christmas dramas apart) give us examples, complete with their music, of types which otherwise existed imperfect. There seems a case, therefore, for examining these dramas and their accompanying music rather closely.

II

Before considering the first group of four dramas, all dealing with St. Nicholas, let us give some attention as to what this particular saint meant to the medieval world. Clearly, he meant a great deal. He was early regarded as the patron saint of travellers; and certainly those who

---

[1] I have been informed that this exceptional *virga* form is to be encountered elsewhere, but I have not yet met with it. The *virga* shape found in the carelessly written *Visitatio*, contained in the thirteenth-century *Tours 927* (fols. 1r.–8v.) looks rather similar sometimes. I imagine this is probably an accident.

travelled by land or sea (particularly by sea) in medieval times, needed all the saintly protection they could get. As the cult permeated Christendom he was felt to be the supernatural guardian and benefactor of all those in need, in peril or under oppression. A wealth of legend grew up concerning his divine interventions.

Very little is historically certain as to his earthly career, apart from the facts that he was a native of Lycia in Asia Minor, and that there he became bishop of Myra in about 325 A.D. Legend speaks of miracles performed during his lifetime, and, after his death, continuing at his tomb at Myra. Although his cult was already established in Europe (or perhaps because of it), certain Italian traders violated his tomb in 1087 and brought the relics to Bari in south Italy, thus establishing a more convenient objective for the St. Nicholas-pilgrimages as far as the West was concerned.

Regarding saint-worship in general, a liturgical phenomenon to be noted from the tenth century onward was the practice of amending certain (sometimes even *all*) of the choral pieces of a particular Canonical Office, and reshaping them in versified forms for the greater glory of the saint whose feast day it happened to be. Such free compositions no doubt afforded to their inventors the same kind of pious and artistic pleasure as was felt by the shapers of tropes and sequences. The many prose *vitae* of the leading saints that were current at the time provided materials, with St. Nicholas having more than his share of attention; and in the versification of the various antiphons and responsories belonging to his Office of December 6th, many of the better known legendary incidents were touched on.

However, regarding the actual dramatization of the St. Nicholas legends, as represented by the four surviving examples, we may, I believe, accept Karl Young's conclusions, which he states in the following terms (II, pp. 310–11):

... We have no evidence, however, that these liturgical treatments of the subject ever developed into drama.

In so far, then, as we can judge from the extant miracle plays, they rest not upon short and summary references to the *vita* such as are found in liturgical embellishments, but directly upon the complete forms of the legends themselves. The plays represent the incidents of the traditional narratives with substantial fidelity, and they appear to have arisen through the application of the dramatic treatment directly to these stories.[1]

---

[1] Young (II, p. 487) has given a lengthy note concerning the early *vitae* of St. Nicholas, together with a list of works dealing with the subject. He remarks:
'As representing the basic sources of the plays treated here I use the ninth-century *Vita a Iohanne Diacono Neapolitano* as first printed in the fifteenth century compilation of Boninus Mombritius. There can be no doubt that this *vita* records the legends in forms typical of Western Europe during the period just preceding the date of the first miracle plays, and its versions of *Tres Filiae, Iconia Sancti Nicholai*, and *Filius Getronis* are as near to the plays in content as are any of the other narrative versions.'
The *Tres Clerici* story, it appears, is not to be found among the early legends. As Karl Young says (p. 328), 'we have no version of it older than the play itself'. Anyway, the story was well known by the late eleventh century.

The first St. Nicholas play in the 'Fleury Playbook' is the *Tres Filiae*, the famous medieval story of an indigent father and his three daughters. In this 'Fleury' version the work is cast in rather elementary forms and is far from satisfying, either dramatically or musically. As the drama opens, *Pater* is heard first, lamenting the state into which he has fallen, and consulting his daughters as to what can be done to remedy it. The eldest of them proposes that they should support him by prostitution, but before an answer can be given, the whole situation is suddenly resolved by a gift of gold being flung through the window. As the family rejoices, a suitor arrives ('with astonishing promptitude', as Karl Young wryly observes). Father and daughter approving of him, he departs with his bride and dowry, which leaves *Pater* once more destitute and lamenting in exactly the same terms as before. The dramatic situation is then twice more repeated, both in the matter of the gold and the providential appearances of the suitors. After the third gift, *Pater* manages to intercept the giver (none other than St. Nicholas himself) and to express his gratitude. He is told to render his thanks to God. A third suitor then appears and is duly given his bride and his gold, and the play ends with a choral performance of the antiphon '*O Christi pietas*', which belongs to the Feast of St. Nicholas.

The rough edges of this drama are all too obvious. Despite the general thanksgiving at the end, we can hardly fail to notice that the poverty-stricken father seems to be left as poor as before, and minus the care of his daughters (this, incidentally, is a technicality which the legend itself does not entirely clarify). Nor can we overlook the repetitiousness and drearily mechanical quality of the work. Karl Young's opinion of the libretto and its shaper is not flattering. 'One longs,' he writes (II, p. 322), 'for the courage to infer that the alacrity with which the suitors scent the dowries, and the uniformity of their wooings, are intended for comic effect! The solemnity of the plodding author's intention, however, is all too obvious.' I see no reason to disagree with Young's assessment.

The text of this 'Fleury' version is printed by Young in II, pp. 316–21.[1] Let us consider it now in rather more detail. It will be found that the work begins with an exordium of three stanzas, the preliminary lament of the father and a reply by the daughters. The form is interesting, employing a familiar hymn-pattern. Numbering the syllables in each line, we find the first two stanzas each resolving into 8,7 : 8,7 : 7 : 8,7. Scholars have in the past been dissatisfied with the text of the third stanza as it stands in the manuscript, and for more than one reason. However, Karl Young prints it as he finds it. When we come to consider the musical settings I shall offer some amendment to the lines.

The main part of the work then follows, and here we find ample evidence for our impressions of plodding repetitiousness. It is made up

---

[1] In the actual Orléans manuscript (pp. 176–82) the texts are written 'straight on' throughout, unless checked by the insertion of rubrics. However, the actual divisions into lines of poetry are indicated by stops (these not necessarily having punctuation significance) and by capital letters. Neither stops nor capital letters are maintained consistently.

of thirty-five stanzas, nearly all identical in their textual pattern; one that consists of five lines in all, four of them with a single rhyme and of ten syllables each, and a final short line of four syllables. This latter occasionally takes on the function of a refrain from stanza to stanza. A few of the stanzas lack one line, some of them two; this apparently by intention.[1]

The whole action divides itself textually into three obvious parts, each concerned with the successive speeches of Father; Daughter (first, second, or third); Father (after the arrival of the gold); Daughter; Suitor; Father (to Daughter); Daughter; Father (to Suitor)—after which, on each occasion, away go the happy pair with their gold.

The second part, obviously, begins with *Pater* renewing his complaint. The second Daughter's three-stanza reply (15, 16, 17) has at least the virtue of bringing new textual matter to old rhythms. But as Daughter, Father, and second Suitor go through the already familiar motions it will be found that stanzas 13 and 14 correspond with stanzas 1 and 2; stanzas 18, 19, 20, 21, 22, and 23 with stanzas 7, 8, 9, 10, 11, and 12. In fact, the scribe did not trouble to write out in full these particular stanzas of the second section, but recalled them merely through the few words (and notes) of successive incipits.

The third section is a mere repetition of what has gone before, with textual variety only in the third Daughter's three stanzas (25, 26, and 27), and broken only by the Father's stanza of thanks to St. Nicholas, and the Saint's reply.

I turn now to the matter of the music. Here it will be found that a similar measure of economy of form has been observed. I give the musical setting of the first stanza of the exordium, rendered rhythmically. The melody will be seen to consist of four main sentences. It will be noted that the second half of the second musical sentence is elaborated to set the single short third line of text, and is also employed for setting the second half of the fourth line of text. In the repetition of this for the second stanza the manuscript gives it in incipit only, a single '*Heu*' and a couple of notes. It will be observed that on the music example I have marked asterisks above certain occasional neumes. This is merely my way of wondering if the scribe at these seemingly analogous places really intended these small note-differences to have been made. My first asterisk (at '*la-men-tum*') marks my reading of an indistinct neume, which is perfectly clear at the corresponding places in the other two stanzas.

The melody is a skilful one. I suspect that it was sung in regular rhythm.

---

[1] These 'reduced' stanzas suffer merely the leaving-out of the fourth line in the case of stanza 9, and in the cases of stanzas 10, 11, and 12 of leaving out both the third and fourth lines, these omissions applying to the corresponding stanzas in the other two sections. They involve only the 'Suitor-Father-Daughter' episode.

In la - men - tum et me - ro - rum ver - sa est le - ti - ci - a quem pre - be - bat o - lim no - bis re - rum ha - bun - dan - ci - - - a. O re - rum in - o - pi - - a! He - u! he - u! pe - ri - - e - runt hu - is vi - te gau - di - - a.

Karl Young's text of the third stanza, beginning '*Finis opum, dum recedunt . . .*' (II, p. 316) shows a textual pattern of 8,7 : 8,7 : 8,7 : 7 : 8,7 : 8,7—two extra double lines as compared with the first two stanzas. The question arises: do we have here a scribal mistake, with two super-fluous lines? If so, which lines will they be? Certainly the double line beginning '*tractat secum*' has come under scholarly suspicion in the matter of sense; also it is one syllable short. Again, the last line but one, beginning '*Heu! heu! perierunt*', might be thought of as having strayed from its rounding-off task in stanzas I and II. But in the manuscript the extra lines have been accommodated plainly enough with musical phrases borrowed from other parts of the setting; and as for the missing syllable from the third double line, there is a corresponding missing neume from the music. It is all very tidy. On the other hand, if these two lines are omitted, then the stanza setting as written out above will fit the remainder very smoothly. The manuscript seems very definite as to its intentions regarding the third stanza, but the distortion certainly appears to be a curious one. I fear that we shall never know the truth of the matter.

What could be called the main tune now follows, a shapely and attractive melody. It had better be, for in the drama it would be heard starting up thirty-five successive times. Like the previous tune (of a much briefer life), it is an Aeolian one; on this occasion transposed, for the B flat as a clef sign is written consistently in the manuscript for the rest of the work. There are four sentences, followed by a briefer fifth. They could be described as A, B, A, B, and ½B. All are linked by a com-mon use of the first four neumes of A—in the cases of lines 3 and 5, in slightly varied form. Once again in repetitions of the tune, one meets in the manuscript with slight differences—extra notes to a neume, small changes of rhythm—trivialities to which it is difficult to apply the term 'variation'. I have once again added some asterisks to certain neumes belonging to the plain version of the melody which is presented with the first stanza. Like the exordium tune, it was probably sung in regular rhythm.

261

In the cases of the first, second, and fourth asterisks the single D is often replaced in later repeats by D,E. The reverse sometimes happens at the third, a single F for the two notes. Finally, at '(*mi-*) *serum*', the rhythms are, more often than not, reversed, giving <u>DE</u> D. One wonders if indeed these small changes had any real reason behind them.

One final point regarding this tune. It is to be found employed as the 'personal' melody of Adeodatus, son of Getron, in the third of the St. Nicholas 'miracles', used whenever the captive youth sings.[1] The four-line stanzas of this particular work are all of ten syllables; thus a last-line adjustment will be found, but there is no doubt as to the tune's identity. Common property, it would seem.

Before leaving '*Tres Filiae*' I must take brief note, as does Karl Young, of another manuscript dealing with the same legend. It comes from Hildesheim,[2] and is of the eleventh to twelfth centuries. It is without anything like the introductory stanzas of the Orléans text, and is also without any musical setting. But of its nineteen stanzas (of the same 10, 10, 10, 4 pattern) fifteen can be found duplicated in the Orléans version. The Hildesheim attempt reveals itself as being even cruder than that of Orléans. The 'Suitor' element is lacking, while St. Nicholas makes one single intervention with a gift of gold, this near the breaking-off of the incomplete text. Neither Karl Young nor Charles Jones (the latter in his *The St. Nicholas Liturgy*—see footnote, p. 256) have anything much to say concerning the Hildesheim manuscript in itself. Jones admits that he has not examined it. Its nature had better be realized. It is in fact a student's rough notebook of no more than eight leaves, the first having suffered 'palimpsest' treatment; altogether, an everyday 'commonplace' book such as many a medieval student might have been found carrying. The writing throughout is by the same hand. The only reason for the sheets having survived is probably the fact that on two inner facing-pages is first the version of *Tres Filiae*, and, following it,

---

[1] Except when he speaks of his native land, when he employs his mother's stanza-melody.
[2] London, *Brit. Mus. Add. MS 22414*, fols. 3v.–4r.

one of *Tres Clerici*, equally primitive in its story-telling by means of uniform 10,10,10,4 type of stanza.

The rest of the Hildesheim manuscript pages are devoted to a variety of matters; brief medical notes—laxatives, antidotes to poisons—also information as to how to distinguish a virgin. Features more worthy of a student are provided by first the brief consideration of a syllogism followed by a short treatise on the abacus. Christopher Hohler, an authoritative writer on liturgical subjects, in a reference to the problems concerned with the St. Nicholas liturgy and the related miracle dramas, brings forward evidence which seems to place the Hildesheim efforts as later than either Karl Young or Charles Jones would date them.[1] He says, in fact (pp. 47–8):

> ... the Fleury and Hildesheim Three Daughters are not successive develop-
> ments of the same play but parallel corruptions of it, and neither text is
> markedly better than the other. From this it should follow that the play
> originated, certainly not at Hildesheim as Mr. Jones suggests, nor yet at
> Fleury or wherever the Fleury manuscript originally came from ... I should
> have thought that its scribe came from the extreme south, say Arles or
> Toulouse. The two manuscripts are, I think, roughly contemporary ... and
> the play should have originated wherever the two scribes both studied ...
> that place should have been in France.

With that I leave *Tres Filiae*, more doubtful than ever as to its origin, and without any belief that it could claim any 'repertoire' companion-ship with (say) the *Visitatio Sepulchri* that shares the same vellum.

III

Tres Clerici has just been met with in connection with the Hildesheim manuscript. In this Hildesheim version the text tells, in the plainest of uniform rhyming stanzas, of the lodging granted to three travelling scholars by a 'Host' and his wife, following their pleas. The guests instantly retire to rest. The two, after some debate, resolve that the sleepers are to be murdered for the sake of their money. This action is apparently carried out in dumb show, although there is no rubric men-tion. The bodies disposed of, the 'Host' and his wife find themselves called on to entertain yet another guest, who demands supper, and 'fresh meat'. When the 'Host' says that he has none, he is told grimly that he has in fact plenty. St. Nicholas then reveals himself and the guilty couple beg for mercy. Through the Saint's prayer, life is restored to the scholars and forgiveness gained for the repentant criminals. At this point, however, the text ends abruptly, and the final items seem to be somewhat disarranged. Since this Hildesheim play is also without its music, we will now leave it and turn to the Orléans version.

---

[1] Christopher Hohler, 'The Proper Office of St. Nicholas and Related Matters with Reference to a Recent Book', *Medium Aevum*, 36 (1967), pp. 40–8.
He is not flattering as to the dramatic qualities of the Hildesheim texts, since he refers to them (p. 46) as 'charades for choirboys'.

Textually, this is not much of an improvement on Hildesheim's. The story is told in nineteen identically-rhythmed stanzas of four lines each, ten syllables per line and mostly rhyming a a b b. However, a preliminary scene can be distinguished in which the scholars are represented as consulting among themselves, apparently on the road outside, before making their appeal to the 'Host'. The wife (*Vetula*) is successfully pictured as formidable, and is appealed to by the scholars as an influence likely to move her husband to accept them. Later, the 'Host' again seeks her advice regarding the admittance of the second caller. Slightly more life is brought to the exchanges through some of the four-line stanzas being halved between two speakers.

The setting to music seems to have been a simple affair. Eighteen of the nineteen stanzas are sung to the same four-sentence Dorian melody. Here it is in rhythmic form:

The musical form appears to be A A B C, three of the sentences concluding with the few notes of an identical cadence. The melody is certainly shapely, but once again we find a setting called on to bear a large number of repetitions. These show a few note-discrepancies, which is perhaps not to be wondered at. One sympathizes with the music-scribe, faced with his seemingly interminable task.

However, after the eighteenth stanza he is given a break. The final one, representing St. Nicholas' prayer, is set by an entirely new melody, still faithful to the Dorian mode but somewhat more melismatic than the main tune. I give it below. Because of the melismas I render it in free rhythm, which may have been the original intention:

The musical form appears again to be A A B C, with a certain amount of transference of brief phrases. Certain blots and smudges on the manuscript page render my own task a little uncertain in places.

Since a manuscript rubric speaks of a 'chorus' as singing '*Te Deum laudamus*', it does seem that we have here the record of an actual performance after a Matins service. But under what conditions, may we wonder? On II, p. 315, Karl Young comments upon the general influence of hymnody upon the successions of uniform stanzas to be found in the two 'miracles' we have been dealing with. Without necessarily agreeing that these works represented mere poems rather than dramas intended for performance, Young was at least ready to entertain such doubts. We have seen that Christopher Hohler is inclined to dismiss the two Hildesheim efforts as being choirboy charades. Could this be a clue? Karl Young has already observed that '. . . a playwright . . . as a schoolboy . . . might have been assigned this or that prose legend for versifying'. Certainly we have heard much of the monastic, and later, cathedral schools of the Middle Ages, which taught their young pupils Latin versification to a very high standard. I have often wondered if what we have here might not in fact be some sort of pedagogical collaboration—a schoolboy's effort set to music by his music master for performance in the choir on 6 December. My own impression is that the musical settings of the two repetitive Orléans works that we have just dealt with, are far more professional than the libretti. However this may be, the plays represent a couple of lucky survivals, which must be placed at the nadir of the 'Playbook' collection.

Karl Young (II, pp. 355–6) prints the text of a manuscript fragment of the twelfth century from Einsiedeln (*Stiftsbibl., MS 34 407*, fol. 2v.–3r.). The lines of hexameters, without any explanatory rubrics, are clearly the concluding part of a *Tres Clerici* drama, beginning with the entry of St. Nicholas, and carrying through the rest of the action to the confessions of the guilty pair and the restoration to life of the scholars. What has survived points to a more detailed and better drama than the other two versions. I have checked up regarding the manuscript and have the assurance of the librarian of the monastic library at Einsiedeln that there is no music notation whatsoever given in the fragment. It would have been interesting to see if the setting showed a similar improvement on the Orléans effort.

IV

After the wooden techniques that we have met with in the dramatic handlings of the first two of the St. Nicholas legends, we come now, in *Iconia Sancti Nicolai*, to two examples of a considerably higher standard of Latin versification, both in imaginative detail and in variety of metre. The first to be considered recalls to our minds the name of its author, an item of information so rarely to be recovered in medieval times. The 'wandering scholar' Hilarius has already been mentioned as the undoubted creator of a 'Daniel' music-drama. His *Ludus super Iconia Sancti Nicolai*, although a scholarly effort, is more modest in its scope.

Once again we have sorrowfully to record that no music of it has come down to us, even though the work was undoubtedly sung.

I have already pointed out that Hilarius, usually supposed to have followed the career of an itinerant scholar, could hardly have brought about an adequate performance of so elaborate a music-drama as his version of *Daniel* with resources that would be likely to amount to no more than those of a travelling jongleur group. He needed, in fact, a large and skilled cast, a large church and a trained liturgical choir, and, if indeed he got his performances with his alternative liturgical con-clusions of either *Te Deum* or *Magnificat*, those conditions must have been met. But after reading through his 'Image of St. Nicholas' one could well conclude that it had been shaped for a most modest presen-tation; two characters only being called on for utterances. These two are *Barbarus*, a rich heathen, who nevertheless possesses an image of the Saint in whose protective powers he has great faith; and the person of St. Nicholas himself. For the purpose of the action a group of 'robbers' are needed, but these carry through their depredations wholly in dumb show. As for the 'Image', the 'production' probably looked for least trouble by having it represented by another living person. No doubt Saint and effigy were made to look as alike as possible.[1]

The action follows the *vita* normally enough but in concise fashion. *Barbarus* announces that he is going on his travels, and that he is placing a chest containing all his wealth under the guardianship of the image of the Saint. Having expressed his faith in that protection, he concludes, with true medieval naïveté, that the Image had better look to it that there is nothing to complain about when he returns.

After his departure the mimed robbery takes place. *Barbarus* returns, discovers his loss, blames the Image, and proceeds to thrash it! Whether or not moved by this, St. Nicholas himself appears to the robbers in their hiding place, complains of the scourging, and threatens to bring them to the gallows if they do not restore the stolen goods immediately. The terrified robbers obey the order, again silently, but no doubt with a great deal of expressive miming. How *Barbarus* missed seeing the return is not explained, but a rubric states that he duly becomes aware of the fact, and joyfully gives the credit to St. Nicholas. Thereupon the Saint appears to him, telling him that it is to God and to Christ that the thanks must be given. In answer *Barbarus* announces his willing-ness to be converted to Christianity.

Such is the somewhat elementary plot, but it gains in literary stature through the playwright's skill in changing his metres with each change of situation, or even emotion, and in making attractive use of vernacular refrains. If only the music could have been recovered, a work well worth staging would surely have been revealed.

---

[1] To judge by the first rubric, which speaks of *'persona Barbari'* and *'persona iconiae'* it does seem that the Image was literally 'impersonated'. In the Orléans work it appears to have been something much smaller; something that could be worn (and concealed) by its owner.

In the manuscript the drama ends with the last words of *Barbarus*. Karl Young, recalling that the other two works by Hilarius are clearly associated with liturgical ceremonies, suggests (II, p. 343) that 'it may be that in copying the *Iconia Sancti Nicolai* the scribe omitted a closing rubric of liturgical significance'. My own speculation is that the absence of *Te Deum* or *Magnificat* may be due to the fact that here we may possibly have an open-air performance, truly goliardic, with perhaps Hilarius in the leading role, Jordanus (or Simon or Hugo)[1] as the Saint, and any of their road companions filling-in the mimed parts.

The Orléans *Iconia* is a more ambitious effort, but marred by stretches of soliloquy too long continued in the same metres and in the same settings. The music scribe once again makes his contributions of what are obviously copying blunders. But, especially in the shorter dialogues, swifter changes of text-metres and melody result in some attractive moments of real music-drama, these chiefly concerned with the three robbers, who really do come alive.

The opening rubric sums up in brief terms the 'argument' of the drama. We learn that the non-Christian is in fact of the Jewish faith. Yet in his opening soliloquy his belief in the merits and good works of St. Nicholas, and the protective powers of his image are stronger than any scepticism he may feel. '*Quem sic bonum me patronum . . .*!' he proclaims from a *sedes* representing his home, with a 'property' chest containing his wealth in the background. I quote text and music of the opening lines, with their quite fascinating rhyme-scheme, these of course addressed to the Image, not the Saint himself:

Judaeus' soliloquy continues for about twenty of these fifteen-syllable lines, with internal rhymes and with paired end-rhymes which we can represent by $\left\{\begin{matrix} a\ a\ b \\ c\ c\ b \end{matrix}\right\}$. Uncertainties as to the total number of lines rests on a couple of discrepancies in the end-rhyme scheme, which has caused scholars to speculate as to lost lines.

The first eleven lines are set by the single musical sentence seen in the example. The music scribe early shows his calibre. The asterisks which I have written above certain notes represent corrections of what I am certain are copying errors.

One small musical change in this first part appears to be deliberate. For the Mixolydian cadence, d' l̲f s-, there is substituted for a while s l t. But before the tune is abandoned the first cadence returns.

---

[1] See Chapter XI, p. 223.

Textually, the fifteen-syllable pattern continues throughout the soliloquy, but at '*Ergo rerum te mearum . . .*' (Young, line 34) there is an interesting sidelight on medieval musicianship. The composer has just written the cadence of the line before (d' l̲f̲ s-); he wishes to change the tune, and seems to have said to himself, 'Why not use the cadence motive as a springboard?' The result is this new melody:

The tune continues for another six lines, hampered by small but all too frequent errors on the part of the music scribe. The last two lines of the soliloquy are for some reason or other given a new melody, but this still Mixolydian.

We must now imagine *Judaeus* taking his departure, confident as to the safety of his treasure chest. No sooner has he gone than the three robbers appear, lamenting their empty pockets and wondering what to do about it, this to the last example of the fifteen-syllable pairs of lines; but to a new tune of their own. It is now that an attempt seems to be made to portray individuals, each contributing his advice and comments. This is especially true of the third robber, who appears to be the shrewdest of the three. It is he who advises caution as they approach the dwelling. It is also he who, when they find the chest too heavy to carry away, discovers that the lock is open. The music, always Mixolydian, has thus far been in no way distinguished, but I feel that the third robber's exaltation as he realizes that the treasure is theirs is well worth recording. I render it in the rhythmic style in which, probably, it was sung:

A rubric informs us that the robbers depart with their spoils, and that *Judaeus* returns and discovers his loss. There now occurs, as an introduction to his lament, the first yell to be set to Gregorian music! Whether it was executed in the strict rhythm here indicated, I have my doubts. Altogether, the strong emotion of the passage would probably mean a rather free rhythmic rendering. The following can be only an approximation:

In the long succession of hexameters that follows, *Judaeus* bewails his sudden descent into poverty, for which he blames his trust in St. Nicholas. Addressing the Image, he warns it that, while he is too weary at the moment, in the morning he intends to scourge it and afterwards burn it!

The music of this extensive item is rather disappointing. There is not the order and balance that is to be found in the setting of *Judaeus'* first item. A few half-achieved attempts at repeated sentences are found, and there are a number of effective instances of *conjunctura*-like downward sweeps of rapid notes, but on the whole the music just drifts. No doubt *Judaeus'* frantic delivery would keep it alive!

The attention turns to the other *sedes*, the robbers' den. To it comes the indignant Saint himself, finding the three busily dividing their plunder. He proceeds to call them 'scoundrels' and 'madmen', and to denounce them in a series of pairs of rhyming lines to a repeated and good quality tune, larded with *conjunctura*-like passages. The melody is somewhat reminiscent of the first two music-sentences from '*Cara michi pignora . . .*' of the drama, *Tres Filiae*, and also Adeodatus' 'personal' tune from *Filius Getronis*. I give it below:

The Saint concludes his denunciation by warning the robbers that if the treasure is not back by the morning he will see that they end up on the gallows. The robbers are left to think it over. The result is a quick patter of mainly single notes as the first two, in turn, wish to hold fast to their booty. But the more sensible third reminds them of their chances of swinging for it. Then comes a unanimous—

---

[1] From this point onwards, for four more lines, the manuscript is inclined to use B flat as a clef sign, at the same time putting in some incidental B flats as an extra precaution.

[2] The text scribe seems to have written '*reliquii*', and to have been given a note for the extra 'i', which seems finally to have been cancelled. I have cancelled the extra note.

We must imagine their doing just that.

One final scene: *Judaeus*, having discovered the return of his property, 'sings loudly' (*'dicat alta voce'*). The setting of four joyful rhyming couplets is an attractive and straightforward melody, rounded off each time by a melismatic *'Gaudeamus!'* This time there is no return of St. Nicholas to receive *Judaeus'* tributes of praise and gratitude, and the next item, fixing the drama as being attached to the liturgy, is the Introit of the Mass of St. Nicholas' Day. Could its first words, *'Statuit ei Dominus testamentum pacis'*, be supposed on this occasion to apply to *Judaeus*?

Various assessments have been made from time to time as to the dramatic value of this particular drama, but seldom has the quality of the music been taken into account. This fact has moved me to find space for more music examples than the dramatic value of the work might justify, as compared with the smooth competence of the major music-dramas of the Orléans collection. Certainly, the brief and lively exchanges between the three robbers are musically delightful at times. Even so, the looseness of structure over a long stretch, apparent in the lament of *Judaeus*, the longueurs of St. Nicholas' denunciation of the robbers, and in each case the frequent melismatic passages, would provide for modern soloists quite formidable tasks. They would have to be trained Gregorian singers. In view of the extensive melismata that occur in each of these solos, I feel that it would be unwise to shackle either item with definite time-signatures, strict rhythmic notations, and 'the tyranny of the bar-line'.[1]

V

The final 'St. Nicholas' drama found in the 'Playbook' is the only known dramatization of this particular 'miracle', *Filius Getronis*. It is remarkable for demanding the assumption of great distances, and, in the course of the action, of the lapse of a year between two happenings. Most remarkable of all is the fact that the composer of the music conceived the idea, not previously met with in the Church music-drama, of allocating to each leading character or group a definite, single melody. To this the particular quatrains would be sung. A momentary and striking exception will be found to have been made to this rule.

The copious Orléans rubrics make the somewhat demanding mise-en-scène quite clear. The *sedes* of the conquest-minded King Marmorinus is on one side of the playing space. There in his 'capital' he sits enthroned with his attendants and soldiers, who are awaiting his military directions. On the other side, in a 'far land', is the city of Excoranda, where there must be imagined such special areas as the Church of St. Nicholas,

---

[1] I have myself transcribed the whole work as for an 'acting-version', and have met with similar attempts. In the treatment of these two particular items, none of them (including my own) has brought much conviction to me.

and the house of the leading citizen Getron, who dwells there with his wife Euphrosina and their young son, Adeodatus.[1] While attending with many others at the Church of St. Nicholas, they find themselves raided by the forces of King Marmorinus. Among those swept away as captives is Adeodatus.

Back at Marmorinus' Court the sturdy youth, now the King's slave-cupbearer, engages Marmorinus in a spirited debate in defence of his faith. After scenes back in Excoranda of Euphrosina's mourning, the attempted comforting by her 'Consolers', and the parents' joint appeal to St. Nicholas, the youth is miraculously 'translated' by the Saint from his task in the King's feast-hall, and delivered to his native city and his home.

It is a good plot. The pity is that it should be unfolded by a text consisting of forty-two identically constructed quatrains, mostly rhyming a a b b (and one with a line left out), with ten syllables to a line every time.

The musician responsible makes a gallant attempt to break the monotony. We will now follow him through the action. It will be apparent that his stanza tunes call very plainly for rhythmic treatment, being quite indistinguishable from the type of melody being sung by the troubadours of the period.

In the opening scene at Marmorinus' Court, we hear first a chorus of the King's armed forces, hailing him and proclaiming their eagerness to serve him; this to their own particular stanza melody (Tune A).[2] It is a Mixolydian one, and 'goes' best, I think, in the second rhythmic mode:

The King replies with his own melody, also **Mixolydian (Tune B)**:

[1] Omitted from the drama plot but found in the *vita* is the information that Getron and Euphrosina were particularly devoted to St. Nicholas, that they caused to be built a church in his honour, and that, lacking a son, they were rewarded for their piety by the birth of Adeodatus (= God-given).

[2] The 'key signature' of one sharp employed here is of course quite arbitrary. It is that used in my own 'acting version' of the music-drama.

gen - tes po - te - rí - tis,   Im - pe - ri - o   me - o   su -
- bi - ci - te;   Re - ·sis - ten - tes vo - bis oc - - ci - di - te.

A remarkable feature of the setting is the use, in the third musical sentence, of a most un-Gregorian trio of appoggiaturas.

The armed forces having moved off, there now occurs one of those 'production' difficulties which crop up elsewhere from time to time in these Church dramas. Nothing is said in the rubrics as to any interval being allowed which would represent the army's period of conquest. As it is, they are back with their King 'by return', with their spoils, announcing that 'many nations' have submitted to him.[1] All this is sung to Tune A. They also produce as one of their captives, Adeodatus ('fair, wise, and noble'), whom they think fitted to be the King's own servant.

The King replies with a stanza of thanks, and then, continuing with Tune B, questions the boy. *Puer* (as he is designated in the manuscript) replies with his own Aeolian music (Tune C):

Ex - co - ran - de prin - ci - pans po - pu - lo,   Pa - ter   me - us,
Get - ron vo - - ca - bu - lo.   De - um   co - lit, cu - ius sunt
ma - ri - a,   Qui fe - cit nos et vos et   o - mni - a

—and the exchanges of stanza tunes accompany a theological squabble as to the respective merits of Apollo and the Christian God. The King closes the debate with understandable sternness, and attention is now switched back to Excoranda and Euphrosina. The latter, having lost sight of her son in the general panic at the church, has searched for him unsuccessfully. She is now represented as uttering a number of stanzas of lament for him. She has of course her own stanza melody (Tune D):

Fi - li   ca - re,   fi - li ca - ris - si - - mi,   Fi - li,   me - e
ma - gna pars   a - ni - me,   Nunc es   no - bis cau - sa tri - sti - - ci -

---

[1] There is a similar situation in 'The Conversion of St. Paul', when after Saul has despatched his men to capture Christians, the next rubric speaks of their return, having discovered a 'great number'.

I have quoted here a later stanza of the lament, since the first version of the melody is a little complicated by three introductory cries of '*Heu!*'. In the course of the successive versions of the tune there are a few note differences. For these I am not inclined to blame the scribe, but conclude that they really are intended as 'variations'.

The lament melody appears at first sight to be in the 'major mode', but the B flat that occurs towards the end, plainly marked in the manuscript, seems to indicate a Mixolydian cadence. It is a good tune, but once again as in others of the St. Nicholas works, in combination with an unchanging textual pattern we get a little too much of it. Euphrosina and her consolers give it to us eleven times without a break.

Karl Young (II, p. 359) remarks that 'the presence of the *consolatrices* and the general form of their dialogue with Euphrosina seem to show that the writer has profited from his acquaintance with the scenes of Rachel in the *Ordo Rachelis*'. He is of course assuming that the individual dramas of the 'Playbook' all stemmed from Fleury, which is no longer thought to be the case. Whoever was the author of *Filius Getronis*, he could have had a number of older models for the employment of a lamenting mother attended by one or more consolers. If indeed he had been acquainted with the 'Playbook' version of 'The Slaying of the Innocents' he would surely have been discouraged by a comparison between the textual and melodic repetitions of his own presentation, and the varied verse-rhythms and the unique musical imagination displayed in the 'Rachel' scenes of the other drama.[1]

Euphrosina's last two stanzas are concerned with an appeal to St. Nicholas to restore her son and her declaration that until she sees him again she will 'no longer partake of meat, or further in wine find joy'. Then, in the midst of a manuscript line, we find that Getron is speaking, obviously to Euphrosina. After a while we gather from his words (and without any assistance from any rubrics) that a year has passed, that the morrow is St. Nicholas' Day, and that they must both attend the feast of the Saint, once more to make an appeal on behalf of their son. Getron's speech occupies four of the usual-style quatrains, and his own tune is of the usual A A B C pattern, and again a Mixolydian one. On this occasion I will give only the first line of this plain and straightforward melody:

[1] See pp. 217–21.

[2] In this case, 'wife', not 'sister': '*soror*' as a term of endearment.

The parents go to the church of St. Nicholas, where Euphrosina 'raises her hands to heaven' and appeals to St. Nicholas, singing four more repeats of her lament tune. Then she goes back to her home, and there now begins something of a producer's headache!

A rubric commands that on returning to her house at the Excoranda *sedes* she must prepare a table bearing bread and wine at which the clergy and the poor of the city may refresh themselves. Meanwhile, from across the playing space, at the '*sedes*' of Marmorinus, the King is heard proclaiming, no doubt with gestures and something of the Herod touch, that he is most frightfully hungry, that he had never been so hungry before in his life, and that his attendants had better move more quickly than they were doing if they don't want him to starve to death! Two stanzas of Tune B occupy this. To Tune A, the attendants now speak of their presenting to the King what we may assume has the appearance of a luxurious feast. He proceeds to eat.

No doubt the idea of the playwright was to contrast the luxury and gluttony at the heathen court with the sober frugality of the Christian meal; this in spite of all the time and organization that would be necessary successfully to maintain the parallel scenes. As for the Excoranda meal, no clue is given as to when and how it was to be cleared from the scene. Anyway, the attention is now firmly turned to Marmorinus. In another of his stanzas he demands wine, together with the presence of his cupbearer. Adeodatus appears, 'sighing grievously' ('*suspiret graviter*'). It may be that his words are not intended to reach the King's ears, for he speaks of his wretched state, and how he can nevermore hope to breathe free breath. The melody that he sings:

He - u! he - u! he - u! mi - chi mi – se - re! Vi - tæ me - æ fi - nem de - si - de - ro!

—represents a unique stroke of medieval musicianship and sensitivity, for it is a quotation. Instead of his own melody he is borrowing his mother's theme, which brings, with thoughts of her, associations of home and freedom. The King's voice strikes in, asking the reason for his sighs. Adeodatus replies boldly with two stanzas speaking of his exile from his own land and his bonds of servitude, but this time in the everyday terms of his own Tune C. 'Alas!' the King replies, mockingly, 'why think on this? I do not wish it, so there is none to release you.'

This is indeed a moment of dramatic irony, for immediately St. Nicholas appears, seizes upon the boy, and transports him, cup in hand, to Excoranda, where he appears before the doors of his own home and the gaze of an astonished citizen, who has not perceived the now vanished Saint, and seems as puzzled regarding the wine-cup as he is with the identity of its bearer.[1] Incidentally, he uses his own personal

[1] In regard to Adeodatus' miraculous transportation, Karl Young speculates 'as to whether the stage properties included some sort of mechanical aids to realism'. The pro-

tune, of A B B C pattern, for his enquiries, although on the first occasion it lacks its second line, probably omitted by the scribe. The citizen hastens to inform Getron that his son is standing at the door; also that the credit is altogether due to St. Nicholas!

A rubric describes the joyful meeting of son and mother. Euphrosina then sings two more ten-syllable quatrains, each to different and new settings, neither particularly distinguished. The first begins:

De - - o no - stro sit laus et glo - ri - a!

—an A A B C musical pattern in the Aeolian mode. There is a similar pattern and mode for the second, beginning:

Sint - que pa - tri no - stro per - pe - tu - e.

Finally, the liturgical antiphon '*Copiose caritatis*' is sung by the chorus, fixing the drama without much doubt to a service on St. Nicholas' Day.

Filius Getronis is an ambitious effort, calling for some startling dramatic effects and for a fairly large number of participants. Also, a remarkable musical device is being tried out; 'leitmotivs', tunes for single ownership. But all this is a great deal marred by the unimaginative, repetitive nature of the libretto, with its everlasting ten syllables to a line. Whatever the composer of the music might have intended towards creating distinctive melodies must surely have been handicapped by that fact.

VI

Passing now to the works that derive from New Testament stories, we find that in *Conversio Pauli Apostoli* we have another example of a libretto consisting of a succession of rhyming quatrains made up of unrelieved ten-syllable lines, hymnology pure and simple. This is offset somewhat by the clarity with which the story is presented, and also by the music which the unknown composer has found for each of the characters. The driving force of the persecutor Saul; the awful majesty of the 'Voice from on high' that leaves him stricken to earth, 'trembling and astonished'; the first apprehensions of Ananias, contrasted with the confidence he expresses when delivering the Lord's message to Saul in

---

ducer, with his demands for large-scale meals and 'invading armies' seems to have had a taste for realism. When one remembers the lowering of Paul from the city walls in a basket, during 'The Conversion of St. Paul', and the travelling 'Star'-candelabra of the Magi, there seems the possibility of some artificial device being used.

his blindness; new-found confidence also, newly-directed, in the converted Saul, as he preaches his sermon 'in a loud voice'—all these and various other emotions are remarkably well conveyed through the slender means of a single vocal line. And this in spite of the monotonous beat of the everlasting ten syllables, which had its effect on the music of some of the other dramas.

No record exists of the work ever having been performed, and no other Church-drama working of the story has ever been found.

The *Conversio* is comparatively generous in regard to rubrics. The first, and lengthiest, makes it clear that the 'station' technique is being used. 'Jerusalem' and 'Damascus' are sites situated well apart, with smaller removes for such localities as 'the house of Ananias' and 'the house of Judas', with a considerable stretch between the two main stations to represent the 'road to Damascus'. A wide area was clearly needed (as in the Herod drama), doubtless comprising a great deal of the nave of whatever monastic or cathedral church it was intended for. Most of the movements of the actors are clearly enough indicated by the rubrics, but some production problems remain. There is of course the matter of the interval between the departure of Saul's followers to hunt down Christians, and their return, which, one way or the other, might seem unbelievably quick work or mean an awkward wait. Did improvised music bridge the gap?

Another question mark must concern *Dominus*. Generations of 'literary' editors have agreed on the assumption of the rubric sentence, '*Tunc rex in alto*', before his first utterance, this fully justified by the Gospel account. It appears likely that the part was sung from an upper gallery, the singer not visible from below, in accordance with what is said as to the party 'hearing a voice, but seeing no man'.

Then there is the representation of Saul's escape from Damascus. Both the Gospel account and the manuscript rubric speak of his being lowered from the city wall in a basket. The modern producer must decide for himself what degree of realism is here to be shown.[1] Other small details would remain to be settled in regard to an actual performance, but since the music is our main consideration, and since the story as related in Acts is well enough known, we will pass immediately to its dramatic rendering.

We meet first Saul himself, addressing his armed followers. In two stanzas and a repeated melody he expresses his loathing for the new Christian sect, and orders his followers to go out into Jerusalem and seize all that they can find of them. This is his first tune, a Dorian one (here transposed up a fourth, with B flat):

---

[1] In the circumstances of a performance of a transcription of this drama by the present writer at Keble College Chapel, Oxford, a few years back, use was made of the tall pulpit. It was faced with cardboard, marked to resemble stone blocks. From the top of this 'Saul' was safely lowered in his basket. In the medieval records of these Church music-dramas, many similar scenic improvisations will be met with.

His followers return, with a couple of prisoners and the news that other Christians have fled to Damascus. They sing cheerfully:

Or perhaps more concisely:

Often enough in these Church dramas duple time seems suitable. Saul now applies to the High Priest at Jerusalem for a letter of authority, so that he may carry on the great work at Damascus. This single stanza-tune is a charming one. I give it at the pitch of the manuscript, but it was probably sung at a higher level:

The High Priest replies with a single stanza and supplies the letter. I will omit his music. It is in the usual Mixolydian strain, with a repeated

[1] The melody as written in the manuscript starts with a B flat as a clef sign, applying to the whole line, which goes as far as '*vobis*'. The next stave, which concludes the item, is without the B flat. I have in the example written the B flats and the precautionary B naturals as accidentals. I have also called attention to what may be a small discrepancy between similar phrases.

277

subtonal cadence which has been repeated enough times in the previous two items. The persecutors set off for Damascus. As they move forward there comes the stroke from the heavens. The leader falls to the ground, the prisoners escape, and the immortal phrase is heard: 'Saul, Saul, why persecutest thou me?' I quote the whole of this dramatic item; a worthy precedent, by several centuries, to Heinrich Schütz's great setting.

Saul, blinded and bewildered, asks whose voice it is that he hears. I give the first phrases of his item in measure, although in performance the whole item would be hesitant and rhythmically disturbed.

Once more the same stern music is heard as Saul is told, 'I am Jesus, whom thou dost persecute . . .'[1]

Helpless, Saul is led away to Damascus. In the same city the Christian, Ananias, lying in his bed, hears from on high the same Voice and the same music. He is told that Saul is in the city and awaits his coming. Understandably, Ananias is apprehensive. His first words are:

—but the Voice reassures him, once again to the same music, and then, in a new passage, tells him of the divine purpose.

Ananias seeks out Saul, and in two stanzas of more resolute music, converts him and also restores his sight. Saul, his energies transferred to a new channel, preaches openly to the people of Damascus:

---

[1] In later appearances of the melody small notational differences are to be seen, the purpose of which is not clear. It is difficult to think of them as 'variations'.

The above is a reading of the first stanza music. The B flat near the end comes as a pleasant touch of colour. Unexpectedly, the composer sets the second stanza of the sermon to a different tune, but it appears to be a close relation.

As a result, the Chief Priest of the synagogue takes action. He calls for the city gates to be guarded, and for Saul to be killed:

—but to no effect. Having escaped from Damascus, Saul is received in Jerusalem by the young Barnabas, who is well informed as to his conversion. Barnabas greets him with a stanza which begins:

—and shows in its first three 'bars' a surprising and inexplicable likeness to the High Priest's outburst. Barnabas, having introduced Saul to the Apostles, sings a final stanza to a new melody, with a quite poetic conclusion regarding the new 'comrade'—'he, who lately fiercest of wolves had seemed, has now changed, to be the most gentle of lambs.'[1]

In this he is probably joined by the chorus of Apostles, who go on to finish the drama by singing the *Te Deum*.

To sum up, it appears to me that here was a composer of resource and imagination. He did well, in spite of the monotonous tread of those incessant ten-syllable lines of the librettist. If only the metres of the texts

[1] This item written a fourth higher than its pitch in the manuscript.

had shown some variety from item to item (and to this opportunity the composer would surely have responded) then we might have gained a little masterpiece of Church music-drama.

VII

The last drama of the 'Playbook' collection is 'The Raising of Lazarus'; the libretto, once again, in stanza form throughout. The narrative follows quite closely the accounts furnished by St. Luke and St. John. Once again we must deplore the fact that a story full of dramatic incident is told in a series of rhyming stanzas of unvarying pattern, two lines of ten syllables each, followed by one of four. The rhyme scheme suggests the pairing of stanzas into a six-line pattern of a a b c c b. The music that is joined to it confirms this, since its course covers the six lines, and, as *the* stanza tune, is the only music employed throughout. I give below in a rhythmic transcription the setting as it applies to the first double-stanza. I give also alternative cadences that are used for the two four-syllable lines (Y). These turn up immediately in following stanza settings. However, the X cadences make occasional returns. To me it seems altogether a haphazard sort of business, with no textual reasons, or any other that I can discover, for the small variations. From time to time there are other slight discrepancies to be found in the repeated music. These appear to arise merely from bad copying.

What happens to the six-line stanza pattern after that, is that it is repeated no fewer than fifty more times! On most occasions the melody is also repeated over the six lines, but exceptions to this occur on the few occasions when one of the characters makes a brief intervention with a single three-line pattern (10 10 4). In these cases it is of course the

---

[1] This example has been transposed up a perfect fourth higher than its pitch in the manuscript, and B flat added as a clef sign.

first half of the melody which is used, but when the succeeding character sings, the first half is used again and the normal pattern resumed.[1]

As for the action,[2] the generous rubrics make it clear that four stations are required, to represent (1) the house of Simon the Pharisee at Bethany, where the anointing of Jesus' feet by a courtesan, as described by St. Luke, takes place; (2) Galilee, to where Jesus withdraws; (3) Jerusalem, whence the friends of Lazarus come;[3] and (4) the place of Lazarus' tomb. It would seem that the Simon *sedes* served also to represent the house of Martha and Mary, sisters of Lazarus at Bethany, where Lazarus sickens and dies. The St. John account identifies the courtesan of the first scene (i.e. Mary Magdalen) with the sister of Martha and Lazarus.

There seems to be no point in retelling here the story of the drama, which, as Karl Young has pointed out, remains very faithful to the two Gospel records. The only real expansions are the laments of the sisters, followed by the consolatory choruses of their brother's friends. The drama closes with the revival of the dead man, and Jesus' order that he shall be freed from his bindings.

The last rubric—'*Et chorus: Te Deum laudamus. Sic finiatur.*'—seems to confirm that the work was planned as a genuine liturgical drama. However, even Karl Young has his doubts. He points out (II, p. 210) that the very opening rubric, '*Incipiant versus*', might indicate that the play is a rhetorical exercise from the monastic school. He speaks of the 'sustained elevation and gravity' of the poem, and of its didactic and theological touches. It appears to me that a monastic school might indeed be the source of the poem. The manuscript presents it in the form of a music-drama through the addition of a single undistinguished stanza-tune.

Justifications for the performability of the drama as it stands have been advanced, on the grounds that medieval audiences, well acquainted with the repetitions of the interminable *chansons de geste*, were quite hardened to what we should think of as intolerable monotony, verbal and musical. I can recall a performance that I once heard of this same music-drama, in which the singing was accompanied by a jongleur-type, mystery-play 'orchestra', the instrumental combinations being varied as the stanzas proceeded. The whole affair was something of the nature of an anachronistic chimaera, but it served to keep the attention of a modern audience. One could give a performance of the work as it stands in the

---

[1] There are two occasions when short sentences are spoken, without music. See Young, II, pp. 200 and 207; these are outside the stanza pattern.

[2] The whole libretto can be seen in Young, II, pp. 199–208.

[3] Fletcher Collins, Jr. however, argues persuasively that only three stations are in fact called for, the reference to Jerusalem providing nothing more than a convenient excuse to take the pharisees offstage after the meal at Simon's. No scene is actually played in the Jerusalem *sedes*. See Collins, *The Production of Medieval Church Music-Drama* (Charlottesville, 1972), p. 168. (*Ed.*)

manuscript, but, to my mind, for no more than curiosity and study purposes.[1]

It is far otherwise, more is the pity, in the case of the only other working of the 'Lazarus' story, found in the manuscript of Hilarius, the goliard scholar, whose other dramatic works we have already examined. In his version, *Suscitacio Lazari*, one meets a different world, that of a practical playwright and a really imaginative poet; and, I suspect, a practical musician as well. But alas, as we have already seen, the manuscript carries no music. If it had, the libretto could not have suffered the imposition of a single stanza tune as a setting, since after the dreary monotony of the 'Playbook' libretto we have a poetic text which, while following no less faithfully the New Testament story (and omitting the somewhat irrelevant foot-anointing incident) yet provides constantly changing metre rhythms. For example, the first few speakers, between them, make use of stanzas of which some show eight-syllable lines, others ten, others seven, and (one fascinating stretch) a pattern of six lines of a 6 6 6 4 5 4 succession, the last three lines consisting of a vernacular refrain. A similar metrical variety prevails throughout.

We may safely assume that the drama was indeed set to music. This granted, then it is equally certain that this music must have conformed in its patterns to the splendid variety of the poetic metres. If the skill of the musical contribution was on a level with the merits of the libretto, then once again we must mourn for the loss of a little masterpiece. The story, well supplied with rubric directions, is made all the more vivid through the changes of metre reflecting the changing emotions of the characters; effects that were no doubt enhanced by the music—music that we can never hope to recover.

VIII

Another checking through of the individual dramatic and musical (especially musical) techniques of the ten music-dramas of the 'Playbook' reinforces my conviction that their apparent associations are due to the haphazard actions of a collector, who 'scooped' his works in very much the same fashion as did the 'jackdaw' arranger of the *Visitatio* from *Tours MS 927*, who secured a great number of his items from here, there, and everywhere. The 'Playbook' then came into being through a uniform copying of the dramas. When and under what circumstances the drama folios were joined with the quite independent liturgical material still seems to be a matter for speculation.

I cannot think that the collector could have belonged to any great monastic centre, where scholarly clerics would be quick to realise the

[1] The unaccompanied *Lazarus* has in fact been performed several times in the United States by Fletcher Collins' group, with intense enthusiasm by the audiences, and was applauded by the monks of the Abbey of St. Benoit de Fleury when performed there in August, 1979 [Ed.]

huge discrepancy of merit between, say, *Officium Stellae* and *Tres Clerici*. If we recall the similar situation with the St. Martial de Limoges manuscript *B.N. 1139* and its unique *Sponsus* (see pp. 148–50), it would seem that for a dramatic work to be included in a monastic library is no guarantee that it originated there or that any practical notice had been taken of it.

IX

Before we leave the twelfth century mention must be made of a formidable work concerned with the theme of the Last Judgement, and particularly with that medieval obsession, the figure of Antichrist. Its libretto is an ambitious one, more than 400 lines of Latin verse, but again we have a case of a text surviving without its music—failing to give justification for its continual use in its rubrics of the verbs '*cantat*' and '*cantant*'.

The original manuscript probably came from the Benedictine monastery at Tegernsee, in Bavaria,[1] and the evidence seems to be that it was written about the year 1160, with a very strong bias in favour of the Emperor Frederick Barbarossa, as against the King of France of the time (Louis VII). It seems doubtful whether the huge, space-demanding drama could have been performed anywhere but in the open air. Its action ranges through all the kingdoms of the world, as the Christian forces resist the powers of Antichrist. Armies march and fight; cities are stormed; prophets are murdered. Finally, just before the advent of the Last Judgement, the heavenly Power intervenes, and Antichrist is struck down.

There seems to be nothing liturgical about the work except for one choral responsory, given only as an incipit, '*Judea et Jerusalem . . .*' but with its identifying and correct service neumes.

The absence of music leaves me with nothing more to do than to speculate that settings would be largely a matter of stanza melodies (three-quarters of the libretto consists of rhyming lines of thirteen syllables); that there is some small amount of dialogue exchanges between individuals; and that I must recommend the reader to peruse Karl Young's pages on the subject, II, pp. 369–96, where the legend of Antichrist is discussed, the text of the Tegernsee drama is given, and the author makes his commentary on the action.

---

[1] Munich, *Staatsbibl., MS lat. 19411*, pp. 6–15. The drama is based on a treatise, *Libellus de Antichristo,* by the monk Adso, dating from the middle of the tenth century.

CHAPTER THIRTEEN

THE THIRTEENTH CENTURY (1)

The Progress of the *Visitatio Sepulchri* dramas
The Zehnsilberspiel

As was attempted in the case of the eleventh and twelfth centuries (see Chapters VII and IX) we will endeavour to assess what effects on the social and religious life of Christendom were brought about by the outstanding happenings of the thirteenth.

As we have observed, in those two extraordinary centuries, the eleventh and twelfth, there appeared an upsurge of enthusiasm for the Christian faith which communicated itself to all classes. Especially was it expressed by the rallying of every country in support of the First Crusade, which proved wholly successful; also by the widespread appreciation and (particularly in France) popular co-operation, given to a new form of religious activity, the creation of cathedrals in the 'Gothic' style, for which France must take the earliest credit. These great town structures, sometimes representing a re-shaping from existing Romanesque buildings, sometimes created almost altogether anew, continued to multiply in numbers during the thirteenth century.

Indeed, France under the firm and shrewd rule of King Philip Augustus (1165–1223) was gaining the cultural ascendancy of Europe. Philip began the new century by re-conquering Normandy from England, and then in 1214 defeating the Emperor Otto IV at Bouvines. Paris, with the growing reputation of its university, was becoming the 'Athens of the North'.

Yet however well matters may have seemed for France, the thirteenth century began for Christendom generally in an atmosphere of disillusion. Already (in 1187) Europe had been rocked by the news that the now more closely united Moslem world under their new leader Saladin had recaptured Jerusalem. The counter which followed, the Third Crusade, had failed. Furthermore, its chief leader, King Richard of England, had actually been arrested on his way home by a fellow-crusader, Leopold of Austria, and sold to the Emperor Henry VI, who released him only after the payment of a heavy ransom.

Meanwhile, in 1198, the vigorous and comparatively young Innocent III, the strongest of the medieval Popes, had succeeded to St. Peter's chair. He himself instigated a new Crusade, the Fourth. It was mostly a French venture (even though Philip Augustus himself was not interested) and was backed by the powerful maritime state of Venice, the trade enemy of Byzantium. In 1204 Christendom was again shaken to learn that this time a Crusade had changed its objective en route, and that the expedition had, instead, stormed and sacked the greatest Christian city of the East, Constantinople itself. The hope of healing the breach between the Greek and Roman Churches was gone for ever, and at first Innocent III raged at the happening. The city remained in Latin control for over fifty years, until a Greek Emperor drove out the invaders. But Byzantine power had been permanently weakened, and in the fifteenth century fell before the conquering Turks. As for Innocent III, he was content in the end to leave the situation as it was presented to him, especially as the Latin rite had been established at Hagia Sophia.

Meanwhile, he had other troubles. It was apparent to him that with the great increase of population (particularly evident in southern France and northern Italy), parochial organization and Christian teaching had suffered widespread decay, and that strange doctrines were rampant. In Languedoc and in many Italian towns, spread by traders, were the tenets of Manichaeism, those of the Cathari, who not only rejected beliefs in the Old Testament but even denied the Incarnation of Christ. For many years the Roman Church had conducted preaching campaigns, particularly in one of the most infected areas, the region of Albi in the south of France. Innocent intensified these activities, but when even he and his legates failed to persuade, he decided on sterner measures, that of a call for a crusade against heresy. He had hoped that Philip Augustus would be persuaded to lead it, but once again the King of France found himself too busy with his own affairs. However, there were plenty of French warriors ready to take part in such a holy and profitable campaign. From 1209 until 1213 battles and massacres gradually wiped out unorthodoxy, leaving Innocent free to continue with his much needed measures for reforming Church organization.

His two successors, Honorius III and Gregory IX, faced a new and disturbing type of secular ruler in Frederick, son of the Emperor Henry VI, early orphaned as the child-ruler of the Norman-founded kingdom of Sicily, the richest and most cosmopolitan state in Europe; and later, established as the Emperor Frederick II. His upbringing was in an atmosphere that shared the cultures of Byzantium and the Moslem Arab civilization. The Christian world, and especially the Papacy, soon realized his scepticism as well as his intellectual attainments. He was in fact in his wide interests, his flashes of cynicism and at times cold-blooded cruelty, a Renaissance prince before the time. '*Stupor mundi*'— 'the wonder of the world'—men called him. He was believed to have stated that 'all the misfortunes of mankind are due to three impostors— Moses, Mohammed, and Christ'. His enemies (they were many) identified him with Antichrist.

For disregarding a Papal command to undertake a Crusade, he was excommunicated. In 1228, however, still under double excommunication, he set out for the Middle East for that purpose, and while he was away Papal troops invaded his Sicilian kingdom. Ironically, the Crusade was actually successful, inasmuch as Frederick was able to negotiate a treaty with Palestine's overlord, the Sultan of Egypt, in 1229. This gave him possession of Jerusalem, together with Nazareth and Bethlehem. He crowned himself King of Jerusalem in the Church of the Holy Sepulchre and soon after returned home, still unshriven, to chase the Papal forces out of his Sicilian territories.[1] Jerusalem remained in Christian hands until 1244, and was then finally lost. Two vain Crusades, the Seventh and Eighth, led by the saintly Louis IX of France, got no further than Egypt.

The uneasy relationship between Pope and Emperor continued, culminating in open war again in 1237. Frederick seemed invincible, forcing Gregory's successor, Innocent IV, to take refuge at Lyons. Then came a bolt from the blue. In 1248 a combination of Italian city states decisively defeated the Imperial forces. Two years later Frederick died. A son and a grandson struggled to maintain their patrimony, but in vain. The Papacy had won the day, but failed to appreciate the realities of the changing times. Towards the end of the thirteenth century Boniface VIII in his Bull, *'Clericus Laicos'*, forbade the taxing of the clergy by any lay authority without his consent. But there were now in Europe secular powers, nationally and centrally governed, ready to react to such a demand. Both the formidable Philip IV ('the Fair') of France and King Edward I of England, although themselves not on the warmest of terms, produced counter-measures that caused Boniface to have second thoughts.

However, just after the turn of the century he took a crucial step, answering the arrest of a French bishop on a charge of treason with the famous Bull, *'Unam Sanctam'*, which declared that it was altogether necessary for salvation that all human creatures should be subject to the Roman pontiff. King Philip's response was drastic and unprecedented. In March 1303 his agent at the head of an armed force actually arrested the Pope at Anagni in Italy. Boniface was soon released, but within a month was dead. The sequel belongs to the fourteenth century, for now began the 'Babylonian Exile' at Avignon, a matter of seventy-five years of French control of the Papacy. The medieval conception of a working partnership between Church and State had proved too difficult for the human nature of both sides, but in demanding single authority the Papacy had overreached itself, having passed the peak of its influence over a secular world, where secular rulers were insisting on solving in their own way what they considered to be secular problems. It is also to be remembered that everywhere in Christendom there was a citizen class of growing prosperity and literacy; one which was more inclined than in the past to question former tenets.

In the exchanges of polemics between Frederick and his successive Papal opponents, the Emperor produced some powerful documents, in

---

[1] Gregory, not at all grateful for the 'delivery', excommunicated Frederick for a third time, on the grounds that he had had friendly relations with the infidels.

the form of letters addressed to his European fellow-princes. Not only did he call for opposition to the Papal policy of absolutism, but he directed attention to the pride and the wealth of the Church, which he held were at the root of its corruption. He proposed a confiscation of that wealth. It was a suggestion that remained long in the minds of secular authorities.

II

We will turn now from the troubled outside world to the quieter atmosphere of monastery and cathedral.[1] A survey of the dramatic activities within the Church during the thirteenth century, as displayed in Appendix Id, appears to show the first signs of a general falling-away of production.[2] The Easter and Christmas tropes of the Mass Introits (the '*Quem quaeritis*' dialogues) are no longer copied. With the exception of two surviving 'third stage' examples, French *Visitatio Sepulchri* production seems confined to brief versions, the idea being, perhaps, that these would cause the minimum of delay in the progress of the Easter liturgy. A striking feature of these thirteenth-century short French manuscripts is their great beauty, most apparent in the execution of the music, always on four-line staves, with clefs. Their appearance is a tribute to the premier position in Christendom that French culture held during the century.

However, in dealing with these brief 'first stage' versions, both French and German, of the thirteenth, and the thirteenth to fourteenth, centuries, I shall emphasise only individual points, since there is so much that is repetitive as we move from one version to another. The fuller library details of the manuscripts are given in Appendix Id. I therefore begin my comments by referring to the French 'first stage' group as consisting of *B.N. 1255*; *Brit. Mus., 37399*; Paris, *Ste. Geneviève 117*.

B.N. 1255, a breviary from an unidentified French monastery, gives us a rare 'prose', '*O quam magno dies ista*', found elsewhere, as far as I am aware, only in a Bourges breviary of 1522, but there without its music. The rhythm of the poetry is that of Adam de St. Victor, the syllable pattern of the lines being 8 7 8 7 . . . (see p. 58). A small proportion of the text, set to a somewhat altered music, is to be found in the *Visitatio* from *Tours 927*, (see p. 295 ff.). The rest of the text and music is conventional; it is a compact and tidy affair.

Brit. Mus. 37399, a Parisian breviary, has a straightforward version which begins with the normal dramatic dialogue, and then is content to

[1] The term 'monastery' is normally applied to a community of 'regular' clergy, living under a 'rule'. Originally, a bishop and his 'secular' cathedral clergy formed a kind of religious community, which, while not actually a 'monastery' per se, was nevertheless referred to on occasions as a *monasterium*. The word had not at first the restricted meaning that it afterwards attained.

[2] It must always be borne in mind that our conclusions have to depend on the documents that have survived. We have a great deal of evidence as to the destructions and 'scrapings' that took place. The proportion of vellum pages lost without trace may have been greater than we realise.

round off with a complete rendering of the *Victimae Paschali* sequence, the dialogue portion used dramatically. This shaping of the 'first stage' type of Sepulchre drama seems to reflect a general practice in the diocese during this period. There is a musical rhyme at the vocative words—rm rd m fm r-, a phrase that seems to come all the way from tenth-century Limoges.

The *Ste. Geneviève 117* version belongs actually to Beauvais. The dialogue is transposed up a fourth from its usual pitch, but we have to assume the B flat until the scribe remembers it midway through. The version is very brief: the dialogue, and then the familiar '*Alleluia, resurrexit Dominus hodie*'. We meet another, and different musical rhyme; rm mr d mfm-d r-. This feature is met with in the slightly earlier *Reims 265* (see p. 158). There are also other musical similarities between the two.

The library details of the thirteenth-century German-derived 'first stage' *Visitatio* dramas can also be seen in Appendix Id. I refer to them here as *Darmstadt 3183*; *Brit. Mus. 23922*; *Rheinau 59*; *Hildesheim 684*; and *Andenne 11*.

Darmstadt 3183, a *rituale*, is hardly worth notice. The dialogue and a couple of antiphons are familiar enough. However, an unusual one, '*Ad sepulcrum Domini gementes venimus, angelus Dei in albis*', is not given its neumes. Music, indeed, is in short supply, enough only to identify the dialogue setting as belonging to St. Gall.

Brit. Mus. 23922, from Strasburg, has unheighted St. Gall neumes, and no advantage over the Darmstadt version except in possessing more stock antiphons including '*Dicant nunc Judaei*'.

A version from the monastery of Rheinau in Switzerland, *Zürich, Rheinau 59*, has nothing to distinguish it but some reasonably full rubrics describing the simple happenings. Being an *ordinarium*, it gives the sung items only in incipit form, but the neumes point to German settings.

A somewhat later (thirteenth- to fourteenth-century) 'first stage' version comes from Hildesheim. It is quite brief and orthodox, with such older antiphons as '*Venite et videte*' and '*Cito euntes*'. However, we have the unusual spectacle of the St. Gall-type settings being written on a four-line stave instead of being expressed as unheighted neumes.

Our final 'first stage' German example comes from Andenne (Belgium) and gives a rare opportunity (in Church drama examples) of meeting the Metz style of music notation. Again the work is very brief; the dialogue, with '*Quis revolvet . . .*' as a beginning, and '*Surrexit Dominus de sepulchro . . .*' to the non-liturgical setting, as a conclusion. There is a unique setting for the two vocative phrases in musical rhyme—rd ms ms r- — for the words '*Christicolae*' and '*caelicolae*'.

Regarding the thirteenth-century examples of the 'second stage' *Visitatios*, I give first abbreviated versions of the details to be found in Appendix Id. These are: *Brit. Mus. Arundel 156*; *Haarlem 258*; *Oxford, Bodl. 202*; *Bodl. 325*; *Bodl. 346*. We may note first that all are German in origin, and that all use the 'revised' dialogue form ('*Quem quaeritis, o tremulae mulieres . . .*'). All make a feature of the display of the grave-clothes, an item that follows naturally on the other common feature, the Race to the Tomb, but not all mention clearly who it is who takes part in this display.

The *Arundel 156* example (from Würzburg) is rather unsatisfactory. It begins with the 'revised' version of the Marys' '*Quis revolvet nobis . . .*'. There follows the normal St. Gall '*Quem quaeritis in sepulchro . . .*' exchange, with its usual '*Non est hic . . .*' sentence. Surprisingly, this is succeeded by another '*Non est hic . . .*', the 'revised' version that usually follows '*Quem quaeritis, o tremulae mulieres . . .*'. It is not given its music. '*Venite et videte . . .*', '*Cito euntes . . .*', and '*Currebant duo simul . . .*' then follow in incipit form, the last-named without music. The Angel and the Marys together then sing the antiphon '*Dicant nunc Judaei . . .*', written in full with its music, after which 'Two Seniors' sing '*Cernitis, o socii . . .*', this again written in full, but without its setting. We must assume from this that the grave clothes are being displayed. The version concludes with the chorus singing '*Surrexit Dominus de sepulchro . . .*' to its liturgical setting. It seems probable to me that the little work represents an uncompleted attempt to change a first stage version into a second stage one.

A South German monastic manuscript (*Oxford, Bodl. MS Misc. Liturg. 202*) gives another not wholly satisfactory version, with un-heighted St. Gall neumes, but with the material, textual and musical, all quite familiar. We meet the 'revised' '*Quis revolvet . . .*'; the '*Quem quaeritis, o tremulae mulieres . . .*' exchanges; and the antiphon '*Venite et videte . . .*'. Peter and John are mentioned as racing to the Tomb to the accompaniment of '*Currebant duo simul . . .*', but thereafter appear to fade out, without any singing of '*Cernitis, o socii . . .*'. The identity of those who retrieve and display the grave-clothes (while everybody sings the liturgical '*Surrexit Dominus de sepulchro . . .*') is not clear. Probably the Marys are intended. An unusual concluding rubric speaks of not only the *Te Deum* being sung, but of tolling bells and the 'populus' singing *Kyrie*.

A manuscript from another unidentified German monastery (*Oxford, Bodl. MS Misc. Liturg. 325*) produces a slightly more extensive version, and rubrics that are more informative. Once again there are unheighted St. Gall neumes, but the setting of the Marys' first item, '*Quis revolvet nobis . . .*' clearly reveals itself as one of the rarer independent versions of the item, one that has the same setting as in the *Cividale CI* Visitatio. After the '*Quem quaeritis, o tremulae mulieres . . .*' exchanges, and '*Venite et videte . . .*', the specially composed item of the Marys, '*Ad monumentum venimus gementes . . .*', is given only in incipit, but with enough neumes to identify the music as coming all the way from the eleventh-century *Einsiedeln, MS 366*. The display of the grave-clothes appears to have taken place twice; by the Marys, and by the *duo seniores* who take part in the Race. The setting of the final item,

'*Surrexit enim sicut . . .*' (given in incipit) is not the liturgical one, but apparently specially composed, and found also in the *Visitatio* from *Klosterneuburg, MS 629*.

The *Visitatio* found in *Oxford, Bodl. MS Misc. Liturg. 346*, need not delay us long. It is a 'reduced' version of our previous *MS 325*, deprived of most of its rubrics but, in spite of the manuscript being a breviary, preserving its St. Gall neumes.

The last of our thirteenth-century 'second stage' *Visitatios* comes from a Haarlem manuscript, *Episcopal Mus. MS 258*. It leads off with what appears to be a rubric error; the Marys would surely not themselves be the singers of the introductory item, '*Maria Magdalena et alia Maria ferebunt diluculo aromata . . .*'. This is the independently composed version of the St. Matthew sentence favoured by a number of German *Visitatios* in preference to very similar liturgical texts, this in spite of the fact that when the number of the Marys happens to be defined it appears to amount to three. A curious circumstance arises after the Angels have made the 'revised' reply '*Non est hic quem quaeritis, sed cito euntes nunciate discipulis eius et Petro . . .*'. The playwright evidently wishes to emphasise this command ('*cito euntes*'); thus the chorus are given the two words as an *incipit*. But the accompanying neumes show that the sentence to be sung is the much earlier '*Cito euntes dicite discipulis quia surrexit Dominus*'; this to quite a different melody from the previous. I have not met elsewhere the juxtaposition of the two different '*Cito euntes*' sentences.

The Marys use as their final antiphon the rarely encountered '*In Galileam Jhesum videbitis, sicut dixit vobis*', to the Hartker setting. There is a processional recession involving the triple elevation of the cross and the exchange between priest and chorus of '*Christus Dominus resurrexit*' and '*Deus gratias*', set very simply.

III

We will now consider the two 'third stage' French *Visitatios* previously mentioned. That from *B.N. MS lat. 904* (fol. 101v.–102r.), a Gradual from Rouen Cathedral, has been commented upon before, inasmuch as when considering the remarkable *Orléans MS 201 Visitatio*, I have spoken of similarities to be found between (non-liturgical) settings of certain texts common to the two works (see pp. 169–70).

But the Rouen version is a modest one beside the highly distinctive Orléans *Visitatio. B.N. 904* begins simply and briefly with the familiar 'approach' sentence of the Marys, '*Quis revolvet . . .*' which (with some individual moments in the setting) brings them face to face with an interrogating Angel outside the Tomb, a structure that is large enough for the Marys to enter.

The dialogue music, as can be ascertained by consulting Chart I of Appendix II, conforms quite closely to a number of French *Visitatio* versions of various dimensions, many of which, like *B.N. 904*, show musical rhymes at the vocative phrases. *B.N. 904's* own version of this is <u>rm</u> <u>mr</u> d <u>mf</u> r -, closest perhaps to the efforts of *Reims MS 265* and *Ste. Geneviève 117*. *B.N. 904* will also be found to belong to the little French group with the (rare) setting of '*Non est hic*' as d r <u>rl</u>. Thereafter, *B.N. 904* does some unusual things. The antiphon sentence '*Venite et videte . . .*' is introduced, not, as had been usual, to act as a recall after a dismissal, but as an invitation to continue forward and enter the Tomb. The music chosen, however, is not that of the liturgical antiphon, but apparently specially composed (and found also in the later 'Dublin Play', and, as far as I am aware, nowhere else).

A rubric instructs the first Angel to move away quickly, but within the Tomb *two* Angels await the Marys. It becomes apparent that the playwright is attempting to reconcile St. Matthew's and St. Mark's accounts (one Angel) with those of St. Luke and St. John (two). But he has another problem; what are the Angels to say to the Marys, the '*Quem quaeritis*' dialogue having been used up? He solves it by anticipating Christ's later question to Mary Magdalen, '*Mulier, quid ploras?*' Mary speaks for all three with the Gospel phrase (from St. John) that we have already found employed in replying to the supposed 'gardener', '(*Quia) tulerunt Dominum meum et nescio ubi posuerunt eum*'. This material is used in the official liturgy, but the various French and German Visitatios that give it to Mary Magdalen unite in disregarding the liturgical music, and in going their own group ways. A brief chart of mine shows me that in the case of *B.N. 904* the setting has for its item-companions those of *Orléans 201*, the (Egmond) 'Dutch Easter Play', and *Tours 927*, all of them almost note for note the same.

B.N. 904's ingenious continuation (imitated by *Tours 927*) is to borrow several verses from St. Luke xxiv and cause the Angels to ask, '*Quem quaeritis viventem cum mortuis? Non est hic, sed surrexit*'; and continue with '*Recordamini qualiter locutus est vobis, . . . et crucifigi, et die tercia resurgere.*' I can only suppose that the straightforward setting is original; it is certainly not the music of the liturgical responsory which employs the verse. *Tours 927* splits the item into three parts and distributes these between the Angels and the Marys, this nearly always to the same music as in *B.N. 904*. *Orléans 201* also takes over the St. Luke verses, but paraphrases them in rhyming, rhythmic lines, set to its own charming measured tune.

Incidentally, the '*Recordamini qualiter . . .*' part of the St. Luke quotation is found also in the *Visitatio* from *St. Quentin, MS 86* of the fourteenth century, a work of considerable length and containing a great deal of vernacular rhyming verse. The music (presumably original) differs from that of *B.N. 904* and *Tours 927*.

In *B.N. 904* there now begin the most dramatic moments of the 'third stage' episode. Christ, as the 'gardener', addresses Mary Magdalen with the Gospel phrase, '*Mulier, quid ploras?*', which the Angel had already appropriated, and adds to it a second question, '*Quem quaeritis?*' *Orléans*

201 has almost exactly the same music; *Tours 927* a similar beginning only. I have, in Chart Four, set out the two questions in comparative form, so that various French, Spanish, and German musical settings may be compared. It is apparent that no use was made by anyone of the liturgical music that set the phrase.

B.N. 904 now passes on to Mary's misapprehension as she implores the supposed gardener to let her know what he has done with the body of Jesus. There was no liturgical music available for the Gospel sentence, and *B.N. 904*'s music seems to represent free composition. After the first few notes the settings as found in *Orléans 201* and the 'Dutch Easter Play' both appear to suggest the same tune. *St. Quentin 86*, even, seems to share some phrases. (However, the German music for the text represents something quite different.)

For the dramatic '*Maria!*'—'*Raboni!*' exchange, *B.N. 904* and *Orléans 201* are closely and effectively allied, the former's setting being:

The (Egmond) 'Dutch Easter Play' version is similar, but spoiled by the intrusive gloss ('*quod dicitur magister*') of the Gospel account. The German (*Zehnsilberspiel*) versions also bring in the gloss, the settings being different and more melismatic.

B.N. 904 then calls on two St. Matthew verses (xxviii: 9–10) for Jesus' final words. The music seems individual, with the setting of *Orléans 201* similar only in moments. The latter actually borrows the music of the first responsory of Easter Day Matins for the two words '*Nolite timere*'.

Finally *B.N. 904* returns to a familiar composition for the Marys' last item of rejoicing, '*Alleluia, resurrexit Dominus . . .*', set to the usual opening notes, l s l s d' s f m f f m̲r̲ -, but thereafter receiving an unusual cutting down of the text.

The 'third stage' *Visitatio* version of Rouen's *B.N. 904* reveals itself as a thoroughly satisfactory presentation of the Easter Sepulchre story told in moderate length. The fact of the existence of other manuscripts of the same version during the thirteenth, fourteenth, and fifteenth centuries bear witness to its acceptability in the Rouen diocese as a practicable proposition. Moreover, in presenting its details, especially its musical details, at some length, I have been moved to call attention to the links that join it so often with the *Visitatio* of *Orléans MS 201*, a more extensive and ambitious work. It will be recalled that I have already noted some musical relationships between the Orléans *Officium Stellae* and the diocese of Rouen.

One more thirteenth-century French *Visitatio* remains to be considered, that from the diocese of Tours, preserved in the city library, (*Tours, Bibl. de la Ville, MS 927*, fol. 1r.–8v.). The manuscript as a whole

---

[1] The d̲'t̲ l̲t̲ t– setting of '*Maria!*' above had been foreshadowed by the previous setting of '*Mulier, quid ploras?*' by both *B.N. 904* and *Orléans 201* as d̲'t̲ l̲t̲ t– l̲s̲ l̲t̲ t–.

is a mid-century miscellany, a gathering together of largely unrelated liturgical items. The drama itself occupies the first few folios, and represents the longest example extant of the *Visitatio Sepulchri*. It is, however, a somewhat peculiar example.

Karl Young, in his survey of the text and production details of the work (I, pp. 438–50) sums up its characteristics in the nutshell of a couple of adjectives—'ambitious' and 'defective'. He goes on to say (p. 449): 'One gathers the impression that the writer, or compiler, had before him a considerable variety of dramatic material, some highly elaborate and some very simple. These resources he seems to have used with avidity, in a desire to incorporate everything that might enlarge and enlighten his own composition. The result is a production very imperfectly articulated, but very generous in its range of scenes and its display of literary forms.'

Karl Young's use of the word 'compiler' is an excellent example of 'le mot juste'. I wholly agree with what he says in regard to this unwieldy and impracticable composition, which seems to me to represent possibly a careless copy of an imperfect original, a great deal of the material having been borrowed from here, there, and everywhere.

Further confirmations of Karl Young's criticisms appear when the music, set down clearly enough in quadrate notation on four stave-lines, is considered in detail, and in comparison with corresponding passages to be found often enough in versions of the Easter dramas that we have already met with.

Before proceeding further with *Tours MS 927*, I have first to call attention to two works that will be new to our consideration. Karl Young has already printed (I, pp. 701–8) all that is extant of a Passion drama of the fourteenth century, belonging to the cathedral of Sulmona, in Italy.[1] The text represents the separate writing-out of the part for a single actor—the sole remains of a Passion drama of obviously major dimensions. No music is given. Fortunately, there are generous rubrics, and these enable us to discover that the lines are those for a minor figure, the 'Fourth Soldier' of Pilate's mercenary guard, one of the party appointed in due course to watch at the Tomb. In point of fact, more often than not the 'Fourth Soldier' blends his words with those of the group, or with the 'Third Soldier'. But the part reaches the respectable total of 226 lines, which hints at a formidable length for the whole work. The text reveals itself as being mainly in stanzas of a pattern much favoured in the period, particularly by the famous poet-composer of sequences, Adam de St. Victor. Although the Sulmona verse shows some occasional variety of metre, using passages with lines of 10, 11, or 12 syllables, it is most of the time in the Victorine pattern that I have previously described,[2] comprising double three-line stanzas, the syllable pattern being 8 8 7 / 8 8 7, and the rhyme scheme a a b c c b.

The rubrics of the Sulmona 'part' also help us to grasp, something

---

[1] *Sulmona, Archivio capitolare di S. Panfilo*, 'Fascicolo 47, n. 9'.
[2] See p. 58.

less than fully, the nature and progress of the 'scenes' which made up the Sulmona Passion as it once stood, with the figures of Jesus, Caiaphas, Herod, Pilate, the Cyrenean cross-bearer, and many other familiar figures all taking part, together with the ubiquitous Soldiers. There come the standard incidents of the Crucifixion, and the drama appears to end with the Resurrection, which moves the Third and Fourth Soldiers to exhort the 'Jewish' onlookers to believe in the Risen Christ.

The other Passion drama to be considered here will not be found in Karl Young's two volumes. In 1936, a few years after the appearance of his work, an Italian scholar, D. M. Inguanez, published the details of a discovery which he had made at the ancient Benedictine monastery of Montecassino. It consisted of the almost complete text of a versified Latin Passion, belonging to the mid-twelfth century, and, without much doubt, a product of the monastery itself.[1] In spite of some patches of partial illegibility it has been found to consist of some 320 lines, which, (apart from the last three, written in the vernacular and representing a lament of the Virgin) are framed, this time wholly so, in stanzas of Victorine verse of the double 8 8 7 pattern. Once again no music is attached.[2] The directing rubrics are generous—even more so than in the case of the Sulmona work. The scenes lead from that of Judas's betrayal of his master through the details of the various trials to the Crucifixion, at which point the drama ends.

The comparatively complete nature of the text supplies a number of 'scenes' that are not apparent in the Sulmona single part. Nevertheless, there are to be distinguished some sixty lines of closely paralleled material common to the two works, which, in relation to the respective manuscript dates, seems to point to a borrowing by Sulmona, or, alternatively, the drawing by each upon some common source. Whatever the answer, we have arrived at the fact of a full-scale Italian dramatic Passion, in existence about or before the mid-twelfth century.

The significance of my mentioning the Montecassino work at this moment is that its discovery, and the obviousness of its material links with the fourteenth-century Sulmona fragment alters somewhat the relation of the latter to the thirteenth-century Tours drama in the matter of the scene of Pilate's Tomb guard, an episode which each of them includes. Before the Montecassino discovery it could be argued that this piece of dramatization *might* have originated with the Tours author, or with the creators of the two extensive thirteenth-century German

[1] An important study, *The Latin Passion Play: Its Origin and Development*, has recently been published by Professor Sandro Sticca, of the New York State University, with the Montecassino work as its main preoccupation. It is printed by the SUNY Press, Albany, N.Y. (1970).

[2] The photographs that I have seen of the original manuscript pages show no sign of any musical notation. Yet the whole work except for its few final lines of 'planctus' consists of a continued succession of stanzas of 'Victorine' verse, 887/887 . . . I cannot think that in the mid-twelfth century any such body of tune-catching poetry intended for performance would have escaped a setting. Adam de St. Victor was already showing how to combine effectively the two arts. Once more I recall a contemporary saying: 'A verse without music is a mill without water.' I believe that in performance the Montecassino 'Passion' was sung.

dramas of the *Zehnsilberspiel* type, that from Klosterneuburg and the Carmina Burana, respectively.[1] But manifestly the existence of the mid-twelfth-century Montecassino work in a highly wrought form, and its close relationship with the texts of the Sulmona fragment, changes the picture. Even though the latter manuscript may belong to the fourteenth century, there seems every reason to expect that the Italian Passion material was in existence before the advent of the Tours drama. Aware of the general methods of the Tours predator, I imagine that he must have 'lifted' it from some such source, even though he might have claimed to be the first French author to use that particular scene.

I shall make some further references to this earliest extant European Passion, that from Montecassino, when, in the next chapter, also devoted to the thirteenth century, we deal with the two German examples of the same type from Benediktbeuern.

We are now ready to consider in detail the *Tours 927 Visitatio* version.

A page, or more, is missing from the beginning, for at the top of the first folio is a line of text, without music, which seems to have come from St. Matthew, the conclusion of the appeal of the chief priests and Pharises to Pilate for a guard on the entrance to the Tomb.[2] The normal text, with its quadrate music notation on four-line staves, then begins: a stanza of Pilate's instructions to his soldiers (Young, II, 2–12).[3] The passage, of twelve lines, starts with a textual pattern, 8 8 7, that suggests the Victorine technique, but after another 8 7 fades into irregular lines that finish with two of 11 and 10 syllables respectively. Contained in the stanza are the phrases, '*Ne furentur illum discipuli et dicant plebi: Surrexit a mortuis.*' This passage occurs also in the two major, *Zehnsilberspiel*-type thirteenth-century *Visitatios* mentioned above, the two German works employing the standard *Zehnsilberspiel* 'Melody III' (see p. 315) for the setting of the stanza that contains it. Tours has a simple setting, formless, except for one line of music that is repeated later.

Next is the Soldiers' item as they move to the Tomb (Young, pp. 13–20). It is an irregular stanza of eight lines which is almost exactly duplicated in the Sulmona version. No comparison of their music is possible, since Sulmona lacks any. The Tours setting, though probably sung in rhythm, is without any clear pattern and is quite undistinguished. I have not met it elsewhere.

Now comes the dramatic happening described by St. Matthew and the Tours rubrics, the descent of the Angel as if in the manner of lightning from heaven. The Soldiers are stricken, to become, at least for the time being, 'as dead men'. Although *Tours*, as we have already noted, is the only French Church drama surviving to give text and music to

---

[1] See pp. 325–32.

[2] The Vulgate phrase is: '*Et erit novissimus error pejor priore*'. The last word is indistinct in the manuscript. The whole relevant section is St. Matthew, xxvii:62–6.

[3] Again I make reference use of the line numberings that Karl Young gives to his printing of the Tours drama libretto, whenever I am considering any passages in detail. His text occupies from pp. 438 to 447 of his first volume.

the setting of the guard, yet two other French *Visitatios*, a 'first stage' type from the Sainte-Chapelle (*Paris, B. de l'Arsenal MS 114*, fol. 73v.–74r.), and a 'third stage' from Coutances (*B.N. MS lat. 1301*, fol. 143v.–145v.), have rubrics directing the episodes of their arrival and striking down, all apparently in dumb show. Both versions are late (fifteenth-century), and neither gives any music.

After the disposal of the guard the three Marys are discerned, with their vessels for the unguents, *'ante hostium ecclesiae'*. Karl Young debates the question as to which side of the church door, within or without, they were supposed to be. I am of the opinion that, in spite of a minimum of actual liturgical items in the work, the 'mise-en-scène' was within a consecrated building, centred round the usual *Sepulchrum:* that is, if the drama was ever performed at all.

What now begins is, at first, a typical *Zehnsilberspiel B* scene (II, 21–52), coming all the way from the twelfth-century *Vich MS 105* (see p. 185 ff.), stanza melody and all. The setting is of course a 'major mode' one. On the ZHN *B, Melody II* chart given on p. 314, the tune as presented by Tours will be found in its small variations from the earliest (Vich) version to be almost identical with that of the 'Dutch Easter Play'. It is a curious fact that the latter writes the melody as starting on G (established as its tonic), and thus has to avoid F natural, for obvious reasons. Tours, starting on F, and able to use B flat, is free to follow Vich in employing the 'leading note' (here, 'E'), and does so.

As for the eight stanzas of this section, the scribe is content to write out the four-sentence stanza-tune only once, a time- and space-saving device that we have met with before in the manuscripts, and which is found imitated in the troubadour's *chansonnier* and the modern hymn book.

After line 51, and the resumption of the music notation, a new figure appears, *Alius Mercator*, his earliest appearance in Church drama, and possibly foreshadowing the 'apprentice' type of later secular drama, and the purveyor of rough humour. Here, however, his questions as to the Marys' needs and his bargaining with them seem wholly serious, (II, 52–65). This section I have not met elsewhere, neither words nor music. The latter is simple, pedestrian, and shows no particular plan. If one tries one can find brief repetitions of a musical phrase in varied forms.

After the Marys have been told by the Merchant in regard to their purchases of spices that *'Mille solidos potestis habere'*, they reply quite happily in unison, with *'Libenter, domine'*. But the music as given in the manuscript is not happily presented for women's voices and for the expression of such amiable emotion. The Merchant's demand had been given an F clef for his bass-range music. The Marys, whose *'Libenter . . .'* reply echoes (imprecisely) the Merchant's last phrase, are given the same F clef and apparently the same deep tessitura. I reproduce it at the same pitch but with a G clef:

The apparent 'lines' of the text of this section seem extremely irregular as regards the successive number of their syllables; thus it seems hopeless to try to bring any sort of rhythmic plan to the music, but we may expect that the phrase, with its diminished fifth leap, was sung at a pitch that suited the voices.

The Marys now move away towards the Tomb. In another brief section (II, 66–9) that has not survived elsewhere, we find one of the Marys mentioning the possibility of their encountering Pilate's guard (a neat link with the first scene), but being heartened by one of her companions. For a change, we have a real musical repetition; the 'reassurance' being set to a shortened version of the 'apprehension' music.

Tours now makes use of material known to a number of other French and French-influenced *Visitatios* for the advancing Marys, mourning as they proceed. This consists of four pairs of lines, beginning respectively: '*Heu! misera, cur contigit . . .*'; '*Heu! redemptio Israel . . .*'; '*Heu! consolatio nostra . . .*'; and '*Iam, iam, ecce . . .*'. These items all appear in the twelfth-century *Madrid, MS 132*, which has Norman musical notation, in the 'appendix' page of the twelfth-century *Visitatio* from *Orléans MS 201*, the thirteenth-century 'Dutch Easter Play', the thirteenth-century *Tours MS 927*, and the fourteenth-century 'Dublin' *Visitatio*, French in origin, now in the Bodleian Library (*MS Rawlinson liturg. d. iv.*). My comparative chart, given to the music of the separate items in each of the manuscript versions, shows me that the settings are all variations on some kind of common source, probably originating somewhere in Normandy;[1] I can afford only one item example:

[1] On p. 156 I have already made mention of *Madrid's* first item; and on p. 172 the whole

The Tours manuscript makes use of all four items for the approach of the Marys. The speech following (I, 78) is that of the single Angel who stands at the Tomb. He declares that Christ is truly risen, and that there is no need for the ointment. Both text and music are new to me. In particular, I think that the setting is a fine example of melodious declamation, growing out of a phrase from the previous item. One would like to think that it originated at Tours.

As the Marys view the empty Sepulchre and retire, they each sing a four-line stanza of comment (II, 80–90). At least, this would be the description if the scribe hadn't left out the fourth line of the second stanza. Again, the music might seem to have consisted of the same pleasant melody for each stanza, except for the fact of the frequent small differences of note-detail in what should have been identical passages. The only explanation seems to lie in the rank carelessness of the scribe. This feature seems to be endemic to the score.

In the fine musical declamation of the next two lines the Angel gives another assurance to the women, and (a new touch to the Sepulchre scene) reveals that he is the Archangel Michael himself. It must perhaps remain uncertain whether Tours can lay claim to the original conception of the worthy material that we have met in the last dozen lines or so, or whether we must imagine some earlier, perished source. But for our next concern (II, 93–9), there can be little doubt whence the ideas derive. This scene of the '*Quem quaeritis*' exchange is quite clearly founded on the unusual pattern that we have already met in the Norman-style *Madrid 132*, and which is also imitated by the 'Dutch Easter Play'.

However, Tours begins the section with an absurdity. Mary Magdalen has seen for herself that the Tomb is empty, has heard from the Archangel that Christ has risen, yet her reply is to wonder 'who will roll away the stone from the door of the sepulchre?'—as if it hadn't already been rolled away! The fact is of course that the jackdaw of Tours had merely picked up one of the prizes he had collected (in this case from *Madrid 132* or a vanished similar source) and, whether or not the addition made any sense, added it to the pile. The imitations of the Madrid passages continue, causing further futilities. Another Mary cries out that the stone *is* rolled away, and that there is a young man in a white garment. Apparently he addresses the Marys, using the trick of *Madrid 132*, leading into the familiar '*Quem quaeritis*' question with a preliminary '*Nolite timere vos, dicite . . .*'. As we have seen, the 'Dutch Easter Play' borrows the same device.

---

of the *Orléans 201*'s 'appendix'. In its own *Visitatio*, Orléans preferred its own series of stanzas for the Mary's first advance, but apparently 'stored' the other verses as a kind of reserve.

[2] On p. 181 I have called attention to the fact that of the two manuscripts concerned with the 'Dutch Easter Play', the earlier, Maastricht one (A), lacks its first folio, and starts abruptly with the Marys' '*Iam, iam, ecce*'. Yet I have also said that the differences to be found throughout between it and the fifteenth-century (B) version amount to not much more than occasional small pitch differences in the music and some different neume groupings. The missing first folio can be reconstructed with confidence from the intact Egmond version.

Both Tours and Madrid have a vocative musical rhyme (*'Chisticolae'* —*'coelicolae'*). I am assuming that the single punctum that spoils it in the case of Tours is the fault of the scribe. The two are also linked by the addition of the word *'quaerimus'* to the Marys' reply, *'Jesum Nazarenum crucifixum . . .'*. Several other French versions include the word, but not at that particular point in the sentence.

As for the next item (II, 100–3), the 'Dutch Easter Play' seems to rob Tours of the credit for the four rhyming lines beginning *'Vultum tristem . . .'*. The two versions agree not only in text, but in the simple and apparently rhythmic setting. *Orléans 201*, as we have already seen, uses exactly the same lyrical verses to dismiss the Marys, but employs its own unique and charming melody.

The new scene that follows is of great dramatic interest. Here, in a French *Visitatio*, is the episode of the Tomb guard reviving, and returning to Pilate, being questioned by him, replying, and then being bribed to remain silent (ll. 104–33). The same happenings are to be found in the two major Sepulchre dramas from Klosterneuberg and Benediktbeuern respectively, but in quite different terms from Tours.[1] With the evidence that has come to light as to well-organized drama involving Pilate and the Tomb guard in monastic circles of eleventh-century Italy, it could be assumed that Tours may have had material to hand about which we know nothing. Possible, but in my opinion less likely, is that someone at Tours wrote the scene.

The Soldiers' first utterances (*'Heu! miseri'* . . .), in seven rhyming but somewhat irregular lines, are set to a formless but pleasantly flowing melody. Pilate's reply and the Soldiers' further speech are in a stricter poetic pattern, and their settings are repeated (with the usual note-discrepancies) in further stanzas.

Pilate's final speech, enjoining silence on the Soldiers as to the happenings at the Tomb, consists of two groups of three lines (l. 127 to end of the section). A new tune is employed, and it should be the same for each group. I am assuming this, since the differences in pitch that occur in places between the two versions of the setting appear to me to be due to the music scribe having omitted to record clef changes.

There follows a very odd happening; the Soldiers are represented as singing *'Tunc erit . . .'* ('Then will be . . .') and with this broken phrase ending the scene!

Since these words were met with at the head of the first folio of the manuscript, and were considered, reasonably enough, to come from the priestly warning to Pilate, as in St. Matthew, xxvii:64, we must apparently think of our scribe, or scribes, as having gone more wildly astray than usual.

A rubric banishes the soldiers and Pilate and indicates Mary Magdalen, alone and near the Sepulchre. Her first words are, *'Heu! me misera! Magnus labor, magnus dolor, magna est tristitia . . .'*. Altogether, one is hardly prepared for her long sorrowfully-worded soliloquy,

[1] See pp. 327–9 and 331.

knowing as she does that the Resurrection has taken place. However, before she has progressed far a sudden familiarity comes into the text, but this is strange to the context. The phrases prove to belong to the beginning of the liturgical sequence, '*O quam magno dies ista . . .*', a rejoicing for the Resurrection; one that we have already met with in the thirteenth-century first stage *Visitatio* from the manuscript *B.N. lat. 1255* (see p. 287). I give below the respective settings of the two lines common to *B.N. lat. 1255* and *Tours 927*. I render the first at the pitch of the manuscript music. Tours' setting I have transposed up a fifth so that exact comparison may be made at a glance. No accidentals are involved: the common source of the music is obvious.

Furthermore, if we now retrace our steps to near the beginning of Mary's solo, it will be found that the music of '*O quam magno . . .*' has been long anticipated in:

This musical sentence is used for the succeeding three lines, and its first five neumes have the trick of cropping up, without any apparent logic, in various later places before the actual appearance of the '*O quam magno . . .*' couplet. Two other single-line melodies are given repeated use, both before and after the actual '*O quam magno . . .*' appearance. One of them is perhaps reminiscent of the third phrase of the Tours music as given on p. 300.

Mary concludes with a thrice-repeated '*Me misera!*' followed by '*Quid agam?*' and '*Heu! tristis, quid dicam?*'. This emotion calls for the appearance of an Angel,[1] to utter the familiar question as to why she should be weeping. Indeed, the Tours Mary is a confirmed pessimist, whom neither Michael nor lesser Angels can move from the standpoint

---

[1] Instead of 'Angelus' the manuscript has 'Jesus', who, it would seem, immediately disappears again. It was Wilhelm Meyer who suggested that 'Angelus' was probably meant. Karl Young says (II, p. 444) 'he may well be right'. I am sure he is.

that she must see her Lord for herself. However, the new scene is as familiar as the first question. Mary's reply, '*Quia tulerunt Dominum . . .*' and indeed the whole of the exchanges, texts and music (ll. 158–63), seem to have been borrowed by Tours, in particular, from *Rouen, B.N. 904,* with but few differences of musical pitch. I have referred before (p. 290) to the coincidences between the Tours and *B.N. 904* manuscripts at this place.

The point is, of course, that the compiler of the Tours version could not resist taking over this considerable further material, however dramatically unnecessary its presence might be, and however the proportions and balance of the work might be disturbed in consequence.

There follows (l. 164) a prayer by Mary Magdalen, with (according to a rubric) her hands raised towards heaven. But near the end of her prose passage she relapses once more into mourning. 'Where is her Lord?' is the constant theme. I do not know if this item represents Tours own effort, or whether it comes from yet unidentified sources. Certainly an unusual rubric follows, when Mary, overcome by her feelings, is represented as sinking to the ground, and being supported by the other two. These sing two lines of attempted comfort, the text and music of which are again new to me.

In this item we have another instance of the unreliability of the music scribe. There is something wrong concerning the clefs of the music of these two lines, as given in the manuscript, since most of the second line of melody appears as if written as a 'tonal sequence', a third below the first-line pitch—an unlikely occurrence. If the F clef is changed to C at the beginning of the second line (at '*de*') and restored at the fourth syllable before the end we discover two identical (as well as charming) lines of music. In my opinion this is how the tune originally stood. One can never really trust the Tours music scribe.

The overall compiler of the Tours *Visitatio* shows himself in no better light just here, either. Mary Magdalen has surely complained enough at this point as to the necessity of seeking her Lord, yet it is thought suitable now to introduce that stock liturgical antiphon, '*Ardens est cor meum . . .*' (the normal liturgical music somewhat simplified) and yet again to bring in an Angel, asking the question '*Quem quaeritis?*' and receiving the reply, '*Viventem cum mortis*', both phrases having been met with not many lines back, in each instance to the music of *B.N. 904.* The best excuse for their appearance here would be to imagine that they were inserted by mistake.

The Angel then considers (ll. 174–6) that the Marys need yet more assurance on the subject of the Resurrection (and who shall blame him for thinking so?). His lines of rhyming verse are set, appropriately enough, to two lines of music belonging to '*O quam magno . . .*'.

Then, for the manuscript itself comes an internal disaster. The Angel's last word at the foot of a page is '*Christus*'; '*videam*' begins another, and it is quickly obvious that although Mary Magdalen is speaking, the exchange is between her and the Apostle Peter. One or more pages must be missing, and it is extremely probable that included in the loss is the Christ-Magdalen scene and the Race to the Tomb, from which latter happening Peter has just returned.

It is interesting to note that the music employed by Mary and Peter for the single lines that they exchange at this resumption (ll. 179–80) is that used by her in her lament before the manuscript break, an example being the setting of the line commencing '*Heu, michi tristi*' (l. 147). Whatever the line was that once preceded Mary's '*Hanc meam . . .*' (l. 179), it must have had the same setting, to judge by the notes attached to its surviving word '*videam*'.[1]

Mary's next two lines to Peter ('*Vade cito . . .*', etc.) are also set to phrases that echo her earlier music. It is of course difficult to decide at times whether the resemblances are intended or are merely fortuitous. With them, the obvious small copying errors continue.

There follows now (ll. 183–94) a not very satisfactory scene between Mary and 'the disciples' (these last-named are not identified). The items consist merely of line incipits, which identify themselves as coming from, respectively, the ancient hymns '*Aurora lucis rutilat*' ('*Tristes erant . . .*') and '*Jesus nostra redemptio*'.

The music scribe leads off with a blunder. The third and fourth neumes of the first line of '*Tristes erant . . .*' are a third too low. When, two items later, Mary Magdalen uses another stanza from the same hymn, the scribe writes the correct version. Between the two comes the first stanza of '*Jesu, nostra redemptio*'. The incipit indicates the normal liturgical tune, somewhat distorted.

Now comes an ambiguous rubric, which speaks of a nameless person entering, clad in a dalmatic and bearing a cross in his hand. Scholars have long decided that Tours has missed out the word 'Jesus'. His speech (ll. 195–7), paraphrasing the account of St. John, is to be found in several of the *Peregrinus* dramas that we have already met with.[2] Tours had decided to add some scenes from this type of drama to its spoils. Its music will be found to follow that of *Madrid 132*, Beauvais (*B.N. 1064*) and *Orléans 201* (the last-named, until it goes its own way, almost exactly note for note). As Tours continues with *Madrid 132* to the end of the item, it shows that, as it climbs to a third above the Madrid music for a while, it has in copying probably missed a change of clef. As a reply to Christ's words by the disciples, Tours follows Madrid and Beauvais in using the non-liturgical setting of '*Surrexit Dominus de sepulchro . . .*'.

However, the section that follows (ll. 201–11) occurs, as far as I am aware, only in Tours. The two appearances of Christ to the disciples, as is usual in the *Peregrinus* dramas, have been telescoped into one, and now doubting Thomas makes his appearance, announcing himself

---

[1] Peter's reply to Mary ('*Dic mihi*') was first actually omitted by the manuscript scribe, but was filled in at the bottom of the page and directed to its proper place by means of asterisks.

[2] See Chapter IX, pp. 185 ff., for accounts of relevant *Peregrinus* dramas.

('*Thomas dicor Didimus*') somewhat in the style of folk-drama. The music seems suspect to me in several places—ugly intervals and discrepancies of pitch in what are probably really repeated musical phrases, and one queer patch caused probably by bringing in a change of clef too early.

The rest of the Tours scene (ll. 212–19) is concerned with the second entry of Christ and his confrontation of Thomas. The texts are stock ones, to be found elsewhere in *Peregrinus* dramas, derived from liturgical antiphons and ultimately from Gospel verses. The music is liturgical, and can be found set out with very few differences of note from p. 390 to p. 393 of the *Antiphonale Romanum* (*infra Hebdom. 1. post Oct. Paschae*).

The concluding portion of the work is conventional. First, Mary Magdalen sings the lyrical part of the Easter sequence *Victimae paschali*, and then 'two disciples' (presumably Peter and John) question her in the usual terms of the second and dialogued part ('*Dic nobis, Maria . . .*'). One final piece of attention must be paid to Tours' wretched music scribe. For the notes of '*Dic nobis, Maria*' he writes, correctly enough:

But when this musical phrase occurs again, at '*Angelicos testes*', he perpetrates this:

How could a scribe with any sort of clerical background have let pass such a passage? In this the most solemn period of the ecclesiastical year, the great Sequence was sung again and again, with the sound of its notes surely engraved deep in the memories of all Christians. It appears to me that the Tours music scribe must have been one of those concerning whom Dom Grégoire Suñol remarked that they understood neither the sense nor the significance of what they were transcribing.

When Mary replies to the question of the disciples as to what she has seen, she indicates in turn Sepulchre, Angels, sudary, and Cross. After scenes that have included appearances of the 'living Christ', two of them to the disciples, we must again feel, more than ever, a sense of anticlimax at the unnecessary marshalling of this minor evidence, and the conventional nature of the disciples' last chorus, '*Credendum est magis*

---

[1] In the case of each example I have transposed the notes a perfect fourth higher than the original.

Wipo of Burgundy's eleventh-century music to the sequence, followed through successive centuries of manuscripts, suffers a few small variations from place to place in such unimportant matters as a *clivis* (passing note) for a *virga*, or vice versa. But the basic line of the melody is always maintained. I have never met another such distortion as Tours gives here.

soli Mariae veraci . . .'. The choral singing of '*Te Deum laudamus*' rounds off the work.

I have made a transcription of the Tours *Visitatio Sepulchri*, as I have of almost all the Church dramas. But I have never contemplated producing an edition that would allow for a practical production of the Tours work. To do so would mean making objections to and attempting to reshape so much that is set down in the obviously incompetent copy of an ill-conceived and ill-constructed edifice built largely from other people's materials. There is also the matter of the hiatus in the manuscript, where almost certainly there stood once the episodes that dealt with the appearance of Christ to Mary Magdalen and the circumstances of the Race to the Sepulchre. To make the action workable all this would have to be reconstructed, and it would have to be a matter of guesswork —quite a lot of guesswork. Doubt could be cast on the overall result, as to whether it really represented the work of a cleric (or clerics) belonging to the diocese of Tours in the thirteenth century.

When I call to mind the lay-out of certain Church dramas of dimensions approaching those of the Tours version[1] and note the intelligent and artistic planning and sense of proportion shown by their clerical creators, I am inclined to wonder if the Tours *Visitatio* ever *did* get to a performance. I find myself imagining, in a great ecclesiastical establishment of the period, scholarly clerical objections to such an unbalanced work; that is, if the present surviving manuscript represents anything near the original intentions of the creators. As it stands it is not a worthy example to put beside the few masterly achievements of medieval musico-dramatic art that have come down to us, and I bracket it with the *Vich MS 105* version (see p. 173 ff.) as being in too tangled and uncertain a condition to be worthy of a reconstruction.

IV

I return now to the subject of the *Zehnsilberspiel*, a type of drama to which I have previously made brief reference (see p. 175 and pp. 178 ff.). Its distinctive stanza items were the bases of some major examples of Sepulchre dramas; these were more prominent in Germany than elsewhere. As we have already found, it is the name of Wilhelm Meyer that is associated with pioneer work in connection with them.[2]

Karl Young (I, pp. 677–8) in the process of introducing the earliest glimpse of the bargaining scene between the Spice Merchant and the Marys, as met with in the twelfth-century *Vich MS 105*, sets out his analysis of Meyer's theories. It seems to me that his précis could not be

[1] Among the few I would include the Orléans *Visitatio*; that from Origny Sainte-Bénoîte (St.Quentin); the Beauvais *Peregrinus*; the Orléans *Officium Stellae* and *Ordo Rachelis*; and of course, the Beauvais *Danielis Ludus*. For a discussion of the St. Quentin *Visitatio*, see pp. 442–7.

[2] W. Meyer, *Gesammelte Abhandlungen zur mittellateinischen Rhythmik*, 2 vols. (Berlin, 1905).

improved on, and I shall quote extensively from it. I pause only to mention that I have already taken note, on p. 179, of the groups of stanzas referred to in this quotation; and have also, on pp. 308–11 below, set out the whole material of the *Zehnsilberspiel* verse-forms. These are free compositions, not merely metrical arrangements of Gospel or liturgical matter. It will be found that the words remain very consistent through the various *Visitatio* versions, even though one or another stanza or set of stanzas may be found omitted, according to the example considered.

I now give Karl Young's summary of the main arguments and theories set out in Meyer's somewhat turgid work:

A discussion of the merchant-scene ... must include some mention of Wilhelm Meyer's intricate inferences concerning the origin of this scene, and concerning the nature of a hypothetical '*Zehnsilberspiel*', of which the action attached to the '*unguentarius*' is an important part. By *Zehnsilberspiel* Meyer means an Easter play containing stanzas of four ten-syllable lines ... In its full *theoretical* form this *Spiel* contains, principally, some six groups of stanzas so in varying metres, as follows:

A. A group of three stanzas, expressing the grief of the three Marys, in lines of fifteen syllables, the stanzas beginning *Heu nobis*, *Jam percusso*, and *Sed eamus* respectively, as seen, for example, in the plays from Engelberg and Rheinau.

B. A group of three stanzas, expressing the intention of buying ointment, in rhyming lines of ten syllables, the stanzas beginning *Omnipotens pater*, *Amisimus enim*, and *Sed eamus unguentum* respectively, as seen, for example, in the plays from Narbonne, Zwickau, and Tours.

C. A group of utterances accompanying the actual purchase of the ointment. Of these the most striking are the five stanzas of ten-syllable lines, beginning respectively *Huc proprius*, *Dic tu nobis*, *Hoc unguentum*, *Aromata pretio*, and *Dabo vobis*. The last two stanzas may be seen in the play from Prague, and all five appear in the play from Benediktbeuern.

D. A group of three stanzas of ten-syllable lines, in which Mary Magdalen expresses her grief. These stanzas begin *Cum venissem*, *En lapis*, and *Dolor crescit* respectively, and they may be seen, for example, in the plays from Engelberg and Cividale.

E. A group of four stanzas in lines of eight syllables, in which Christ expounds the Resurrection to Mary Magdalen, and lays his command upon her. The stanzas begin respectively *Prima quidem*, *Haec priori*, *Ergo noli*, and *Nunc ignaros*, and they may be seen, for example, in the plays from Engelberg and Einsiedeln.

F. A single stanza of ten-syllable lines—either the one beginning *Vere vidi* or that beginning *Galilaeam omnes*—in which Mary Magdalen makes her announcement to the disciples, or to others.[1]

Meyer observes that, whereas groups A, B, and C—which are concerned with the merchant-scene—are found in plays from France, groups D, E, and F—associated with the scene between Christ and Mary Magdalen—are not regularly found there. The combination of all three groups, A, B, and C,

---

[1] A small correction is needed here. Both stanzas are employed by *Klosterneuberg MS 574.*

sometimes found in France, does not occur in Germany,[1] a normal German arrangement being a combination of groups A, D, E, and F. From these general facts Meyer infers the following:

(1) At the time when a French cleric added to the *Visitatio* a scene between Christ and Mary Magdalen, another French cleric invented a merchant-scene; and since neither the Bible nor the liturgy provided speeches for such a dramatic invention, the author used secular metrical forms, and composed group A for the entrance of the Marys, group B for their journey to the tomb, and group C for their dialogue with the merchant.

(2) A play containing groups A, B, and C, along with the Christ-Magdalen scene, was carried from France to Germany; and upon the model of A, B, and C, a German writer embellished the Christ-Magdalen scene, the result being groups D, E, and F. For the sake of solemnity and contrast, this writer composed the four stanzas of Christ, group E, in lines of eight syllables. Thus the *Zehnsilberspiel* was brought to its theoretically complete form in Germany.

Although certain of Meyer's ingenious *obiter dicta* cannot be taken very seriously, the general outline of his argument is theoretically acceptable. There are good reasons for believing that the ten-syllable line arose first in France, and was used there dramatically before it was cultivated in Germany. Meyer's general theory of the origin of the *Zehnsilberspiel* in France and of its completion in Germany accords well enough with the known facts and with the extant texts. His general view will, perhaps, be regarded by most students of the subject as an unproved possibility.

The present writer will now take up the tale. I must call attention first of all to the use by Meyer and Karl Young of the terms 'hypothetical' and '*theoretically* complete' as applied to the *Zehnsilberspiel*. They are each implying, it would appear, that they have not met with an example of the form which includes stanzas from every one of the six different sets of groups (A to F) as set out above. If the chart on pp. 308–11 is consulted, it will be seen that they were very nearly right—but not quite. The fifteenth-century *Visitatio* from Wolfenbüttel, contained in *MS Helmst 965*, which both writers seem to have missed, does indeed comply with the full requirements for being considered as a 'practical' example, inasmuch as it draws on all six sections. However, the late date of the manuscript robs it of any significance when it comes to discussing 'origins'.[2]

Karl Young is also concerned with another writer on the same subject, K. Dürre, to whom I have already referred on p. 173 as framing a 'merchant-scene' theory out of the opening four-line stanza of the disordered *Vich MS 105 Visitatio*. This eight-syllable, single rhyme item prefaces the widely used '*Omnipotens pater altissime . . .*' group, and in both its text and music appears to me not to 'belong' in style to the more familiar composition. The '*Omnipotens pater . . .*' stanza, with its music, we have already seen (p. 174). I will now set down the opening four-line

---

[1] This statement, as I shall show, is not wholly accurate.

[2] For a more extensive discussion of this manuscript, see pp. 389 ff.

stanza in question, with its music in modern free notation:[1]

E – ā – mus mir – ram   e – me – 're
Let us go forth to   pur – chase myrrh,

cum li – qui – do   a – ro – ma – te
with oint – ment of the sweetest o – dour

ut va – le – a – mus   un – ge – re
that will al – low us   to a – noint

cor – pus dat – um se – pul – tu – re
the bo – dy destin'd for bu – – ri – al

I have no doubt whatsoever that the setting was sung in regular rhythm, possibly in 'second rhythmic mode'; and what a well-balanced and charming little tune emerges!

I quote Karl Young again (I, p. 682):

Dürre infers that the merchant-scene originated from the procession of the Marys to a side-altar to receive their vessels from an attendant, and that to accompany this act were composed, either in Spain or in France, the first four eight-syllable lines in the text before us. These four lines, he thinks are probably the original literary kernel of the merchant-scene, and had, at first, no connection with Meyer's *Zehnsilberspiel*. Later, some cleric composed the stanzas of 10-syllable lines (5–33). The first of these stanzas (ll. 5–8) was composed upon the model of 10-syllable prayer-formulas, such as *Omnipotens sempiterne Deus*. The third stanza (ll. 13–16) was probably inspired by the original 8-line stanza. The figure of the *mercator*, Dürre infers, may show the influence of the merchant who appears in the dramatic *Sponsus*; or possibly, the Easter merchant-scene was the earlier, and is itself reflected in *Sponsus*.

It does not appear that Dürre seriously invalidates Meyer's general theory. He merely points to what he considers an earlier form of the merchant-scene, in which were spoken only four 8-syllable lines. His indication may, or may not, be significant. Although I am complimented by Dürre's attaching so much importance to a text that I was the first to publish, I cannot regard his contentions as proved.

I feel myself more inclined to favour Dürre's ideas than does Karl Young. The latter mentions (I, p. 402) that rubric details in several *Visitatio* dramas suggest such a scene as the handing over of the vessels, and he cites the *Visitatio* from Toul, where the Marys make a special detour to a side altar for the purpose of receiving them. The regular

---

[1] I have once more transposed the original pitch of a musical example up a fourth, so that it may fit comfortably on to a G stave. I have written it in modern free rhythm notation, which preserves very clearly the details of the neume groupings. But as I have said before, the composition would surely have been sung in troubadour-like fashion.

N

rhythms and balancing phrases of both the text and its music suggest that whatever actions took place were conceived dramatically, serving to launch the Marys on their way, and by its own example suggesting further verbal and musical invention. I can readily imagine a later cleric, seeking to create a 'bargaining' scene, being charmed with both the text of the stanza and its setting, and being unable to resist including it as a preface to his own efforts. The fact is obvious that it has served to inspire the third stanza of the *Zehnsilberspiel B* section that follows—'*Sed eamus unguentum emere . . .*'—although some modification was needed to accommodate a new syllable pattern and a new tune. It appears to me that Dürre has made a very interesting and feasible suggestion. I have, myself, never met either the four-line stanza or its music before, and have reproduced the latter in a 'free-rhythm' form in the hope that somebody more widely versed in medieval music than I may have encountered it elsewhere, a piece of information that might prove useful.

Returning to a consideration of the *Zehnsilberspiel* form as a whole, I now propose to set out the whole of the stanza-material mentioned in our previous references to the six groups. In the case of each group I also identify the *Visitatios* in which the particular group is to be found employed. Certain of the versions, owing to the lateness of their appearance in the medieval centuries, have not yet received my detailed attention. Two versions, the 'Dutch Easter Play' and Wolfenbüttel *MS Helmst 965*, are not mentioned in standard Church drama writings, including those of Karl Young.

ZEHNSILBERSPIEL

A. *The Lament of the Marys*
(as they approach the Sepulchre)   All three stanzas in:

Syllables

1. Heu! nobis internas mentes	8	*Engelberg 314*[1]	
quanti pulsant gemitus	7	*Rheinau XVIII*[2]	
Pro nostra consolatore,	8	*Einsiedeln 300*[3]	
quo privamur misere,	7	*Nuremberg 22923*[4]	
Quem crudelis Judeorum	8	*Zwickau XXXVI.I.24 (B)*[5]	
morti debit populus	7	*Wolfenbüttel Helmst 965*[6]	
		Munich 4660a (Benediktbeuern)[7]	

[1] See pp. 369–70.   [2] See pp. 317–9.   [3] See pp. 179–81.   [4] See pp. 316–9.
[5] There are three *Visitatio* versions in this manuscript, all closely allied, the last two, however, containing a large vernacular element. I refer to them as A, B, and C. See pp. 406–9.
[6] See pp. 389–94.   [7] See pp. 330–2.

2. Iam percusso ceu pastore,
     oves errant misere;
   Sic magistro descendente
       turbantur discipuli.
   Atque nos absente eo,
     dolor tenet nimius.

3. Sed eamus et ad eius
       properemus tumulum;
   Si dileximus viventem,
     diligamus mortuum.

Cividale CI[1]

In *St. Quentin 86*[2] only stanzas 2 and 3 are given. A much amended version of the first stanza is sung by the Marys towards the end of the work; this is in prose.

B. *A Prayer and the Decision to Buy Ointment*

1. Omnipotens Pater altissime,   10
     Angelorum rector mitissime,   10
   Quid faciemus non miserrime   10
     Heu, quantus est noster dolor! 9

2. Amisimus enim solatium,
     Jhesum Christum, Mariae
       filium;
   Ipse erat nostra solatio.
     Heu, quantus est noster dolor!

3. Sed eamus unguentum emere,
     Quo Dominum possimus
       unguere,
   Ipse erat nostra redemptio.
     Heu, quantus est noster dolor!

All three stanzas in:
Vich 105[3]
Zwickau A
Zwickau B (no music)
Zwickau C
Wolfenbüttel Helmst 965
Tours 927[4]
Dutch Easter Play[5]
St. Quentin 86 (in vernacular)
Narbonne (incipits only: no music).

C. *The Buying of the Ointment*
   (The Marys bargain with the Merchant)

1. Aromata precio querimus,   10
     Corpus Jesu ungere volumus; 10
   Aromata sunt odorifera   10
   Sepulture Christi memoria.   10

2. Huc propius flentes accedite,
     Et ungentum si vultis, emite,
   Aliter nusquam portabitis.
     Vere quantus est dolor vester! 9

The given stanzas do not represent all the existing metrical material concerned with this episode, but these are the most prominent. The first five are found in the Benediktbeuern MS.

Other occurrences are:
Wolfenbüttel 965, st. 2, 3, 4, 5
Prague VI.G.10a,[6] st. 1, 4.
Klosterneuberg 574,[7] st. 1, 4.

---

[1] See pp. 370–2.   [2] See pp. 364–9.   [3] See pp. 173–8.   [4] See pp. 292–304.
[5] See pp. 181–5.   [6] See pp. 374.   [7] See pp. 325–30.

3. Dic tu nobis, mercator iuvenis,
Hoc ungentum si tu vendideris,
Dic precium, pro quanto dederis.
Heu, quantus est dolor noster!

Prague VI.G.3b,[1] 1st stanza.

(Other Prague MSS without music not considered here.)

4. Dabo vobis ungenta optima,
Salvatoris ungere vulnera,
Sepulture eius in memoriam
Et nomini eius ad gloriam.

Vich 105 and *Tours 927*, varied workings of the same material.

St. Quentin 86—an extension of the scene in the vernacular.

5. Hoc ungentum si vultis emere,
Auri talentum michi tradite;
Aliter nusquam portabitis.
Vere quantus sit dolor vester!

Another stanza, sung by the Merchant, and found in the Vich and Tours manuscripts, should be mentioned.

6. Mulieres, michi intendite,
Hoc unguentum si vultis emere,
Datur genus mire potentie.
(Marys) Heu, quantus est noster dolor!

D. *The Lament of Mary Magdalen*

1. Cum venissem ungere mortuum, 10
Monumentum inveni vacuum. 10
Heu! nescio recte discernere 10
Ubi possim magistrum
querere. 10

A 'constant' set. All three stanzas found in the following:
Engelberg 314
Rheinau XVIII
Einsiedeln 300
Zwickau A & C
Zwickau B (no music)
Cividale C I
Klosterneuberg 574
Wolfenbüttel H. 965

2. Dolor crescit, tremunt precordia
De magistri pii absencia,
Qui salvavit me plenam viciis,
Pulsis a me septem demoniis.

3. En, lapis est vere depositus,
Qui fuerat cum signo positus.
Munierat locum militibus;
Locus vacat, illis absentibus.

E. *Christ's Words to Mary Magdalen*

1. Prima quidem suffragia
Stola tulit carnalia 8
Exhibendo communia 8
Se per nature munia. 8
(Mary) Sancte Deus! 8

All four verses found in the following:
Engelberg 314
Rheinau XVIII
Einsiedeln 300
Zwickau A & C

2. Hec priori dissimilis,
   Hec est incorruptibilis,
   Que dum fuit passabilis.
   Iam non erit solubilis.
   (Mary) Sancte fortis!

Zwickau B (no music)
Nuremberg 22928
Wolfenbüttel H. 965

3. Ergo noli me tangere,
   Nec ultra velis plangere,
   Quem mox in puro sydere
   Cernes ad Patrem scandere.
   (Mary) Sancte immortalis,
          miserere nobis!

4. Nam ignaros huius rei
   Fratres certos reddes mei;
   In Galyleam, dic, ut eant,
   Et me viventem videant.

F. *Mary Magdalen's Announcement to
   the Disciples, or to the other Marys*

1. Vere vidi Dominum vivere,   10
   Nec dimisit me pedes tangere;   10
   Discipulos oportet credere,   10
   Quod ad Patrem velit
                     ascendere.   10

Both stanzas used in:
Klosterneuberg 574

2. Galyleam omnes adibitis;
   Ibi Jesum vivium vidibitis;
   Quem post mortem vivum non
                        vidimus,
       Nos ibidem visuros credimus.

First only in:
Zwickau A & C
Cividale C I
Wolfenbüttel H. 965
Second only in:
St. Florian XI, 434[1]
(together with '*En, angeli*', below.)

(G.)
An additional stanza associated in the
St. Florian example with '*Galyleam
omnes*' above, is here given. Its usual
employment is by the Marys after their
dismissal by the Angels:

Used by the Marys after their
dismissal by the Angels in:
Klosterneuberg 574
Rheinau XVIII
Engelberg 314
Einsiedeln 300

En, angeli aspectum vidimus,   10
   Et responsum eius audivimus,   10
Qui testatur Dominim vivere;   10
   Sic oportet te, Symon, credere. 10

Used by the Marys (together with
'*Galyleam omnes*') as a reply to
'*Dic nobis*', in the St. Florian
example.

Since the great majority of the *Visitatio* versions containing *Zehnsilberspiel* stanzas give also musical settings to them, the melodies that
now accompany these verses must now be considered. I recall what I
have already said on p. 178—that there appear to have been six stanza
melodies employed throughout the type; these, like the rhyming

---

[1] See p. 387.

stanzas, reasonably consistent from one version to another. In the main, the individual melodies tend to remain faithful to their particular set of stanzas, but a certain amount of cross-borrowing will have to be noted. Any doubts and misunderstandings will, I hope, be cleared up by the chart which can be consulted on p. 319.

There will, then, be stanza-groups A to G, catered for by what I shall term Melodies I to VI. In the various original manuscripts the musical notations are presented in various ways. When one is lucky, one finds notes of quite definite pitch, sometimes (happily) on a four-line stave; sometimes carefully heighted above a horizontal line of known pitch-value; sometimes as a line of unheighted neumes. In the case of the last-named, their readings often rest on no more than a 'highly probable' basis.

From the succession of stanza-groups that have been set out above it should be clear what particular manuscript versions are available for consultation in each case.

On my own personal charts I have set out in comparative form every musical setting available to me of every stanza-group. It is manifestly impossible for me to reproduce all this material within the limits of this book. I have therefore had to devise some limits to reproduction. In the first case, that of Group A, Melody I, there are nine musical versions, four of them in unheighted neumes. I am proposing to set out the first stanza of the group with the earliest appearance of the melody in neumes; the earliest staved version; and the latest staved version.[1] These comprise, (a) *Einsiedeln, Stiftsb. MS 300*, pp. 93–4 (twelfth to thirteenth century); (b) *Engelberg, Stiftsb. MS 314*, f. 75v.–78v. (fourteenth century); (c) *Zwickau, Ratsschulb. MS B*, f. 7r.–10v. (sixteenth century). The six musical phrases that set the first stanza, given below, could be said to consist of the pattern a b c d c d. It will be seen that between the fourteenth-century Engelberg and the sixteenth-century Zwickau melodic versions, there is only a general resemblance at the start, but in the third sentence onward the settings are plainly united.

As for the music of the second and third stanzas, the general plan seems to have been to set the first half-line to a new phrase (X), while the remaining five half-lines re-employ the first stanza material, b c d c d. It is curious to observe Engelberg leaving its originally simple b material in the later stanzas and foreshadowing Zwickau's version. If I had the space I could call attention to various discrepancies and actual differences to be found here and there among the settings, but there is no doubt in my mind that there was a single source to the musical material associated with the three stanzas of ZHN A.

---

[1] I should have used as the earliest staved version, *Cividale, Museo Reale MS C1*, had not its first A stanza been missing owing to the loss of a manuscript page. Also I make no use in this instance of *St. Quentin MS 86*, since it does not present the group in the normal fashion.

'ZEHNSILBERSPIEL'

A. MELODY I (First Stanza):

Zehnsilberspiel B and its Melody II we have already met with on p. 174, in connection with *Vich 105* and the first manuscript appearance of the composition. The three ten-syllable stanzas have but that single stanza-tune, in the 'major key'. I will chart some of the remaining examples, none of which show much variation. In point of fact, the Vich version of the melody is not only the earliest surviving but also the most melismatic of all.

ZHN. B, MELODY II (All three Stanzas) :

Regarding the above three versions of the tune, the 'Dutch Easter Play' has already received notice (p. 181) as starting on G instead of the usual F, this pitch being possible owing to the fact that the leading note of the 'major key' melody is never called for. The Wolfenbüttel scribe starts on F and writes in the B flats for the first two sentences; but leaves them for the singer to supply in the last two. The St. Quentin example, which uses vernacular translations a great deal, is curious. In its version of '*Omnipotens* . . .' ('*Peres trestous puissans* . . .') (see Young, I, p. 413) it wrenches the rhythm of the three 10-syllable lines with refrain into four shorter vernacular lines with refrain, yet endeavours at the same time to keep to the original melody! Like the 'Dutch Easter Play' it starts the tune on G.

In the case of *Zehnsilberspiel C*, not only is the material employed by the versions much less constant, but we are concerned with three different melodies. One of them happens to be Melody II. The simple solution as to a setting found by such versions as *Vich 105*, *Tours 927*, *St. Quentin*, and *Wolfenbüttel* was to carry forward the music of ZHN B into the following scene, the number of syllables to the line still being 10. A new tune crops up in four versions, those from Prague, *MSS VI G 3b*, and *10a* (identical),[1] and from the Benediktbeuern and *Klosterneuburg 574 Visitatios*,[2] the last two having their music in unheighted neumes, but their close association with each other and the Prague melody clearly evident. I chart them below:

ZHN. C, MELODY III (First Stanza) :

Prague, MS G.3b employs the fourth, '*Dabo vobis . . .*' verse, but is unique in using for this occasion the setting which I shall soon be presenting as Melody VI.

The Benediktbeuern version, which employs five of the given verses, abandons Melody I after the first one, and gives other sets of neumes for the remainder. In the cases of three of them, these almost certainly represent Melody II. We have already found this happening in regard to *Vich 105*, *Tours 927* and others. The neumes of the remaining Benediktbeuern stanza ('*Dabo vobis . . .*') I cannot at present interpret.

But Melody III is also met with apart from the Merchant episode. The Klosterneuburg version uses it a great deal in scenes where the soldiers are concerned, and, in company with *Cividale MS C.1*, and the Wolfenbüttel and Zwickau (A & C) manuscripts, employs it as a setting for '*Vere vidi Dominum vivere . . .*' (ZHN F). A curious point about the Zwickau and Wolfenbüttel versions of the melody is that the setting of the first two words is, in each case, not the usual one, but borrowed from the music of ZHN D ('*Cum venissem . . .*'). After these first few notes both manuscripts revert to Melody III. Why this should be so I have no idea; I can merely record it.

[1] See pp. 372–4.   [2] See pp. 325–32.

The music of *Zehnsilberspiel* D, the lament of Mary Magdalen, as shown in the eight examples that I have (five of them line-versions), indicates a single strophic melody, with not very much variation in the various manuscripts. Three settings of the first verse are given, and these I have chosen to indicate the maximum amount of discrepancy. The music I shall term Melody IV.

ZHN. D, MELODY IV (First Stanza):

In three examples, *Engelberg 314*, *Einsiedeln 300*, and *Rheinau XVIII*, the verse beginning '*En, angeli aspectum . . .*' is found set to Melody IV. Its position, immediately previous to '*Cum venissem . . .*' in each case, seems to have invited this. '*En angeli aspectum . . .*' also appears in a 'second stage' example, *St. Florian, MS 434*, where it is set to an entirely different melody.

Zehnsilberspiel E, comprising the four stanzas which the risen Christ addresses to the Magdalen, has only one setting, which I term Melody V. I know of six extant manuscripts showing this music, three on staves and three in neume form. Of these latter, the *Nuremberg MS 22923* has suffered some defacement. *Engelberg 314* and *Wolfenbüttel 965*, two-line versions, will serve as representative examples:

ZHN. E, MELODY V (First Stanza):

316

In the case of the Wolfenbüttel version, stanzas 3 and 4 each prefer for their last word ('*scandere*' and '*videant*' respectively) the music employed by the Engelberg manuscript, i.e. fm rm m-. Stanzas 3 and 4 of the Engelberg version have a few notes which differ from corresponding places in the first two. These may represent errors in copying, and anyway the general effect is that of a common strophic setting. The remaining versions, *Rheinau XVIII*, *Einsiedeln 300*, *Zwickau MSS A & C of XXXVI, 1. 24*, and *Nuremberg 22923*, agree in having a normal standard melody, but the fourth stanza music consists of the *second* half of the melody (starting t m t d) and used twice over.

As will be seen from the stanzas of ZHN E, set out on pp. 310–11, Mary utters each of her three adoring phrases, '*Sancte Deus!*; *Sancte fortis!*' after each of the first three stanzas of Christ. The words are, of course, liturgical, to be found in the Roman Gradual (*Feria VI in Parasceve, ad Missam Praesanctificatorum*). The music of the versions, however, is not that of the liturgy. It will be sufficient if I give the neumes of *Einsiedeln 300* (twelfth to thirteenth centuries) and the staved notes of the fifteenth-century *Wolfenbüttel 965*, since the versions using the settings differ only in quite small details.

Two somewhat footloose stanzas used by Mary Magdalen to tell of her meeting with the risen Christ I have named as *Zehnsilberspiel* F. In point of fact they come together, as far as I know, only in Klosterneuberg 574. In this manuscript the first, '*Vere vidi . . .*', is set to Melody IV, while the second, '*Galyleam omnes . . .*', although immediately succeeding the other, has the same music as is associated with it in a fifteenth-century, 'second stage' Visitatio from *St. Florian, MS 474*. This I shall term Melody VI. I give below the settings from these two manuscripts:

ZHN. F, MELODY VI

Much more will be seen of Melody VI when the extensive Easter drama from Klosterneuberg, *MS 574,* is considered more fully. One surprising use of it is worthy of mention. In the Prague manuscript *G. 10a,* showing a *Visitatio* (see p. 374), two verses of Section C appear, the Marys using '*Aromata precio . . .*' and the Merchant replying with '*Dabo vobis . . .*'. The first stanza is set to Melody III, a usual practice, but '*Dabo vobis . . .*' to Melody VI is, as far as I am aware, an altogether unique occurrence.

It must also be noted that the remaining single appearances of '*Vere vidi . . .*' in the *Cividale CI,* Zwickau, and Wolfenbüttel manuscripts are associated with Melody III. In the cases of the last two there is the curious fact that the first few notes undoubtedly belong to Melody VI.

Regarding the Marys' 'additional' stanza, beginning '*En angeli aspectum vidimus . . .*', and which I have labelled as 'G', I can here summarize the musical information concerning it by saying that it is set to Melody IV in the versions from Engelberg, Rheinau, and Einsiedeln, and Melody VI in those from St. Florian and Klosterneuburg 574.

I give below in tabular form a concise summary of the relationships between the various stanza groups and the melodies that are associated with them.

Notes on the table opposite:

[1] The capital letters refer to the stanza groups (see pp. 330 ff.), and the Roman numbers to the melodies as set out, I to VI. In the case of Section C I have given in small figures the number of the stanzas employed in each particular drama. In Section F the letters 'v' and 'g' refer to the uses of the stanzas beginning, respectively, '*Vere vidi*' and '*Galyleam omnes*'.

[2] This Benediktbeuern detail is not quite correctly described. Stanza 1 ('*Aromata precio*') is set to Melody III, three others to Melody II, and '*Dabo vobis*' to unheighted neumes that I cannot identify.

[3] Other melodies (as far as I know, unique to Wolfenbüttel) are given to some of its vernacular stanzas.

ZEHNSILBERSPIEL[1]

Century	MS	Stanza Groups and Melody Numbers					'Vere vidi' and 'Gal. omnes'	'En angeli aspectum'
12th	Vich 105		BII	CII (3, 6, 5)				IV
12–13th	Einsiedeln 300	AI			DIV	EV		IV
12–13th and 15th	'Dutch Easter Play'		BII	CII	DIV	EV		
13th	Klosterneuberg 574			CIII (1, 4)	DIV		F { IV(v.) VI(g.) }	VI
13th	Benediktbeuern (Mch. 4660a)	AI		CIII & II (1 to 5)[2]	DIV	EV		
13th	Rheinau XVIII	AI			DIV	EV		IV
13th	Nuremberg 22923	AI			DIV	EV		
13th	Tours 927		BII	CII (3, 6, 5)				
14th	Engelberg 314	AI			DIV	EV		IV
14th	Cividale C I	AI			DIV		FIII(v.)	
14th	St. Quentin 86	AI (modified)	BII (vernacular)	CII (vernacular)	DIV		FIII(v.)	
14th	Prague VI.G.3b			CIII (1)				
14th	Prague G. 10a			C { III(1) VI(4) }				
15th	Wolfenbüttel H. 9653	AI	BII	CII (3, 5)	DIV	EV	FIV(v.)	
15th	St. Florian XI 434							
16th	Zwickau XXXVI, A & C		BII		DIV	EV	FVI(g.)	VI
16th	Zwickau XXXVI, B	AI			DIV	EV	FIII(v.)	
		AI	B (no music)	C { III(1) VI(4) }	D (no music) E (no music)			

For the sake of completeness I add details of a few more versions which include one or another of these stanza groups but without giving the music. I have omitted some Prague examples which follow those above in using C only. The texts of all these given are mostly incipits.

15th (?)	Narbonne		B			
15th	Barking (Oxf. Un. Coll. MS 169)	A(1)				
15th	St. Gall 448	A			D	E
15th	Wolfenbüttel MS Aug. 84	A			D(1)	E	F(v.)

A glance at our main list of texts and melodies will show objections to certain of Meyer's statements as set down by Karl Young, and re-quoted on my pp. 305–6. For example, the combination of A, B, and C does occur in Germany, and as often as it does in France, that is, once in each case. Moreover, the German (Wolfenbüttel) example is the more satisfactory of the two, since the Section C stanzas of St. Quentin are in French and are not literal translations. I have already called attention to the fact that the Wolfenbüttel version, although very largely in the vernacular, contains every one of the sections detailed, in Latin verse. Thus it is a unique example of the 'complete' *Zehnsilberspiel*. Meyer seems mistaken, also, in saying that the combination of the groups A, D, E, and F represents a normal German arrangement. It would seem to be mostly A, D, and E only, with the frequent addition of the '*En, angeli vidimus . . .*' stanza, set to one or another of the melodies.

The origin of the merchant-scene in France, or in some French-influenced region, seems borne out by the appearance of the B and C material in the twelfth-century Vich manuscript set to Melody II. This setting survives through the centuries and is never challenged in Section B, while holding its own against later intruders in C.

That Sections D, E, and F were composed in Germany is probable enough by reason of their distribution in the manuscripts, but if additional confirmation were wanted, it can be found in the fact that the melodies employed, III, IV, and V, do not appear in any French versions.

But I feel less satisfied with Meyer's contention that the three stanzas of Section A were composed in France and taken to Germany. The only French version containing Section A is to be found in the St. Quentin manuscript of the fourteenth century. In this the Marys sing as their opening lament the second and third stanzas only. The setting reveals itself as a transposed and tortured version of Melody I, with some scattered B flat accidentals which would probably be better employed for clef purposes. A variation of the first stanza, however, appears towards the end of the work, sung by the three Marys after Christ has departed (see p. 368). It is in prose form, and is as follows: '*Eya! nobis internas mentes pulsat gaudium pro nostro consolatore, quem gaudemus hodie cum triumpho victorie a mortuis resurgere.*' The music accompanying it is a further altered and distorted version of the original stanza-setting. Evidently, then, this transfer of a passage, much amended, and finally changed from verse to prose is a later re-shaping of the original form. Throughout the numerous German examples (one of them, *Einsiedeln 300*, dating from the twelfth or early thirteenth century) the three stanzas are consistent, and there is very little divergence in the various versions of the melody. No other surviving French manuscript contains these stanzas. The fifteenth-century Barking *Visitatio* shows the first stanza (and that only) in its normal form as found in the German manuscripts. It would seem then, that although the ten-syllable stanza type probably first arose in France, this particular group of stanzas was of German composition.

I shall now, in the following chapter, discuss those five or so major German examples of the *Visitatio Sepulchri* belonging to the thirteenth century which made common use of the *Zehnsilberspiel* framework.

CHAPTER FOURTEEN

THE THIRTEENTH CENTURY (2)

The *Zehnsilberspiel* Easter dramas
The Benediktbeuern 'Passion' dramas
Peregrinus dramas. Dramas of the
Christmas season

THE thirteenth-century *Visitatio Sepulchri* examples that remain to be dealt with are all German in origin, and all of them examples of the *Zehnsilberspiel* type, each making use in its own way of the common texts and music.

We begin with the version from the monastery of Rheinau in Switzerland.[1] Although the closely-packed text is supplied with a setting of no more than unheighted St. Gall style neumes, the whole of the music can be given a staved interpretation, with no more than a few instances of doubt. Links between Rheinau and the fourteenth-century *Engelberg MS 314* will become apparent when we meet with the music of the latter. Once again I shall refer the reader to Karl Young's readings of the texts (I, pp. 385–9).

After a generous first rubric, which sets the scene and makes some attempt to detail the costuming, a choral 'antiphon' is sung, describing the intentions of the Marys. An incipit only, '*Maria Magdalena*' with its unheighted neumes, is given. These neumes, which appear to indicate d m̲f̲s̲ s ' s f̲m̲ f̲s̲ s-, make it necessary to correct Karl Young's reading of the text of the rest of the item, since this music, as *Engelberg 314* makes plain, belongs to a non-liturgical composition, the text of which continues as '. . . *et Maria Jacobi et Salome sabbato quidem . . .*' and gives us the right number of Marys for the cast.

The movement of the Marys to the Tomb is straightforward—the three stanzas of the ZHN A to Melody I, the neumes interpreting themselves quite happily. The Marys' pause before the Tomb ('*Quis revolvet nobis lapidem . . .*') is non-liturgical and again German, a setting used by *Einsiedeln 300*, *Melk 1094*, and *Klosterneuberg 574*.

But the identity of the dialogue at the Tomb which follows is quite unexpected, since *Rheinau XVIII*, unlike the rest of the German *Zehnsilberspiel* group, chooses to use the older form of the St. Gall '*Quem quaeritis*' dialogue, musical rhyme and all, instead of the '*Quem quaeritis, O tremulae mulieres . . .*' version.

Both items that follow, '*Venite et videte . . .*' and '*Ad monumentum*

---

[1] *Zurich, Zentralbibl., Rheinau XVIII*, pp. 282–3 (a *lectionarium*).

venimus . . .', are set to their usual music, the former liturgical (Hartker), the latter specially composed, but employed by centuries of *Visitatio* versions. Thence onward the Rheinau drama runs for some distance a parallel course with the fourteenth-century *Engelberg 314*. Both share what seems to be an unnecessarily early introduction of the Apostle Peter, in order to justify the use by Mary Magdalen of ZHN G—the '*En angeli aspectum . . .*' stanza. Apparently Peter disappears again, and then comes Mary's lament: '*Cum venissem ungere . . .*'—all three stanzas of ZHN D, set to Melody IV, which, by the way, had been employed for '*En angeli aspectum . . .*'.

For the first moments of the Christ-Magdalen exchange, Rheinau unaccountably leaves without neumes the 'Gardener's' first question, '*Mulier, quid ploras?*' But the '*Maria'*–'*Rabbi*' ('*Rabboni*') setting that it gives belongs firmly to Einsiedeln of the twelfth to thirteenth centuries and Zwickau of the sixteenth. Christ's '*Noli me tangere . . .*', except for a couple of notes, comes again straight from *Einsiedeln 300*.

Use now is made of ZHN E with Melody V, as Christ expounds the Resurrection to Mary ('*Prima quidem . . .*') and the latter intersperses her adoring phrases ('*Sancte Deus*', etc.) after each of the stanzas. Rheinau, in each of the settings, shows in its neumes a general conformity with the standard melodies.

Christ then departs, and Mary returns to the Sepulchre to the sound of the lyrical first part of '*Victimae Paschali*'. The interrogation of Mary by the chorus then follows, but is interrupted by an unusual feature, the 'race' to the Sepulchre by Peter and John, accompanied not by the usual choral performance of '*Currebant duo simul . . .*' but by their own singing of three stanzas of the ancient hymn, '*Jhesu, nostra redemptio . . .*', while they are in full flight! This must have raised an interesting production problem. As for the normal '*Currebant duo simul . . .*', this is employed (uniquely) to fill the moments of the entry of the disciples into the Tomb and their recovery of the grave-clothes. There come performances of three more liturgical pieces; the anti-Jewish '*Dicant nunc Judaei . . .*', the 'verse' ('*Quod enim vivit . . .*') from the antiphon, '*Christus resurgens . . .*', and the antiphon '*Surrexit enim sicut . . .*'.

To round off, and to lead to the '*Te Deum laudamus*', we have the choral singing of the last two sections of '*Victimae Paschali*', the first of which ('*Credendum est magis . . .*') is no longer in the Roman service books. There is a final mention of the blessing of the 'populus' who have turned up to witness the performance.

This version, with its generous and informative rubrics, must no doubt have been successful dramatically. The common *Zehnsilberspiel* material is on the whole well handled, in spite of what seems an unnecessary dragging in of Peter and '*En angeli aspectum . . .*'. There might also be the criticism that the final piling up of secondary evidence as to the Resurrection tends to fall rather flat, occurring as it does after the actual appearance of the living Christ. But this criticism applies to most of the *Zehnsilberspiel* versions.

The Nuremberg example[1] (Young, I, pp. 397–401), although much of its material is 'stock', has excellent and graphic rubrics as to actions, tones of voice, and intentions. Young (I, p. 401) calls attention to several such instances, as well as the unusual action on the part of a playwright—that of deliberately *altering* a word of the liturgy. When Mary sings the '*Victimae paschali*' sentence concerning the belief that Christ had risen from the grave, the word '*Scimus*' is found altered (uniquely) to '*Scio*', making the matter personal to her.

Nuremberg's music is set down in St. Gall unheighted neumes. Most but not all of these neumes are capable of being interpreted on staves. It leads off with a faulty item. The first choral antiphon is worded '*Maria Magdalena et alia Maria . . .*', one of the type mentioning only two Marys, its identity confirmed by its neumes; this (unlike Rheinau XVIII's choice) being unsuitable for a work which immediately afterwards mentions three Marys.

The opening lament of the women (ZHN A to Melody I); the ubiquitous free composition, '*Ad monumentum venimus . . .*'; and the similar type '*Quis revolvet nobis ab ostio lapidem . . .*' have very recognizable versions of their usual melodies. The '*Quem quaeritis*' exchange follows, but this time in the more usual form found among the *Zehnsilberspiel* group—'*Quem quaeritis, o tremulae mulieres . . .*', etc. Quite normal is the setting of the free composition, '*Ad monumentum venimus . . .*'.

The next item, '*Heu! redemptio Israhel, ut quid mortem sustinuit . . .*', is familiar enough, but its presentation unique. Its music is recognizable, but it is sung, without its other associated verses, by the three Marys in turn. Also, between the singing of the individual Marys, the chorus strikes in with two successive sentences ('*Maria plorans . . .*' and '*Non sufficiens . . .*') which, as far as I am aware, are unique to *Visitatio* versions. They may be ancient responses, but I cannot interpret the neumes in either case.

The exchanges between the risen Christ and Mary are couched in the usual terms, including the unfortunate use of the Biblical gloss '*quod dicitur magister*'. It is strange to think that the playwright who could make a number of subtle and unusual points in his drama should be so imitative in this matter. Although on this particular page the manuscript is badly rubbed and damaged in places, rendering some of the stanza words and a number of the neumes illegible, it is clear that the music of the items is on familiar lines.

The rest of the drama consists of entirely recognizable material. ZHN E, to Melody V, Christ's address to Mary, is carried through with one exceptional feature; the three groups of Mary's interspersed words, '*Sancte fortis . . .*', etc., are here sung continuously, after the third of Christ's stanzas.

Apparently, Christ then disappears, and we have the arrival of the two disciples, singing the hymn, '*Jhesu, nostra redemptio . . .*', the stanzas

[1] Nuremberg, *Germanisches Nationalmuseum, MS 22923*, fols. 105v.–107v.

given in incipit form but the usual setting apparent. On this occasion they make no attempt to race while singing it!

Thereafter, we meet with the whole of '*Victimae paschali*' in incipit form, with, in the second part, the disciples questioning Mary, and the chorus striking in with the last line of the sequence.

Then, rather late in the day for it to matter, the disciples race to the Tomb to the usual choral singing of '*Currebant duo simul . . .*', recover the grave-clothes and display them to the choir, while singing the non-liturgical '*Cernitis, o socii . . .*' to the usual music. Then comes the antiphon '*Surrexit enim sicut . . .*', but before the choir proceeds to the '*Te Deum*' there occurs the rubric '*Populo interim acclamante*', followed by the phrase '*Christ ist erstanden*', together with neumes. Undoubtedly these three words represent an incipit—an invitation for the populace to participate in this famous vernacular hymn.[1]

I turn now to the two closely linked German *Zehnsilberspiel* dramas of the thirteenth century, to which I have already made reference. The first to be considered is the manuscript from the Augustinian canonry of Klosterneuberg.[2]

The relevant section, the last in the manuscript, is called *Ordo Paschalis*, and occupies four and a half closely written pages, the speeches for the most part being accompanied by 'campo aperto' German neumes. These, seemingly, having in the past been neglected, I have myself transcribed them from photographs of the original pages. Much material can be readily recognized, and *Zehnsilberspiel* verses and melodies play their parts. It is a moot point, indeed, as to whether some of the ZHN melodies here employed do not appear for the very first time.[3] The earliest effective editor of the manuscript, H. Pfeiffer, once suggested that the drama was arranged by a member of the fraternity at Klosterneuberg in 1204, for the special benefit of Duke Leopold VI, who paid an Easter visit to the monastery in that year. This statement may be no more than a speculation.

Regarding the unheighted neumes of the work, I have one great regret—that I cannot interpret those of the melody (apparently a mildly melismatic one) to which the Roman guard sing their five stanzas while making a circuit of the Tomb. A few other brief passages which baffle me I shall detail in due course. But the fact remains that the music of the Klosterneuberg *Visitatio* could, for performance purposes, be almost wholly restored, thanks to evidence drawn from other manuscripts. I shall, in the course of tracing the progress of the work, identify the various melodies.

---

[1] See pp. 162–3 (Chapter IX) for the text and music of a stanza of this hymn. The Nuremberg version is slightly more elaborate than usual in its settings of the third word.

[2] *Klosterneuberg, Stiftsbibl., MS 574*, fols. 142v.–144v. The first important editing of the text was undertaken by H. Pfeiffer in 1908, revised in 1913. It has had further editorial attention from Karl Young (I, pp. 421–32). In each case the criticisms were based on considerations of the text only.

[3] This is always a dangerous kind of speculation, since more of these Church dramas have perished, probably, than have survived. (This, of course, represents another speculation.)

A striking feature concerning the Klosterneuberg *Visitatio* is that text and music seem to show the work of two separate scribes. Furthermore, there is the bewildering fact that a large portion of the text together with its neumes has been written twice over, and that all this waste of valuable vellum occurs in order that one of the sections may change its place in the order of events. Through these repetitions and the placings of a couple of none too obvious square brackets, the net result is a correction which ensures that (I quote Karl Young) 'the negotiations of the high priests and the soldiers are disposed of before the occurrence of more significant incidents in which the soldiers are not concerned' (I, p. 430). Since Karl Young has again numbered the lines of text in his transcriptions, I shall again take advantage of the fact for the purposes of reference.

The opening rubric speaks first of Pilate, who enters to the choral singing of a 'responsory', given in incipit form as '*Ingressus Pilatus . . .*' Karl Young points out that the only known liturgical responsory ('*Ingressus Pilatus cum Jesu in praetorium . . .*'—Hartker, p. 9) hardly fills the bill. In any case the incipit has no neumes. There follows a brief exchange between the priests and Pilate concerning the former's wish to have a guard on the Tomb. The first four stanzas (ll. 1–16) are set to ZHN Melody III. The playwright apparently now thinks some kind of relief necessary in the music, since the priests, offering bribes to the soldiers, do so to ZHN Melody VI. The soldiers' reply-stanza returns to Melody III, and then, as they march round the Tomb expanding the theme '*Non credimus Christum resurgere . . .*' (ll. 25–44) they do so to the tune that I have regretfully described to myself as Melody 'X'.

There now appears the sword-bearing angel, smiting down the guard and singing a passage which begins, '*Alleluia; Resurrexit victor ab infernis . . .*' (ll. 45–60). Once again the neumes might have proved insoluble but for the fact that a fifteenth-century 'first stage' *Visitatio* from Melk[1] reproduces the passage, with its music in Gothic notation on four-line staves. The Melk syllable-groupings do not always coincide with those of Klosterneuberg, but there is no doubt that they represent the same basic setting.

As the soldiers lie stricken, a brief version of the Merchant Scene (II, 61–8) begins; actually two stanzas of ZHN C, set to the hard-worked Melody III. Incidentally, it could be remarked that *Klosterneuberg* is living up to the title of '*Zehnsilberspiel*', since thus far we have had very little else other than ten-syllable lines.

Familiar material continues, this time in prose. The '*Quis revolvet . . .*' question has rather a special setting, found in such versions as *Einsiedeln 300*, *Rheinau XVIII*, and more especially in *Melk 1094*, and *St. Florian VI 434*, the last-named of the fifteenth century and the 'second stage' (see my pp. 387–8).

The less usual question and reply at the Tomb (ll. 70–1) replaces the normal '*Quem quaeritis*' exchange. The text turns up also in the *B.N. 904*

---

[1] Melk, *Stiftsbibl.*, MS *1094*, fols. 35r.–38v. (fifteenth century). See my p. 387.

and *Tours 927* versions, but I cannot see any connections between their settings and the simple neumes given here. The Angel's passage which follows, '*Nolite expavescere . . .*' (ll. 71–4), is found almost exactly reproduced in the two fifteenth-century versions from St. Florian and Melk. There is a similar near-agreement in the case of the music.

After the Angel returns to the Sepulchre and before the Marys can report this to the disciples there occurs a surprising scribal insertion. Half way through the rubric that we have just reached, between the words '*Sepulchrum*' and '*Tunc*', a scribe has inserted a right-angled bracket (⌐). The intended effect of this, apparently, coupled with a similar, but reversed, bracket (¬), met with 49 lines further on, is to cancel—wipe out—all the material between the brackets and start afresh afterwards. As regards Karl Young's Volume I, one could reckon as non-existent p. 424 from the rubric word '*Tunc*' to the end of the page, together with the whole of p. 425. The second bracket, if transferred to Karl Young's transcription, would be sited, conveniently enough, after the very last word on p. 425 ('*credimus*').

The same textual scribe now makes a new start. Instead of Mary encountering the disciples with ZHN G, Melody VI, the scene is abandoned, to be used later. In Young's volume, we find ourselves at the top of p. 426. The Roman guards have revived and have returned to the High Priests to report. The six four-line stanzas (every line of ten syllables!) are, as far as I am aware, unique to this manuscript (ll. 124–47).

But the music is not. The first stanza of the soldiers, '*Nobis autem . . .*' is set to ZHN, Melody III, but by way of a change, the second uses ZHN, Melody VI. The *Pontifices* think this a good idea and reply ('*Que refertis . . .*' and '*Morem nobis . . .*'), employing the same tune twice more, and at the same time offering further bribes to the guards for the spreading of false news, i.e., that the disciples have stolen the body.

The guards react as expected, but in the manuscript a scribal crisis is apparent. The writing out of the text on fol. 143v., together with its neumes, finishes half-way along the second line of the soldiers' first stanza, at '*sparsim*' (l. 140). Looking across to the manuscript's fol. 144r. we discover that new hands have taken over, both in regard to texts and music, and that in the middle of a line of poetry. One can but wonder as to the sudden change. Was it anything to do with the contretemps concerned with the pages of repetition? The first script seemed clear enough, but the neume writing may perhaps have been thought unusually sprawling. Certainly the new music scribe used less ink for his neumes, and a smaller, more upright and more St. Gall-like style of notation. He had ideas of his own, as well. It is amusing to note that the setting of the stanza that was taken over by the new hands, and which for a line and a half consisted of ZHN, Melody VI, was promptly amended by the newcomer, and for the remainder of the stanza is quite plainly Melody III. And yet, for the second and last of the soldiers' stanzas ('*In ruinam . . .*') the music undoubtedly returns to Melody VI!

We come now (l. 148) to the re-writing of the bracket-cancelled part. The rubric, *'Tunc Mariae . . .'*, is written again, and the cancelled part takes on its new look. Comparing the two versions one finds in the second a few differences, both textual and musical. We may assume these, perhaps, to be scribal corrections or errors of copying, as we choose. I shall take note of a few cases.

The Marys, in their new placing, now greet the disciples with *'En angeli aspectum . . .'* to the second music scribe's version of Melody VI. The reply of Peter and John (ll. 152–3), a goliard-style rhythm and a welcome change from ten syllables, appears unique. I am not able to transcribe its neumes.[1] The pair then hasten to the Tomb, without, however, the usual antiphon comment from the choir, and share in the recovery of the grave-clothes. Their words to each other, *'Monumentum inveni vacuum . . .'* (we are back with ten syllables) is repeated in slightly amended form as they return to the main body of the disciples. Both stanzas use Melody III.

Mary Magdalen now enters alone to the empty scene and begins her three-stanza lament, ZHN D, to Melody IV (ll. 162–73). It is followed by an insertion not found in the first writing-out, the widely encountered two lines beginning, *'Heu! redemptio Israel . . .'*. The scribe has not chosen to add the usual neumes.

The normal texts of the Christ-Magdalen scene now commence, but whoever was writing out the music was beginning to tire of his task rather more quickly than his predecessor, and from now on I shall frequently have to refer back to the first setting-down of the neumes, since we now meet with items which the second scribe has left without their music, for no apparent reason.

The often employed text (*'Quia*) *tulerunt Dominum meum . . .'* has collected several Church-drama settings and a couple of liturgical ones, but Klosterneuberg's neumes are difficult to reconcile with any of them.[2] On the other hand, the music of *'Domine, si tu sustulisti eum . . .'* and *'Noli me tangere . . .'* (l. 179 & l. 183) seems close to a number of other German settings.

There now occurs a notable feature, no less than a dramatic version of the Harrowing of Hell. After Christ's gentle rebuff of Mary (*'Noli me tangere . . .'*) two Angels appear and precede Christ on his path *ad Infernum*. How all the dramatic actions which now occur were stage-managed we have no clue. However, we have already met with the traditional legend of the Harrowing of Hell, which had found expression in the apocryphal Gospel of Nicodemus, and had been associated with the last four verses of the 24th Psalm. Both sources inspired the semi-

[1] Could they indicate some kind of adaptation of Melody VI to the changed verbal rhythms?

[2] Chart IV affords comparisons between the musical settings of the brief but highly dramatic exchanges between Christ and Mary Magdalen, as treated by a number of French and German versions. It will be seen that Klosterneuberg's melismatic music shows no resemblance to that of any of the others here shown, except perhaps that found in the fourteenth-century *Cividale MS CI*. Even this appears somewhat distant.

dramatic *Elevatio* ceremony, and that of a consecration of a church, as well as the famous antiphon, '*Cum rex gloriae . . .*'.

It is the last-named composition that the first Klosterneuberg writing-out makes use of. The two Angels are directed to sing it as a processional song, and the first words, with the standard antiphon neumes, are given as an incipit. Some of the Psalm phrases are employed in the dialogue between Christ, breaking down the gates, and *Diabolus* within. From the antiphon is taken the cry of the worthy souls, anticipating the delivery that Christ would bring to them from the common fate of all mankind since Adam's fall.

It is strange that the second writing out should call on the Angels to sing the liturgical antiphon '*Surrexit Christus et illuxit populo suo . . .*' instead of (more to the point) '*Cum rex gloriae . . .*'. However, it comes into line with the first after this, including the use of the antiphon phrase, '*Advenisti, desiderabilis!*' and continues so, except for the fact that the second music scribe, after writing the neumes of '*Surrexit Christus . . .*', resigns his task from there on.[1]

How exactly the Harrowing scene is closed is not apparent. However, we are immediately presented with the Marys singing the stanzas '*Vere vidi Dominum . . .*' and '*Galileam omnes adibitis . . .*', the latter addressed to the '*Apostoli*' (ZHN F), both of them sung to Melody IV (ll, 194–201).[2]

The remainder of the drama relies almost altogether on familiar material. The Apostles, who have been 'murmuring' the hymn '*Jesu, nostra redemptio . . .*' (this rubric is worth noting) now break out eagerly with the '*Dic nobis . . .*' question of '*Victimae paschali*', replied to by Mary Magdalen, with the 'Apostles' concluding the sequence from '*Credendum est magis . . .*' onward.

There follows the usual '*Cernitis, o socii . .*' that accompanies the display of the grave-clothes. Both the latter action and Mary's 'sequence' evidence might have been considered unimportant by an audience who had previously witnessed a representation of the resurrected Christ.

A problem remains, the singing by the chorus of the antiphon '*Currebant duo simul . . .*' normally associated with the Race to the Sepulchre. It is surely misplaced here (l, 218).

On the previous line an incipit indicates the singing of an antiphon. It may turn out to be one found on p. 230 of Hartker's Antiphonale, but in the absence of neumes there is no proof. Anyway, it is now obsolete. Finally, the cantor begins the general singing of the vernacular '*Crist der ist erstanden*'.

Although there is no mention of '*Te Deum laudamus*', it does seem probable that the drama was performed in the monastic church, but not necessarily in the traditional position at the end of Easter Matins. Perhaps Pfeiffer's suggestion as to a special 'celebrity' performance is a sound one.

---

[1] The second scribe must be awarded another censure. In his copying he misses out the *Diabolus* question, '*Quis est iste rex gloriae?*', that is given in the first account.

[2] This fact is of course gained from the *first* writing out.

In spite of all the imperfections revealed in regard to the writing down, the Klosterneuberg version is a very important one. In it, certain materials may have appeared for the first time, such as the ZHN C stanza, '*Dabo vobis . . .*', and perhaps the two settings, Melody III and VI. Other originalities appear to be the goliardic and sceptical lines of Peter and John (ll, 79–80), as well as the break away from the normal '*Quem quaeritis*' exchanges in the sepulchre scene. Some very graphic rubrics will also be noted.

The shortcomings that the manuscript reveals in the matter of setting-down may have been largely righted in actual performance. If so, a moving example of medieval music-drama would have been revealed.

The next version to be considered is an incomplete one, but indeed a close companion of Klosterneuberg's. It is to be found in the famous thirteenth-century manuscript known as the *Carmina Burana*. Of this Karl Young says (I, p. 432):

> This varied collection of poems—joyous and sober, pious and licentious—is preserved in a manuscript of the late thirteenth century, found in the year 1803 at the Bavarian monastery of Benediktbeuern. It may have been the repertory of wandering scholars, or, more probably, the valued possession of a monastic community which desired to have its own anthology of the vivacious literary inventions of the *vagantes*.

Bound up with the rest are the two leaves that contain the Sepulchre drama.[1] They are cut at the top and damaged at the edges, but the very clear text, closely written, with 'campo aperto' German neumes, has not suffered at all.

A remarkable feature about this version is that a great deal of the material—more than half the lines in fact—is found in the Klosterneuberg drama, set to very much the same music. In spite of this borrowing, the Benediktbeuern version contains a good deal that seems to be original. Once again it is not possible to restore the music in absolute completeness, for neumes that baffled me in the Klosterneuberg version appear once more. Again I have to content myself with noting the familiar melodies. Again, I give Karl Young's numberings of the lines of verse.

The first scene is close to that of Klosterneuberg's, but is indeed an improvement on it. The opening rubrics are more informative, and reveal the presence of new figures, Pilate's wife and the *Assessores*, apparently a body of counsellors. The first phrase, '*Cantatis Matutinis in die Paschae . . .*', makes the liturgical attachment of the drama certain. Again the ambiguous '*Ingressus Pilatus*' incipit occurs, again without music. The first two stanzas, sung by the Priests and Pilate respectively, are almost exactly as in Klosterneuberg. Melody III is employed in both versions, with Melody VI as a contrast.[2] But some changes occur; the

---

[1] Munich, *Staatsbibl.*, *MS lat. 4660a, Carmina Burana saec. xiii*, fols. Vr.–VIv.

[2] It is to be noted in the course of a consideration of the manuscript that when successive stanza texts are given the same tune, there are often small discrepancies to be met with between successive reproductions of neume settings, such as could not possibly be explained as 'variations'. We have met with such instances before.

Assessores take over a stanza belonging to the Priests in the Kloster-neuberg drama, and also, freshly composed stanzas are employed. Another new feature is the introduction of a body of Jews (Young, p. 433, ll, 22–5). Their rhythmic, 'goliardic' verses are set to a melody that I much regret not being able to identify, for the passage, in what might be called '*Stabat Mater*' rhythm, undoubtedly provides an attractively dramatic few moments.

The scene continues, after Pilate's '*En habetis . . .*' (Melody III), with stanzas not previously encountered. These include the incident of the Jews bribing the Soldiers. However, the music remains familiar, Melody III relieved by Melody VI. The last lines of the Jews, sung while handing over the money, abandon the 'ten syllables' for a more irregular pattern, set to neumes that I cannot interpret (ll. 44–5).

There follows now something of a return to Klosterneuberg. The Soldiers depart to the Sepulchre, the stanza '*Defensores erimus . . .*' is sung to Melody III, and then come the five stanzas (ll. 50–69), with their refrain '*Schawe propter insidias*', set to neumes closely resembling those of the Klosterneuberg version. The rubrics make it clear that each of the five soldiers is to be allotted a solo verse, with (probably) the refrain sung in chorus. I am inclined to think that this is what happened in the Klosterneuberg version, in this instance the practice being taken as a matter of course. The Church drama is able to show plenty of examples of this device.

Once again the striking down of the Soldiers is enacted, this time by two Angels, to music closely resembling that of Klosterneuberg, and interpretable from the Melk *Visitatio*. But the material is briefer and slightly rearranged.

It would seem that Benediktbeuern had later ambitions regarding this scene, since on the top margin of fol. VIr., partly destroyed by a trimming of the vellum, is an added passage in another hand, with some added neumes. This insertion, possibly more of a reminder than a worked-out episode, seems to suggest that somebody or other was seeking to drama-tize the actual Resurrection, with sung texts for an Angel and Christ ('*dominica persona*'), the latter assuming the guise of a gardener prepara-tory to encountering Mary Magdalen. Anyway, the scene is now abruptly changed.

Most of what follows will be found to be familiar. The 'Ointment purchase' scene of the Marys (ZHN C) now begins (ll. 80–99). Benedikt-beuern is exceptional in employing all five stanzas, leading off with Melody III, followed by a couple of uses of Melody II. But when the *Apotecarius* employs the '*Dabo vobis . . .*' stanza, he sings it to an un-familiar setting.

A new figure appears in the bargaining, the Apothecary's wife, singing the stanza, '*Hoc unguentum . . .*' to Melody II. The Apothecary also provides a novelty. Apparently well aware of Christ as the Saviour, he courteously indicates to the Marys the right road to the Sepulchre. His lines, varied in rhythm and set to a simple melody almost wholly in single notes, comes as a welcome relief from the long stretches of ten-syllable verse.

Once more familiar material appears: ZHN A, Melody I, the lament of the Marys as they approach the Tomb (ll. 105–12). Unusually, on this occasion the normal order of the stanzas is not preserved. It is succeeded by the lament stanza, '*Iam, iam, ecce* . . .', found elsewhere in a few *Visitatios* such as the 'Dublin Play',[1] *Tours 927*, the Dutch Easter Play, and in the 'Appendix' to the *Orléans MS 201* version. The often used item at the Sepulchre, '*Quis revolvet nobis lapidem* . . .', also sung by the Marys, has a setting that is more French than German in its simplicity, but appears to show no similarity to any of the several different settings that the sentence receives. It has certainly none to the melismatic version from Klosterneuberg. It is preceded by the three-fold cry by the Marys of '*O Deus*' (l. 115), a trick that is normally French.

Amazingly, the Sepulchre scene now terminates, with no sign of any Angels to question the Marys. We are presented with the scene of the Soldiers' return to Pilate and the Jews. The remaining material is in close parallel with Klosterneuberg's relevant stanzas (ll. 119–end). The two first stanzas, '*Visionem gravem* . . .' to Melody VI, and '*Nobis autem* . . .' to Melody III, represent a reversal of the order in which they occur in the Klosterneuberg version. Finally, as the bottom of the page is reached, we are given three lines of the Priests' stanza, '*Que refertis verba* . . .', set to Melody III. No more leaves of the work survive.

It seems clear that this version, although drawing heavily on the Klosterneuberg drama, is not a mere copy of it, for what has been borrowed has in some places been improved by skilful augmentations. Possible French influences have already been commented upon, but, in addition, there remains a proportion of what seems to be original thought, both literary and musical. Regretfully, we must leave the problem of how the work was continued and concluded as being an insoluble one.

II

We come now to the two examples of the *Peregrinus* drama which survive from the thirteenth century. The first, a processional, was written down at Rouen Cathedral,[2] and as we might expect from Rouen, written down very beautifully, with informative rubrics and a musical setting in quadrate notation on a four-line stave. Our regrets must be for the brevity of the version (coming as it does much later in time, it would seem, than the splendid *Peregrinus* from Beauvais), and also for the curious manner of its termination.

---

[1] See my pp. 358–62.
[2] *Rouen, Bibl. de la Ville, MS 222*, fols. 43v.–45r. The text can be seen in Karl Young, I, pp. 461–2.

We have already in Chapter IX (pp. 185–8) dealt with the basic features of the *Peregrinus* type of drama. The beginning of the Rouen example is true to the pattern. The drama is staged on Easter Monday; the hour is that of mid-Vespers. The liturgical ceremony has been interrupted by the appearance of the two 'disciples', dressed as wayfarers singing the hymn '*Jesu, nostra redemptio . . .*' on their way to 'Emmaus'; the 'inn' being a temporary structure erected in the nave. There comes the Stranger, bare-footed, clad in alb and amice, and bearing a cross. The opening dialogue is once more an exchange of the St. Luke-derived antiphons, set to the usual liturgical swift recitative. After the normal couple of questions and answers, Rouen passes straight to the Stranger's denunciation, '*O stulti et tardi . . .*'. On this occasion Rouen's music strays at times from the Hartker setting to which other *Peregrinus* versions largely conform.

The Rouen continuation is disappointing. Several sung items used by other versions are disregarded, the actions detailed in rubrics. There comes the disciples' invitation to enter the 'inn at Emmaus'. The item is one shared by most of the surviving *Peregrinus* versions, the first sentence, '*Mane nobiscum . . .*', being a liturgical antiphon; the continuation '*Sol vergens . . .*' is an invention, found earlier in the Beauvais, the Orléans, and the Madrid twelfth-century versions. In the cases of both the antiphon and the invented passage, all the extant versions using them employ very much the same music. In the Supper scene Rouen once again relies on dumb show, carefully detailed in lengthy rubrics. The disciples utter no more than '*Nonne cor nostrum . . .*', the usual liturgical antiphon employed after Christ's disappearance to express their amazement and joy, having now realized his identity.

It is difficult to grasp the logic of what Rouen chooses to do next. The disciples are now standing outside the 'inn': Mary Magdalen appears suddenly in the near-by pulpit and is immediately questioned by the two in the familiar terms of the '*Victimae paschali*' sequence.[1] Her 'stock' replies are accompanied by displays of the grave-clothes. Karl Young (I, p. 462) justly remarks on the sense of anticlimax that this episode brings.

The other surviving *Peregrinus* of the thirteenth century is written on the two sides of a single leaf included with the *Carmina Burana* group.[2] The page has most of the one margin torn away, but the written material itself has survived remarkably. The rubrics are adequate. The music, written to the sung texts throughout, consists of unheighted St. Gall neumes, but an examination of these reveals everywhere settings that are wholly liturgical. As Karl Young puts it (I, p. 466), 'The dependence of the entire play upon this choir book [i.e., the *liber responsalis*] is astonishing'. I have myself compared the sung items of the drama with

---

[1] Rouen does not seem to have made use of the '*Victimae paschali*' dialogue as a concluding item in any of the several *Visitatio* manuscripts produced by the cathedral.

[2] *Munich, Staatsbibl., MS lat. 4660a, Carmina Burana (Fragmenta Burana)*, fols. viir.–viiv.

their antiphon counterparts to be found in that monumental source, Hartker's *Antiphonale*, and can bear witness that Karl Young's words are borne out in respect to the music as well as the texts.

One notes that at the opening of the drama the disciples are directed to sing, instead of the usual '*Jesu, nostra redemptio . . .*' hymn, the 'resurrection' antiphon, '*Surrexit Christus et illuxit populo suo . . .*', which rather anticipates the revelation soon to come to them, and gives them little excuse for the 'sadness' noted by the Stranger. However, the real excuse seems to be that the playwright was needing the '*Jesu, nostra redemptio . . .*' hymn as a rounding-off item.

The playwright dismisses the Emmaus road and inn-supper episodes in the same brief manner as does the Rouen version. Then, possessing a wealth of relevant antiphons for the purpose,[1] he concentrates on producing a couple of confused scenes, founded on antiphons, representing the two appearances of Christ to his assembled disciples, togther with the episode of 'doubting Thomas'. The drama really concludes with the singing of the hymn, '*Jesu, nostra redemptio . . .*'; nevertheless, the same style of text and neume writing continues with an episode that seems to have no relevance, carried through by 'the Mother of the Lord', two Angels, and two of the Marys. Who sings the next passage is not clear. '*Egredimini et videte, filiae Syon . . .*' is drawn from the Song of Solomon and has no relevance to the *Peregrinus* drama. The rest of the text as printed by Karl Young, together with its neumes, is written by a quite different hand, and may, I believe, be disregarded.

III

I turn now to consider two thirteenth-century Passion dramas from the *Carmina Burana* manuscript of Benediktbeuern, to which I have already made reference on p. 295, while considering the important and comparatively recent discovery of the twelfth century Passion at Montecassino.

The text of the first (*Ludus Breviter de Passione*)[2] is printed by Karl Young, with his commentary (I, pp. 514–18). He describes the work as 'a brief and rudimentary dramatic sketch' (p. 518). The actions range widely—from the Last Supper, Judas' Betrayal, the Trial before Pilate, the Crucifixion (with the Virgin Mother's Lament), and finally, a mention of the episode of Joseph of Arimathea. The text, however, is comparatively short, being composed entirely of borrowed material, mainly literal excerpts from the four Gospels.

It is to be noted that, unlike what is frequently found, the borrowed Gospel phrases are not in themselves liturgical antiphons, and thus the opportunity for ready-made musical settings has not been presented. In fact, the whole brief drama, the text only of which is given, would appear

---

[1] Karl Young, I, pp. 688–9, has listed the texts of the antiphons to be found in Hartker's *Liber responsalis*, which were made use of by playwrights concerned with the *Peregrinus* drama.

[2] *Munich, Staatsbibl., MS lat. 4660a, fols. iiiv.–ivv.*

to have been performed as a *spoken* work, the only musical touch being the lament sung by the Virgin before the Cross. This is not identified in the text, but was probably the widely known '*Planctus ante nescia . . .*', which was written as a brief incipit (and out of place) in the manuscript.

The '*Breviter*' is a poor sort of effort.[1] Karl Young has characterized its dialogue as 'wooden', and points out that a considerable part of its action is in pantomime. However, if it was actually produced, it must have called for ample space and a considerable number of actors.

The second Passion from the *Carmina Burana* is a very different affair.[2] Regarding the collection of libretto material, the same plan is followed as in the '*Ludus breviter . . .*'; all four evangelists are called on directly to contribute passages which could serve as the bases for dialogue. However, in the case of this more extensive work there is much dramatic and textual invention, particularly in the episodes concerned with, respectively, Mary Magdalen and the Virgin Mother. Also, we meet with a great deal of invented vernacular poetry, this representing not translation of Latin stanzas, but new and interesting material. There is some use of liturgical texts for choral purposes, set to liturgical music, but the proportion is small.

Although Karl Young calls the work 'disordered', and points out several places where its construction is inclined to creak, I feel that he, like generations of other commentators who have considered only the texts of these works, has not taken into account the *music*—its merits, and what would have been its effects on a medieval audience in performance. The 'Passion' is a most impressive work, set throughout to music, and using the contrasting devices of recitative and arietta, full of brilliant, intricate, and effective vocal invention, which must have in places called for all the resources of technique and musical memory that its skilled singers had mastered.[3]

I have presented a photograph of fol. 108r. of the manuscript.[4] It will be seen that the scribal music placed above the text (in not too exact a fashion at times) consists of unheighted St. Gall-type neumes.[5] Let us recall that the main information conveyed by such a notation as it stands tells us how many individual musical notes there are to each syllable of the text. We are not informed in any way what the actual

---

[1] It has occurred to me to wonder whether '*Ludus Breviter . . .*' represents a preliminary shaping of a *Carmina Burana* 'Passion' which was considered unsatisfactory and not further proceeded with, one piece of evidence being that the addition of the neume music was not attempted. Could it be that the second and far more worthy 'Passion' was assumed to be *Carmina Burana*'s 'official' one?

[2] *Munich, Staatsbibl., MS lat. 4660, fols. 107r.–112v.*

[3] Some few and brief blank stretches where there should obviously have been neumes must, I believe, be blamed on scribal negligence.

[4] See Plate IX.

[5] The usual practice was for a verbal text to be written first, and for the music notation to be supplied afterwards by the specialist music scribe. The duality of the procedure is sometimes made evident when the music scribe has obviously found that he has not been given sufficient space above a syllable to accommodate the length of a melismatic passage, and is compelled to stray on above the next syllable, tucking the music for the latter underneath.

pitches of the notes are, nor whether the tune is in free rhythm or is intended to have a regularly recurrent pattern. It is only when we have identified the melody in some way, usually as existing elsewhere in some diastematic or staved form, that we can really have a working version of it.

In the case of the present Passion, while the neume incipits of the few liturgical pieces seem to indicate the standard liturgical settings such as are found in Hartker and other early service books, the vast majority of the settings of the biblical texts used in the action seem to indicate original composition, perhaps unique to the *Carmina Burana*. In some of the dramatic dialogues, such as that between Jesus and Pilate, the notes are almost wholly *punctum* and *virga*, swift exchanges of free-rhythm, single-note syllables. In others of the single-sentence dialogues we meet with occasional two- or three-note neumes (the 'neumatic' style). But when strong emotion is called for, expressed in rhyming poetry, whether Latin or German, then we encounter elaborate melismatic passages, and the presence of a first-class *coloratura* soloist.

I am venturing to transcribe the neumes of a typical melismatic passage, in an attempt to illustrate the kinds of vocal technique that was expected from the leading singers, such as 'Mary Magdalen', 'Jesus', and the 'Mother of the Lord'. In the instance below the scene is at the Cross; the Virgin Mary is uttering her lament in a series of vernacular stanzas, all in elaborate settings. I give the second of them, chiefly because it has four lines, and not six like the first.

Den sihe ich ie-mer-li-chen an Lat i-uch er-bar-men, wip un-de-man.

lat iwer ou-gen se-hen dar un-de-nemt der mar-ter reh-te war.

As far as I am aware, the 'composed' melodies that turn up in the Passion have not been given their firm melodic line in modern times. I have not been able to accomplish this task myself, but, as I review the work, I shall do my best to define their nature and quality. In my discussion of the text, I shall continue to use Karl Young's line numberings, as they appear in his transcription, I, pp. 518–38.

The opening 16 lines of the libretto are occupied, first, by the entries of the participants—Pilate, Herod, and their trains, the Priests, the Merchant, and Mary Magdalen. There is little doubt that the groups would, initially, keep apart, each to their own 'station'. Nothing is said as to the site. Obviously a large space was required, and this may well have been that of a church building. The entries are accompanied by the choral singing of the responsory '*Ingressus Pilatus . . .*'. Karl Young has doubts as to the identity of this responsory, of which only the two opening words are given, but the accompanying group of neumes seems to identify it as coinciding with that given by Hartker, p. 9.

Immediately after, Christ appears, no doubt well apart from the other groups, and in a series of short sentences, summons to him the two 'fishermen', Peter and Andrew. Was any realism attempted, one wonders, regarding the shores of Galilee and the fishing nets? Swiftly following, come two more brief episodes, the restoring of the blind man's sight, and the calling (from his tree) of Zacchaeus the taxgatherer, who offers a brief justification of himself. All these sentence-long exchanges are set to neumes that seem to indicate 'free-rhythm' and a mildly ornate style.

From line 35 onward there occurs a 'Palm Sunday' episode, rather hazy as to its intentions. The texts of two antiphons are provided, to be sung presumably by a liturgical chorus, and there is mention of boys with olive branches. More definite (line 36) is the Pharisee's dinner-invitation to Jesus. Its terms, and Christ's acceptance, are manifest inventions, texts and music, as are the four short lines of verse added by the host. All this music is slightly ornate, and all probably in 'free-rhythm', including the stanza.

There now comes very much of a change of direction. Interest is turned to Mary Magdalen in her role as a succesful harlot—and proud of it. She occupies our attention now for quite a long portion of the work (ll. 41–151). We follow her career, which starts under the firm control of *Diabolus*, to her gradual repentance, guided by the influence of an Angel, and her tear-stained appearance at the feet of Christ at the dinner-table.

The highlight of the episode, or at least the first part of it, must surely be her exultant song:

> Mundi delectatio   dulcis est et grata;
> Eius conversatio   suavis et ornata . . .
>
> (ll. 41–2)

—which continues to eight lines and may have been the success of the show, since the playwright-producers insisted on finding, later in the scene, two more opportunities for Mary to repeat the stanza.

But what *was* the melody? One fact is apparent. The neume notation shows that the eight lines are set in pairs, AB AB . . ., so that we need only to know the first two musical sentences.[1] But nothing more is presented except lines of unheighted neumes.

For a long time now my question has been, 'Will no one tell me what she sings?', but as far as I am aware no scholar has yet come up with the answer in modern notation. I suspect it to have been a fine vigorous number, nothing 'plaintive' about it.[2]

The bargaining with the Merchant for cosmetics follows (ll. 50–75).

---

[1] There are a few small differences in detail between the neume settings from one pair of lines to another. These are at times (obviously) scribal slips, or due to the need for liquescent effects between consonants.

[2] The example that follows below is no doubt a perfectly futile exercise, but it represents a wish-fulfilment on my part. I have been moved to attempt a reading of the neumes which at least conforms to their syllable groupings and the rise and fall of the vocal line. For the

The rhyming stanzas which Mary and he interchange, first in Latin, later in the vernacular, appear to be set to relatively simple music, but almost certainly measured. Then an Angel appears, and in a stanza that is more elaborate both in textual rhythm and music, makes mention of Jesus of Nazareth, but Mary's defiant reply is '*Mundi delectatio . . .*'.

Further 'professional' matters follow—the appearance of a lover ('*Amator*'), and again the Merchant. These stanzas, though rhythmic, involve tunes that are mostly single-note. Once again (l. 96) the Angel intervenes with his earlier stanza, '*O Maria Magdalene . . .*'.

Once again Mary's reply is '*Mundi delectatio . . .*', but immediately and dramatically comes the change of heart. Her stanza (l. 98), '*Heu! vita praeterita, vita plena malis . . .*' is set to much more elaborate music, as is the Angel's 'gospel' comment concerning the rejoicing in heaven 'over one sinner that repenteth . . .'.

Mary's visit to the Merchant is this time for a different purpose; *Diabolus* and *Amator* disappear, and Mary journeys to the Pharisee's house dressed in black, and purchases her ointment on the way.

It is odd to observe that the stanza interchange between Mary and the Merchant is this time conducted in terms of ZHN C. The two different melodies, mildly neumatic, seem to me to show no similarities to the stock *Zehnsilberspiel* ones.

An interruption by the chorus (l. 116) is one of several places where multi-voice comments are offered, serving to describe what is happening in the action.

Mary's stanza, as she approaches Jesus weeping, is set to the same melismatic music as '*Hinc ornatus saeculi . . .*' (l. 105), but the two vernacular verses which follow have been left without their music.

The anointing takes place, and there follow now the comments by the host, by Judas, and by Jesus himself, all of them sentences taken from Matthew and Luke and given simple free settings. Jesus, in a verse-paraphrase, then tells the parable of the two debtors (l. 135), again in a simple rhythmic setting. Finally, he dismisses Mary, in a highly melismatic passage, with the assurance that her sins are forgiven her.

Mary departs, singing two vernacular stanzas of, strangely enough, a

---

melody I have chosen the Aeolian mode, together with the (iambic) second rhythmic mode, which here, I believe, gives the right sprightliness to the song.

[Mary Magdalen]

(Fast)

Mun-di de-lec-ta-ti - o dul-cis est et gra - - ta;

E - ius con-ver - sa-ti - o su - a-vis et or - na - - - ta.

338

highly emotional lament. Commenting on this, Karl Young, (I, p. 535) speaks of it as supporting the view that the whole Magdalen scene 'was originally an independent piece, somewhat imperfectly fitted to its present surroundings'. The stanzas each have the same musical setting, the vocal pyrotechnics of which must have been well worth listening to.

There follows now the episode of the Raising of Lazarus, with Mary Magdalen present as the sister of Martha and the dead man. A good deal of music is missing from the Gospel texts that are used for the dialogue. Altogether, it is difficult to visualize a successful scene.

However, the episode which follows, that of the Garden of Gethsemane and the betrayal, must have been effective, founded as it was on passages from St. Matthew's account; sometimes in plain prose, sometimes paraphrased into verse with rhythmic settings. Here is what must have been a very moving moment. If only we could recall the melody to which Jesus' prayer was set!

Pa – ter, si fi – e – ri po – test, tran – se – at a me ca – lix is – te ... (etc.)

The episode of the arrest of Jesus makes use of St. John's account, but the simple music does not follow that of the *liturgical* Passion of St. John of Good Friday. Comparative musical simplicity is maintained through the scenes of Peter's denial and the successive interrogations by Herod and Pilate, with the prose set mainly by virga and punctum. A rubric makes mention of the hanging of Judas, *Diabolus* lending a hand; this was no doubt done in dumb show.

A rubric also details the Crucifixion. A curious point is that the inscription recorded by St. Luke, '*Iesus Nazarenus, rex Iudeorum*', is actually given simple neumes, and is apparently sung by Pilate, who proceeds to snub Jewish protests with '*Quod scripsi, scripsi!*'

There now comes the scene of the Virgin before the Cross and a complete change of musical style. The four stanzas of lament that she sings are extremely melismatic. I have on p.336 already given a quotation from the item. As she continues, familiar Latin rhyming texts appear— '*Flete, fideles animae . . .*'; '*Triste spectaculum . . .*'; and '*Mi, Iohannes, planctum move . . .*'. The use of the sequence '*Planctus ante nescia . . .*' is also hinted at, and the presence of St. John confirmed by his being called on to sing a rhythmic, rhyming quatrain, '*O Maria, tantum noli . . .*'

Normally, the verb used in connection with the utterances of the actors is '*cantet*', but on some few occasions '*dicat*' is used, possibly to show that expression is more important than the exact pitch of the notes. Examples can be seen during Jesus' dying moments (ll. 291–5), where the neumes are no more than single notes.

His last cry of '*Ely, Ely, lama sabactany . . .!*' ('*dicit clamando*') has no music.

o

The few remaining items, mingled Latin and vernacular sentences, are strictly in single notes. They include Longinus' declaration of faith, and the mockery of the Jews.

This (on fol. 111r.; Young, l. 305) seems to represent the end of the drama, something of a fading-out. Irrelevant matter continues for a couple or so of pages, and then there turn up a pair of eight-line stanzas that might have been of use to the drama. They are headed, '*Cantus Joseph ab Arimathia*' and represent the traditional plea of Joseph and Pilate's reply. The setting (the usual unheighted neumes) is obviously rhythmic, mildly ornate, and (if some neume discrepancies are passed over) has the same tune for each stanza.

I have dwelt to some length on the nature and techniques of the music of what is clearly a somewhat disordered work. But a major one: Karl Young, in a flash of perception, called it 'an episodical religious opera'. An opera it is. We do not know how good, and the likelihood is that we never shall, for unless the secret of the neumes can be unlocked, and singers assembled such as performed with ease the pyrotechnics of the vocal score, we shall not be able to gauge the part that the music would play in the emotional impact of the work on an audience.

For assessment, the bare text is a poor substitute.

IV

I turn once more to the Christmas season, and to an interest which to this point we have seen expressed dramatically only as an episode in several of the 'Magi-Herod' dramas.

The *Officium Pastorum*, a separate dramatization of St. Luke's account of the angelic revelation to the shepherds, and of their journey to the manger at Bethlehem, has already been discussed in Chapter VI, pp. 102–4, where I have traced its development from the trope '*Quem quaeritis in praesepe* . . .', which was early to be found prefacing the Introit of the Third Mass of Christmas Day. The Christmas trope itself, as I have already shown, represented a verbal dialogue clearly founded on the still older Easter Introit trope, '*Quem quaeritis in sepulchro* . . .'. I was emphatic, however, in pointing out that the music of the Christmas trope was a separate invention.

As I have also mentioned, a further piece of invention was required of the shaper of the Christmas dialogue. While his Easter model could claim Gospel authority in giving speech to his Marys at the Sepulchre, St. Luke's shepherds were mute, and encountered no questioners at the Manger. I have already indicated the solution which was arrived at, the adoption of a tradition of the second century, which spoke of two mid-wives (*obstetrices*) as being present at the *praesepe*. This identification was apparently felt even before the dialogue had been dramatized. When this last step occurred the drama is not found, as is the trope, preceding the Introit of the Third Mass of Christmas Day (the *Magna Missa*), but that of the First (or 'Midnight') Mass, in which rite the costumed Shepherds took over various liturgical duties.

Although the vernacular mystery plays of Europe (including England) made much of the story of the Shepherds, it would appear that church music-drama had considerably less enthusiasm for the theme in isolation, to judge by the small number of surviving examples. The coming of the Kings to the Manger, together with their encounter with Herod on the way, apparently made a much more dramatic story. However, in half a dozen versions of the Magi drama the Shepherds were allowed a subordinate inclusion, mostly in being questioned by the Kings while *returning* from the Manger. Only in the longest of the group, from the Orléans manuscript, are they permitted their own stage approach to the Virgin and Child.

As for the Shepherds' own separate music-drama, it so happens that there has come down to us in a form which makes a complete acting-version possible, one single example only. Its original home (it dates of course from the thirteenth century) was Rouen Cathedral, but it is now to be found in the Bibliothèque Nationale. *MS lat. 904*, fol. 11v.–12v. A couple or so other Rouen manuscripts show substantially the same libretto (and, incidentally, some useful additional rubrics) but it is only *MS 904* which supplies the musical setting.[1]

Our consideration must now be for the last-named, beautifully written in regard to both text and music. The latter is set out in free rhythm on a four-line stave in mature French quadrate notation, with C and F clefs.

Speculating on how the little work was originally produced, and surveying the information given by the several Rouen manuscripts, we gather that the only real 'property' was the *praesepe*, or manger, but nothing is ever said as to its construction. We are told, though, that it contained the 'figures' of the Virgin and Child. The Rouen evidence is that these were effigies, but a thirteenth-century Padua version (without music) may intend them to be actually living. In certain other dramas, dealing with the slaying of the Innocents, Joseph is shown taking Mary and the Child to Egypt and bringing them back after all danger had passed, which seems to suggest instances of the Virgin, if not the Child, being represented by a living person. As for the position of the *praesepe*, although all the Rouen texts place it behind the main altar, it is located in the choir in the Padua version, and definitely well into the nave in the case of the Magi drama of *Orléans 201*. In other instances of its mention the site is not stated. There seems to have been a general agreement that it should be curtained in some fashion, Mother and Child being kept hidden until revealed by the Midwives. Costuming, as one might expect from the close proximity of actual Church rites, consisted of modified uses of liturgical garments. The Rouen scheme was for the Angels to have albs and amices, the Shepherds tunics and amices, the Midwives

---

[1] Details of these other Rouen manuscripts, containing basically the same version with useful rubrics, can be found in Karl Young's II, pp. 12–16 and 428–9.

dalmatics. One secular touch is allowed; the Shepherds are to carry staves. Rouen is generous regarding the number of Shepherds—no less than five! But the Padua play keeps to the number usually found in the Christmas trope, that is, two. The Magi dramas are no help, for though the *Pastores* make brief appearances in some of them, no number is mentioned. In modern performances we might settle for the traditional number, three, as found in the mystery plays and graphic representations.

Rouen leaves us in no doubt as to when the drama begins—immediately *after* the *Te Deum* of Matins and itself leading straight on to link up with the Introit of the 'Midnight Mass'.[1]

The construction of the *MS 904* drama can be very simply analysed. Its core is the trope of the Christmas Introit ('*Quem quaeritis in praesepe . . .*'), its text unchanged from that of the group of Limoges tropers of the tenth and eleventh centuries, its music almost so. Round this St. Luke's account is shaped, with musical settings in plainchant style for the passages of direct speech given by the Evangelist (vs. 10, 11, 12, 14, and 15). A third element is a lyrical one. Two short rhyming poems, commencing respectively with '*Pax in terris nunciatur . . .*' and '*Salve, virgo singularis . . .*' are employed. The musical settings of each appear to call for rhythmic interpretation, and both appear to be original compositions, unique to Rouen. A short, free-rhythm passage beginning '*Alleluia, iam scimus . . .*' belongs to the original Christmas Introit tropes, but here, in the drama, it is separated from the rest of the exchanges and placed at the very end, so that it may act as a bridge to the Mass Introit which follows, the first words of which are, '*Dominus dixit ad me . . .*'.

We will now consider the little work item by item. A first rubric introduces us to a scene that we have met before, a dramatization of St. Luke, ii: 10–12, which describes the appearance of the Angel 'in the heights', bringing his news to the Shepherds in the fields. In Chapter X, (pp. 204–5), I have already discussed the remarkable similarity between the settings of certain items found in this Rouen 'Shepherds' Play' and the 'Magi-Herod' drama from *Orléans 201*. These, the Angel's '*Nolite timere . . .*' and the Shepherds' '*Transeamus usque Bethleem . . .*' (both of which represent free composition), are so close as to cause us to assume that we are dealing with one and the same composition. Even more remarkable is the matter of the music of the respective settings of the Midwives' question at the Manger. The first four words, '*Quem quaeritis in praesepe . . .*' are in each case set (and this uniquely) to the Easter music of '*Quem quaeritis in sepulchro . . .*'. As we have seen, all this has led me to speculate on the probability of the splendid 'Magi-

---

[1] Situated as the little drama is, as an insertion between the end of Matins and the Mass Introit, it seems improbable to me that in the original performances any attempt would be made to introduce instrumental sounds of any sort. In a transcription of the work which I once made (*Officium Pastorum, A Thirteenth-Century Music-Drama*, O.U.P., 1967), I did in fact add some passages for chamber-organ and bell-chimes. Certainly, in my preface I said that these were mere suggestions, but I rather wish now that I'd left them out altogether.

Herod' (*Officium Stellae*) drama of *Orléans 201* having its origin in the diocese of Rouen.

Be that as it may, the two dramas decline to agree as to the music of a '*Gloria in excelsis* . . .' sung by the attendant Angels. Neither setting is liturgical.

The Shepherds now set off to Bethlehem, singing a travel song of six quatrains,[4] shaped in the familiar 8 7 8 7 pattern. I imagine that it was intended to be sung rhythmically.

As I have mentioned above, it appears in no other Church music-drama. I quote the first quatrain with its music, the latter transcribed in first mode rhythm:

Of the remaining stanzas, the second is set much more melismatically, the third returns to the quiet melody of the first, while the music of the last is once again more complicated rhythmically, suggesting a free flourish towards the close. It may conceivably have gone something like this:

There follows the '*Transeamus* . . .' passage which coincides with the Orléans item, which brings them to the Manger and the question of the Midwives:

Except for the doubtful pitch of the liquescent, coinciding in its first eight notes with the Orléans *Officium Stellae* version, each, as we have

---

[4] In the last quatrain (see Young, II, p. 18) the third line is written with only four syllables. Karl Young is probably right in repeating these syllables to complete the line, even though the original manuscript is quite definite in omitting both text and setting at this point.

[1] In this example I have transposed the original pitch of the music down a fourth. If it were not an anachronistic assumption, the opening musical phrases might be thought to suggest tonic followed by dominant harmony.

[2] In the manuscript the word 'coelo' has been omitted. However, the two notes of its setting are there.

[3] This note, which I give as G, is written ambiguously in the manuscript. It could be the tone above.

seen, borrows the music from the Easter '*Quem quaeritis*' question before returning to the normal Christmas trope music. '*Salvatorem Christum Dominum . . .*' of the Shepherds, together with '*Adest hic parvulus . . .*' and '*Ecce virgo . . .*' of the Midwives (the latter after they have drawn back the curtain) have all been encountered, with their settings, in numerous trope versions.

There follows a lyric of considerable charm, the two stanzas sung by the Shepherds as they kneel before the Mother and Child. As far as I am aware the composition is unique to this work, but I print here my transcription of the first stanza with its music (set in the second rhythmic mode) in case any scholar better informed than I in regard to medieval music has met the melody elsewhere. It rings very much like a folk tune, and is in the 'major' mode.

After the Shepherds have risen from their knees and turned away, the acted drama swiftly ends. They sing (to the choir) the usual concluding Christmas trope sentence, '*Iam vere scimus Christum natum . . .*', and move to join the service as the Introit of the First Mass of Christmas begins. Thereafter they take over various liturgical tasks, as detailed by the rubrics.

The *Officium Pastorum* of Rouen appears to me to be a model example of how an invented Church drama could be fitted into an official liturgical ceremony with perfect appositeness and dignity.

V

I pass now to the wider type of Christmas drama, the *Officium Stellae* of the Three Kings and Herod. For our first thirteenth-century example we need not move from our Rouen manuscript *B.N. MS lat. 904*, this time seeking fol. 28v.–30r. At such a flourishing diocese as that of Rouen it is remarkable to find that its contribution to the type (we can only judge by what has survived) is of such general discussion of the origin and diffusion of the *Officium Stellae* type.[1] As I have already indicated, the Rouen version is put on record in several surviving manuscripts of the thirteenth and fourteenth centuries, of which *B.N. 904* is the only one to

[1] See Chapter VIII, pp. 124ff., and for the *B.N. 904* version in particular, pp. 126–8.

include its music. The aim of the version, one might guess, was to give some extra emphasis to the Oblation ceremony of the Christmas Mass, by introducing the dramatic figures of the Three Kings, realistically attired, and following a no less realistic Star, reaching the Manger without any interruption by Herod,[1] to display their impressive and traditional gifts at the altar of the Holy Cross. Immediately after, other clergy and members of the congregation come forward to the altar with their own gifts.

There follow the usual final features—the Magi's slumber, the angelic warning, and the hurried departure of the Three, which, in reality ends with their re-entering the choir to bear their parts in the Mass itself.

In my opinion, the Rouen version represents an individual editing of material, texts and music, already widely known, which is adapted, and subordinated, to the needs of an important ceremonial item, the Oblation. But in a Christendom which has produced a number of major and independent versions of the Magi-Herod story, I cannot imagine that Rouen would have been content, for festive occasions, with the modest effort such as that of *B.N. MS lat. 904* represents. Recalling the evidence which I have already advanced as to the close textual and musical links between the Rouen *Officium Pastorum* and the *Officium Stellae* from *Orléans MS 201*, I must repeat once again my belief that the latter may have had its origin in the Rouen region!

I have already mentioned (p. 135) the thirteenth-century *Officium Stellae* from Laon,[2] which adds to the Magi-Herod story in unbroken performance the episode of the slaying of the Innocents. If Karl Young's transcription of the text (II, pp. 103–6) is consulted, it will be seen that almost all the items texts are familiar, including the usual Magi-Herod 'core' (see my pp. 127–8). The manuscript, however, is unfortunately devoid of its music. While most of the settings could, with confidence, be restored, it is regrettable that the one outstanding and unique item of the Laon version must remain so deprived. This is a four-line rhyming stanza ('*Multi reges . . .*') addressed by Joseph to the Magi, a unique moment as far as the Church dramas are concerned.

The succeeding episode concerned with the slaying of the Innocents is a dull one, not aided by Laon's consistent economy in regard to rubric directions. '*Quare non defendis . . .*', the appeal of the children to the Angel as their slayers appear, and the Angel's reply, '*Adhuc sustinete modicum tempus . . .*' are both adapted from the text of a liturgical responsory, these items being unique to the Orléans and Laon drama versions. The appeal of the mourning Rachel and the efforts of her 'Consolers' are shaped in rhyming verse, mostly borrowed, it would seem, from the powerful scene as staged by *Orléans 201*. Rachel's entry stanza text is taken from a sequence, '*Celsa pueri . . .*'. I cannot of course answer for the music. The succeeding exchanges between Rachel and her

---

[1] Herod, missing as a character, is represented by his mention in one of the liturgical responsories, '*Interrogabat Magos . . .*', sung by the choir in procession.

[2] Laon, *B. de la Ville, MS 263*, fols. 149r.–151r.

consolers are mainly in the terms, (and probably the music) of the Orléans version. Again, at '*Quam beata . . .*' the '*Celsa pueri . . .*' sequence is drawn upon, while a couple of Rachel's concluding lines, beginning '*Planctus nostrum . . .*' again represent a sequence borrowing, this time from '*Misit Herodes innocentum . . .*'. No attempt is apparently made to represent the children's restoration to life.

A feature which (among others) Laon shares with the Orléans version is the recollection of a verse from the Gospel of St. John, '*Ecce, Agnus Dei . . .*'.[1] Each version not only uses the verse to sing about the 'Lamb of God', but produces an actual lamb to which to address the song. The Orléans lamb is a good deal more mobile than that of Laon. While the Orléans item is set to a charming and apparently original rhythmic tune, we are left, unfortunately, with no knowledge as to how Laon set it.

To sum up: the Laon 'double drama' seems to be of no great merit; this is especially true of its second part. It appears to lack the dramatic spark, and thus we need not mourn that the lack of its music makes its revival impracticable.

VI

'The Christmas Play from Benediktbeuern' is Karl Young's name for the attempt, found in the *Carmina Burana*, to shape a dramatic work that should comprehend the main themes of the Christmas Season.[2]

Once again at Benediktbeuern we meet with a considerable drama the bulk of which consists of rhyming stanzas, these showing some variety of poetic pattern. There are a number of contributions by a liturgical chorus, one reason for imagining that the work, if it were performed at all, was staged in the wide spaces of a large church nave. Most of the material sung by the chorus consisted of liturgical antiphons and responsories—these, from the evidence of the neumes, seeming to show affinity with the settings found in the Antiphonale of Hartker.

Regarding the vocal settings of the libretto—as in the case of the 'Passion' drama (see pp. 334–40)—the music notation given is no more than unheighted St. Gall neumes, which need some previous knowledge of the melodies concerned for their elucidation. Since most of the action is maintained in the form of groups of rhyming Latin stanzas, the tunes set to these appear to be similarly rhythmic. They are 'neumatic' in style with virga and punctum prevailing, but with occasional vocal flourishes. Once again, the unfortunate music scribe is frequently not given enough vellum space for his melismatic displays, and the resultant welter is sometimes difficult to sort out.

As for the prose passages, usually appearing to be set more elab-

---

[1] As Karl Young points out, each version would be reminded of the sentence from the fact of its occurring in the liturgical epistle of the day.

[2] *Munich, Staatsbibl., MS lat. 4660*, fols. 99r.–104v. Karl Young (II, f.p. 72) reproduces a photograph of fol. 99r. of the manuscript.

orately, we shall find that these are, often enough, liturgical in origin, with liturgical music. But a proportion of them seem, musically, to represent free composition.

However, the saddest feature of this particular *Carmina Burana* drama is that something seems to have gone wrong with the task of the music scribe. With the exception of the setting of one stanza (ll. 95–102),[1] the neumes of which have not been filled in, all is well to begin with, for the first seven folios. But with the beginning of fol. 102v. the music fails completely, halfway through a stanza (line 336) and remains missing until line 510. There comes a half-hearted re-appearance of the neumes for a few items, then again a banishment, this time to the end of the work. Of a total of 575 lines of libretto, roughly 350 have been given their musical settings. Manifestly, the rest should have received the same treatment, but the scribe never got down to the task.

It appears to me that, with so much absent of that obviously very important feature—the music, the manuscript as it stands could not represent the source for a practical, 'acting' version. In the course of his commentary on the drama, Karl Young (II, p. 196) mentions the opinion held by some critics that, with all the exceptional demands for realism that the rubrics appear to call for, the work was not intended for actual production upon a stage, but rather for private reading—in fact, 'an academic literary exercise', as the author puts it.

In opposition to that idea, however, is, all the time and trouble spent by the music-scribe in writing out about two-thirds of the elaborate neume settings, and then not finishing the task. As far as I know, there is no record of any actual performance of the work, at Benediktbeuern or elsewhere. I therefore suggest that the unfinished state of the music was due to the fact that whoever had arranged for its writing-out had decided, for one reason or another, that no staging was possible. Somewhere, perhaps, an apprehensive 'cantor-producer' may have given a sigh of relief.

On his pages 190–6 Karl Young has analysed and commented on each stage of the dramatic text. There would be no point in my attempting anything like the same task. My efforts must be towards discovering what can be learned from a consideration of the music, this in spite of the handicap of dealing for most of the time with unheighted and unrealizable neumes.

In the opening scene we meet with a familiar theme, that of the 'Prophets', prophesying the coming of Christ. The assembly appears to be sited in a church nave, and on this occasion they are presided over by St. Augustine himself, the supposed author of the famous sermon.[2]

There is an unusually modest number of them, of which Isaiah is the first to make his contribution. His double quatrain is set by what is obviously a rhythmic, measured tune, its melodic scheme being

---

[1] I am once more taking advantage of the fact that Karl Young (II, pp. 172–90) has numbered libretto lines.

[2] See my pp. 149–52, where the *Ordo Prophetarum* of B.N., *MS lat. 1139* is discussed.

a b a b c d c d. There follow what appear to be a couple of antiphon incipits, sung probably by the soloist himself, the second showing the liturgical music of Hartker, the other, not. Then Daniel contributes his two stanzas. Conveniently enough, the music of Isaiah's stanza is borrowed as a setting for both of them.[1] The singer rounds off his stanza with two liturgical antiphons, '*Ecce virgo concipiet . . .*', and '*Dabit illi Dominus*'.

Next, we have the advent of the freely-gesticulating Sybil, a widely appreciated classical figure surviving into the medieval age. She sings four stanzas of eight lines each, six syllables to the line. The setting appears to be a new one, and to be the same for each stanza, if the occasional neume discrepancy is disregarded. The tune must have been a measured one, mostly single notes, varied in almost every line by a *climacus*. The Sybil's final contribution comes from the 'Augustinian sermon', and, in the manuscript, consists of no more than an incipit, *Judicii signum: Tellus. . . .* The few neumes given in the manuscript seem to hint at one of the several melodies, attached to this 'Song of the Sybil', extant at the time.[2]

Ju – di – ci – i   si – gnum: Tel – lus ...

'Aaron' now offers his contribution, and is given as a choral introduction a liturgical antiphon that speaks of his 'flowering rod'. The actor concerned was obviously a fluent soloist, since his two rhyming 15-syllable lines are set by a number of vocal flourishes. His three four-line stanzas that follow have somewhat simpler settings.

For our last 'prophet' episode we are given a somewhat sketchy version of the meeting of Balaam and his ass with the sworded Angel. The Angel's reply to Balaam's 'cursing' speech imitates its construction and deliberately borrows its music. Balaam departs, singing the 'prophetic' antiphon '*Orietur stella ex Jacob . . .*', and with it the whole *Ordo Prophetarum* section ends.

There now begin (K.Y., line 79) the antics of *Archisynagogus*, the chief of the Jewish sceptics, and an early example of the semi-buffoon in drama. Indignantly, and with exaggerated gestures he protests against the statements of the prophets in two eight-line, seven-syllable stanzas. From the evidence of the neumes the first, with occasional melismas, has an unusually repetitive melody-pattern of ab ab ab ab, while the second

---

[1] Even in this mainly well-written Benediktbeuern manuscript I meet with problems when it comes to successive writings-out of the same melody by the music-scribe. Small discrepancies occur—for example, a *climacus*, with three falling *punctum* notes reproduced with two only. I refuse to believe the 'variations' excuse so often advanced to account for what is more likely to have been scribal carelessness.

There are other places in the manuscript that have uncertainties, due to rubbings and smears.

[2] See H. Anglès, *La música a Catalunya fins al segle XIII*, 1935, table f.p. 294.

stanza appears to change the tune and give lines of neumes that seem to show only one repetition.

Then comes an odd intrusion (line 95). The 'Boy Bishop' enters, soberly to inform everyone that *Archisynagogus*' arguments will be refuted by St. Augustine himself. No music is supplied for his utterance of an eight-line rhyming stanza. Perhaps he was intended to *speak* it, and was not going to be entrusted with any singing.[1] Whatever the case, he immediately disappears without any further display of his 'office' and is seen no more.

The music immediately resumes, as the Prophets, as a body, add their pleas for Augustine to intervene, this in an eight-line stanza. The tune is organized in the familiar pattern of ab ab cd cd. Augustine replies with a different eight-line melody. Both are 'neumatic', i.e. with only occasional compound neumes. There now begins the debate between Augustine and *Archisynagogus* (Young, ll. 119–206).

Karl Young comments to some length on the material of the disputation. I will content myself with technical details. The first (six-syllable) stanza seems to be set by a new melody, but again to the tune-pattern, ab ab cd cd. The exchanges that follow between the Saint and *Archisynagogus* occupy over 70 lines of rhyming verse, and every single line is of seven syllables.[2] *Archisynagogus* now contributes five successive stanzas, which, if one could be sure of all the neume details being written correctly, seem to indicate the same measured tune repeated four more times.

Augustine's 'sober and discreet' single-stanza reply includes three long drawn out melismas, music not met with before. But astonishingly, *Archisynagogus* retorts with a stanza (ll. 176–183) set to the same music. Augustine's next two stanzas are intended to overwhelm *Archisynagogus* objections, the second containing the striking analogy so much approved by Young (II, p. 193). The music, however, is something of a puzzle to me. The neumes of the first stanza seem to indicate a new tune, but although there are similarities to be found in the unheighted notation of the second, one hesitates to believe that the settings are the same.

We are on safer ground with the next item, and very impressive it is. The Saint breaks out into the first verse of the famous (and here most suitable) sequence, St. Bernard's *'Laetabundus exultet fidelis chorus, alleluia!'* The composition is taken up by the Prophets, and sung to the end, *alternatim*. A rather humorous touch is supplied by *Archisynagogus*, who caps the Prophets' phrase *'Res miranda!'* by (no doubt) bawling, but to the same music, *'Res neganda!'*. Augustine tries to insist, with another *'Res miranda!'* but *Archisynagogus* is quite irrepressible. However, the sequence continues, to the sequence music, the Saint and

---

[1] The fact that the rubric of the Boy Bishop uses *'dicat'* is no argument. *'Dicat'* has just been employed for the singing of Balaam's Angel and for *Archisynagogus*.

[2] Except for *Archisynagogus*' first (vocative) line, *'O Augustine'*, which is two syllables and two neumes short. Probably a textual omission.

the Prophets taking alternate verses and finally combining to sing together the last two sections (*Infelix propera* . . .)[1]

The scene ends with Augustine's solo singing of an anti-Semitic passage beginning: '*Discant* [*sic*] *nunc Judaei* . . .'. One expects the familiar antiphon, '*Dicant nunc Judaei* . . .', one that we have several times encountered, but it proves to be a new composition, unique, but founded on the old model. Some resemblance might be traced between the first few neumes of the manuscript and the Hartker setting, but any further musical link is not to be found. *Archisynagogus* continues with his derisive antics during the 'antiphon' singing, and then apparently departs, to raise trouble elsewhere.

There follows what might be described as the beginning of a new 'act'. We are now concerned with the Annunciation—with the Angel and the Virgin. Their exchanges are in incipit form, taken mainly from the liturgy of the Feast of the Annunciation. Some of the neume incipits are familiar, some not. A couple of the text incipits are without music; the second of them (line 246) not yet interpreted to the satisfaction of scholars.

Mary briefly encounters Elizabeth; they exchange liturgical antiphons, and then Mary rounds off the scene by singing the *Magnificat* to what appears to be a simple chant-tone.

The next episode is described by Karl Young as 'a pantomime representation of the Nativity itself, the details of which are left to speculation' (II, p. 193). There follows a choral comment by the liturgical choir —the antiphon '*Hodie Christus natus est* . . .', sung to the Hartker music.

The 'Star' having appeared, the three Kings make their appearance. This scene compares unfavourably with the vivacity and variety of similar 'Magi' episodes that we have already considered. The first King utters four eight-line, seven-syllable stanzas, with the same meausred melody for each stanza. Next, the second King takes over with four more such stanzas. There is a change of melody, and in spite of some small neume discrepancies, I am assuming that the same music fitted all four. As it happens, the second stanza contains *ten* lines, but already, without any musical references, the French scholar Du Meril had queried the inclusion of the last two lines (299–300). Altogether, a textual and musical scribal muddle seems to have occurred here. As one might expect, the third King now joins the debate, with *his* contribution of four eight-line, seven-syllable stanzas, and a new tune. The latter at least brings some momentary variety, since the setting involves three long melismatic passages of over a dozen notes to a syllable. Karl Young's opinion of the versified speeches of the scene, which, he says, 'are somewhat appalling in their prolixity and pedantry' (p. 193), seems to me to be entirely just. No lightening of the situation, I imagine, came from the music.

---

[1] Two of the normal verses, '*Sicut sidus radium* . . .' and '*Neque sidus radio* . . .', are omitted by Benediktbeuern.

It was in the third King's third stanza that disaster struck the manuscript from the point of view of being a 'practical' document. Halfway through a line (336), and turning over to a new page (102v.), the music-scribe, for one reason or another, abandoned his task. For more than three closely-written manuscript pages long stretches of the rhyming stanzas exchanged by various characters remain without their settings. There comes a brief neume resumption as I have already mentioned, but this soon fades.

The absence of the music cancels any hope of relieving the monotony of the long line of identically constructed stanzas concerned with the reception of the three by Herod's '*nuncio*', and his passing of the messages to Herod, who is highly indignant. The only break in the rhythmic monotony is that Herod is allowed to express his anger in lines of alternate seven and six syllables, but just for the moment![1]

Certainly there is another gleam at this point, the entry of *Archisynagogus* with his followers, in the role of the crafty counsellor. Herod addresses him as '*magister*', and accepts his advice to conceal his hostility and to send the Kings on their way to the Manger. But once again a long succession of seven-syllable lines is established as the three are received and despatched.

The appearance of the Shepherds, together with *Angelus* and *Diabolus*, prepares us for a scene of the type that we have already found carried out at Benediktbeuern in the case of Mary Magdalen. The Angel actually employs a six-syllable stanza, and the Shepherds a '7–6' one, but *Angelus*, *Diabolus*, and *Pastores* round off the phase of no music with a final group of seven-syllable stanzas.

With the singing of '*Gloria in excelsis Deo . . .*' by the Shepherds (as met with in Hartker), the writing down of the neumes is resumed. The scribal style is closely the same, but whether indeed it was the same scribe I cannot be sure. The Shepherds then express their intention of proceeding to Bethlehem in yet another seven-syllable stanza, set in simple 'single-note-to-the-syllable' fashion. Whoever wrote out the stream of *virgae* and *puncta*, it wasn't the original scribe.

A somewhat perfunctory and unsatisfactory scene at the Manger follows, when successively the Shepherds and the Kings offer their adoration and the latter present their gifts.

The neumes written above the sentences concerned all point to the use of liturgical music (as found in Hartker). There comes the 'dream-warning' by the Angel, but his incipit is without neumes.

The Kings not having returned to the Court, we find Herod and *Archisynagogus* taking counsel together, once again in seven-syllable stanzas, but without their music. The antiphon incipit, '*Tu Bethlehem . . .*', sung by *Archisynagogus*, is certainly given brief neumes, but this is the expiring effort. Herod orders the slaughter of the Children in one more

---

[1] Some very occasional eight-syllable lines appear in print, but these are due to the suggestions of 'text' editors, who seem sometimes to forget that, with the principle of repeated stanza-tunes being often employed, scribes tended to keep their scansions uniform

neumeless seven-syllable stanza, and the Mothers lament to what might have been quite an interesting composition (with a '*heu, heu, heu!*' refrain), if only its music had been preserved.

We are then given a description of Herod's horrible death and the succession of his son, Archelaus, all of which was no doubt carried through in some form of dumb show. Finally come some sentences from Joseph and from Mary, concerned with the Holy Family's (rather tardy) flight to Egypt. Karl Young calls attention to the fact that Mary's two hexameters (beginning '*Omnia dura pati...*') are identically the same as found in the *Ordo Rachelis* of Freising (II, p. 195). It is a great pity that Benediktbeuern has not supplied the neumes for the two lines. I have before me those of the Freising version—quite melismatic at times. It would be interesting to see whether the two settings also coincided.

I must repeat my opinion that the work could never have been intended merely as a literary exercise. The music written for it is, in places, demanding of the highest vocal skill and fluency, such as would be found only at a well-established ecclesiastical centre. When one surveys the enormous demands made on the memory and vocal fluency of the soloists concerned (this revealed only in part), and when one realizes that most of the tunes were *not* liturgical (and thus familiar), but very likely newly composed, the magnitude of the task of production looms very large in imagination.

I return to the reluctant conclusion that the manuscript represents an abandoned effort. I will change my mind only when some unambiguous record turns up of a performance, or when another 'producer's' copy is found to have survived, with all its neumes filled in.

VII

With the end of the thirteenth century the high summer of the Church music-drama movement was passing. In the previous chapter we have already reviewed the factors which in Christendom gradually undermined the foundations of the 'Age of Faith'. Town and countryside, Church and secular governments all faced new and more severe trials in the four-teenth century. It is to this century that we now turn.

CHAPTER FIFTEEN

THE FOURTEENTH CENTURY

IN the period that we are now approaching, medieval Christendom found itself facing a decline. Ever since the eleventh century the gradual onset of more favourable material conditions had caused the population totals of Europe to rise, but by the end of the thirteenth century the food supply was not able to show a corresponding increase. Outworn agricultural methods and bad harvests led, in the first decades of the new century, to famine and epidemics.

Then came war, more continuous war, to bring even greater misery and famine to Northern Europe. At the turn of the century Philip the Fair of France opened a series of campaigns in Flanders, a setback to the prosperity of one of the most industrious regions of Europe. Even worse, in 1338 there began the so-called Hundred Years' War between France and England, each with its allies. Fought over by national and by mercenary troops, France's economy was gradually wrecked. After a while the plague of professional plunderers spread to Italy, Germany, and Spain. Throughout the period rival German princes strove for the doubtful privilege of the Imperial title.[1]

In the last years of the 1340s came a more terrible scourge, the Black Death, a frightful answer to the problems of over-population. Between a fifth and a third of the people of Christendom perished in a disaster which created multiple social and material problems that could expect no immediate solution. The effect upon every level of the population of all these changed conditions was profound. As C. T. Wood puts it:

Everywhere people became subject to wild and unreasoning terrors ...
Belief in witchcraft reached new heights; frenzied bacchanals and orgies flourished in every land; writers and artists began to introduce a new theme in their works, The Dance of Death.[2]

Froissart mentions in his chronicles a sight that was apparently common on the European roads of the mid-century, that of the 'penitents', who, walking in procession, practised flagellation upon each other, using scourges which terminated with metal.

[1] For both Germany and Italy the lack of a settled central authority meant centuries of delays for the achievement of their nationhood.
[2] C. T. Wood, *The Age of Chivalry* (New York, 1970), p. 141.

In 1358 the oppressed and starving peasants of France broke into savage rebellion (the 'Jacquerie'), and were crushed with equal savagery. A similar English revolt followed in 1381.

From J. Huizinga's now classical work, *The Waning of the Middle Ages*, I quote one of his opinions concerning the period:

So violent and motley was life, that it bore the mixed smell of blood and roses. The men of that time always oscillated between the fear of hell and the most naïve joy, between cruelty and tenderness, between harsh asceticism and insane attachment to the delights of this world, between hatred and goodness, always running to extremes.[1]

The consolations of religion may not have proved as reassuring as in past centuries. We have already taken note of the clash between Pope Boniface VIII and powerful secular interests. It led, after 1305, to the seventy years of 'Babylonian Exile' at Avignon,[2] with the head of the Western Church under the political control of the French monarchy. There a succession of Popes remained until 1377. In that year Gregory XI returned to Rome, but soon died there. A Roman conclave elected Urban VI, but Avignon's cardinals replied with their own Clement VII, and the scandal of a divided Christendom continued until 1417. During the Great Schism, as it was called, not only the King of France, but the rulers of Scotland, Spain, and Portugal, together with a number of German princes, had looked to Avignon rather than to Rome for their Pope.

II

In such a climate can we be surprised that the flow of newly-created Latin dramas of the Church, with their refined and subtle music, showed a remarkable drying-up of production?—that is, as far as can be judged by what has survived.

A glance at Appendix Ii, listing the works written down in the four-teenth century, reveals that while the *Visitatio Sepulchri* type maintains examples of its 'three stages', it would seem that, apart from the evidence of these efforts, the heart has largely gone out of the whole move-ment. Two other exceptions must be noted: the Cividale *Planctus Mariae*, sung before a representation of the Cross by the four characters detailed by St. John (xix: 25–6), a remarkably melodious work; and the elaborate production of the 'Presentation of the Blessed Virgin Mary . . . ' by Philippe de Mézières, previously mentioned. Other than these, fourteenth-century Church drama's interests rest on very little else than the *Visitatio Sepulchri* type.

Even here there is obvious reliance on the past in both French and German 'first-stage' examples. One bright spot among those of the

---

[1] J. Huizinga, *The Waning of the Middle Ages* (London, 1924), p. 18.
[2] Avignon was in fact a Papal possession, but was uncomfortably close to French territory.

'second-stage' is the so-called 'Dublin Play', in which a more vital mind is apparent. Regarding 'third-stage' *Visitatios*, that from St. Quentin is of importance. It borrows much, but is well organized dramatically, and is a brave attempt to blend together Latin and vernacular texts. Finally we have German *Zehnsilberspiel* examples, with a version from Cividale showing some signs of musical originality. I deal first with 'first-stage' *Visitatios* from French sources.

We will consider a brief and simple one from a Châlons-sur-Marne breviary,[1] which might well represent a re-copying from an eleventh-century source—the straightforward dialogue between the Angels and the Marys rounded off promptly by the latter announcing the Resurrection by means of the standard French composition, '*Alleluia, resurrexit Dominus, hodie resurrexit . . .*', but, according to the rubric, not to 'the clergy', but '*ad populum*'. In spite of the extreme beauty of the scribal work in the manuscript I suspect a couple of slips in setting down the familiar music.

There are some other points in the version which need consideration. The first is the intrusion of the word '*quaerimus*' into the reply of the Marys ('*Jhesum Nazarenum quaerimus crucifixum . . .*'). It is a rare circumstance, but has occurred as early as in the tenth- to eleventh-century version from Prüm (*B.N. MS lat 9448*), as well as in other examples such as *Paris, B. de l'Arsenal MS 595* (fourteenth century), *Cambrai 75* (eleventh century) and *Metz 452* (eleventh to twelfth century). There is a common musical setting—s f r- or s f̲m̲ r-.[2]

Another unusual feature linking the versions that we have just mentioned is a wholly musical one. The age-old phrase of the dialogue, '*Non est hic!*', set, ever since the Limoges *B.N. MS lat. 1240*, to the ringing r̲l 1 l̲t̲d̲'-, is by a number of later French *Visitatios*, including those we have just mentioned, ranged at a lower pitch, as d (or d̲r) r r̲l-.

The previously mentioned *Paris, Arsenal MS 595*,[3] is very obviously closely connected with *B.N. MS lat. 1269*, since it comes also from Châlons and is identical in text and almost identical in setting. We note that this time the Marys are directed to address their announcement to the choir. Also to be noted is the addition in the bottom left-hand column, apparently by the same scribe, of the rubrics and incipits for the singing of the sequence, '*Victimae paschali*'. Here, it is apparently designed to take the place of '*Alleluia, resurrexit Dominus . . .*' as an alternative conclusion, since the words '*Te Deum*' are written again, at the end of it. Once again homage must be paid to the beauty of the scribal work, both textual and musical. Quadrate plainsong notation on the four-line stave, as we know it, has reached perfection.

---

[1] Paris, *B.N. MS lat. 1269*, fols. 279r.–279v.

[2] *Madrid 132* and *Tours 927*, both of which we have already dealt with, employ '*quaerimus*' in the dialogue reply, but in the reverse order ('. . . *crucifixum quaerimus*') and with different music.

[3] Paris, *Bibl. de l'Arsenal, MS 595*, fol. 164v., another breviary (described in Young, I, pp. 610–11).

Our next example takes us back to Rouen and a somewhat unusual 'first-stage' example;[1] once again beautifully written, but totally lacking in rubrics except for the single word *PROSA* which heads five lines of verse, all to a single 'e' rhyme and representing a type of short sequence. It precedes the '*Quis revolvet . . .*' question of the Marys, and is worthy of notice, not only for its general attractiveness, but also because the settings of the first halves of the first and second lines represent a musical quotation—the first eight notes of the famous sequence '*Victimae paschali*'. The obvious assumption is that it was sung by the liturgical chorus as a form of introduction. However, Karl Young is unwilling to accept it as part of the *Visitatio* on the ground that its theme, the Resurrection, is not a good accompaniment to the entrance of the yet uninformed Marys (I, p. 600). Against this, we may recall a number of instances of medieval insensitivity in such matters.[2] Anyway, the little composition is well worth putting on record here as an example of medieval tunefulness, and of the use of the resource of reminiscence:

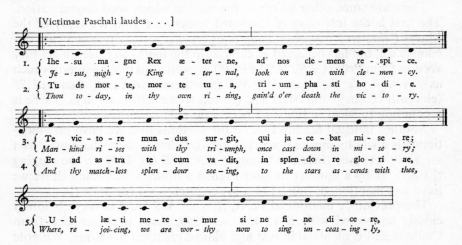

[Victimae Paschali laudes . . .]

1. { Ihe - .su .ma - gne Rex æ - ter - ne, ad' nos cle - mens re - .spi - ce.
   { *Je - sus, migh - ty King e - ter - nal, look on us with cle - men - cy.*

2. { Tu de mor - te, mor - te tu - a, tri - um - pha - sti ho - di - e.
   { *Thou to - day, in thy own ri - sing, gain'd o'er death the vic - to - ry.*

3. { Te vic - to - re mun - dus sur - git, qui ja - ce - bat mi - se - re;
   { *Man - kind ri - ses with thy tri - umph, once cast down in mi - se - ry;*

4. { Et ad as - tra te - cum va - dit, in splen - do - re glo - ri - ae,
   { *And thy match-less splen - dour see - ing, to the stars as - cends with thee,*

5. { .U - bi læ - ti me - re - a - mur si - ne fi - ne di - ce - re,
   { *Where, re - joi-cing, we are wor - thy now to sing un - ceas - ing - ly,*

The '*Alleluia*' is melismatic, and certainly effective:

Al - le - - - - - - - - lu - ia!

The first words of the Marys consist of the cry of '*O Deus*' (found in a few French versions as a preliminary to the '*Quis revolvet . . .*' question set to liturgical music). The first two sentences of the dialogue are

[1] Rouen, *B. de la Ville*, MS 252, fols. 101v.–102r., a *Liber responsoralis* (described in Young, I, pp. 599–600).

[2] E.g. in *Daniel* it will be recalled that the chorus of legates bringing the prophet to King Darius mention that they are celebrating the Nativity that ransomed all mankind from death. They go on to speak, as in the past tense, of the delivery of Daniel himself from the lions' jaws, which assurance would no doubt later comfort him. They conclude with a last reference to the 'Virgin-born'.

reminiscent of Limoges in their settings, but '*Non est hic*' is, surprisingly, given the rarer music—d̲r r r̲l- —that we have just been encountering. The treatment of what should have been a straightforward French composition, '*Alleluia, resurrexit Dominus . . .*' is irregular, with the normal music somewhat reshaped. There follow several liturgical antiphons, set to their usual music, but one item, beginning '*Ite, nuntiate fratribus meis . . .*', is out of the ordinary. It is, as far as I am aware, unique to this version, both text and music. As Karl Young has pointed out, the use of '*me*' and '*meis*' could suggest that the presence of Christ has been called for, but in the absence of rubrics no further conclusions can be firmly drawn.

Immediately before the '*Te Deum*' comes one last and melismatic '*alleluia*', the music of which proves to be the same as that which rounds off the '*Prosa*'. This appears to show that perhaps '*Ihesu magne rex aeterne . . .*' was thought of as part of the *Visitatio* entity.

The next French version to be considered is surely a re-copying of a survival from earlier centuries. *B.N. MS lat. 784*, fol. 106v.,[1] has already been mentioned in an earlier chapter (see p. 112) as showing links with the '*Quem quaeritis*' of that problem manuscript *B.N. MS lat. 1139*. One might assume the *B.N. 784* reading to represent a 'corrected' version of that belonging to *B.N. 1139* (they both derive, supposedly, from the Limoges monastery of St. Martial), since the texts coincide, except for the *B.N. 1139* omission of a whole sentence, and (in my opinion) several other miscopyings and, probably, omissions of clef changes in both the versions. It has already been noted that they share the use of a French trope, '*Ubi est Christus . . . sepulchrum.*'

There would seem to be no need for me to repeat what I have already said concerning the *B.N. 784* version, except to underline the opinion that its music setting of the dialogue is based on that of the trope version as found in *B.N. 887*, the earliest surviving French example of a musical rhyme at the vocative phrases. In my opinion the *B.N. 887* reading of the 'rhyme': mr̲ d̲l, d̲t, d̲r̲d r-, would have been reproduced in the other two versions, but for the blunders of the respective scribes.

I turn now to German 'first-stage' versions; the first from Darmstadt.[2] The notation is Gothic, on a four-line stave with clefs, crystal-clear. In spite of the very German notation the dialogue is cast in the older form ('*Quem quaeritis in sepulchro . . .*'), and the brief work is rounded off by an exchange of antiphons, between Angels and Marys, Marys and the choir, without any aid from rubrics. All but one of the antiphons are quite familiar, the rarer one being '*Et recordate sunt verborum eius . . .*' (Hartker, p. 232).

---

[1] Described by Karl Young, I, p. 271. As has already been mentioned (p. 112) Young describes it as belonging to the thirteenth to fourteenth centuries, but Solesmes, on the evidence of the music notation, favours the fourteenth to fifteenth. This odd notation, square notes, carefully heighted round a single horizontal line which proves to represent F, is, as far as I know, unique to the Church music-drama movement.

[2] Darmstadt, *Landesbibl., MS 545*, fols. 57v.–58r.—a *cantuale*.

A version from Cologne[1] is, within its brief dimensions, the answer to a music paleographer's prayer. The four-line stave, besides having its clefs, has the C line coloured yellow, the F line red, and the others brown! The notation itself is of the '*Hufnagel*' variety, but contrives to show all the small details, such as *quilismas* and the exact pitch of liquescents. However, no originality emerges. The dialogue (transposed up a fourth, by the way, like that of *Darmstadt 545*) is of the normal St. Gall type, and the introductory '*Quis revolvet . . .*', the '*Venite et videte . . .*', together with the concluding '*Surrexit Dominus de sepulchro . . .*', are all normal liturgical antiphons with their normal music. No new wings are being tried out.

Very much the same remark may be made concerning a version from Cividale Cathedral.[2] It is a competent and well rubricated work, beautifully written, the square plainchant notation, on this occasion, being provided with a stave of five lines. Although in Northern Italy, Cividale was in a German region of influence, and in this version employed the 'revised' German-style dialogue text and setting ('*Quem quaeritis, o tremulae mulieres . . .*'). Once again, as we consider the items, we are on familiar ground, even though the Marys' first question, '*Quis revolvet nobis ab ostio lapidem . . .*', is a variation of and an expansion of the more usually employed Hartker antiphon, to a different music. I have met with over thirty German *Visitatio* versions that make use of the new text, together with non-liturgical settings which clearly represent small variations on a common, specially composed melody.

After the dialogue the Angel's invitation, '*Venite et videte . . .*', is to its usual liturgical music, as is the Marys' final '*Surrexit Dominus de sepulchro . . .*'. The preceding happenings—the recovery of the grave-clothes followed by their display to the choir—are accompanied by the women singing the items '*Ad monumentum venimus gementes . . .*' and '*Cernitis, O socii . . .*', by the fourteenth century long established, and sung to standardized settings. Once again it might be felt that in the fourteenth century, types of Easter drama that took neither too much liturgical time nor trouble were being the most favoured.

III

However, when we turn to the first and only example of a 'second stage' *Visitatio* drama belonging to the French regions (see Young, I, pp. 347–50) we are given reason for revising the opinion just expressed. The manuscript in which this work is contained is a Processional belonging to the church of St. John the Evangelist in Dublin, and is now in the

---

[1] London, *Brit. Mus. Add. MS 31913*, fols. 263v.–264r.—a breviary (see Young, I, p. 593).

[2] Just before the last war this manuscript had been reported lost for many years (by Karl Young and others). As a result of my requests, the library authorities were good enough to institute another search. This led to its re-discovery. I am a little uncertain as to its present shelf details (*Cividale, Museo Archeologico Nazionale, Codex XLI*, folio *138v.*).

Bodleian Library.[1] It is familiarly known as the 'Dublin Play', and I have in previous pages more than once referred to it in passing. It clearly has links of some sort with the splendid twelfth-century *Visitatio* from *Orléans 201*, with *Madrid 132*, and perhaps with the 'Dutch Easter Play'. There seems in it something of the same vitality, the same seeking after originality that one finds in the Orléans *Visitatio* and the two great Beauvais music-dramas. The version is beautifully written, generously informative in its rubrics, and with its square music notation clearly set out on four-line staves. The sporadic insertions of B flats may represent later additions.

The first rubric speaks of three persons, suitably attired to represent the Marys, seeking Jesus and entering in turn, each carrying a pyx to represent a box of ointment. Each sings a brief lament, which brings us instantly in touch with the Orléans *Visitatio*, since the stanzas correspond with the first three of the latter—except that the second and third are interchanged, as well as a phrase or so. Certainly these particular texts are, as far as I am aware, unique to the two versions. It is less easy to have opinions concerning the respective settings. I am inclined to think that the Orléans tune was a 'home product', consistent through the three stanzas, except for that extraordinary, 'un-Gregorian' flourish of falling thirds which I have put on record on pp. 165–6. In the case of the 'Dublin Play' the stanza settings are untidily alike, but show very little resemblance to the more attractive line of the Orléans musical phrases.

But with the fourth 'Dublin' stanza a new situation arises. The first line begins, '*Heu! misere cur contigit . . .*' and recalls the actions of several other French versions, which make use of some, or all, of the pairs of lines which appear in the Orléans *Visitatio* in the form of a kind of appendix to the drama, a 'reserve' lament for the Marys, as it were. I have put on record, on p. 297, one of these stanzas, as it appears in five separate French versions. A musical family likeness is apparent in all of them.

The 'Dublin Play' follows with '*Heu! consolatio nostra . . .*'. This I have also charted, and find less agreement on this occasion among the musical settings. Dublin's is somewhat distant from that of Orléans, and Madrid's from both. In fact, Dublin's closest musical companion for the time being is the Dutch (Egmond) Easter Play. A new feature is the use of the stanza by two German *Zehnsilberspiel Visitatios*, *Nuremberg 22923* (neumes only) and the sixteenth-century example from Zwickau. Curiously enough, the setting of the last-named is nearest to that of the 'Orléans appendix' than any other.

'*Heu! redemptio Israhel . . .*' (with some disagreements as to the exact wording of the sentence) involves the same manuscripts, together with the addition of the fifteenth-century *Zehnsilberspiel* from Wolfenbüttel, *MS Helmst 65*. Here, there seems to be a kind of family feeling between

---

[1] Oxford, *Bibl. Bodl., MS Rawlinson Liturg. d.iv.*, fols. 130r.–132r. A more or less exact reproduction is to be found in Archbishop Marsh's Library in Dublin, *MS Z.4.2.20*, fol. 59r.–61r.

359

the settings of all the versions concerned, including the German ones, although I should not like to be specific regarding the pitches of the unheighted neumes of *Nuremberg 22923*.

The chorus '*Iam, iam ecce . . .*' of the 'Dublin' Marys is found elsewhere only in the 'Orléans appendix', the Dutch (Egmond) drama, *Tours 927*, and, surprisingly, in the Benediktbeuern (*Carmina Burana*) *Visitatio*. The Egmond and Tours settings are manifestly closely allied with that of Dublin; the Orléans version is less close. The simple and unheighted neumes of the Benediktbeuern manuscript afford very little evidence.

The last three Dublin stanzas, divided between the Marys and sung in turn before they reach the Sepulchre, can be matched only in the Orléans version. Each item, '*Condumentis aromatum . . .*', '*Nardi vetet commixtio . . .*', and '*Sed nequimus hoc patrare . . .*', is textually the same: but I can see no links between their respective musical settings; here each version has gone its own way. If the two melodies of '*Sed nequimus . . .*' are rhythmed, two delightful and quite different troubadour-like compositions result.

The Sepulchre dialogue now begins, with a single Angel framing the question in unusual terms—'*Quem quaeritis ad sepulcrum . . .?*' This small departure from the usual '*in sepulchro . . .*' is found in *Madrid 132*, but as far as I am aware, nowhere else.[1] Another noticeable feature—a musical rhyme of r̲m̲ r̲d̲ m f̲m̲ r- —is found between the vocative phrases. *Madrid 132* has almost the same, but its first vocative '*O*' is missing. However, this particular musical rhyme is found also in Paris, *Arsenal, MS 1169*, *B.N. MS lat. 1235* (*MS 1169*'s counterpart in a stave version), *B.N. MS lat. 9449*, and *B.N. MS lat. 12044*. One notes that Dublin remembers that a single Angel is involved, and alters '*caelicolae*' to '*caelicola*'.

Also, the playwright was not going to be content with the stock reply, '*Non est hic*'. It is here replaced[2] by a re-shaping, text and music, which may owe something to the thirteenth-century Rouen *Visitatio, B.N. MS lat. 904*.[3] The respective passages have much in common. In particular, the '*Venite et videte . . .*' sentence, as it is treated here, is unique to these two works. The music owes nothing to either the antiphon '*Venite et videte . . .*' (Hartker, p. 226) or the sentence contained in the Easter responsory '*Angelus Domini descendit . . .*' and appears to represent free composition. As Karl Young points out, '*Venite et videte . . .*', so often used in its antiphon form as the second and awkward recall of the already dismissed Marys, is here moved forward to a more suitable place, immediately after the Angel's announcement of the Resurrection.

While the (Rouen) *MS 904* version is content to close with the singing of the standard French trope, '*Resurrexit Dominus . . .*', to, in the main, its usual setting,[4] Dublin's free treatment of the composition is appar-

---

[1] I await any correction on this point, about which I am uneasy.
[2] See Young, I, p. 349.   [3] See my pp. 290–2.   [4] See my p. 292.

ently unique and quite successful. Modifying the text, and plainly attracted by the normal ringing opening, it sets about repeating the phrase:

l s l s d' s͟f m͟f͟m   r   f f mr-
Al-le-lu-ya, re-sur-re - xit Do-mi-nus . . .

and then going its own way.

The sentence that follows, and with which the Angel dismisses the Marys, is '*Et euntes dicite discipulis eius et Petro quia surrexit.*' This appears to be borrowed from the 'verse' of the Easter responsory '*Maria Magdalene et altera Maria . . .*' as it appears in Hartker, p. 232.[1] A slightly amended version of the same sentence also occurs in the 'Dutch Easter Play', but the respective settings have nothing to do with each other, nor with the liturgical music.

As far as I am aware, the rhyming couplet which Dublin now gives to the Marys as they depart from the Sepulchre is unique to that version. It appears to drop easily into rhythmic form, a 'major mode' tune that seems well worth reproducing:

E – ya! per-ga-mus pro-pe-re man-da-tum hoc per-fi-ce-re.

There comes now the episode which justifies the description of the 'Dublin Play' as belonging to Karl Young's 'second stage'. But Dublin has its own individuality. The appearance of the two disciples is prefaced by a careful rubric description of their appearances and costuming. They are to be barefooted: the tunic of John is white, and he carries a palm branch; Peter's tunic is red, and he bears a symbolic key. The first Mary breaks the news of the Resurrection by the simple means of singing the lyrical first part of the sequence '*Victimae paschali*'. The disciples question her with '*Dic nobis . . .*'; she replies with the '*Sepulchrum Christi viventes . . .*' sentence, after which the other two add, in turn, '*Angelicos testes . . .*' and '*Surrexit Christus . . .*'. The news sends the two disciples running to the Sepulchre, but without the oft-employed choral accompaniment of the choral antiphon '*Currebant duo simul . . .*'; (the passage is merely quoted in a rubric).[2] Finally, it is the disciples who, returning reassured, proclaim, '*Credendum est magis soli Mariae veraci . . .*'.[3]

Dublin's reshaping of this episode is dramatically natural and quite individual, and reflects credit on whoever was responsible for the drama.

---

[1] The 'verse' of this responsory as given in the modern Roman service book is a different one ('*Et valde mane una sabbatorum . . .*'—see Young, I, p. 601). A four-line stave interpretation of the Hartker neumes of its '*Cito euntes dicite . . .*' can be found in the breviary, *Brit. Mus. Add. MS 37399*, fol. 238v.

[2] The only mention of the grave-clothes is the formal one, contained in the Sequence.

[3] Karl Young's objection to the introduction of the phrase '. . . *soli Mariae veraci . . .*' on the grounds that all three Marys replied to the disciples, seems to me to be a frail one, since, each being heard in turn, each was in turn believed in.

It is left now to the chorus to round off the work by singing the last lines of the sequence, the satisfying belief that '*Scimus Christum surrexisse a mortuis vere . . .*'.

In my opinion, the 'Dublin Play', showing as it does a number of instances of originality in text and setting, together with a clear sense of dramatic feeling, is well worth a practical revival.

When it comes to considering fourteenth-century German examples of the 'second stage' *Visitatio* type, we meet with some disappointment. The verdict must be 'no progress' from the pattern of familiar items that we have encountered as belonging to the thirteenth century.[1] The five versions I am considering are from: (i) Munich (*Staatsbibl.*) *MS lat. 6423*; (ii) Munich, *MS lat. 16141*; (iii) Klosterneuberg (*Stiftsbibl.*) *MS 629*; (iv) Klosterneuberg *MS 1213*; and (v) Prague, *Narodni Museum, MS XV.A.10*.[2]

Munich 6423 is contained on a single torn page.[3] The items, '*Quis revolvet . . .*' (the independent, not the Hartker version), the dialogue '*Quem quaeritis, O tremulae mulieres . . .*', the Marys' '*Ad monumentum . . .*', '*Cernitis, O socii . . .*' for the display of the grave-clothes, all now represent familiar settings, even though, originally, specially composed tunes. The music is in unheighted but easily transcribable St. Gall neumes. There is no mention of Peter and John running their race, but the choral singing of the antiphon '*Currebant duo simul*' seems to presuppose this, especially as the grave-clothes are represented as being recovered. However, the drama of the situation is marred by the fact that it is the liturgical figure of *Plebanus* who receives them and who sings '*Cernitis, O socii . . .*'. A rare final rubric is to be noted, a call for the 'clash' of bells at the singing of '*Te Deum*'.

Munich 16141 (see Young, I, pp. 634–5) gives us the same items with very much the same neume music, but with the minimum of rubrics— merely the naming of characters. However, on this occasion it is definitely Peter and John who sing '*Cernitis, O socii . . .*'.

Klosterneuberg 629[4] presents four-line staved music, in Gothic notation, with B flats scrupulously added. The same items, with closely corresponding settings, are present, but with the addition of some liturgical items. Karl Young, rightly, complains once more of the discrepancy between the opening antiphon, '*Maria Magdalena et alia Maria . . .*' and the fact of *three* Marys taking part in the drama. The playwright has also yielded to that old temptation, after the Angel has dismissed the Marys, of using the antiphon '*Venite et videte . . .*' for what, dramatically, seems to be an unnecessary recall. However, immediately after, a rubric definitely banishes both Angel and Marys from the scene, leaving it clear for the race; after which Peter and John display the grave-clothes they have retrieved.

---

[1] See Chapter XIII, pp. 288–90.   [2] See Appendix Ie for full library details.
[3] The manuscript is mentioned in passing in Young, I, p. 308 note 1. The text itself, taken from Einsiedeln, *Stiftsbibl.*, *MS 81*, fol. 141v. (fifteenth century), is printed on pp. 308–9.
[4] Mentioned briefly by Young, I, p. 317 note 1.

There are two liturgical items to conclude, '*Surrexit enim sicut dixit Dominus . . .*' and the rather sour '*Dicant nunc Judaei . . .*'. Klosterneuberg's music for '*Surrexit enim . . .*', like that for most of the numerous *Visitatio* versions that use the item, is not that of the (Hartker) liturgical antiphon, but what appears to be an independent composition, which seems to have arisen first in the eleventh century.

There is little to be said regarding the *ordinarium, Klosterneuberg 1213*.[1] On the same plan as the last version, the items are in *incipit* form, with no sign of their settings. Only at the end is something exceptional. A verse of the vernacular German song, '*Christ ist erstanden . . .*', turns up, one that I have already reproduced and commented upon on pp. 162–3. The neumes that are written above this vernacular text (the only music of the version) I frankly cannot reconcile with the tune that I have given there. They may, of course, represent a more melismatic version of it. If the *populus* mentioned in the final rubric joined with the clerics in the singing of it, they would have done well indeed!

I pass now to the last of the fourteenth-century 'second-stage' group, that from Prague, *Narodni Museum*[2] *MS XV, A. 10*. The musician will be intrigued by the unusual, angular, semi-Gothic notation, written on what is frequently a five-line stave. But we meet with no more than the usual texts set to more or less normal music.[3] By way of a change, this is a version which, having employed the responsory '*Maria Magdalena et alia Maria . . .*' as a choral introduction, is consistent enough to insist on two Marys only taking part in the drama. After the Marys leave the Sepulchre to the usual '*Ad monumentum venimus gementes . . .*' a '*Victimae paschali*' dialogue scene succeeds, all sentences reduced to incipits, the questioner being, unfortunately for drama, the priestly celebrant himself. A 'single Mary' gives the three-sentence statement of the tomb-evidence, and the chorus proceeds to round off the sequence.

We must assume that the two disciples have been listening to what *Prima Maria* and the chorus have had to say, and that this starts them on the Race. Meanwhile it is the celebrant who begins the singing of the '*Currebant duo simul . . .*' antiphon. The grave-clothes having been recovered, the two disciples lay them on an altar, the celebrant then taking and kissing them.

There is a balanced and graceful musical ending:

---

[1] The text is given in Young, I, pp. 329–30.   [2] The text is given in Young, I, pp. 344–5.

[3] A striking example among the items is the widely-used '*Quis revolvet nobis ab hostio lapidem quem tegere sanctum venimus sepulchrum*'. It is a non-liturgical, mainly German composition, developed from a previously existing antiphon, but with quite different music. It must have appeared some time in the eleventh century. I have charted more than thirty examples of it. There is no doubt that throughout it represents one single basic tune, but the variations on it are numerous, and fascinating. At times a sudden leap in the range of a version causes me to suspect a missing clef-change. The melody is in the Phrygian (mi) mode, starting (as in *Udine, MS F. 25*) with l,s, d rm m mrd rm . . . but the majority of the ver-

Quis re-vol-vet no-bis—

sions transpose the tune up a fourth. Some put in the necessary B flat, some don't trouble. One version (*Graz, MS I. 1459*, of the sixteenth century) raises its version a fifth, relying on the fact that the tune does not touch the seventh of the normal scale.

It may be thought that the latter part of the work was ruled more by considerations of ceremonial than those of drama.

It appears to me that of this undistinguished group of fourteenth-century German *Visitatios*, that from the monastery of Klosterneuberg (*MS 629*) would prove to be the most satisfactory in performance.

I turn now to fourteenth-century examples of the 'third stage' *Visitatio Sepulchri*, and to the version belonging to the nunnery at Barking, Essex.[1] It owes its existence to the organizing zeal of the formidable Abbess, Lady Katherine Sutton, to whom we have already referred (p. 14), in connection with her own particular version of the *Elevatio* ceremony.

The Barking *Visitatio*, as we have it, must be looked upon with a great deal of regret, since it is one of the few known examples of English Church music-drama, but has come down to us with most of its texts in incipit form, and stripped totally of its music. Moreover, while some of the items hinted at by these incipits are familiar, and could be restored with their probable music, many others represent the start of what must remain totally unknown sentences. These might well have supplied us with some novel dialogue exchanges.

I can do no more, therefore, except refer to Karl Young's account of the *Visitatio* (I, pp. 381–5), which says all that can be said in the absence of the music.[2]

The French *Visitatio* from the nunnery of Origny-Sainte-Bénoîte near St. Quentin, now to be considered, is even more out of the ordinary than the Barking version—and also a good deal longer.[3] Concerning it, Karl Young remarks:

---

[1] Now in the library of University College, Oxford, *MS 169*, pp. 121–4. The whole manuscript is an *ordinarium*, written in the fifteenth century, but I have placed the *Visitatio* in the fourteenth, since Lady Katherine Sutton was in command at Barking from 1363 to 1376. Karl Young (II, p. 411) quotes a rubric passage inspired by the Abbess as to the didactic value of the dramas.

[2] I would dearly have liked to know if the music of '*Heu, dolor* . . .', sung by the Marys in the Barking work, had anything to do with the beautiful and otherwise unique setting of the '*Heu, dolor! Heu, quam dira* . . .' of Mary Magdalen's lament in the twelfth-century *Visitatio* of *Orléans 201*.

[3] In Karl Young's day the library details were—*St. Quentin, B. de la Ville MS 86*, pp. 609–25 (a '*Miscellanea*'), but when I sought photographs of the pages, I found that it was from the Bibliothèque Nationale, Paris, that I had to obtain them. Young prints the text in I, pp. 412–19.

This MS is the 'Livre du Trésor' of the abbey, put into French and revised under the direction of the abbess Isabelle d'Acy (1286–1324) . . . The translation into French seems to have been made in 1286, and additions to have been included in the fourteenth century.[1]

The St. Quentin version contains no scene which in some form or other has not previously been encountered. Its unusual length is due to the considerable extension of some of these scenes. In it we shall meet a fair amount of the vernacular, sometimes in the form of translations of familiar Latin verses, sometimes representing free composition. The rubrics are written in French throughout. The script, which is apparently in a single hand throughout, is a beautiful one. Only for a few brief moments does the music fail to accompany the sung texts. It is written on a four-line stave with clefs, and for most of the time consists of bold square plainchant notation. A curious fact is that the notation, to begin with, is in rather indifferent Norman style, but persists only for a few lines. Authority may not have liked it, and may have insisted on the change, which may perhaps have involved a change of music-scribe.[2]

The drama is given no definite start. There are signs of extensive erasures on its first page (p. 609), at the top of which several incipits of responsories have survived, none relevant to the *Visitatio*. Of the latter, very little is missing, it would seem, for the first words are a rubric description of the formal processional entry of the Marys, with the priest and the choir.

Karl Young, in his transcription of the text of the work, has on this occasion again numbered the lines of the text. I shall take advantage of this fact for reference purposes.

From the opening rubric we learn that Mary Magdalen is already provided with her box of ointment; thus it is the other two only who seek the spice merchant. In spite of the definite understanding as to their number we encounter the contradictory sentence, '*Maria Magdalena et alia Maria . . .*'. This is not the actual responsory as found in Hartker and surviving in modern Roman service books, but one of the three other 'unofficial' compositions that we have already encountered. St. Quentin has a familiar setting. More recognizable material follows (Young, ll. 4–10)—the second and third stanzas of ZHN A, set to a somewhat re-shaped but recognizable version of Melody I. What happens to the first stanza ('*Heu, nobis internas mentes . . .*') we shall discover later.[3]

---

[1] Young, I, p. 684. A bibliography of previous studies of and references to the manuscript is given there.

[2] It seems more likely that the original scribe himself made the adjustment, under orders. As a professional music-scribe (as he probably was) he would command more than one style. Three manuscript pages further on there comes a lapse. The melismatic music for the first syllable of '*He - las!*' turns up in Norman notation, hastily and untidily altered back to quadrate. The word had, in a previous stanza, already been set in the 'approved' style.

[3] B flats are inserted in the manuscript setting in somewhat casual fashion. I conclude that the flat should be a clef sign throughout the item, indicating transposition.

An original feature is the interspersed comment by the choir ('*Dominus quærentes* . . .') taken from the opening sentence. Another novelty is the free versification of the oft-encountered item ('*Quis revolvet nobis lapidem* . . .') (ll. 12–14), the setting being the music of the two previous stanzas. Seeing that the Marys have not yet reached the Merchant, let alone approached the Tomb, the reason for the insertion of this stanza seems obscure.

The Marys now prepare for the purchase of the ointment, and although the verses are in French, they will be readily recognized as deriving from the familiar '*Omnipotens Pater* . . .' stanzas (ZHN B). The music, too, is once again an old acquaintance, Melody II, but repeated without break with what might for modern ears be thought of as appalling persistence, for the whole of the scene, sixteen uniform stanzas (ll. 16–75). The St. Quentin version of the tune will be seen set out on p. 314. The music scribe at this point got himself in a tangle, trying apparently to save space, and reduced for a brief while to writing some of the notes of the tune on a single line!

After the first two stanzas the scene is concerned with the Spice Merchant and the 'other two' Marys, seeking to emulate the Magdalen in possessing ointment. The Merchant greets them with a stanza which may have been modelled on that beginning '*Mulieres michi intendite* . . .', found in *Vich 105* (see p. 175). Indeed, the twelfth-century version may have suggested a great deal that follows, but as the scene progresses we meet with what seems to be fresh literary composition, particularly after the price has been settled and the Marys invite the Merchant to accompany them to the Sepulchre! His initial reluctance, followed by a speech that seems to point to his subsequent conversion, appear to be special inventions, certainly adding to the interest of the scene.

Melody II continues all through these matters, both sides employing it. But the Merchant's stanzas are reduced to three lines (using a, a, b of the tune) since he has no occasion to make use of the Marys' refrain. '*Helas! verrons le nous iamais!*'

On one single occasion the Marys strike in with it (K.Y., I, p. 40), adding it to his stanza. This is after he has stated that the ointment they desire will cost them five gold pieces: whereupon he hastily offers a cheaper line! This, however, is rejected; only the best will do. The playwright's touch here is very human, and unique among the Church dramas.

As the three come to the Sepulchre, they sing two stanzas (ll. 76–81), which again seem peculiar to this drama. Their model, however, is the first stanza of the ZHN A lament ('*Heu, nobis internas mentes* . . .'), missing from the beginning of the work; this doubly proved by the fact that the musical setting is the St. Quentin version of Melody I.

Next, the '*Quis revolvet* . . .' item once more appears, but this time in its usual prose form, a recognizable setting and in a more appropriate position. Two Angels are encountered at the Sepulchre, St. John's account apparently being borne in mind. Another novelty; the familiar

'*Quemquaeritis*' dialogue is transformed into original verse. The question, the reply, and the assurance of Christ's resurrection are recast in the form of three groups of two lines, set to a single melody that seems to be specially composed for this work (ll. 83–8). I have not met it elsewhere. The '*Venite et videte...*' invitation is incorporated into the second speech of the Angels. Another interesting feature is the stage direction as to the gradual revelation of the empty Tomb.

I give below the two lines of music which set the three pairs of verses. I render them in free rhythm, but they were probably sung in measured fashion. I have not met the melody elsewhere, and have set it down in case anyone better informed than I can cast further light on its origin.

The '*Heu, infelices! quid agimus...*' of the Marys that follows (ll. 89–90) has a setting which seems to be a somewhat twisted version of what *St. Quentin 86* has already made of ZHN A, Melody I.

The Angels' answer, '*Recordamini qualiter...*' is found in both the Rouen and Tours versions, but to a different free-rhythm setting. St. Quentin's may be original, as may be the music to '*Infelix ego misera!*' sung by Mary Magdalen alone, after the other two have departed from the Sepulchre.

There now begins a familiar dramatic scene, that between the Angels and Mary Magdalen. We have met the text items that commence it frequently enough (ll. 95–9). The music of '*Mulier, quid ploras?*' clearly derives from that of the twelfth-century *Vich 105* version, and no other, but the remainder of these brief exchanges, text and music, appear to be liturgical. After this the Angels and Mary settle to sing alternate rhyming stanzas to each other, in the vernacular; no less than eight of them (ll. 100–35). The Angels use a straightforward (probably rhythmic) Mixolydian melody, one that I have not encountered before.

Musically it is an a a b a pattern.

Each of Mary's stanza replies uses for its setting the first (repeated) line of music as given above. Then follow two more lines of a refrain lament, thus:

Musically this is an a a b c d pattern.

This textual and musical scheme continues to the total of eight stanzas, when apparently, the Angels disappear and are replaced by the risen Christ. Familiar texts follow, but Christ's final question '*Mulier, quid ploras . . .?*' and the '*Maria*'–'*Raboni*' exchange have what seems to be individual, though simple, music. The St. John passage, '*Domine, si tu sustulisti eum . . .*' has a setting which has much in common with that of the *Rouen 904* version, but the three successive items, '*Noli me tangere . . .*', '*Avete vos . . .*', and '*Ite nuntiate fratribus . . .*' (ll. 141–6), seem to represent independent invention, or at least, adaptation.

Meanwhile, the other two Marys have returned, and receive with Mary Magdalen the instructions of Christ, the St. Matthew verse, '*Ite, nuntiate fratribus meis . . .*'; one employed also by the Orléans and Rouen dramas, but to a different music.

Christ having departed, there now occurs a curious item (ll. 147–8). Having omitted from the beginning the first stanza of ZHN A ('*Heu! nobis internas mentes . . .*') the playwright introduces here an adaptation of the text, set to a somewhat altered version of the St. Quentin writer's own idea of Melody I. The Marys' '*Ad monumentum venimus . . .*', which immediately follows, is altogether familiar.

The '*Victimae paschali*' sequence is now introduced and given an original arrangement. The three Marys are met by Peter and John, whose impatience for news is shown by a rubric. They '*prendent le manche le Magdelainne au peu de lons . . .*', and put to her the usual questions. Having received the usual replies,[1] rendered with appropriate gestures; they then interrupt the course of the sequence to race to the Sepulchre, accompanied by the usual singing of '*Currebant duo simul . . .*'. The interval before their return with the grave-clothes is filled by the singing of the remainder of the sequence verses. It is the two Disciples who render '*Cernitis, o socii . . .*', while the Marys kneel to kiss the clothes.

A final careful stage-direction orders that these shall be returned to

---

[1] Mary Magdalen speaks of her sight of the Risen Christ, while the lesser evidence is left to the other two, the anticlimax thus being rendered, perhaps, somewhat less noticeable.

the Sepulchre by the Disciples, while the Marys sing '*ceste anteune*'. At this point the text breaks off and the work is left unfinished, but manifestly near its conclusion. The term '*anteune*' can hardly refer to the '*Te Deum*'; we must assume some familiar antiphon such as '*Surrexit Dominus de sepulchro . . .*', or '*Alleluia, resurrexit Dominus hodie . . .*'. We must also recall that there is no guarantee that the '*Te Deum*' was there in any case. Also, the loss of the text at the beginning has deprived us of the chance of seeing whether the version was preceded by the responsory '*Dum transisset . . .*'. Thus, these two landmarks and any others being absent, there is no proof that the drama was performed in a church building after Matins at all. However, we may recall that the work's unusual dimensions are due to the extensions of two quite familiar scenes, and that basically it is framed like many another 'third-stage' *Visitatio*. I think that there can be little doubt that the nunnery of Origny-Sainte-Bénoîte made good practical use within its chapel of the artistic treasure which it possessed. Viewing the drama as a whole, we are aware of a writer, arranger, and musician of ability and dramatic imagination. The versifications are skilful and varied in form, and we have noted quite a number of instances of independent thinking.

Modern audiences might not appreciate the repetitions of stanza pattern and melody involved in the scenes between the Marys and the Merchant, the Angels and the Magdalen, but medieval listeners, more accustomed to such longueurs, would undoubtedly have taken such situations in their stride. We must include *St. Quentin 86* as being among the most successful of the Church music-dramas; one surely worthy of revival.

I turn now to the fourteenth-century *Engelberg 314*, which I have previously mentioned when dealing with the thirteenth-century Zürich (*Rheinau*) *MS XVIII*.[1] The Engelberg manuscript apparently owes much of its content to the earlier *Visitatio*, or to material very close to it. The chief new value of *Engelberg 314* is the fact that it gives us a complete musical setting of the texts, on a four-line stave with clefs, and, where necessary, B flats. The German neume-forms are to my mind rather ugly, but nevertheless quite clear in intention. Moreover, they serve to interpret the unheighted St. Gall neumes of *Rheinau XVIII*, and to confirm the fact that the latter's first antiphon incipit ('*Maria Magdalena . . .*') was indeed intending to speak of *three* Marys.[2]

Engelberg 314 follows Rheinau's example in using ZHN A, Melody I for the first three-stanza lament, but transposing the setting a fourth higher. They disagree regarding the independent composition, '*Quis revolvet nobis lapidem . . .*'; Rheinau prefers the older version with its characteristic music, Engelberg the newer version. There now comes the Sepulchre exchanges. In the case of Rheinau we have already remarked the fact that the monastery, an important German centre, chose to retain the older form of question, '*Quem quaeritis in sepulchro . . .*', with its traditional music. Engelberg prefers '*Quem quaeritis, o tremulae*

---

[1] See pp. 316–17. The text is printed in Young, I, pp. 375–7. [2] Young, pp. 375–7.

mulieres . . .' but cannot escape the ancient spell, for the music for the first two words is: r ḷ,dt, dṛd r-, before conforming to the usual setting of the revised dialogue. Engelberg follows Rheinau in dragging in the unnecessary recall of the Marys through the use of the ancient antiphon '*Venite et videte . . .*'. But in the next item it is Engelberg's own responsibility for striking an immediate exultant note through the singing by all three Marys (*alta voce*) of '*Surrexit Dominus de sepulchro . . .*'. This early rejoicing does not chime well with all the doubts, weeping, and lamenting soon to follow.

Like Rheinau, Engelberg now introduces a *Zehnsilberspiel* stanza, '*En angeli aspectum . . .*' (to Melody IV), which Mary apparently addresses to Peter, whose early appearance on the scene is vouched for by *Rheinau XVIII*. He seems quickly to have faded out again, since Melody IV is immediately employed for the ZHN D set of stanzas, the Magdalen's solitary lament, which is interrupted by the appearance of the disguised Christ.

His question, and Mary's '*Domine, si tu sustulisti eum . . .*', show some moments of possible musical independence. But Engelberg follows Rheinau and several other German *Visitatios* in causing Christ to sing '*Maria*' three times, in a somewhat florid setting. Mary's reply is marred by the rentention of the Vulgate gloss, '. . . *quod dicitur magister.*'

The items now proceed in familiar fashion, for, after a normal setting of '*Noli me tangere . . .*' we meet with the four stanzas of ZHN E, set to Melody V and interspersed with Mary's phrases of adoration. The work then ends abruptly with a blank four-line stave, above which are written the words '*Chorus Victimae paschali laudes*'. There is no more on the page, and no further sign in the manuscript of any continuation of the work.

When one compares this unsatisfactory finish with what *Rheinau XVIII* had to say after this point (which was a great deal), one is inclined to assume that the Engelberg copying was left incomplete.

We move to northern Italy for our next fourteenth-century 'third stage' *Visitatio*, but to a centre, Cividale, which we have already seen to have been under German influence.

MS CI, now in the Museo Archeologico Nazionale, is a processional that once belonged to the famous Cathedral of Cividale. As for the *Visitatio* (fol. 77r.–79r.), the text is finely written, and the square music notation, on four-line staves with C and F clefs, end-of-line 'directs', and all necessary B flats, beautifully so.[1]

Unfortunately, the first page of the *Visitatio* is missing, but we can readily recognize the first word we have, '*pastore*' (and its music), as belonging near the beginning of the second stanza of ZHN A, set to Melody I.[2] While making use of a great deal of common material, texts,

---

[1] The text is given in Young, I, pp. 378–80.

[2] I have in this item corrected a pitch error by the music scribe. Especially in these longer works containing repetitions of tunes such errors are very obvious, and I do not always remark on them.

and music, Cividale omits the Race to the Sepulchre episode, and provides a couple of sections which, in both texts and music, seem to be duite unique.

After the first laments, the '*Quis revolvet . . .*' question is given one of its usual settings, while the first exchange, '*Quem quaeritis, o tremulae mulieres . . .*', and '*Iesum Nazarenum . . .*', follows the familiar German pattern.

But what comes next is a remarkable piece of artistic imagination. Instead of the usual prose reply by the Angel, beginning '*Non est hic . . .*', we meet a poetic paraphrase of ten short lines ('*Nolite metuere . . .*') which possess the rhythmic vitality of a goliard poem. (See Karl Young, I, p. 379). The music, in free style with some melismatic passages, is, as far as I am aware, original, and in my opinion very attractive. The setting of the fourth line is that of the sixth; and the fifth, that of the seventh. Otherwise, there is no repetition of musical phrases. Karl Young, on his pages 380–1, makes a further point. The last couple of lines, '*. . . Michi si non creditis, videte sepulchrum!*' ('*. . . If you doubt my word, you may believe the testimony of your own eyes!*'), enables the Angel to introduce in a much more natural fashion than usual, the familiar antiphon command, '*Venite et videte . . .*'.

The Marys having come to the Tomb and censed it, the Angel continues with the same style of original poetic paraphrase, this time of the familiar prose passage, '*Ite, dicite discipulis eius . . .*'. The music of six of its eight short lines has been borrowed from the '*Nolite metuere . . .*' paraphrase. Refreshing originality! But with the Marys' '*Ad monumentum venimus . . .*' we are back to a familiar item, both in text and music.

Mary Magdalen is now alone, and again all is familiar. In spite of the angelic assurances she is unconvinced, and proceeds to utter the three stanzas of ZHN D, Melody IV. There comes the interruption of the disguised Jesus, who sings one of the most splendidly lyrical of all musical passages in Church drama. As far as I am aware, it is unique to the Cividale version. I quote it below, transposed up a fourth for its better accommodation on a G clef stave:

Mu — — li — er, quid plo — — — — — — — ras?

There follows the prose sentence '*Quia tulerunt Dominum meum . . .*'. Settings of this text, including liturgical ones, are many and various, but I find Cividale's not easy to duplicate in any of its phrases.

Christ now reveals his identity in the usual way, by the single gentle word, '*Maria!*', but this is achieved musically in striking fashion, by re-employing the phrase that had previously set '*Mulier*':

Ma — — — ri — a!

There comes Mary's high-pitched cry, as she runs to his feet:

More Cividale originalities follow.

In most *Visitatio* examples of the longer sort, there succeeds, as Christ's gentle repulse, the prose passage '*Noli me tangere . . .*'. There are several musical settings, in group agreement, but Cividale will have none of them and goes its own way; once again paraphrasing, and producing two rhyming couplets (Young, I, p. 380). These are set to a somewhat melismatic tune, of a a b a' pattern, one that I have not met before.

Apparently Christ then retires, leaving Mary alone. She sings the ZHN F stanza, '*Vere vidi Dominum vivere . . .*', used elsewhere only by *Klosterneuberg 574*, and two later Visitatios from Zwickau and Wolfenbüttel. The two last-named agree with Cividale in setting the stanza to Melody III. Curiously enough, the unfamiliar melody of the previous item, the pattern of which I spoke of in terms of a a b a', commences in a fashion very reminiscent of Melody III.

Mary's '*Vere vidi . . .*' is addressed not to the two disciples, who are not represented in the work, but to the chorus. No doubt it could be said that these represented the body of the disciples, but something of drama is here lost.

The '*Victimae paschali*' finish, as presented, falls somewhat flat. The chorus ask the 'single Mary' the usual '*Dic nobis, quid vidisti . . .*' question, and receive the usual three-sentence reply, with its evidence so unimportant when following Christ's actual appearance. The final two sentences of the sequence are sung by the chorus, with a concluding '*Alleluia*'. The rest of the page (about a third) is left blank, without any trace of a '*Te Deum*' incipit.

In spite of the somewhat tame ending, we have met with competent, and at times original, dramatic writing, both in the matter of texts and music settings—with some outstanding instances in the case of the latter. The version is surely worthy of a revival in performance.[1]

To conclude our review of fourteenth century 'third stage' *Visitatios* I consider a small group, all closely similar, which appear to have belonged to a Prague convent of nuns, the number extant being probably seven. I will content myself with examining in detail only the version from *MS VI. G. 3b* (fol. 84r.–90r.), from a processional now in the University Library at Prague.[2] The version is clearly written, and is given satisfactory rubrics and a complete musical setting in Gothic neumes on a four-line stave. Similar versions of this group are not so well treated, only one other having its music. This Prague conception

---

[1] In April 1939 I supervised a performance of this work in the King's Weigh Chapel, London, under the auspices of the Plainsong and Medieval Music Society.

[2] The whole text of this Prague version can be seen in Karl Young, I, pp. 402–5.

contains a number of originalities, and also, even when employing familiar texts, frequently insists on what appears to be its own particular musical invention.

At the very start we find something unusual. In the first rubric we are told of the entry of the Lady Abbess, followed by Mary Magdalen and three other Marys, to the choral singing of the Easter responsory, '*Dum transisset sabbatum . . .*', which tells of the purchase of the spices. Immediately after, the Marys are to be seen carrying out the action, accepting, and no doubt appearing to pay for, unguents from a silent 'Merchant'. We have already seen in ZHN C how this 'purchase' scene could be handled. *Prague VI.G.3b* is content with a single stanza, '*Aromata precio quaerimus . . .*', a stanza which, incidentally, is found only in the Prague group and in the longer Klosterneuburg and Benediktbeuern versions, sung to Melody III.

What follows in the next six items—the antiphon comment of the choir;[1] the doubts of the Marys as they approach the Tomb; the later style '*Quem quaeritis . . .*', '*Non est hic . . .*' exchange; the '*Venite et videte . . .*' antiphon; the invented '*Ad monumentum venimus . . .*' of the Marys—are all familiar, and are given familiar settings. Unusual is the introduction of the liturgical antiphon, '*Noli flere Maria . . .*' (used also by St. Quentin and the Orléans *Visitatio*). Prague's music comes straight from Hartker's Antiphonal. Another rarely employed antiphon text follows, sung by the convent; '*Maria stabat ad monumentum . . .*'.[2]

All the texts of the Christ-Magdalen exchanges will be found to be familiar, from '*Tulerunt Dominum meum . . .*' to '*Noli me tangere . . .*', but again it is surprising to find that the music appears to belong to Prague alone; that is, as far as my seekings are concerned. The '*Maria*'— '*Raboni*' setting is interesting, and as far as I know, unique.

I again transpose:

—Mary borrowing part of Christ's music.

When, in '*Noli me tangere . . .*' the word '*Maria*' occurs, it is set to the same phrase as that of '*Raboni*'.

The next item is seldom seen in Church drama. '*Venit Maria*

---

[1] As Karl Young points out (p. 405) the singular inappropriateness of the antiphon '*Maria Magdalena et alia Maria . . .*' is apparent, both in relation to the numbers of the Marys and the rubric details of the purchase. In point of fact, the mystery of the four Marys is never elucidated. We may perhaps conclude that Prague, most exceptionally, wanted it that way.

[2] Professor Lipphardt notes that this antiphon belongs to the late '*Historia*' [*officium*] *Sanctae Mariae Magdalenae* (13th century) [*Ed.*].

annuncians . . .' might be classed as an antiphon, since the text turns up in Hartker, but Prague's setting is quite different.[1]

There follows a '*Victimae paschali*' exchange between the Magdalen and a '*Cantrix*' (!), carried through in pedestrian fashion, with the chorus rounding off the sequence.

An unusual feature follows, the singing by a priest of '*Christus Dominus resurrexit . . .*'. The text is found also in *Haarlem MS 258* (see p. 290), but Prague's setting is much more elaborate.

Finally, there occurs a rather untidy finish. The inclusion of the choral antiphon '*Currebant duo simul . . .*' leads us to guess that a Race to the Sepulchre takes place, but no rubric helps us. Two priests display the grave clothes and sing '*Cernitis, o socii . . .*', to the usual music, after which the convent concludes the drama with the 'German' setting of '*Surrexit Dominus de sepulchro . . .*'.

In three of the remaining Prague manuscripts there is to be found a feature not present in the version that we have just considered. This is an utterance for the Spice Merchant, '*Dabo vobis unguenta optima . . .*', in reply to Mary's verse '*Aromata precio . . .*'. It is in fact one of the more rarely occurring ZHN C stanzas, but we have already encountered it in the two extensive thirteenth-century *Visitatios* from Klosterneuberg and Benediktbeuern.[2] In each of the latter cases it is set to Melody III. As two of the three Prague versions referred to above are without their music, I turn to the *MS VI, G. 10a* (fol. 149r.–153v.) from the same library, and belonging apparently to the turn of the century. We find that this version, and thus probably all the Prague manuscripts, prefer to set the stanza to the less often employed Melody VI.

The texts and music of *MS VI. G. 10a* are so similar to those of the earlier *MS VI. G. 3b* as to make it apparent that the Prague convent was quite settled in its mind as to what it preferred as a *Visitatio Sepulchri*.

With these Prague versions, we conclude our survey of fourteenth-century *Visitatio* versions. There are other scattered items of evidence as to fourteenth-century performances of *Visitatio*-type Church dramas, even though the actual written work concerned has not come down to us; also, indications that some individual dramas existed in a number of slightly modified versions. Again, it may be that there are fourteenth-century *Visitatio* manuscripts in existence which have escaped my attention. It seems undeniable, however, that Appendix Ie points to a falling away in Christendom of a general interest in Latin Church music-dramas, even those of the Easter Sepulchre.

IV

As for the post-Easter activities of the fourteenth century, I can report only one newly-written version of a *Peregrinus*, this occurring in a breviary used at Saintes in Western France. Fortunately, it has retained

---

[1] Also from the *Historia Sanctae Mariae Magdalenae*, see footnote p. 373 [*Ed.*].
[2] See pp. 330 and 331.

its music, written in square notation on a four-line stave (*B.N., MS lat. 16309*, fol. 604r.–605r.).[1] Although so late in appearance, it actually represents the simplest form of the *Peregrinus* type that has survived. The little work, showing no relationship to the liturgical items immediately surrounding it, must surely be a copy of a much older version now perished. I have referred to it in the course of my general discussion of the *Peregrinus* type on pp. 185–98, where I also give some details as to reported performances in various countries of this form of drama.

After the *Peregrinus* happenings the next major event of the season we might expect to see dramatized would be the Ascension, described in the first chapter of the Acts of the Apostles. But, as Karl Young observes (I, p. 483), what we meet with in liturgical records proves to be overwhelmingly concerned 'merely with symbolic or mimetic acts accompanying the authorized forms of worship'.

Recalling that so fruitful source, the '*Quem quaeritis in sepulchro . . .*' exchange, and also the question of the 'two men in white apparel' who 'stood by' at the Ascension, one might well have expected the trope which indeed actually arose to a brief existence, '*Quem creditis super astra ascendisse, o Christicolae?*', to have shaped itself into an actual dramatic representation of the Ascension, and that in wide use. I have already reproduced the two sentences of the exchange between Angels and apostles, together with their musical settings as recovered from that curious miscellany, *B.N., (N.A.) MS 1235* (see pp. 86–7). The debt of this trope to the parent '*Quem quaeritis*' is evident, the more so when the music is examined and it is seen that although the melodic line is in the main, different, the composer has been unable to resist developing a musical rhyme at the vocative phrases which seems to owe a debt to Limoges. Limoges also happens to have at least two other tropers of the late tenth and the eleventh centuries which contain an Ascension trope, but these are set to a different music. The *British Museum MS Cotton Caligula, AXIV* (fol. 18r.) also has an Ascension trope; the music, in Anglo-Saxon neumes, appears to be quite different again from the other settings. It does not seem that the Ascension trope inspired that single-minded drive which produced the *Visitatio Sepulchri*, and the almost standardized text and music for its central dialogue.

Ascension Day is celebrated on the Thursday following the fifth Sunday after Easter, and, as Karl Young has shown (I, pp. 483–4), all over Christendom, especially in the fifteenth and sixteenth centuries, the event was recalled in the course of the liturgy of the day in various symbolic ways, culminating vividly in places with the drawing up of an effigy of Christ through the church roof.

Karl Young prints in full (I, pp. 484–88) the text of a ceremony from fourteenth-century Moosburg.[2] This is a far more ambitious effort, and, since it is given 'living' characters—the impersonations of the apostles,

---

[1] The text is given in Young, I, pp. 453–8.
[2] Munich, *Staatsbibl., MS lat. 9469*, fols. 72v.–73v.

the Virgin Mary and two Angels, all suitably costumed and exchanging dialogue—we must grant that here we have true drama, one drawback being the necessity of representing Christ in no more than effigy. Another disadvantage is the fact that the text is an *ordinarium*; as a result not a note of the sung texts is written in. However, it is clear that no original composition was being attempted, and that the music would have proved to have come wholly from the choir books; in which case, I am assuming that Karl Young has said all that there is to be said regarding this rare attempt to create an Ascension drama.

V

From Clermont-Ferrand cathedral comes a single fourteenth-century example of the Christmas '*Quem quaeritis in praesepe . . .*' dialogue, a breviary version (without its music) placed after the '*Te Deum*' of Matins and directed to lead straight into the first Mass of Christmas Day.[1] The rubrics speak of *Pastores*, and this may hint at impersonation, and an actual dramatic performance as a preface to the Introit of the Mass.

In the previous chapter (see pp. 344–5) I have spoken of the singularly modest thirteenth-century production by the diocese of Rouen of a 'Magi' drama, brief in action and closely woven into the Oblation ceremony of the Epiphany Mass. I have mentioned also that to judge by the several surviving 'repeats' of the text (no other version except that of *B.N. MS lat. 904* has its music given), a fair amount of use must have been made of it in the Normandy of the thirteenth to fifteenth centuries. In the fourteenth century there appears a version that must nowadays be described as *Rouen, Bibl. de la Ville, MS 384*, fol. 38v.–39v. As I have indicated, there is no music, but the manuscript being an ordinarium, the accompanying rubrics are unusually generous, and serve to assist any attempts to revive the *B.N. 904* version.

VI

An important and unique Crucifixion drama remains to be considered.[2] We can be sure of giving it its correct name, since its first rubric states: '*Hic incipit Planctus Mariae et aliorum in die Parasceven . . .*'. The 'others' in this Good Friday drama consist of Mary Magdalen, Mary the mother of James, and the youthful St. John.[3] The single scene is concerned only with their laments, addressed among themselves, to the (presumed)

[1] Paris, *B.N., MS lat. 1274*, fol. 40v. The text is given in Young, II, p. 12.

[2] *Cividale, Museo Archeologico Nazionale, MS CI*, fols. 74r.–76v., a Processional of the fourteenth century, belonging originally to the *Cividale* Cathedral. The text is given in Young, I, pp. 506–13.

[3] But see Karl Young, I, p. 513 and my pp. 380–1 in the matter of the speaker of Item 17 ('*Consolare, Domina . . .*').

effigy of Christ upon the Cross, and even at times to the 'people' supposedly assembled at the Crucifixion. It is however the Virgin Mother who dominates the scene. Of the score of stanza items uttered, she bears the major part, singing more lines than those of the rest put together.

In the matter of Passion dramas there has already been mention in Chapter XIII of the incomplete 'Sulmona fragment', the text of which, framed in rhyming stanzas, Karl Young has reprinted (I, pp. 701–8). I have noted on pp. 293–4 its links with the recently discovered and far more important text, that of a mid-twelfth-century Passion from the monastery of Montecassino in Italy. A large number of the incidents of the Passion story, we found, were related in the Montecassino work, which makes use throughout of the double 887 pattern of the Victorine sequence verse. But as we have noted, neither manuscript had managed to retain the music settings which must undoubtedly have once accompanied this type of 'sequence' poetry.

The Cividale *Planctus Mariae* had less ambitions in regard to time and space. It begins with the assembling of the four before the Cross, and ends when the Virgin Mother, overcome with grief, sinks into the supporting arms of her friends. But the idea of the mourning Mother at the Cross (put into immortal shape by the '*Stabat Mater*' sequence) had produced many '*Planctus*' poems during the Middle Ages, these growing in number with the increasing cult of the Virgin. The Cividale work is the most striking of the few surviving examples, which from their dialogue form and other evidence, seem to have been meant for dramatic use—most probably for inclusion in the Good Friday ceremony of the Adoration of the Cross, in which there also occur the striking *Improperia*, the 'reproaches', supposedly spoken by Christ himself.

The only Gospel reference to the assembly of the faithful few at the Cross is St. John xix: 25–27, a brief narrative bare of any mention of lament. However, medieval imagination and an apocryphal gospel created the figure of the mourning Mother. Normally, the *Planctus* was either for the Virgin Mary alone; or in dialogue with Christ; or with John; or with both the other two, Christ committing his Mother to the care of John as related in the latter's own Gospel. The Cividale version is unique in employing four participants, their identities coinciding with the Gospel account.[1]

In my discussion of this text I shall once again make use of Karl Young's line numberings for reference. It is apparent that the text is divided into twenty separate items, each headed by the name of the performer of the item. The actual manuscript is a beautifully written one,[2] the music being in square notation on a four-line stave, with 'directs' and added B flats. The work begins with no more heading than the rubric that I have already mentioned. It breaks off before the end owing to a

[1] But see p. 381.

[2] Karl Young (I, f.p. 506), gives as Plate XII a reproduction of the Cividale drama's first manuscript page.

missing page, and item no. 20 is left incomplete, a deficiency which is partly reparable.

Complete originality can certainly not be claimed for the libretto of the Cividale *Planctus*, since nearly half the lines in its score of stanzas can be found, identical or closely related, in the *planctus* '*Flete, fideles animae . . .*', a work of a dozen stanzas written in the thirteenth century or earlier.[1] This poem belonged apparently to the Virgin alone, imagined as uttered at the foot of the Cross. One of its stanzas gives an intact version of Cividale's incomplete Item 20. It is, however, without music, although undoubtedly some kind of setting would once have existed.

Cividale, for all its care in naming each speaker, contains possible scribal errors: for example, the incongruous intrusion of John into No. 8 ('*Triste spectaculum . . .*'), where according to the manuscript he takes over from the Virgin Mary in mid-sentence.

A striking and unique feature of the Cividale version is the multiplicity of its rubric stage-directions. In this short, almost static drama there are no less than seventy-nine of them, written in a tiny script above the text and mingling with the music staves. Numerous different hand and arm gestures and body movements are called for, together with embraces and kneelings. The playwright was apparently trying to arrange for the drama to produce itself!

Alone among surviving dramatic laments at the Cross, Cividale has preserved its musical setting. As usual, this consists of no more than a single line of vocal melody. Thanks to the immaculate notation the pitches of the notes are never in question, but there is little doubt that what we are dealing with is not 'plain' chant, but music as rhythmic in intention as the verse to which it is joined.

The libretto poem assembled for the Cividale *Planctus*—(and 'assembled' seems to be the operative word)—comprises in my opinion the most rhythmically varied of all such to be met with among the medieval Church dramas. Soon after the start of the work, when the passage '*Ergo quare, fili care . . .*' (borrowed from the earlier *planctus* mentioned above) begins to appear, so also does the familiar Victorine 887 887 verse patterns so much overworked in other Passion poems. But not for long; a glance at the Karl Young text will reveal what rhythmic variety there is in the lines of the successive items, ready to guide the melodies of the settings into a similar artistic variety.

While more often than not in the progress of the work a new text-item means a new tune there are a number of exceptions to this practice. Of particular interest is the subsequent handling of the music to which the passage '*Ergo quare . . .*' referred to above is set (Item 2; Young, ll. 9–13). The melody was perhaps inherited, like the text, from the older poem but it is later put to notable use. I give the setting as it occurs in the second item—its first appearance. I have myself given a first-rhythmic-mode reading to the music:

---

[1] The text is printed in full by Karl Young (I, pp. 498–9).

The third item ('*Rex celestis . . .*') is sung by St. John to a new melody but the fourth ('*Munda caro . . .*'), that of Mary Jacobi, has for its setting a repeat of the '*Ergo quare . . .*' tune, unchanged but for the fact that in the manuscript it is now pitched a fifth higher.[1]

A general survey of the music will now reveal that this tune could be thought of as an early example of what later ages have termed the '*idée fixe*'. On at least four more occasions we are reminded of its presence. In Item 10 (St. John's '*O Maria mater . . .*') the tune is extended and given a different cadence. In Item 9 (the Virgin Mother's '*Mi, Johannes . . .*') the extension is longer and employs new material.

In Item 15 ('*Quis est hic . . .*') Mary Jacobi gives once more a simple rendering of the tune, all the more effective in its plainness since it follows long and elaborate solos (Items 12 and 13) by the Virgin Mother and by Mary Magdalen, and again a despairing one by the Virgin, who, striking her breast and in an emotional climax, utters her cry of:

Immediately after (Item 16), the Virgin makes a plain use of the '*idéé*' once more in the striking stanza '*O vos omnes qui transitis per viam . . .*', concluding with the '*Heu me!*' lament. Incidentally, at the end of her '*Fili me, carissime . . .*' item (No. 18), she repeats the '*Heu me! misera Maria!*' lament, but this time increasing the emotion by raising the pitch of the passage ($\underline{d}'\underline{r}'$ m' $\underline{d}'\underline{t}'$ d' - 1 . . .).

I have been fortunate in having seen, under cathedral conditions, a number of performances by professional singers of a transcription of this work.[2] On some technical points I may well have given opportunities

---

[1] This fact, together with other manuscript evidence concerning the tessitura of the Virgin Mother's music, caused me to decide when making a transcription of the work that if the other Marys were to be sopranos, the Virgin Mother must be cast as a contralto, or at least a mezzo.

[2] The transcription, *Planctus Mariae*, is published by Oxford University Press (London, 1965). I made some suggestions there regarding possible support for the voices by means of chamber organ and chime bells, but I am not enthusiastic for the idea. I should like to say once again that I believe that 'voices alone' would probably represent the authentic original conditions. I also supplied a portion of a relevant thirteenth-century motet as an 'introduction'. I suggest that this also might be dispensed with, the four 'actors' merely entering silently.

for criticism, but the impact on the hearers was, I believe, that here was a drama charged with passionate human feeling. To me, also, the device of the '*idée fixe*' was a success. The item '*Ergo quare, fili care . . .*' in itself was a tragic question, and I can imagine that the playwright-composer was intending to remind us at intervals of that bewildered '*quare?*' which was haunting the thoughts of all the mourners, by his repeated use of the musical theme.

There are other transferences of melody. John, in No. 19, sings the tune that he has already employed in No. 3. The Virgin's setting of '*Qui timor . . .*' in Item 14 (1. 85) is used by Mary Magdalen in Item 17, but without the lament section with which the former ends.

There are two 'pairs' of settings. The first, John's '*Fleant materna viscera . . .*'[1] (Item no. 5), is balanced by the Virgin's no. 6, '*Flete, fideles animae . . .*'. The settings differ by a few notes only, which is fortunate, since a word ('*matris*') is obviously missing from No. 5, and the twin score supplies the absent music. The other 'pair' comprise Nos. 12 and 13 and represent the most ambitious solos of the work. The first, the Virgin's impassioned cavatina ('*O Maria Magdalena . . .*'; ll. 64–75) extends in my transcription to 55 bars of triple time. Mary Magdalena in reply ('*Mater Jesu crucifixi . . .*'; ll. 76–80) and using much the same musical material, but with omissions and modifications, confines her answer to 28 bars. For the transcriber the possession of two very similar settings here was fortunate, since the scribe's intentions regarding accidentals are not always clear, and some useful comparisons were possible.

Two particularly beautiful and shapely melodies are the settings of No. 8 ('*Triste spectaculum . . .*') and No. 11 ('*O, Pater benigne . . .*'). The latter derives a number of its musical phrases from the former, with differences of rhythm brought about by differences of text accents.

A few other problems remain to be mentioned. In the same No. 8 the Virgin recalls the prophecy as to the sword that 'shall pierce through thy own soul', and, a rubric directing her to 'point to an angel', she declares 'he it is who foretold it; this is the sword which pierces through me'. It is all very puzzling. Perhaps the sworded angel was a near-by effigy; but in any case, it was Simeon, not an angel, who made the prophecy (St. Luke ii: 35).

There is also the matter of the incomplete final item (No. 20; '*O mentes perfidas . . .*'), incomplete at the bottom of a manuscript page, with the next leaf, which undoubtedly saw the end of the work, missing. I have already mentioned the possibility of completing the stanza text from another *planctus*. But this unfortunately did not solve the music problem, since '*Flete, fideles . . .*' is without its setting. However, a comparison of the surviving 13 bars of music of No. 20 with the first 13 bars of No. 18 ('*Fili mi . . .*') reveal so close a similarity as to encourage the idea of fitting the remaining and borrowed text of No. 20 to the rest

---

[1] In the manuscript, Item no. 5 is set down quite unmistakably to be sung by John. Some previous literary editors have remarked that the text belongs more fittingly to one of the 'lesser' Marys.

of the music of No. 18, certainly a smooth enough task. I fancy that this represents a near-correct guess.

Finally, a paleographical matter: Karl Young, commenting on the drama on p. 513, says: 'Particularly noteworthy is the increase of the number of speakers to five'. I can only assume that he is bearing in mind the *'Consolare, Domina . . .'* stanza (No. 17) addressed by a 'lesser Mary' to the Virgin. He prints the speaker's name as *'Maria sola'*, but he gives as a footnote Coussemaker's reading of the second word, which the latter makes out to be *'Salome'*. It would thus seem that he accepts this sudden advent of a new character into the cast. Certainly I have no more than a photograph of the manuscript page in front of me (albeit a very clear one), but, in my opinion, the word *'sola'* (not *'Salome'*) can be traced. But further illegible smearings follow, impossible to interpret. I should have thought that No. 17 belongs best to Mary Magdalen. The Virgin has just sung. Before her Mary Jacobi has had her second chance of a solo. It seems surely to be the Magdalen's turn, before the Virgin's last powerful *'Heu me . . .'* lament. For the new figure of Mary Salome to be brought in at this late point just to sing a single short solo, seems to me very unlikely.

Even so, with all the doubts and perhaps some unsolved problems, the Cividale *Planctus Mariae* constitutes a medieval work of art and is worthy of modern revival. Here is something more than drama—real music-drama—drama with the pitches of its emotions heightened through its partnership with purposeful styles of melody.

I have already made mention of another remarkable fourteenth-century work concerned with the Virgin, the 'Presentation of the Blessed Virgin Mary at the Temple',[1] the brain-child of that highly gifted French nobleman, Philippe de Mézières. I have spoken of the extraordinary wealth of stage directions which the original manuscript supplied, and which Karl Young has printed in full, together with the drama-text. The work has also received attention from Hardin Craig (pp. 78–9), and particularly from Grace Frank.[2] From her pages may be read an account of the painstaking production details, while Karl Young has summarized the action of the drama (II, pp. 242–4), making mention of the moments of medieval humour which occur—the rough treatment of the chained and howling Lucifer by the sworded Archangel and the fleeing from the building of the outfaced and weeping Synagoga. The latter incident was apparently expected to cause 'laughter in church', which was duly allowed for.

But the fact remains that the whole of the textual material, with the exception of one item, is liturgical in nature. Also, there is no note of musical notation in the manuscript, which may indicate that all that was sung was a matter of routine knowledge.

---

[1] *Festum Praesentationis Beatae Mariae Virginis.* The full dramatic ceremony is given in Young, II, pp. 227–42. For my discussion of it with particular regard to the question of instruments in medieval performances, see pp. 250–1.

[2] Grace Frank, *The Medieval French Drama* (Oxford, 1954), pp. 64–5 and 70–3.

We have already made note of the two *Pulsatores*, who were the only musicians present, and have discovered that they were likely to have been players of portative organs. Their main task, it seems, was to supply '*conductus*' music during the various movements of the actors from place to place. No clue is given as to what they were supposed to play.

However, there was another important task for them, the non-liturgical item mentioned above. In an effort to move the listening populace to devotion ('*ad excitandum populum ad devotionem*'), a secular *cantilena* was performed, but its identity is not disclosed (see my p. 251).

Undoubtedly we have here a true drama acted out by impersonated characters. It must have been an impressive and moving spectacle, but we have no hint of invented and dramatic melody such as was present in the Cividale *Planctus Mariae* and which would add another dimension to the emotions of the dramatic text and action.

Further fourteenth-century dramas concerning the Virgin deal with the Annunciation. Karl Young (II, pp. 245–6) has an informative section on this type of observance through the centuries, where liturgy mingles with symbolism and the use of effigies. He prints the text (II, p. 247) from a Cividale manuscript,[1] a processional. It would appear that the action, carried out by Mary, Elizabeth, and an Angel, with the official deacon supplying the liturgical matter, was performed in the open air, the procession returning to the building to sing the '*Te Deum*'. There are readings from the Gospel and plainchant for the liturgical items, but one delightful invented interlude, the singing of a single three-line stanza by Elizabeth, addressed to Mary and, surely, delivered rhythmically:

Sal - ve ca - ra, De - o gra - ta, te sa - lu - to, sis be - a - - ta; Te - cum sit - que Do - mi - nus.

Karl Young also prints the text of a fourteenth-century Annunciation from the cathedral library of Padua (II, pp. 248–50),[2] and describes the drama, which is given ample stage directions in the manuscript. The vocal music represents no more than familiar plainchant, but there occurs a rare mention, a call for the tolling of a heavy tower bell—in this case to summon the company from their dinner to the drama. At the very conclusion comes another rare piece of information. The '*Magnificat*' (Mary's own song) is to be performed *alternatim*; that is, the organ and the chorus will render the verses alternately throughout.

---

[1] *Cividale, Museo Archeologico Nazionale, MS CII*, fols. 69v.–71r.
[2] *Padua, Bibl. Capit. MS C 56*, fols. 36v.–39r. The numberings of the pages do not agree with those given by Karl Young. However, these are the (amended) figures which I see on the photos of the manuscript which I possess. Evidently a re-numbering has taken place in the Padua library.

One more drama of the Virgin Mary surviving from the fourteenth century remains to be considered, that of the 'Purification' feast of February 2nd. Karl Young (II, pp. 250–5) ranges over numerous medieval records that reveal how the story told by St. Luke of the Presentation of the infant Jesus at the Temple, forty days after the Nativity, and which was celebrated at first as a feast of the Son, gradually changed its emphasis in favour of the Mother. He prints (II, pp. 253–5), as the best example of a genuine drama on the subject, a text from earlier pages of the same manuscript belonging to Padua Cathedral,[1] and afterwards describes the action. As he observes, the work may be characterized as a genuine play in the form of an elaborate dumb-show, in which the action is accompanied by the singing of appropriate liturgical pieces.

Once again there is no more for me to add concerning the musical side, except that again a tolling bell summons the participants, and that the singing of the final '*Gloria Patri*' is to be performed *alternatim*, between organ and chorus.

---

[1] *Padua, Bibl. Capit., MS C 56*, fols. 15r.–17v. What I have said in a previous footnote in the case of the other Padua manuscript regarding the revision of page numberings applies also here.

CHAPTER SIXTEEN

THE FIFTEENTH CENTURY

THE closing years of the fourteenth century found western Christendom still in a divided state. Also, a new kind of criticism of the Church was beginning to make a noticeable impact. John Wycliffe (1320–84), a learned English churchman, and a famous debater, preacher, and writer, began in his later years to dare to question matters of doctrine. Also, he helped in a translation of the Latin Bible into the vernacular, and organized his 'poor priests' to spread his ideas from the rectory at Lutterworth to the length and breadth of England. Often it would have gone ill with him but for the protection given him by friends in high places, who supported him for their own political ends. The 'Lollard' movement, as it came to be called, continued, comparatively unsuccessfully, in England for a century and a half, with Church authorities, supported by such kings as Henry IV, V, and VII, taking occasional stern measures against the new heresy.

It was otherwise on the Continent. Scholars who came to England from Bohemia in the train of Anne, Richard II's queen, took eagerly to Wycliffe's writings, and bore them back to Europe, where his ideas started to spread. Under the leadership of John Hus (1373–1415), sometime rector of Prague University and a follower of Wycliffe's teachings, a movement began which had an eventual influence on Martin Luther and the shaping of the Reformation.

With the first two decades of the fifteenth century came desperate efforts on the part of responsible leaders, ecclesiastical and secular, to bring about a return to normal and dignified conditions in the higher levels of Church government. The first important event was the calling of the Council of Constance (1414–18). As it happened, one of its earliest acts was to summon John Hus before it. In spite of a safe-conduct given him by the Emperor Sigismund, he was tried and condemned for heresy, and suffered death by fire. The same Council ordered the bones of John Wycliffe to be disinterred and burnt. Of more practical use was the Council's healing of the Great Schism. The deposition of no less than three 'Popes', each denouncing the other two, became necessary, and in the end there came the establishment once more, back in Rome, of a single and undisputed Vicar of Christ.

Although for a great part of the fifteenth century disintegration of the old order continued, yet economic recovery from the sad conditions of the fourteenth was evident. New outlooks, also, began to be apparent. With the waning of the 'age of chivalry' romantic impulses tended to be replaced by greater common-sense, but developed often enough to the cunning and duplicity found in many a Renaissance ruler.

In 1415 Henry V of England revived the Anglo-French struggle which had ended in the third quarter of the previous century with the recovery by France of most of her occupied territories. In Henry is to be seen a ruler of this new age, efficient, determined, and coldly realistic (rejecting, for example, such 'chivalric' ideas as challenges to single combat). After his early victories and his early death, the English cause once again turned towards failure, the French revival sparked off by the appearance of one of the most wonderful and inexplicable figures in all history. Joan of Arc was filled with all the passionate religious beliefs of the Age of Faith. Yet in practical affairs her instinctive, common-sense realism belonged to the new era. After something over a year of decisive triumphs she was captured and delivered to a court of French and Burgundian ecclesiastics. According to the lights of the time her trial was a fair one, conducted by a conscientious body of men. By them she was found guilty of heresy and witchcraft. She was handed over to the English authorities to be burnt in the market-place at Rouen.

But her task was accomplished. French military confidence had returned in full measure. Before the middle of the century all that remained of the English foothold was Calais and its 'pale'.

Joan at her trial made plain her belief that she was 'not bound to submit her words and deeds to the Church Militant or to any other than to God'. This was a voice from the new age. Yet (and here I quote the words of Charles T. Wood)[1]:

. . . Joan's was not the world of Machiavelli and the Renaissance, and neither was it that of Luther. Dying serene in the faith that 'God helping me, today I shall be with Him in Paradise', she was the last of the medieval saints. And though her career did much to end chivalry, our memory of her does much to preserve it.

Five and a half centuries later the Church which had condemned her did indeed canonize her as a saint.

II

It is impossible to imagine that the degradation of the Roman Church at its highest levels did not have some impact on the monastic life, and that of the secular clergy in close contact with the laity. But would this offer any explanation for the falling away in production of Latin Church dramas through the fifteenth century, confined as they were almost entirely to the *Visitatio Sepulchri* type? To me a more likely reason would

[1] C. T. Wood, *The Age of Chivalry* (New York, 1970), p. 150.

be the final triumph of the vernacular, spoken religious drama, as far as the growing body of intelligent laity were concerned.[1]

From the time of the twelfth-century *Mystère d'Adam* onwards, vernacular drama had gone from strength to strength. Whatever interest the laity may have taken in the Church Latin dramas as spectacles, they were probably not much concerned with the fact that the more or less incomprehensible texts were all sung in one form or another of expressive melody. The striking subtleties in the music of these works, of which we have taken note from time to time, were realized, probably, by only a small minority of listeners, while in the open-air drama the citizen, as a change from the plain tones of everyday speech, met with incidental music, vocal and instrumental, that was probably more to his taste.

We shall find in the lengthier Church dramas of the fifteenth and sixteenth centuries a manifest anxiety on the part of the clerical play-wrights to *explain* to the lay portion of their audiences the gist of what the sung Latin texts were saying. The outside dramatic activities were perhaps bringing an influence to bear.

Turning to actual manuscript versions written (or re-copied) in the fifteenth century, we will consider first some unambitious 'first stage' *Visitatios*.

The first fifteenth-century 'first stage' *Visitatio* that I mention is an imperfect one, and something of a curiosity—*Paris, B.N. MS 1123*.[2] A *processionale*, it consists of no more than an introductory and identi-fying rubric, followed by the three usual dialogue sentences and no more. The first and third are given their music, neatly written in square notation on four-line staves with clefs, but '*Jesum Nazarenum . . .*' is left unset. The page itself (25) is out of place, and its back (25v.) has been left blank, as if the copying were to be continued. From certain similari-ties in the music, I am inclined to believe that the version is closely related to that found in *Brit. Mus., Add. MS 37399* (see pp. 287–8), one of a group that makes great use of the sequence '*Victimae paschali*'. Possibly it was intended that this should be copied on the blank page. Both versions set the first vocative ('*O Christicolae*') to the notes rm rd m fm r-. *MS 37399* repeats the music for '*o caelicolae*', making a musical rhyme. If only *B.N. MS 1123* had given its music at this point the question of relationships might have been really settled.

A brief Bamberg *Visitatio*[3] has a long ancestry, being a copy of our previously mentioned *Bamberg MS 22*, with its remarkable five intro-ductory rhyming lines, these given an echo effect in their settings (see pp. 158–9). *MS 27*, through its heavy 'nail' notation on four-line staves,

---

[1] Concerning the 'gradual transference of religious drama from ecclesiastical to secular auspices', Karl Young remarks (II, p. 421): 'The change came about not through peremptory legislation, but, if we may judge by the results, through the natural desire of both playwright and audience for an increase in the scope of the performances, for an enrichment of content, and for the use of the vernacular.'

[2] *Paris, B.N. MS lat. 1123*, fol. 25r.

[3] *Bamberg, Staatsbibl., MS 27* (Ed. I, p. 13), fol. 170r. (This version is mentioned as a variant to *Bamberg 22* in Young, I, p. 584).

furnishes the clues to *MS 22*'s unheighted neumes, but does not show the artistry of the earlier version, which runs the last two lines together in unbroken fashion, and then, at the very end, effectively combines their echoes.

A processional from Melk[1] is worthy of notice because of its introduction of the ten-syllable verses beginning '*Resurrexit victor ab infernis . . .*'. This rare composition has already been mentioned (on p. 326) in connection with the *Visitatios* from *Klosterneuberg 574* and *Munich 4660 a*. The Melk version, its German notation being on a four-line stave, proved useful for deciphering the unheighted neumes of the older manuscripts. The verses served also to replace the normal '*Non est hic . . .*' reply by the Angel. They are followed by a prose passage beginning '*Nolite expavescere . . .*' which contains much familiar textual material, but cast in a form that is found elsewhere in two other versions only, the above-mentioned *Klosterneuberg 574* and the fifteenth-century *Visitatio* from St. Florian[2] (see below, pp. 387–8). The three musical settings seem very largely to agree, the Melk melody being a transposed version of that of St. Florian. The Klosterneuberg version is of course in unheighted neumes only. I can trace no earlier origin for the melody, which together with the text seems to represent original composition.

We come now to a brief and unenterprising version from Amberg,[3] with nothing new to note in text or music, except the fact that the first two sentences of the '*Quem quaeritis*' dialogue are transcribed up a fourth, and the '*Non est hic . . .*' setting transposed down again. The version, in clumsy 'nail' notation, probably represents a re-copying of a much earlier manuscript.

I leave fifteenth-century 'first stage' versions with a reference to a manuscript from Brescia in Lombardy which intrigued Karl Young (see I, pp. 221–2). On the face of it we have here a brief dramatic *Visitatio Sepulchri* set down to lead into the Introit of the Easter Mass, with the costumed and impersonating 'Marys' going on to sing the tropes of the Introit, which are given in the text. The version, strange as it is, must be accepted as it stands, but as Karl Young points out, its late date makes it likely that here we have an arrangement arising from mere imitation of the Sepulchre dramas, which had for long been associated with Easter Matins. Incidentally, the version is an *ordinarium*, written mostly in incipits and without its music.

Moving to some 'second stage' versions, we meet first the St. Florian version. The manuscript pages are beautifully written, with Gothic music notation on four lines. The work begins with some originalities of treatment. The main characters—the Angel, the three Marys, and the two Apostles—are given separate choral notice of their entrances and movements to their respective places, relevant liturgical items being

---

[1] *Melk, Stiftsbibl., MS 1094*, fols. 35r.–38v. The text is given by Young in I, pp. 619–20.

[2] *St. Florian, Stiftsbibl., MS XI 434*, fols. 165r.–170r. The text is given in Young, I, pp. 365–7.

[3] *Munich, Staatsbibl., MS lat. 2988*, fols. liv:–lv:. The text is given in Young, I, p. 584.

sung. As we have previously realized, the '*Nolite expavescere . . .*' sentences from St. Mark, set to specially composed music, replace the normal '*Quem quaeritis*' exchange.

Other novelties, peculiar to St. Florian, occur with the appearance of the questioning Apostles. The Marys reply to them with, first, the ZHN G stanza ('*En angeli . . .*') and then with the second of ZHN F ('*Galyleam omnes . . .*'). The version then returns to routine, with a quite usual succession of items, including the Race to the Tomb, and familiar final choruses. We note, however, a mention of the 'populus' and of '*Crist ist erstanden . . .*'. The item is given in incipit but with a decorated version of the normal opening music (r d r f͟s͟r f͟m͟r). Could it be that the onlookers were thought worthy to be entrusted with the singing of a whole stanza?

Another brief Prague version,[1] again neatly written, and with German neumes, has nothing out of the ordinary to say. Once again we have the Hartker antiphon, '*Maria Magdalena et altera Maria . . .*' preceding the appearance of *three* Marys. Also, there seems to be some scribal carelessness in dealing with the problem of the B flats in the 'revised' version of '*Quis revolvet nobis ab hostio lapidem . . .*'. Their correct placing can be seen from the settings given in other Prague versions and in Cividale's two manuscripts, CI and XLI. Both in this item and in the '*Quem quaeritis, o tremulae mulieres . . .*' dialogue it would be better to give B flats as clef signs. Rubrics are of the briefest; the 'race' is indicated by nothing more than the '*Currebant duo simul . . .*' antiphon; while the final '*Dic nobis . . .*' exchanges between Mary Magdalen and the chorus (*not* the disciples) are no more than a series of incipits. '*Crist ist erstanden . . .*' is given in incipit, this time with the usual notes, r d r f͟s͟ r-.

A 'second stage' version from Cracow[2] is contained in a manuscript from the cathedral library. This gives the bulk of a brief work, together with its music, Gothic notation on four lines. In his discussion of the manuscript Karl Young comments on the adequate and careful rubrics supplied. As for the missing music of the first two items, we may note that the '*Maria Magdalena . . .*' sentence as given is not the liturgical responsory but a widely employed example of free composition, and its setting safely known. The manuscript refers to it incorrectly as an 'antiphon'. Although we meet with no way of checking the point, it would appear that only two Marys were employed. The other item, '*Quis revolvet . . .*', can also have its music duly restored. As for the rest of the little work, there is no touch of originality anywhere. All is inherited.

As a final 'second stage' example, I present one of a group that are all very similar in content; this, from Augsburg, having the advantage of its music, and being an early example of liturgical text and music in printed form.[3]

[1] *Prague, University Library, MS I.D. 20*, fol. 69v.

[2] *Cracow, Bibl. Capit. MS 85*, fols. 116v.–117r. (A.D. 1471). The text is given in Young, I, pp. 316–18. Lipphardt reports that the manuscript has been renumbered and is now *MS 53* [Ed.].   [3] *Obsequiale sive Benedictionale . . .* (Augsburg, A.D. 1499), fols. 32v.–34v.

The manuscript pages show first, tightly packed, a full set of rubrics with the texts given as incipits, and then, with much reduced rubrics, the text items in full, their settings in ponderous printed Gothic notation on four-line staves. Karl Young prints both sections on p. 645 of his first volume, without, of course, the music. But so entirely 'stock' is the whole brief work that this could be supplied not too inaccurately by anyone acquainted with certain German *Visitatio Sepulchri* settings of the period. I should mention that the first (*ordinarium*) section speaks of the final singing of '*Victimae paschali*' and '*Crist ist erstanden*'. These are not referred to in the second writing-out, with music.

Of the 'third stage' dramas belonging to the century, that from Barking Abbey has already been dealt with (see p. 364). Its rubrics make it clear that first performances took place during the rule (A.D. 1363–76) of that forceful Abbess, the Lady Katherine Sutton. The surviving manuscript, therefore, would appear to be a re-writing, which at least implies a wish to keep the work alive in the new century, even if only in *ordinarium* form.

Another disappointing 'third stage' survival comes from Coutances, again an *ordinarium*.[1] No music is given, and the reasons for its mention here depend first on the inclusion of the phrase '*Adam novus veterem*', a probable reference (and, if so, unique) to the splendid 'sequence' of fifteen lines found in the twelfth-century *Peregrinus* in *Orléans 201*, where it is given a powerful musical setting (see p. 193).

The other Coutances interest is the inclusion of the incident (reported by St. Matthew) of the setting of an armed Roman guard around the Tomb of Christ, 'lest his disciples come by night, and steal him away . . .', culminating with their being smitten by (in this case) two Angels. The 'lightning' was apparently represented by candelabra of ten candles each. Coutances does not give its 'soldiers' any opportunity for revival and retirement, as does, for example, the version from *Klosterneuberg 574*; insisting, apparently, that they shall remain 'as dead men' until the advent of '*Te Deum laudamus*'.

The last of the 'third stage' dramas is a very different affair. The *Visitatio* from Wolfenbüttel[2] has, strangely enough, escaped the attention of a number of scholars, including Wilhelm Meyer, E. K. Chambers, and Karl Young, and, as far as I am aware, its full importance has not been realized. I have already referred, on p. 306, to the fact that in this particular version all six groups of stanzas needed by Meyer to transform his 'hypothetical' *Zehnsilberspiel* into reality are there, complete with their musical settings, as a reference to the chart on p. 319 will testify.

I write with photographs of the manuscript pages in front of me. Both the text and the curious Gothic-style music notation are wretchedly set down, but regarding the former the task is lightened by the fact that we have before us a very orthodox Latin libretto, whose musical settings are

---

[1] *Paris B.N. MS lat. 1301*, fols. 143v.–145v. Karl Young prints the text, with the incipits expanded, in I, pp. 408–10.

[2] *Wolfenbüttel, MS Helmst. 965*, fols. 181r.–192r.

nearly all instantly identifiable, and subject to no more than the usual small variations of pitch and grouping.

But what complicates the whole picture is the fact that the work contains a great deal of material other than this—rhyming German verse, in fact, and rather more German verse than Latin. As we shall see, the vernacular poetry sometimes paraphrases the Latin stanza which has preceded it, sometimes offers a further comment. Also, such poetry is sometimes sung, either to a borrowed tune, one already in use with a Latin text, or to an independent one. At other times the text is simply spoken. Altogether, the Wolfenbüttel drama represents a stage when clerical playwrights were realizing more clearly the necessity of bringing to the lay listeners, unschooled in Latin, a better idea of what such dramas were all about, while still holding to the same traditional framework.

In spite of the hundreds of lines involved there is no evidence to suggest that the drama was performed anywhere but within church walls. The first sung item to be written down (on fol. 181r.) together with its liturgical music, is the last responsory of Easter Matins, '*Dum transisset sabbatum . . .*'. I now propose to trace the course of the work, item by item. The *Dramatis Personae* are: (1) the three Marys, with the Magdalen, as usual in the leading part, and to be identified by the rubric *Tertia Maria*; (2) the 'Spice Merchant' (with the doubtful presence of a young assistant); (3) no fewer than three Angels; (4) the Risen Christ (*Salvator*); and finally (5) 'Doubting Thomas'. Rubrics comprise little more than the names of the characters, with, at times, some assistance as to whether a passage is sung or spoken, through the use of the rubric verbs '*cantat*' and '*dicit*'.

Immediately after the responsory the First Mary sings the first stanza of ZHN A ('*Heu, nobis internas . . .*'), to Melody I—six lines in the pattern 87 87 87.

She follows it immediately with six lines in the vernacular, which, if not a strict translation, certainly interprets the sentiments.[1] From later evidence I do not doubt that the vernacular stanza was merely spoken, and that no attempt was made to adjust Melody I to it. (It could be done!)

Next, we have the ZHN A '*Iam percusso . . .*' stanza, sung by the second Mary, followed by the third, singing '*Sed eamus . . .*'. In each case a German stanza is interspersed, the second a reasonable paraphrase of its Latin predecessor. The third, however, is longer and of a different pattern as compared with '*Sed eamus . . .*', and, while introduc-

---

[1] I attempt on this occasion to justify this statement by giving, side by side, a translation of the ZHN A first stanza (see p. 308), and also one of the vernacular verses that follow, ('*O wê uns dren'vil armen . . .*'):

Alas! how great within our hearts	O how wretched are we three;
the grief and lamentation.	May God have mercy on us
Because of him our Comforter	Since that we have lost the One
we grieve in desolation.	Who was born to comfort us;
Him the evil ones of Jewry	Whom the wretched Jewish people
put to death with cruelty.	Caused to hang upon a Cross.

ing the subject of the buying of the ointment, does so in rather different terms.

ZHN B, the prayer and the decision to buy ointment, is represented by two of the usual stanzas, '*Omnipotens Pater . . .*' and '*Amisimus enim . . .*', set to Melody II, but these seem to have very little relationship with the associated vernacular poetry; e.g., after the three Marys have sung in chorus what can be rendered as:

> Almighty and most exalted Father,
> most gentle ruler of th'angelic host,
> What are we most wretched ones now to do . . .

—Mary Magdalen's subsequent speech in German amounts to no more than: 'Our grief and suffering are very great: this is the cause of our deep distress.' The next and lengthier vernacular stanza is similarly independent.

The drama then moves to ZHN C, the buying of the ointment, but without any change to the music of the Latin stanzas, Melody II continuing in use. The Merchant now appears, and sings the second of the stanza groups, '*Huc proprius flentes . . .*'.[1] As it happens, his following speech is fairly close to a paraphrase of the Latin. The usual exchanges continue, with one of the spoken stanzas actually supplied with the verb '*dicit*'. Later in the work more rubric use is made of '*cantat*' and '*dicit*', but very haphazardly.

As the bargaining progresses we meet a new feature, all the Marys singing a stanza in German (in which they seek a 'very special' ointment), the text set to a Lydian mode melody that I have not encountered before, and which seems to me quite attractive. I give the music, in what might have been its rhythmic rendering:

> Sa - ge uns, cra - mer, le - ve vrunt, is dy van ar - ze di - ge icht kunt,
> *Tell us, good mer - chant, dear - est friend, do you know much of me - di - cal lore,*
>
> ed - der hes - tu ien - nige sal - ve gût, dâr na so steit uns de mût?
> *or have you sup - plies of that fine salve which we ear - nest - ly de - sire?*

Now comes a curious rubric, '*Ad robin*', and a spoken quatrain from the Marys beginning, '*Wilkome, leve iungelin . . .*', followed by another appeal for medical information. Is this a case of an appearance of the figure of the 'apprentice'? However, there seems no further evidence of him, and it appears to be the Merchant who continues the exchanges by using for a sung stanza in German the melody that I have set out above. Then, surprisingly, the Marys break in ('*ad invicem cantant*') with what Wolfenbüttel has up to this point refused to employ, the ZHN line

[1] Oddly enough, the Marys' first stanza, '*Aromata precio quaerimus . . .*', is omitted.

'*Heu, quantus est noster dolor!*',[1] of which other *Zehnsilberspiel* dramas made great use in their B and C sections.

The bargainings continue, spoken in the vernacular. The Merchant accepts the offer of three gold byzants for the precious ointment, and assures the Marys that they have got good value for their money! The Marys depart, singing of their intention to anoint the sacred flesh. Their words are set by a brief melody in the major mode which is new to me.

But thereafter Wolfenbüttel comes down to a solid level of tradition. The Marys approach the Tomb singing '*Quis revolvet . . .*' to familiar music, while Mary Magdalen's spoken text is almost a paraphrase of the Latin. During the Tomb exchanges the Latin items follow the usual '*Quem quaeritis, o tremulae mulieres . . .*' pattern. The interspersed vernacular verses vary between mere rough paraphrases and attempts to bring in further scripture-derived details. For instance, after the singing by the Angels of the brief antiphon '*Venite et videte . . .*' the vernacular lines spoken by the Third Angel amount to: 'Come, that you may see and relate the truth. He is not here; he has arisen and has gone to Galilee.'

After the usual '*Ad monumentum venimus . . .*' (a good deal expanded in the German commentary by Mary Magdalen) the two other Marys sing in Latin two stanzas of the ancient hymn '*Jhesu, nostra redemptio . . .*' to the liturgical tune. After a vernacular comment by the second Mary, Mary Magdalen takes over the hymn tune, which is adapted to fit her two stanzas in German in which she laments her sins, bringing in the familiar phrase as to her having been possessed by seven devils. Her singing then merges into the usual three stanzas of her lament, ZHN D, set by the normal Melody IV. In succession we have '*Cum venissem . . .*', '*En lapis est . . .*' and '*Dolor crescit . . .*', interspersed with her speaking and singing vernacular verses. The music of the German-sung stanzas consists of adaptations of Melody IV, not always a happy arrangement, while the vernacular texts in general seem to work out somewhat dull and repetitive. Mary's last sung lament is, surprisingly, '*Heu! redemptio Israel, ut quid mortem sustinuit.*' Normally, this sentence is found in company with several other such bewailings, in a number of both French and German *Visitatios*.

There now occurs the standard 'gardener' scene, between '*Salvator*' and Mary Magdalen. The music is at times individual, but showing some similarities to the Zwickau version. The vernacular, invented speeches in this scene are particularly trite. Instead of leaving alone Christ's tender and revealing sung word, '*Maria!*', the playwright directs him to add, in speech, 'Mary, it is I, your Comforter. You are free of all your sins!'

Now follows the '*Prima quidem suffragia . . .*' stanzas; in other words, ZHN E, set to Melody V. The Risen Christ addresses the usual four

---

[1] On p. 314 I have set out three examples of ZHN B, Melody II. One of them is the Wolfenbüttel version. Here, I have restored the 'lament' line to the place where it really belonged.

Latin stanzas to the Magdalen, and the latter makes the usual comments. Once again there is a cluttering of vernacular verses, this time more to the point as fair translations. With the spoken words (I translate), 'Woman, I will soon see that day on which I shall ascend to my Father', the Saviour departs, and Mary is left to sing the stanza '*Vere vidi Dominum . . .*' (ZHN F). This is set to a version of Melody IV, which is close to that used by the Cividale *CI* and Zwickau dramas. Mary immediately sings a vernacular version of the Latin, the same tune being adapted to the German text.

Then comes a long passage of thirty-nine lines in rhyming German couplets, spoken by Mary Magdalen, and beginning: 'I shall proclaim consolation to all sinners . . .'. It is obviously a verse-sermon, aimed at the lay audience. It speaks of the Crucifixion, the Resurrection, the Ascension, and of Christ's promise of the Second Coming. Then, without any questioning disciples, and alone, she proceeds to sing the lyrical first part of the '*Victimae paschali*' sequence, this divided into two items with her spoken paraphrases of the Latin interspersed. The rubrics '*cantat*' and '*dicit*' are freely used in these later pages.

At the moment when we expect an interruption by Peter and John, putting the question, '*Dic nobis, Maria . . .*' (the normal continuation of the sequence in these dramas) we meet with a very different situation. The new entrant is 'doubting Thomas', with whom Mary exchanges a series of spoken, rhyming couplets in German, the whole scene a piece of down-to-earth invention. Thomas says bluntly, 'Mary, hold your noise!', and questions the idea of a dead man lying in a grave and then arising on the third day. Mary is equally acrid. 'Silence, you unbelieving Thomas!' she says, 'You talk such nonsense!', and proceeds to offer to take him to where the Saviour is, to see for himself.

Jesus is found, greets Thomas, and invites him to touch his wounds. Thomas's surrender is complete. He has seen and is convinced. Once again a drama makes effective use of St. John, xx:29!

It would seem that then both the Saviour and Thomas leave the scene, and are replaced by the other two Marys. We now have the '*Victimae paschali*' scene completed in Wolfenbüttel's own unique way, since it is the lesser Marys who take the places of the usual Apostles, and proceed to address the Magdalen, singing the '*Dic nobis . . .*' question and then obligingly proceeding to translate it into German speech. Mary Magdalen, replying with '*Sepulchrum viventis . . .*', follows the same curious procedure. All continue with the rest of the questioning and replies found in the Sequence, each item being followed up by a spoken paraphrase in the vernacular.

As I have remarked before, all this minor evidence as to the Lord's survival should surely have been made secondary to a proclamation by Mary Magdalen to whomever she was trying to convince, that she herself had seen and spoken to him.

It is she who concludes the work, singing the sequence line, '*Surrexit Christus, spes mea . . .*', and adding a final spoken couplet to the effect that

> God my Comforter has risen
> And has gone to Galilee.

There is no sign of a '*Te Deum*'. The last words are a rubric, '*Et sic est finis*'.

Wolfenbüttel MS Helmst 965 gives us a monumental work. If, as the evidence seems to show, it was performed within church walls, then it must have put considerable demands upon available liturgical time, and apparently it was thought to be worth this privilege. It is unique in the amount of trouble that it takes to keep the secular portion of the audience, largely unlearned in Latin, informed as to what the actors were saying. One notes in particular the long vernacular speech of Mary Magdalen which summarizes much of the Easter story, with emphasis on the forgiveness of sins for the truly repentant. In a Christendom of the fifteenth century, where the open-air 'mystery' dramas, spoken in the vernacular, were widespread in all countries, it would seem that clerical authorities had awakened to the need of such clarifications in the performances of Church music-dramas. Certainly it marks a concession on the part of a single version towards the use of the vernacular that goes much farther than any similar such work. We might even think of it as a desperate effort towards keeping alive what was taking on the appearance of a fast-fading movement. However this may be, we must surely consider this work as a remarkable one, the result of some keen, and at times, original thinking.

III

Having considered Easter Sepulchre manuscripts that were written in the fifteenth century and have survived from that time, we discover that, when we seek other types of liturgical drama belonging to the same period, there is very little to find. The most outstanding is the second writing-down of that curious mélange, the so-called 'Dutch Easter Play'. Obviously, it is closely based on the twelfth-century version, which attempted (not really successfully, I believe) to blend dramatically two different themes, the actions at the Easter Sepulchre and on the road to Emmaus. However, I have already discussed both manuscript versions at length, on pp. 181–5.

What I mention next is strictly not a liturgical work at all. I refer to the so-called 'Shrewsbury Fragments', certain pages from a fifteenth-century manuscript which is now in the Library of the Shrewsbury School, Stafford (England), where it is listed as *MS VI* (*Mus. iii, 42.*). The relevant pages are fol. 38r.–42v.[1] Karl Young, concerned only with the texts, devotes many pages of valuable comment to the questions

---

[1] The rest of the pages of the manuscript (it ends at fol. 43r.) are devoted to the writing-down of various processional pieces, with a couple or so of responsories and proses. *Triplex* singing is mentioned.

that inevitably arise from their strange nature (see Young, II, pp. 514–23).

It appears that the dramatic material is no more than a *single* actor's part (with 'cues')—the lines for his participation in three separate dramas, in which he is cast for, respectively (and all this has a familiar ring), the 'Third Shepherd', the 'Third Mary', and one of the 'two Disciples' (on the road to Emmaus). We are of course easily able to identify the *Officium Pastorum, Visitatio Sepulchri*, and *Peregrinus*, but what we meet with for most of the single part is Northern English vernacular, with touches of Midland dialect, in regular rhythmic lines rhyming ab, ab . . .; spoken, not sung, and spoken in the everyday language that every citizen in the region would be able to appreciate. However, in the course of each of the dramas there occur passages in the Church's own tongue such as we have met with so often before. There are ten such brief insertions, sung by the characters or by the chorus, of which four have not had their music set down. There also occur four Latin stanzas which I have not met with elsewhere. My task must be to examine the musical settings that are written in, to see if any significant conclusions may be drawn from them.

The first point that I must make is that the music of the 'Fragments', on a five-line stave with the usual clefs, and with B flat sometimes supplied as a stave sign, displays the 'measured' forms of the *Ars Nova* age, those used for writing the rhythmic intricacies of the polyphonic music of that period. I recognize only one melody given in the manuscript, that employed by the Third Shepherd in singing '*Transeamus usque Bethlehem . . .*'.[1] The melody seems to agree approximately with the setting found in the *Officium Stellae* of *Orléans 201* and in the Rouen *Officium Pastorum, B.N. MS lat. 904.*[2]

As for the rest, the Latin sentences may be familiar, but the musical settings certainly are not! Let us continue with the 'Shepherds' Play'. Soon after the '*Transeamus . . .*' passage the text hints at the scene at the Manger. At this point Karl Young (II, p. 516) calls our attention to an asterisk (the work, probably, of a later hand) which directs us to p. 42v., where, it would seem, there was a small area of spare vellum. Here is to be found the Latin reply of the Shepherd to the Midwives at the Manger, the text just as it is found in the Christmas trope version, as well as in the *Rouen 904* and *Orléans 201* shapings of the scene. Karl Young quite rightly prints the sentence as belonging to fol. 38v. Probably, the Midwives have just asked their question, '*Quem quaeritis in praesepe? Pastores, dicite!*', and are getting their reply. But what the Third Shepherd is singing will be seen to be, from the given notation, nothing to do with the unison, free-rhythm melody invented for the Christmas trope and the Church music-drama versions. It is clearly one part of a quite

---

[1] The Shrewsbury manuscript writes '*Bethelem*'.

[2] Two other *Officium Stellae* versions, that from Freising of the eleventh century, and that from Brussels, of the twelfth, have brief neume incipits that do not seem to agree with the French music.

elaborate polyphonic setting of the text, in as many parts as there were Shepherds, and in the sophisticated 'de Vitris' notation with occasional red-ink colouring given to the breves.[1] In the absence of the other two Shepherds' parts, nothing further can be said, except that, in the background, there must have been a trained and skilful composer.

We pass to the next drama fragment with a very definite manuscript rubric as to its identity, '*Officium Resurreccionis in die Pasche*'. Immediately, the Third Mary is found to be singing the familiar line, '*Heu, redempcio Israel! Ut quid mortem sustinuit.*' No music is supplied. Karl Young conjectures that the other two Marys will already have sung the two other pairs of lines which normally precede the given pair, but there is no guarantee that this was so. It has already been noted, in the Wolfenbüttel *Visitatio*, how this same utterance appeared quite in isolation. The lack of music is much to be deplored here. It might have proved to have been a free-rhythm melody, sung as a solo, and perhaps showing musical links with a number of earlier *Visitatios*. However, when after more vernacular verses, '*Iam, iam, ecce, iam properamus . . .*' turns up, followed by the even more familiar '*O Deus! Quis revolvet nobis lapidem . . .*', the music notation tells us in each case that we have here, yet again, concerted and polyphonic efforts by the three actors. It would seem that, immediately after, the Marys offered in turn some vernacular verses—clarifications of the situation, since we have the Third saying:

> . . . Some succour soon he will us send
> At help to lift away this lid.[2]

After this, the '*Quem quaeritis*' encounter must have taken place, since the 'Third Mary's' next quatrain speaks of the angelic information that they have just received.

The next speech of our actor, which apparently winds up the play, is a double quatrain rhyming throughout 'ab, ab . . .' and beginning:

> Christ is risen, witness we
> By tokens that we have seen this morn . . .

—with later references to the fact that he will be found in Galilee. However, the eight-line stanza is prefaced by two familiar Latin lines:

> *Surrexit Christus, spes nostra;*[3]
> *Praecedet vos in Galileam.*

---

[1] This is no place to expound knotty and largely irrelevant problems concerned with medieval polyphonic notation. However, any reader who wishes for information as to the several significations that could be attached to the appearances of *red* notes on a stave may consult Gustave Reese, *Music in the Middle Ages*, p. 345. Notes coloured thus appeared in French measured notation early in the fourteenth century. Reese remarks that this use survived until well into the fifteenth century, especially in England.

[2] This suggests a 'sepulchre' of a chest-like or 'cavity' nature, rather than a structure which imitated the Holy Sepulchre at Jerusalem, with a door that was closed by a stone.

[3] In the liturgy—'*mea*', not '*nostra*'. This adjustment is often found in the dramas using the Sequence.

I speculate—did the Third Mary, before speaking the vernacular stanza, actually *sing* the '*Victimae paschali*' music of the Latin lines, or join with the other two in doing so? They were all three trained musicians. One would think that it could hardly happen otherwise. The great Sequence in its majestic setting permeated the season's liturgy, and must have sung in the minds of all worshippers, especially in those of trained musicians.

A line is now found drawn across the manuscript, marking the end of the Sepulchre drama. No title is given to the *Peregrinus* that follows, but the first rubric introduces 'disciples, singing together' ('*Discipuli insimul cantent*'). It is never made clear in the manuscript which of the two, 'Cleophas' or his companion ('Luke'?), takes over the written text. Karl Young chooses 'Cleophas' but admits mere conjecture. Whoever assumed it, he is given an immediate and testing musical assignment. Four rhyming lines in Latin, previously unknown to me, and commencing '*Infidelis incursum populi . . .*', are set to an elaborately rhythmic notation which presumably blends with a vocal part sung by the other disciple. This, and the exchanges of spoken vernacular stanzas that follow, tell of the tribulations of the followers of Jesus, and the need for flight. The two discuss the situation and their intention of going to Emmaus.

Prefixing one of 'Cleophas' ' vernacular stanzas, but being given no scribal distinction from the rest of the lines, there occurs another Latin intrusion, St. Luke xxiv:20 ('*Et quomodo tradederunt eum . . .*'). Unlike earlier passages from the St. Luke chapter which were made use of, together with their liturgical music, in all surviving examples of the *Peregrinus* drama this verse occurs in other such versions only in those contained in *Orléans 201* and *Madrid 132* and *289*. There is no known liturgical antiphon from which the music (which all three supply) could have been borrowed. However, the simple free-rhythm settings have manifestly a common derivation. It may have been *Orléans 201* (with the most complete version of the Vulgate text) which conceived it, but we can make no comparison between the Orléans and Shrewsbury musical settings, for the latter's (if indeed the texts were sung) are not given.

But like Orléans, and unlike the two Madrid versions, Shrewsbury gives the verse in full. The fact might appear as a link between the 'Fragments' and earlier dramatic activities in Northern France, but certainly a vague one that must not be presumed on too far, until stronger evidence as to the make-up of Latin dramas of the medieval Church in England has been discovered.

A stanza later 'Cleophas' has another Gospel quotation to make, from St. Luke, xxiv:25 of the same chapter ('*Dixerunt etiam . . .*'). None of the other *Peregrinus* versions uses it, although the best of them, from Beauvais, has paraphrased it in the course of a long and splendid invented passage. Shrewsbury, unfortunately, supplies no music.

It is now apparent that the 'Stranger' has appeared, and that the unwitting disciples are telling him all about himself. St. Luke's verse 29 ('*Mane nobiscum, quoniam advesperascit . . .*') is now sung by the two, and represents the disciples' invitation to share with them the hospitality of the inn at which they have arrived. The verse is also a liturgical antiphon (see Hartker, p. 234). All the surviving *Peregrinus* dramas make use of it, also borrowing the liturgical music, but Shrewsbury has something quite different. Once more our actor has to sing a measured, flowing and probably subordinate part in an 'ars nova' setting of the text, on four-line staves.

At some time during the vernacular stanzas that follow, Jesus must have allowed himself to be recognized, before 'vanishing out of sight'. The disciples speak their bewilderment, and then once more we meet with Latin. '*Quid agamus, vel dicamus . . .*' they sing, and again a rhythmic flowing part is provided. I give our actor-disciple's last spoken words, as he endeavours to calm his companion's agitation:[1]

> We saw him wholly, hide and hue,
> > Therefore be still, and stint your strife.
> That it was Christ full well we knew;
> > He cut our bread withouten knife!

A hymn is then sung, and proves to be the last stanza of the service hymn '*Ad coenam agni*'. It can be seen with its music in *Antiphonale Romanum, Hymni Antiqui*, p. 19. The plainchant setting seems to bear no relationship to the Shrewsbury notation, which is once again measured and complicated.

Two final lines in Latin then occur ('*Frater Thoma, causa tristicie . . .*'), also set to measured music; referring obviously to 'doubting Thomas', but doing no more than hinting at the possibility of an additional episode dealing with him.

I turn back now to the very first sung item of the 'Fragments', the single music-part which set the Gospel words, '*Transeamus usque Bethlehem . . .*'. As we have observed, the part is in the complicated *measured* notation of the period. In dealing with the remainder of the measured music parts set down for this single actor I spoke of them as showing no features that could link them with the known liturgical settings of the particular Latin words. But in this case I must call attention to the fact that the music of '*Transeamus usque Bethlehem . . .*' as written in the Shrewsbury manuscript appears to be a rhythmed version of the plainchant tune, only slightly varied in pitch details. I write down a portion of the item as it appears in the Shrewsbury manuscript:

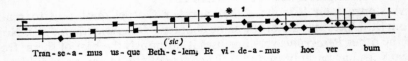

Tran-se-a-mus us-que Beth-e-lem; Et vi-de-a-mus hoc ver—bum
(*sic*)

---

[1] I have slightly modernized some of the spelling.

quod   fac – tum · est . . .

—and ask that it should be compared with the music example to be found on p. 205, where the same passage, from, respectively, the Orléans *Officium Stellae* and the Rouen *Officium Pastorum* are being compared in regard to their music. It appears to me therefore that we have here an example of a plainsong (free rhythm) melody being deliberately turned into a rhythmic one, for the purpose of combining it with other rhythmic parts to form a polyphonic setting.[2]

The three dramas contained in the Fragments that are sketched by the single 'part' give no clue as to the conditions under which they were performed. Even if all was done in the open air, attracting a large citizen audience, the hand of the Church is still very obviously present. The poet responsible for the lively vernacular lines (as far as we have them) was a skilled and experienced manipulator of his rhyming verse; while the nature of the music makes it clear that the composer, producing 'up-to-date' polyphonic part-writing, and the actor-singers, interpreting it, were professionally-trained people, such as still would be found only in the service of the Church.

Yet, as in the case of the Wolfenbüttel *Visitatio*, the Church was learning that Latin was not enough, and that the sung speech-music, skilled as it was, was passing over the heads of the secular audiences, who were becoming more and more accustomed to the cut and thrust of spoken, vernacular dialogue, and content to take their music in no more than incidental and background fashion.

IV

Little remains of surviving fifteenth-century manuscripts detailing dramatic activities of the Church.

Karl Young (I, pp. 503–6) reports an Adoration of the Cross ceremony recorded in a Regensburg manuscript.[3] The latter is an *ordinarium*; no music is given, and speeches are in incipit form. Undoubtedly in the course of the action the Virgin and St. John were impersonated, and undoubtedly they exchanged metrical laments. But in the absence of any

---

[1] Regarding my footnote on p. 396 concerning the '*ars nova*' use of 'red' notes—the notes in the above music example marked with an asterisk were, in the manuscript, written with red ink.

[2] Concerning this matter, in 1966 I wrote to Dom Anselm Hughes, editor of Vol. II of the *New Oxford History of Music*. I sent him copies of the relevant material. In his reply he confirmed my opinion as to the example being a detached single part of a polyphonic setting. He said also that he knew of other examples of plainsong being taken and turned into a metrical polyphonic part; a not altogether uncommon practice. He instanced the '*triplex*', '*Crucifixum in carne*', from the liturgical pieces found in another part of the same manuscript.

[3] *Munich, Staatsbibl., MS lat. 26947*, fols. 116r.–117v.

musical notation nothing more can be added to what Karl Young has already said.

To round off the century, as it were, there is the curious survival of a brief Christmas dialogue from the cathedral of Clermont-Ferrand,[1] a '*Quem quaeritis in praesepe . . .*' placed after the Matins *Te Deum*, and leading straight into the First Mass of Christmas, with insufficient evidence as to whether the exchanges represent a trope or a dramatization. However, in Chapter XV (p. 376) we have previously encountered an almost identical version from the same cathedral (also without its music) but with more evidence as to impersonation being indeed intended.

[1] *Clermont-Ferrand, B. de la Ville, MS 67*, fol. 28v. The text is given in Young, II, pp. 11–12.

CHAPTER SEVENTEEN

THE SIXTEENTH CENTURY

The last of the church
music-dramas

ALTHOUGH the single control of the Church of Rome had been achieved once more, in the first half of the sixteenth century large areas of Germany were moving towards a reorganization in religious worship, following the lead given by the formidable Wittenberg scholar, Martin Luther (1483–1546), who found ample materials for his attacks on the still corrupt hierarchy. He appeared to have support from a high proportion of his fellow countrymen, and to him Germany owed a translation of the whole Bible into the vernacular.

Not until the mid-forties did the Church of Rome rally its resources effectively, but when the reaction came, it proved a powerful one. It was aided in its 'Counter-Reformation' by a newly established and highly efficient body, 'The Society of Jesus'—the Jesuits. While the Council of Trent (1545–63) cleansed abuses as never before, the Jesuits won back for Rome much territory that had appeared lost to the Protestant reformers.

However, since our particular concern is with the Church music-dramas, and since that movement in the sixteenth century was very obviously doomed, there seems no need here to pursue further matters concerned with the social and political conditions of the period.

Ever since Wycliffe, 'reformers' had denounced the religious dramas in no uncertain terms, as well as any other features of the traditional liturgy that seemed to them symbolic or dramatic, and therefore 'idolatrous'. But as one result of the policies of the Council of Trent, even the former tolerant supporters of the orderly Latin dramas within the Church turned against them. In company with many well-loved sequences, tropes, and similar comparatively recent intrusions, they were removed from the official service books. The changes and removals took time, but the Council was determined to return to the greater liturgical simplicity of earlier centuries.

We will now consider what dramatic material did manage to survive in service books of the Church of Rome belonging to the sixteenth century.

A few 'first-stage' *Visitatio* versions survive, to be written down again as for continued use. One from Hildesheim[1] is a reproduction of *MS 684* from the same monastery, one that has already been noted as belonging to the thirteenth to fourteenth centuries. It might well have come from the tenth. Its simplicity shows nothing new either in text or music.

An example from St. Gall,[2] showing the 'revised' '*Quem quaeritis*' in its usual musical terms plus the '*Venite et videte . . .*' antiphon is almost devoid of rubrics and apparently out of place in the manuscript. Its chief interest is in illustrating how the art of the scribe had degenerated in regard to the setting down of both text and music, owing probably to the spread of the art of printing. Examples of printed *Visitatios* are now to be found in Germany, the music in heavy Gothic 'nail' notation.

One of these printed versions comes from a service book from Constance, dated A.D. 1597 and now in the British Museum.[3] It is also one of those few existing *Visitatio* versions whose rubrics show that it was to be performed *before* the Office of Matins, in a place where it was in danger of clashing with the symbolic Easter ceremony of the *Elevatio*. In discussing the relatively small number of dramas that use this arrangement, Karl Young cites several instances of mild incongruity in the combining of these two ceremonies, whose themes are historically separated in time (I, pp. 301–6). The Constance *Visitatio* clearly reflects this incongruity: from a procession to the Sepulchre for the purpose of elevating the Sacrament we are abruptly switched over to the '*Quem quæritis*' interrogation.

The textual material of the Constance version contains no surprises, except perhaps for the presence of *three* Angels for the interrogation, and the use of a relatively rare liturgical antiphon, '*Et recordate sunt verborum eius . . .*'. It is also to be noted that the choir, not the Marys, announce the Resurrection, and that there are a few notes of unfamiliar pitch in the St. Gall setting of the dialogue. Texts and music of the antiphons '*Venite et videte . . .*' and '*Surrexit Dominus de sepulchro . . .*' are strictly liturgical.

A very curious version of the '*Quem quaeritis*' exchanges survives in a Venetian service book of 1579,[4] where the familiar question and replies are employed during a '*Tollite portas . . .*' ceremony. An ecclesiastical party is apparently assembled outside the church doors. When these latter are struck and the demand for opening made, the retort from within takes the form of the '*Quem quaeritis*' question. The normal exchanges continue, but with the conclusion of '*Ite, nunciate quia*

[1] *Hildesheim, Beverinische Bibl., MS 697*, fol. 182v. (See Young, I, p. 585.)

[2] *St. Gall, Stiftsbibl., MS 392*, pp. 109–10. (See Young, I, p. 581.)

[3] *Benedictionale Ecclesiae et Diocoesis Constantiensis, Constance*, pp. 183–7 (*Brit. Mus.*). (See Young, I, p. 301.)

[4] *London, Brit. Mus. MS Legg. 51 (Liber Sacerdotalis—Venice 1579 A.D.)*, fols. 265r.–267r. I cannot find any reference to this manuscript in the pages of Karl Young.

surrexit a mortuis' the doors are opened and the outside party enter, to be met with the antiphon, '*Venite et videte locum ubi positus . . .*'. Thereafter, the priest proclaims '*Surrexit Christus*' to the chorus and the populace, while the chorus replies '*Deo gratias*'. Later, the Marian antiphon '*Regina caeli . . .*' is sung. It is a strange fact that while the two antiphons have fairly normal liturgical settings, the music given to the '*Quem quaeritis*' passages (set down in unmistakable square notation on four lines with clefs) is badly distorted. One could imagine that whoever wrote it down had no previous acquaintance with its Dorian mode tradition.[1]

Passing to 'second-stage' *Visitatio* versions we soon meet once again the disposition to rely on past forms. An example from the famous monastery of St. Lambrecht at Graz[2] in S. Austria proves to be little other than a later edition of the version that has already been considered on pp. 172–4. This, from Graz, *MS II 798* of the twelfth century, is much more generous in its rubrics, and enables us to follow the monastic performance in close detail. But *MS I 1459*, its music written on four-line staves, has already enabled us to interpret the unheighted neumes of the earlier version. What differences they indicate between the settings are minor ones and without significance.

The *MS I. 1459 Visitatio* chooses deliberately to include the third responsory of Matins '*Dum transisset sabbatum, Maria Magdalena et Maria Jacobi et Salome . . .*'), together with its music written out in full, as part of the drama, which follows faithfully the plan laid down by the earlier version. Once again we find each Mary in turn relating a sentence from the '*Victimae paschali*' sequence.[3] Then, after the Race to the Tomb, the three take over the grave-clothes for display. Both versions call for the singing of '*Crist ist erstanden*', in the case of the earlier version accompanied by the rubric '*plebe conclamante*'. The contribution of *MS I. 1459* seems to have been a more formal one, by the chorus, but no mention is made of the twelfth century vernacular cry of '*Giengen dreie vrovven . . .*'.

The rest of the surviving 'second-stage' *Visitatios* are all German, all of the same general pattern, and all examples of the new enterprise of printing both texts and music. They occur in the liturgical *Agendas* issued during the course of the century by various leading dioceses. From that of Salzburg a number of examples have survived. I mention first that printed in 1511.[4] It appears to include the responsory '*Dum transisset . . .*' as being within the drama action, and writes it out in full with its music. The item '*Maria Magdalena et altera Maria . . .*' follows. Then we meet the stock items '*Quis revolvet nobis . . .*' and the 'revised'

---

[1] The time was fast approaching when the deplorable Medicean Edition of the Chant would appear, to wreck its traditions for a couple of centuries or more.

[2] *Graz, Universitätsbibl., MS I. 1459*, fols. 54r.–56v. (See Young, I, p. 360.)

[3] In the case of *MS I. 1459* incipits only of each sentence were given, without any music. But this was quite a safe piece of labour-saving.

[4] *Agenda Salisburgense, anni 1511*, fols. 58v.–60v. (See Young, I, p. 638.) There is a copy in the British Museum.

exchanges, beginning with '*Quem quaeritis, o tremulae mulieres . . .*', these succeeded by the Marys' '*Ad monumentum venimus . . .*'. The Race then occurs, to the usual '*Currebant duo simul . . .*' of the chorus, after which the recovered grave-clothes are displayed by Peter and John. The secular onlookers are then allotted an incipit of '*Crist ist erstanden . . .*' to the usual simple notes, but without any evidence as to how much of the composition they are to sing. The version is rounded off by a choral rendering of the ancient Easter antiphon '*Surrexit enim sicut dixit Dominus . . .*', the music given being used by quite a number of German examples through the centuries. Only a few St. Gall manuscripts seem to employ the liturgical setting found in Hartker. The Salzburg version, unusually, makes no attempt to use the sequence '*Victimae paschali*'.

There is one curious musical feature that concerns the settings of the '*Quem quaeritis*' exchange sentences. The original music scribe, no doubt carrying in his head the usual Phrygian mode ('mi') settings of the sentences,[1] and perhaps seeking to raise their pitch, has realized that the passage could be written as having B as its modal 'final' instead of E, since the note immediately below the final is not wanted. He thus starts:

in what to a modern reader might seem like 'Key G', but keeps his 'mode' intact by not being called on to touch F in any of the 'exchange' passages.

A much later edition of the same *Agenda* (A.D. 1575)[2] reveals no significant differences in either music or texts, but once again the '*Quem quaeritis*' section shows an interesting musical feature. Instead of the upward transposition of the fifth shown in the 1511 version, the later one gives the more usual lift of a fourth, writing in a careful B flat as a clef sign throughout the exchanges. Both versions resume the normal pitch for the setting of '*Ad monumentum venimus . . .*' and onward. While each uses the same setting for '*Quis revolvet nobis . . .*', this needing a B flat throughout, the 1575 version is careful to give it as a clef sign, while the earlier one relies apparently on the suggestions of *musica ficta*. Neither supplies more than the minimum of rubric directions.

An *Agenda* from the diocese of Passau, dating from 1514,[3] has little that is not familiar. There is the embarrassing responsory that mentions only two Marys as being present; a '*Quis revolvet nobis . . .*' that needs B flats for its setting throughout (to judge by *Cividale MS CI* and similar versions); and a '*Quem quaeritis . . .*' section that suffers the same neglect. Another scribal (or perhaps, printer's) error is a wrongly placed

---

[1] See Chapter VII, pp. 120–1, regarding the '*Quem quaeritis*' 'revised' version.
[2] *Agenda Salisburgense, A.D. 1575*, pp. 264–72. There is a copy in the British Museum.
[3] *Agenda Pataviensis, A.D. 1514*, fols. 91v.–93v. There is a copy in the British Museum.

clef for the first set of stave lines of the familiar setting to '*Ad monumentum venimus . . .*'.

For the rest of the version all is familiar, including the Race, and the disciples' display of the grave-clothes. Passau chooses to employ the dramatic part of '*Victimae paschali*' as a conclusion, the chorus questioning and the Marys replying in unison. A textual incipit calls for '*Crist ist erstanden*'.

The next to be considered, from a Bamberg *Agenda* of 1587,[1] has no new features to show, but appears to be very carefully prepared, and has generous performance rubrics. We learn, for instance, that all the roles were filled by choirboys. Actions and tones of voice are vividly detailed. One striking example of delivery concerns the singing of '*Cernitis, o socii . . .*'. The direction is '*cantent etiam querula voce*'; in other words, the disciples are to express their disappointment and bewilderment. 'Is this all we can learn?' they seem to be implying. But immediately the chorus retort strongly with '*Surrexit Dominus de sepulchro, qui pro nobis pependit in ligno!*'. They have realized the situation more swiftly than have Peter and John.

Other rubrics reveal that the *Sepulchrum Christi* is here a curtained-off area, in which a white sudary is lying to represent the grave-clothes. No mention is made of the singing of the antiphon '*Currebant duo simul . . .*' to accompany the Race. In view of the care taken in the production we may assume that this was really meant. It was an omission that was seldom followed. Bamberg seems to have thought, as we are inclined to do, that its absence was a dramatic gain.

The opening rubric mentions the singing of the responsory '*Dum transisset . . .*', but there is fortunately no sign of '*Maria Magdalena et alia Maria . .* '; thus consistency regarding the number of the Marys has in this instance been preserved.

The final rubric speaks of the general singing of '*cantilenas paschales Germanicas*', including, no doubt, '*Crist ist erstanden*'.

Such types of 'second-stage' *Visitatios* seem to have been quite plentiful in Germany at this time. As a concluding example I make note of one from Augsburg, a printed service book of A.D. 1580.[2] There are only a couple of textual differences between it and the Bamberg version just considered. The Augsburg one omits '*Venite et videte . . .*' and brings back the choral '*Currebant duo simul . . .*' of the Race episode. But apart from these items they are musically identical; amazingly so.[3] The two versions must have been linked in some way.

Augsburg concludes by calling for a performance of the whole of '*Victimae paschali*'. This portion lies, apparently, outside the action of the drama, and is purely a liturgical matter, but the disposition called

---

[1] *Agenda Bambergensia, Ingolstadt, A.D. 1587*, pp. 597–604. (See Young, I, p. 323.) There is a copy in the British Museum.

[2] *Ritus Ecclesiastici Augustensis Episcopatus* (Dillingen, 1580), pp. 593 to (nominally) 598. In point of fact, whoever was responsible for numbering the original pages printed pp. 595 and 596 twice over. (See Young, I, pp. 351–2.) There is a copy in the British Museum.

[3] The music differs in one place only, in the groupings (not the pitch) of three notes.

for is unique. The whole of the sequence is to be sung, but at the conclusion of each verse a verse from '*Crist ist erstanden*' is to be interspersed. No music is written down for the two compositions, nor
(information that would have been very welcome) any details as to the
stanzas of the vernacular hymn to be sung. Two other Augsburg
Visitatio versions are to be found together in another printed service
book.[1] These merely echo the '*Ritus*' details.

It is evident that throughout the sixteenth century there was a widespread desire in Germany to make use of a style of brief Easter drama
that included the vivid incident of the race to the Tomb. It is also clear
that the movement was one of flagging vitality, the material based on
long established forms.

We meet now a major 'third-stage' *Visitatio Sepulchri*, a last example
of the *Zehnsilberspiel* form.[2] At Zwickau in Saxony a manuscript is preserved holding three successive versions of the work. I shall give my
main consideration to the first, since the other two appear to be re-
arrangements or reshapings of it, providing translations into the vernacular, either as additions to, or substitutes for, the Latin rhyming
texts. The details of the whole manuscript are given below;[3] I have
named the versions 'A', 'B', and 'C' respectively.

I consider now version A, which introduces the three Marys ('*ad
modum honestarum Mulierum*') with a reference to the responsory '*Dum
transisset . . .*' but then writing out the text and music only of its verse
('*Et valde mane . . .*').[4] The first actual dramatic item, accompanying the
Marys' progress, is the quite apposite hymn, '*Jhesu, nostra redemptio . . .*'.
Three stanzas are sung, allotted to each of the three in turn, and given
their normal settings. In their advance the Marys now make use of
ZHN B ('*Omnipotens Pater altissime . . .*'), treating its three stanzas in
the same fashion, and employing Melody II. Just as we are expecting a
'Merchant Scene' with its bargaining (ZHN C) we find that this has
been dispensed with, and an explanation of the Marys' intentions offered
by employing the non-liturgical item, '*Maria Magdalena et alia Maria
ferebant diluculo aromata Dominum quaerentes in monumento*'. Only the
first two words of the item were written down, but their music identifies
the item and shows it to have the same setting as the corresponding
items in *Passau, A.D. 1514*, and *Prague XV.A.10*. But it also has the
result of being at variance with the plain statement of both rubrics and
previous responsory that three Marys were involved. We have seen this
discrepancy arising all too often. However, onward for a while from
'*Quis revolvet nobis . . .*' through the '*Quem quaeritis*' exchanges (with no

---

[1] *Obsequiale sive Benedictionale . . . Augustensem, A.D. 1499*, fols. 32v.–34v. There is a
copy in the British Museum.

[2] See the ZHN Chart on p. 319.

[3] *Zwickau, Ratsschulbibl., MS XXXVI, I. 24, Visitationes Sepulchri*, fols. 1r.–16r. The
version to which we are giving main attention occupies fols. 1r.–6r. I have termed it version A.
Fol. 6v. is blank. Version B occupies 7r.–10v. Version C starts immediately after the conclusion of B and continues to fol. 16r. Karl Young (I, pp. 669–73), deals with the text of
version A; mentioning the others on p. 683.

[4] We note the use of the organ to introduce the responsory.

fewer than four Angels) to '*Ad monumentum venimus . . .*' all is quite normal, both texts and music. The latter again shows affinities with the Prague and Passau settings. One notes that the pitches of '*Venite et videte . . .*' and '*Ad monumentum venimus . . .*' are both unusual, the former at a fifth below, the latter at a fourth above their normal level.

Having stated the situation in '*Ad monumentum venimus . . .*', the three seem now temporarily to part company. Mary Magdalen proceeds to another altar to mourn alone in terms of ZHN D, all three stanzas, and set to Melody IV. Returning, she sings the lament that we have noted first in the 'appendix' of the *Visitatio* from *Orléans 201* (beginning '*Heu, redemptio Israhel . . .*'). The music given is close to that of Orléans and a number of other versions.

There now occurs the 'Christ-Magdalen' scene, shaped in the usual fashion but with, strangely enough, no mention of the sacred name. The rubrics merely mention *plebanus*, i.e. the priest who took the part. The music of the exchanges, as in most other versions, shows a certain independence, while at times offering parallels with the Wolfenbüttel version. It is strange to find Zwickau adding to Mary's glad cry of '*Raboni!*' the gloss, '*quod dicitur magister*'.[1]

Plebanus then addresses Mary, singing the four stanzas of the '*Prima quidem suffragia . . .*' composition (ZHN E to the usual Melody V). Mary, as usual, intersperses the adoring comments, '*Sancte Deus!*', '*Sancte fortis!*', and '*Sancte et immortalis, miserere nobis!*', the music of which is given with very little variation in similar German versions. The actual four stanzas of ZHN E are set down in the manuscript as incipits; first lines only, without their music. At the conclusion of the item, Mary leaves *plebanus* and hastens back to the other two, to deliver the news to them by means of the stanza, '*Vere vidi Dominum vivere . . .*' (ZHN F), set here to Melody III.

Still addressing the other two, she passes on to the lyrical first part of the sequence '*Victimae paschali*'. When the '*Dic nobis . . .*' section is reached, it is neither the two disciples nor the chorus who put the twice repeated question and receive the three sentences of the Magdalen's reply, but most unusually, the other two Marys. Finally, the chorus joins with the two Marys in rounding off the sequence with '*Credendum est magis soli Mariae . . .*'.

Only after this do 'two deacons' appear, and, to the choral sounds of '*Currebant duo simul . . .*', enact the Race. The grave-clothes recovered, they display them while singing '*Cernitis, o socii . . .*'. *Plebanus superius* then begins the antiphon, '*Surrexit Dominus de sepulchro . . .*', this completed by the choir. Unusually, it is the same ecclesiastic who gives the lead for '*Crist ist erstanden . . .*'. The '*Te Deum*' follows; a rubric mentions that this is introduced by the organ. The co-operation of the laity is apparently called for in these later antiphons. Incidentally, after the conclusion of '*Victimae paschali*' the rest of the items are given only in

---

[1] The Vulgate '*Raboni*' is given in the manuscript as '*Rabi*'.

textual incipits, and without any of their settings, which indeed would be well enough known.

I have already mentioned the fact that the four stanzas of ZHN E ('*Prima quidem . . .*') were given only in incipit form. The scribe seems to have had misgivings regarding this, since, after the conclusion of the work and on fol. 5v. and 6r. he writes the '*Mulier, quid ploras . . .*' sentences again (apparently merely as a guide) and then records every word and every note of music of '*Prima quidem . . .*' in full.

The Zwickau 'A' drama as it stands appears to be a competent and actable piece of work. However, the presence of the other two versions in the manuscript seems to suggest that there was some contemporary dissatisfaction with it. Possibly it was felt that it had not followed the trend displayed in such major German *Visitatios* as *Wolfenbüttel, Helmst, MS 965*, in introducing translations of the Latin items together with original vernacular verse into the framework of the drama. Versions B and C do exactly that, at considerable length. Version C, for example, offers us, besides a number of invented German stanzas, the original and then a complete translation of the three stanzas of '*Jhesu, nostra redemptio . . .*' adapted to the original music. Version B, discovering that version A had omitted the usual ZHN opening laments of the Marys ('*Heu, nobis internas mentes . . .*'; '*Iam percusso . . .*'; and '*Sed eamus et ad eius . . .*'), inserts all three stanzas with their music,[1] and provides vernacular translations, again adapted to the original melodies.

Karl Young (I, p. 683) mentions versions B and C of Zwickau, but speaks of them (with others) as having a large vernacular element 'which excludes them from extended treatment at present'. As far as I am aware, he did not return to them. Obviously, these two versions are approaching the 'transitional' type, and having made note of some examples of the music that still linked them with the Church, I will follow Karl Young in abandoning further attention to them.

In an era of swiftly changing religious tendencies the lengthy Church type of *Visitatio Sepulchri*, with sung Latin texts set to alternations of free-rhythm and measured music, was undoubtedly on the way out. The citizen attracted to religious drama found it presented more and more in the form of spoken prose dialogue, in the vernacular, and in the open air. Yet in the region of Zwickau (in the little town of Köstritze) there was born in the last quarter of the sixteenth century the great German composer Heinrich Schütz, who can surely be said to have preserved some of the characteristics of the Church music-drama style, including the use of single-line, unaccompanied chant. Late in his life he wrote three Passions on the lines of the liturgical ones, relating the events strictly in terms of the vernacular Gospel accounts, the German texts set to a free unaccompanied recitative of his own devising, based on plainchant technique. At intervals he interspersed four-part unaccompanied choruses, settings of speeches or comments arising from actions in the story. Except for the first and last, these choral items kept strictly

---

[1] Zwickau's settings can be seen on my p. 313.

to Gospel words. As in the case of the Church works, Schütz's recitatives were denied every resource but those of the uttered word and the single line of the reinforcing chant-melody. Certainly in his choruses vocal harmony and contrapuntal part-writing produced their emotional effects, but no sounds of any instrument, no other colour but that of the voice, were allowed anywhere to intrude. The Zwickau *Visitatio Sepulchri* and other works must still have been in practical existence in his time. Could he have met with such examples, and been influenced by them in adopting an austerity so uncharacteristic of the Renaissance?

III

In the course of our survey of centuries of dramatic activities within the medieval Church, we have noted a number of border-line cases, where the use of symbolism in the course of a ceremony has appeared to cause it to hover on the verge of becoming true drama—or actually achieving that stage, with no more aid than that of relevant liturgical texts and their music. Some few last examples of such productions are noted below, as belonging to the sixteenth century.

I mention first an ambitious observance on the Feast of the Ascension, carried through at Bamberg.[1] There were no definite actors, but a clerical assembly headed by an officiating priest who supervised the ceremonial drawing-up of an effigy of Christ, from a small platform up to and through an opening in the church roof. Preceding this came various prayers and liturgical sung items, as well as the censing and sprinkling of the image. Another picturesque effect followed, when choirboys, already stationed in the roof, asked the angelic question (as in Acts, i:12) and received a reply from the chorus below; all this in terms of an antiphon of the day. A number of other liturgical items rounded off the ceremony, which included other objective features such as the casting down of fragments of wafer and drops of water. At the end the witnessing populace were given the chance of singing the vernacular hymn, '*Christ fuhr gen Himmel*'. However picturesque the incidents, it must nevertheless be concluded that all was liturgical and symbolic, and that here was no true drama.

I mention also another sixteenth-century text, quoted by Karl Young (I, p. 696), the manuscript of which I have not seen.[2] It describes very much the same ceremony, but is of interest to me inasmuch as it makes mention of the use of musical instruments. It speaks of responsories and hymns as being performed by chorus and organ. In what manner is not stated, but later, in connection with the '*Benedictus*', the familiar word '*alternatim*' is employed. Between actions, also, trumpeters sound their

---

[1] *Agenda Bambergensia, Ingolstadt*, pp. 627–35 (A.D. 1587). There is a copy in the British Museum, also containing the 'second stage' *Visitatio* already referred to in this chapter. See Karl Young, I, p. 694 for the 'Ascension' text. The music is entirely liturgical.

[2] *Berlin, Staatsbibl., MS theo. Lat. qu. 87b*, fols. 44v.–46v.

instruments, and with the raising of the image and the descent of the wafers comes the sound of thunder; this latter effected by the roll of a drum ('*tympanum*'). Opportunity is given also for the chiming of 'all the bells'.

The Easter season concluding with the feast of Pentecost, Whit Sunday in medieval Christendom was celebrated by ceremonies that recalled the descent of the Holy Spirit upon the apostles, as recorded in Chapter 2 of the Acts. The Third Person of the Trinity was represented in medieval iconography as taking the form of a dove. Thus in many of the recorded ceremonies we find that a dove, actual or artificial, plays its part in appearing through the inevitable roof-orifice, as is still done in Florence. Other objects of symbolic import—e.g., flowers, perfumes, and even burning tow ('cloven tongues as of fire') were also sent down. Karl Young (I, pp. 489–91) records a number of accounts of such ceremonies, concluding with that of another Bamberg manuscript.[1] I can do nothing better than to call attention to his commentary. He concludes: 'Clearly such ceremonies are not lacking in theatrical effect, and one feels that they ought to have achieved something more positive in the way of impersonation and drama . . . But of such developments the observances under review gave no evidence. The impressive theme of Pentecost was not effectually dramatized'.

Myself, I find a further interest in the Halle Pentecost account, which shows a Renaissance interest in bringing solo instrumental colour into the proceedings. The sounds of trumpeters and pipe-players are mentioned, as well as an ambitious '*alternando*' scheme for performing the famous hymn, '*Veni creator . . .*', whereby the organist completed the first verse, and the chorus the second; then the trumpeters sound again before the organist proceeds to the third.

I conclude with a brief mention of a sixteenth-century Halle Assumption,[2] which carries through the symbolic drawing up of an effigy of the Virgin 'to heaven', to the accompaniment of joyful music from the organ and also trumpeters (or pipe-players). The action is preceded and followed by sung liturgical items, and no further details as to the instrumental music are given.[3]

---

[1] *Bamberg, Staatsbibl., MS 119 (Ed. VI. 3)*, fols. 114r.–114v. (Halle, A.D. 1532).

[2] *Bamberg, Staatsbibl., MS lit. 119 (Ed. VI. 3)*, fols. 166v.–167r. (A.D. 1532) (see Young, II, pp. 255–6).

[3] Further information concerning Assumption practices in Spain has been gained by R. B. Donovan (*Liturgical Drama in Medieval Spain*); indeed, a good deal of new knowledge concerning the medieval liturgical drama in general in that country. Speaking of ceremonies at the Cathedral in Valencia in connection with the feasts of Pentecost and the Assumption, he calls attention to a remarkable piece of 'stage machinery' known as the *Ara Coeli*. I give the author's own description of it (pp. 145–6):

'The "aracoeli" was a sort of mechanical lift which moved back and forth between "heaven" and "earth" in spectacular fashion, carrying statues, and at times the actors themselves. It was associated chiefly with the Blessed Virgin. In the final scene of the Assumption performance, it transported her (a statue) to heaven; in the Christmas piece it brought down from the upper part of the church an image of the Virgin and Child. Still today at Elche the "aracoeli" performs its function in the famous Assumption play, one of the few medieval dramatic productions which has survived to modern times.'

IV

With the sixteenth century we reach the end of the Medieval music-drama movement. Although *vernacular* religious drama of one sort or another would continue everywhere in the Renaissance centuries, the Latin plays seemed doomed to oblivion—a doom rendered official by the Tridentine reforms, which banished from the service books the last traces of liturgical drama. With it, alas, was banished also the music, single-strand music that showed often enough a dramatic awareness and resource that has not yet even today received the appreciation it deserves.

CHAPTER EIGHTEEN

CONCLUSION

I propose in this final chapter to take a general survey of the Latin music-dramas of the medieval Church. In doing so, I shall endeavour to summarize the features and qualities which sustained them for several centuries, until in the end, as we have seen, they met with an era that had no further use for them.

I

Let me begin by recalling some of the major objectives of this study, and also some of its major results. As I have said before, I believe that the musical evidence that I have been able to bring forward has (to begin with) added an important amount to our knowledge of the medieval drama in general; it has solved a number of previously puzzling problems concerning medieval stagecraft; but above all, it has shown that an outstanding dramatic resource existed in them such as can hardly be imagined by the shapers of spoken drama—that of musical suggestion; and this of high dramatic and emotional power. Its quality was absolute; its effectiveness upon the listener as an individual depended upon what response was possible from within him. Hence, it was an art to be appreciated fully only by a minority—a fact that was brought home many centuries later to another imagination intent on music-drama: that of Richard Wagner. On this point I shall have more to say later.

A matter which I think must be considered as settled is the single origin (as an act of original composition) of the Easter trope which was the germ of Christendom's dramatic revival, '*Quem quaeritis in sepulchro?*'. The employment of the musical 'comparative chart' shows beyond doubt that it must have spread from some single source, and acquired its local variants from the accidents of time and distance.

We have seen often enough, in comparing dramas that have items of text held in common, how clinching is the evidence of a comparison of the musical notations when seeking to establish 'relationships'. Karl Young did not foresee that such items as liturgical antiphons and responsories left in ambiguous *incipit* form could be identified if the start of the notations were also supplied. I recall such matters as the debate on '*Resurrexit*' or '*Resurrexi*', and the 'abbreviated form' theory.[1]

By the same means, the interesting fact has emerged that, while the 'Christmas' trope '*Quem quaeritis in praesepe . . .*' established its dialogue text in imitation of the Easter one, its music was an original act of composition. But, once established (*B.N. MS lat. 1118* is an early example), the setting, normally constant throughout Christendom, showed a few interesting lapses when, momentarily, the influence of the older music associated with the two words '*Quem quaeritis*' proved too strong. In the case of *Engelberg, MS 314*, the *Visitatio* of which makes use of the revised dialogue, '*Quem quaeritis, o tremulae mulieres . . .?*', the first five-word phrase is actually shaped to the Easter music, and only afterwards takes up the usual revised setting. More important is the fact of a similar substitution having taken place in, respectively, the *Officium Pastorum* of Rouen (*B.N. MS lat. 904*), and the *Officium Stellae* of *Orléans 201*. Each work employs the Easter music for its setting of '*Quem quaeritis in praesepe . . .?*'. This, combined with other textual similarities, clinched by their settings, seems in my opinion to make it likely that the Orléans drama really belonged originally to the diocese of Rouen.[2]

I have relied on musical evidence to establish that in the '*Quem quaeritis*' dialogue the apparent absence of a vocative '*o*' before the word '*Christicolae*' could yet allow for its insertion in performance.[3]

An occasional feature (which would not be apparent were no more than the texts of the dramas consulted) is the 'musical rhyme', which, as we have seen, occurs when the two vocative words '*Christicolae*' and '*caelicolae*' have, note for note, the same setting. These are minority occurrences, but usually indicate that the dramas concerned may show further links with each other.[4]

Regarding the similarities that I have shown exist between the '*Quem quaeritis*' versions belonging respectively to *B.N. MS lat. 1240* and the *Winchester Troper*, my arguments, it will be remembered, rely very much on musical evidence, particularly on the music of those identical tropes which are attached to their respective Mass Introits.[5]

I recall as a particularly clear example of the unique value of musical evidence, the clues which enabled me to 'explain' the line of unheighted, close-packed, melismatic St. Gall neumes, which Karl Young queried in the *Visitatio, Bamberg MS 22*, belonging to the end of the eleventh century. I was fortunate in also possessing photographs of *Bamberg MS 27*, of the fifteenth century, whose *Visitatio* proved almost identical in text, and which had decipherable music. From a comparison of the two manuscripts the fact emerged that here was an early example of the 'echo' device, one side of a choir singing a phrase, which, in reply, was vocalized to a vowel sound by the other.[6]

---

[1] See Chapter V, pp. 68–71 and Chapter VI, pp. 98–100.   [2] See Chapter X, pp. 203–6.
[3] See Chapter V, pp. 80–1.   [4] See Chapter V, pp. 78–9.
[5] See Chapter VI, pp. 93–8.   [6] See Chapter IX, pp. 158–9 and Young, I, p. 585.

For reasons of space I must neglect further recollections as to the discovery of facts that no amount of study of the text alone could have revealed. Another equally valuable result of our attention to the music however, is the re-discovery of the artistic subtleties which the original composers brought to it, and which surely must have given additional pleasure to the more informed and sensitive members of a medieval audience. One of the most straightforward of satisfactions for a musically minded listener is to hear a fine song-tune, well sung. As we have found, the liturgical dramas abound with such items, lyrical, rhyming passages, set to what must be interpreted as balanced, rhythmic melodies. Here I suffer from an embarrassment of riches, and can spare no more than a few such recollections. One of my favourites, in *Daniel*, is Belshazzar's solo, '*Qui scripturam hanc legeret . . .*', as he promises rewards to the interpreter of the writing, as fine a tune as any trouvère could show.[1] Among this group I include lyrical melodies that are sung in unison by two or three voices, and this includes the '*Sed nequimus hoc patrare . . .*' of the three Marys at the Tomb, in the *Visitatio* from *Orléans 201.*[2] In the same manuscript occurs the Magi's '*Caldaei sumus . . .*', and Archelaus' stirring '*Salve, pater . . .*'.[3] Freer in construction, but particularly attractive, is Mary Magdalen's solitary and mournful solo, '*Heu, dolor . . .*'.[4] A most effective lyric is the setting of the sequence '*Quem non praevalent . . .*', sung by the Magi as they set off for the Manger. It proves to be not the ancient sequence melody, but a specially composed, rhythmic one.[5] Two examples of contrasting emotion clearly expressed in the music can be seen in successive solos by 'doubting Thomas', in the Beauvais *Peregrinus*—'*Nisi fixurum . . .*' and '*O, Jesu Domine . . .*'. The first well supports a defiant scepticism, the second a complete submission, as Thomas lies prostrate at Jesus' feet.[6] A brief but powerful solo is that of the Virgin Mother in the *Planctus Mariae* from Cividale. Her '*Heu, me . . . misera Maria!*' lament is given an extra force when it is repeated later at a higher pitch and slightly elaborated, a notable device.[7] Also most effective are the solo interchanges of rejoicing by the three Marys near the end of the Orléans *Visitatio* ('*Resurrexit hodie . . .*', '*Frustra signas lapidem . . .*', etc.).[8] Many more examples of outstanding melodic beauty could be quoted. I recall that earliest medieval setting of a famous passage, 'Saul, Saul, why persecutest thou me . . .?' from 'The Conversion of St. Paul', the singer probably unseen, and placed in the triforium gallery. Having heard it sung in performance, I have concluded that it is as dramatically effective in its way as Schütz's great setting.[9]

---

[1] See Chapter XI, p. 236.
[2] Chapter IX, pp. 166–7.
[3] Chapter X, pp. 207 and 208.
[4] Chapter IX, p. 168.
[5] Chapter X, p. 210.
[6] Chapter IX, pp. 197–8. I can vouch for the effectiveness of the emotional contrast, having heard excellent renderings of the two items during a performance of the work in Guildford Cathedral in 1965.
[7] Chapter XV, p. 379.
[8] Chapter IX, p. 171.
[9] See Chapter XII, p. 278. I attended a performance in Keble College Chapel at Oxford in September 1968.

Sometimes, when a lyrical, rhyming item occurs, it will be found to have been, as it were, led up to by more animated passages of rapid plainchant. I recall the opening scene of the Beauvais *Peregrinus*, when the two wayfarers are challenged by the Stranger. Their early exchanges are Gospel passages which happen also to be liturgical antiphons, happily familiar, probably, to the medieval listener. But these, on this occasion, lead in quite natural fashion to a series of invented rhyming passages, set to specially composed and quite charming rhythmic music. As I have previously remarked, here is *recitativo secco*, followed by *arietta*, and turning up considerably earlier in musical history than the Italian shapings of that useful device.[1]

Karl Young, apologizing in his Preface for not dealing with the 'melodies' of the dramas, speaks of the 'originalities' which a study of them might reveal. We have already seen a number of instances of his hopes being fulfilled. I recall one of the most striking, of which students of medieval music in general should take note. In 'The Slaying of the Innocents', from *Orléans 201*, the pleading cadence phrase used by the anguished mothers is taken over by Rachel in her following Lament, and repeatedly woven into her first solo in a most musically resourceful fashion, an early example of a dramatic use of a musical 'motif'.[2] An even subtler instance of this occurs in the *Orléans 201, Officium Stellae*, where the brief phrase which sets the key word '*stella*' is allowed to dominate the scene, occurring again and again as the musical setting to different, (but relevant) clauses.[3]

Continuing with *Orléans 201*, let us recall the imaginative treatment of what should have been the '*Non est hic . . .*' reply in the *Visitatio* drama. It begins by setting the first two words, '*Quid, Christicolae*', to a rhythmic variation of the '*Quem quaeritis in sepulchro?*' music, continues independently with '*viventem quaeritis cum mortuis?*', and then, having reached '*Non est hic*', sets the words to the usual upward leap. Thereafter, text and music break free, and continue in an original and melodious fantasy upon the usual ideas. It is a passage of really artistic imagination.[4]

The device whereby a character is associated with a distinctive item of melody (sometimes termed a 'reminiscence theme') is given prominence in some musical histories as having been employed successfully in the opera, *Richard, Coeur-de-Lion* (1784), by the French composer, Grétry. In this work, Blondel sometimes sings his 'personal' tune, sometimes plays it on his violin. This trick is held to be the precursor of the Wagnerian *leitmotif*. But as we have already seen,[5] far earlier than Grétry's day, the unknown composer of the music of the *Filius Getronis* was giving each of his leading characters or groups, their own particular

---

[1] Chapter IX, pp. 194–5.

[2] Chapter X, pp. 217–8. I witnessed the effectiveness of the device in the course of a New York performance in 1963.

[3] Chapter X, p. 206.   [4] Chapter IX, p. 167.

[5] See Chapter XII, pp. 270–5.

stanza-melody, adding also the refinement of causing the captive youth, when mourning for home, to borrow his mother's melody for the purpose.

Another example of the musical resource of 'reminiscence' is to be found in *B.N. MS lat. 252* (Rouen), where the opening phrase of the introductory Prosa ('*Jesu, magne Rex aeterne . . .*') is set to the unmistakable first eight notes of the sequence, '*Victimae paschali*'.[1]

A musical subtlety can be perceived in the Cividale *Planctus Mariae*, where a phrase sung by the Virgin as the setting of '*Ergo quare, fili care, pendes ita . . .?*' is employed four times by later soloists for other and different texts, representing, apparently, a questioning *idée fixe* that must have possessed them all—'Why indeed . . . dost thou hang thus, when thou art life itself?'[2]

II

As my final reflection, I return now to what to me is one of the most intriguing of the liturgical music dramas, the eleventh-century *Officium Stellae* from the cathedral of Freising. I have already pointed out that this battered manuscript page contains, at a remarkably early date, almost all the features, texts and music, which in the subsequent centuries were to be found so closely followed in succeeding versions of varying dimensions of the same type. The questions raised by this curious situation I have endeavoured to discuss fully in Chapter VIII. However, I speak of the drama again, since it shows very well some of the essential differences separating the Church music-dramas from the vernacular types of the outside world, which as we have found were by the fourteenth century offering the Latin plays a stiff (and ultimately fatal) competition. In vernacular drama the details of a particular story were followed through in scenes of *spoken* verse, the standards and the rhythmic variety of which varied with the abilities of the poet-dramatists. Generally speaking, what music there was mostly took the form of inserted songs (although in the most flourishing days of the citizens' 'mystery' plays, especially in France, introductory and incidental instrumental music by jongleur 'orchestras' was freely employed).[3] Clearly, however, music played a supplementary rather than a primary role.

On the other hand, what the Freising *Officium Stellae* accomplished was early to find a formula, taken up by many a later music-drama, for the telling of a swift-moving dramatic narrative in equally swift-moving

[1] Chapter XV, p. 356.   [2] Chapter XV, pp. 378–9.

[3] Concerning the terms 'miracle' and 'mystery' plays, Grace Frank writes (*Medieval French Drama*, Oxford, 1954, p. 162):

'It is obvious that the modern distinction between the words "miracle" and "mystery"— the first now usually applied to miracles of the Virgin and to miracles or lives of the saints, the second to plays with Biblical themes—did not obtain in the Middle Ages. In England "miracle play" came to be the generic term for all religious plays, in France "*mystère*" could refer to saint plays, dumb shows, and later even to non-religious texts (in 1548 we hear of *mystères profanes*).'

music, the two forming equal halves of the play's overall artistic design. If Karl Young's text is consulted, it will be seen how quickly the prose exchanges move. Sometimes the lines are brief liturgical phrases, employed because they happen to be relevant (antiphons, responsories, and the like, set to their liturgical music), sometimes freely-invented ones with specially composed music. With regard to these latter, we have found certain of them common to the whole 'Magi' movement, with the possibility of their having actually originated in Freising.

One such item is Freising's pungent exchange between the Magi and Herod: '*Caldaei sumus; pacem ferimus . . .*'.[1] It is my great regret that I cannot interpret the music. (As we have seen, *Orléans 201* borrows the stanza and gives it a beautiful setting.[2] Freising's is different, possibly simpler, but still, I believe, rhythmic.) After Herod has consulted his advisers (who reply in hexameters), we have the King's cross-examination of the three Magi, and here his use of the short, original prose sentences, mostly to single notes, as he hurls his savage questions at them in turn, brings an excellent sense of verisimilitude to the dramatic scene. This trick of a succession of prose sentences, followed by an occasional lyrical item, re-appears, as we have seen, in many other samples of medieval music-drama—and with good reason! For here, without a doubt, we have text and music working hand in hand to create a powerful dramatic effect.

Seeking for a vernacular, spoken drama dealing with the same subject to place in comparison with the Freising example, it occurs to me that probably the version best known to English readers would be the late-medieval 'Coventry' drama, enacted by the 'Shearmen and Tailors' of that city.[3] Rhymed throughout in middle-English spoken verse, the play contains a Herod after the average citizen audience's own heart, together with the celebrated stage direction, 'Here Erode ragis in the pagond and in the strete also.' Furthermore, we meet with three inserted songs, one of them the charming chordal part-song, '*Lully, lulla, thow littel tine child . . .*'—the 'Coventry Carol'. It will be recalled that the Freising drama's references to the 'Innocents' stopped short with Herod's wild threats, and that the 'Slaughter' was reserved for another Freising drama of a somewhat later date and rather different style of content.[4] Coventry's remaining incidents move straight forward, with the approach of the soldiers, the attempted resistance of the mothers (one of them brandishing a pot-ladle), the massacre, the report of the Flight into Egypt, and Herod's final baffled rage. It is all spoken; no doubt very vigorously and effectively, but with no further musical colouring.

As it happens, Freising's (separate) 'Slaughter' is rather an unsatisfactory affair. It will be remembered that I have already discussed it,

---

[1] See Chapter VIII, p. 131.   [2] See Chapter X, p. 207.
[3] Hardin Craig, ed., *Two Coventry Corpus Christi Plays* (Early English Text Society, extra series, 2nd edn., 1957, p. 87).
[4] See Chapter X, pp. 211–4.

spending most of my words in emphasising its dramatic faults. The straightforward Coventry treatment, as drama, shines by comparison. But neither effort, liturgical or vernacular, in representing the grief of Rachel, belongs to the same world as that scene of tense drama and musical mastery, her lament, as contained in *Orléans 201*, with its beautiful, sorrow-stirring melody. Here we find liturgical drama attaining its full potential, as it were; reaching those depths of intense beauty and profundity which it, uniquely, seems capable of touching.

In case I may seem to be too much emphasising the merits of the Latin Church dramas as against those of the medieval secular world, concerning which I can claim no expert knowledge, let me make clear that, rightly or wrongly, I consider the latter in most aspects as an independent dramatic movement, equally devoted to the service of the Christian faith, but indeed, one that had adapted better to the social conditions of the changing Europe of the late Middle Ages. We have noted how, even as early as the fourteenth century, a great deal of the heart seemed to have gone out of the whole Church movement, with the exception of the *Visitatio* type. This same century, incidentally, marked the emergence—in fact, the *explosion*—of the English vernacular mystery cycles, which, while covering much of the same material as the older Church dramas, revealed in their overall concept, design, and expansiveness a striking independence.[1] In France, too, vernacular drama was very much the rising star, having achieved considerable sophistication as early as the mid-twelfth century.[2] By the fifteenth century we see Latin drama at the edge of capitulation: in the (comparatively few) surviving *Visitatios* the anxiety of the Church playwrights to *explain* Latin passages by adding vernacular verse-translations is made very manifest.

In the end, there is no manner of doubt that the man of the street and market place had made it very plain that he preferred his own plain, local speech to a Latin which, however sonorous in its sung form, had the disadvantages of being largely incomprehensible. As for the melodic subtleties that permeated the whole art of the liturgical music-drama, and which I have dwelt upon so closely and so often, he was probably never even aware of most of them, and was no doubt wholly satisfied to take his music in incidental and 'background' form. Under the handicaps then, of a specialized language and a specialized music, this great artistic movement, born, as it were, before its time, faded, died, and was forgotten.

---

[1] For a thorough discussion of the relationship between liturgical and cycle drama, see Rosemary Woolf, *The English Mystery Plays* (University of California Press, 1972), pp. 3–24. The dramatic artistry of the English cycle play is extensively discussed in V. A. Kolve, *The Play Called Corpus Christi* (Stanford University Press, 1966).

[2] I think particularly of the Anglo-Norman *Le Jeu d'Adam* (c. 1150), *La Seinte Resureccion* (c. 1180), and the masterful end-of-the-century play by Jean Bodel, *Le Jeu de Saint Nicolas*. For a thorough discussion of the vernacular French drama, see Grace Frank, *Medieval French Drama*, of which mention has already been made in footnote 3, p. 416 [*Ed.*].

APPENDIX

SURVIVING MANUSCRIPTS

This setting-out, century by century, of the identities of the surviving manuscripts of the Latin Church music-dramas which have retained their musical settings, amounts to a brief historical survey of the rise, progress, and decline of the various types. It is also a catalogue of the photographs of these manuscripts, which, being in the possession of the present writer, are the basic materials upon which the evidences advanced in this book are founded. To the name of each manuscript there have been added details that will identify it at the library where at present it is to be found.[1]

The numbers in bold type at the end of entries refer to pages in this book where the manuscript is discussed or referred to.

Ia   **The Tenth Century**

i THE 'QUEM QUAERITIS' TROPE
of the Introit of the Mass of Easter

France

Paris, B.N. MS lat. 1240 (Troper from St. Martial de Limoges), fol. 30v., **66–78, 93–4, 96–8, 138, 413**

Paris, B.N. MS lat. 1118 (Troper from Auch or Toulouse), fol. 40v., **72–3, 75–6, 77N., 94, 138**

Germany and Switzerland

St. Gall, Stiftsbibliothek MS 484 (Troper), p. 111, **67, 78–81, 82, 84, 85, 113–14, 117, 118, 183, 322**

St. Gall, Stiftsbibliothek MS 339 (Gradual), pp. 106–7

St. Gall, Stiftsbibliothek MS 391 (Antiphonal of Hartker), pp. 37–8

ii VISITATIO SEPULCHRI
The dramatization (at the end of Matins) of the 'Quem Quaeritis' dialogue

England

Oxford, Bodleian Library MS 775 (The 'Winchester Troper'), fols. 17r.–17v.[2], **93–8, 413**

iii THE 'QUEM QUAERITIS IN PRAESEPE' TROPE
of the Introit of the third Mass of Christmas

---

[1] The photographs of these manuscripts, assembled by Dr. Smoldon, are now in the Library of London University [Ed.].

Mention is occasionally made in the catalogue of certain manuscripts (mostly of the *Ordinarium* type) which, though of interest for one or another reason, have not been supplied by their scribes with their musical notations. Generally speaking, I have not troubled to obtain photographs of these, and in the lists that follow have marked them with the sign *.

[2] See also *Regularis Concordia* of St. Ethelwold, which has text and full stage directions but no music; see above, p. 68.

P

France

Paris, B.N. MS lat. 1118 (Troper from Auch or Toulouse), fols. 8v.–9r., **86, 103, 105, 115, 413**

Ib   **Tenth to Eleventh Century**
i 'QUEM QUAERITIS' EASTER TROPE

France

Paris, Bibliothèque de l'Arsenal MS 1169 (Troper from Autun), fols. 18v.–19r., **67, 69, 80, 85, 117N., 118, 360**
Apt, Bibliotheca Capitolina MS 18(4) (Troper), fols. 33v.–34r., **69, 71, 72, 75–6, 94**
Apt, Bibliotheca Capitolina MS 17(5) (Troper), **71, 75–6**

Germany

Vienna, Nationalbibliothek MS 1888 ('*Miscellanea*' from Mainz), fol. 103r.

ii VISITATIO SEPULCHRI

Germany

Bamberg, Staatsbibliothek MS lit. 5 (Troper from Reichenau), Ed. V, 9, fols. 45r.–45v., **86, 100–1, 120**
Paris, B.N. MS lat. 9448 (Troper from Prüm), fol. 33v., **86, 101**

Ic   **The Eleventh Century**
i 'QUEM QUAERITIS' EASTER TROPES

France

Paris, B.N. MS lat. 1084 (Troper of St. Martial de Limoges), fols. 64v.–65r., **75–6**
Paris, B.N. MS lat. 1871 (Nouvelle acquisition) (Troper from Aurillac), fol. 13v., **76, 77N.**
Paris, B.N. MS lat. 1119 (Troper of St. Martial de Limoges), fols. 21r.–21v., **75–6, 77N., 94**
Paris, B.N. MS lat. 1120 (Troper of St. Martial de Limoges), fols. 20v.–21r., **73N., 75–6, 77N., 94**
Paris, B.N. MS lat. 1121 (Troper of St. Martial de Limoges), fols. 11v.–12r.
Paris, B.N. MS lat. 909 (Troper of St. Martial de Limoges), fols. 21v.–22r.
Paris, B.N. MS lat. 779 (Troper of St. Martial de Limoges, *not* from Arles as sometimes stated), fols. 35r.–36v., **76, 77N.**
Paris, B.N. MS lat. 887 (Troper of Aurillac), fol. 19r., **69, 73N., 76N., 77N., 111–12, 357**
Oxford, Bodleian Library MS Douce 222 (Troper from Novalesa but probably French), fols. 18r.–19r., **113**

Germany and Switzerland

St. Gall, Stiftsbibliothek MS 381 (Troper), p. 247
St. Gall, Stiftsbibliothek MS 376 (Troper), p. 197, **81, 118**
St. Gall, Stiftsbibliothek MS 387 (Breviary), pp. 57–8
Oxford, Bodleian Library MS Selden Supra 27 (Troper from Heidenheim), fols. 69v.–70r., **116, 118**
Zurich, Zentralbibliothek Rheinau MS 97 (Troper), pp. 16–17

Italy

Verona, Biblioteca Capitolina MS 107 (Troper), fol. 11r., **114**
Rome, Biblioteca Angelica MS 123 (BIII.18) (Troper), fol. 48v.
Ivrea, Biblioteca Capitolina MS 60 (Troper), fol. 70v. [?], **87, 114**
Turin, Biblioteca Reale MS G.V. 20 (Gradual-Troper), fol. 96r. [?], **114**
Monza, Biblioteca Capitolina MS C13/76 (Gradual-Troper), fols. 98v.–99r., **114–15**
ii VISITATIO SEPULCHRI
Stage I (Marys and Angels only)

England

Cambridge, Corpus Christi College MS 473 (an eleventh-century version of the 'Winchester Troper'), fol. 27v., **96**

France

Paris, B.N. MS lat. 9449 (Troper from Nevers), fol. 34r., **80, 102**N., **117, 155, 205**N., **360**

Cambrai, Bibliothèque de la Ville MS 75 (Gradual-Troper from Arras), fol. 11v., **80, 101, 116–17**

Spain

London, B.M. MS 30848, fol. 125v. ⎱ duplicate versions from a Breviary from Silos,
London, B.M. MS 30850, fol. 106v. ⎰ the latter with fuller rubrics, **80, 117**

Germany

Berlin, Staatsbibliothek MS theo. Lat. 4°.11, fols. 45v.– ⎫ duplicate versions of
46r.   ⎬ a Gradual from Min-
Berlin, Staatsbibliothek MS theo. lat. 4°.15, fol. 120r. ⎭ den **81, 118**

Paris, B.N. MS lat. 10510 (Troper from Echternach), fol. 11r., **118**

iii 'QUEM QUAERITIS IN PRAESEPE'

France

Paris, B.N. MS lat. 1119 (Troper of St. Augustin de Limoges), fol. 4r., **104, 115**

Paris, B.N. MS lat. 1121 (Troper of St. Martial de Limoges), fols. 2r.–2v., **104**

Paris, B.N. MS lat. 1084, fols. 53v.–54r., **104**

Paris, B.N. MS lat. 887 (Troper of Aurillac), fol. 9v., **104**

Oxford, Bodleian Library MS Douce 222 (Troper from Novalesa but probably French), fols. 6r.–6v., **104**

Italy

Ivrea, Biblioteca Capitolina MS 60 (Troper), fol. 10v., **104**

Ivrea Biblioteca Capitolina MS 91(LX)

Verona, Biblioteca Capitolina MS 107 (Troper), **104**

iv 'MAGI' MUSIC-DRAMA OF ADVENT
The Three Kings and Herod

France

Paris, Bibliothèque Mazarin MS 1708 (*Liber Responsorialis* from Nevers), fol. 81v., **129**

Paris, B.N. MS lat. 16819 (*Lectionarium* from Compiègne), fols. 49r.–49v., **128**N., **129, 130, 199, 200**

Germany

Munich, Staatsbibliothek MS lat. 6264a ('miscellany' from Freising), fol. 1[1], **129, 130–4, 199, 200, 202, 204, 416–17**

v THE SLAYING OF THE INNOCENTS

Germany

Munich, Staatsbibliothek MS lat. 6264a ('miscellany' from Freising),) fol. 27[2], **134–5, 211–14, 417–18**

Paris, B.N. MS lat. 1139 (from the Troper of St. Martial de Limoges), fol. 32v.[3], **135–7**

vi SPONSUS

France

Paris, B.N. MS lat. 1139 (from the Troper of St. Martial de Limoges), fols. 53r.–55v.[4], **139–49**

vi THE PROCESSION OF PROPHETS

France

Paris, B.N. MS lat. 1139 (from the Troper of St. Martial de Limoges), fols. 55v.–58r., **149–52**

---

[1] The first folio only belongs to the eleventh century.
[2] Folio 27 belongs to the eleventh to twelfth century.
[3] A dialogue between the mourning Rachel and an Angel.
[4] A *mystère* dramatizing the parable of the Wise and Foolish Virgins.

Id **Eleventh to Twelfth Century**
i 'QUEM QUAERITIS' EASTER TROPE
France

Paris, B.N. MS lat. 1139 (from the Troper of St. Martial de Limoges), fol. 53r.[1], 76N., **111–13, 176, 357**

Italy

Vercelli, Biblioteca Capitolina MS 56 (Missal), fol. 87v., **114, 155N.**
Modena, Biblioteca Capitolina MS O.1.7 (Troper), fol. 102v.
Piacenza, Biblioteca Capitolina MS 65 (Gradual-Troper), fol. 235v., **114**

Spain

Vich, Museo MS 105 (formerly 111) (Troper), fol. 2r., **173**
Huesca, Biblioteca Capitolina MS 4 (*Hymnarium-Troparium*), fols. 123–4, **76, 94**
ii VISITATIO SEPULCHRI
Stage I
Germany

Munich, Staatsbibliothek MS lat. 14083 (Troper), fols. 89r.–89v., **118, 123**
Munich, Staatsbibliothek MS lat. 14765 (*Consuetude*), fols. 93v.–94r., **118–19, 123**
Metz, Bibliotheca Municipalis MS 452 (Troper), fol. 25r., **101**
Zurich, Zentralbibliothek MS 65 (*Liber Responsoralis* from Solothurn), p. 103, **119**
Einsiedeln, Stiftsbibliothek MS 366 (*Fragmenta Liturgica*), pp. 55–6, **79, 85, 119, 120–2, 123, 289**

Ie **The Twelfth Century**
i 'QUEM QUAERITIS' EASTER TROPE
Italy

Benevento, Biblioteca Capitolina MS 27 (Troper of Benevento), fol. 47v., **154**
Benevento, Biblioteca Capitolina MS VI, 38
Monza, Biblioteca Capitolina MS K.11 (Gradual-Troper), fols. 60r.–60v., **154**
Vercelli, Biblioteca Capitolina MS 161 (Gradual-Troper of Vercelli), fol. 121r., **115, 154**
Vercelli, Biblioteca Capitolina MS 146 (Gradual-Troper), fol. 109r., **154, 156**
Vercelli, Biblioteca Capitolina MS 162 (Gradual-Troper), fol. 191v., **154, 156**
Turin, Biblioteca Nazionale MS F IV18 (Troper from Bobbio), fol. 85v. [Turin MS 897], **114, 154**
ii VISITATIO SEPULCHRI
(a) Stage I
France

Paris, B.N. MS lat. 1235 (Nouvelle acquisition) (Gradual-Troper from Nevers), fol. 205r., **80, 102N., 117, 155, 156, 205N., 360**
Paris, B.N. MS lat. 12044 (Gradual-Troper from Fossata), fols. 100r.–100v., **156, 360**
Madrid, Biblioteca Nacional MS C.132 (Gradual; Norman-Sicilian), fols. 102v.–103r., **156–7, 165, 172, 182, 183, 184, 185, 297, 298, 359, 360**

Netherlands

Utrecht, Bibliotek van de Rijksuniversiteit MS 407 (*Liber Responsalis* from Utrecht), fol. 116v., **157**
Germany and Switzerland

St. Gall, Stiftsbibliothek MS 360 (*Versus* from St. Gall), pp. 31–2
Munich, Staatsbibliothek MS lat. 14845 (*Hymnarium-Prosarium*), fols. 94r.–94v., **158**
Munich, Staatsbibliothek MS lat. 23037 (Breviary), fol. 176v., **157**
Oxford, Bodleian Library MS Misc. lit. 297 (Breviary), fol. 111r.
Stuttgart, Landesbibliothek MS 4° 36 (*Liber Responsalis*), fols. 122v.–123v., **157**

---

[1] Some writers assume that the '*Quem Quaeritis*' of *Paris, B.N. MS lat. 1139* is a *Visitatio*. There is no proof of this. I agree with Karl Young in treating it as a trope; see above, p. 112.

Italy

Udine, Biblioteca Arcivescovile MS F 25 (*Liber Responsalis* from Treviso), fols. 94v.–95r., **122N., 157, 363N.**
(b) Stage II

Germany

Vienna, Nationalbibliothek MS lat. 1890 (Breviary), fols. 163r.–163v., **122, 160–1**
Graz, Universitätsbibliothek MS II 798 (Breviary), fols. 52r.–53r., **161–3**
(c) Stage III

France

Orléans, Bibliothèque de la Ville MS 201, pp. 220–2[1], **156, 164, 165–73, 178, 180, 182, 290, 291, 292, 297, 299, 332, 359, 360, 414**

Spain

Vich, Museo MS 105 (Troper), fols. 58v.–62r., **112–13, 164, 173–8, 180, 182, 187, 296, 304, 306–7, 309, 310, 313, 315, 319, 366**
iii 'QUEM QUAERITIS IN PRAESEPE'

France

Paris, B.N. MS lat. 1235 (Nouvelle acquisition) (Gradual-Troper from Nevers), fols. 183v.–184r., **104, 105N., 115, 199**

Italy

Turin, Biblioteca Nazionale MS F IV18 (Troper from Bobbio), fols. 9v.–10r., **104, 199**
iv MAGI

France

Paris, B.N. MS lat. 1235 (Nouvelle acquisition) (Gradual-Troper from Nevers), fols. 198r.–199v.[2], **104, 125, 127, 199**
Montpellier, MS H.304, **126, 201, 209**
Madrid, Biblioteca Nacional MS 289 (Troper); Norman-Sicilian, fols. 107v.–110r., **125, 199–200**
Orléans, Bibliothèque de la Ville MS 201, **125, 130, 131, 203–11, 255N., 341, 342–3, 395, 413, 415**

Belgium

Brussels, Bibliothèque des Bollandistes MS 299 (*Evangelium* from Bilsen), fols. 179v.–180v., **129N., 130, 131, 132N., 133, 202–3, 204**
v SLAYING OF THE INNOCENTS

France

Orléans, Bibliothèque de la Ville MS 201, pp. 214–20[3], **135, 214–21, 255N., 415, 418**
vi PEREGRINUS

France

Madrid, Biblioteca Nacional MS C.132 (Norman-Sicilian), fols. 105v.–108r., **186, 187, 190–1, 302, 397**
Madrid, Biblioteca Nacional MS 289 (Troper; Norman-Sicilian), fols. 117–18, **186, 188–90, 191, 397**
Paris, B.N. MS lat. 1064 (Nouvelle acquisition) (from Beauvais Cathedral), fols. 8r.–11v., **186, 188, 189, 194–8, 255, 302, 414**
Orléans, Bibliothèque de la Ville MS 201, pp. 225–30, **186, 189, 191–4, 302, 389, 397**
vii OLD TESTAMENT DRAMAS

---

[1] Kept with the rest of the 'Playbook' at the end of the twelfth-century file. Page numbers given here and subsequently for *Orléans, Bibliothèque de la Ville MS 201* refer to the 'Playbook'.
[2] Confused sentences.
[3] Independent of *Magi.*

France

(1) *Daniel* (Beauvais)
London, B.M. MS Egerton 2615, fols. 95r.–108r., **132, 224–9, 234–45, 252–5, 356N., 414**
(2) *Daniel* (written by Hilarius)
Paris, B.N. MS lat. 11331, fols. 12v.–16r., **223–4, 225–6**
(3) *Isaac and Rebecca*
Vorau, MS 233*¹, **221–2**
viii NEW TESTAMENT DRAMAS

France

(1) *Raising of Lazarus*
Orléans, Bibliothèque de la Ville MS 201, pp. 197–213, **280–2**
(2) *Raising of Lazarus* (written by Hilarius)
Paris, B.N. MS lat. 11331, fols. 9r.–10v.*, **281–2**
(3) *Conversion of St. Paul*
Orléans, Bibliothèque de la Ville MS 201, pp. 230–3, **275–80, 414**
ix MIRACLES OF ST. NICHOLAS
(1) *The Three Daughters*

France

Orléans, Bibliothèque de la Ville MS 201, pp. 176–82, **259–62, 263, 269**

Germany

London, B.M. MS 22414 (from Hildesheim; eleventh–twelfth century), fols. 3r.–4r.*, **262–3**
(2) *The Three Clerks*

France

Orléans, Bibliothèque de la Ville MS 201, pp. 183–7, **264–5**

Germany

London, B.M. MS 22414 (from Hildesheim), fol. 4r.*, **263**
(3) *Image of St. Nicholas*

France

Orléans, Bibliothèque de la Ville MS 201, pp. 188–96, **265, 267–70**
(4) *Image of St. Nicholas* (written by Hilarius)
Paris, B.N. NS lat. 11331, fols. 11r.–12r.*, **266–7**
(5) *Son of Getron*

France

Orléans, Bibliothèque de la Ville MS 201, pp. 196–205, **269, 270–5, 415–16**

If **Twelfth to Thirteenth Century**
i 'QUEM QUAERITIS' EASTER TROPE

Spain

Vich, Museo MS 32 (Troper from Bobbio), fol. 48v., **112–13, 116, 154, 155, 176**
ii VISITATIO SEPULCHRI
(a) Stage I

France

Reims, Bibliothèque de la Ville MS 265 (Gradual), fol. 22v., **80, 117, 158, 288, 291**

Germany

Bamberg, Staatsbibliothek MS 22 (Gradual), fol. 128r., **158–9, 172, 413**
(b) Stage III

Netherlands

The Hague, Royal Library MS 76F3, fol. 1 and fol. 14², **181–5**

---

¹ Part of the text only with indecipherable neumes; see Young, vol. II, pp. 258–66.
² See below, Ik, p. 429.

Appendix. Surviving Manuscripts

Germany

Einsiedeln, Stiftsbibliothek MS 300 (*Liber Responsalis*), pp. 93–4, **178–81, 308, 310, 311, 312–13, 316, 317, 319, 321**

iii MAGI

Germany

London, B.M. MS 23922 (*Liber Responsalis* from Strasburg), fols. 8v.–11r.

iv LAST JUDGEMENT
(Anti-Christ)

Germany

Munich, Staatsbibliothek MS 19411, fols. 6–15*[1], **283**

Ig   **The Thirteenth Century**

i VISITATIO SEPULCHRI
(a) Stage I

France

Paris, B.N. MS lat. 1255 (Breviary), fols. 151v.–152r., **287, 300**
Paris, Ste. Geneviève MS 117 (*Liber Responsalis*), fol. 101r., **80, 117**N., **287, 288, 291**

Germany

Darmstadt, Landesbibliothek MS 3183 (*Rituale*), pp. 108–9, **288**
London, B.M. Add. MS 23922 (*Liber Responsalis*), fols. 41v.–42v., **119, 288**
Zurich, Zentralbibliothek MS Rheinau 59 (*Ordinarium*), pp. 112–13, **99, 288**
(b) Stage II

Germany

Haarlem, Episcopal Museum MS 258 (Breviary), fol. 45v., **288, 290, 374**
London, B.M. BS Arundel 156 (Gradual), fol. 35r., **288, 289**
Oxford, Bodleian Library MS Misc. Liturg. 202 (Breviary), fols. 72v.–73r., **288, 289**
Oxford, Bodleian Library MS Misc. Liturg. 325 (*Ordinarium*), fols. 82r.–82v., **121**N., **288, 289**
Oxford, Bodleian Library MS Misc. Liturg. 346 (Breviary), fols. 114v., **288, 290**
(c) Stage III (and extensions)

France

Paris, B.N. MS lat. 904 (Gradual), fols. 101v.–102v., **96–7, 169, 170, 182, 290–2, 301, 326, 360, 368**
Tours, Bibliothèque de la Ville MS 927 (*Miscellanea*), fols. 1r.–8v., **156, 157**N., **165, 170, 182, 257**N., **282, 291, 292, 304, 309, 310, 315, 319, 326, 332, 360**

Germany

Zurich, Zentralbibliothek MS Rheinau XVIII (*Lectionarium*), pp. 282–3‡[2], **308, 310, 311, 316, 317, 319, 322–3, 369–70**
Nuremberg; Nationalmuseum MS 22923 (*Liber Responsalis*), fols. 105v.–107v.‡, **121**N., **162, 165, 308, 311, 316, 317, 319, 324–5, 359**
Klosterneuburg, Stiftsbibliothek MS 574 (*Miscellanea*), fols. 142v.–144v.‡, **305**N., **309, 310, 311, 315, 317–18, 319, 322, 325–30, 372, 387, 389**
Munich, Staatsbibliothek MS lat. 4660a (*Carmina Burana*), fols. vr.–viv.‡, **308, 319, 330–2, 360**

ii MAGI

France

Paris, B.N. MS lat. 904 (Gradual from Rouen), fols. 28v.–30r.[3], **126–8, 133, 344–5, 376**
Laon, Bibliothèque de la Ville MS 263 (Troper), fols. 149r.–151r.[4], **126, 129, 214**N., **345–6**

iii SLAYING OF THE INNOCENTS

[1] See Young, II, p. 371.
[2] The sign ‡ denotes *Zehnsilberspiel*.
[3] See also Rouen 384 (fourteenth-century) which has no music but plentiful rubrics.
[4] In this Troper, the *Magi* and *Slaying of the Innocents* dramas are shown in continuous form. Although no music is given it was obviously used.

425

France

Laon, Bibliothèque de la Ville MS 263 (Troper), fols. 149r.–151r.*, **135**

iv PEREGRINUS

France

Rouen, Bibliothèque de la Ville MS 222 (Processional), fols. 43v.–45r., **186, 332–3**

Germany

Munich, Staatsbibliothek MS lat. 4660a (*Carmina Burana*), fols. viir.–viiv., **186, 189, 333–4**

v PASSION DRAMA

Germany

Munich, Staatsbibliothek MS lat. 4660a (*Carmina Burana*), fols. iii.v–iv.v.*¹, **334–5**
Munich, Staatsbibliothek MS lat. 4660 (*Carmina Burana*), fols. 107r.–112v.², **335–40**

vi OFFICIUM PASTORUM

France

Paris, B.N. MS lat. 904 (Gradual from Rouen), fols. 11v.–12v.³, **204–6, 341–4, 395, 413**

vii CHRISTMAS DRAMA

Germany

Munich, Staatsbibliothek MS lat. 4660 (*Carmina Burana*), fols. 99r.–104v.⁴, **346–52**

viii OLD TESTAMENT DRAMA

France

Joseph and his Brethren
Laon, Bibliothèque de la Ville MS 263 (Troper), fols. 151r.–153v.*⁵

Ih   **Thirteenth to Fourteenth Century**

i VISITATIO SEPULCHRI
(a) Stage I

France

London, B.M. Add. MS 37399 (Breviary), fols. 236v.–237r., **156, 287, 361N., 386**

Germany

Hildesheim, Beverinische Bibliothek MS 684 (Breviary), fol. 245v., **288**
Andenne, Biblioteca Capitolina MS 11 (Missal), fol. 125r., **288**

Ii   **The Fourteenth Century**

i VISITATIO SEPULCHRI
(a) Stage I

France

Paris, B.N. MS lat. 1269 (Breviary), fols. 279r.–279v., **102, 355**
Paris, Bibliothèque de l'Arsenal MS 595 (Breviary-Missal), fol. 164v., **102, 355**
Rouen, Bibliothèque de la Ville MS 252 (*Liber Responsalis*), fols. 101v.–102r., **157, 356–7**

Germany

Darmstadt, Landesbibliothek MS 545 (*Cantuale*), fols. 57v.–58r., **357**
Cividale, Museo Archeologico Nazionale MS 1.VII (Processional), **358**

---

¹ Brief, but considerable space needed; a great deal of the action is in pantomime.
² A major work. Unheighted neumes for most of text; Gospel texts, liturgical items and invented passages. The first appearance of *Angelus* versus *Diabolus*.
³ See above, note 15.
⁴ Includes Prophets, Annunciation, Birth of Christ, Magi, Herod, Shepherds, Innocents, Flight into Egypt. The music is in neumes, but not throughout; long and prolix stanzas are set to melismatic tunes.
⁵ Incomplete; written wholly in rhyming stanzas which are rhythmically varied; there are no liturgical pieces and no evidence as to circumstances of production; there is much pantomime.

London, B.M. Add. MS 31913 (Breviary), fols. 263v.–264r., **358**
St. Gall, Stiftsbibliothek MS 384 (Breviary), p. 240
(b) Stage II

France
Oxford, Bodleian Library MS Rawlinson Liturg. d.IV (Processional; the 'Dublin Play'), fols. 130r.–132r., **156, 160, 165, 170, 254, 291, 297, 332, 358–61**

Germany
Munich, Staatsbibliothek MS lat. 6423 (*Liber Responsorialis*), fol. 1v., **362**
Munich, Staatsbibliothek MS lat. 16141 (*Liber Responsorialis*), fols. 76v.–77r., **362**
Klosterneuberg, Stiftsbibliothek MS 1213 (*Ordinarium*), fols. 83r.–83v., **162, 362, 363**
Klosterneuberg, Stiftsbibliothek MS 629, fols. 103v.–105r., **290, 362, 364**
Prague, Národni Museum MS XVA.10 (Breviary), fols. 192r.–192v., **362, 363, 406**
(c) Stage III (and extensions)

England
Oxford, University College MS 169 (*Ordinarium*; the 'Barking Drama' (1363–1376); MS of fifteenth century), pp. 121–4*, **164, 320, 364, 389**

France[1]
St. Quentin, Bibliothèque de la Ville MS 86 (*Miscellanea*), pp. 609–25, **120, 122N., 178, 182, 291, 309, 310, 312N., 314, 315, 319, 320, 364–9**

Germany
Engelberg, Stiftsbibliothek MS 314 (*Collectio cantil.*), fols. 75v.–78v.‡, **121, 308, 310, 311, 312–13, 316–17, 319, 322, 369–70, 413**
Cividale, Museo Archeologico Nazionale MS CI (Processional), fols. 77r.–79v.‡, **309, 310, 311, 312N., 319, 370–2**
Prague, Veřejná a Universitní Knihovna MS VI.G.36 (Processional), fols. 84r.–90r.[2], **309, 310, 315, 319, 372–4**

ii MAGI

France
Rouen, Bibliothèque de la Ville MS 384 (*Ordinarium*), fols. 38v.–39v.*[3], **188, 376**

iii PEREGRINUS
Paris, B.N. MS lat. 16309 (from a Saintes Breviary), fols. 604r.–605r.[4], **186, 188, 374–5**

iv OFFICIUM PASTORUM

France
Paris, B.N. MS lat. 1274 (from Clermont-Ferrand), fol. 40v., **376**

v ASCENSION

Germany
Munich, Staatsbibliothek MS lat. 9469 (from Moosburg), fols. 72v.–73v.*[5], **375–6**

vi PLANCTUS MARIAE

Italy
Cividale, Museo Archeologico Nazionale MS CI (Processional), fols. 74r.–76v., **354, 376–82, 414, 416**

vii DRAMAS OF THE BLESSED VIRGIN MARY
(1) *The Presentation of the Blessed Virgin Mary at the Temple*

---

[1] In *Avranches, Bibliothèque de la Ville MS 214*, pp. 236–8, there is a 'third stage' *Visitatio*, the sentences mostly incipits and with no music but showing a French-style work with some resemblances to *Rouen MS 904* previously discussed (see above, notes 15 and 21) but with some unique incipits.

[2] Two other *Visitatios* (both *Ordinariums*) from the same library represent similar versions but are without their musical settings.

[3] No music given but this work is a parallel of *Paris, B.N. MS lat. 904* (Gradual) of the thirteenth century.

[4] The simplest of the *Peregrinus* versions, possibly copied from an earlier MS.

[5] Includes Twelve Apostles, the Blessed Virgin Mary, two Angels; an *image* of Christ was drawn through the roof. All dialogue from liturgical sources.

France
Paris, B.N. MS lat. 17730*[1], **250–2, 381–2**
(2) *The Annunciation*
Italy
Cividale, Museo Archeologico Nazionale MS CII (Processional), fols. 69v.–71r.[2], **382**
Padua, Biblioteca Capitolina MS C.56 (Processional), fols. 36v.–38r.[3], **249, 382**
(3) *The Purification*
Italy
Padua, Biblioteca Capitolina MS C.56 (Processional), fols. 15r.–17v.[4], **249, 383**

Ij   **Fourteenth to Fifteenth Century**
VISITATIO SEPULCHRI
Stage I
France
Paris, B.N. MS lat. 784 (*Liber Responsalis*), fol. 106v., **112–13, 148, 357**

Ik   **The Fifteenth Century**
i VISITATIO SEPULCHRI
(a) Stage I
France
Paris, B.N. MS lat. 1123 (Processional), fol. 25r., **386**
Germany
Munich, Staatsbibliothek MS lat. 2988 (*Liber Responsorialis*), fols. liv v.–lv r.
Bamberg, Staatsbibliothek MS lat. 27 (Ed.I.13) (*Liber Responsalis*), fols. 170r., **158, 386–7, 413**
Melk, Stiftsbibliothek MS 1094 (Processional), fols. 35r.–38v., **322, 326, 332, 387**
Italy
Brescia, Biblioteca Civica Queriniana MS H.vi.11 (*Ordinarium*), fol. 30r.*[5], **387**
(b) Stage II
Germany
London, B.M. I.A.6780 (printed; *Augsburg Obsequale*, 1499), fols. 32v.–35r.
Cracow, Biblioteca Capitolina MS 85 (*Liber Responsalis anni 1471*), fols. 116v.–117r., **388**
Prague, Veřejná a Universitní Knihovna MS ID.20 (*Liber Responsorialis*), fol. 69v., **388**
St. Florian, Stiftsbibliothek MS XI 434 (*Liber Benedictionum*), fols. 165r.–170r., **311, 316, 317–18, 319, 326, 387–8**
(c) Stage III (and extensions)

[1] This MS was written by the French nobleman Philippe de Mézières. The Virgin is represented as a child of 3 years. Based on apocryphal gospels, the story was traditional, from the east; the feast was recognized by the Eastern Church. Philippe de Mézières met it in Venice around 1370. Although no music is given, two instrumentalists (playing portative organs?) are mentioned.
[2] The Virgin Mary, Elizabeth, and an Angel are represented. The texts and music are liturgical except for a brief verse.
[3] Acted, but to liturgical texts and music. The '*Magnificat*' was sung *alternatim*.
[4] The Virgin, the Child Jesus, Joseph, Anne, four Prophets, three Angels are all represented. The Child is 'presented' at the 'Temple'. The action is dramatically done but the text and music are liturgical. The folio numbers for this *Purification* and for the Padua *Annunciation* (above) differ from those printed by Karl Young, They are, however, those marked on the photographs of the MS pages sent to me by the Padua librarian.
[5] This trope version, which leads straight into the '*Resurrexi* . . .' introit of the Easter Mass, has nevertheless rubrics which seem to indicate a dramatic treatment of the '*Quem quaeritis*' exchanges. Unfortunately, no music is given,

Appendix. Surviving Manuscripts

Germany
Wolfenbüttel, Herzog-August Bibliothek MS Helmst 965, fols. 181r.–192r.‡[1], **121, 306, 308, 309, 310, 311, 314, 315, 316–17, 319, 320, 359, 372, 389–94, 408**

England
Oxford, University College MS 169 (*Ordinarium*; fifteenth-century MS of the 'Barking Drama' (1363–1376)), pp. 121–4*, **389**

France
Paris, B.N. MS lat. 1301 (*Ordinarium* from Coutances), fols. 143v.–145v.*[2], **296, 389**

ii SHEPHERDS
Introit Trope of the first Mass of Christmas

France
Clermont-Ferrand, Bibliothèque de la Ville MS 67 (Breviary), fol. 28v.*[3], **400**

iii DRAMATIC PLANCTUS

Germany
Munich, Staatsbibliothek MS lat. 26947 (*Ordinarium* from Regensburg), fols. 116r.–117v.[4], **399**

iv MISCELLANEOUS

Netherlands
The Hague, Royal Library MS 71 J70 (*Hymnarium*; sometimes known as the 'Dutch Easter Play'), fols. 163v.–170r.[5], **156, 170, 178, 181–5, 191, 291, 292, 296, 298, 299, 309, 314, 319, 332, 359, 360, 394**

England
Shrewsbury, Shrewsbury School Library MS VI (Music iii, 42) (the 'Shrewsbury Fragments'), fols. 38r.–39r.[6], **187, 394–9**

II   The Sixteenth Century
i VISITATIO SEPULCHRI
(a) Stage I

Germany
Hildesheim, Beverinische Bibliothek MS 697 (*Liber Responsorialis*), fol. 182v., **402**
St. Gall, Stiftsbibliothek MS 392 (*Liber Responsorialis*), pp. 109–10, **121, 402**

Italy
London, B.M. Legg. 51 (Printed Service Book: *Liber Sacerdotalis*, Venice 1579), fols. 265r.–267r., **402–3**
London, B.M. (Printed Service Book: *Benedictionale Ecclesiae*, Constance 1597), pp. 183–7, **402**
(b) Stage II

Germany
Graz, Universitätsbibliothek MS I.1459 (Processional *anni* 1571), fols. 54r.–56v., **363N., 403**

---

[1] A 'complete' example of a *Zehnsilberspiel*, plus a good number of vernacular stanzas.

[2] Although no music is written in, it is of interest because of the rubrics describing the striking down of the soldiers guarding the tomb.

[3] It is not certain whether impersonation was intended in this trope.

[4] This involves a *Planctus* used during an Adoration of the Cross ceremony, which included impersonations of the Virgin Mary and St. John.

[5] A comprehensive Easter drama, incorporating a Wayfarers' scene (*Peregrinus*); it is really a repeat of an earlier, and now incomplete, MS of the twelfth to thirteenth century; see above, Appendix If, p. 424.

[6] These pages, known generally as the 'Shrewsbury Fragments', represent the setting down of a single actor's part, written in rhyming verse in the vernacular of a northern English dialect. The dramas involved represent transitional forms of a *Pastores*, a *Visitatio*, and a *Peregrinus*. All the vernacular lines were spoken by the actor playing 'Third Shepherd', 'Third Mary', and the second of the two 'Wayfarers'. A few passages of brief and familiar Latin sentences, set to *Ars Nova*, measured notation, seem to point to harmonized singing, the surviving parts being subordinate ones.

The following four *Visitatio* versions are all printed German service books and all to be found at the British Museum:

Salzburg, *Agenda* for 1511, fols. 58v.–60v.[1], **403–4**

Passau, *Agenda* for 1514, fols. 91v.–93v., **404–5, 406**

Dillingen, *Ritus Ecclesiastici* . . . for 1580, pp. 594–8[2], **405–6**

Ingolstadt, *Agenda Bambergensia* for 1587, pp. 597–604, **405**

(c) Stage III

Germany

Zwickau, Ratsschulbibliothek MS XXXVI I.24 (*Visitationes Sepulchri*), [A] fols. 1r.–6r.‡[3], **308, 309, 310, 311, 312–13, 315, 316, 319, 359, 372, 406–9**

ii MISCELLANEOUS

(1) *Ascension*

Germany

Ingolstadt, *Agenda Bambergensia* for 1597, pp. 627–35[4], **409**

(2) *Pentecost*

Germany

Bamberg, Staatsbibliothek MS lit. 119 (from Halle, 1532), fols. 114r. and v.[5], **250, 410**

(3) *Assumption of the Blessed Virgin Mary*

Germany

Bamberg, Staatsbibliothek MS lit. 119 (from Halle, 1532), fols. 166v.–167r.[6], **249, 410**

---

[1] A Salzburg *Agenda* for 1575 (pp. 264–72) shows no more than a few variants.

[2] There are actually *seven* pages; the original printer used the numbering 595–6 twice over.

[3] In the same MS are two more writings-out (B, fols. 7r–10v.; and C fols. 10v.–16r.) of a very normal *Zehnsilberspiel* version. B and C provide either substitutes for Latin texts or additions to them, in the vernacular.

[4] The material is wholly liturgical. Use is made of an effigy, and some miming; also chorus and organ, and trumpets and drums for interval music. The Bamberg *Agenda* copy in the British Museum was destroyed during the last war. I was fortunate in having made a copy of the page concerned.

[5] The material is wholly liturgical, and the action symbolic rather than dramatic. Use is made of an organ and two large bells with interval music from trumpets and pipes.

[6] The material is wholly liturgical, and the action symbolic rather than dramatic, with instrumental music as in the Bamberg Ascension ceremony (see above, note 4).

CHART   THREE

The Revised 'Quem Quaeritis' Exchange

[Some Examples of Its Setting]

CHART TWO

A comparative chart of the music of the Easter 'Quem quaeritis' dialogue, concerned with **A** German versions from St. Gall and allied centres : **B** Italian versions : **C** Spanish versions. Examples that through the use of one or more horizontal clef lines cause the pitch of the notes to be more or less certain are marked with an L. Versions stemming from St. Gall are almost invariable in their use of musical rhymes at the vocative phrases.

Text: Quem quae-ri-tis in se-pul-chro, o Chri-sti-co-lae? Je-sum Na-za-re-num cru-ci-fi-xum, o cae-li-co-lae. Non est hic; sur-re-xit si-cut pre-di-xe-rat. I-te, num-ti-a-te qui-a sur-re-xit de se-pul-chro

A St. Gall

St. Gall 484 (c. 950 A.D.)	See Plate I. The earliest surviving trope version of the St. Gall type. Music written in unheighed St. Gall neumes, as are most of the earlier St. Gall versions.
Berlin 4°. 15 (11th cent.)	Music in unheighed neumes. The MS. showed a vocative 'o' for Christicolae. A comparison with the neumes of MS. 484 will show why I supplied the 'o' for the latter.
Einsiedeln 366 (11th-12th cent.)	See Plate VIII. The key to the early St. Gall neume version.
Utrecht 407 (12th cent.)	The music on a four-line stave Gothic notation, with clefs. This, and all remaining St. Gall examples, can be read with confidence.
Andenne 11 (13th-14th cent.)	Metz music notation.
Darmstadt 545 (14th cent.)	Gothic notation. A confirmation of the fact that the liquescent note of Quem is 'do'.
Brit. Mus. 81913 (14th cent.) (Cologne)	Gothic notation.
Bamberg 27 (15th cent.)	Gothic notation. Almost exactly the same as an unheighed neume version of the 12th-13th cent., Bamberg 22.
Constance, printed Service book (16th cent.) (in Brit. Mus.)	Music, printed Gothic.

B Italian

Vercelli 162 (Early 12th cent.)	Somewhat uncertain heighting of Primitive Italian neumes, but the very unusual second neume (r m r) appears to be the scribe's intention : as does the omission of the second vocative phrase.
Vercelli 56 (Early 12th cent.)	Central Italy neumes, set round a single line with an F clef.
Modena, O.i.7 (11th-12th cent.)	See Plate VI, Central Italy neumes set round a single line with an F clef. End of line 'directa'.
Piacenza 65 (Late 12th cent.)	Norman neumes. See Plate VII.
Turin, F. iv. 18 (12th cent.)	Milanese notation. Single line with use of F, C and A clefs. Many fainter lines used to identify pitch of notes. Plenty of B flats.
Monza, K.11 (13th cent.)	A strange 'oblong' notation. Thick F line with a number of lesser ones when needed. The setting of the first two words unique.
Benevento 27 (12th cent.)	Beneventan notation round an F line that soon peters out. Music helped by 'directa' and hindered by obliteration.

C Spanish

Brit. Mus. 30850 (Silos, 11th cent.)	Visigothic notation, very carelessly heighted notation. Numerous doubtful places on the transcription.
Santiago (12th cent.)	A torn and stained fragment that had been used as a binding for another MS. It shows a 12th century Visisenite, French in style. Aquitanian notation, single F line with directs. Much damaged.
Vich 32 (12th-13th cent.)	Catalonian notation. F and C lines, with 'directs'. Altogether clear.

CHART ONE

THE MUSIC OF THE 'QUEM QUERITIS' DIALOGUE:

A as occurring in various early Limoges tropers and manuscripts from other centres influenced by the Limoges style. All settings were originally in either unheighted, or approximately heighted neumes, and for the definitive versions given here, depend often on the techniques of comparison. The exact pitches of the liquescents throughout the whole chart, often appear uncertain. None of the versions give any clue as to the pitch of the first note.

B as occurring in other (or later) French manuscripts, independent of the Limoges influence. All the examples given below are stave versions, and the identity of their notes almost wholly certain. Four of the eight are at the Dorian pitch; starting on D: the other four are transposed up a fourth in the original manuscripts, the necessary B flat sometimes written in, sometimes just left to the singer to supply.

A

- B.N. 1240 (933-36 A.D.)
- Bibl. Bodl. 775 (W.T. c. 980 A.D.)
- B.N. 1118 (c. 988-96 A.D.)
- B.N. 1084 (10th-11th cent.)
- Apt 4 (10th-11th cent.)
- B.N. (N.A.) 1871 (11th cent.)
- B.N. 1119 (11th cent.)
- B.N. 909 (11th cent.)
- B.N. 1121 (11th cent.)
- B.N. 779 (11th cent.)
- B.Bodl. Douce 222
- B.N. 887 (11th cent.)
- B.N. 1139 (11th-12th cent.)
- Hyesca 4 (Spain, 11th-12th cent.)

B

- B.N. 12044 (12th cent.)
- B.N. 904 (13th cent.)
- Reims 265 (12th-13th cent.)
- Paris, B. St. Geneviève 117 (13th cent.)
- Brit. Mus. Add. MS. 37399 (13th-14th cent.)
- Rouen, B. de la Ville 252 (14th cent.)
- Paris B. l'Arsenal 595 (14th cent.)
- B.N. 784 (14th-15th cent.)

Quem quæ - ri - tis in se - pul - chro, o Chri - sti - co - læ?

Non est hic; sur - re - xit si - cut præ - di - xe - rat: I - te, nun - ti - a - te qui - a sur - re - xit

di - cen - tes

nearly a musical rhyme

(a musical rhyme)

Omitted

(The scribe must have failed to copy a change of clef)

notes missing from reproduction through careless photography

Blank

THE MUSIC OF THE 'QUEM QUERITIS' DIALOGUE: A

THE MUSIC OF THE 'QUEM QUERITIS' DIALOGUE: B

The earliest surviving version of the music is found in Einsiedeln, MS. 366, of the eleventh to twelfth centuries.
A constant setting is apparent throughout the forty or more surviving examples having their music. The mode is Phrygian, closing on E, but some versions are found transposed up a fourth, with B flat (written or understood). I have rendered all the given examples at that pitch, in order to facilitate comparisons.

CHART FOUR
THE CHRIST - MAGDALEN EXCHANGE

Rheinau XVIII lacks neumes for these sentences

* Damaged places– reading uncertain.

Ma — — — ri — a! Ra — bo — ni! (quod dicitur magister.)

(Christ: — — — — —) (Mary: — — — —)

[Both 'Maria' and 'Raboni' written three times, but no music given.]

Missing pages

Ma — — — ri — a! Rab — — — bi! (quod di - ci - tur ma - gi-ster.)

(3 times)

(?)* (3 times)

(once only)

(3 times) (Rab — — — bi)

(once only) (Ra — bo — — ni)

(once)

(once) (sic)

(once) (sic)

(3 times) (Rab — — —bi)

435

WORKS CITED

Albrecht, Otto E., *Four Latin Plays of St. Nicholas*, Philadelphia, 1935.

Analecta Hymnica Medii Aevi, ed. G. M. Dreves, C. Blume, and H. Bannister, 55 vols., Leipzig, 1866–1922.

Angles, Higini, *La Musica a Catalunya fins al segle XIII*, Barcelona, 1935.

Anglo-French Sequelae, ed. from the papers of H. M. Bannister by Dom Anselm Hughes, Plainsong and Medieval Music Society, London, 1934.

Antiphonale du B. Hartker (*St. Gall, MSS 390–391*), facsimile edition in *Paléographie musicale*, iie série, i, Solesmes, 1900.

Apel, Willi, *Gregorian Chant*, London, 1958.

Aubry, Pierre, *Trouvères et troubadours*, Paris, 1909.

Beck, J., *La Musique des troubadours*, Paris, 1910.

Bowles, Edmund, 'The Role of Musical Instruments in Medieval Sacred Drama,' *Musical Quarterly*, January, 1959.

    'Were Musical Instruments used in the Liturgical Service during the Middle Ages?' *Galpin Society Journal*, X, May, 1957.

Brooks, N. C., 'Eine liturgisch-dramatische Himmelfahrtsfeier,' *Zeitschrift für deutsches Altertum*, lxxi (1925), pp. 91–6.

    'The Lamentations of Mary in the Frankfurt Group of Passion Plays,' *Journal of English and Germanic Philology*, iii (1900–1901), pp. 415–30.

    'Neue lateinische Osterfeiern,' *Zeitschrift für deutsches Altertum*, l (1908), pp. 297–312.

    'Some New Texts of Liturgical Easter Plays,' *Journal of English and Germanic Philology*, viii (1909), pp. 463–88.

    'Osterfeiern aus Bamberger und Wolfenbüttler Handschriften,' *Zeitschrift für deutsches Altertum*, lv (1914), pp. 52–61.

    'A Rheinau Easter Play of the late XVIth Century,' *Journal of English and German Philology*, xxvi (1927), pp. 226–36.

    The Sepulchre of Christian Art and Liturgy, University of Illinois Studies in Language and Literature, vii, No. 2, Urbana, 1921.

Chansonnier Cangé, ed. J. Beck, 2 vols., Paris and Philadelphia, 1927.

Chailley, Jacques, 'Le drame liturgique médiéval à Saint Martial de Limoges,' *Revue d'Histoire du Théâtre*, 7 (1955), pp. 127–44.

    L'Ecole Musicale de Saint Martial de Limoges jusqu'à la fin du XIᵉ siècle, Paris, 1960.

Chambers, E. K., *The Mediaeval Stage*, London, 1903.

Clark, J. M., *The Abbey of St. Gall*, Cambridge, 1926.

Corbin, Solange, 'Le Manuscrit 201 d'Orléans—Drames liturgiques dits de Fleury,' *Romania*, 36 (1953), pp. 1–43.

Coulton, G. G., 'Monasticism: its Causes and Effects,' *Harmsworth Universal History*.

Coussemaker, E. de, *Drames liturgiques du moyen âge*, Rennes, 1860. Reprinted, Geneva, 1975.

Craig, Hardin, *English Religious Drama of the Middle Ages*, London, 1955.

Creizenach, W., *Geschichte des neuern Dramas*, 2nd ed., 3 vols., Halle, 1911–23.

Davis, R. H. C., *A History of Medieval Europe*, London, 1957.

Donovan, Richard, *The Liturgical Drama in Medieval Spain*, Toronto, 1958.

Frank, Grace, *The Medieval French Drama*, Oxford, 1954.

Gennrich, F., *Trouvadours, Troubères, Minne- und Meistergesang*, Köln, 1953.

Gerbert, M., *De Cantu et Musica Sacra*, 2 vols., St. Blasien, 1774.

Grove, G., *Dictionary of Music and Musicians*, 5th ed., ed. E. Blom, 9 vols., 1954.

Handschin, Jacques, 'The Two Winchester Tropers,' *Journal of Theological Studies*, XXXVII (1936.)

    'Trope, Sequence, and Conductus,' *New Oxford History of Music*, II, London, 1967.

Hardison, O. B., *Christian Rite and Christian Drama in the Middle Ages*, Baltimore, 1965.

Harrison, Frank L., *Music in Medieval Britain*, London, 1958.

Historical Antholology of Music, ed. A. T. Davison and W. Apel, Vol. 1, Cambridge, Mass., 1949.

Hohler, Christopher, 'The Proper Office of St. Nicholas, and Related Matters with Reference to a Recent Book,' *Medium Aevum*, 36 (1967), pp. 40–8.

Hughes, David, 'Further Notes on the Grouping of the Aquitainian Tropers,' *Journal of the American Musicological Society*, 19 (1966), pp. 3–12.

Huizinga, J., *The Waning of the Middle Ages*, London, 1924.

Jones, Charles W., *The Saint Nicholas Liturgy and its Literary Relationships*, Berkeley, 1963.

Jungmann, J. A., *The Mass of the Roman Rite*, translated by Francis A. Brunner, 2 vols., New York, 1951.

Klapper, J., 'Der Ursprung der lateinischen Osterfeiern,' *Zeitschrift für Deutsche Philologie*, L (1923), pp. 46–58.

Lange, C., *Die lateinischen Osterfeiern*, Munich, 1887.

Liber Usualis, ed. Benedictines of Solesmes, 1950.

Lipphardt, W., *Die Weisen der lateinischen Osterspiele des 12. und 13. Jahrhunderts*, Kassel, 1948.

Liuzzi, Ferdinando, 'L'Espressione Musicale nel Dramma liturgico,' *Studi Medievali*, 2 (1929), pp. 74–109.

    La Lauda e i primordi della melodia italiana, 2 vols., Rome, 1934.

    'Le Vergini savie et le Vergini folli,' *Studi Medievali*, Nuova Serie III (1930), pp. 82–109.

Luzarche, V., *Office de Pâques ou de la Resurrection*, Tours, 1856.

Martene, E., *De Antiquis Ecclesiae Ritibus*, 4 vols., Venice, 1788.

Meyer, W., *Gesammelte Abhandlung zur mittelateinischen Rythmik*, 2 vols., Berlin, 1905.

Migne, J. B., *Patrologiae Cursus Completus: Patrologia Latina*, 221 vols., Paris, 1844–64.

Milchsack, G., *Die Oster- und Passionsspiele, I, die lateinischen Osterfeiern*, Wolfenbüttel, 1880.

Misset, E., and Pierre Aubry, eds., *Les Proses d'Adam de Saint Victor*, Paris, 1900.

New Oxford History of Music, Vol. II, Early Medieval Music up to 1300, ed. Dom Anselm Hughes, London, 1967.

Paléographie musicale: les manuscrits de chant grégorien, ambrosien, mozarabe, gallican publiés en fac-similés phototypiques par les Bénédictines de Solesmes, Solesmes or Tournai, 1889ff.

Reese, Gustave, *Music in the Middle Ages,* New York, 1940.

Regularis Concordia, ed. Dom Thomas Symons, London and New York, 1953.

Schönemann, Oskar, *Der Sündenfall und Marienklage,* Hanover, 1855.

Schubiger, A., *Die Sängerschule St. Gallens,* 1858.

    Musikalischen Spicileglen, Berlin, 1876.

Sepet, M., *Origines catholiques du théâtre moderne,* Paris, 1904.

Smits van Waesberghe, Jos., 'A Dutch Easter Play,' *Musica Disciplina,* VII (1953), pp. 15–37.

    Cymbala (Bells in the Middle Ages), Rome, 1951.

Sticca, Sandro, *The Latin Passion Play: its Origin and Development,* Albany (State University of New York Press), 1970.

Strunk, Oliver, *Source Readings in Music History,* vol. 1, New York, 1950.

Suñol, Dom Gregory, *Introduction à la Paléographie Musicale Grégorienne,* Paris, 1935.

Thomas, L.-P., *Le 'Sponsus' (Mystère des vierges sages et des vierges folles),* Paris, 1951.

Wagner, Peter, *Introduction to the Gregorian Melodies,* translated by Agnes Orme and E. G. P. Wyatt, Plainsong and Medieval Music Society, London, 1901.

Villetard, H., *L'Office de Pierre de Corbeil,* 1907.

Winchester Troper, ed. W. H. Frere, London, 1894.

Wood, Charles F., *The Age of Chivalry,* London, 1970.

Young, Karl, *The Drama of the Medieval Church,* 2 vols., Oxford, 1933.

SUPPLEMENTARY BIBLIOGRAPHY

Compiled by Cynthia Bourgeault

The following is offered as a highly selective list of major studies in the field of liturgical drama which have appeared since Smoldon's death, or with which he was unacquainted. In compiling this list, I have drawn heavily upon the researches of two scholars, C. Clifford Flanigan and Walther Lipphardt; for a more substantive bibliography, I urge readers to consult their works first hand (Flanigan, 'The Liturgical Drama and its Tradition: A Review of Scholarship 1965–75,' *Research Opportunities in Renaissance Drama*, xviii and xix (1975 and 1976); Lipphardt, *Lateinische Osterfeiern und Osterspiele*, Berlin and New York, 1975)—particularly strong in German and Continental sources). I would like also to call special attention to Andrew Hughes' excellent bibliography, *Medieval Music: The Sixth Liberal Art* (Toronto, 1974), which has apparently escaped notice by both Flanigan and Lipphardt, and which is rich and superbly well organized.

Arlt, Wulf, *Ein Festoffizium des Mittelalters aus Beauvais in seiner liturgischen und musicalischen Bedeutung*, Köln, 1970.

Axton, Richard, *European Drama of the Early Middle Ages*, London, 1974.

Bischoff, Bernhard, ed. (completing the work of Otto Schumann), *Carmina Burana: Die Trink- und Spielerlieder—Die geistlichen Dramen*, Heidelberg, 1970.

Blank, Richard, *Sprache und Dramaturgie*, Humanistische Bibliothek, Abhandlungen und Texte, Munich, 1969.

Brandel, R., 'Some Unifying Devices in the Religious Music Drama of the Middle Ages,' *Aspects of Medieval and Renaissance Music*, New York, 1966, pp. 40–48.

Collins, Fletcher, jr., *Medieval Church Music-Dramas: A Repertory of Complete Plays*, Charlottesville (University of Virginia Press), 1976.

   The Production of Medieval Church Music-Dramas, Charlottesville (University of Virginia Press), 1972.

Corbin, Solange, 'Un jeu liturgique d'Hérode,' *Mittellateinisches Jahrbuch*, 8, 1973.

Corpus Antiphonalium Officii (*CAO*), ed. René-Jean Hesbert, 4 vols., Rome (Herder), 1963–70.

Crocker, Richard, 'The Troping Hypothesis,' *Musical Quarterly*, 52 (1966), pp. 183–203.

de Boor, Helmut, 'Das holländische Osterspiele,' *Acta Germanica*, 3 (1968), pp. 47–62.

   Die Textgeschichte der lateinische Osterfeiern (Hermaea: Germanistische Forschungen, NF 22), Tübingen, 1967.

Dolan, Diane, *Le drame liturgique de Pâques en Normandie et en Angleterre au moyen âge*, Paris, 1975.

Donnat, L., 'Recherches sur l'influence de Fleury au x.–xi. siècle,' *Actes et memoires de la Semaine d'Etudes Medievales de St. Benoit-sur-Loire*, Orléans and Tours, 1970.

Donovan, Richard B., 'Two Celebrated Centers of Medieval Liturgical Drama: Fleury and Ripol,' *The Medieval Drama and its Claudelian Revival*, ed. E. Catherine Dunn, Tatiana Fotitch, and Bernard M. Peebles, Washington, D.C., 1970, pp. 41–51.

Dunn, E. Catherine, 'Voice Structure in the Liturgical Drama: Sepet Reconsidered,' in *Medieval English Drama: Essays Critical and Contextual*, ed. Jerome Taylor and Alan H. Nelson, Chicago, 1972, pp. 44–63.

Evans, Paul, 'Some Reflections on the Origin of the Trope,' *Journal of the American Musicological Society*, 14 (1961), pp. 119–30.

    The Early Trope Repertory of St. Martial de Limoges, Princeton, 1970.

Flanigan, C. Clifford, 'The Liturgical Context of the *Quem quaeritis* Trope,' *Comparative Drama*, Vol. 8, No. 1 (*Studies in Medieval Literature in Honor of William L. Smoldon on his 82nd Birthday*), spring, 1974.

    'The Roman Rite and the Origins of the Liturgical Drama,' *University of Toronto Quarterly*, 43 (1974). pp. 263–84.

    'The Liturgical Drama and its Tradition: A Review of Scholarship 1965–75,' *Research Opportunities in Renaissance Drama*, Part I: Vol. XVIII (1975), pp. 81–102; Part II, Vol. XIX (1976), pp. 109–36.

Hallinger, K., 'Die Provenienz der Consuetudo Sigiberti,' *Medievalia Litteraria, Festschrift fur H. de Boor zum 80. Geburtstag*, Munich, 1971.

Hardison, O. B., 'Gregorian Easter Vespers and Early Liturgical Drama,' *The Medieval Drama and its Claudelian Revival*, ed. E. Catherine Dunn, Tatiana Fotitch, and Bernard M. Peebles, Washington, D.C., 1970.

Heitz, Carol, *Recherches sur les rapports entre architecture et liturgie à l'époque carolingienne*, Paris, 1963.

Hughes, Andrew, *Medieval Music: The Sixth Liberal Art*, Toronto, 1974.

Hughes, David G., 'The First Magdalene Lament of the Tours Easter Play,' *Journal of the American Musicological Society*, 29 (1976), pp. 276–83.

Husmann, Heinrich, 'Sinn und Wesen der Tropen veranschaulicht an den Introitustropen des Weihnachtsfestes,' *Archiv. für Musikwissenschaft*, 16 (1959), pp. 135–47.

    'Tropen- und Sequenzenhandschriften,' *Répertoire Internationale des Sources Musicales (RISM)*, Series B v, Vol. 1, Munich and Duisburg, 1964.

Konigson, Elie, *L'espace théâtrale médiéval*, Paris, 1975.

Lipphardt, Walther, *Das Herodesspiel von Le Mans nach den Handschriften Madrid Bibl. Nac. 288 und 289 (XI. und XII. Jahrhundert)*, 1965.

    Lateinische Osterfeiern und Osterspiele, Vol. 1, Berlin and New York, 1975.

    'Liturgische Dramen,' in *Die Musik in Geschichte und Gegenwart (MGG)*, ed. Friedrich Blume, Vol. VIII, Kassel, 1960, pp. 1010–51.

    'Die Mainzer *Visitatio Sepulchri*', in *Medievalia Litteraria: Festschrift für H. de Boor zum 80. Geburtstag*, Munich, 1971.

    'Die *Visitatio Sepulchri* (III Stufe) von Geinrode,' *Daphnis, Zeitschrift für mittlere deutsche Litteratur*, I (1972), pp. 1–14.

'Liturgical and Secular Elements in Medieval Liturgical Drama,' *Report of the Tenth Congress, Ljubljana, 1967*, ed. Dragotin Cvetko, Kassel, 1970, pp. 271–83.

McGee, Timothy J., 'The Liturgical Placements of the *Quem quaeritis* Dialogue,' *Journal of the American Musicological Society*, 29 (1976), pp. 1–29.

Odelman, Eva, 'Comment a-t-on appelé les tropes? Observations sur les rubriques des tropes des Xe et XIe siècles,' *Cahiers de Civilisation Médiévale*, 18 (1975), pp. 15–36.

Smits van Waesberghe, Josef, 'Das Nürnberger Osterspiel,' *Festschrift für Joseph Schmidt-Görg zum 60. Geburtstag*, Bonn, 1957.

Sponsus: Dramma della vergini prudenti e delle vergini stolte, ed. D'Arco Silvio Avalle and Raffello Monterosso, Milan and Naples, 1965.

Stemmler, Theo, *Liturgische Feiern und Geistliche Spiele: Studien zu Erscheinungsformen des Dramatische in Mittelalter*, Tübingen, 1970.

Sticca, Sandro, 'Drama and Spirituality in the Middle Ages,' *Medievalia et Humanistica*, NS (1973), pp. 69–78.

Stevens, John, 'Music in Some Early Medieval Plays', *Studies in the Arts: Proceedings of the St. Peter's College Literary Society*, ed. Francis Warner, Oxford (Basil Blackwell), 1968, pp. 21–40.

Werner, W., 'Studien zu den Passions- und Osterspielen in ihrem Übergang vom Latein zur Volkssprache,' *Philologische Studien und Quellen*, 18, Berlin, 1963.

Wickham, Glynne, *Shakespeare's Dramatic Heritage*, London, 1969.

Woolf, Rosemary, *The English Mystery Plays*, Berkeley, 1972.

A SMOLDON BIBLIOGRAPHY

The major scholarly works and performing editions of
William L. Smoldon

SCHOLARLY WORKS

'The Easter Sepulchre Music Drama,' *Music and Letters*, XXVII (1946), pp. 1–17.

'Liturgical Drama,' *New Oxford History of Music*, Vol. II, ed. Dom Anselm Hughes, London, 1954, pp. 175–219.

'The Music of the Medieval Church Drama,' *Musical Quarterly*, 48 (1962), pp. 476–97.

'Medieval Lyrical Melody and the Latin Church Dramas,' *Musical Quarterly*, 51 (1954), pp. 507–17.

'The Melodies of Music in Medieval Church-Drama and their Significance,' *Comparative Drama*, 2 (1968), pp. 185–209. Reprinted with extensive revisions in *Medieval English Drama: Essays Critical and Contextual*, ed. Jerome Taylor and Alan H. Nelson, Chicago, 1972, pp. 64–80.

'Liturgical Music-Drama,' *Grove's Dictionary of Music and Musicians*, Vol. 5 (1954), pp. 317–43.

'The Origins of the '*Quem quaeritis*' and the Easter Sepulchre Music Drama as demonstrated by their Musical Settings,' *The Medieval Drama*, ed. Sandro Sticca, Albany, N.Y., 1970, pp. 121–54.

Cvetko, Dragotin, ed., 'Liturgical and Secular Elements in Medieval Liturgical Drama,' *Report of the Tenth Congress, Ljubljana, 1967*, Kassel, 1970, pp. 271–83.

PERFORMING EDITIONS

The Play of Daniel: a Medieval Liturgical Drama, London, The Plainsong and Medieval Music Society, 1960.

Herod, A Medieval Nativity Play, London and New York, 1960.

The Play of Herod, a Twelfth Century Musical Drama, ed. Noah Greenberg and William L. Smoldon, (OUP), New York, 1965.

Officium Pastorum (The Shepherds at the Manger), London (OUP), 1967.

Peregrinus, London (OUP), 1965.

Planctus Mariae, London (OUP), 1965.

Sponsus (The Bridegroom), London (OUP), 1972.

Visitatio Sepulchri, London (OUP), 1964.

FESTSCHRIFTS

Studies in Medieval Literature in Honor of William L. Smoldon on his 82nd Birthday (Comparative Drama, Vol. 8, No. 1), spring, 1974.

442

INDEX

Compiled by Cynthia Bourgeault

443

447